69

The Editor

STEWART J. COOKE is Faculty Lecturer in English at McGill University. He is associate editor of *The Collected Plays of Frances Burney* and co-editor of *The Early Journals and Letters of Fanny Burney.*

EVELINA

AUTHORITATIVE TEXT
CONTEXTS AND CONTEMPORARY REACTIONS
CRITICISM

A NORTON CRITICAL EDITION

Frances Burney
EVELINA,
or,
The History of a Young Lady's Entrance into the World

AUTHORITATIVE TEXT

CONTEXTS AND

CONTEMPORARY REACTIONS

CRITICISM

Edited by

STEWART J. COOKE
MCGILL UNIVERSITY

W • W • NORTON & COMPANY • *New York* • *London*

The text of this book is composed in Electra
with the display set in Bernhard
Composition and Manufacturing by
The Maple-Vail Book Manufacturing Group
Cover illustration: Thomas Gainsborough, *The Honorable Mrs. Graham.*
National Gallery of Scotland, Edinburgh, Scotland, Great Britain. Reprinted
by permission of Art Resource.

Library of Congress Cataloging-in-Publication Data

Burney, Fanny, 1752–1840.
Evelina, or, The history of a young lady's entrance into the world:
authoritative text, contexts and contemporary reactions, criticism
/Frances Burney; edited by Stewart J. Cooke.
p.   cm.—(A Norton critical edition)
Includes bibliographical references (p.).

ISBN 0-393-97158-9 (pbk.)

1. England—Social life and customs—18th century—Fiction.
2. Young women—England—Fiction.   I. Cooke, Stewart J.   II. Title.
III. Title: History of a young lady's entrance into the world.
PR3316.A4E8   1997
823'.6—DC21
96-54869

W. W. Norton & Company, Inc., 500 Fifth Avenue, New York, N.Y. 10110
www.wwnorton.com

W. W. Norton & Company Ltd., Castle House, 75/76 Wells Street,
London W1T 3QT

4 5 6 7 8 9 0

Contents

Preface

The author of *Evelina* learned of its publication accidentally, when her unsuspecting stepmother read aloud at the breakfast table the following advertisement:

> *This day was published,* In three volumes, 12 mo. price seven shillings and sixpence sewed, or nine shillings bound, EVELINA; Or, A YOUNG LADY'S ENTRANCE into the WORLD. Printed for T. Lowndes, No 77, in Fleet street.
>
> (*London Evening Post,* 27–29 Jan. 1778)

Among those present, only Charlotte and Susanna Burney were aware of the significance of the event, but even they could have had no inkling how much and how quickly it was to transform their sister's life. Burney's "frolic"—the clandestine writing of the novel in a feigned hand and the cloak-and-dagger negotiations with the publisher Thomas Lowndes—could not remain a secret for long once "the Literary World was favoured with the first publication of the ingenious, learned, & most profound Fanny Burney," as she playfully phrased it in her journal. The critics were unanimous in their praise of the anonymous novel, and the reading public was captivated. Edmund Burke, the statesman and writer, could not put it down and stayed up all night to finish it; Sir Joshua Reynolds, the painter, offered £50 for the identity of the author; Richard Brinsley Sheridan, the playwright, thought its author should write a comedy for the stage; and the Great Cham of literary society, Samuel Johnson himself, compared it favorably to the novels of Samuel Richardson and Henry Fielding. Within months, it was considered unfashionable not to have read the book or have met the twenty-six-year-old author.

Burney's stock dropped off considerably in the following century, occasioned perhaps by her rather self-serving publication of her father's *Memoirs* and the critics' myopic and hostile response to her fourth novel, *The Wanderer* (see below, p. 369). Nonetheless, if nineteenth-century critics are less kind in their reception of Burney's work, one need look no further than Jane Austen's fiction to see how profound was her influence on subsequent novelists. In both subject matter and style, Burney is one of the important links between the eighteenth-century novel and the nineteenth-century novel, and it is fitting that the merit and importance of her novels have once again come to be recognized.

By the end of 1779, *Evelina* (for which Burney received only 20 guineas plus £10 for the third edition) had gone through four editions with a fifth pirated edition appearing in Dublin. After reading the proofs, Burney had sent Lowndes a list of changes and corrections, which were printed as an errata sheet in the first edition and incorporated, with further changes, into the second and third editions, published on 26 October 1778 (though with the imprint date of 1779) and 26 February 1779 respectively. This text is based on the third edition, which incorporates all of Burney's changes and is the first to use the expanded subtitle "The History of a Young Lady's Entrance into the World." It attempts to reproduce Burney's text exactly, except for the occasional obvious misspelling, duplicated word, or punctuation error, which have been silently corrected. It makes no concessions to consistency.

I am indebted to past editors of *Evelina*, particularly Margaret Anne Doody and Edward A. Bloom, whose annotations were always informative and useful, even those with which I disagreed. I should also like to thank Mariopi Spanos for many hours of photocopying and proofreading and Jacqueline Reid-Walsh for guiding me to the relevant dance manuals. Finally, I wish to dedicate this book to my late wife, Ruth Neufeld, who helped me prepare the proposal. Without her tireless devotion, this edition would never have gotten on the drawing board, least of all off it.

The Text of
EVELINA

To ——— ———[1]

Oh author of my being!—far more dear
  To me than light, than nourishment, or rest,
Hygieia's[2] blessings, Rapture's burning tear,
  Or the life blood that mantles in my breast!

If in my heart the love of Virtue glows,
  'T was planted there by an unerring rule;
From thy example the pure flame arose,
  Thy life, my precept—thy good works, my school.

Could my weak pow'rs thy num'rous virtues trace,
  By filial love each fear should be repress'd;
The blush of Incapacity I'd chace,
  And stand, recorder of thy worth, confess'd:

But since my niggard stars that gift refuse,
  Concealment is the only boon I claim;
Obscure be still the unsuccessful Muse,
  Who cannot raise, but would not sink, thy fame.

Oh! of my life at once the source and joy!
  If e'er thy eyes these feeble lines survey,
Let not their folly their intent destroy;
  Accept the tribute—but forget the lay.

---

1. To Dr. Charles Burney (1726–1814), Frances Burney's father.
2. Personified health in Greek mythology, usually said to be the daughter of Asclepius, the god of healing.

To the Authors of the Monthly and Critical Reviews.[1]

Gentlemen,

The liberty which I take in addressing to You the trifling production of a few idle hours, will, doubtless, move your wonder, and, probably, your contempt. I will not, however, with the futility of apologies, intrude upon your time, but briefly acknowledge the motives of my temerity: lest, by a premature exercise of that patience which I hope will befriend me, I should lessen its benevolence, and be accessary to my own condemnation.

Without name, without recommendation, and unknown alike to success and disgrace, to whom can I so properly apply for patronage, as to those who publicly profess themselves Inspectors of all literary performances?

The extensive plan of your critical observations,—which, not confined to works of utility or ingenuity, is equally open to those of frivolous amusement,—and yet worse than frivolous, dullness,—encourages me to seek for your protection, since,—perhaps for my sins!—it entitles me to your annotations. To resent, therefore, this offering, however insignificant, would ill become the universality of your undertaking, though not to despise it may, alas! be out of your power.

The language of adulation, and the incense of flattery, though the natural inheritance, and constant resource, from time immemorial, of the Dedicator, to me offer nothing but the wistful regret that I dare not invoke their aid. Sinister views would be imputed to all I could say; since, thus situated, to extol your judgment, would seem the effect of art, and to celebrate your impartiality, be attributed to suspecting it.

As Magistrates of the press, and Censors for the public,—to which you are bound by the sacred ties of integrity to exert the most spirited impartiality, and to which your suffrages should carry the marks of pure, dauntless, irrefragable truth—to appeal for your Mercy, were to solicit your dishonour; and therefore,—though 'tis sweeter than frankincense,—more grateful to the senses than all the odorous perfumes of Arabia,—and though

> It droppeth like the gentle rain from heaven
> Upon the place beneath,——[2]

---

1. For their respective reviews of *Evelina*, see below, pp. 359–61.
2. Should be "droppeth as"; Shakespeare, *The Merchant of Venice* (4.1.185–86).

4

I court it not! to your justice alone I am entitled, and by that I must abide. Your engagements are not to the supplicating author, but to the candid public, which will not fail to crave

The penalty and forfeit of your bond.[3]

No hackneyed writer, inured to abuse, and callous to criticism, here braves your severity;—neither does a half-starv'd garretteer,

Oblig'd by hunger—and request of friends,—[4]

implore your lenity: your examination will be alike unbiassed by partiality and prejudice:—no refractory murmuring will follow your censure, no private interest be gratified by your praise.

Let not the anxious solicitude with which I recommend myself to your notice, expose me to your derision. Remember, Gentlemen, you were all young writers once, and the most experienced veteran of your corps, may, by recollecting his first publication, renovate his first terrors, and learn to allow for mine. For, though Courage is one of the noblest virtues of this nether sphere, and, though scarcely more requisite in the field of battle, to guard the fighting hero from disgrace, than in the private commerce of the world, to ward off that littleness of soul which leads, by steps imperceptible, to all the base train of the inferior passions, and by which the too timid mind is betrayed into a servility derogatory to the dignity of human nature; yet is it a virtue of no necessity in a situation such as mine; a situation which removes, even from cowardice itself, the sting of ignominy;—for surely that courage may easily be dispensed with, which would rather excite disgust than admiration! Indeed, it is the peculiar privilege of an author, to rob terror of contempt, and pusillanimity of reproach.

Here let me rest,—and snatch myself, while I yet am able, from the fascination of Egotism,—a monster who has more votaries than ever did homage to the most popular deity of antiquity; and whose singular quality is, that while he excites a blind and involuntary adoration in almost every individual, his influence is universally disallowed, his power universally contemned, and his worship, even by his followers, never mentioned but with abhorrence.

In addressing you jointly, I mean but to mark the generous sentiments by which liberal criticism, to the utter annihilation of envy, jealousy, and all selfish views, ought to be distinguished.

I have the honour to be,
GENTLEMEN,
Your most obedient
Humble servant,
* * * * * *.

3. Changed from "my bond"; *The Merchant of Venice* (4.1.207).
4. Alexander Pope, *Epistle to Dr. Arbuthnot* (44).

Preface

IN the republic of letters, there is no member of such inferior rank, or who is so much disdained by his brethren of the quill, as the humble Novelist: nor is his fate less hard in the world at large, since, among the whole class of writers, perhaps not one can be named of which the votaries are more numerous but less respectable.

Yet, while in the annals of those few of our predecessors, to whom this species of writing is indebted for being saved from contempt, and rescued from depravity, we can trace such names as Rousseau, Johnson,[1] Marivaux, Fielding, Richardson, and Smollet,[2] no man need blush at starting from the same post, though many, nay, most men, may sigh at finding themselves distanced.

The following letters are presented to the public—for such, by novel writers, novel readers will be called,—with a very singular mixture of timidity and confidence, resulting from the peculiar situation of the editor; who, though trembling for their success from a consciousness of their imperfections, yet fears not being involved in their disgrace, while happily wrapped up in a mantle of impenetrable obscurity.

To draw characters from nature, though not from life, and to mark the manners of the times, is the attempted plan of the following letters. For this purpose, a young female, educated in the most secluded retirement, makes, at the age of seventeen, her first appearance upon the great and busy stage of life; with a virtuous mind, a cultivated understanding, and a feeling heart, her ignorance of the forms, and inexperience in the manners, of the world, occasion all the little incidents which these volumes record, and which form the natural progression of the life of a young woman of obscure birth, but conspicuous beauty, for the first six months after her Entrance into the world.

Perhaps were it possible to effect the total extirpation of novels, our young ladies in general, and boarding-school damsels in particular, might profit from their annihilation: but since the distemper they have spread seems incurable, since their contagion bids defiance to the medicine of advice or reprehension, and since they are found to baffle all the mental

---

1. However superior the capacities in which these great writers deserve to be considered, they must pardon me that, for the dignity of my subject, I here rank the authors of Rasselas and Eloise as Novelists. [Burney's note]

2. Jean-Jacques Rousseau (1712–78), author of La Nouvelle Héloïse, ou Julie (1761); Samuel Johnson (1707–84), author of The History of Rasselas, Prince of Abyssinia (1759); Pierre Carlet de Chamblain de Marivaux (1688–1763), author of La Vie de Marianne (1731–41) and Le Paysan parvenu (1735–36); Henry Fielding (1707–54), author of Shamela (1741), Joseph Andrews (1742), Jonathan Wild (1743), Tom Jones (1749), and Amelia (1751); Samuel Richardson (1689–1761), author of Pamela (1740–41), Clarissa (1747–48), and Sir Charles Grandison (1753–54); Tobias Smollett (1721–71), author of Roderick Random (1748), Peregrine Pickle (1751), Ferdinand Count Fathom (1753), Sir Launcelot Greaves (1760–62), and Humphry Clinker (1771).

art of physic, save what is prescribed by the slow regimen of Time, and bitter diet of Experience, surely all attempts to contribute to the number of those which may be read, if not with advantage, at least without injury, ought rather to be encouraged than contemned.

Let me, therefore, prepare for disappointment those who, in the perusal of these sheets, entertain the gentle expectation of being transported to the fantastic regions of Romance, where Fiction is coloured by all the gay tints of luxurious Imagination, where Reason is an outcast, and where the sublimity of the Marvellous, rejects all aid from sober Probability. The heroine of these memoirs, young, artless, and inexperienced, is

No faultless Monster that the world ne'er saw,[3]

but the offspring of Nature, and of Nature in her simplest attire.

In all the Arts, the value of copies can only be proportioned to the scarcness of originals: among sculptors and painters, a fine statue, or a beautiful picture, of some great master, may deservedly employ the imitative talents of younger and inferior artists, that their appropriation to one spot, may not wholly prevent the more general expansion of their excellence; but, among authors, the reverse is the case, since the noblest productions of literature are almost equally attainable with the meanest. In books, therefore, imitation cannot be shunned too seduously; for the very perfection of a model which is frequently seen, serves but more forcibly to mark the inferiority of a copy.

To avoid what is common, without adopting what is unnatural, must limit the ambition of the vulgar herd of authors: however zealous, therefore, my veneration of the great writers I have mentioned, however I may feel myself enlightened by the knowledge of Johnson, charmed with the eloquence of Rousseau, softened by the pathetic powers of Richardson, and exhilarated by the wit of Fielding, and humour of Smollet, I yet presume not to attempt pursuing the same ground which they have tracked; whence, though they may have cleared the weeds, they have also culled the flowers, and though they have rendered the path plain, they have left it barren.

The candour of my readers, I have not the impertinence to doubt, and to their indulgence I am sensible I have no claim: I have, therefore, only to entreat, that my own words may not pronounce my condemnation, and that what I have here ventured to say in regard to imitation, may be understood, as it is meant, in a general sense, and not be imputed to an opinion of my own originality, which I have not the vanity, the folly, or the blindness, to entertain.

Whatever may be the fate of these letters, the editor is satisfied they will meet with justice; and commits them to the press, though hopeless of fame, yet not regardless of censure.

3. Changed from "A faultless monster, which the World ne'er saw"; John Sheffield (1647–1721), Duke of Buckingham and Normanby, *An Essay on Poetry* (1682).

VOLUME I

Letter I.

LADY HOWARD TO THE REV. MR. VILLARS.

Howard Grove, Kent.[1]

Can any thing, my good Sir, be more painful to a friendly mind, than a necessity of communicating disagreeable intelligence? Indeed, it is sometimes difficult to determine, whether the relator or the receiver of evil tidings is most to be pitied.

I have just had a letter from Madame Duval; she is totally at a loss in what manner to behave; she seems desirous to repair the wrongs she has done, yet wishes the world to believe her blameless. She would fain cast upon another the odium of those misfortunes for which she alone is answerable. Her letter is violent, sometimes abusive, and that of *you!* — *you*, to whom she is under obligations which are greater even than her faults, but to whose advice she wickedly imputes all the sufferings of her much-injured daughter, the late Lady Belmont. The chief purport of her writing I will acquaint you with; the letter itself is not worthy your notice.

She tells me that she has, for many years past, been in continual expectation of making a journey to England, which prevented her writing for information concerning this melancholy subject, by giving her hopes of making personal inquiries; but family occurrences have still detained her in France, which country she now sees no prospect of quitting. She has, therefore, lately used her utmost endeavours to obtain a faithful account of whatever related to her *ill-advised* daughter; the result of which giving her *some reason* to apprehend that, upon her death-bed, she bequeathed an infant orphan to the world, she most graciously says, that if *you*, with whom *she understands* the child is placed, will procure authentic proofs of its relationship to her, you may send it to Paris, where she will properly provide for it.

This woman is, undoubtedly, at length, self-convicted of her most unnatural behaviour: it is evident, from her writing, that she is still as vulgar and illiterate as when her first husband, Mr. Evelyn, had the weakness to marry her; nor does she at all apologise for addressing herself to me, though I was only once in her company.

---

1. Kent is a maritime county in the southeast of England; Howard Grove is fictional.

Her letter has excited in my daughter Mirvan, a strong desire to be informed of the motives which induced Madame Duval to abandon the unfortunate Lady Belmont, at a time when a mother's protection was peculiarly necessary for her peace and her reputation. Notwithstanding I was personally acquainted with all the parties concerned in that affair, the subject always appeared of too delicate a nature to be spoken of with the principals; I cannot, therefore, satisfy Mrs. Mirvan otherwise than by applying to you.

By saying that you *may* send the child, Madame Duval aims at *conferring*, where she most *owes* obligation. I pretend not to give you advice; you, to whose generous protection this helpless orphan is indebted for every thing, are the best and only judge of what she ought to do; but I am much concerned at the trouble and uneasiness which this unworthy woman may occasion you.

My daughter and my grandchild join with me in desiring to be most kindly remembered to the amiable girl; and they bid me remind you, that the annual visit to Howard Grove, which we were formerly promised, has been discontinued for more than four years.

> I am, dear Sir,
> with great regard,
> Your most obedient friend and servant,
> M. Howard.

Letter II.

MR. VILLARS TO LADY HOWARD.

Berry Hill, Dorsetshire.[1]

Your Ladyship did but too well foresee the perplexity and uneasiness of which Madame Duval's letter has been productive. However, I ought rather to be thankful that I have so many years remained unmolested, than repine at my present embarrassment; since it proves, at least, that this wretched woman is at length awakened to remorse.

In regard to my answer, I must humbly request your Ladyship to write to this effect: "That I would not, upon any account, intentionally offend Madame Duval, but that I have weighty, nay unanswerable reasons for detaining her grand-daughter at present in England; the principal of which is, that it was the earnest desire of one to whose Will she owes implicit duty. Madame Duval may be assured that she meets with the utmost attention and tenderness; that her education, however short of my wishes, almost exceeds my abilities; and I flatter myself, when the time arrives that she shall pay her duty to her grand-mother, Madame Duval will find no reason to be dissatisfied with what has been done for her."

1. Dorset is a maritime county on the south coast of England; Berry Hill is fictional.

Your Ladyship will not, I am sure, be surprised at this answer. Madame Duval is by no means a proper companion or guardian for a young woman; she is at once uneducated and unprincipled; ungentle in temper, and unamiable in her manners. I have long known that she has persuaded herself to harbour an aversion for me—Unhappy woman! I can only regard her as an object of pity!

I dare not hesitate at a request from Mrs. Mirvan, yet, in complying with it, I shall, for her own sake, be as concise as I possibly can; since the cruel transactions which preceded the birth of my ward, can afford no entertainment to a mind so humane as her's.

Your Ladyship may probably have heard, that I had the honour to accompany Mr. Evelyn, the grandfather of my young charge, when upon his travels, in the capacity of a tutor. His unhappy marriage, immediately upon his return to England, with Madame Duval, then a waiting-girl at a tavern, contrary to the advice and entreaties of all his friends, among whom I was myself the most urgent, induced him to abandon his native land, and fix his abode in France. Thither he was followed by shame and repentance; feelings which his heart was not framed to support: for, notwithstanding he had been too weak to resist the allurements of beauty, which nature, though a niggard to her of every other boon, had with a lavish hand bestowed on his wife; yet he was a young man of excellent character, and, till thus unaccountably infatuated, of unblemished conduct. He survived this ill-judged marriage but two years. Upon his death-bed, with an unsteady hand, he wrote me the following note:

"My friend! forget your resentment, in favour of your humanity;—a father, trembling for the welfare of his child, bequeaths her to your care. O Villars! hear! pity! and relieve me!"

Had my circumstances permitted me, I should have answered these words by an immediate journey to Paris; but I was obliged to act by the agency of a friend, who was upon the spot, and present at the opening of the will.

Mr. Evelyn left to me a legacy of a thousand pounds, and the sole guardianship of his daughter's person till her eighteenth year conjuring me, in the most affecting terms, to take the charge of her education till she was able to act with propriety for herself; but in regard to fortune, he left her wholly dependent on her mother, to whose tenderness he earnestly recommended her.

Thus, though he would not, to a woman low-bred and illiberal as Mrs. Evelyn, trust the conduct and morals of his daughter, he nevertheless thought proper to secure to her the respect and duty which, from her own child, were certainly her due; but, unhappily, it never occurred to him that the mother, on her part, could fail in affection or justice.

Miss Evelyn, Madam, from the second to the eighteenth year of her life, was brought up under my care, and, except when at school, under my roof. I need not speak to your Ladyship of the virtues of that excellent young creature. She loved me as her father; nor was Mrs. Villars less valued by her; while to me she became so dear, that her loss was little less afflicting than that which I have since sustained of Mrs. Villars herself.

At that period of her life we parted; her mother, then married to Monsieur Duval, sent for her to Paris. How often have I since regretted that I did not accompany her thither! protected and supported by me, the misery and disgrace which awaited her, might, perhaps, have been avoided. But, to be brief—Madame Duval, at the instigation of her husband, earnestly, or rather tyrannically, endeavoured to effect a union between Miss Evelyn and one of his nephews. And, when she found her power inadequate to her attempt, enraged at her non-compliance, she treated her with the grossest unkindness, and threatened her with poverty and ruin.

Miss Evelyn, to whom wrath and violence had hitherto been strangers, soon grew weary of such usage; and rashly, and without a witness, consented to a private marriage with Sir John Belmont, a very profligate young man, who had but too successfully found means to insinuate himself into her favour. He promised to conduct her to England—he did.—O, Madam, you know the rest!—Disappointed of the fortune he expected, by the inexorable rancour of the Duvals, he infamously burnt the certificate of their marriage, and denied that they had ever been united!

She flew to me for protection. With what mixed transports of joy and anguish did I again see her! By my advice she endeavoured to procure proofs of her marriage;—but in vain: her credulity had been no match for his art.

Every body believed her innocent, from the guiltless tenor of her unspotted youth, and from the known libertinism of her barbarous betrayer. Yet her sufferings were too acute for her tender frame, and the same moment that gave birth to her infant, put an end at once to the sorrows and the life of its mother.

The rage of Madame Duval at her elopement, abated not while this injured victim of cruelty yet drew breath. She probably intended, in time, to have pardoned her, but time was not allowed. When she was informed of her death, I have been told, that the agonies of grief and remorse, with which she was seized, occasioned her a severe fit of illness. But, from the time of her recovery to the date of her letter to your Ladyship, I had never heard that she manifested any desire to be made acquainted with the circumstances which attended the death of Lady Belmont, and the birth of her helpless child.

That child, Madam, shall never, while life is lent me, know the loss she has sustained. I have cherished, succoured, and supported her, from her earliest infancy to her sixteenth year; and so amply has she repaid my care and affection, that my fondest wish is now circumscribed by the desire of bestowing her on one who may be sensible of her worth, and then sinking to eternal rest in her arms.

Thus it has happened that the education of the father, daughter, and grand-daughter, has devolved on me. What infinite misery have the two first caused me! Should the fate of the dear survivor be equally adverse, how wretched will be the end of my cares—the end of my days!

Even had Madame Duval merited the charge she claims, I fear my fortitude would have been unequal to such a parting; but, being such as she is, not only my affection, but my humanity recoils, at the barbarous idea of deserting the sacred trust reposed in me. Indeed, I could but ill support her former yearly visits to the respectable mansion at Howard Grove; pardon me, dear Madam, and do not think me insensible of the honour which your Ladyship's condescension confers upon us both; but so deep is the impression which the misfortunes of her mother have made on my heart, that she does not, even for a moment, quit my sight, without exciting apprehensions and terrors which almost overpower me. Such, Madam, is my tenderness, and such my weakness!—But she is the only tie I have upon earth, and I trust to your Ladyship's goodness not to judge of my feelings with severity.

I beg leave to present my humble respects to Mrs. and Miss Mirvan; and have the honour to be,

Madam, your Ladyship's most obedient
and most humble servant,
ARTHUR VILLARS.

Letter III.
[Written some months after the last.]

LADY HOWARD TO THE REV. MR. VILLARS.

Dear and Rev. Sir,   Howard Grove, March 8.

Your last letter gave me infinite pleasure: after so long and tedious an illness, how grateful to yourself and to your friends must be your returning health! You have the hearty wishes of every individual of this place for its continuance and increase.

Will you not think I take advantage of your acknowledged recovery, if I once more venture to mention your pupil and Howard Grove together? Yet you must remember the patience with which we submitted to your desire of not parting with her during the bad state of your health, though it was with much reluctance we forbore to solicit her company. My grand-daughter, in particular, has scarce been able to repress her eagerness to again meet the friend of her infancy; and for my own part, it is very strongly my wish to manifest the regard I had for the unfortunate Lady Belmont, by proving serviceable to her child;

which seems to me the best respect that can be paid to her memory. Permit me, therefore, to lay before you a plan which Mrs. Mirvan and I have formed, in consequence of your restoration to health.

I would not frighten you;—but do you think you could bear to part with your young companion for two or three months? Mrs. Mirvan proposes to spend the ensuing spring in London, whither, for the first time, my grandchild will accompany her: Now, my good friend, it is very earnestly their wish to enlarge and enliven their party by the addition of your amiable ward, who would share, equally with her own daughter, the care and attention of Mrs. Mirvan. Do not start at this proposal; it is time that she should see something of the world. When young people are too rigidly sequestered from it, their lively and romantic imaginations paint it to them as a paradise of which they have been beguiled; but when they are shown it properly, and in due time, they see it such as it really is, equally shared by pain and pleasure, hope and disappointment.

You have nothing to apprehend from her meeting with Sir John Belmont, as that abandoned man is now abroad, and not expected home this year.

Well, my good Sir, what say you to our scheme? I hope it will meet with your approbation; but if it should not, be assured I can never object to any decision of one who is so much respected and esteemed as Mr. Villars, by

His most faithful, humble servant,
M. Howard.

Letter IV.

MR. VILLARS TO LADY HOWARD.

Berry Hill, March 12.

I am grieved, Madam, to appear obstinate, and I blush to incur the imputation of selfishness. In detaining my young charge thus long with myself in the country, I consulted not solely my own inclination. Destined, in all probability, to possess a very moderate fortune, I wished to contract her views to something within it. The mind is but too naturally prone to pleasure, but too easily yielded to dissipation: it has been my study to guard her against their delusions, by preparing her to expect,— and to despise them. But the time draws on for experience and observation to take the place of instruction: If I have, in some measure, rendered her capable of using one with discretion, and making the other with improvement, I shall rejoice myself with the assurance of having largely contributed to her welfare. She is now of an age that happiness is eager to attend,—let her then enjoy it! I commit her to the protection of your Ladyship, and only hope she may be found worthy half the goodness I am satisfied she will meet with at your hospitable mansion.

Thus far, Madam, I chearfully submit to your desire. In confiding my ward to the care of Lady Howard, I can feel no uneasiness from her absence, but what will arise from the loss of her company, since I shall be as well convinced of her safety as if she were under my own roof;—but, can your Ladyship be serious in proposing to introduce her to the gaieties of a London life? Permit me to ask, for what end, or what purpose? A youthful mind is seldom totally free from ambition; to curb that, is the first step to contentment, since to diminish expectation, is to increase enjoyment. I apprehend nothing more than too much raising her hopes and her views, which the natural vivacity of her disposition would render but too easy to effect. The town-acquaintance of Mrs. Mirvan are all in the circle of high life; this artless young creature, with too much beauty to escape notice, has too much sensibility to be indifferent to it; but she has too little wealth to be sought with propriety by men of the fashionable world.

Consider, Madam, the peculiar cruelty of her situation; only child of a wealthy Baronet, whose person she has never seen, whose character she has reason to abhor, and whose name she is forbidden to claim; entitled as she is to lawfully inherit his fortune and estate, is there any probability that he will *properly* own her? And while he continues to persevere in disavowing his marriage with Miss Evelyn, she shall never, at the expence of her mother's honour, receive a part of her right, as the donation of his bounty.

And as to Mr. Evelyn's estate, I have no doubt but that Madame Duval and her relations will dispose of it among themselves.

It seems, therefore, as if this deserted child, though legally heiress of two large fortunes, must owe all her rational expectations to adoption and friendship. Yet her income will be such as may make her happy, if she is disposed to be so in private life; though it will by no means allow her to enjoy the luxury of a London fine lady.

Let Miss Mirvan, then, Madam, shine in all the splendor of high life; but suffer my child still to enjoy the pleasures of humble retirement, with a mind to which greater views are unknown.

I hope this reasoning will be honoured with your approbation; and I have yet another motive which has some weight with me; I would not willingly give offence to any human being, and surely Madame Duval might accuse me of injustice, if, while I refuse to let her grand-daughter wait upon her, I consent that she should join a party of pleasure to London.

In sending her to Howard Grove, not one of these scruples arise; and therefore Mrs. Clinton, a most worthy woman, formerly her nurse, and now my housekeeper, shall attend her thither next week.

Though I have always called her by the name of Anville, and reported in this neighbourhood that her father, my intimate friend, left her to my guardianship, yet I have thought it necessary she should herself be acquainted with the melancholy circumstances attending her birth; for, though I am very desirous of guarding her from curiosity and impertinence, by concealing her name, family, and story, yet I would not leave it in the power of chance, to shock her gentle nature with a tale of so much sorrow.

You must not, Madam, expect too much from my pupil. She is quite a little rustic, and knows nothing of the world; and though her education has been the best I could bestow in this retired place, to which Dorchester,[1] the nearest town, is seven miles distant, yet I shall not be surprised if you should discover in her a thousand deficiencies of which I have never dreamt. She must be very much altered since she was last at Howard Grove,—but I will say nothing of her; I leave her to your Ladyship's own observations, of which I beg a faithful relation; and am,

Dear Madam,
with great respect,
Your obedient and most humble servant,
ARTHUR VILLARS.

Letter V.

MR. VILLARS TO LADY HOWARD.

Dear Madam,   March 18.

This letter will be delivered to you by my child,—the child of my adoption,—my affection! Unblest with one natural friend, she merits a thousand. I send her to you, innocent as an angel, and artless as purity itself: and I send you with her the heart of your friend, the only hope he has on earth, the subject of his tenderest thoughts, and the object of his latest cares. She is one, Madam, for whom alone I have lately wished to live; and she is one whom to serve I would with transport die! Restore her but to me all innocence as you receive her, and the fondest hope of my heart will be amply gratified.

A. VILLARS.

Letter VI.

LADY HOWARD TO THE REV. MR. VILLARS.

Dear and Rev. Sir,   Howard Grove.

The solemn manner in which you have committed your child to my care, has in some measure dampt the pleasure which I receive from the trust, as it makes me fear that you suffer from your compliance, in which case I shall very sincerely blame myself for the earnestness with which I

---

1. The capital of Dorset, six miles north of Weymouth.

have requested this favour; but remember, my good Sir, she is within a few days summons, and be assured I will not detain her a moment longer than you wish.

You desire my opinion of her.

She is a little angel! I cannot wonder that you sought to monopolize her. Neither ought you, at finding it impossible.

Her face and person answer my most refined ideas of complete beauty: and this, though a subject of praise less important to you, or to me, than any other, is yet so striking, it is not possible to pass it unnoticed. Had I not known from whom she received her education, I should, at first sight of so perfect a face, have been in pain for her understanding; since it has been long and justly remarked, that folly has ever sought alliance with beauty.

She has the same gentleness in her manners, the same natural graces in her motions, that I formerly so much admired in her mother. Her character seems truly ingenuous and simple; and, at the same time that nature has blessed her with an excellent understanding, and great quickness of parts, she has a certain air of inexperience and innocency that is extremely interesting.

You have no reason to regret the retirement in which she has lived; since that politeness which is acquired by an acquaintance with high life, is in her so well supplied by a natural desire of obliging, joined to a deportment infinitely engaging.

I observe with great satisfaction a growing affection between this amiable girl and my grand-daughter, whose heart is as free from selfishness or conceit, as that of her young friend is from all guile. Their regard may be mutually useful, since much is to be expected from emulation, where nothing is to be feared from envy. I would have them love each other as sisters, and reciprocally supply the place of that tender and happy relationship, to which neither of them have a natural claim.

Be satisfied, my good Sir, that your child shall meet with the same attention as our own. We all join in most hearty wishes for your health and happiness, and in returning our sincere thanks for the favour you have conferred on us.

I am, Dear Sir,
Your most faithful servant,
M. Howard.

Letter VII.

Howard Grove, March 26.

Be not alarmed, my worthy friend, at my so speedily troubling you again; I seldom use the ceremony of waiting for answers, or writing with any regularity, and I have at present immediate occasion for begging your patience.

Mrs. Mirvan has just received a letter from her long-absent husband, containing the welcome news of his hoping to reach London by the beginning of next week. My daughter and the Captain have been separated almost seven years, and it would therefore be needless to say what joy, surprise, and consequently confusion, his, at present, unexpected return has caused at Howard Grove. Mrs. Mirvan, you cannot doubt, will go instantly to town to meet him; her daughter is under a thousand obligations to attend her; I grieve that her mother cannot.

And now, my good Sir, I almost blush to proceed;—but, tell me, may I ask—will you permit—that your child may accompany them? Do not think us unreasonable, but consider the many inducements which conspire to make London the happiest place at present she can be in. The joyful occasion of the journey; the gaiety of the whole party, opposed to the dull life she must lead if left here, with a solitary old woman for her sole companion, while she so well knows the cheerfulness and felicity enjoyed by the rest of the family,—are circumstances that seem to merit your consideration. Mrs. Mirvan desires me to assure you, that one week is all she asks, as she is certain that the Captain, who hates London, will be eager to revisit Howard Grove: and Maria is so very earnest in wishing to have the company of her friend, that, if you are inexorable, she will be deprived of half the pleasure she otherwise hopes to receive.

However, I will not, my good Sir, deceive you into an opinion that they intend to live in a retired manner, as that cannot be fairly expected. But you have no reason to be uneasy concerning Madame Duval; she has not any correspondent in England, and obtains no intelligence [1] but by common report. She must be a stranger to the name your child bears; and, even should she hear of this excursion, so short a time as a week, or less, spent in town upon so particular an occasion, though previous to their meeting, cannot be construed into disrespect to herself.

Mrs. Mirvan desires me to assure you, that if you will oblige her, her *two* children shall equally share her time and her attention. She has sent a commission to a friend in town to take a house for her; and while she waits for an answer concerning it, I shall for one from you to our petition. However, your child is writing herself, and that, I doubt not, will more avail than all we can possibly urge.

My daughter desires her best compliments to you *if*, she says, you will grant her request, but *not else*.

Adieu, my dear Sir,—we all hope every thing from your goodness.

M. Howard.

---

1. Information or news.

Letter VIII.

Howard Grove, March 26.

This house seems to be the house of joy; every face wears a smile, and a laugh is at every body's service. It is quite amusing to walk about, and see the general confusion; a room leading to the garden is fitting up for Captain Mirvan's study. Lady Howard does not sit a moment in a place; Miss Mirvan is making caps; every body so busy!—such flying from room to room!—so many orders given, and retracted, and given again!—nothing but hurry and perturbation.

Well but, my dear Sir, I am desired to make a request to you. I hope you will not think me an incroacher; Lady Howard insists upon my writing!—yet I hardly know how to go on; a petition implies a want,—and have you left me one? No, indeed.

I am half ashamed of myself for beginning this letter. But these dear ladies are so pressing—I cannot, for my life, resist wishing for the pleasures they offer me,—provided you do not disapprove them.

They are to make a very short stay in town. The Captain will meet them in a day or two. Mrs. Mirvan and her sweet daughter both go;—what a happy party! Yet I am not *very* eager to accompany them: at least, I shall be contented to remain where I am, if you desire that I should.

Assured, my dearest Sir, of your goodness, your bounty, and your indulgent kindness, ought I to form a wish that has not your sanction? Decide for me, therefore, without the least apprehension that I shall be uneasy, or discontented. While I am yet in suspense, perhaps I may *hope*, but I am most certain, that when you have once determined, I shall not repine.

They tell me that London is now in full splendour. Two Play-houses are open,—the Opera-House,—Ranelagh,—and the Pantheon.[1]—You see I have learned all their names. However, pray don't suppose that I make any point of going, for I shall hardly sigh to see them depart without me; though I shall probably never meet with such another opportunity. And, indeed, their domestic happiness will be so great,—it is natural to wish to partake of it.

I believe I am bewitched! I made a resolution when I began, that I would not be urgent; but my pen—or rather my thoughts, will not suffer

---

1. The two playhouses are Covent Garden Theater, first opened in 1732, and Drury Lane Theater, built in 1663. The Haymarket Opera House or King's Theater, built by Sir John Vanbrugh in 1705, produced Italian opera. Ranelagh, a pleasure garden in Chelsea that opened in 1742, contained a garden, an ornamental lake, a canal, a Chinese pavilion, and a rotunda where refreshments were served. The Pantheon, in Oxford Street, designed to be the "winter Ranelagh," opened in 1772; it offered concerts, ridottos, and masquerades and contained rooms for cards and refreshments. See Ben Weinreb and Christopher Hibbert, eds., *The London Encyclopaedia* (Bethesda, MD: Adler, 1983).

me to keep it—for I acknowledge, I must acknowledge, I cannot help wishing for your permission.

I almost repent already that I have made this confession; pray forget that you have read it, if this journey is displeasing to you. But I will not write any longer; for the more I think of this affair, the less indifferent to it I find myself.

Adieu, my most honoured, most reverenced, most beloved father! for by what other name can I call you? I have no happiness or sorrow, no hope or fear, but what your kindness bestows, or your displeasure may cause. You will not, I am sure, send a refusal, without reasons unanswerable, and therefore I shall cheerfully acquiesce. Yet I hope—I hope you will be able to permit me to go!

> I am,
> With the utmost affection,
> gratitude, and duty,
> Your
> EVELINA.

I cannot to you sign Anville and what other name may I claim?

Letter IX.

MR. VILLARS TO EVELINA.

Berry Hill, March 28.

To resist the urgency of entreaty, is a power which I have not yet acquired: I aim not at an authority which deprives you of liberty, yet I would fain guide myself by a prudence which should save me the pangs of repentance. Your impatience to fly to a place which your imagination has painted to you in colours so attractive, surprises me not; I have only to hope that the liveliness of your fancy may not deceive you: to refuse, would be raising it still higher. To see my Evelina happy, is to see myself without a wish: go then, my child, and may that Heaven, which alone can, direct, preserve, and strengthen you! To That, my love, will I daily offer prayers for your felicity; O may it guard, watch over you! defend you from danger, save you from distress, and keep vice as distant from your person as from your heart! And to Me, may it grant the ultimate blessing of closing these aged eyes in the arms of one so dear—so deservedly beloved!

ARTHUR VILLARS.

Letter X.

EVELINA TO THE REV. MR. VILLARS.

Queen-Ann-Street,[1] London, Saturday, April 2.

This moment arrived. Just going to Drury-Lane theatre. The celebrated Mr. Garrick performs Ranger.[2] I am quite in extacy. So is Miss Mirvan. How fortunate, that he should happen to play! We would not let Mrs. Mirvan rest till she consented to go, her chief objection was to our dress, for we have had no time to *Londonize* ourselves; but we teized her into compliance, and so we are to sit in some obscure place, that she may not be seen. As to me, I should be alike unknown in the most conspicuous or most private part of the house.

I can write no more now. I have hardly time to breathe—only just this, the houses and streets are not quite so superb as I expected. However, I have seen nothing yet, so I ought not to judge.

Well, adieu, my dearest Sir, for the present; I could not forbear writing a few words instantly on my arrival; though I suppose my letter of thanks for your consent is still on the road.

Saturday night.

O my dear Sir, in what raptures am I returned! Well may Mr. Garrick be so celebrated, so universally admired—I had not any idea of so great a performer.

Such ease! such vivacity in his manner! such grace in his motions! such fire and meaning in his eyes!—I could hardly believe he had studied a written part, for every word seemed to be uttered from the impulse of the moment.

His action—at once so graceful and so free!—his voice—so clear, so melodious, yet so wonderfully various in its tones—such animation!— every look *speaks!*

I would have given the world to have had the whole play acted over again. And when he danced—O how I envied Clarinda![3] I almost wished to have jumped on the stage and joined them.

I am afraid you will think me mad, so I won't say any more; yet I really believe Mr. Garrick would make you mad too, if you could see him. I intend to ask Mrs. Mirvan to go to the play every night while we stay in town. She is extremely kind to me, and Maria, her charming daughter, is the sweetest girl in the world.

---

1. A street in the West End, near Wimpole and Harley Streets; built from 1723 onward on the Portland Estate (*London Encyclopaedia* 628).
2. David Garrick (1717–79), the most celebrated actor of his day, was a family friend of the Burneys. Ranger is the hero of *The Suspicious Husband* (1747), a comedy by Benjamin Hoadly (1706–57), written to showcase Garrick's talents.
3. The heroine of *The Suspicious Husband.*

I shall write to you every evening all that passes in the day, and that in the same manner as, if I could see, I should tell you.

Sunday.

This morning we went to Portland chapel, and afterwards we walked in the Mall of St. James's Park, which by no means answered my expectations: it is a long straight walk, of dirty gravel, very un-easy to the feet; and at each end, instead of an open prospect, nothing is to be seen but houses built of brick. When Mrs. Mirvan pointed out the *Palace* to me[4]—I think I was never much more surprised.

However, the walk was very agreeable to us; every body looked gay, and seemed pleased and the ladies were so much dressed, that Miss Mirvan and I could do nothing but look at them. Mrs. Mirvan met several of her friends. No wonder, for I never saw so many people assembled together before. I looked about for some of *my* acquaintance, but in vain for I saw not one person that I knew, which is very odd, for all the world seemed there.

Mrs. Mirvan says we are not to walk in the Park again next Sunday, even if we should be in town, because there is better company in Kensington Gardens.[5] But really if you had seen how much every body was dressed, you would not think that possible.

Monday.

We are to go this evening to a private ball, given by Mrs. Stanley, a very fashionable lady of Mrs. Mirvan's acquaintance.

We have been *a shopping*, as Mrs. Mirvan calls it, all this morning, to buy silks, caps, gauzes, and so forth.

The shops are really very entertaining, especially the mercers;[6] there seem to be six or seven men belonging to each shop, and every one took care, by bowing and smirking, to be noticed; we were conducted from one to another, and carried from room to room, with so much ceremony, that at first I was almost afraid to go on.

I thought I should never have chosen a silk, for they produced so many I knew not which to fix upon and they recommended them all so strongly, that I fancy they thought I only wanted persuasion to buy every thing they shewed me. And, indeed, they took so much trouble, that I was almost ashamed I could not.

4. St. Paul's, Great Portland Street, a chapel of ease to the parish of St. Marylebone, built in 1765–66 (Henry B. Wheatley and Peter Cunningham, *London Past and Present* [London, 1891] 3: 62); Pall Mall, a fashionable street near St. James's Park, built in 1661; the Palace or Buckingham House, at the west end of St. James's Park, built for John Sheffield, the Duke of Buckingham and Normanby, in 1702–5. George III bought the property in 1762, and in 1775 the house was transferred to Queen Charlotte for life; thereafter, it was known as the Queen's House. Buckingham Palace was later built on the site (*The London Encyclopaedia* 101–2).
5. Expansive gardens attached to Kensington Palace, west of the City. Queen Caroline (1683–1737) had the original gardens extended by an additional three hundred acres in Hyde Park. Its "Broad Walk" was a fashionable, and exclusive, promenade.
6. Textile dealers.

At the milliners,[7] the ladies we met were so much dressed, that I should rather have imagined they were making visits than purchases. But what most diverted me was, that we were more frequently served by men than by women; and such men! so finical, so affected! they seemed to understand every part of a woman's dress better than we do ourselves; and they recommended caps and ribbands with an air of so much importance, that I wished to ask them how long they had left off wearing them.

The dispatch with which they work in these great shops is amazing, for they have promised me a compleat suit of linen[8] against the evening.

I have just had my hair dressed.[9] You can't think how oddly my head feels; full of powder and black pins, and a great *cushion* on the top of it. I believe you would hardly know me, for my face looks quite different to what it did before my hair was dressed. When I shall be able to make use of a comb for myself I cannot tell for my hair is so much entangled, *frizled* they call it, that I fear it will be very difficult.

I am half afraid of this ball to-night for, you know, I have never danced but at school; however, Miss Mirvan says there is nothing in it. Yet I wish it was over.

Adieu, my dear Sir; pray excuse the wretched stuff I write perhaps I may improve by being in this town, and then my letters will be less unworthy your reading. Mean time, I am,

> Your dutiful and affectionate,
> though unpolished,
> EVELINA.

Poor Miss Mirvan cannot wear one of the caps she made, because they dress her hair too large for them.

Letter XI.

EVELINA IN CONTINUATION.

Queen-Ann-Street, April 5, Tuesday morning.

I have a vast deal to say, and shall give all this morning to my pen. As to my plan of writing every evening the adventures of the day, I find it impracticable; for the diversions here are so very late, that if I begin my letters after them, I could not go to bed at all.

We past a most extraordinary evening. A *private* ball this was called, so I expected to have seen about four or five couple; but Lord! my dear Sir, I believe I saw half the world! Two very large rooms were full of

---

7. Dealers in women's hats and trimmings.
8. A linen gown.
9. Immense hairdos, sometimes two- to three-feet high and sporting decorations, were then fashionable.

company; in one, were cards for the elderly ladies, and in the other, were the dancers. My mamma Mirvan, for she always calls me her child, said she would sit with Maria and me till we were provided with partners, and then join the cardplayers.

The gentlemen, as they passed and repassed, looked as if they thought we were quite at their disposal, and only waiting for the honour of their commands; and they sauntered about, in a careless indolent manner, as if with a view to keep us in suspense. I don't speak of this in regard to Miss Mirvan and myself only, but to the ladies in general; and I thought it so provoking, that I determined, in my own mind, that, far from humouring such airs, I would rather not dance at all, than with any one who should seem to think me ready to accept the first partner who would condescend to take me.

Not long after, a young man, who had for some time looked at us with a kind of negligent impertinence, advanced, on tiptoe, towards me; he had a set smile on his face, and his dress was so foppish, that I really believe he even wished to be stared at; and yet he was very ugly.

Bowing almost to the ground, with a sort of swing, and waving his hand with the greatest conceit, after a short and silly pause, he said, "Madam—may I presume?"—and stopt, offering to take my hand. I drew it back, but could scarce forbear laughing. "Allow me, Madam," (continued he, affectedly breaking off every half moment) "the honour and happiness—if I am not so unhappy as to address you too late—to have the happiness and honour—"

Again he would have taken my hand, but, bowing my head, I begged to be excused, and turned to Miss Mirvan to conceal my laughter. He then desired to know if I had already engaged myself to some more fortunate man? I said No, and that I believed I should not dance at all. He would keep himself, he told me, disengaged, in hopes I should relent; and then, uttering some ridiculous speeches of sorrow and disappointment, though his face still wore the same invariable smile, he retreated.

It so happened, as we have since recollected, that during this little dialogue, Mrs. Mirvan was conversing with the lady of the house. And very soon after another gentleman, who seemed about six-and-twenty years old, gayly, but not foppishly, dressed, and indeed extremely handsome, with an air of mixed politeness and gallantry, desired to know if I was engaged, or would honour him with my hand. So he was pleased to say, though I am sure I know not what honour he could receive from me; but these sort of expressions, I find, are used as words of course, without any distinction of persons, or study of propriety.

Well, I bowed, and I am sure I coloured; for indeed I was frightened at the thoughts of dancing before so many people, all strangers, and, which was worse, *with* a stranger; however, that was unavoidable, for though I looked round the room several times, I could not see one person that I knew. And so, he took my hand, and led me to join in the dance.

The minuets were over before we arrived, for we were kept late by the milliner's making us wait for our things.

He seemed very desirous of entering into conversation with me; but I was seized with such a panic, that I could hardly speak a word, and nothing but the shame of so soon changing my mind, prevented my returning to my seat, and declining to dance at all.

He appeared to be surprised at my terror, which I believe was but too apparent: however, he asked no questions, though I fear he must think it very strange; for I did not choose to tell him it was owing to my never before dancing but with a school-girl.

His conversation was sensible and spirited; his air and address were open and noble; his manners gentle, attentive, and infinitely engaging; his person is all elegance, and his countenance, the most animated and expressive I have ever seen.

In a short time we were joined by Miss Mirvan, who stood next couple to us. But how was I startled, when she whispered me that my partner was a nobleman! This gave me a new alarm; how will he be provoked, thought I, when he finds what a simple rustic he has honoured with his choice! one whose ignorance of the world makes her perpetually fear doing something wrong!

That he should be so much my superior every way, quite disconcerted me; and you will suppose my spirits were not much raised, when I heard a lady, in passing us, say, "This is the most difficult dance I ever saw."

"O dear, then," cried Maria to her partner, "with your leave, I'll sit down till the next."

"So will I too, then," cried I, "for I am sure I can hardly stand."

"But you must speak to your partner first," answered she; for he had turned aside to talk with some gentlemen. However, I had not sufficient courage to address him and so away we all three tript, and seated ourselves at another end of the room.

But, unfortunately for me, Miss Mirvan soon after suffered herself to be prevailed upon to attempt the dance; and just as she rose to go, she cried, "My dear, yonder is your partner, Lord Orville, walking about the room in search of you."

"Don't leave me then, dear girl!" cried I; but she was obliged to go. And now I was more uneasy than ever; I would have given the world to have seen Mrs. Mirvan, and begged of her to make my apologies; for what, thought I, can I possibly say to him in excuse for running away? he must either conclude me a fool, or half mad; for any one brought up in the great world, and accustomed to its ways, can have no idea of such sort of fears as mine.

My confusion increased when I observed that he was every where seeking me, with apparent perplexity and surprise; but when, at last, I saw him move towards the place where I sat, I was ready to sink with shame and distress. I found it absolutely impossible to keep my seat, because I could not think of a word to say for myself, and so I rose, and walked hastily towards the card-room, resolving to stay with Mrs. Mirvan the rest of the evening, and not to dance at all. But before I could find her, Lord Orville saw and approached me.

He begged to know if I was not well? You may easily imagine how much I was embarrassed. I made no answer, but hung my head, like a fool, and looked on my fan.

He then, with an air the most respectfully serious, asked if he had been so unhappy as to offend me?

"No, indeed!" cried I: and, in hopes of changing the discourse, and preventing his further inquiries, I desired to know if he had seen the young lady who had been conversing with me?

No;—but would I honour him with any commands to her?

"O by no means!"

Was there any other person with whom I wished to speak?

I said *no*, before I knew I had answered at all.

Should he have the pleasure of bringing me any refreshment?

I bowed, almost involuntarily. And away he flew.

I was quite ashamed of being so troublesome, and so much *above* myself as these seeming airs made me appear; but indeed I was too much confused to think or act with any consistency.

If he had not been swift as lightning, I don't know whether I should not have stolen away again; but he returned in a moment. When I had drunk a glass of lemonade, he hoped, he said, that I would again honour him with my hand, as a new dance was just begun. I had not the presence of mind to say a single word, and so I let him once more lead me to the place I had left.

Shocked to find how silly, how childish a part I had acted, my former fears of dancing before such a company, and with such a partner, returned more forcibly than ever. I suppose he perceived my uneasiness; for he intreated me to sit down again, if dancing was disagreeable to me. But I was quite satisfied with the folly I had already shewn, and therefore declined his offer, tho' I was really scarce able to stand.

Under such conscious disadvantages, you may easily imagine, my dear Sir, how ill I acquitted myself. But, though I both expected and deserved to find him very much mortified and displeased at his ill fortune in the choice he had made, yet, to my very great relief, he appeared to be even contented, and very much assisted and encouraged me. These people in high life have too much presence of mind, I believe, to *seem* disconcerted, or out of humour, however they may feel: for had I been the person of the most consequence in the room, I could not have met with more attention and respect.

When the dance was over, seeing me still very much flurried, he led me to a seat, saying that he would not suffer me to fatigue myself from politeness.

And then, if my capacity, or even if my spirits had been better, in how animated a conversation might I have been engaged! it was then I saw that the rank of Lord Orville was his least recommendation, his understanding and his manners being far more distinguished. His remarks upon the company in general were so apt, so just, so lively, I am almost surprised myself that they did not re-animate me; but indeed I was too well convinced of the ridiculous part I had myself played before so nice[1] an observer, to be able to enjoy his pleasantry: so self-compassion gave me feeling for others. Yet I had not the courage to attempt either to defend them, or to rally in my turn, but listened to him in silent embarrassment.

When he found this, he changed the subject, and talked of public places, and public performers; but he soon discovered that I was totally ignorant of them.

He then, very ingeniously, turned the discourse to the amusements and occupations of the country.

It now struck me, that he was resolved to try whether or not I was capable of talking upon *any* subject. This put so great a constraint upon my thoughts, that I was unable to go further than a monosyllable, and not even so far, when I could possibly avoid it.

We were sitting in this manner, he conversing with all gaiety, I looking down with all foolishness, when that fop who had first asked me to dance, with a most ridiculous solemnity, approached, and after a profound bow or two, said, "I humbly beg pardon, Madam,—and of you too, my Lord,—for breaking in upon such agreeable conversation—which must, doubtless, be more delectable—than what I have the honour to offer—but—"

I interrupted him—I blush for my folly,—with laughing; yet I could not help it; for, added to the man's stately foppishness, (and he actually took snuff between every three words) when I looked around at Lord Orville, I saw such extreme surprise in his face,—the cause of which appeared so absurd, that I could not for my life preserve my gravity.

I had not laughed before from the time I had left Miss Mirvan, and I had much better have cried then; Lord Orville actually stared at me; the beau, I know not his name, looked quite enraged. "Refrain—Madam," (said he, with an important air,) "a few moments refrain!—I have but a sentence to trouble you with.—May I know to what accident I must attribute not having the honour of your hand?"

"Accident, Sir!" repeated I, much astonished.

"Yes, accident, Madam—for surely,—I must take the liberty to

---

1. Exact, precise.

observe—pardon me, Madam,—it ought to be no common one—that should tempt a lady—so young a one too,—to be guilty of ill-manners."

A confused idea now for the first time entered my head, of something I had heard of the rules of an assembly;[2] but I was never at one before,—I have only danced at school,—and so giddy and heedless I was, that I had not once considered the impropriety of refusing one partner, and afterwards accepting another. I was thunderstruck at the recollection: but, while these thoughts were rushing into my head, Lord Orville, with some warmth, said, "This Lady, Sir, is incapable of meriting such an accusation!"

The creature—for I am very angry with him—made a low bow, and, with a grin the most malicious I ever saw, "My Lord," said he, "far be it from me to *accuse* the lady, for having the discernment to distinguish and prefer—the superior attractions of your Lordship."

Again he bowed, and walked off.

Was ever any thing so provoking? I was ready to die with shame. "What a coxcomb!" exclaimed Lord Orville; while I, without knowing what I did, rose hastily, and moving off, "I can't imagine," cried I, "where Mrs. Mirvan has hid herself!"

"Give me leave to see," answered he. I bowed and sat down again, not daring to meet his eyes; for what must he think of me, between my blunder, and the supposed preference?

He returned in a moment, and told me that Mrs. Mirvan was at cards, but would be glad to see me; and I went immediately. There was but one chair vacant, so, to my great relief, Lord Orville presently left us. I then told Mrs. Mirvan my disasters, and she good-naturedly blamed herself for not having better instructed me, but said she had taken it for granted that I must know such common customs. However, the man may, I think, be satisfied with his pretty speech, and carry his resentment no farther.

In a short time, Lord Orville returned. I consented, with the best grace I could, to go down another dance, for I had had time to recollect myself, and therefore resolved to use some exertion, and, if possible, appear less a fool than I had hitherto done; for it occurred to me that, insignificant as I was, compared to a man of his rank and figure; yet, since he had been so unfortunate as to make choice of me for a partner, why I should endeavour to make the best of it.

The dance, however, was short, and he spoke very little; so I had

---

2. See G. M. S. Chivers, *A Pocket Companion to French and English Dancing* (London, 1821): "Any lady refusing to dance with a Gentleman, if disengaged, will be under the penalty of not joining the next two dances" (36). See also Timothy Dow Adams, "To Know the Dancer from the Dance," *Studies in the Novel* 14 (1982):

> To accept one dance actually meant to accept two, and the rules of society required that a woman who turned down a proposal from one partner must not dance with another. That an acceptance usually carried with it an obligation for two dances becomes more important when we realize that two dances could easily take up a large part of the evening. (55)

no opportunity of putting my resolution in practice. He was satisfied, I suppose, with his former successless efforts to draw me out: or, rather, I fancied, he had been inquiring *who I was*. This again disconcerted me, and the spirits I had determined to exert, again failed me. Tired, ashamed, and mortified, I begged to sit down till we returned home, which I did soon after. Lord Orville did me the honour to hand me to the coach, talking all the way of the honour *I* had done *him!* O these fashionable people!

Well, my dear Sir, was it not a strange evening? I could not help being thus particular, because, to me, every thing is so new. But it is now time to conclude. I am, with all love and duty,

Your
EVELINA.

Letter XII.

EVELINA IN CONTINUATION.

Tuesday, April 5.

There is to be no end to the troubles of last night. I have this moment, between persuasion and laughter, gathered from Maria the most curious dialogue that ever I heard. You will, at first, be startled at my vanity; but, my dear Sir, have patience!

It must have passed while I was sitting with Mrs. Mirvan in the card-room. Maria was taking some refreshment, and saw Lord Orville advancing for the same purpose himself; but he did not know her, though she immediately recollected him. Presently after, a very gay-looking man, stepping hastily up to him, cried, "Why, my Lord, what have you done with your lovely partner?"

"*Nothing!*" answered Lord Orville, with a smile and a shrug.

"By Jove," cried the man, "she is the most beautiful creature I ever saw in my life!"

Lord Orville, as he well might, laughed; but answered, "Yes, a pretty modest-looking girl."

"O my Lord!" cried the madman, "she is an angel!"

"A *silent* one," returned he.

"Why ay, my Lord, how stands she as to that? She looks all intelligence and expression."

"A poor weak girl!" answered Lord Orville, shaking his head.

"By Jove," cried the other, "I am glad to hear it!"

At that moment, the same odious creature who had been my former tormentor, joined them. Addressing Lord Orville with great respect, he said, "I beg pardon, my Lord,—if I was—as I fear might be the case—rather too severe in my censure of the lady who is honoured with your protection—but, my Lord, ill-breeding is apt to provoke a man."

"Ill-breeding!" cried my unknown champion, "impossible! that elegant face can never be so vile a mask!"

"O Sir, as to that," answered he, "you must allow *me* to judge; for though I pay all deference to your opinion—in other things—yet I hope you will grant—and I appeal to your Lordship also—that I am not totally despicable as a judge of good or ill-manners."

"I was so wholly ignorant," said Lord Orville, gravely, "of the provocation you might have had, that I could not but be surprised at your singular resentment."

"It was far from my intention," answered he, "to offend your Lordship; but, really, for a person who is nobody, to give herself such airs,—I own I could not command my passions. For, my Lord, though I have made diligent enquiry—I cannot learn who she is."

"By what I can make out," cried my defender, "she must be a country parson's daughter."

"He! he! he! very good, 'pon honour!" cried the fop,—"well, so I could have sworn by her manners."

And then, delighted at his own wit, he laughed, and went away, as I suppose, to repeat it.

"But what the deuce is all this?" demanded the other.

"Why a very foolish affair," answered Lord Orville; "your Helen[1] first refused this coxcomb, and then—danced with me. This is all I can gather of it."

"O Orville," returned he, "you are a happy man!—But, *ill-bred?*—I can never believe it! And she looks too sensible to be *ignorant.*"

"Whether ignorant or mischievous, I will not pretend to determine, but certain it is, she attended to all *I* could say to her, though I have really fatigued myself with fruitless endeavors to entertain her, with the most immovable gravity; but no sooner did Lovel begin his complaint, than she was seized with a fit of laughing, first affronting the poor beau, and then enjoying his mortification."

"Ha! ha! ha! why there's some *genius* in that, my Lord, though perhaps rather—*rustick.*"

Here Maria was called to dance, and so heard no more.

Now tell me, my dear Sir, did you ever know any thing more provoking? *"A poor weak girl!"* *"ignorant or mischievous!"* What mortifying words! I am resolved, however, that I will never again be tempted to go to an assembly. I wish I had been in Dorsetshire.

Well, after this, you will not be surprised that Lord Orville contented himself with an enquiry after our healths this morning, by his servant, without troubling himself to call;[2] as Miss Mirvan had told me he would: but perhaps it may be only a country custom.

1. Helen of Troy; a compliment to Evelina's beauty.
2. Gentlemen customarily called upon their dance partners the next morning to enquire after their healths. They might, as Orville does here, merely send a servant with a calling card.

I would not live here for the world. I care not how soon we leave town. London soon grows tiresome. I wish the captain would come. Mrs. Mirvan talks of the opera for this evening; however, I am very indifferent about it.

Wednesday morning.

Well, my dear Sir, I have been pleased against my will, I could almost say, for I must own I went out in very ill-humour, which I think you cannot wonder at: but the music and the singing were charming; they soothed me into a pleasure the most grateful, the best suited to my present disposition in the world. I hope to persuade Mrs. Mirvan to go again on Saturday. I wish the opera was every night. It is, of all entertainments, the sweetest, and most delightful. Some of the songs seemed to melt my very soul. It was what they call a *serious* opera, as the *comic* first singer was ill.

To-night we go to Ranelagh. If any of those three gentlemen who conversed so freely about me should be there——but I won't think of it.

Thursday morning.

Well, my dear Sir, we went to Ranelagh. It is a charming place, and the brilliancy of the lights, on my first entrance, made me almost think I was in some enchanted castle, or fairy palace, for all looked like magic to me.

The very first person I saw was Lord Orville. I felt so confused! —but he did not see me. After tea, Mrs. Mirvan being tired, Maria and I walked round the room alone. Then again we saw him, standing by the orchestra. We, too, stopt to hear a singer. He bowed to me; I courtesied, and I am sure I coloured. We soon walked on, not liking our situation: however, he did not follow us; and when we passed by the orchestra again, he was gone. Afterwards, in the course of the evening, we met him several times; but he was always with some party, and never spoke to us, tho' whenever he chanced to meet my eyes, he condescended to bow.

I cannot but be hurt at the opinion he entertains of me. It is true, my own behavior incurred it—yet he is himself the most agreeable and, seemingly, the most amiable man in the world, and therefore it is that I am grieved to be thought ill of by him: for of whose esteem ought we to be ambitious, if not of those who most merit our own?—But it is too late to reflect upon this now. Well, I can't help it;—However, I think I have done with assemblies!

This morning was destined for *seeing sights*, auctions, curious shops, and so forth; but my head ached, and I was not in a humour to be amused, and so I made them go without me, though very unwillingly. They are all kindness.

And now I am sorry I did not accompany them, for I know not what to do with myself. I had resolved not to go to the play tonight; but I believe I shall. ~~In short, I hardly care whether I do or n~~ot.

*   *   *   *   *

I thought I had done wrong! Mrs. Mirvan and Maria have been half the town over, and so entertained!—while I, like a fool, stayed at home to do nothing. And, at an auction in Pall-mall, who should they meet but Lord Orville! He sat next to Mrs. Mirvan, and they talked a great deal together: but she gave me no account of the conversation.

I may never have such another opportunity of seeing London; I am quite sorry that I was not of the party; but I deserve this mortification, for having indulged my ill-humour.

Thursday night.

We are just returned from the play, which was King Lear, and has made me very sad. We did not see any body we knew.

Well, adieu, it is too late to write more.

Friday.

Captain Mirvan is arrived. I have not spirits to give an account of his introduction, for he has really shocked me. I do not like him. He seems to be surly, vulgar, and disagreeable.

Almost the same moment that Maria was presented to him, he began some rude jests upon the bad shape of her nose, and called her a tall, ill-formed thing. She bore it with the utmost good humour; but that kind and sweet-tempered woman, Mrs. Mirvan, deserved a better lot. I am amazed she would marry him.

For my own part, I have been so shy, that I have hardly spoken to him, or he to me. I cannot imagine why the family was so rejoiced at his return. If he had spent his whole life abroad, I should have supposed they might rather have been thankful than sorrowful. However, I hope they do not think so ill of him as I do. At least, I am sure they have too much prudence to make it known.

Saturday night.

We have been to the opera, and I am still more pleased than I was on Tuesday. I could have thought myself in paradise, but for the continual talking of the company around me. We sat in the pit,[3] where every body was dressed in so high a style, that, if I had been less delighted with the performance, my eyes would have found me sufficient entertainment from looking at the ladies.

I was very glad I did not sit next the Captain, for he could not bear

---

3. The area near the stage; at the opera, seats in the pit were both fashionable and expensive.

the music, or singers, and was extremely gross in his observations on both. When the opera was over, we went into a place called the coffee-room, where ladies as well as gentlemen, assemble. There are all sorts of refreshments, and the company walk about, and *chat* with the same ease and freedom as in a private room.

On Monday we go to a ridotto,[4] and on Wednesday we return to Howard Grove. The Captain says he won't stay here to be *smoked with filth* any longer; but, having been seven years *smoked with a burning sun*, he will retire to the country, and sink into a *fair-weather chap*.

Adieu, my dear Sir.

Letter XIII.

EVELINA IN CONTINUATION.

My dear Sir,   Tuesday, April 12.

We came home from the ridotto so late, or rather, so early, that it was not possible for me to write. Indeed we did not go,—you will be frightened to hear it,—till past eleven o'clock: but nobody does. A terrible reverse of the order of nature! We sleep with the sun, and wake with the moon.

The room was very magnificent, the lights and decorations were brilliant, and the company gay and splendid. But I should have told you, that I made many objections to being of the party, according to the resolution I had formed. However, Maria laughed me out of my scruples, and so once again—I went to an assembly.

Miss Mirvan danced a minuet, but I had not the courage to follow her example. In our walks I saw Lord Orville. He was quite alone, but did not observe us. Yet, as he seemed of no party, I thought it was not impossible that he might join us; and tho' I did not wish much to dance at all,—yet, as I was more acquainted with him than with any other person in the room, I must own I could not help thinking it would be infinitely more desirable to dance again with him, than with an entire stranger. To be sure, after all that had passed, it was very ridiculous to suppose it even probable, that Lord Orville would again honour me with his choice; yet I am compelled to confess my absurdity, by way of explaining what follows.

Miss Mirvan was soon engaged; and, presently after, a very fashion-

---

4. "An entertainment, or social assembly, consisting of music or dancing" *(Oxford English Dictionary)*. Dr. Burney, quoting the *Freeholder's Journal* for 14 February 1772, writes: "In 1772, a new species of entertainment was advertised at the Opera-house, called a *Ridotto* [or Redoute]: 'it was opened with twenty-four select songs, which lasted about two hours; after which the company passed over a bridge, from the pit to the stage, where a duke and duchess led up the ball: the hours were the same as at a masquerade' " (A *General History of Music,* ed. Frank Mercer [New York: Dover, 1957] 2: 995).

able, gay-looking man, who seemed about 30 years of age, addressed himself to me, and begged to have the honour of dancing with me. Now Maria's partner was a gentleman of Mrs. Mirvan's acquaintance; for she had told us it was highly improper for young women to dance with strangers, at any public assembly. Indeed it was by no means my wish so to do; yet I did not like to confine myself from dancing at all; neither did I dare refuse this gentlemen, as I had done Mr. Lovel, and then, if any acquaintance should offer, accept him: and so, all these reasons combining, induced me to tell him—yet I blush to write it to you!—that I was *already engaged*; by which I meant to keep myself at liberty to dance or not, as matters should fall out.

I suppose my consciousness betrayed my artifice, for he looked at me as if incredulous; and, instead of being satisfied with my answer, and leaving me, according to my expectation, he walked at my side, and, with the greatest ease imaginable, began a conversation, in the free style which only belongs to old and intimate acquaintance. But, what was most provoking, he asked me a thousand questions concerning *the partner to whom I was engaged*. And, at last, he said, "Is it really possible that a man whom you have honoured with your acceptance, can fail to be at hand to profit from your goodness?"

I felt extremely foolish, and begged Mrs. Mirvan to lead to a seat, which she very obligingly did. The Captain sat next her, and, to my great surprise, this gentleman thought proper to follow, and seat himself next to me.

"What an insensible!" continued he; "why, Madam, you are missing the most delightful dance in the world! The man must be either mad, or a fool—Which do you incline to think him yourself?"

"Neither, Sir," answered I in some confusion.

He begged my pardon for the freedom of his supposition, saying, "I really was off my guard, from astonishment that any man can be so much and so unaccountably his own enemy. But where, Madam, can he possibly be?—has he left the room?—or has not he been in it?"

"Indeed, Sir," said I peevishly, "I know nothing of him."

"I don't wonder that you are disconcerted, Madam, it is really very provoking. The best part of the evening will be absolutely lost. He deserves not that you should wait for him."

"I do not, Sir," said I, "and I beg you not to—"

"Mortifying, indeed, Madam," interrupted he, "a lady to wait for a gentleman:—O fie!—careless fellow!—what can detain him?— Will you give me leave to seek him?"

"If you please, Sir," answered I, quite terrified lest Mrs. Mirvan should attend to him, for she looked very much surprised at seeing me enter into conversation with a stranger.

"With all my heart," cried he; "pray, what coat has he on?"

"Indeed I never looked at it."

"Out upon him!" cried he; "What! did he address you in a coat not worth looking at?—What a shabby wretch!"

How ridiculous! I really could not help laughing, which, I fear, encouraged him, for he went on.

"Charming creature!—and can you really bear ill usage with so much sweetness?—Can you, *like patience on a monument*,[1] smile in the midst of disappointment?—For my part, though I am not the offended person, my indignation is so great, that I long to kick the fellow round the room!—unless, indeed,—(hesitating and looking earnestly at me,) unless, indeed—it is a partner of your own *creating*?"

I was dreadfully abashed, and could not make any answer.

"But no!" cried he, (again, and with warmth,) "it cannot be that you are so cruel! Softness itself is painted in your eyes:—You could not, surely, have the barbarity so wantonly to trifle with my misery."

I turned away from this nonsense, with real disgust. Mrs. Mirvan saw my confusion, but was perplexed what to think of it, and could not explain to her the cause, lest the Captain should hear me. I therefore proposed to walk, she consented, and we all rose; but, would you believe it? this man had the assurance to rise too, and walk close by my side, as if of my party!

"Now," cried he, "I hope we shall see this ingrate.—Is that he?"—pointing to an old man, who was lame, "or that?" And in this manner he asked me of whoever was old or ugly in the room. I made no sort of answer; and when he found that I was resolutely silent, and walked on, as much as I could, without observing him, he suddenly stamped his foot, and cried out, in a passion, "Fool! ideot! booby!"

I turned hastily toward him: "O, Madam," continued he, "forgive my vehemence, but I am distracted to think there should exist a wretch who can slight a blessing for which I would forfeit my life!—O! that I could but meet him! I would soon—But I grow angry: pardon me, Madam, my passions are violent, and your injuries affect me!"

I began to apprehend he was a madman, and stared at him with the utmost astonishment. "I see you are moved, Madam," said he, "generous creature!—but don't be alarmed, I am cool again, I am indeed,—upon my soul I am,—I entreat you, most lovely of mortals! I entreat you to be easy."

"Indeed, Sir," said I very seriously, "I must insist upon your leaving me; you are quite a stranger to me, and I am both unused, and averse to your language and your manners."

This seemed to have some effect on him. He made me a low bow, begged my pardon, and vowed he would not for the world offend me.

"Then, Sir, you must leave me," cried I.

"I am gone, Madam, I am gone!" with a most tragical air; and he

1. "She sate like Patience on a monument, / Smiling at grief" (Shakespeare, *Twelfth Night* 2.4.114–15).

marched away, a quick pace, out of sight in a moment; but before I had time to congratulate myself, he was again at my elbow.

"And could you really let me go, and not be sorry?—Can you see me suffer torments inexpressible, and yet retain all your favour for that miscreant who flies you?—Ungrateful puppy!—I could bastinado him!"

"For Heaven's sake, my dear," cried Mrs. Mirvan, "who is he talking of?"

"Indeed—I do not know, Madam," said I, "but I wish he would leave me."

"What's all that there?" cried the Captain.

The man made a low bow, and said, "Only, Sir, a slight objection which this young lady makes to dancing with me, and which I am endeavouring to obviate. I shall think myself greatly honoured, if you will intercede for me."

"That lady, Sir," said the Captain coldly, "is her own mistress." And he walked sullenly on.

"You, Madam," said the man, (who looked delighted, to Mrs. Mirvan,) "you, I hope, will have the goodness to speak for me."

"Sir," answered she gravely, "I have not the pleasure of being acquainted with you."

"I hope when you have, Ma'am," cried he, (undaunted) "you will honour me with your approbation; but, while I am yet unknown to you, it would be truly generous in you to countenance me; and, I flatter myself, Madam, that you will not have cause to repent it."

Mrs. Mirvan, with an embarrassed air, replied, "I do not at all mean, Sir, to doubt your being a gentleman,—but—"

"But *what*, Madam?—that doubt removed, why a *but?*"

"Well, Sir," said Mrs. Mirvan (with a good humoured smile,) "I will even treat you with your own plainness, and try what effect that will have on you: I must therefore tell you, once for all——"

"O pardon me Madam!" interrupted he, eagerly, "you must not proceed with those words, *once for all*; no, if I have been too *plain*, and though a *man*, deserve a rebuke, remember, dear ladies, that if you *copy*, you ought in justice, to *excuse* me."

We both stared at the man's strange behaviour.

"Be nobler than your sex," continued he, turning to me, "honour me with one dance, and give up the ingrate who has merited so ill your patience."

Mrs. Mirvan looked with astonishment at us both. "Who does he speak of, my dear?—you never mentioned——"

"O, Madam!" exclaimed he, "he was not worth mentioning—it is pity he was ever thought of; but let us forget his existence. One dance is all I solicit. Permit me, Madam, the honour of this young lady's hand; it will be a favour I shall ever most gratefully acknowledge."

"Sir," answered she, "favours and strangers have with me no connection."

"If you have hitherto," said he, "confined your benevolence to your intimate friends, suffer me to be the first for whom your charity is enlarged."

"Well, Sir, I know not what to say to you,—but—"

He stopt her *but* with so many urgent intreaties, that she at last told me, I must either go down one dance, or avoid his importunities by returning home. I hesitated which alternative to chuse; but this impetuous man at length prevailed, and I was obliged to consent to dance with him.

And thus was my deviation from truth punished; and thus did this man's determined boldness conquer.

During the dance, before we were too much engaged in it for conversation, he was extremely provoking about *my partner*, and tried every means in his power to make me own that I had deceived him; which, though I would not so far humble myself as to acknowledge, was, indeed, but too obvious.

Lord Orville, I fancy, did not dance at all; he seemed to have a large acquaintance, and joined several different parties: but you will easily suppose I was not much pleased to see him, in a few minutes after I was gone, walk towards the place I had just left, and bow, to and join Mrs. Mirvan!

How unlucky I thought myself, that I had not longer withstood this stranger's importunities! The moment we had gone down the dance, I was hastening away from him; but he stopt me, and said that I could by no means return to my party, without giving offence, before we had *done our duty of walking up the dance*.[2] As I know nothing at all of these rules and customs I was obliged to submit to his directions; but I fancy I looked rather uneasy, for he took notice of my inattention, saying, in his free way, "Whence that anxiety?—Why are those lovely eyes perpetually averted?"

"I wish you would say no more to me, Sir," (cried I peevishly,) "you have already destroyed all my happiness for this evening."

"Good Heaven! what is it I have done?—How have I merited this scorn?"

"You have tormented me to death; you have forced me from my friends, and intruded yourself upon me, against my will, for a partner."

"Surely, my dear Madam, we ought to be better friends, since there seems to be something of sympathy in the frankness of our dispositions.—And yet, were you not an angel—how do you think I could brook such contempt?"

2. In a country dance, the couple, after "going down the dance" or dancing between two rows of dancers, must "walk up the dance" or return to their place while other couples take their turns.

"If I have offended you," cried I, "you have but to leave me—and O how I wish you would!"

"My dear creature," (said he, half laughing) "why where could you be educated?"

"Where I most sincerely wish I now was!"

"How conscious you must be, all beautiful that you are, that those charming airs serve only to heighten the bloom of your complexion!"

"Your freedom, Sir, where you are more acquainted, may perhaps be less disagreeable; but to *me*—"

"You do me justice," (cried he, interrupting me) "yes, I do indeed improve upon acquaintance; you will hereafter be quite charmed with me."

"Hereafter, Sir, I hope I shall never—"

"O hush!—hush!—have you forgot the situation in which I found you?—Have you forgot, that when deserted, I pursued you,—when betrayed, I adored you?—but for me—"

"But for you, Sir, I might, perhaps, have been happy."

"What then, am I to conclude that, *but for me,* your *partner* would have appeared?—poor fellow!—and did my presence awe him?"

"I wish *his* presence, Sir, could awe *you!*"

"His presence!—perhaps then you see him?"

"Perhaps, Sir, I do;" cried I, quite wearied of his raillery.

"Where?—where?—for Heaven's sake show me the wretch!"

"Wretch, Sir!"

"O, a very savage!—a sneaking, shame-faced, despicable puppy!"

I know not what bewitched me—but my pride was hurt, and my spirits were tired, and—in short—I had the folly, looking at Lord Orville, to repeat, "*Despicable*, you think?"

His eyes instantly followed mine; "Why, is *that* the gentleman?"

I made no answer; I could not affirm, and I would not deny;—for I hoped to be relieved from his teizing, by his mistake.

The very moment we had done what he called our duty, I eagerly desired to return to Mrs. Mirvan.

"To your *partner* I presume, Madam?" said he, very gravely.

This quite confounded me; I dreaded lest this mischievous man, ignorant of his rank, should address himself to Lord Orville, and say something which might expose my artifice. Fool! to involve myself in such difficulties! I now feared what I had before wished, and therefore, to *avoid* Lord Orville, I was obliged myself to *propose* going down another dance, though I was ready to sink with shame while I spoke.

"But your *partner*, Ma'am?" (said he, affecting a very solemn air) "perhaps he may resent my detaining you: if you will give me leave to ask his consent——"

"Not for the universe."

"Who is he, Madam?"

I wished myself a hundred miles off. He repeated his question,—
"What is his name?"

"Nothing—nobody—I don't know.—"

He assumed a most important solemnity; "How!—not know?—Give
me leave, my dear Madam, to recommend this caution to you; Never
dance in public with a stranger,—with one whose name you are unacquainted with,—who may be a mere adventurer,—a man of no character,—consider to what impertinence you may expose yourself."

Was ever anything so ridiculous? I could not help laughing, in spite
of my vexation.

At this instant, Mrs. Mirvan, followed by Lord Orville, walked up to
us. You will easily believe it was not difficult for me to recover my gravity; but what was my consternation, when this strange man, destined to
be the scourge of my artifice, exclaimed, "Ha! my Lord Orville!—I protest I did not know your Lordship. What can I say for my usurpation?—
Yet, faith, my Lord, such a prize was not to be neglected."

My shame and confusion were unspeakable. Who could have supposed or foreseen that this man knew Lord Orville? But falsehood is not
more unjustifiable than unsafe.

Lord Orville—well he might,—looked all amazement.

"The philosophic coldness of your Lordship," continued this odious
creature, "every man is not endowed with. I have used my utmost
endeavours to entertain this lady, though I fear without success; and
your Lordship will not be a little flattered, if acquainted with the difficulty which attended my procuring the honour of only one dance."
Then, turning to me, who was sinking with shame, while Lord Orville
stood motionless, and Mrs. Mirvan astonished,—he suddenly seized my
hand, saying, "Think, my Lord, what must be my reluctance to resign
this fair hand to your Lordship!"

In the same instant, Lord Orville took it of him; I coloured violently,
and made an effort to recover it. "You do me too much honour, Sir,"
cried he, (with an air of gallantry, pressing it to his lips before he let it
go) "however, I shall be happy to profit by it, if this lady," (turning to
Mrs. Mirvan) "will permit me to seek for her party."

To compel him thus to dance, I could not endure, and eagerly called
out, "By no means—not for the world!—I must beg——"

"Will you honour *me*, Madam, with your commands," cried my tormentor; "may *I* seek the lady's party?"

"No, Sir," answered I, turning from him.

"What *shall* be done, my dear?" said Mrs. Mirvan.

"Nothing, Ma'am;—any thing, I mean——"

"But do you dance, or not? you see his Lordship waits."

"I hope not,—I beg that—I would not for the world—I am sure I
ought to—to——"

I could not speak; but that confident man, determined to discover whether or not I had deceived him, said to Lord Orville, who stood suspended, "My Lord, this affair, which, at present, seems perplexed, I will briefly explain;—this lady proposed to me another dance,—nothing could have made me more happy—I only wished for your Lordship's permission; which, if now granted, will, I am persuaded, set every thing right."

I glowed with indignation. "No, Sir—It is your absence, and that alone, can set everything right."

"For Heaven's sake, my dear," (cried Mrs. Mirvan, who could no longer contain her surprise,) "what does all this mean?—were you pre-engaged?—had Lord Orville——"

"No, Madam," cried I, "only—only I did not know that gentleman,—and so—and so I thought—I intended—I——"

Overpowered by all that had passed, I had not strength to make my mortifying explanation;—my spirits quite failed me, and I burst into tears.

They all seemed shocked and amazed.

"What is the matter, my dearest love?" cried Mrs. Mirvan, with the kindest concern.

"What have I done?" exclaimed my evil genius, and ran officiously for a glass of water.

However, a hint was sufficient for Lord Orville, who comprehended all I would have explained. He immediately led me to a seat, and said, in a low voice, "Be not distressed, I beseech you; I shall ever think my name honoured by your making use of it."

This politeness relieved me. A general murmur had alarmed Miss Mirvan, who flew instantly to me; while Lord Orville, the moment Mrs. Mirvan had taken the water, led my tormentor away.

"For Heaven's sake, dear Madam," cried I, "let me go home,—indeed, I cannot stay here any longer."

"Let us all go," cried my kind Maria.

"But the Captain—what will he say—I had better go home in a chair."

Mrs. Mirvan consented, and I rose to depart. Lord Orville and that man both came to me. The first, with an attention I but ill merited from him, led me to chair,[3] while the other followed, pestering me with apologies. I wished to have made mine to Lord Orville, but was too much ashamed.

It was about one o'clock. Mrs. Mirvan's servants saw me home.

And now,—what again shall ever tempt me to an assembly? I dread to hear what you will think of me, my most dear and honoured Sir: you will need your utmost partiality, to receive me without displeasure.

This morning Lord Orville has sent to enquire after our healths: and

3. A sedan or enclosed chair for one person, carried on poles by two men.

Sir Clement Willoughby, for that, I find, is the name of my persecutor, has called: but I would not go down stairs till he was gone.

And now, my dear Sir, I can somewhat account for the strange, provoking, and ridiculous conduct of this Sir Clement last night; for Miss Mirvan says, he is the very man with whom she heard Lord Orville conversing at Mrs. Stanley's, when I was spoken of in so mortifying a manner. He was pleased to say he was glad to hear I was a fool, and therefore, I suppose, he concluded he might talk as much nonsense as he pleased to me: however, I am very indifferent as to his opinion;—but for Lord Orville,—if then he thought me an ideot, now, I am sure, he must suppose me both bold and presuming. Make use of his name!— what impertinence!—he can never know how it happened,—he can only imagine it was from an excess of vanity;—well, however, I shall leave this bad city to-morrow, and never again will I enter it!

The Captain intends to take us to-night to the Fantocini.[4] I cannot bear that Captain; I can give you no idea how gross he is. I heartily rejoice that he was not present at the disagreeable conclusion of yesterday's adventure, for I am sure he would have contributed to my confusion; which might perhaps have diverted him, as he seldom or never smiles but at some other person's expence.

And here I conclude my London letters,—and without any regret; for I am too inexperienced and ignorant to conduct myself with propriety in this town, where everything is new to me, and many things are unaccountable and perplexing.

Adieu, my dear Sir; Heaven restore me safely to you! I wish I was to go immediately to Berry Hill; yet the wish is ungrateful to Mrs. Mirvan, and therefore I will repress it. I shall write an account of the Fantocini from Howard Grove. We have not been to half the public places that are now open, though I dare say you will think we have been to all. But they are almost as innumerable as the persons who fill them.

Letter XIV.

EVELINA IN CONTINUATION.

Queen-Ann-Street, April 13.

How much will you be surprised, my dearest Sir, at receiving another letter from London of your Evelina's writing! But, believe me, it was not my fault, neither is it my happiness, that I am still here: our journey has been postponed by an accident equally unexpected and disagreeable.

We went last night to see the Fantocini, where we had infinite entertainment from the performance of a little comedy, in French and Italian, by puppets, so admirably managed, that they both astonished and

4. A puppet show.

diverted us all, except the Captain, who has a fixed and most prejudiced hatred of whatever is not English.

When it was over, while we waited for the coach, a tall elderly woman brushed quickly past us, calling out, "My God, what shall I do?"

"Why what *would* you do?" cried the Captain.

"*Ma foi, Monsieur,*"[1] answered she, "I have lost my company, and in this place I don't know nobody."

There was something foreign in her accent, though it was difficult to discover whether she was an English or a French woman. She was very well dressed, and seemed so entirely at a loss what to do, that Mrs. Mirvan proposed to the Captain to assist her.

"Assist her!" cried he, "ay, with all my heart; — let a link-boy[2] call her a coach."

There was not one to be had, and it rained very fast.

"*Mon Dieu*" exclaimed the stranger, "what shall become of me? *Je suis au desespoir!*"[3]

"Dear Sir," cried Miss Mirvan, "pray let us take the poor lady into our coach. She is quite alone, and a foreigner — —."

"She's never the better for that," answered he: "she may be a woman of the town,[4] for anything you know."

"She does not appear such," said Mrs. Mirvan, "and indeed she seems so much distressed, that we shall but follow the golden rule, if we carry her to her lodgings."

"You are mighty fond of new acquaintance," returned he, "but first let us know if she be going our way."

Upon enquiry, we found that she lived in Oxford Road, and, after some disputing, the Captain, surlily, and with a very bad grace, consented to admit her into his coach; though he soon convinced us, that he was determined she should not be too much obliged to him, for he seemed absolutely bent upon quarrelling with her: for which strange inhospitality, I can assign no other reason, than that she appeared to be a foreigner.

The conversation began, by her telling us, that she had been in England only two days; that the gentlemen belonging to her were Parisians, and had left her, to see for a hackney-coach,[5] as her own carriage was abroad; and that she had waited for them till she was quite frightened, and concluded that they had lost themselves.

"And pray," said the Captain, "why did you go to a public place without an Englishman?"

"*Ma foi*, Sir," answered she, "because none of my acquaintance is in town."

1. "Faith, Sir."
2. A boy with a torch who ran ahead of the chair to light the way.
3. "My God . . . I am in despair!"
4. A prostitute.
5. A carriage kept for hire.

"Why then," said he, "I'll tell you what; your best way is to go out of it yourself."

"*Pardi,*[6] *Monsieur,*" returned she, "and so I shall; for, I promise you, I think the English a parcel of brutes; and I'll go back to France as fast as I can, for I would not live among none of you."

"Who wants you?" cried the Captain: "do you suppose, Madam French, we have not enough of other nations to pick our pockets already? I'll warrant you, there's no need for you for to put in your oar."

"Pick your pockets, Sir! I wish nobody wanted to pick your pockets no more than I do; and I'll promise you, you'd be safe enough. But there's no nation under the sun can beat the English for ill-politeness; for my part, I hate the very sight of them, and so I shall only just visit a person of quality or two, of my particular acquaintance, and then I shall go back again to France."

"Ay, do;" cried he, "and then go to the devil together, for that's the fittest voyage for the French and the quality."

"We'll take care, however," cried the stranger, with great vehemence, "not to admit none of your vulgar, unmannered English among us."

"O never fear," (returned he coolly) "we shan't dispute the point with you; you and the quality may have the devil all to yourselves."

Desirous of changing the subject of a conversation which now became very alarming, Miss Mirvan called out, "Lord, how slow the man drives!"

"Never mind, Moll," said her father, "I'll warrant you he'll drive fast enough tomorrow, when you are going to Howard Grove."

"To Howard Grove!" exclaimed the stranger; "why *mon Dieu*, do you know Lady Howard?"

"Why, what if we do?" answered he; "that's nothing to you; she's none of *your* quality, I'll promise you."

"Who told you that?" cried she, "you don't know nothing about the matter; besides, you're the ill-bredest person ever I see; and as to your knowing Lady Howard, I don't believe no such a thing; unless, indeed, you are her steward."

The Captain, swearing terribly, said, with great fury, "*you* would much sooner be taken for her wash-woman."

"Her wash-woman, indeed!—Ha, ha, ha!—why you han't no eyes; did you ever see a wash-woman in such a gown as this?—besides, I'm no such mean person, for I'm as good as Lady Howard, and as rich too; and besides, I'm now come to England to visit her."

"You may spare yourself that there trouble," said the Captain, "she has paupers enough about her already."

"Paupers, Mr.!—no more a pauper than yourself, nor so much nei-

6. An attenuated form of "pardieu," i.e., "by God."

ther;—but you are a low, dirty fellow, and I shan't stoop to take no more notice of you."

"Dirty fellow!" (exclaimed the Captain, seizing both her wrists) "hark you, Mrs. Frog, you'd best hold your tongue, for I must make bold to tell you, if you don't, that I shall make no ceremony of tripping you out of the window; and there you may lie in the mud till some of your *Monseers* come to help you out of it."

Their encreasing passion quite terrified us; and Mrs. Mirvan was beginning to remonstrate with the Captain, when we were all silenced by what follows.

"Let me go, villain that you are, let me go, or I'll promise you I'll get you put to prison for this usage; I'm no common person, I assure you, and, *ma foi*, I'll go to Justice Fielding[7] about you; for I'm a person of fashion, and I'll make you know it, or my name i'n't Duval."

I heard no more: amazed, frightened, and unspeakably shocked, an involuntary exclamation of *Gracious Heaven!* escaped me, and, more dead than alive, I sunk into Mrs. Mirvan's arms. But let me draw a veil over a scene too cruel for a heart so compassionately tender as yours; it is sufficient that you know this supposed foreigner proved to be Madame Duval,—the grandmother of your Evelina!

O, Sir, to discover so near a relation in a woman who had thus introduced herself!—what would become of me, were it not for you, my protector, my friend, and my refuge?

My extreme concern, and Mrs. Mirvan's surprise, immediately betrayed me. But, I will not shock you with the manner of her acknowledging me, or the bitterness, the *grossness*—I cannot otherwise express myself,—with which she spoke of those unhappy past transactions you have so pathetically related to me. All the misery of a much injured parent, dear, though never seen, regretted, though never known, crowded so forcibly upon my memory, that they rendered this interview—one only excepted—the most afflicting I can ever know.

When we stopt at her lodgings, she desired me to accompany her into the house, and said she could easily procure a room for me to sleep in. Alarmed and trembling, I turned to Mrs. Mirvan. "My daughter, Madam," said that sweet woman, "cannot so abruptly part with her young friend; you must allow a little time to wean them from each other."

"Pardon me, Ma'am," answered Madame Duval, (who, from the time of her being known, somewhat softened her manners) "Miss can't possibly be so nearly connected to this child as I am."

"No matter for that," cried the Captain, (who espoused my cause to satisfy his own pique, though an awkward apology had passed between

---

7. Sir John Fielding (d. 1780), blind half-brother of Henry Fielding. He was appointed to the magistracy for Westminster in 1751 and for Middlesex in 1754.

them) "she was sent to us, and so, dy'e see, we don't chuse for to part with her."

I promised to wait upon her at what time she pleased the next day, and, after a short debate, she desired me to breakfast with her, and we proceeded to Queen-Ann-street.

What an unfortunate adventure! I could not close my eyes the whole night. A thousand times I wished I had never left Berry Hill; however, my return thither shall be accelerated to the utmost of my power; and, once more in that abode of tranquil happiness, I will suffer no temptation to allure me elsewhere.

Mrs. Mirvan was so kind as to acccompany me to Madame Duval's house this morning. The Captain too, offered his service, which I declined, from a fear she should suppose I meant to insult her.

She frowned most terribly upon Mrs. Mirvan, but she received me with as much tenderness as I believe she is capable of feeling. Indeed, our meeting seems really to have affected her; for when, overcome by the variety of emotions which the sight of her occasioned, I almost fainted in her arms, she burst into tears, and said, "Let me not lose my poor daughter a second time!" This unexpected humanity softened me extremely; but she very soon excited my warmest indignation, by the ungrateful mention she made of the best of men, my dear, and most generous benefactor. However, grief and anger mutually gave way to terror, upon her avowing the intention of her visiting England was to make me return with her to France. This, she said, was a plan she had formed from the instant she had heard of my birth, which, she protested, did not reach her ears till I must have been twelve years of age; but Monsieur Duval who, she declared, was the worst husband in the world, would not permit her to do any thing she wished: he had been dead but three months, which had been employed in arranging certain affairs, that were no sooner settled, than she set off for England. She was already out of mourning, for she said nobody here could tell how long she had been a widow.

She must have been married very early in life; what her age is, I do not know; but she really looks to be less than fifty. She dresses very gaily, paints very high, and the traces of former beauty are still very visible in her face.

I know not when, or how, this visit would have ended, had not the Captain called for Mrs. Mirvan, and absolutely insisted upon my attending her. He is become, very suddenly, so warmly my friend, that I quite dread his officiousness. Mrs. Mirvan, however, whose principal study seems to be healing those wounds which her husband inflicts, appeased Madame Duval's wrath, by a very polite invitation to drink tea and spend the evening here. Not without great difficulty was the Captain prevailed upon to defer his journey some time longer; but what could be done? it would have been indecent for me to have quitted town the very instant I discovered that Madame Duval was in it; and to have stayed here solely under her protection—Mrs. Mirvan, thank Heaven, was too kind for such a thought. That she should follow us to Howard Grove, I almost equally dreaded; it is, therefore determined that we remain in London for some days, or a week: though the Captain has declared that the *old French hag*, as he is pleased to call her, shall fare never the better for it.

My only hope, is to get safe to Berry Hill; where, counselled and sheltered by you, I shall have nothing more to fear. Adieu, my ever dear and most honoured Sir! I shall have no happiness till I am again with you!

Letter XV.

MR. VILLARS TO EVELINA.

Berry Hill, April 16.

In the belief and hope that my Evelina would ere now have bid adieu to London, I had intended to have deferred writing, till I heard of her return to Howard Grove; but the letter I have this moment received, with intelligence of Madame Duval's arrival in England, demands an immediate answer.

Her journey hither equally grieves and alarms me: how much did I pity my child, when I read of a discovery at once so unexpected and unwished! I have long dreaded this meeting and its consequence; to claim you, seems naturally to follow acknowledging you: I am well acquainted with her disposition, and have for many years foreseen the contest which now threatens us.

Cruel as are the circumstances of this affair, you must not, my love, suffer it to depress your spirits; remember, that while life is lent me, I will devote it to your service; and, for future time, I will make such provision as shall seem to me most conducive to your future happiness. Secure of my protection, and relying on my tenderness, let no apprehensions of Madame Duval disturb your peace; conduct yourself towards her with all the respect and deference due to so near a relation, remembering always, that the failure of duty on her part, can by no means justify any neglect on yours: indeed, the more forcibly you are struck with improprieties and misconduct in another, the greater should be your observance and diligence to avoid even the shadow of similar errors. Be careful, therefore, that no remissness of attention, no indifference of obliging, make known to her the independance I assure you of; but when she fixes the time for her leaving England, trust to me the task of refusing your attending her: disagreeable to myself I own it will be, yet to you, it would be improper, if not impossible.

In regard to her opinion of me, I am more sorry than surprised at her determined blindness; the palliation which she feels the want of, for her own conduct, leads her to seek for failings in all who were concerned in those unhappy transactions which she has so much reason to lament. And this, as it is the cause, so we must, in some measure, consider it as the excuse of her inveteracy.

How grateful to me are your wishes to return to Berry Hill! your lengthened stay in London, and the dissipation in which I find you are involved, fill me with uneasiness. I mean not however that I would have you sequester yourself from the party to which you belong, since Mrs. Mirvan might thence infer a reproof which your youth and her kindness would render inexcusable. I will not, therefore, enlarge upon this subject, but content myself with telling you, that I shall heartily rejoice when I hear of your safe arrival at Howard Grove, for which place I hope you will be preparing at the time you receive this letter.

I cannot too much thank you, my best Evelina, for the minuteness of your communications; continue to me this indulgence, for I should be miserable if in ignorance of your proceedings.

How new to you is the scene of life in which you are now engaged,—balls—plays—operas—ridottos—Ah, my child! at your return hither, how will you bear the change? My heart trembles for your future tranquillity.—Yet I will hope every thing from the unsullied whiteness of your soul, and the native liveliness of your disposition.

I am sure I need not say, how much more I was pleased with the mistakes of your inexperience at the private ball, than with the attempted adoption of more fashionable manners at the ridotto. But your confusion and mortifications were such as to entirely silence all reproofs on my part.

I hope you will see no more of Sir Clement Willoughby, whose conversation and boldness are extremely disgustful to me. I was gratified by the good-nature of Lord Orville, upon your making use of his name, but I hope you will never again put it to such a trial.

Heaven bless thee, my dear child, and grant that neither misfortune nor vice may ever rob thee of that gaiety of heart which, resulting from innocence, while it constitutes your own, contributes also to the felicity of all who know you!

ARTHUR VILLARS.

Letter XVI.

EVELINA TO THE REV. MR. VILLARS.

Queen-Ann-Street, Thursday morning, April 14.

Before our dinner was over yesterday, Madame Duval came to tea: though it will lessen your surprise, to hear that it was near five o'clock, for we never dine till the day is almost over. She was asked into another room, while the table was cleared, and then was invited to partake of the desert.

She was attended by a French gentleman, whom she introduced by the name of Monsieur Du Bois: Mrs. Mirvan received them both with her usual politeness; but the Captain looked very much displeased, and after a short silence, very sternly said to Madame Duval, "Pray who asked you to bring that there spark with you?"

"O," cried she, "I never go no-where without him."

Another short silence ensued, which was terminated by the Captain's turning roughly to the foreigner, and saying, "Do you know, *Monseer*, that you are the first Frenchman I ever let come into my house?"

Monsieur Du Bois made a profound bow. He speaks no English, and understands it so imperfectly, that he might, possibly, imagine he had received a compliment.

Mrs. Mirvan endeavoured to divert the Captain's ill-humour, by starting new subjects; but he left to her all the trouble of supporting them, and leant back in his chair in gloomy silence, except when any opportunity offered of uttering some sarcasm upon the French. Finding her efforts to render the evening agreeable were fruitless, Mrs. Mirvan proposed a party to Ranelagh. Madame Duval joyfully consented to it, and the Captain, though he railed against the dissipation of the women, did not oppose it, and therefore Maria and I ran up stairs to dress ourselves.

Before we were ready, word was brought us that Sir Clement Willoughby was in the drawing-room. He introduced himself under the pretence of enquiring after all our healths, and entered the room with the easy air of an old acquaintance; though Mrs. Mirvan confesses that he seemed embarrassed, when he found how coldly he was received, not only by the Captain, but by herself.

I was extremely disconcerted at the thoughts of seeing this man again, and did not go downstairs till I was called to tea. He was then deeply engaged in a discourse upon French manners with Madame Duval and the Captain, and the subject seemed so entirely to engross him, that he did not, at first, observe my entrance into the room. Their conversation was supported with great vehemence; the Captain roughly maintaining the superiority of the English in every particular, and Madame Duval warmly refusing to allow of it in any; while Sir Clement exerted all his powers of argument and of ridicule to second and strengthen whatever was advanced by the Captain: for he had the sagacity to discover, that he could take no method so effectual for making the master of the house his friend, as to make Madame Duval his enemy: and indeed, in a very short time, he had reason to congratulate himself upon his successful discernment.

As soon as he saw me, he made a most respectful bow, and hoped I had not suffered from the fatigue of the ridotto: I made no other answer than a slight inclination of the head, for I was very much ashamed of that whole affair. He then returned to the disputants, where he managed the argument so skillfully, at once provoking Madame Duval, and delighting the Captain, that I could not forbear admiring his address, though I condemned his subtlety. Mrs. Mirvan, dreading such violent antagonists, attempted frequently to change the subject; and she might have succeeded, but for the interposition of Sir Clement, who would not suffer it to be given up, and supported it with such humour and satire, that he seems to have won the Captain's heart; though their united forces so enraged and overpowered Madame Duval, that she really trembled with passion.

I was very glad when Mrs. Mirvan said it was time to be gone. Sir Clement arose to take leave; but the Captain very cordially invited him to join our party: he *had* an engagement, he said, but would give it up to have that pleasure.

Some little confusion ensued in regard to our manner of setting off; Mrs. Mirvan offered Madame Duval a place in her coach, and proposed that we four females should go all together: however, this she rejected, declaring she would by no means go so far without a gentleman, and wondering so polite a lady could make *so English* a proposal. Sir Clement Willoughby said his chariot[1] was waiting at the door, and begged to know if it could be of any use. It was, at last, decided, that a hackney-coach, should be called for Monsieur Du Bois and Madame Duval, in which the Captain, and, at his request, Sir Clement, went also; Mrs. and Miss Mirvan and I had a peaceful and comfortable ride by ourselves.

I doubt not but they quarrelled all the way; for when we met at Ranelagh, every one seemed out of humour: and, though we joined parties, poor Madame Duval was avoided as much as possible by all but me.

The room was so very much crowded, that, but for the uncommon assiduity of Sir Clement Willoughby, we should not have been able to procure a box (which is the name given to the arched recesses that are appropriated for tea-parties) till half the company had retired. As we were taking possession of our places, some ladies of Mrs. Mirvan's acquaintance stopped to speak to her, and persuaded her to *take a round*[2] with them. When she returned to us, what was my surprise, to see that Lord Orville had joined her party! The ladies walked on; Mrs. Mirvan seated herself, and made a slight, though respectful, invitation to Lord Orville to drink his tea with us; which, to my no small consternation, he accepted.

I felt a confusion unspeakable at again seeing him, from the recollection of the ridotto adventure: nor did my situation lessen it, for I was seated between Madame Duval and Sir Clement, who seemed as little

---

1. A coach was a large four-wheeled, enclosed carriage, pulled by either four or six horses; a chariot was a light four-wheeled, enclosed carriage.
2. Walk once around the place.

as myself to desire Lord Orville's presence. Indeed, the continual wrangling and ill-breeding of Captain Mirvan and Madame Duval, made me blush that I belonged to them. And poor Mrs. Mirvan and her amiable daughter had still less reason to be satisfied.

A general silence ensued after he was seated: his appearance, from different motives, gave a universal restraint to every body. What his own reasons were for honouring us with his company, I cannot imagine, unless, indeed, he had a curiosity to know whether I should invent any new impertinence concerning him.

The first speech was made by Madame Duval, who said, "It's quite a shocking thing to see ladies come to so genteel a place as Ranelagh with hats on; it has a monstrous vulgar look: I can't think what they wear them for. There is no such a thing to be seen in Paris."

"Indeed," cried Sir Clement, "I must own myself no advocate for hats; I am sorry the ladies ever invented or adopted so tantalizing a fashion; for, where there is beauty, they only serve to shade it, and, where there is none, to excite a most unavailing curiosity. I fancy they were originally worn by some young and whimsical coquet."

"More likely," answered the Captain, "they were invented by some wrinkled old hag, who'd a mind for to keep the young fellows in chace, let them be never so weary."

"I don't know what you may do in England," cried Madame Duval, "but I know in Paris no woman need n't be at such a trouble as that, to be taken very genteel notice of."

"Why, will you pretend for to say," returned the Captain, "that they don't distinguish the old from the young there as well as here?"

"They don't make no distinguishments at all," said she; "they're vastly too polite."

"More fools they!" cried the Captain, sneeringly.

"Would to Heaven," cried Sir Clement, "that, for our own sakes, we Englishmen too were blest with so accommodating a blindness!"

"Why the devil do you make such a prayer as that?" demanded the Captain: "them are the first foolish words I've heard you speak; but I suppose you're not much used to that sort of work. Did you ever make a prayer before, since you were a sniveler?"

"Ay, now," cried Madame Duval, "that's another of the unpolitenesses of you English, to go to talking of such things as that: now in Paris, nobody never says nothing about religion, no more than about politics."

"Why then," answered he, "it's a sign they take no more care of their souls than of their country, and so both one and t'other go to old Nick."

"Well, if they do," said she, "who's the worse, so long as they don't say nothing about it? it's the tiresomest thing in the world to be always talking of them sort of things, and nobody that's ever been abroad troubles their heads about them."

"Pray then," cried the Captain, "since you know so much of the matter, be so good as to tell us what they *do* trouble their heads about?—hay, Sir Clement! ha'n't we a right to know that much?"

"A very comprehensive question," said Sir Clement, "and I expect much instruction from the lady's answer."

"Come, Madam," continued the Captain, "never flinch; speak at once; don't stop for thinking."

"I assure you I am not going," answered she; "for as to what they *do* do, why they've enough to do, I promise you, what with one thing or another."

"But *what, what* do they do, these famous *Monseers?*" demanded the Captain; "can't you tell us? do they game?—or drink?—or fiddle?—or are they jockeys?—or do they spend all their time in flummering[3] old women?"

"As to that, Sir,—but indeed I shan't trouble myself to answer such a parcel of low questions, so don't ask me no more about it." And then, to my great vexation, turning to Lord Orville, she said, "Pray, Sir, was you ever in Paris?"

He only bowed.

"And pray, Sir, how did you like it?"

This *comprehensive* question, as Sir Clement would have called it, though it made him smile, also made him hesitate; however, his answer was expressive of his approbation.

"I thought you would like it, Sir, because you look so like a gentleman. As to the Captain, and as to that other gentleman, why they may very well not like what they don't know: for I suppose, Sir, you was never abroad?"

"Only three years, Ma'am," answered Sir Clement, drily.

"Well, that's very surprising! I should never have thought it: however, I dare say you only kept company with the English."

"Why pray, who *should* he keep company with?" cried the Captain: "what, I suppose you'd have him ashamed of his own nation, like some other people not a thousand miles off, on purpose to make his own nation ashamed of him?"

"I'm sure it wou'd be a very good thing if you'd go abroad yourself."

"How will you make out that, hay, Madam? come, please to tell me, where wou'd be the good of that?"

"Where! why a great deal. They'd make quite another person of you."

"What, I suppose you'd have me learn to cut capers?—and dress like a monkey?—and palaver[4] in French gibberish?—hay, would you?—And powder, and daub, and make myself up, like some other folks?"

"I would have you learn to be more politer, Sir, and not to talk to ladies in such a rude, old-fashion way as this. You, Sir, as have been in

3. Flattering.
4. To speak flatteringly.

Paris" (again addressing herself to Lord Orville) "can tell this English gentleman how he'd be despised, if he was to talk in such an ungenteel manner as this, before any foreigners. Why there isn't a hair-dresser, nor a shoe-maker, nor nobody, that would n't blush to be in your company."

"Why look ye, Madam," answered the Captain, "as to your hair-pinchers and shoe-blacks, you may puff off their manners, and welcome; and I am heartily glad you like 'em so well; but as to me, since you must needs make so free of your advice, I must e'en tell you, I never kept company with any such gentry."

"Come, ladies and gentlemen," said Mrs. Mirvan, "as many of you as have done tea, I invite to walk with me." Maria and I started up instantly; Lord Orville followed; and I question whether we were not half round the room ere the angry disputants knew that we had left the box.

As the husband of Mrs. Mirvan had borne so large a share in this disagreeable altercation, Lord Orville forbore to make any comments upon it; so that the subject was immediately dropt, and the conversation became calmly sociable, and politely chearful, and, to every body but me, must have been highly agreeable:—but, as to myself, I was so eagerly desirous of making some apology to Lord Orville for the imperti-nence of which he must have thought me guilty at the ridotto, and yet so utterly unable to assume sufficient courage to speak to him concern-ing an affair in which I had so terribly exposed myself, that I hardly ventured to say a word all the time we were walking. Besides, the knowl-edge of his contemptuous opinion, haunted and dispirited me, and made me fear he might possibly misconstrue whatever I should say. So that, far from enjoying a conversation which might, at any other time, have delighted me, I continued silent, uncomfortable, and ashamed. O Sir, shall I ever again involve myself in so foolish an embarrassment? I am sure that if I do, I shall deserve yet greater mortification.

We were not joined by the rest of the party till we had taken three or four turns around the room, and then, they were so quarrelsome, that Mrs. Mirvan complained of being fatigued, and proposed going home. No one dissented. Lord Orville joined another party, having first made an offer of his services, which the gentlemen declined, and we pro-ceeded to an outward room, where we waited for the carriages. It was settled that we should return to town in the same manner we came to Ranelagh, and, accordingly, Monsieur Du Bois handed Madame Duval into a hackney-coach, and was just preparing to follow her, when she screamed, and jumpt hastily out, declaring she was wet through all her clothes. Indeed, upon examination, the coach was found to be in a dismal condition; for the weather proved very bad, and the rain had, though I know not how, made its way into the carriage.

Mrs. and Miss Mirvan, and myself, were already disposed of as before; but no sooner did the Captain hear this account, than, without any ceremony, he was so civil as to immediately take possession of the vacant seat in his own coach, leaving Madame Duval and Monsieur Du Bois to take care of themselves. As to Sir Clement Willoughby, his own chariot was in waiting.

I instantly begged permission to offer Madame Duval my own place, and made a motion to get out; but Mrs. Mirvan stopped me, saying that I should then be obliged to return to town with only the foreigner, or Sir Clement.

"O never mind the old Beldame," cried the Captain, "she's weatherproof, I'll answer for her; and besides as we are all, I hope, *English*, why she'll meet with no worse than she expects from us."

"I do not mean to defend her," said Mrs. Mirvan; "but indeed, as she belongs to our party, we cannot, with any decency, leave the place, till she is, by some means, accommodated."

"Lord, my dear," cried the Captain, whom the distress of Madame Duval had put into very good humour, "why she'll break her heart, if she meets with any civility from a filthy Englishman."

Mrs. Mirvan, however, prevailed, and we all got out of the coach, to wait till Madame Duval could meet with some better carriage. We found her, attended by Monsieur Du Bois, standing amongst the servants, and very busy in wiping her negligee, and endeavouring to save it from being stained by the wet, as she said it was a new Lyons silk.[5] Sir Clement Willoughby offered her the use of his chariot, but she had been too much piqued by his raillery to accept it. We waited some time, but in vain, for no hackney-coach could be procured. The Captain, at last, was persuaded to accompany Sir Clement himself, and we four females were handed into Mrs. Mirvan's carriage, though not before Madame Duval had insisted upon our making room for Monsieur Du Bois, to which the Captain only consented in preference to being incommoded by him in Sir Clement's chariot.

Our party drove off first. We were silent and unsociable; for the difficulties attending this arrangement had made every one languid and fatigued. Unsociable, I must own, we continued; but very short was the duration of our silence, as we had not proceeded thirty yards before every voice was heard at once,—for the coach broke down! I suppose we concluded of course, that we were all half killed, by the violent shrieks that seemed to come from every mouth. The chariot was stopped, the servants came to our assistance, and we were taken out of the carriage, without having been at all hurt. The night was dark and wet; but I had scarce touched the ground, when I was lifted suddenly from it, by Sir Clement Willoughby, who begged permission to assist me, though he did not wait to have it granted, but carried me in his arms back to Ranelagh.

5. Negligee: a loose gown; Lyons silk: expensive silk from Lyons, France.

He enquired very earnestly if I was not hurt by the accident? I assured him I was perfectly safe, and free from injury, and desired he would leave me, and return to the rest of the party, for I was very uneasy to know whether they had been equally fortunate. He told me he was happy in being honoured with my commands, and would joyfully execute them; but insisted upon first conducting me to a warm room, as I had not wholly escaped being wet. He did not regard my objections, but made me follow him to an apartment, where we found an excellent fire, and some company waiting for carriages. I readily accepted a seat, and then begged he would go.

And go, indeed, he did; but he returned in a moment, telling me that the rain was more violent than ever, and that he had sent his servants to offer their assistance, and acquaint *the Mirvans* of my situation. I was very mad that he would not go himself; but as my acquaintance with him was so very slight, I did not think proper to urge him contrary to his inclination.

Well, he drew a chair close to mine, and, after again enquiring how I did, said, in a low voice, "You will pardon me, Miss Anville, if the eagerness I feel to vindicate myself, induces me to snatch this opportunity of making sincere acknowledgments for the impertinence with which I tormented you at the last ridotto. I can assure you, Madam, I have been a true and sorrowful penitent ever since; but—shall I tell you honestly what encouraged me to——"

He stopt; but I said nothing, for I thought instantly of the conversation Miss Mirvan had overheard, and supposed he was going to tell me himself what part Lord Orville had borne in it; and really I did not wish to hear it repeated. Indeed, the rest of his speech convinces me that such was his intention; with what view, I know not, except to make a merit of his defending me.

"And yet," he continued, "my excuse may only expose my own credulity, and want of judgment and penetration. I will, therefore, merely beseech your pardon, and hope that some future time——"

Just then, the door was opened by Sir Clement's servant, and I had the pleasure of seeing the Captain, Mrs. and Miss Mirvan, enter the room.

"O ho," cried the former, "you have got a good warm birth[6] here; but we shall beat up your quarters.[7] Here, Lucy, Moll, come to the fire, and dry your trumpery.[8] But, hey-day,—why where's old Madame French?"

"Good God," cried I, "is not Madame Duval then with you?"

"With me! No,—thank God."

I was very uneasy to know what might have become of her, and, if they would have suffered me, I should have gone out in search of her

6. Berth.
7. Arouse or disturb; visit unceremoniously.
8. Trifles, trash.

myself; but all the servants were dispatched to find her, and the Captain
said we might be very sure her *French beau* would take care of her.

We waited some time without any tidings, and were soon the only
party in the room. My uneasiness increased so much that Sir Clement
now made a voluntary offer of seeking her. However, the same moment
that he opened the door with this design, she presented herself at it,
attended by Monsieur Du Bois.

"I was this instant, Madam," said he, "coming to see for you."

"You are mighty good, truly," cried she, "to come when all the mischief's over."

She then entered,—in such a condition!—entirely covered with mud,
and in so great a rage, it was with difficulty she could speak. We all
expressed our concern, and offered our assistance,—except the Captain,
who no sooner beheld her, than he burst out into a loud laugh.

We endeavoured, by our enquiries and condolements, to prevent her
attending to him; and she was, for some time, so wholly engrossed by
her anger and her distress, that we succeeded without much trouble.
We begged her to inform us how this accident had happened. "How!"
repeated she,—"why it was all along of your all going away,—and there
poor Monsieur Du Bois—but it was n't his fault,—for he's as bad off as
me."

All eyes were then turned to Monsieur Du Bois, whose clothes were
in the same miserable plight with those of Madame Duval, and who,
wet, shivering, and disconsolate, had crept to the fire.

The Captain laughed yet more heartily; while Mrs. Mirvan, ashamed
of his rudeness, repeated her enquiries to Madame Duval; who
answered, "Why, as we were a-coming along, all in the rain, Monsieur
Du Bois was so obliging, though I'm sure it was an unlucky obligingness
for me, as to lift me up in his arms, to carry me over a place that was
ancle-deep in mud; but instead of my being ever the better for it, just as
we were in the worst part,—I'm sure I wish we had been fifty miles
off,—for, somehow or other, his foot slipt,—at least, I suppose so,—
though I can't think how it happened, for I'm no such great weight,—
but, however that was, down we both came together, all in the mud;
and the more we tried to get up, the more deeper we got covered with
the nastiness—and my new Lyons negligee, too, quite spoilt!—however,
it's well we got up at all, for we might have laid there till now, for aught
you all cared; nobody never came near us."

This recital put the Captain into an extacy; he went from the lady to
the gentleman, and from the gentleman to the lady, to enjoy alternately
the sight of their distress. He really shouted with pleasure; and, shaking
Monsieur Du Bois strenuously by the hand, wished him joy of having
touched English ground; and then he held a candle to Madame Duval,
that he might have a more complete view of her disaster, declaring
repeatedly, that he had never been better pleased in his life.

The rage of poor Madame Duval was unspeakable; she dashed the candle out of his hand, stamped upon the floor, and, at last spat in his face.

This action seemed immediately to calm them both, as the joy of the Captain was converted into resentment, and the wrath of Madame Duval into fear; for he put his hands upon her shoulders, and gave her so violent a shake, that she screamed out for help; assuring her, at the same time, that if she had been one ounce less old, or less ugly, she should have had it all returned on her own face.

Monsieur Du Bois, who had seated himself very quietly at the fire, approached them, and expostulated very warmly with the Captain; but he was neither understood nor regarded, and Madame Duval was not released, till she quite sobbed with passion.

When they were parted, I entreated her to permit the woman who has charge of the ladies cloaks to assist in drying her clothes; she consented, and we did what was possible to save her from catching cold. We were obliged to wait in this disagreeable situation near an hour, before a hackney-coach could be found; and then we were disposed in the same manner as before our accident.

I am going this morning to see poor Madame Duval, and to enquire after her health, which I think must have suffered by her last night's misfortunes; though, indeed, she seems to be naturally strong and hearty.

Adieu, my dear Sir, till to-morrow.

Letter XVII.

EVELINA IN CONTINUATION.

Friday morning, April 15.

Sir Clement Willoughby called here yesterday at noon, and Captain Mirvan invited him to dinner. For my part, I spent the day in a manner the most uncomfortable imaginable.

I found Madame Duval at breakfast in bed, though Monsieur Du Bois was in the chamber; which so much astonished me, that I was, involuntarily, retiring, without considering how odd an appearance my retreat would have, when Madame Duval called me back, and laughed very heartily at my ignorance of foreign customs.[1]

The conversation, however, very soon took a more serious turn; for she began, with great bitterness, to inveigh against the *barbarous brutality of that fellow the Captain*, and the horrible ill-breeding of the English in general, declaring she should make her escape with all expedition from so *beastly a nation*. But nothing can be more strangely

---

1. French ladies, unlike English ladies, received both male and female visitors while still in bed.

absurd, than to hear politeness recommended in language so repugnant to it as that of Madame Duval.

She lamented, very mournfully, the fate of her Lyons silk, and protested she had rather have parted with all the rest of her wardrobe, because it was the first gown she had bought to wear upon leaving off her weeds.[2] She has a very bad cold, and Monsieur Du Bois is so hoarse, he can hardly speak.

She insisted upon my staying with her all day, as she intended, she said, to introduce me to some of my own relations. I would very fain have excused myself, but she did not allow me any choice.

Till the arrival of these relations, one continued series of questions on her side, and of answers on mine, filled up all the time we passed together. Her curiosity was insatiable; she enquired into every action of my life, and every particular that had fallen under my observation, in the lives of all I knew. Again, she was so cruel as to avow the most inveterate rancour against the sole benefactor her deserted child and grand-child have met with; and such was the indignation her ingratitude raised, that I would actually have quitted her presence and house, had she not, in a manner the most peremptory, absolutely forbid me. But what, good Heaven! can induce her to such shocking injustice? O my friend and father! I have no command of myself when this subject is started.

She talked very much of taking me to Paris, and said I greatly wanted the polish of a French education. She lamented that I had been brought up in the country, which, she observed, had given me a very *bumpkinish air*. However, she bid me not despair, for she had known many girls much worse than me, who had become very fine ladies after a few years residence abroad; and she particularly instanced a Miss Polly Moore, daughter of a chandler's-shop[3] woman, who, by an accident not worth relating, happened to be sent to Paris, where, from an aukward, ill-bred girl, she so much improved, that she has since been taken for a woman of quality.

The relations to whom she was pleased to introduce me, consisted of a Mr. Branghton, who is her nephew, and three of his children, the eldest of which is a son, and the two younger are daughters.

Mr. Branghton appears about forty years of age. He does not seem to want a common understanding, though he is very contracted and prejudiced: he has spent his whole time in the city,[4] and I believe feels a great contempt for all who reside elsewhere.

His son seems weaker in his understanding, and more gay in his tem-

---

2. A widow's mourning apparel.
3. A candle-maker's shop.
4. The area formerly within the walls of medieval London, bounded by the Thames to the south, the Inns of Court and Temple Bar to the west, and the Tower to the east. Associated with wealth and vulgarity and home primarily to the mercantile classes, the City was shunned by the people of fashion, who preferred the residential areas to the west ("the Town").

per; but his gaiety is that of a foolish, over-grown school-boy, whose mirth consists in noise and disturbance. He disdains his father for his close attention to business, and love of money, though he seems himself to have no talents, spirit, or generosity, to make him superior to either. His chief delight appears to be tormenting and ridiculing his sisters, who, in return, most heartily despise him.

Miss Branghton, the eldest daughter, is by no means ugly, but looks proud, ill-tempered, and conceited. She hates the city, though without knowing why; for it is easy to discover she has lived no where else.

Miss Polly Branghton is rather pretty, very foolish, very ignorant, very giddy, and, I believe, very good-natured.

The first half-hour was allotted to *making themselves comfortable*, for they complained of having had a very dirty walk, as they came on foot from Snow Hill,[5] where Mr. Branghton keeps a silversmith's shop; and the young ladies had not only their coats to brush, and shoes to dry, but to adjust their head-dress, which their bonnets had totally discomposed.

The manner in which Madame Duval was pleased to introduce me to this family, extremely shocked me. "Here, my dears," said she, "here's a relation you little thought of: but you must know my poor daughter Caroline had this child after she run away from me,—though I never knew nothing of it, not I, for a long while after; for they took care to keep it a secret from me, though the poor child has never a friend in the world besides."

"Miss seems very tender-hearted, aunt," said Miss Polly, "and to be sure she's not to blame for her mama's undutifulness, for she could n't help it."

"Lord no," answered she, "and I never took no notice of it to her; for indeed, as to that, my own poor daughter was n't so much to blame as you may think, for she'd never have gone astray, if it had not been for that meddling old parson I told you of."

"If aunt pleases," said young Mr. Branghton, "we'll talk o' somewhat else, for Miss looks very uneasy-like."

The next subject that was chosen, was the age of the three young Branghtons and myself. The son is twenty; the daughters upon hearing that I was seventeen, said that was just the age of Miss Polly; but their brother, after a long dispute, proved that she was two years older, to the great anger of both sisters, who agreed that he was very ill-natured and spiteful.

When this point was settled, the question was put, Which was tallest?—We were desired to measure, as the Branghtons were all of different opinions. None of them, however, disputed my being the tallest in the company, but, in regard to one another they were extremely quarrelsome: the brother insisted upon their measuring *fair*, and not with *heads*

5. A winding, narrow, and steep street, which ran from Holborn Bridge to Newgate (*London Past and Present* 3: 259–60).

and *heels*; but they would by no means consent to lose those privileges of our sex, and therefore the young man was *cast*,[6] as shortest; though he appealed to all present upon the injustice of the decree.

This ceremony over, the young ladies began, very freely, to examine my dress, and to interrogate me concerning it. "This apron's your own work, I suppose, Miss? but these sprigs a'nt in fashion now. Pray, if it is not impertinent, what might you give a yard for this lutestring?[7]—Do you make your own caps, Miss?—" and many other questions equally interesting and well-bred.

They then asked me *how I liked London?* and whether I should not think the country a very *dull place*, when I returned thither? "Miss must try if she can't get a good husband," said Mr. Branghton, "and then she may stay and live here."

The next topic was public places, or rather the theatres, for they knew of no other; and the merits and defects of all the actors and actresses were discussed: the young man here took the lead, and seemed to be very conversant on the subject. But during this time, what was my concern, and, suffer me to add, my indignation, when I found, by some words I occasionally heard, that Madame Duval was entertaining Mr. Branghton with all the most secret and cruel particulars of my situation! The eldest daughter was soon drawn to them by the recital; the youngest and the son still kept their places, intending, I believe, to divert me, though the conversation was all their own.

In a few minutes, Miss Branghton, coming suddenly up to her sister, exclaimed, "Lord, Polly, only think! Miss never saw her papa!"

"Lord, how odd!" cried the other; "why then, Miss, I suppose you would n't know him?"

This was quite too much for me; I rose hastily, and ran out of the room: but I soon regretted I had so little command of myself, for the two sisters both followed, and insisted upon comforting me, notwithstanding my earnest entreaties to be left alone.

As soon as I returned to the company, Madame Duval said, "Why, my dear, what was the matter with you? why did you run away so?"

This question almost made me run again, for I knew not how to answer it. But, is it not very extraordinary, that she can put me in situations so shocking, and then wonder to find me sensible of any concern?

Mr. Branghton junior now enquired of me, whether I had seen the Tower, or St. Paul's church?[8] and upon my answering in the negative, they proposed making a party to shew them to me. Among other ques-

6. Defeated.
7. Sprigs: designs imitating sprigs or young shoots, embroidered on textile fabrics; lutestring: "glossy, silk fabric" (*OED*).
8. The Tower of London, begun by William I and completed by Edward I, encloses an area of eighteen acres and has served at various times as a palace, a prison, and a place of execution. St. Paul's Cathedral, the fifth cathedral to be built on the site (the fourth was destroyed in the Great Fire of London in 1666), was designed by Christopher Wren (1632–1723).

tions, they also asked if I had ever seen *such a thing as an Opera?* I told them I had. "Well," said Mr. Branghton, "I never saw one in my life, so long as I've lived in London, and I never desire to see one, if I live here as much longer."

"Lord, Papa," cried Miss Polly, "why not? you might as well for once, for the curiosity of the thing: besides, Miss Pomfret saw one, and she says it was very pretty."

"Miss will think us very vulgar," said Miss Branghton, "to live in London, and never have been to an Opera; but it's no fault of mine, I assure you Miss, only Papa don't like to go."

The result was, that a party was proposed, and agreed to, for some early opportunity. I did not dare contradict them; but I said that my time, while I remained in town, was at the disposal of Mrs. Mirvan. However, I am sure I will not attend them, if I can possibly avoid so doing.

When we parted, Madame Duval desired to see me the next day; and the Branghtons told me, that the first time I went towards Snow Hill, they should be very glad if I would call upon them.

I wish we may not meet again till that time arrives.

I am sure I shall not be very ambitious of being known to any more of my relations, if they have any resemblance to those whose acquaintance I have been introduced to already.

Letter XVIII.

EVELINA IN CONTINUATION.

I had just finished my letter to you this morning, when a violent rapping at the door made me run down stairs; and who should I see in the drawing room, but—Lord Orville!

He was quite alone, for the family had not assembled to breakfast. He enquired first of mine, then of the health of Mrs. and Miss Mirvan, with a degree of concern that rather surprised me, till he said he had just been informed of the accident we had met with at Ranelagh. He expressed his sorrow upon the occasion with the utmost politeness, and lamented that he had not been so fortunate as to hear of it in time to offer his services. "But, I think," he added, "Sir Clement Willoughby had the honour of assisting you?"

"He was with Captain Mirvan, my Lord."

"I had heard of his being of your party."

I hope that flighty man has not been telling Lord Orville he only assisted *me!* however, he did not pursue the subject, but said, "This accident, though extremely unfortunate, will not, I hope, be the means of frightening you from gracing Ranelagh with your presence in future?"

"Our time, my Lord, for London, is almost expired already."

"Indeed! do you leave town so very soon?"

"O yes, my Lord, our stay has already exceeded our intentions."

"Are you, then, so particularly partial to the country?"

"We merely came to town, my Lord, to meet Captain Mirvan."

"And does Miss Anville feel no concern at the idea of the many mourners her absence will occasion?"

"O, my Lord,—I'm sure you don't think—" I stopt there, for, indeed, I hardly knew what I was going to say. My foolish embarrassment, I suppose was the cause of what followed;—for he came to me, and took my hand, saying, "I *do* think, that whoever has once seen Miss Anville, must receive an impression never to be forgotten."

This compliment,—from Lord Orville,—so surprised me, that I could not speak; but felt myself change colour, and stood for some moments, silent, and looking down: however, the instant I recollected my situation, I withdrew my hand, and told him that I would see if Mrs. Mirvan was not dressed. He did not oppose me, so away I went.

I met them all on the stairs, and returned with them to breakfast.

I have since been extremely angry with myself for neglecting so excellent an opportunity of apologizing for my behaviour at the ridotto: but, to own to the truth, that affair never once occured to me during the short *tête-à-tête* which we had together. But, if ever we should happen to be so situated again, I will certainly mention it; for I am inexpressibly concerned at the thought of his harbouring an opinion that I am bold or impertinent, and I could almost kill myself for having given him the shadow of a reason for so shocking an idea.

But was not it very odd that he should make me such a compliment? I expected it not from him;—but gallantry, I believe, is common to all men, whatever other qualities they may have in particular.

Our breakfast was the most agreeable meal, if it may be called a *meal*, that we have had since we came to town. Indeed, but for Madame Duval I should like London extremely.

The conversation of Lord Orville is really delightful. His manners are so elegant, so gentle, so unassuming, that they at once engage esteem, and diffuse complacence. Far from being indolently satisfied with his own accomplishments, as I have already observed many men here are, though without any pretensions to his merit, he is most assiduously attentive to please and to serve all who are in his company; and, though his success is invariable, he never manifests the smallest degree of consciousness.

I could wish that *you*, my dearest Sir, knew Lord Orville, because I am sure you would love him; and I have felt that wish for no other person I have seen since I came to London. I sometimes imagine, that when his youth is flown, his vivacity abated, and his life is devoted to retirement, he will, perhaps, resemble him whom I most love and honour. His present sweetness, politeness, and diffidence, seem to promise in future the same benevolence, dignity, and goodness. But I must not expatiate upon this subject.

When Lord Orville was gone,—and he made but a very short visit,— I was preparing, most reluctantly, to wait upon Madame Duval; but Mrs. Mirvan proposed to the Captain, that she should be invited to dinner in Queen-Ann-street; and he readily consented, for he said he wished to ask after her Lyons negligee.

The invitation is accepted, and we expect her every moment. But to me, it is very strange, that a woman, who is the uncontrolled mistress of her time, fortune, and actions, should chuse to expose herself voluntarily to the rudeness of a man who is openly determined to make her his sport. But she has very few acquaintance, and, I fancy, scarce knows how to employ herself.

How great is my obligation to Mrs. Mirvan, for bestowing her time in a manner so disagreeable to herself, merely to promote my happiness! every dispute in which her undeserving husband engages, is productive of pain, and uneasiness to herself; of this I am so sensible, that I even besought her not to send to Madame Duval, but she declared she could not bear to have me pass all my time, while in town, with her only. Indeed she could not be more kind to me, were she your daughter.

Letter XIX.

EVELINA IN CONTINUATION.

Saturday morning, April 16.

Madame Duval was accompanied by Monsieur Du Bois. I am surprised that she should chuse to introduce him where he is so unwelcome; and, indeed, it is strange that they should be so constantly together: though I believe I should not have taken notice of it, but that Captain Mirvan is perpetually rallying me upon my *grandmama's beau.*

They were both received by Mrs. Mirvan with her usual good-breeding; but the Captain, most provokingly, attacked her immediately, saying, "Now, Madam, you that have lived abroad, please to tell me this here; Which did you like best, the *warm room* at Ranelagh, or the *cold bath* you went into afterwards? though, I assure you, you look so well that I should advise you to take another dip."

"*Ma foi*, Sir," cried she, "nobody asked for your advice, so you may as well keep it to yourself: besides, it's no such great joke to be splashed, and to catch cold, and spoil all one's things, whatever you may think of it."

"*Splashed*, quoth-a!—why I thought you were soused all over.— Come, come, don't mince the matter, never spoil a good story; you know you had n't a dry thread about you—'Fore George, I shall never think on't without hallowing! such a poor forlorn, draggle-tailed—*gentlewoman!* and poor *Monseer* French, here, like a drowned rat, by your side!—"

"Well, the worse pickle we was in, so much the worser in you not to help us, for you knowed where we were fast enough, because, while I laid in the mud, I'm pretty sure I heard you snigger; so it's like enough you jostled us down yourself, for Monsieur Du Bois says, that he is sure he had a great jolt given him, or he should n't have fell."

The Captain laughed so immoderately, that he really gave me also a suspicion that he was not entirely innocent of the charge; however, he disclaimed it very peremptorily.

"Why then," continued she, "if you did n't do that, why did n't you come to help us?"

"Who, I?—what, do you suppose I had forgot I was an *Englishman*, a filthy, beastly *Englishman?*"

"Very Well, Sir, very well; but I was a fool to expect any better, for it's all of a piece with the rest; you know you wanted to fling me out of the coach-window, the very first time ever I see you: but I'll never go to Ranelagh with you no more, that I'm resolved; for I dare say, if the horses had runn'd over me, as I laid in that nastiness, you'd never have stirred a step to save me."

"Lord, no, to be sure, Ma'am, not for the world! I know your opinion of our nation too well, to affront you by supposing a *Frenchman* would want *my* assistance to protect you. Did you think that *Monseer* here, and I, had changed characters, and that he should pop you into the mud, and I help you out of it? Ha, ha, ha!"

"O, very well, Sir, laugh on, it's like your manners; however, if poor Monsieur Du Bois had n't met with that unlucky accident himself, I should n't have wanted nobody's help."

"O, I promise you, Madam, you'd never have had mine; I knew my distance better and as to your being a little ducked, or so, why, to be sure, *Monseer* and you settled that between yourselves; so it was no business of mine."

"What, then, I suppose you want to make me believe as Monsieur Du Bois served me that trick o'purpose?"

"O' purpose! ay, certainly, who ever doubted that? Do you think a *Frenchman* ever made a blunder? If he had been some clumsy-footed *English* fellow, indeed, it might have been accidental: but what the devil signifies all your hopping and capering with your dancing-masters, if you can't balance yourselves upright?"

In the midst of this dialogue, Sir Clement Willoughby made his appearance. He affects to enter the house with the freedom of an old acquaintance, and this very *easiness*, which, to me, is astonishing, is what most particularly recommends him to the Captain. Indeed, he seems very successfully to study all the humours of that gentleman.

After having heartily welcomed him, "You are just come in time, my boy," said he, "to settle a little matter of a dispute between this here gentlewoman and I; do you know, she has been trying to persuade me, that she did not above half like the ducking *Monseer* gave her t'other night."

"I should have hoped," (said Sir Clement, with the utmost gravity) "that the friendship subsisting between that lady and gentleman, would have guarded them against any actions professedly disagreeable to each other; but, probably, they might not have discussed the matter previously; in which case, the gentleman, I must own, seems to have been guilty of inattention, since, in my humble opinion, it was his business first to have enquired whether the lady preferred soft, or hard ground, before he dropt her."

"O very fine, Gentlemen, very fine," cried Madame Duval, "you may try to set us together by the ears as much as you will; but I'm not such an ignorant person as to be made a fool of so easily; so you need n't talk no more about it, for I sees into your designs."

Monsieur Du Bois, who was just able to discover the subject upon which the conversation turned, made his defence, in French, with great solemnity: he hoped, he said, that the company would at least acknowledge, he did not come from a nation of brutes, and consequently, that to wilfully offend any lady, was, to him, utterly impossible; but that, on the contrary, in endeavouring, as was his duty, to save and guard her, he had himself suffered, in a manner which he would forbear to relate, but which, he greatly apprehended, he should feel the ill effects of for many months; and then, with a countenance exceedingly lengthened, he added, that he hoped it would not be attributed to him as national prejudice, when he owned that he must, to the best of his memory, aver, that his unfortunate fall was owing to a sudden but violent push, which, he was shocked to say, some malevolent person, with a design to his injury, must certainly have given him; but whether with a view to mortify him, by making him let the lady fall, or whether merely to spoil his clothes, he could not pretend to determine.

This disputation was, at last, concluded by Mrs. Mirvan's proposing that we should all go to Cox's Museum.[1] Nobody objected, and carriages were immediately ordered.

In our way down stairs, Madame Duval, in a very passionate manner, said, "*Ma foi*, if I would n't give fifty guineas only to know who gave us that shove!"

This Museum is very astonishing, and very superb; yet, it afforded me but little pleasure, for it is a mere show, though a wonderful one.

---

1. A museum of mechanical works of art in precious and semiprecious stones set up in Spring Gardens in 1772 by the jeweller and silversmith James Cox (d. 1792?) of Shoe Lane, Fleet Street. The collection, consisting of fifty-six pieces and valued at £197,000, was sold by lottery in 1775. See *London Encyclopaedia* 206.

Sir Clement Willoughby, in our walk round the room, asked me what my opinion was of this brilliant *spectacle?*

"It is very fine, and very ingenious," answered I, "and yet—I don't know how it is—but I seem to *miss something.*"

"Excellently answered!" cried he, "you have exactly defined my own feelings, though in a manner I should never have arrived at. But I was certain your taste was too well formed, to be pleased at the expence of your understanding."

"*Pardi,*" cried Madame Duval, "I hope you two is difficult enough! I'm sure if you don't like this, you like nothing; for it's the grandest, prettiest, finest sight that ever I see, in England."

"What," (cried the Captain with a sneer) "I suppose this may be in your French taste? it's like enough, for it's all *kickshaw*[2] work. But, pr'ythee, friend," (turning to the person who explained the devices) "will you tell me the *use* of all this? for I'm not enough of a conjurer to find it out."

"Use, indeed!" (repeated Madame Duval disdainfully) "Lord, if every thing's to be useful!—"

"Why, Sir, as to that, Sir," said our conductor, "the ingenuity of the mechanism,—the beauty of the workmanship,—the—undoubtedly, Sir, any person of taste may easily discern the utility of such extraordinary performances."

"Why then, Sir," answered the Captain, "your person of taste must be either a coxcomb, or a Frenchman; though, for the matter of that, 'tis the same thing."

Just then, our attention was attracted by a pine-apple, which, suddenly opening, discovered a nest of birds, who immediately began to sing. "Well," cried Madame Duval, "this is prettier than all the rest! I declare, in all my travels, I never see nothing eleganter."

"Hark ye, friend," said the Captain, "hast never another pine-apple?"

"Sir?—"

"Because, if thou hast, pr'ythee give it us without the birds; for, d'ye see, I'm no Frenchman, and should relish something more substantial."

This entertainment concluded with a concert of mechanical music: I cannot explain how it was produced, but the effect was pleasing. Madame Duval was in extasies; and the Captain flung himself into so many ridiculous distortions, by way of mimicking her, that he engaged the attention of all the company; and, in the midst of the performance of the Coronation Anthem[3] while Madame Duval was affecting to beat time, and uttering many expressions of delight, he called suddenly for salts, which a lady, apprehending some distress, politely handed to him, and which, instantly applying to the nostrils of poor Madame Duval,

2. Frivolous, trifling.
3. "Zadock the Priest," by George Frideric Handel (1685–1759), composed for the coronation of George II (1727).

she involuntarily snuffed up such a quantity, that the pain and surprise made her scream aloud. When she recovered, she reproached him, with her usual vehemence; but he protested he had taken that measure out of pure friendship, as he concluded, from her raptures, that she was going into hysterics. This excuse by no means appeased her, and they had a violent quarrel; but the only effect her anger had on the Captain, was to encrease his diversion. Indeed, he laughs and talks so terribly loud in public, that he frequently makes us ashamed of belonging to him.

Madame Duval, notwithstanding her wrath, made no scruple of returning to dine in Queen-Ann-street. Mrs. Mirvan had secured places for the play at Drury-Lane Theatre, and, though ever uneasy in her company, she very politely invited Madame Duval to be of our party; however, she had a bad cold, and chose to nurse it. I was sorry for her indisposition, but I knew not how to be sorry she did not accompany us, for she is—I must not say what, but very unlike other people.

Letter XX.

EVELINA IN CONTINUATION.

Our places were in the front row of a side-box. Sir Clement Willoughby, who knew our intention, was at the door of the Theatre, and handed us from the carriage.

We had not been seated five minutes, before Lord Orville, who we saw in the stage-box,[1] came to us; and he honoured us with his company all the evening. Miss Mirvan and I both rejoiced that Madame Duval was absent, as we hoped for the enjoyment of some conversation, uninterrupted by her quarrels with the Captain: but I soon found that her presence would have made very little alteration, for so far was I from daring to speak, that I knew not where even to look.

The play was Love for Love[2] and though it is fraught with wit and entertainment, I hope I shall never see it represented again, for it is so extremely indelicate,—to use the softest word I can,—that Miss Mirvan and I were perpetually out of countenance, and could neither make any observations ourselves, nor venture to listen to those of others. This was the more provoking, as Lord Orville was in excellent spirits, and exceedingly entertaining.

When the Play was over, I flattered myself I should be able to look about me with less restraint, as we intended to stay the farce;[3] but the curtain had hardly dropped, when the box-door opened, and in came Mr. Lovel, the man by whose foppery and impertinence I was so

---

1. Side boxes were located along the sides of the theater, stage boxes—the most expensive seats in the theater—over the proscenium.
2. A comedy by William Congreve (1670–1729), first produced in 1695.
3. Plays were often followed by a shorter farce.

much teized at the ball where I first saw Lord Orville.

I turned away my head, and began talking to Miss Mirvan, for I was desirous to avoid speaking to him;—but in vain, for as soon as he had made his compliments to Lord Orville and Sir Clement Willoughby, who returned them very coldly, he bent his head forward, and said to me, "I hope, Ma'am, you have enjoyed your health since I had the honour—I beg ten thousand pardons, but I protest I was going to say the honour of *dancing* with you—however, I mean the honour of *seeing* you dance?"

He spoke with a self-complacency that convinced me he had studied this address, by way of making reprisals for my conduct at the ball: I therefore bowed slightly, but made no answer.

After a short silence, he again called my attention, by saying, in an easy, negligent way, "I think, Ma'am, you was never in town before?"

"No, Sir."

"So I did presume. Doubtless, Ma'am, every thing must be infinitely novel to you. Our customs, our manners, and *les etiquettes de nous autres*,[4] can have very little resemblance to those you have been used to. I imagine, Ma'am, your retirement is at no very small distance from the capital?"

I was so much disconcerted at this sneering speech, that I said not a word; though I have since thought my vexation both stimulated and delighted him.

"The air we breathe here, however, Ma'am," (continued he, very conceitedly) "though foreign to that you have been accustomed to, has not, I hope, been at variance with your health?"

"Mr. Lovel," said Lord Orville, "could not your *eye* have spared that question?"

"O, my Lord," answered he, "if *health* were the only cause of a lady's bloom, my eye, I grant, had been infallible from the first glance; but—"

"Come, come," cried Mrs. Mirvan, "I must beg no insinuations of that sort; Miss Anville's colour, as you have successfully tried, may, you see, be heightened;—but I assure you, it would be past your skill to lessen it."

"'Pon honour, Madam," returned he, "you wrong me; I presumed not to infer that *rouge* was the only succedaneum for health; but, really, I have known so many different causes for a lady's colour, such as flushing,—anger,—*mauvaise honte*,[5]—and so forth, that I never dare decide to which it may be owing."

"As to such causes as them there," cried the Captain, "they must belong to those that they keep company with."

4. "Our etiquette."
5. "Shame" or "dishonour."

"Very true, Captain," said Sir Clement; "the natural complexion has nothing to do with the occasional sallies of the passions, or any accidental causes."

"No, truly," returned the Captain, "for now here's me, why I look like any other man, just now; and yet, if you were to put me in a passion, 'fore George you'd soon see me have as fine a high colour as any painted Jezabel in all this place, be she never so bedaubed."

"But," said Lord Orville, "the difference of natural and of artificial colour seems to me very easily discerned; that of Nature is mottled, and varying; that of art, *set*, and *too* smooth; it wants that animation, that glow, that *indescribable something* which, even now that I see it, wholly surpasses all my powers of expression."

"Your Lordship," said Sir Clement, "is universally acknowledged to be a *connoisseur* in beauty."

"And you, Sir Clement," returned he, "an *enthusiast*."

"I am proud to own it," cried Sir Clement; "in such a cause, and before such objects, enthusiasm is simply the consequence of not being blind."

"Pr'ythee a truce with all this palavering," cried the Captain, "the women are vain enough already; no need for to puff 'em up more."

"We must all submit to the commanding officer," said Sir Clement, "therefore, let us call another subject. Pray, Ladies, how have you been entertained with the play?"

"Want of entertainment," said Mrs. Mirvan, "is its least fault; but I own there are objections to it, which I should be glad to see removed."

"I could have ventured to answer for the Ladies," said Lord Orville, "since I am sure this is not a play that can be honoured with their approbation."

"What, I suppose it is not sentimental enough!" cried the Captain, "or else it is too good for them; for I'll maintain it's one of the best comedies in the language, and has more wit in one scene, than there is in all the new plays put together."

"For my part," said Mr. Lovel, "I confess I seldom listen to the players: one has so much to do, in looking about and finding out one's acquaintance, that, really, one has no time to mind the stage. Pray,"—(most affectionately fixing his eyes upon a diamond ring on his little finger) "pray—what was the play to-night?"

"Why, what the D——l," cried the Captain, "do you come to the play without knowing what it is?"

"O yes, Sir, yes, very frequently: I have no time to read play-bills; one merely comes to meet one's friends, and shew that one's alive."

"Ha, ha, ha!—and so," cried the Captain, "it costs you five shillings a night just to shew you're alive! Well, faith, my friends should all think me dead and underground, before I'd be at that expence for 'em. Howsomever, this here you may take from me,—they'll find you out fast enough, if you've anything to give 'em.—And so you've been here all this time, and don't know what the play was?"

"Why, really, Sir, a play requires so much attention,—it is scarce possible to keep awake, if one listens;—for, indeed, by the time it is evening, one has been so fatigued, with dining,—or wine,—or the house,[6]—or studying,—that it is—it is perfectly an impossibility. But, now I think of it, I believe I have a bill in my pocket; O, ay, here it is—Love for Love, ay,—true, ha, ha,—how could I be so stupid!"

"O, easily enough, as to that, I warrant you," said the Captain; "but, by my soul, this is one of the best jokes I ever heard! Come to a play, and not know what it is!—Why, I suppose you would n't have found it out, if they had *fob'd* you off with a scraping of fidlers, or an opera?—Ha! ha! ha!—Why now, I should have thought you might have taken some notice of one *Mr. Tattle* that is in this play!"

This sarcasm, which caused a general smile, made him colour: but, turning to the Captain with a look of conceit, which implied that he had a retort ready, he said, "Pray, Sir, give me leave to ask,—what do *you* think of *one Mr. Ben*, who is also in this play?"

The Captain, regarding him with the utmost contempt, answered in a loud voice, "Think of him!—why I think he's a *man!*" And then, staring full in his face, he struck his cane on the ground, with a violence that made him start. He did not, however, chuse to take any notice of this; but, having bit his nails some time in manifest confusion, he turned very quick to me, and in a sneering tone of voice, said, "For my part, I was most struck with the *country* young lady, Miss Prue; pray what do *you* think of her, Ma'am?"[7]

"Indeed, Sir," cried I, very much provoked, "I think—that is, I do not think any thing about her."

"Well, really, Ma'am, you prodigiously surprise me!—*mais, apparemment ce n'est qu'un façon de parler?*[8]—though I should beg your pardon, for probably you do not understand French?"

I made no answer, for I thought his rudeness intolerable; but Sir Clement, with great warmth, said, "I am surprised that you can suppose such an object as Miss Prue would engage the attention of Miss Anville even for a moment."

"O Sir," returned this fop, " 'tis the first character in the piece!—so well drawn,—so much the thing!—such true country-breeding,—such rural ignorance!—ha! ha! ha!—'tis most admirably hit off, 'pon honour!"

I could almost have cried, that such impertinence should be levelled at me; and yet, chagrined as I was, I could never behold Lord Orville

---

6. The House of Commons.
7. Mr. Tattle: a gossiping fop; Mr. Ben: a young sailor; Miss Prue: a boisterous country girl. All are characters in *Love for Love*.
8. "But apparently it's only a manner of speaking."

Evelina

and this man at the same time, and feel any regret for the cause I had given of displeasure.

"The only female in the play," said Lord Orville, "worthy of being mentioned to these ladies is Angelica."[9]

"Angelica," cried Sir Clement, "is a noble girl; she tries her lover severely, but she rewards him generously."

"Yet, in a trial so long," said Mrs. Mirvan, "there seems rather too much consciousness of her power."

"Since my opinion has the sanction of Mrs. Mirvan," added Lord Orville, "I will venture to say, that Angelica bestows her hand rather with the air of a benefactress, than with the tenderness of a mistress. Generosity without delicacy, like wit without judgment, generally give as much pain as pleasure. The uncertainty in which she keeps Valentine,[1] and her manner of trifling with his temper, give no very favourable idea of her own."

"Well, my Lord," said Mr. Lovel, "it must, however, be owned, that uncertainty is not the *ton* among our ladies at present; nay, indeed, I think they say,—though, faith," taking a pinch of snuff, "I hope it is not true—but they say, that *we* now are most shy and backward."

The curtain then drew up, and our conversation ceased. Mr. Lovel, finding we chose to attend to the players, left the box. How strange it is, Sir, that this man, not contented with the large share of foppery and nonsense which he has from nature, should think proper to affect yet more! for what he said of Tattle and of Miss Prue, convinced me that he really had listened to the play, though he was so ridiculous and foolish as to pretend ignorance.

But how malicious and impertinent in this creature to talk to me in such a manner! I am sure I hope I shall never see him again. I should have despised him heartily as a fop, had he never spoken to me at all; but now, that he thinks proper to resent his supposed ill-usage, I am really quite afraid of him.

The entertainment was, The Deuce is in Him,[2] which Lord Orville observed to be the most finished and elegant *petite piece* that was ever written in English.

In our way home, Mrs. Mirvan put me into some consternation, by saying it was evident, from the resentment which this Mr. Lovel harbours of my conduct, that he would think it a provocation sufficiently important for a duel, if his courage equalled his wrath.

I am terrified at the very idea. Good Heaven! that a man so weak and frivolous should be so revengeful! However, if bravery would have excited him to affront Lord Orville, how much reason have I to rejoice,

9. The heroine of *Love for Love.*
1. The hero of *Love for Love.*
2. A two-act farce by George Colman, the elder (1732–94), first performed as an afterpiece at Drury Lane, 4 November 1763.

that cowardice makes him contented with venting his spleen upon me! But we shall leave town soon, and, I hope, see him no more.

It was some consolation to me, to hear, from Miss Mirvan, that, while he was speaking to me so cavalierly, Lord Orville regarded him with great indignation.

~~But, really, I think there ought to be a book, of the laws and customs *à-la-mode*, presented to all young people upon their first introduction into public company.~~

To-night we go to the opera, where I expect very great pleasure. We shall have the same party as at the play; for Lord Orville said he should be there, and would look for us.

Letter XXI.

EVELINA IN CONTINUATION.

I have a volume to write of the adventures of yesterday.

In the afternoon,—at Berry Hill, I should have said the *evening*, for it was almost six o'clock,—while Miss Mirvan and I were dressing for the opera, and in high spirits from the expectation of great entertainment and pleasure, we heard a carriage stop at the door, and concluded that Sir Clement Willoughby, with his usual assiduity, was come to attend us to the Haymarket; but, in a few moments, what was our surprise, to see our chamber-door flung open, and the two Miss Branghtons enter the room! They advanced to me with great familiarity, saying, "How do you do, cousin?—so we've caught you at the glass!—well, I'm determined I'll tell my brother of that!"

Miss Mirvan, who had never before seen them, and could not, at first imagine who they were, looked so much astonished, that I was ready to laugh myself, till the eldest said, "We're come to take you to the opera, Miss; papa and my brother are below, and we are to call for your grand-mama as we go along."

"I am very sorry," answered I, "that you should have taken so much trouble, as I am engaged already."

"Engaged! Lord, Miss, never mind that," cried the youngest, "this young lady will make your excuses, I dare say; it's only doing as one would be done by, you know."

"Indeed, Ma'am," said Miss Mirvan, "I shall myself be very sorry to be deprived of Miss Anville's company this evening."

"Well, Miss, that is not so very good-natured in you," said Miss Bran-ghton, "considering we only come to give our cousin pleasure; it's no good to us; it's all upon her account; for we came, I don't know how much round about to take her up."

"I am extremely obliged to you," said I, "and very sorry you have lost so much time; but I cannot possibly help it, for I engaged myself without knowing you would call."

"Lord, what signifies that?" said Miss Polly, "you're no old maid, and so you need n't be so very formal: besides, I dare say those you are engaged to a'n't half so near related to you as we are."

"I must beg you not to press me any further, for I assure you it is not in my power to attend you."

"Why we came all out of the city on purpose: besides, your grand-mama expects you;—and pray, what are we to say to her?"

"Tell her, if you please, that I am much concerned,—but that I am pre-engaged."

"And who to?" demanded the abrupt Miss Branghton.

"To Mrs. Mirvan,—and a large party."

"And, pray, what are you all going to do, that it would be such a mighty matter for you to come along with us?"

"We are all going to—to the opera."

"O dear, if that be all, why can't we go altogether?"

I was extremely disconcerted at this forward and ignorant behaviour, and yet their rudeness very much lessened my concern at refusing them. Indeed, their dress was such as would have rendered their scheme of accompanying our party impracticable, even if I had desired it; and this, as they did not themselves find out, I was obliged, in terms the least mortifying I could think of, to tell them.

They were very much chagrined, and asked where I should sit?

"In the pit," answered I.

"In the pit!" repeated Miss Branghton, "well, really, I must own I should never have supposed that my gown was not good enough for the pit: but come, Polly, let's go; if Miss does not think us fine enough for her, why to be sure she may chuse."

Surprised at this ignorance, I would have explained to them that the pit at the opera required the same dress as the boxes; but they were so much affronted, they would not hear me, and, in great displeasure, left the room, saying they would not have troubled me, only they thought I should not be so proud with my own relations, and that they had at least as good a right to my company as strangers.

I endeavoured to apologize, and would have sent a long message to Madame Duval; but they hastened away without listening to me; and I could not follow them down stairs, because I was not dressed. The last words I heard them say, were, "Well, her grand-mama will be in a fine passion, that's one good thing."

Though I was extremely mad at this visit, yet I so heartily rejoiced at their going, that I would not suffer myself to think gravely about it.

Soon after, Sir Clement actually came, and we all went down stairs. Mrs. Mirvan ordered tea; and we were engaged in a very lively conversation, when the servant announced Madame Duval, who instantly followed him into the room.

Her face was the colour of scarlet, and her eyes sparkled with fury.

She came up to me with a hasty step, saying, "So, Miss, you refuses to come to me, do you? And pray who are you, to dare to disobey me?"

I was quite frightened;—I made no answer;—I even attempted to rise, and could not, but sat still, mute and motionless.

Every body but Miss Mirvan seemed in the utmost astonishment; and the Captain, rising and approaching Madame Duval, with a voice of authority, said, "Why how now, Mrs. Turkey-Cock, what's put you into this here fluster?"

"It's nothing to you," answered she, "so you may as well hold your tongue, for I sha'n't be called to no account by you, I assure you."

"There you're out, Madam Fury," returned he, "for you must know I never suffer any body to be in a passion in my house, but myself."

"But you *shall*," cried she, in a great rage, "for I'll be in as great a passion as ever I please, without asking your leave, so don't give yourself no more airs about it. And as for you, Miss," again advancing to me, "I order you to follow me this moment, or else I'll make you repent it all your life." And, with these words, she flung out of the room.

I was in such extreme terror, at being addressed and threatened in a manner to which I am so wholly unused, that I almost thought I should have fainted.

"Don't be alarmed, my love," cried Mrs. Mirvan, "but stay where you are, and I will follow Madame Duval, and try to bring her to reason."

Miss Mirvan took my hand, and most kindly endeavoured to raise my spirits: Sir Clement, too, approached me, with an air so interested in my distress, that I could not but feel myself obliged to him; and, taking my other hand, said, "For Heaven's sake, my dear Madam, compose yourself: surely the violence of such a wretch ought merely to move your contempt; she can have no right, I imagine, to lay her commands upon you, and I only wish that you would allow *me* to speak to her."

"O no! not for the world!—indeed, I believe,—I am afraid—I had better follow her."

"Follow her! Good God, my dear Miss Anville, would you trust yourself with a mad woman? for what else can you call a creature whose passions are so insolent? No, no; send her word at once to leave the house, and tell her you desire that she will never see you again."

"O Sir! you don't know who you talk of!—it would ill become me to send Madame Duval such a message."

"But *why*," cried he, (looking very inquisitive,) "*why* should you scruple to treat her as she deserves?"

I then found that his aim was to discover the nature of her connection with me; but I felt so much ashamed of my near relationship to her, that I could not persuade myself to answer him, and only entreated that he would leave her to Mrs. Mirvan, who just then entered the room.

Before she could speak to me, the Captain called out, "Well, Goody, what have you done with Madame French? is she cooled a little? cause if she be n't, I've just thought of a most excellent device to bring her to."

"My dear Evelina," said Mrs. Mirvan, "I have been vainly endeavouring to appease her; I pleaded your engagement, and promised your future attendance: but I am sorry to say, my love, that I fear her rage will end in a total breach (which I think you had better avoid) if she is any further opposed."

"Then I will go to her, Madam," cried I, "and, indeed, it is now no matter, for I should not be able to recover my spirits sufficiently to enjoy much pleasure *any* where this evening."

Sir Clement began a very warm expostulation and entreaty, that I would not go; but I begged him to desist, and told him, very honestly, that, if my compliance were not indispensably necessary, I should require no persuasion to stay. He then took my hand, to lead me down stairs; but the Captain desired him to be quiet, saying he would 'squire me himself, "because," he added, (exultingly rubbing his hands) "I have a wipe[1] ready for the old lady, which may serve her to *chew* as she goes along."

We found her in the parlour. "O, you're come at last, Miss, are you? — fine airs you give yourself, indeed! — *ma foi*, if you had n't come, you might have stayed, I assure you, and have been a beggar for your pains."

"Heyday, Madam," cried the Captain, (prancing forward, with a look of great glee,) "what, a'n't you got out of that there passion yet? why then, I'll tell you what to do to cool yourself; call upon your old friend, *Monseer* Slippery, who was with you at Ranelagh, and give my service to him, and tell him, if he sets any store by your health, that I desire he'll give you such another souse as he did before: he'll know what I mean, and I'll warrant you he'll do't for my sake."

"Let him, if he dares!" cried Madame Duval; "but I sha'n't stay to answer you no more; you are a vulgar fellow, — and so, child, let us leave him to himself."

"Hark ye, Madam," cried the Captain, "you'd best not call names, because, d'ye see, if you do, I shall make bold to shew you the door."

She changed colour, and saying, "*Pardi*, I can shew it myself," hurried out of the room, and I followed her into a hackney coach. But, before we drove off, the Captain, looking out of the parlour window, called out "D'ye hear, Madam, don't forget my message to *Monseer*."

You will believe our ride was not the most agreeable in the world; indeed, it would be difficult to say which was least pleased, Madame Duval or me, though the reasons of our discontent were so different: however, Madame Duval soon got the start of me; for we had hardly turned out of Queen-Ann-street, when a man, running full speed, stopt the coach. He came up to the window, and I saw he was the Captain's

1. A cutting remark or jeer.

servant. He had a broad grin on his face, and panted for breath.
Madame Duval demanded his business; "Madam," answered he, "my
master desires his compliments to you, and—and—and he says he
wishes it well over with you. He! he! he!—"

Madame Duval instantly darted forward, and gave him a violent blow
on the face; "Take that back for your answer, sirrah," cried she, "and
learn to grin at your betters another time. Coachman, drive on!"

The servant was in a violent passion, and swore terribly; but we were
soon out of hearing.

The rage of Madame Duval was greater than ever, and she inveighed
against the Captain with such fury, that I was even apprehensive she
would have returned to his house, purposely to reproach him, which
she repeatedly threatened to do: nor would she, I believe have hesitated
a moment, but that, notwithstanding her violence, he has really made
her afraid of him.

When we came to her lodgings, we found all the Branghtons in the
passage, impatiently waiting for us, with the door open.

"Only see, here's Miss!" cried the brother.

"Well, I declare I thought as much!" said the younger sister.

"Why, Miss," said Mr. Branghton, "I think you might as well have
come with your cousins at once; it's throwing money in the dirt, to pay
two coaches for one fare."

"Lord, father," cried the son, "make no words about that; for I'll pay
for the coach that Miss had."

"O, I know very well," answered Mr. Branghton, "that you're always
more ready to spend than to earn."

I then interfered, and begged that I might myself be allowed to pay
the fare, as the expense was incurred upon my account; they all said *no*,
and proposed that the same coach should carry us on to the opera.

While this passed, the Miss Branghtons were examining my dress,
which, indeed, was very improper for my company; and, as I was
extremely unwilling to be so conspicuous amongst them, I requested
Madame Duval to borrow a hat or bonnet for me of the people of the
house. But she never wears either herself, and thinks them very *English*
and barbarous; therefore she insisted that I should go full dressed, as I
had prepared myself for the pit, though I made many objections.

We were then all crowded into the same carriage; but when we
arrived at the opera-house, I contrived to pay the coachman. They made
a great many speeches; but Mr. Branghton's reflection had determined
me not to be indebted to him.

If I had not been too much chagrined to laugh, I should have been
extremely diverted at their ignorance of whatever belongs to an opera.
In the first place they could not tell at what door we ought to enter, and
we wandered about for some time, without knowing which way to turn:

they did not chuse to apply to me, though I was the only person of the party who had ever before been at an opera; because they were unwilling to suppose that their *country cousin*, as they were pleased to call me, should be better acquainted with any London public place than themselves. I was very indifferent and careless upon this subject, but not a little uneasy at finding that my dress, so different from that of the company to which I belonged, attracted general notice and observation.

In a short time, however, we arrived at one of the door-keeper's *bars*. Mr. Branghton demanded for what part of the house they took money? They answered the pit, and regarded us all with great earnestness. The son then advancing, said "Sir, if you please, I beg that I may treat Miss."

"We'll settle that another time," answered Mr. Branghton, and put down a guinea.

Two tickets of admission were given to him.

Mr. Branghton, in his turn, now stared at the door-keeper, and demanded what he meant by giving him only two tickets for a guinea.

"Only two, Sir!" said the man, "why, don't you know that the tickets are half a guinea each?"

"Half a guinea each!" repeated Mr. Branghton, "why, I never heard of such a thing in my life! And pray, Sir, how many will they admit?"

"Just as usual, Sir, one person each."

"But one person for half a guinea!—why I only want to sit in the pit, friend."

"Had not the ladies better sit in the gallery, Sir; for they'll hardly choose to go into the pit with their hats on?"

"O, as to that," cried Miss Branghton, "if our hats are too high we'll take them off when we get in. I sha'n't mind it, for I did my hair on purpose."

Another party then approaching, the door-keeper could no longer attend to Mr. Branghton, who, taking up the guinea, told him it should be long enough before he'd see it again, and walked away.

The young ladies, in some confusion, expressed their surprise that their *papa* should not know the Opera prices, which, for their parts, they had read in the papers a thousand times.

"The price of stocks," said he, "is enough for me to see after; and I took it for granted it was the same thing here as at the playhouse."

"I knew well enough what the price was," said the son, "but I would not speak, because I thought perhaps they'd take less, as we're such a large party."

The sisters both laughed very contemptuously at this idea, and asked him if he ever heard of *people's abating*[2] any thing at a public place?

"I don't know whether I have or no," answered he; "but I am sure if they would, you'd like it so much the worse."

2. Reducing the price.

"Very true, Tom," cried Mr. Branghton; "tell a woman that any thing is reasonable, and she'll be sure to hate it."

"Well," said Miss Polly, "I hope that Aunt and Miss will be of our side, for Papa always takes part with Tom."

"Come, come," cried Madame Duval, "if you stand talking here, we sha'n't get no place at all."

Mr. Branghton then enquired the way to the gallery, and, when we came to the door-keeper, demanded what was to pay.

"The usual price, Sir," said the man.

"Then give me change," cried Mr. Branghton, again putting down his guinea.

"For how many, Sir?"

"Why—let's see,—for six."

"For six, Sir? why, you've given me but a guinea."

"*But* a guinea! why how much would you have? I suppose it i'n't half a guinea a piece here too?"

"No, Sir, only five shillings."

Mr. Branghton again took up his unfortunate guinea, and protested he would submit to no such imposition. I then proposed that we should return home, but Madame Duval would not consent, and we were conducted, by a woman who sells books of the opera, to another gallery-door, where, after some disputing, Mr. Branghton at last paid, and we all went up stairs.

Madame Duval complained very much of the trouble of going so high, but Mr. Branghton desired her not to hold the place too cheap; "for, whatever you may think," cried he, "I assure you I paid pit price; so don't suppose I come here to save my money."

"Well, to be sure," said Miss Branghton, "there's no judging of a place by the outside, else, I must needs say, there's nothing very extraordinary in the stair case."

But, when we entered the gallery, their amazement and disappointment became general. For a few instants, they looked at one another without speaking, and then they all broke silence at once.

"Lord, Papa," exclaimed Miss Polly, "why you have brought us to the one-shilling gallery!"[3]

"I'll be glad to give you two shillings, though," answered he, "to pay. I was never so fooled out of my money before, since the hour of my birth. Either the door-keeper's a knave, or this is the greatest imposition that ever was put upon the public."

"*Ma foi,*" cried Madame Duval, "I never sat in such a mean place in all my life;—why it's as high!—we sha'n't see nothing."

"I thought at the time," said Mr. Branghton, "that three shillings was an exorbitant price for a place in the gallery, but as we'd been asked so

---

3. The gallery at the top of the auditorium, containing the cheapest seats.

much more at the other doors, why I paid it without many words; but then, to be sure, thinks I, it can never be like any other gallery, we shall see some *crinkum-crankum*[4] or other for our money;—but I find it's as arrant a take-in as ever I met with."

"Why it's as like the twelve penny gallery at Drury-Lane," cried the son, "as two peas are one to another. I never knew father so bit before."

"Lord," said Miss Branghton, "I thought it would have been quite a fine place,—all over I don't know what,—and done quite in taste."

In this manner they continued to express their dissatisfaction till the curtain drew up; after which, their observations were very curious.

They made no allowance for the customs, or even for the language, of another country, but formed all their remarks upon comparisons with the English theatre.

Notwithstanding my vexation at having been forced into a party so very disagreeable, and that, too, from one so much—so very much the contrary—yet, would they have suffered me to listen, I should have forgotten every thing unpleasant, and felt nothing but delight in hearing the sweet voice of Signor Millico,[5] the first singer; but they tormented me with continual talking.

"What a jabbering they make!" cried Mr. Branghton; "there's no knowing a word they say. Pray what's the reason they can't as well sing in English?—but I suppose the fine folks would not like it, if they could understand it."

"How unnatural their action is!" said the son; "why now who ever saw an Englishman put himself in such out-of-the-way postures?"

"For my part," said Miss Polly, "I think it's very pretty, only I don't know what it means."

"Lord, what does that signify?" cried her sister; "mayn't one like a thing without being so very particular?—You may see that Miss likes it, and I don't suppose she knows more of the matter than we do."

A gentleman, soon after, was so obliging as to make room in the front row for Miss Branghton and me. We had no sooner seated ourselves, than Miss Branghton exclaimed, "Good gracious! only see!—why, Polly, all the people in the pit are without hats, dressed like anything!"

"Lord, so they are," cried Miss Polly, "well, I never saw the like!—it's worth coming to the Opera, if one saw nothing else."

I was then able to distinguish the happy party I had left; and I saw that Lord Orville had seated himself next to Mrs. Mirvan. Sir Clement had his eyes perpetually cast towards the five-shilling gallery, where I suppose he concluded that we were seated; however, before the Opera was over, I have reason to believe that he had discovered me, high and

4. "Anything full of twists and turns, or intricately or fancifully elaborated" (*OED*).
5. Guiseppe Millico (1737–1802), Italian castrato soprano, composer, and singing teacher. Dr. Burney called him a "judicious performer, and worthy man . . . whose voice had received its greatest beauties from art" (*History of Music* 2: 877–78).

distant as I was from him. Probably he distinguished me by my head-dress.

At the end of the first act, as the green curtain dropped, to prepare for the dance, they imagined that the Opera was done; and Mr. Branghton expressed great indignation that he had been *tricked* out of his money with so little trouble. "Now, if any Englishman was to do such an impudent thing as this," said he, "why he'd be pelted;—but here, one of these outlandish gentry may do just what he pleases, and come on, and squeak out a song or two, and then pocket your money without further ceremony."

However, so determined he was to be dissatisfied, that, before the conclusion of the third act, he found still more fault with the Opera for being too long, and wondered whether they thought their singing good enough to serve us for supper.

During the symphony of a song of Signor Millico's, in the second act, young Mr. Branghton said, "It's my belief that that fellow's going to sing another song!—why there's nothing but singing!—I wonder when they'll speak."

This song, which was slow and pathetic, caught all my attention, and I lean'd my head forward to avoid hearing their observations, that I might listen without interruption, but, upon turning round, when the song was over, I found that I was the object of general diversion to the whole party; for the Miss Branghtons were tittering, and the two gentlemen making signs and faces at me, implying their contempt of my affectation.

This discovery determined me to appear as inattentive as themselves; but I was very much provoked at being thus prevented enjoying the only pleasure, which, in such a party, was within my power.

"So, Miss," said Mr. Branghton, "you're quite in the fashion, I see;—so you like Operas? well, I'm not so polite; I can't like nonsense, let it be never so much the taste."

"But pray, Miss," said the son, "what makes that fellow look so doleful while he's singing?"

"Probably because the character he performs is in distress."

"Why then I think he might as well let alone singing till he's in better cue: it's out of all nature for a man to be piping when he's in distress. For my part, I never sing but when I'm merry; yet I love a song as well as most people."

When the curtain dropt, they all rejoiced.

"How do *you* like it?"—and "How do *you* like it?" passed from one to another with looks of the utmost contempt. "As for me," said Mr. Branghton, "they've caught me once, but if ever they do again, I'll give 'em leave to sing me to Bedlam [6] for my pains: for such a heap of stuff never

6. Hospital of St. Mary of Bethlehem for lunatics.

did I hear; there is n't one ounce of sense in the whole Opera, nothing but one continued squeaking and squalling from beginning to end."

"If I had been in the pit," said Madame Duval, "I should have liked it vastly, for music is my passion; but sitting in such a place as this, is quite unbearable."

Miss Branghton, looking at me, declared, that she was not *genteel* enough to admire it.

Miss Polly confessed, that, if they would but sing *English* she would like it *very well.*

The brother wished he could raise a riot in the house; because then he might get his money again.

And, finally, they all agreed, that it was *monstrous dear.*

During the last dance, I perceived, standing near the gallery-door, Sir Clement Willoughby. I was extremely vexed, and would have given the world to have avoided being seen by him: my chief objection was, from the apprehension that he wou'd hear Miss Branghton call me *cousin.* — I fear you will think this London journey has made me grow very proud, but indeed this family is so low-bred and vulgar, that I should be equally ashamed of such a connexion in the country, or anywhere. And really I had already been so much chagrined that Sir Clement had been a witness of Madame Duval's power over me, that I could not bear to be exposed to any further mortification.

As the seats cleared, by parties going away, Sir Clement approached nearer to us; the Miss Branghtons observed with surprise, what a fine gentleman was come into the gallery, and they gave me great reason to expect, that they would endeavour to attract his notice, by familiarity with me, whenever he should join us; and so, I formed a sort of plan to prevent any conversation. I'm afraid you will think it wrong; and so I do myself now, — but, at the time, I only considered how I might avoid immediate humiliation.

As soon as he was within two seats of us, he spoke to me, "I am very happy, Miss Anville, to have found you, for the Ladies below have each an humble attendant, and therefore I am come to offer my services here."

"Why then," cried I, (not without hesitating) "if you please, — I will join them."

"Will you allow me the honour of conducting you?" cried he eagerly; and, instantly taking my hand, he would have marched away with me; but I turned to Madame Duval, and said, "As our party is so large, Madam, if you will give me leave, I will go down to Mrs. Mirvan, that I may not croud you in the coach."

And then, without waiting for an answer, I suffered Sir Clement to hand me out of the gallery.

Madame Duval, I doubt not, will be very angry, and so I am with myself, now, and therefore I cannot be surprised: but Mr. Branghton, I

am sure, will easily comfort himself, in having escaped the additional
coach expense of carrying me to Queen-Ann-street: as to his daughters,
they had no time to speak, but I saw they were in utter amazement.

My intention was to join Mrs. Mirvan, and accompany her home. Sir
Clement was in high spirits and good humour; and, all the way we
went, I was fool enough to rejoice in secret at the success of my plan;
nor was it till I got down stairs, and amidst the servants, that any difficulty occurred to me of meeting with my friends.

I then asked Sir Clement how I should contrive to acquaint Mrs.
Mirvan that I had left Madame Duval?

"I fear it will be almost impossible to find her," answered he; "but
you can have no objection to permitting me to see you safe home."

He then desired his servant, who was waiting, to order his chariot to
draw up.

This quite startled me; I turned to him hastily, and said that I could
not think of going away without Mrs. Mirvan.

"But how can we meet with her?" cried he; "you will not chuse to go
into the pit yourself; I cannot send a servant there; and it is impossible
for *me* to go and leave you alone."

The truth of this was indisputable, and totally silenced me. Yet, as
soon as I could recollect myself, I determined not to go in his chariot,
and told him I believed I had best return to my party up stairs.

He would not hear of this; and earnestly entreated me not to withdraw
the trust I had reposed in him.

While he was speaking, I saw Lord Orville, with several ladies and
gentlemen, coming from the pit passage: unfortunately, he saw me too,
and, leaving his company, advanced instantly towards me, and, with an
air and voice of surprise, said, "Good God, do I see Miss Anville!"

I now most severely felt the folly of my plan, and the awkwardness of
my situation; however, I hastened to tell him, though in a hesitating
manner, that I was waiting for Mrs. Mirvan: but what was my disappointment, when he acquainted me that she was already gone home!

I was inexpressibly distressed; to suffer Lord Orville to think me satisfied with the single protection of Sir Clement Willoughby, I could not
bear; yet I was more than ever averse to returning to a party which I
dreaded his seeing. I stood some moments in suspense, and could not
help exclaiming, "Good Heaven, what can I do!"

"Why, my dear Madam," cried Sir Clement, "should you be thus
uneasy?—you will reach Queen-Ann-street almost as soon as Mrs. Mirvan, and I am sure you cannot doubt being as safe."

I made no answer, and Lord Orville then said, "My coach is here;
and my servants are ready to take any commands Miss Anville will honour me with for them. I shall myself go home in a chair, and therefore ———"

How grateful did I feel for a proposal so considerate, and made with so much delicacy! I should gladly have accepted it, had I been permitted, but Sir Clement would not let him even finish his speech; he interrupted him with evident displeasure, and said, "My Lord, my own chariot is now at the door."

And just then the servant came, and told him the carriage was ready. He begged to have the honour of conducting me to it, and would have taken my hand, but I drew it back, saying, "I can't—I can't indeed! pray go by yourself—and as to me, let me have a chair."

"Impossible!" (cried he with vehemence) "I cannot think of trusting you with strange chairmen,—I cannot answer it to Mrs. Mirvan,—come, dear Madam, we shall be home in five minutes."

Again I stood suspended. With what joy would I then have compromised with my pride, to have been once more with Madame Duval and the Branghtons, provided I had not met with Lord Orville! However, I flatter myself that he not only saw but pitied my embarrassment, for he said in a tone of voice unusually softened, "To offer my services in the presence of Sir Clement Willoughby would be superfluous; but I hope I need not assure Miss Anville how happy it would make me to be of the least use to her."

I courtsied my thanks. Sir Clement, with great earnestness, pressed me to go; and while I was thus uneasily deliberating what to do, the dance, I suppose, finished, for the people crowded down stairs. Had Lord Orville then repeated his offer, I would have accepted it notwithstanding Sir Clement's repugnance; but I fancy he thought it would be impertinent. In a very few minutes I heard Madame Duval's voice, as she descended from the gallery. "Well," cried I hastily, "if I must go—" I stopt, but Sir Clement immediately handed me into his chariot, called out "Queen-Ann-street," and then jumped in himself. Lord Orville, with a bow and a half smile, wished me good night.

My concern was so great, at being seen and left by Lord Orville in so strange a situation, that I should have been best pleased to have remained wholly silent during our ride home: but Sir Clement took care to prevent that.

He began by making many complaints of my unwillingness to trust myself with him, and begged to know what could be the reason? This question so much embarrassed me, that I could not tell what to answer, but only said, that I was sorry to have taken up so much of his time.

"O Miss Anville," (cried he, taking my hand) "If you knew with what transport I would dedicate to you not only the present but all the future time allotted to me, you would not injure me by making such an apology."

I could not think of a word to say to this, nor to a great many other equally fine speeches with which he ran on, though I would fain have withdrawn my hand, and made almost continual attempts; but in vain, for he actually grasped it between both his, without any regard to my resistance.

Soon after, he said that he believed the coachman was going the wrong way, and he called to his servant, and gave him directions. Then again addressing himself to me, "How often, how assiduously have I sought an opportunity of speaking to you, without the presence of that brute, Captain Mirvan! Fortune has now kindly favoured me with one, and permit me," again (seizing my hand) "permit me to use it, in telling you that I adore you."

I was quite thunderstruck at this abrupt and unexpected declaration. For some moments I was silent, but, when I recovered from my surprise, I said, "Indeed, Sir, if you were determined to make me repent leaving my own party so foolishly, you have very well succeeded."

"My dearest life," cried he, "is it possible you can be so cruel? Can your nature and your countenance be so totally opposite? Can the sweet bloom upon those charming cheeks, which appears as much the result of good-humour as of beauty—"

"O, Sir," cried I, interrupting him, "this is very fine; but I had hoped we had had enough of this sort of conversation at the Ridotto, and I did not expect you would so soon resume it."

"What I then said, my sweet reproacher, was the effect of a mistaken, a profane idea, that your understanding held no competition with your beauty; but now, now that I find you equally incomparable in both, all words, all powers of speech, are too feeble to express the admiration I feel of your excellencies."

"Indeed," cried I, "if your thoughts had any connexion with your language, you would never suppose that I could give credit to praise so very much above my desert."

This speech, which I made very gravely, occasioned still stronger protestations, which he continued to pour forth, and I continued to disclaim, till I began to wonder that we were not in Queen-Ann-street, and begged he would desire the coachman to drive faster.

"And does this little moment," cried he, "which is the first of happiness I have ever known, does it already appear so very long to you?"

"I am afraid the man has mistaken the way," answered I, "or else we should ere now have been at our journey's end. I must beg you will speak to him."

"And can you think me so much my own enemy?—if my good genius has inspired the man with a desire of prolonging my happiness, can you expect that I should counter-act its indulgence?"

I now began to apprehend that he had himself ordered the man to go a wrong way, and I was so much alarmed at the idea, that, the very instant it occurred to me, I let down the glass, and made a sudden effort to open the chariot-door myself, with a view of jumping into the street;

but he caught hold of me, exclaiming, "For Heaven's sake, what is the matter?"

"I—I don't know," cried I, (quite out of breath) "but I am sure the man goes wrong, and if you will not speak to him, I am determined I will get out myself."

"You amaze me," answered he, (still holding me) "I cannot imagine what you apprehend. Surely you can have no doubts of my honour?"

He drew me towards him as he spoke. I was frightened dreadfully, and could hardly say, "No, Sir, no,—none at all,—only Mrs. Mirvan,—I think she will be uneasy."

"Whence this alarm, my dearest angel?—What can you fear?—my life is at your devotion, and can you, then, doubt my protection?"

And so saying, he passionately kissed my hand.

Never, in my whole life, have I been so terrified. I broke forcibly from him, and, putting my head out of the window called aloud to the man to stop. Where we then were, I know not, but I saw not a human being, or I should have called for help.

Sir Clement, with great earnestness, endeavoured to appease and compose me; "If you do not intend to murder me," cried I, "for mercy's, for pity's sake, let me get out!"

"Compose your spirits, my dearest life," cried he, "and I will do everything you would have me." And then he called to the man himself, and bid him make haste to Queen-Ann-street. "This stupid fellow," continued he, "has certainly mistaken my orders; but I hope you are now fully satisfied."

I made no answer, but kept my head at the window, watching which way he drove, but without any comfort to myself, as I was quite unacquainted with either the right or the wrong.

Sir Clement now poured forth abundant protestations of honour, and assurances of respect, entreating my pardon for having offended me, and beseeching my good opinion: but I was quite silent, having too much apprehension to make reproaches, and too much anger to speak without.

In this manner we went through several streets, till at last, to my great terror, he suddenly ordered the man to stop, and said, "Miss Anville, we are now within twenty yards of your house; but I cannot bear to part with you, till you generously forgive me for the offence you have taken, and promise not to make it known to the Mirvan's."

I hesitated between fear and indignation.

"Your reluctance to speak, redoubles my contrition for having displeased you, since it shews the reliance I might have on a promise which you will not give without consideration."

"I am very, very much distressed," cried I, "you ask a promise which you must be sensible I ought not to grant, and yet dare not refuse."

"Drive on!" cried he to the coachman; —— "Miss Anville, I will not compel you; I will exact no promise, but trust wholly to your generosity."

This rather softened me; which advantage he no sooner perceived, than he determined to avail himself of, for he flung himself on his knees, and pleaded with so much submission, that I was really obliged to forgive him, because his humiliation made me quite ashamed: and, after that, he would not let me rest till I gave him my word that I would not complain of him to Mrs. Mirvan.

~~My own folly and pride, which had put me in his power, were pleas which I could not but attend to in his favour.~~ However, I shall take very particular care never to be again alone with him.

When, at last, we arrived at our house, I was so overjoyed, that I should certainly have pardoned him then, if I had not before. As he handed me up stairs, he scolded his servant aloud, and very angrily, for having gone so much out of the way. Miss Mirvan ran out to meet me, —— and who should I see behind her, but Lord Orville!

All my joy now vanished, and gave place to shame and confusion; for I could not endure that he should know how long a time Sir Clement and I had been together, since I was not at liberty to assign any reason for it.

They all expressed great satisfaction at seeing me, and said they had been extremely uneasy and surprised that I was so long coming home, as they had heard from Lord Orville that I was not with Madame Duval. Sir Clement, in an affected passion, said that his booby of a servant had misunderstood his orders, and was driving us to the upper end of Piccadilly. For my part, I only coloured, for though I would not forfeit my word, I yet disdained to confirm a tale in which I had myself no belief.

Lord Orville, with great politeness, congratulated me, that the troubles of the evening had so happily ended, and said, that he had found it impossible to return home, before he enquired after my safety.

In a very short time he took leave, and Sir Clement followed him. As soon as they were gone, Mrs. Mirvan, though with great softness, blamed me for having quitted Madame Duval. I assured her, and with truth, that for the future I would be more prudent.

The adventures of the evening so much disconcerted me, that I could not sleep all night. I am under the most cruel apprehensions, lest Lord Orville should suppose my being on the gallery-stairs with Sir Clement was a concerted scheme, and even that our continuing so long together in his chariot, was with my approbation, since I did not say a word on the subject, nor express any dissatisfaction at the coachman's pretended blunder.

Yet his coming hither to wait our arrival, though it seems to imply some doubt, shews also some anxiety. Indeed Miss Mirvan says, that he appeared *extremely* anxious, nay uneasy and impatient for my return. If I did not fear to flatter myself, I should think it not impossible but that he had a suspicion of Sir Clement's design, and was therefore concerned for my safety.

What a long letter is this! however, I shall not write many more from London; for the Captain said this morning, that he would leave town on Tuesday next. Madame Duval will dine here to-day, and then she is to be told his intention.

I am very much amazed that she accepted Mrs. Mirvan's invitation, as she was in such wrath yesterday. I fear that to day I shall myself be the principal object of her displeasure; but I must submit patiently, for I cannot defend myself.

Adieu, my dearest Sir. Should this letter be productive of any uneasiness to you, more than ever shall I repent the heedless imprudence which it recites.

Letter XXII.

EVELINA IN CONTINUATION.

Monday morning, April 18.

Mrs. Mirvan has just communicated to me an anecdote concerning Lord Orville, which has much surprised, half pleased, and half pained me.

While they were sitting together during the opera, he told her that he had been greatly concerned at the impertinence which the young lady under her protection had suffered from Mr. Lovel; but that he had the pleasure of assuring her, she had no future disturbance to apprehend from him.

Mrs. Mirvan, with great eagerness, begged he would explain himself, and said she hoped he had not thought so insignificant an affair worthy his serious attention.

"There is nothing," answered he, "which requires more immediate notice than impertinence, for it ever encroaches when it is tolerated." He then added, that he believed he ought to apologize for the liberty he had taken of interfering, but that, as he regarded himself in the light of a *party concerned*, from having had the honour of dancing with Miss Anville, he could not possibly reconcile to himself a patient neutrality.

He then proceeded to tell her, that he had waited upon Mr. Lovel the morning after the play; that the visit had proved an amicable one, but the particulars were neither entertaining nor necessary; he only assured her, Miss Anville might be perfectly easy, since Mr. Lovel had engaged his honour never more to mention, or even to hint at what had passed at Mrs. Stanley's assembly.

Mrs. Mirvan expressed her satisfaction at this conclusion, and thanked him for his polite attention to her young friend.

"It would be needless," said he, "to request that this affair may never transpire, since Mrs. Mirvan cannot but see the necessity of keeping it inviolably secret; But I thought it incumbent upon me, as the young lady is under your protection, to assure both you and her of Mr. Lovel's future respect."

Had I known of this visit previous to Lord Orville's making it, what dreadful uneasiness would it have cost me! Yet that he should so much interest himself in securing me from offence, gives me, I must own, an internal pleasure greater than I can express; for I feared he had too contemptuous an opinion of me, to take any trouble upon my account. Though, after all, this interference might rather be to satisfy his own delicacy, than from thinking well of me.

But how cool, how quiet is true courage! Who, from seeing Lord Orville at the play, would have imagined his resentment would have hazarded his life?[1] yet his displeasure was evident, though his real bravery and his politeness equally guarded him from entering into any discussion in our presence.

Madame Duval, as I expected, was most terribly angry yesterday; she scolded me for I believe two hours, on account of having left her, and protested she had been so much surprised at my going, without giving her time to answer, that she hardly knew whether she was awake or asleep. But she assured me, that if ever I did so again, she would never more take me into public. And she expressed an equal degree of displeasure against Sir Clement, because he had not even spoken to her, and because he was always of the Captain's side in an argument. The Captain, as bound in honour, warmly defended him, and then followed a dispute in the usual style.

After dinner, Mrs. Mirvan introduced the subject of our leaving London. Madame Duval said she should stay a month or two longer. The Captain told her she was welcome, but that he and his family should go into the country on Tuesday morning.

A most disagreeable scene followed. Madame Duval insisted upon keeping me with her; but Mrs. Mirvan said, that as I was actually engaged on a visit to Lady Howard, who had only consented to my leaving her for a few days, she could not think of returning without me.

Perhaps if the Captain had not interfered, the good-breeding and mildness of Mrs. Mirvan might have had some effect upon Madame Duval; but he passes no opportunity of provoking her, and therefore made so many gross and rude speeches, all of which she retorted, that, in conclusion, she vowed she would sooner go to law, in right of her relationship, than that I should be taken away from her.

I heard this account from Mrs. Mirvan, who was so kindly considerate as to give me a pretence for quitting the room, as soon as this dispute

1. Lord Orville challenged Lovel to a duel, which was forestalled when Lovel agreed to discontinue insulting Evelina.

began, lest Madame Duval should refer to me, and insist on my obedience.

The final result of the conversation was, that, to soften matters for the present, Madame Duval should make one in the party for Howard Grove, whither we are positively to go next Wednesday. And though we are none of us satisfied with this plan, we know not how to form a better.

Mrs. Mirvan is now writing to Lady Howard, to excuse bringing this unexpected guest, and to prevent the disagreeable surprise, which must, otherwise, attend her reception. This dear lady seems eternally studying my happiness and advantage.

To-night we go to the Pantheon, which is the last diversion we shall partake of in London, for to-morrow ———

*   *   *   *   *

This moment, my dearest Sir, I have received your kind letter.

If you thought us too dissipated the first week, I almost fear to know what you will think of us this second; — however, the Pantheon this evening will probably be the last public place which I shall ever see.

The assurance of your support and protection in regard to Madame Duval, though what I never doubted, excites my utmost gratitude: how, indeed, cherished under your roof, the happy object of your constant indulgence, how could I have borne to become the slave of her tyrannical humours? — pardon me that I speak so hardly of her, but, whenever the idea of passing my days with her occurs to me, the comparison which naturally follows, takes from me all that forbearance, which, I believe, I owe her.

You are already displeased with Sir Clement: to be sure, then, his behaviour after the Opera will not make peace with you. Indeed, the more I reflect upon it, the more angry I am. I was entirely in his power, and it was cruel in him to cause me so much terror.

O my dearest Sir, were I but worthy the prayers and the wishes you offer for me, the utmost ambition of my heart would be fully satisfied! but I greatly fear you will find me, now that I am out of the reach of your assisting prudence, more weak and imperfect than you could have expected.

I have not now time to write another word, for I must immediately hasten to dress for the evening.

Letter XXIII.

EVELINA IN CONTINUATION.

Queen-Ann-Street, Tuesday, April 19.

There is something to me half melancholy in writing an account of our last adventures in London; however, as this day is merely appropriated to packing, and preparations for our journey, and as I shall shortly have no more adventures to write, I think I may as well complete my town journal at once. And, when you have it all together, I hope, my dear Sir, you will send me your observations and thoughts upon it to Howard Grove.

About eight o'clock we went to the Pantheon. I was extremely struck with the beauty of the building, which greatly surpassed whatever I could have expected or imagined. Yet, it has more the appearance of a chapel than of a place of diversion; and, though I was quite charmed with the magnificence of the room, I felt that I could not be as gay and thoughtless there as at Ranelagh, for there is something in it which rather inspires awe and solemnity, than mirth and pleasure. However, perhaps it may only have this effect upon such a novice as myself.

I should have said, that our party consisted only of Captain, Mrs. and Miss Mirvan, as Madame Duval spent the day in the city:—which I own I could not lament.

There was a great deal of company; but the first person we saw was Sir Clement Willoughby. He addressed us with his usual ease, and joined us for the whole evening. I felt myself very uneasy in his presence; for I could not look at him, nor hear him speak, without recollecting the chariot adventure; but to my great amazement, I observed that he looked at *me* without the least apparent discomposure, though certainly he ought not to think of his behaviour without blushing. I really wish I had not forgiven him, and then he could not have ventured to speak to me any more.

There was an exceeding good concert, but too much talking to hear it well. Indeed I am quite astonished to find how little music is attended to in silence; for though every body seems to admire, hardly any body listens.

We did not see Lord Orville, till we went into the tea-room, which is large, low, and under ground, and serves merely as a foil to the apartments above; he then sat next to us; he seemed to belong to a large party, chiefly of ladies; but, among the gentlemen attending them, I perceived Mr. Lovel.

I was extremely irresolute whether or not I ought to make any acknowledgments to Lord Orville for his generous conduct in securing me from the future impertinence of that man; and I thought, that as he had seemed to allow Mrs. Mirvan to acquaint me, though no one else, of the measures which he had taken, he might, perhaps, suppose me ungrateful if silent: however, I might have spared myself the trouble of deliberating, as I never once had the shadow of an opportunity of speaking unheard by Sir Clement. On the contrary, he was so exceedingly officious and forward, that I could not say a word to any body, but instantly he bent his head forward, with an air of profound attention, as if I had addressed myself wholly to him: and yet, I never once looked at him, and would not have spoken to him on any account.

Indeed, Mrs. Mirvan, herself, though unacquainted with the behaviour of Sir Clement after the opera, says it is not right for a young woman to be seen so frequently in public with the same gentleman; and, if our stay in town was to be lengthened, she would endeavour to represent to the Captain the impropriety of allowing his constant attendance; for Sir Clement, with all his *easiness*, could not be so eternally of our parties, if the Captain was less fond of his company.

At the same table with Lord Orville, sat a gentleman,—I call him so only because he *was* at the same table,—who, almost from the moment I was seated, fixed his eyes steadfastly on my face, and never once removed them to any other object during tea-time, notwithstanding my dislike of his staring, must, I am sure, have been very evident. I was quite surprised, that a man whose boldness was so offensive, could have gained admission into a party of which Lord Orville made one; for I naturally concluded him to be some low-bred and uneducated man; and I thought my idea was indubitably confirmed, when I heard him say to Sir Clement Willoughby, in an *audible whisper,*—which is a mode of speech very distressing and disagreeable to by-standers,—"For Heaven's sake, Willoughby, who is that lovely creature?"

But what was my amazement, when, listening attentively for the answer, though my head was turned another way, I heard Sir Clement say, "I am sorry I cannot inform your Lordship, but I am ignorant myself."

Lordship!—how extraordinary! that a *nobleman*, accustomed, in all probability, to the first rank of company in the kingdom, from his earliest infancy, can possibly be deficient in *good manners*, however faulty in morals and principles! Even Sir Clement Willoughby appeared modest in comparison with this person.

During tea, a conversation was commenced upon the times, fashions, and public places, in which the company of both tables joined. It began by Sir Clement's enquiring of Miss Mirvan, and of me, if the Pantheon had answered our expectations.

We both readily agreed that it had greatly exceeded them.

"Ay, to be sure," said the Captain, "why you don't suppose they'd confess they did n't like it, do you? Whatever's the fashion, they must like of course;—or else I'd be bound for it they'd own, that there never was such a dull place as this here invented."

"And has, then, this building," said Lord Orville, "no merit that may serve to lessen your censure? Will not your eye, Sir, speak something in its favour?"

"Eye!" cried the Lord, (I don't know his name,) "and is there any eye here, that can find pleasure in looking at dead walls or statues, when such heavenly living objects as I now see demand all their admiration?"

"O, certainly," said Lord Orville, "the lifeless symmetry of architecture, however beautiful the design and proportion, no man would be so mad as to put in competition with the animated charms of nature: but when, as to-night, the eye may be regaled at the same time, and in one view, with all the excellence of art, and all the perfection of nature, I cannot think that either suffer by being seen together."

"I grant, my Lord," said Sir Clement, "that the cool eye of unimpassioned philosophy may view both with equal attention, and equal safety; but, where the heart is not so well guarded, it is apt to interfere, and render, even to the eye, all objects but one insipid and uninteresting."

"Aye, aye," cried the Captain, "you may talk what you will of your eye here, and your eye there, and, for the matter of that, to be sure you have two,—but we all know they both squint one way."

"Far be it from me," said Lord Orville, "to dispute the *magnetic* power of beauty, which irresistibly draws and attracts whatever has soul and sympathy: and I am happy to acknowledge, that though we have now no *gods* to occupy a mansion professedly built for them,[1] yet we have secured their *better halves*, for we have *goddesses* to whom we all most willingly bow down." And then, with a very droll air, he made a profound reverence to the ladies.

"They'd need be goddesses with a vengeance," said the Captain, "for they're mortal dear to look at. Howsomever, I should be glad to know what you can see in e'er a face among them that's worth half a guinea for a sight."

"Half a guinea!" exclaimed that same Lord, "I would give half I am worth for a sight of only *one*, provided I make my own choice. And, prithee, how can money be better employed than in the service of fine women?"

"If the ladies of his own party can pardon the Captain's speech," said Sir Clement, "I think he has a fair claim to the forgiveness of all."

"Then you depend very much, as I doubt not but you may," said Lord Orville, "upon the general sweetness of the sex;—but, as to the ladies of the Captain's party, they may easily pardon, for they cannot be hurt."

"But they must have a devilish good conceit of themselves, though," said the Captain, "to believe all that. Howsomever, whether or no, I should be glad to be told, by some of you, who seem to be knowing in them things, what kind of diversion can be found in such a place as this here, for one who has had, long ago, his full of face-hunting?"

Every body laughed, but nobody spoke.

"Why look you there, now," continued the Captain, "you're all at a dead stand![2]—not a man among you can answer that there question. Why, then, I must make bold to conclude, that you all come here for no manner of purpose but to stare at one another's pretty faces;—

1. A Pantheon, from the Greek *pan* ("all") and *theos* ("god"), is a temple dedicated to all the gods.
2. A standstill.

though, for the matter of that, half of 'em are plaguy ugly;—and, as to t'other half,—I believe it's none of God's manufactory."

"What the ladies may come hither for, Sir," said Mr. Lovel, (stroking his ruffles, and looking down,) "it would ill become *us* to determine; but as to we men, doubtless we can have no other view, than to admire them."

"If I be n't mistaken," cried the Captain, (looking earnestly in his face,) "you are that same person we saw at Love for Love t'other night; be n't you?"

Mr. Lovel bowed.

"Why, then, Gentlemen," continued he, with a loud laugh, "I must tell you a most excellent good joke;—when all was over, as sure as you're alive, he asked what the play was! Ha, ha, ha!"

"Sir," said Mr. Lovel, colouring, "if you were as much used to a town life as I am,—which, I presume, is not precisely the case,—I fancy you would not find so much diversion from a circumstance so common."

"Common! what, is it common?" repeated the Captain; "why then, 'fore George, such chaps are more fit to be sent to school, and well disciplined with a cat o' nine tails, than to poke their heads into a play-house. Why, a play is the only thing left, now-a-days, that has a grain of sense in it; for as to all the rest of your public places, d'ye see, if they were all put together, I would n't give *that* for 'em!" snapping his fingers. "And now we're talking of them sort of things, there's your operas,—I should like to know, now, what any of you can find to say for them."

Lord Orville, who was most able to have answered, seemed by no means to think the Captain worthy an argument, upon a subject concerning which he had neither knowledge nor feeling: but, turning to us, he said, "The ladies are silent, and we seem to have engrossed the conversation to ourselves, in which we are much more our own enemies than theirs. But," addressing himself to Miss Mirvan and me, "I am most desirous to hear the opinions of these young ladies, to whom all public places must, as yet, be new."

We both, and with eagerness, declared that we had received as much, if not more pleasure, at the opera than any where: but we had better have been silent; for the Captain, quite displeased, said, "What signifies asking them girls? Do you think they know their own minds yet? Ask 'em after any thing that's called diversion, and you're sure they'll say it's vastly fine;—they are a set of parrots, and speak by rote, for they all say the same thing: but ask 'em how they like making puddings and pies, and I'll warrant you'll pose 'em. As to them operas, I desire I may hear no more of their liking such nonsense; and for you, Moll," to his daughter, "I charge you, as you value my favour, that you'll never again be so impertinent as to have a taste of your own before my face. There are fools enough in the world, without your adding to their number. I'll have no daughter of mine affect them sort of megrims.[3] It is a shame they a'n't put down; and if I'd my will, there's not a magistrate in this town but should be knocked of the head for suffering them. If you've a mind to praise any thing, why you may praise a play, and welcome, for I like it myself."

This reproof effectually silenced us both for the rest of the evening. Nay, indeed, for some minutes it seemed to silence every body else; till Mr. Lovel, not willing to lose an opportunity of returning the Captain's sarcasm, said, "Why, really Sir, it is but natural to be most pleased with what is most familiar, and, I think, of all our diversions, there is not one so much in common between us and the country, as a play. Not a village but has its barns and comedians; and as for the stage business, why it may be pretty equally done any where; and even in regard to *us*, and the *canaille*[4] confined as we all are within the semi-circle of a theatre, there is no place where the distinction is less obvious."

While the Captain seemed considering for Mr. Lovel's meaning, Lord Orville probably with a view to prevent his finding it, changed the subject to Cox's Museum, and asked what he thought of it?

"Think!—" said he, "why I think as how it i'n't worth thinking about. I like no such *jemcracks*.[5] It is only fit, in my mind, for monkeys,—though, for aught I know, they too might turn up their noses at it."

"May we ask your Lordship's own opinion?" said Mrs. Mirvan.

"The mechanism," answered he, "is wonderfully ingenious: I am sorry it is turned to no better account; but its purport is so frivolous, so very remote from all aim at instruction or utility, that the sight of so fine a shew, only leaves a regret on the mind, that so much work, and so much ingenuity, should not be better bestowed."

"The truth is," said the Captain, "that in all this huge town, so full as it is of folks of all sorts, there i'n't so much as one public place, besides the play-house, where a man, that's to say, a man who *is* a man, ought not to be ashamed to shew his face. T'other day they got me to a ridotto; but I believe it will be long enough before they get me to another. I knew no more what to do with myself, than if my ship's company had been metamorphosed into Frenchmen. Then, again, there's your famous Ranelagh, that you make such a fuss about;—why what a dull place is that!—it's the worst of all."

"Ranelagh dull!"—"Ranelagh dull!"—was echoed from mouth to mouth and all the ladies, as if of one accord, regarded the Captain with looks of the most ironical contempt.

"As to Ranelagh," said Mr. Lovel, "most indubitably, though the price is plebeian, it is by no means adapted to the plebeian taste. It requires a certain acquaintance with high life, and—and—and something of—

---

3. Whims or fancies.
4. Rabble or mob.
5. Gimcracks, knickknacks, or useless ornaments; also applied to mechanical contrivances.

of—something *d'un vrai goût*, to be really sensible of its merit. Those whose—whose connections, and so forth, are not among *les gens comme il faut*, can feel nothing but *ennui* at such a place as Ranelagh."[6]

"Ranelagh!" cried Lord ——, "O, 'tis the divinest place under heaven, —— or, indeed,—for aught I know ——"

"O you creature!" cried a pretty, but affected young lady, patting him with her fan, "you sha'n't talk so; I know what you are going to say; but, positively, I won't sit by you, if you're so wicked."

"And how can one sit by you, and be good?" said he, "when only to look at you is enough to make one wicked—or wish to be so?"

"Fie, my Lord!" returned she, "you are really insufferable. I don't think I shall speak to you again these seven years."

"What a metamorphosis," cried Lord Orville, "should you make a patriarch of his Lordship!"

"Seven years!" said he, "dear Madam, be contented with telling me you will not speak to me *after* seven years, and I will endeavour to submit."

"O, very well, my Lord," answered she, "pray date the end of our speaking to each other as early as you please, I'll promise to agree to your time."

"You know, dear Madam," said he, sipping his tea, "you know I only live in your sight."

"O yes, my Lord, I have long known that. But I begin to fear we shall be too late for Ranelagh this evening."

"O no, Madam," said Mr. Lovel, looking at his watch, "it is but just past ten."

"No more!" cried she, "O then we shall do very well."

All the ladies now started up, and declared they had no time to lose.

"Why what the D——l," cried the Captain, leaning forward with both his arms on the table, "are you going to Ranelagh at this time of night?"

The ladies looked at one another, and smiled.

"To Ranelagh?" cried Lord ——, "Yes, and I hope you are going too; for we cannot possibly excuse these ladies."

"I go to Ranelagh?—if I do, I'll be ——."

Every body now stood up, and the stranger Lord, coming round to me, said, "*You* go, I hope?"

"No, my Lord, I believe not."

"O you cannot, must not be so barbarous." And he took my hand, and ran on, saying such fine speeches and compliments, that I might almost have supposed myself a goddess, and him a pagan, paying me adoration. As soon as I possibly could, I drew back my hand; but he frequently, in the course of conversation, contrived to take it again,

6. *D'un vrai goût*: "of a true taste"; *les gens comme il faut*: "genteel people"; *ennui*: "boredom."

though it was extremely disagreeable to me; and the more so, as I saw that Lord Orville had his eyes fixed upon us, with a gravity of attention that made me uneasy.

And, surely, my dear Sir, it was a great liberty in this lord, notwithstanding his rank, to treat me so freely. As to Sir Clement, he seemed in misery.

They all endeavoured to prevail with the Captain to join the Ranelagh party; and this Lord told me, in a low voice, that *it was tearing his heart out* to go without me.

During this conversation, Mr. Lovel came forward, and assuming a look of surprise, made me a bow, and enquired how I did, protesting, upon his honour, that he had not seen me before, or would sooner have paid his respects to me.

Though his politeness was evidently constrained, yet I was very glad to be thus assured of having nothing more to fear from him.

The Captain, far from listening to their persuasions of accompanying them to Ranelagh, was quite in a passion at the proposal, and vowed he would sooner go to the *Black-hole in Calcutta.*[7]

"But," said Lord ——, "if the *ladies* will take their tea at Ranelagh, you may depend upon our seeing them safe home, for we shall all be proud of the honour of attending them."

"May be so," said the Captain; "but I'll tell you what, if one of these places be n't enough for them to-night, why to-morrow they shall go to ne'er a one."

We instantly declared ourselves very ready to go home.

"It is not for yourselves that we petition," said Lord ——, "but for *us*; if you have any charity, you will not be so cruel as to deny us; we only beg you to prolong our happiness for a few minutes,—the favour is but a small one for you to grant, though so great a one for us to receive."

"To tell you a piece of my mind," said the Captain, surlily, "I think you might as well not give the girls so much of this palaver: they'll take it all for gospel. As to Moll, why she's well enough, but nothing extraordinary, though, perhaps, you may persuade her that her pug-nose is all the fashion: and as to the other, why she's good white and red to be sure; but what of that?—I'll warrant she'll moulder away as fast as her neighbours."

"Is there," cried Lord ——, "another man in this place, who, seeing such objects, could make such a speech?"

"As to that there," returned the Captain, "I don't know whether there be or no, and, to make free, I don't care; for I sha'n't go for to model myself by any of these fair-weather chaps, who dare not so much as say their souls are their own,—and, for aught I know, no more they ben't.

---

7. Referring to a small cell at Fort William, Calcutta, in which 146 Europeans were imprisoned by Suraj-ud-daulah, the Nawab of Bengal, on the night of 21 June 1756. Because of the stifling heat, only 23 of them survived the night.

I'm almost as much ashamed of my countrymen as if I was a French-man, and I believe in my heart there i'n't a pin to chuse between them; and, before long, we shall hear the very sailors talking that lingo, and see never a swabber without a bag and a sword."[8]

"He, he, he!—well, 'pon honour," cried Mr. Lovel, "you gentlemen of the ocean have a most severe way of judging."

"Severe! 'fore George, that is impossible; for, to cut the matter short, the men, as they call themselves, are no better than monkeys; and as to the women, why they are mere dolls. So, now you've got my opinion of this subject; and so I wish you good night."

The ladies, who were very impatient to be gone, made their courtsies, and tripped away, followed by all the gentlemen of their party, except the Lord before mentioned, and Lord Orville, who stayed to make enquiries of Mrs. Mirvan concerning our leaving town; and then saying, with his usual politeness, something civil to each of us, with a very grave air, he quitted us.

Lord —— remained some minutes longer, which he spent in making a profusion of compliments to me, by which he prevented my hearing distinctly what Lord Orville said, to my great vexation, especially as he looked—I thought so, at least,—as if displeased at his particularity of behaviour to me.

In going to an outward room, to wait for the carriage, I walked, and could not possibly avoid it, between this nobleman and Sir Clement Willoughby; and, when the servant said the coach stopped the way, though the latter offered me his hand, which I should much have pre-ferred, this same Lord, without any ceremony, took mine himself; and Sir Clement, with a look extremely provoked, conducted Mrs. Mirvan.

In all ranks and all stations of life, how strangely do characters and manners differ! Lord Orville, with a politeness which knows no inter-mission, and makes no distinction, is as unassuming and modest, as if he had never mixed with the great, and was totally ignorant of every qualification he possesses; this other Lord, though lavish of compli-ments and fine speeches, seems to me an entire stranger to real good-breeding; whoever strikes his fancy, engrosses his whole attention. He is forward and bold, has an air of haughtiness towards men, and a look of libertinism towards woman; and his conscious quality seems to have given him a freedom in his way of speaking to either sex, that is very little short of rudeness.

When we returned home, we were all low-spirited; the evening's entertainment had displeased the Captain, and his displeasure, I believe, disconcerted us all.

And here I thought to have concluded my letter; but, to my great surprise, just now we had a visit from Lord Orville. He called, he said,

---

8. Swabber: a sailor of low rank whose duty it is to swab the decks; a bag and sword: both the bag-wig, the back hair of which was enclosed in a bag, and the sword are marks of a gentleman.

to pay his respects to us before we left town, and made many enquiries concerning our return; and, when Mrs. Mirvan told him we were going into the country without any view of again quitting it, he expressed his concern in such terms—so polite, so flattering, so serious—that I could hardly forbear being sorry myself. Were I to go immediately to Berry Hill, I am sure I should feel nothing but joy;—but, now we are joined by this Captain, and by Madame Duval, I must own I expect very little pleasure at Howard Grove.

Before Lord Orville went, Sir Clement Willoughby called. He was more grave than I had ever seen him, and made several attempts to speak to me in a low voice, and to assure me that his regret upon the occasion of our journey, was entirely upon my account. But I was not in spirits, and could not bear to be teazed by him. However, he has so well paid his court to Captain Mirvan, that he gave him a very hearty invitation to the Grove. At this, he brightened,—and, just then, Lord Orville took leave.

No doubt but he was disgusted at this ill-timed, ill-bred partiality; for surely it was very wrong to make an invitation before Lord Orville, in which he was not included! I was so much chagrined, that, as soon as he went, I left the room; and I shall not go down stairs till Sir Clement is gone.

Lord Orville cannot but observe his assiduous endeavours to ingratiate himself into my favour; and does not this extravagant civility of Captain Mirvan, give him reason to suppose, that it meets with our general approbation? I cannot think upon this subject, without inexpressible uneasiness;—and yet, I can think of nothing else.

Adieu, my dearest Sir. Pray write to me immediately. How many long letters has this one short fortnight produced! More than I may, probably, ever write again: I fear I shall have tired you with reading them; but you will now have time to rest, for I shall find but little to say in future.

And now, most honoured Sir, with all the follies and imperfections which I have thus faithfully recounted, can you, and with unabated kindess, suffer me to sign myself

Your dutiful
and most affectionate
EVELINA?

Letter XXIV.

MR. VILLARS TO EVELINA.

Berry Hill, April 22.

How much do I rejoice that I can again address my letters to Howard Grove! My Evelina would have grieved had she known the anxiety of my mind, during her residence in the great world. My apprehensions have been inexpressibly alarming; and your journal, at once exciting and relieving my fears, has almost wholly occupied me, since the time of your dating it from London.

Sir Clement Willoughby must be an artful designing man; I am extremely irritated at his conduct. The passion he pretends for you has neither sincerity nor honour; the manner and the opportunities he has chosen to declare it, are bordering upon insult.

His unworthy behaviour after the opera, convinces me, that, had not your vehemence frightened him, Queen-Ann-street would have been the last place whither he would have ordered his chariot. O my child, how thankful am I for your escape! I need not now, I am sure, enlarge upon your indiscretion and want of thought, in so hastily trusting yourself with a man so little known to you, and whose gaiety and flightiness should have put you on your guard.

The nobleman you met at the Pantheon, bold and forward as you describe him to be, gives me no apprehension; a man who appears so openly licentious, and who makes his attack with so little regard to decorum, is one who, to a mind such as my Evelina's, can never be seen but with the disgust which his manners ought to excite.

But Sir Clement, though he seeks occasion to give real offence, contrives to avoid all appearance of intentional evil. He is far more dangerous, because more artful; but I am happy to observe, that he seems to have made no impression upon your heart, and therefore a very little care and prudence may secure you from those designs which I fear he has formed.

Lord Orville appears to be of a better order of beings. His spirited conduct to the meanly impertinent Lovel, and his anxiety for you after the opera, prove him to be a man of sense and of feeling. Doubtless, he thought there was much reason to tremble for your safety, while exposed to the power of Sir Clement; and he acted with a regard to real honour, that will always incline me to think well of him, in so immediately acquainting the Mirvan family with your situation. Many men of this age, from a false and pretended delicacy to a friend, would have quietly pursued their own affairs, and thought it more honourable to leave an unsuspecting young creature to the mercy of a libertine, than to risk his displeasure by taking measures for her security.

Your evident concern at leaving London, is very natural, and yet it afflicts me. I ever dreaded your being too much pleased with a life of dissipation, which youth and vivacity render but too alluring; and I almost regret the consent for your journey, which I had not the resolution to withhold.

Alas, my child, the artlessness of your nature, and the simplicity of your education, alike unfit you for the thorny paths of the great and busy world. The supposed obscurity of your birth and situation, makes you liable to a thousand disagreeable adventures. Not only my views, but my hopes for your future life, have ever centered in the country. Shall I own to you, that, however I may differ from Captain Mirvan in other respects, yet my opinion of the town, its manners, inhabitants, and diversions, is much upon a level with his own? Indeed it is the general harbour of fraud and of folly, of duplicity and of impertinence; and I wish few things more fervently, than that you may have taken a lasting leave of it.

Remember, however, that I only speak in regard to a public and dissipated life; in private families, we may doubtless find as much goodness, honesty, and virtue, in London as in the country.

If contented with a retired station, I still hope I shall live to see my Evelina the ornament of her neighbourhood, and the pride and delight of her family: giving and receiving joy from such society as may best deserve her affection, and employing herself in such useful and innocent occupations as may secure and merit the tenderest love of her friends, and the worthiest satisfaction of her own heart. Such are my hopes, and such have been my expectations. Disappoint them not, my beloved child, but chear me with a few lines, that may assure me, this one short fortnight spent in town, has not undone the work of seventeen years spent in the country.

ARTHUR VILLARS.

Letter XXV.

EVELINA TO THE REV. MR. VILLARS.

Howard Grove, April 25.

No, my dear Sir, no, *the work of seventeen years* remains such as it was, ever unworthy your time and your labour, but not more so now,—at least I hope not,—than before that fortnight which has so much alarmed you.

And yet, I must confess, that I am not half so happy here at present as I was ere I went to town: but the change is in the place, not in me. Captain Mirvan and Madame Duval have ruined Howard Grove. The harmony that reigned here, is disturbed, our schemes are broken, our way of life is altered, and our comfort is destroyed. But do not suppose *London* to be the source of these evils; for, had our excursion been any where else, so disagreeable an addition to our household, must have caused the same change at our return.

I was sure you would be displeased with Sir Clement Willoughby, and therefore I am by no means surprised at what you say of him: but for Lord Orville—I must own I had greatly feared, that my weak and imperfect account would not have procured him the good opinion which he so well deserves, and which I am delighted to find you seem to have of him. O Sir, could I have done justice to the merit of which I believe him possessed;—could I have painted him to *you* such as he appeared to *me*,—then, indeed, you would have had some idea of the claim which he has to your approbation!

After the last letter which I wrote in town, nothing more passed previous to our journey hither, except a very violent quarrel between Captain Mirvan and Madame Duval. As the Captain intended to travel on horseback, he had settled that we four females should make use of his coach. Madame Duval did not come to Queen-Ann-street, till the carriage had waited some time at the door, and then, attended by Monsieur Du Bois, she made her appearance.

The Captain, impatient to be gone, would not suffer them to enter the house, but insisted that we should immediately get into the coach. We obeyed; but were no sooner seated, than Madame Duval said, "Come, Monsieur Du Bois, these girls can make very good room for you; sit closer, children."

Mrs. Mirvan looked quite confounded, and M. Du Bois, after making some apologies about crowding us, actually got into the coach, on the side with Miss Mirvan and me. But no sooner was he seated, than the Captain, who had observed this transaction very quietly, walked up to the coach door, saying, "What, neither with your leave, nor by your leave?"

M. Du Bois seemed rather shocked, and began to make abundance of excuses; but the Captain neither understood nor regarded him, and, very roughly, said, "Look'ee, *Monseer*, this here may be a French fashion, for aught I know,—but Give and Take is fair in all nations; and so now, d'ye see, I'll make bold to shew you an English one."

And then, seizing his wrist, he made him jump out of the coach.

M. Du Bois instantly put his hand upon his sword, and threatened to resent this indignity. The Captain, holding up his stick, bid him draw at his peril. Mrs. Mirvan, greatly alarmed, got out of the coach, and, standing between them, entreated her husband to re-enter the house.

"None of your clack!" cried he, angrily, "what the D——l, do you suppose I can't manage a Frenchman?"

Meantime, Madame Duval called out to M. Du Bois, "*Eh, laissez-le, mon ami, ne le corrigez pas; c'est une vilaine bête qui n'en vaut pas la peine.*"

"*Monsieur le Capitaine,*" cried M. Du Bois, "*voules-vouz bien me demander pardon?*" [1]

"O ho, you demand pardon, do you?" said the Captain, "I thought as much; I thought you'd come to;—so you have lost your relish for an English salutation, have you?" strutting up to him with looks of defiance.

A crowd was now gathering, and Mrs. Mirvan again besought her husband to go into the house.

1. "Eh, laissez-le . . .": "Oh, let him be, my friend, don't correct him; he is a nasty beast who is not worth the trouble"; "Monsieur le Capitaine . . .": "Captain, would you please apologize?"

"Why what a plague is the woman afraid of?—did you ever know a Frenchman that could not take an affront?—I warrant, *Monseer* knows what he is about;—don't you, *Monseer?*"

M. Du Bois, not understanding him, only said, "*plaît-il, Monsieur?*" [2]

"No, nor *dish* me, neither," answered the Captain; "but, be that as it may, what signifies our parleying here? If you've any thing to propose, speak at once; if not, why let us go on our journey without more ado."

"*Parbleu, je n'entends rien, moi!*" [3] cried M. Du Bois, shrugging his shoulders, and looking very dismal.

Mrs. Mirvan then advanced to him, and said, in French, that she was sure the Captain had not any intention to affront him, and begged he would desist from a dispute which could only be productive of mutual misunderstanding, as neither of them knew the language of the other.

This sensible remonstrance had the desired effect, and M. Du Bois, making a bow to every one, except the Captain, very wisely gave up the point, and took leave.

We then hoped to proceed quietly on our journey; but the turbulent Captain would not yet permit us. He approached Madame Duval with an exulting air, and said, "Why how's this, Madam? what, has your champion deserted you? why I thought you told me, that you old gentlewomen had it all your own way, among them French sparks?"

"As to that, Sir," answered she, "it's not of no consequence what you thought; for a person who can behave in such a low way, may think what he pleases for me, for I sha'n't mind."

"Why, then, Mistress, since you must needs make so free," cried he, "please to tell me the reason why you took the liberty for to ask any of your followers into my coach, without my leave? Answer me to that."

"Why then, pray, Sir," returned she, "tell me the reason why you took the liberty to treat the gentleman in such a unpolite way, as to take and pull him neck and heels out? I'm sure he had n't done nothing to affront you, nor nobody else; and I don't know what great hurt he would have done you, by just sitting still in the coach, he would not have eat it."

"What, do you think, then, that my horses have nothing to do, but to carry about your snivelling Frenchmen? If you do, Madam, I must make bold to tell you, you are out, for I'll see 'em hang'd first."

"More brute you, then! for they've never carried nobody half so good."

"Why, look'ee, Madam, if you must needs provoke me, I'll tell you a piece of my mind; you must know, I can see as far into a mill-stone as another man: and so, if you thought for to fobb me off with one of your

2. "Pardon me, Sir?"
3. "To be sure, I understand nothing!" "Parbleu" is a euphemistic variant of "pardieu."

smirking French puppies for a son-in-law, why you'll find yourself in a hobble, that's all."[4]

"Sir, you're a ————— but I won't say, what;—but I protest, I had n't no such a thought, no more had n't Monsieur Du Bois."

"My dear," said Mrs. Mirvan, "we shall be very late."

"Well, well," answered he, "get away then; off with you, as fast as you can, it's high time. As to Molly, she's fine lady enough in all conscience; I want none of your French chaps to make her worse."

And so saying, he mounted his horse, and we drove off. And I could not but think with regret of the different feelings we experienced upon leaving London, to what had belonged to our entering it!

During the journey Madame Duval was so very violent against the Captain, that she obliged Mrs. Mirvan to tell her, that, when in her presence, she must beg her to chuse some other subject of discourse.

We had a most affectionate reception from Lady Howard, whose kindness and hospitality cannot fail of making every body happy, who is disposed so to be.

Adieu, my dearest Sir. I hope, though I have hitherto neglected to mention it, that you have always remembered me to whoever has made any enquiry concerning me.

Letter XXVI.

EVELINA TO THE REV. MR. VILLARS.

Howard Grove, April 27.

O my dear Sir, I now write in the greatest uneasiness! Madame Duval has made a proposal which terrifies me to death, and which was as unexpected, as it is shocking.

She had been employed for some hours this afternoon in reading letters from London, and, just about tea-time, she sent for me into her room, and said, with a look of great satisfaction, "Come here, child, I've got some very good news to tell you: something that will surprise you, I'll give you my word, for you ha'n't no notion of it."

I begged her to explain herself; and then, in terms which I cannot repeat, she said she had been considering what a shame it was to see me such a poor country, shame-faced thing, when I ought to be a fine lady; and that she had long, and upon several occasions, blushed for me, though she must own the fault was none of mine: for nothing better could be expected from a girl who had been so immured. However, she assured me she had, at length, hit upon a plan, which would make quite another creature of me.

---

4. "I can see as far into a millstone . . .": "I am as smart as the next man," generally used "in ironical commendation of pretended extraordinary acuteness" (*OED*), "in a hobble": in an awkward or perplexing situation.

I waited, without much impatience, to hear what this preface led to; but I was soon awakened to more lively sensations, when she acquainted me, that her intention was to prove my birthright; and to claim, by law, the inheritance of my real family!

It would be impossible for me to express my extreme consternation, when she thus unfolded her scheme. My surprise and terror were equally great, I could say nothing; I heard her with a silence which I had not the power to break.

She then expatiated very warmly upon the advantages I should reap from her plan; talked in a high style of my future grandeur; assured me how heartily I should despise almost every body and every thing I had hitherto seen; predicted my marrying into some family of the first rank in the kingdom; and, finally, said I should spend a few months in Paris, where my education and manners might receive their last polish.

She enlarged also upon the delight she should have, in common with myself, from mortifying the pride of certain people, and shewing them that she was not to be slighted with impunity.

In the midst of this discourse, I was relieved by a summons to tea. Madame Duval was in great spirits; but my emotion was too painful for concealment, and every body enquired into the cause. I would fain have waived the subject, but Madame Duval was determined to make it public. She told them, that she had it in her head to *make something of me*, and that they should soon call me by another name than that of Anville, and yet that she was not going to have the child married, neither.

I could not endure to hear her proceed, and was going to leave the room; which, when Lady Howard perceived, she begged Madame Duval would defer her intelligence to some other opportunity; but she was so eager to communicate her scheme, that she could bear no delay, and therefore they suffered me to go without opposition. Indeed, whenever my situation or affairs are mentioned by Madame Duval, she speaks of them with such bluntness and severity, that I cannot be enjoined a task more cruel than to hear her.

I was afterwards acquainted with some particulars of the conversation by Miss Mirvan, who told me that Madame Duval informed them of her plan with the utmost complacency, and seemed to think herself very fortunate in having suggested it; but soon after, she accidentally betrayed, that she had been instigated to the scheme by her relations the Branghtons, whose letters, which she received to-day, first mentioned the proposal. She declared that she would have nothing to do with any *round-about ways*, but go openly and instantly to law, in order to prove my birth, real name, and title to the estate of my ancestors.

How impertinent and officious, in these Branghtons, to interfere thus in my concerns! You can hardly imagine what a disturbance this plan has made in the family. The Captain, without enquiring into any particulars of the affair, has peremptorily declared himself against it, merely because it has been proposed by Madame Duval, and they have battled the point together with great violence. Mrs. Mirvan says she will not even *think*, till she hears your opinion. But Lady Howard, to my great surprise, openly avows her approbation of Madame Duval's intention: however, she will write her reasons and sentiments upon the subject to you herself.

As to Miss Mirvan, she is my second self, and neither hopes nor fears but as I do. And as to *me*,—I know not what to say, nor even what to wish; I have often thought my fate peculiarly cruel, to have but one parent, and from that one to be banished for ever;—while, on the other side, I have but too well known and felt the propriety of the separation. And yet, you may much better imagine than I can express, the internal anguish which sometimes oppresses my heart, when I reflect upon the strange indifferency, that must occasion a father never to make the least enquiry after the health, the welfare, or even the life of his child!

O Sir, to *me*, the loss is nothing!—greatly, sweetly, and most benevolently have you guarded me from feeling it; but for *him*, I grieve indeed!—I must be divested, not merely of all filial piety, but of all humanity, could I ever think upon this subject, and not be wounded to the soul.

Again I must repeat, I know not what to *wish*: think for me, therefore, my dearest Sir, and suffer my doubting mind, that knows not which way to direct its hopes, to be guided by your wisdom and unerring counsel.

Evelina.

Letter XXVII.

Lady Howard to the Rev. Mr. Villars.

Dear Sir,   Howard Grove

I cannot give a greater proof of the high opinion I have of your candour, than by the liberty I am now going to take, of presuming to offer you advice, upon a subject concerning which you have so just a claim to act for yourself: but I know you have too unaffected a love of justice, to be partially tenacious of your own judgment.

Madame Duval has been proposing a scheme which has put us all in commotion, and against which, at first, in common with the rest of my family, I exclaimed; but upon more mature consideration, I own my objections have almost wholly vanished.

This scheme is no other than to commence a law-suit with Sir John Belmont, to prove the validity of his marriage with Miss Evelyn; the necessary consequence of which proof, will be securing his fortune and estate to his daughter.

And why, my dear Sir, should not this be? I know that, upon first hearing, such a plan conveys ideas that must shock you; but I know, too, that your mind is superior to being governed by prejudices, or to opposing any important cause on account of a few disagreeable attendant circumstances.

Your lovely charge, now first entering into life, has merit which ought not to be buried in obscurity. She seems born for an ornament to the world. Nature has been bountiful to her of whatever she had to bestow; and the peculiar attention you have given to her education, has formed her mind to a degree of excellence, that, in one so young, I have scarce ever seen equalled. Fortune, alone, has hitherto been sparing of her gifts; and she, too, now opens the way which leads to all that is left to wish for her.

What your reasons may have been, my good Sir, for so carefully concealing the birth, name, and pretensions of this amiable girl, and forbearing to make any claim upon Sir John Belmont, I am totally a stranger to; but, without knowing, I respect them, from the high opinion I have of your character and judgment: but I hope they are not insuperable; for I cannot but think, that it was never designed, for one who seems meant to grace the world, to have her life devoted to retirement.

Surely Sir John Belmont, wretch as he has shewn himself, could never see his accomplished daughter, and not be proud to own her, and eager to secure her the inheritance of his fortune. The admiration she met with in town, though merely the effect of her external attractions, was such, that Mrs. Mirvan assures me, she would have had the most splendid offers, had there not seemed to be some mystery in regard to her birth, which, she was well informed, was assiduously, though vainly, endeavoured to be discovered.

Can it be right, my dear Sir, that this promising young creature should be deprived of the fortune, and rank of life, to which she is lawfully entitled, and which you have prepared her to support and to use so nobly? To despise riches, may, indeed, be philosophic, but to dispense them worthily, must, surely, be more beneficial to mankind.

Perhaps a few years, or, indeed, a much shorter time, may make this scheme impracticable: Sir John, though yet young, leads a life too dissipated for long duration; and, when too late, we may regret that something was not sooner done; for it will be next to impossible, after he is gone, to settle or prove any thing with his heirs and executors.

Pardon the earnestness with which I write my defense of this affair; but your charming ward has made me so warmly her friend, that I cannot be indifferent upon a subject of such importance to her future life.

Adieu, my dear Sir;—send me speedily an answer to this remonstrance, and believe me to be, &c.

M. HOWARD.

Letter XXVIII.

MR. VILLARS TO LADY HOWARD.

Berry Hill, May 2.

Your letter, Madam, has opened a source of anxiety to which I look forward with dread, and which to see closed, I scarcely dare expect. I am unwilling to oppose my opinion to that of your Ladyship, nor indeed, can I, but by arguments which, I believe, will rather rank me as a hermit, ignorant of the world, and fit only for my cell, than as a proper guardian, in an age such as this, for an accomplished young woman. Yet, thus called upon, it behoves me to explain, and endeavour to vindicate, the reasons by which I have been hitherto guided.

The mother of this dear child,—who was led to destruction by her own imprudence, the hardness of heart of Madame Duval, and the villany of Sir John Belmont,—was once, what her daughter is now, the best beloved of my heart; and her memory, so long as my own holds, I shall love, mourn and honour! On the fatal day that her gentle soul left its mansion, and not many hours ere she ceased to breathe, I solemnly plighted my faith, *That her child if it lived, should know no father, but myself, or her acknowledged husband.*

You cannot, Madam, suppose that I found much difficulty in adhering to this promise, and forbearing to make any *claim* upon Sir John Belmont. Could I feel an affection the most paternal for this poor sufferer, and not abominate her destroyer? Could I wish to deliver to *him*, who had so basely betrayed the mother, the helpless and innocent offspring, who, born in so much sorrow, seemed entitled to all the compassionate tenderness of pity?

For many years, the *name* alone of that man, accidentally spoken in my hearing, almost divested me of my Christianity, and scarce could I forbear to execrate him. Yet I sought not, neither did I desire, to deprive him of his child, had he, with any appearance of contrition, or, indeed, of humanity, endeavoured to become less unworthy such a blessing;— but he is a stranger to all parental feelings, and has with a savage insensibility, forborne to enquire even into the existence of this sweet orphan, though the situation of his injured wife was but too well known to him.

You wish to be acquainted with my intentions.—I must acknowledge, they were such as I now perceive would not be honoured with your Ladyship's approbation: for though I have sometimes thought of presenting Evelina to her father, and demanding the justice which is her due, yet, at other times, I have both disdained and feared the application; disdained, lest it should be refused, and feared, lest it should be accepted!

Lady Belmont, who was firmly persuaded of her approaching dissolution, frequently and earnestly besought me, that if her infant was a female, I would not abandon her to the direction of a man so wholly unfit to take the charge of her education; but, should she be importunately demanded, that I would retire with her abroad, and carefully conceal her from Sir John, till some apparent change in his sentiments and conduct should announce him less improper for such a trust. And often would she say, "Should the poor babe have any feelings correspondent with its mother's, it will have no want, while under your protection." Alas! she had no sooner quitted it herself, than she was plunged into a gulph of misery, that swallowed up her peace, reputation, and life.

During the childhood of Evelina I suggested a thousand plans for the security of her birth-right;—but I as oftentimes rejected them. I was in a perpetual conflict, between the desire that she should have justice done her, and the apprehension that, while I improved her fortune, I should endanger her mind. However, as her character began to be formed, and her disposition to be displayed, my perplexity abated; the road before me seemed less thorny and intricate, and I thought I could perceive the right path from the wrong: for, when I observed the artless openness, the ingenuous simplicity of her nature; when I saw that her guileless and innocent soul fancied all the world to be pure and disinterested as herself, and that her heart was open to every impression with which love, pity, or art might assail it;—then did I flatter myself, that to follow my own inclination, and to secure her welfare, was the same thing; since, to expose her to the snares and dangers inevitably encircling a house of which the master is dissipated and unprincipled, without the guidance of a mother, or any prudent and sensible female, seemed to me no less than suffering her to stumble into some dreadful pit, when the sun was in its meridian. My plan, therefore, was not merely to educate and to cherish her as my own, but to adopt her the heiress of my small fortune, and to bestow her upon some worthy man, with whom she might spend her days in tranquility, chearfulness, and good-humour, untainted by vice, folly, or ambition.

So much for the time past. Such have been the motives by which I have been governed; and I hope they will be allowed not merely to account for, but also to justify, the conduct which has resulted from them. It now remains to speak of the time to come.

And here, indeed, I am sensible of difficulties which I almost despair of surmounting according to my wishes. I pay the highest deference to your Ladyship's opinion, which it is extremely painful to me not to concur with; yet, I am so well acquainted with your goodness, that I presume to hope it would not be absolutely impossible for me to offer such arguments as might lead you to think with me, that this young creature's chance of happiness seems less doubtful in retirement, than it would be in the gay and dissipated world: but why should I perplex your Ladyship with reasoning that can turn to so little account? for, alas! what arguments, what persuasions can I make use of, with any prospect of success, to such a woman as Madame Duval? Her character, and the violence of her disposition, intimidate me from making the attempt: she is too ignorant for instruction, too obstinate for entreaty, and too weak for reason.

I will not, therefore, enter into a contest from which I have nothing to expect but altercation and impertinence. As soon would I discuss the effect of sound with the deaf, or the nature of colours with the blind, as aim at illuminating with conviction a mind so warped by prejudice, so much the slave of unruly and illiberal passions. Unused as she is to controul, persuasion would but harden, and opposition incense her. I yield, therefore, to the necessity which compels my reluctant acquiescence, and shall now turn all my thoughts upon considering of such methods for the conducting this enterprize, as may be most conducive to the happiness of my child, and least liable to wound her sensibility.

The law-suit, therefore, I wholly and absolutely disapprove.

Will you, my dear Madam, forgive the freedom of an old man, if I own myself greatly surprised, that you could, even for a moment, listen to a plan so violent, so public, so totally repugnant to all female delicacy? I am satisfied your Ladyship has not weighed this project. There was a time, indeed, when, to assert the innocence of Lady Belmont, and to blazon to the world the *wrongs*, not *guilt*, by which she suffered, I proposed, nay attempted, a similar plan: but then, all assistance and encouragement was denied. How cruel to the remembrance I bear of her woes, is this tardy resentment of Madame Duval! She was deaf to the voice of Nature, though she has hearkened to that of Ambition.

Never can I consent to have this dear and timid girl brought forward to the notice of the world by such a method; a method, which will subject her to all the impertinence of curiosity, the sneers of conjecture, and the stings of ridicule. And for what?—the attainment of wealth, which she does not want, and the gratification of vanity, which she does not feel.—A child to appear against a father!—no, Madam, old and infirm as I am, I would even yet sooner convey her myself to some remote part of the world, though I were sure of dying in the expedition.

Far different had been the motives which would have stimulated her unhappy mother to such a proceeding; all her felicity in this world was irretrievably lost; her life was become a burthen to her, and her fair fame, which she had early been taught to prize above all other things, had received a mortal wound: therefore, to clear her own honour, and to secure from blemish the birth of her child, was all the good which Fortune had reserved herself the *power* of bestowing. But even this last consolation was with-held from her!

Let milder measures be adopted; and—since it must be so,—let application be made to Sir John Belmont; but as to a law-suit, I hope, upon this subject, never more to hear it mentioned.

With Madame Duval, all pleas of delicacy would be ineffectual; her scheme must be opposed by arguments better suited to her understanding. I will not, therefore, talk of its impropriety, but endeavour to prove its inutility. Have the goodness, then, to tell her, that her own intentions would be frustrated by her plan, since, should the law-suit be commenced, and even should the cause be gained, Sir John Belmont would still have it in his power, and, if irritated, no doubt in his inclination, to cut off her grand-daughter with a shilling.

She cannot do better, herself, than to remain quiet and inactive in the affair: the long and mutual animosity between her and Sir John, will make her interference merely productive of debates and ill-will. Neither would I have Evelina appear till summoned. And as to myself, I must wholly decline *acting*, though I will, with unwearied zeal, devote all my thoughts to giving counsel: but, in truth, I have neither inclination nor spirits adequate to engaging personally with this man.

My opinion is, that he would pay more respect to a letter from your Ladyship upon this subject, than from any other person. I, therefore advise and hope, that you will yourself take the trouble of writing to him, in order to open the affair. When he shall be enclined to see Evelina, I have for him a posthumous letter, which his much-injured lady left to be presented to him, if ever such a meeting should take place.

The views of the Branghtons, in suggesting this scheme, are obviously interested; they hope, by securing to Evelina the fortune of her father, to induce Madame Duval to settle her own upon themselves. In this, however, they would probably be mistaken, for little minds have ever a propensity to bestow their wealth upon those who are already in affluence, and, therefore, the less her grand-child requires her assistance, the more gladly she will give it.

I have but one thing more to add, from which, however, I can by no means recede: my word so solemnly given to Lady Belmont, that her child should never be owned[1] but with her self, must be inviolably adhered to.

> I am, dear Madam, with great respect,
> Your Ladyship's most obedient servant,
> ARTHUR VILLARS.

Letter XXIX.

MR. VILLARS TO EVELINA.

Berry Hill, May 2.

How sincerely do I sympathise in the uneasiness and concern which my beloved Evelina has so much reason to feel! The cruel scheme in agitation is equally repugnant to my judgment and my inclination,—yet to

1. Acknowledged.

oppose it, seems impracticable. To follow the dictates of my own heart, I should instantly recall you to myself, and never more consent to your being separated from me; but the manners and opinion of the world demand a different conduct. Hope, however, for the best, and be satisfied you shall meet with no indignity; if you are not received into your own family as you ought to be, and with the distinction that is your due, you shall leave it for ever; and, once, again restored to my protection, secure your own tranquillity, and make, as you have hitherto done, all the happiness of my life!

ARTHUR VILLARS.

Letter XXX.

EVELINA TO THE REV. MR. VILLARS.

Howard Grove, May 6.

The die is thrown, and I attend the event in trembling! Lady Howard has written to Paris, and sent her letter to town, to be forwarded in the ambassador's packet, and in less than a fortnight, therefore, she expects an answer. O Sir, with what anxious impatience shall I wait its arrival! upon it seems to depend the fate of my future life. My solicitude is so great, and my suspence so painful, that I cannot rest a moment in peace, or turn my thoughts into any other channel.

Deeply interested as I now am in the event, most sincerely do I regret that the plan was ever proposed: methinks it *cannot* end to my satisfaction; for either I must be torn from the arms of my *more* than father,— or I must have the misery of being finally convinced, that I am cruelly rejected by him who has the natural claim to that dear title; which, to write, mention, or think of, fills my whole soul with filial tenderness.

The subject is discussed here eternally. Captain Mirvan and Madame Duval, as usual, quarrel whenever it is started: but I am so wholly engrossed by my own reflections, that I cannot even listen to them. My imagination changes the scene perpetually; one moment, I am embraced by a kind and relenting parent, who takes me to that heart from which I have hitherto been banished, and supplicates, through me, peace and forgiveness from the ashes of my mother!—at another, he regards me with detestation, considers me as the living image of an injured saint, and repulses me with horror!—But I will not afflict you with the melancholy phantasms of my brain, I will endeavour to compose my mind to a more tranquil state, and forbear to write again, till I have, in some measure, succeeded.

May Heaven bless you, my dearest Sir! and long, long may it continue you on earth, to bless

Your grateful
EVELINA!

Letter XXXI.

Sir,   Howard Grove, May 5.

You will, doubtless, be surprised at receiving a letter from one who had for so short a period the honour of your acquaintance, and that at so great a distance of time; but the motive which has induced me to take this liberty, is of so delicate a nature, that were I to commence making apologies for my officiousness, I fear my letter would be too long for your patience.

You have, probably, already conjectured the subject upon which I mean to treat. My regard for Mr. Evelyn and his amiable daughter was well known to you: nor can I ever cease to be interested in whatever belongs to their memory or family.

I must own myself somewhat distressed in what manner to introduce the purport of my writing; yet, as I think that, in affairs of this kind, frankness is the first requisite to a good understanding between the parties concerned, I will neither torment you nor myself with punctilious ceremonies, but proceed instantly and openly to the business which occasions my giving you this trouble.

I presume, Sir, it would be superfluous to tell you, that your child resides still in Dorsetshire, and is still under the protection of the Reverend Mr. Villars, in whose house she was born: for, though no enquiries concerning her have reached his ears, or mine, I can never suppose it possible you have forborne to make them. It only remains, therefore, to tell you, that your daughter is now grown up; that she has been educated with the utmost care, and the utmost success; and that she is now a most deserving, accomplished, and amiable young woman.

Whatever may be your view for her future destination in life, it seems time to declare it. She is greatly admired, and, I doubt not, will be very much sought after: it is proper, therefore, that her future expectations, and your pleasure concerning her, should be made known.

Believe me, Sir, she merits your utmost attention and regard. You could not see and know her, and remain unmoved by those sensations of affection which belong to so near and tender a relationship. She is the lovely resemblance of her lovely mother;—pardon, Sir, the liberty I take in mentioning that unfortunate lady, but I think it behoves me, upon this occasion, to shew the esteem I felt for her; allow me, therefore, to say, and be not offended at my freedom, that the memory of that excellent lady has but too long remained under the aspersions of calumny; surely it is time to vindicate her fame!—and how can that be done in a manner more eligible, more grateful to her friends, or more honourable to yourself, than by openly receiving as your child, *the daughter of the late Lady Belmont?*

The venerable man who has had the care of her education, deserves your warmest acknowledgments, for the unremitting pains he has taken, and attention he has shewn, in the discharge of his trust. Indeed she has been peculiarly fortunate in meeting with such a friend and guardian: a more worthy man, or one whose character seems nearer to perfection, does not exist.

Permit me to assure you, Sir, she will amply repay whatever regard and favour you may hereafter shew her, by the comfort and happiness you cannot fail to find in her affection and duty. To be owned *properly* by you, is the first wish of her heart; and I am sure, that to merit your approbation will be the first study of her life.

I fear that you will think this address impertinent; but I must rest upon the goodness of my intention to plead my excuse.

I am, Sir,
Your most obedient humble servant,
M. Howard.

VOLUME TWO

Letter I.

EVELINA TO THE REV. MR. VILLARS.

Howard Grove, Kent, May 10.

Our house has been enlivened to-day by the arrival of a London visitor; and the necessity I have been under of concealing the uneasiness of my mind, has made me exert myself so effectually, that I even think it is really diminished; or, at least, my thoughts are not so totally, so very anxiously occupied by one only subject as they lately were.

I was strolling this morning with Miss Mirvan, down a lane about a mile from the grove, when we heard the trampling of horses; and, fearing the narrowness of the passage, we were turning hastily back, but stopped upon hearing a voice call out, "Pray, Ladies, don't be frightened, for I will walk my horse." We turned again, and then saw Sir Clement Willoughby. He dismounted, and approaching us, with the reins in his hand, presently recollected us. "Good Heaven," cried he, with his usual quickness, "do I see Miss Anville?—and you too, Miss Mirvan?"

He immediately ordered his servant to take charge of his horse, and then, advancing to us, took a hand of each, which he pressed to his lips, and said a thousand fine things concerning his good fortune, our improved looks, and the charms of the country, when inhabited by such rural deities. "The town, Ladies, has languished since your absence,—

or, at least, I have so much languished myself, as to be absolutely insensible to all it had to offer. One refreshing breeze, such as I now enjoy, awakens me to new vigour, life, and spirit. But I never before had the good luck to see the country in such perfection."

"Has not almost every body left town, Sir?" said Miss Mirvan.

"I am ashamed to answer you, Madam—but indeed it is as full as ever, and will continue so, till after the birth-day.[1] However, you Ladies were so little seen, that there are but few who know what it has lost. For my own part, I felt it too sensibly, to be able to endure the place any longer."

"Is there any body remaining there, that we were acquainted with?" cried I.

"O yes, Ma'am." And then he named two or three persons we have seen when with him; but he did not mention Lord Orville, and I would not ask him, lest he should think me curious. Perhaps, if he stays here some time, he may speak of him by accident.

He was proceeding in this complimentary style, when we were met by the Captain; who no sooner perceived Sir Clement, than he hastened up to him, gave him a hearty shake of the hand, a cordial slap on the back, and some other equally gentle tokens of satisfaction, assuring him of his great joy at his visit, and declaring he was as glad to see him as if he had been a messenger who brought news that a French ship was sunk. Sir Clement, on the other side, expressed himself with equal warmth, and protested he had been so eager to pay his respects to Captain Mirvan, that he had left London in its full lustre, and a thousand engagements unanswered, merely to give himself that pleasure.

"We shall have rare sport," said the Captain, "for do you know the old French-woman is among us? 'Fore George, I have scarce made any use of her yet, by reason I have had nobody with me that could enjoy a joke: howsomever, it shall go hard but we'll have some diversion now."

Sir Clement very much approved of the proposal; and we then went into the house, where he had a very grave reception from Mrs. Mirvan, who is by no means pleased with his visit, and a look of much discontent from Madame Duval, who said to me, in a low voice, "I'd as soon have seen Old Nick as that man, for he's the most impertinentest person in the world, and is n't never of my side."

The Captain is now actually occupied in contriving some scheme which, he says, is *to play the old Dowager off;*[2] and so eager and delighted is he at the idea, that he can scarcely constrain his raptures sufficiently to conceal his design, even from herself. I wish, however, since I do not dare put Madame Duval upon her guard, that he had the delicacy not to acquaint me with his intention.

1. King George III's birthday, June 4, which marked the end of the London season.
2. To cause Madame Duval to display herself disadvantageously.

Letter II.

May 13th.

The Captain's operations are begun,—and, I hope, ended; for indeed, poor Madame Duval has already but too much reason to regret Sir Clement's visit to Howard Grove.

Yesterday morning, during breakfast, as the Captain was reading the news-paper, Sir Clement suddenly begged to look at it, saying he wanted to know if there was any account of a transaction, at which he had been present the evening before his journey hither, concerning a poor Frenchman, who had got into a scrape which might cost him his life.

The Captain demanded particulars; and then Sir Clement told a long story, of being with a party of country friends, at the Tower, and hearing a man call out for mercy in French; and that when he enquired into the occasion of his distress, he was informed, that he had been taken up upon suspicion of treasonable practices against the government. "The poor fellow," continued he, "no sooner found that I spoke French, than be besought me to hear him, protesting that he had no evil designs; that he had been but a short time in England, and only waited the return of a Lady from the country, to quit it for ever."

Madame Duval changed colour, and listened with the utmost attention.

"Now, though I by no means approve of so many foreigners continually flocking into our country," added he, addressing himself to the Captain, "yet I could not help pitying the poor wretch, because he did not know enough of English to make his defence: however, I found it impossible to assist him, for the mob would not suffer me to interfere. In truth, I am afraid he was but roughly handled."

"Why, did they duck him?" said the Captain.

"Something of that sort," answered he.

"So much the better! so much the better!" cried the Captain, "an impudent French puppy!—I'll bet you what you will he was a rascal. I only wish all his countrymen were served the same."

"I wish you had been in his place, with all my soul!" cried Madame Duval, warmly;—"but pray, Sir, did n't nobody know who this poor gentleman was?"

"Why, I did hear his name," answered Sir Clement, "but I cannot recollect it,"

"It was n't—it was n't—Du Bois?" stammered out Madame Duval.

"The very name!" answered he, "yes, Du Bois, I remember it now."

Madame Duval's cup fell from her hand, as she repeated "Du Bois! Monsieur Du Bois, did you say?"

"Du Bois! why that's *my* friend," cried the Captain, "that's *Monseer Slippery*, i'n't it?—Why he's plaguy fond of sousing work; howsomever, I'll be sworn they gave him his fill of it."

"And I'll be sworn," cried Madame Duval, "that you're a—but I don't believe nothing about it, so you need n't be so overjoyed, for I dare say it was no more Monsieur Du Bois than I am."

"I thought at the time," said Sir Clement, very gravely, "that I had seen the gentleman before, and now I recollect, I think it was in company with you, Madame."

"With *me*, Sir!" cried Madame Duval.

"Say you so!" said the Captain, "why then, it must be he, as sure as you're alive!——Well but, my good friend, what will they do with poor *Monseer?*"

"It is difficult to say," answered Sir Clement, very thoughtfully, "but I should suppose, that if he has not good friends to appear for him, he will be in a very unpleasant situation; for these are serious sort of affairs."

"Why do you think they'll hang him?" demanded the Captain.

Sir Clement shook his head, but made no answer.

Madame Duval could no longer contain her agitation; she started from her chair, repeating, with a voice half choaked, "Hang him!—they can't,—they shan't,—let them at their peril!—however, it's all false, and I wont believe a word of it;—but I'll go to town this very moment, and see M. Du Bois myself;—I wont wait for nothing."

Mrs. Mirvan begged her not to be alarmed; but she flew out of the room, and up stairs into her own appartment. Lady Howard blamed both the gentlemen for having been so abrupt, and followed her. I would have accompanied her, but the Captain stopped me; and, having first laughed very heartily, said he was going to read his commission to his ship's company.

"Now, do you see," said he, "as to Lady Howard, I sha'nt pretend for to enlist her into my service, and so I shall e'en leave her to make it out as well as she can; but as to all you, I expect obedience and submission to orders; I am now upon a hazardous expedition, having undertaken to convoy a crazy vessel to the shore of Mortification; so, d'ye see, if any of you have any thing to propose, that will forward the enterprize,—why speak and welcome; but if any of you, that are of my chosen crew, capitulate, or enter into any treaty with the enemy,—I shall look upon you as mutinying, and turn you adrift."

Having finished this harangue, which was interlarded with many expressions, and sea-phrases, that I cannot recollect, he gave Sir Clement a wink of intelligence, and left us to ourselves.

Indeed, notwithstanding the attempts I so frequently make of writing some of the Captain's conversation, I can only give you a faint idea of his language; for almost every other word he utters, is accompanied by an oath, which, I am sure, would be as unpleasant for you to read, as for me to write. And, besides, he makes use of a thousand sea-terms, which are to me quite unintelligible.

Poor Madame Duval sent to enquire at all probable places, whether she could be conveyed to town in any stage-coach: but the Captain's servant brought her for answer, that no London stage would pass near Howard Grove till to-day. She then sent to order a chaise; but was soon assured, that no horses could be procured. She was so much inflamed by these disappointments, that she threatened to set out for town on foot, and it was with difficulty that Lady Howard dissuaded her from this mad scheme.

The whole morning was filled up with these enquiries. But, when we were all assembled to dinner, she endeavoured to appear perfectly unconcerned, and repeatedly protested that she gave not any credit to the report, as far as it regarded M. Du Bois, being very certain that he was not the person in question.

The Captain used the most provoking efforts to convince her that she deceived herself; while Sir Clement, with more art, though not less malice, affected to be of her opinion; but, at the same time that he pretended to relieve her uneasiness, by saying that he doubted not having mistaken the name, he took care to enlarge upon the danger to which the *unknown gentleman* was exposed, and expressed great concern at his perilous situation.

Dinner was hardly removed, when a letter was delivered to Madame Duval. The moment she had read it, she hastily demanded from whom it came. "A country boy brought it," answered the servant, "but he would not wait."

"Run after him this instant!" cried she, "and be sure you bring him back. *Mon Dieu! quel avanture! que ferai-je?*" [1]

"What's the matter? what's the matter?" said the Captain.

"Why nothing,—nothing's the matter. *O mon Dieu!*"

And she rose, and walked about the room.

"Why, what—has *Monseer* sent to you?" continued the Captain: "is that there letter from him?"

"No,—it i'n't;—besides, if it is, it's nothing to you."

"O then, I'm sure it is! Pray now, Madame, don't be so close; come, tell us all about it,—what does he say? how did he relish the horse-pond?—which did he find best, sousing *single* or *double?*—'Fore George, 'twas plaguy unlucky you was not with him!"

"It's no such a thing, Sir," cried she, very angrily, "and if you're so very fond of a horse-pond, I wish you'd put yourself into one, and not be always a thinking about other people's being served so."

The man then came in, to acquaint her they could not overtake the boy. She scolded violently, and was in such perturbation, that Lady

1. "My God! What a mess! What shall I do?"

Howard interfered, and begged to know the cause of her uneasiness, and whether she could assist her?

Madame Duval cast her eyes upon the Captain and Sir Clement, and said she should be glad to speak to her Ladyship, without so many witnesses.

"Well, then, Miss Anville," said the Captain, turning to me, "do you and Molly go into another room, and stay there till Mrs. Duval has opened her mind to us."

"So you may think, Sir," cried she, "but who's fool then? no, no, you need n't trouble yourself to make a ninny of me, neither, for I'm not so easily taken in, I'll assure you."

Lady Howard then invited her into the dressing-room, and I was desired to attend her.

As soon as we had shut the door, "O my Lady," exclaimed Madam Duval, "here's the most cruellest thing in the world has happened!— but that Captain is such a beast, I can't say nothing before him,—but it's all true! poor M. Du Bois is tooked up!"

Lady Howard begged her to be comforted, saying that, as M. Du Bois was certainly innocent, there could be no doubt of his ability to clear himself.

"To be sure, my Lady," answered she, "I know he is innocent; and to be sure they'll never be so wicked as to hang him for nothing?"

"Certainly not;" replied Lady Howard, "you have no reason to be uneasy. This is not a country where punishment is inflicted without proof."

"Very true, my Lady; but the worst thing is this; I cannot bear that that fellow, the Captain, should know about it; for if he does, I sha'n't never hear the last of it;—no more won't poor M. Du Bois."

"Well, well," said Lady Howard, "shew me the letter, and I will endeavour to advise you."

The letter was then produced. It was signed by the clerk of a country justice; who acquainted her, that a prisoner, then upon trial for suspicion of treasonable practices against the government, was just upon the point of being committed to jail, but having declared that he was known to her, this clerk had been prevailed upon to write, in order to enquire if she really could speak to the character and family of a Frenchman who called himself Pierre Du Bois.

When I heard the letter, I was quite amazed at its success. So improbable did it seem, that a foreigner should be taken before a *country* justice of peace, for a crime of so dangerous a nature, that I cannot imagine how Madame Duval could be alarmed, even for a moment. But, with all her violence of temper, I see that she is easily frightened, and, in fact, more cowardly than many who have not half her spirit; and so little does she reflect upon circumstances, or probability, that she is continually the dupe of her own—I ought not to say *ignorance*, but yet, I can think of no other word.

I believe that Lady Howard, from the beginning of the transaction, suspected some contrivance of the Captain, and this letter, I am sure, must confirm her suspicion: however, though she is not at all pleased with his frolick, yet she would not hazard the consequence of discovering his designs: her looks, her manner, and her character, made me draw this conclusion from her apparent perplexity; for not a word did she say, that implied any doubt of the authenticity of the letter. Indeed there seems to be a sort of tacit agreement between her and the Captain, that she should not appear to be acquainted with his schemes; by which means she at once avoids quarrels, and supports her dignity.

While she was considering what to propose, Madame Duval begged to have the use of her Ladyship's chariot, that she might go immediately to the assistance of her friend. Lady Howard politely assured her, that it would be extremely at her service; and then Madame Duval besought her not to own to the Captain what had happened, protesting that she could not endure he should know poor M. Du Bois had met with so unfortunate an accident. Lady Howard could not help smiling, though she readily promised not to *inform* the Captain of the affair. As to me, she desired my attendance; which I was by no means rejoiced at, as I was certain she was going upon a fruitless errand.

I was then commissioned to order the chariot.

At the foot of the stairs I met the Captain, who was most impatiently waiting the result of the conference. In an instant we were joined by Sir Clement. A thousand enquiries were then made concerning Madame Duval's opinion of the letter, and her intentions upon it: and when I would have left them, Sir Clement, pretending equal eagerness with the Captain, caught my hand, and repeatedly detained me, to ask some frivolous question, to the answer of which he must be totally indifferent. At length, however, I broke from them; they retired into the parlour, and I executed my commission.

The carriage was soon ready and Madame Duval having begged Lady Howard to say she was not well, stole softly down stairs, desiring me to follow her. The chariot was ordered at the garden-door; and when we were seated, she told the man, according to the clerk's directions, to drive to Mr. Justice Tyrell's, asking, at the same time, how many miles off he lived?

I expected he would have answered that he knew of no such person; but, to my great surprise, he said, "Why 'Squire Tyrell lives about nine miles beyond the park."

"Drive fast, then," cried she, "and you sha'n't be no worse for it."

During our ride, which was extremely tedious, she tormented herself with a thousand fears for M. Du Bois's safety; and piqued herself very much upon having escaped unseen by the Captain, not only that she avoided his triumph, but because she knew him to be so much M. Du Bois's enemy, that she was sure he would prejudice the Justice against him, and endeavour to take away his life. For my part, I was quite ashamed of being engaged in so ridiculous an affair, and could only think of the absurd appearance we should make upon our arrival at Mr. Tyrell's.

When we had been out near two hours, and expected every moment to stop at the place of our destination, I observed that Lady Howard's servant, who attended us on horseback, rode on forward till he was out of sight, and soon after returning, came up to the chariot-window, and delivering a note to Madame Duval, said he had met a boy, who was just coming with it to Howard Grove, from the Clerk of Mr. Tyrell.

While she was reading it, he rode round to the other window, and, making a sign for secrecy, put into my hand a slip of paper, on which was written, "Whatever happens, be not alarmed,—for *you* are safe—though you endanger all mankind!"

I readily imagined that Sir Clement must be the author of this note, which prepared me to expect some disagreeable adventure: but I had no time to ponder upon it, for Madame Duval had no sooner read her own letter, than, in an angry tone of voice, she exclaimed, "Why now what a thing is this! here we're come all this way for nothing!"

She then gave me the note, which informed her, that she need not trouble herself to go to Mr. Tyrell's as the prisoner had had the address to escape. I congratulated her upon this fortunate incident; but she was so much concerned at having rode so far in vain, that she seemed less pleased than provoked. However, she ordered the man to make what haste he could home, as she hoped, at least, to return before the Captain should suspect what had passed.

The carriage turned about, and we journeyed so quietly for near an hour, that I began to flatter myself we should be suffered to proceed to Howard Grove without further molestation, when suddenly, the footman called out, "John, are we going right?"

"Why, I a'n't sure," said the coachman, "but I'm afraid we turned wrong."

"What do you mean by that, Sirrah?" said Madame Duval, "why if you lose your way, we shall be all in the dark."

"I think we should turn to the left," said the footman.

"To the left!" answered the other; "No, no, I'm partly sure we should turn to the right."

"You had better make some enquiry," said I.

"*Ma foi*," cried Madame Duval, "we're in a fine hole, here!—they neither of them know no more than the post. However, I'll tell my Lady, as sure as you're born, so you'd better find the way."

"Let's try this lane," said the footman.

"No," said the coachman, "that's the road to Canterbury; we had best go straight on."

"Why that's the direct London road," returned the footman, "and will lead us twenty miles about."

"*Pardi*," cried Madame Duval, "why they won't go one way nor t'other! and, now we're come all this jaunt for nothing, I suppose we shan't get home to-night!"

"Let's go back to the public-house," said the footman, "and ask for a guide."

"No, no," said the other, "if we stay here a few minutes, somebody or other will pass by: and the horses are almost knocked up already."

"Well, I protest," cried Madame Duval, "I'd give a guinea to see them sots both horse-whipped! As sure as I'm alive, they're drunk! Ten to one but they'll overturn us next!"

After much debating, they, at length, agreed to go on, till we came to some inn, or met with a passenger who could direct us. We soon arrived at a small farm-house, and the footman alighted, and went into it.

In a few minutes he returned, and told us we might proceed, for that he had procured a direction; "But," added he, "it seems there are some thieves hereabouts; and so the best way will be for you to leave your watches and purses with the farmer, who I know very well, and who is an honest man, and a tenant of my Lady's."

"Thieves!" cried Madame Duval, looking aghast, "the Lord help us!—I've no doubt but we shall be all murdered!"

The farmer came up to us, and we gave him all we were worth, and the servants followed our example. We then proceeded, and Madame Duval's anger so entirely subsided, that, in the mildest manner imaginable, she intreated them to make haste, and promised to tell their Lady how diligent and obliging they had been. She perpetually stopped them, to ask if they apprehended any danger; and was, at length, so much overpowered by her fears, that she made the footman fasten his horse to the back of the carriage, and then come and seat himself within it. My endeavours to encourage her were fruitless; she sat in the middle, held the man by the arm, and protested that if he did but save her life, she would make his fortune. Her uneasiness gave me much concern, and it was with the utmost difficulty I forbore to acquaint her that she was imposed upon; but the mutual fear of the Captain's resentment to me, and of her own to him, neither of which would have any moderation, deterred me. As to the footman, he was evidently in torture from restraining his laughter, and I observed that he was frequently obliged to make most horrid grimaces, from pretended fear, in order to conceal his risibility.

Very soon after, "The robbers are coming!" cried the coachman.

The footman opened the door, and jumped out of the chariot.

Madame Duval gave a loud scream.

I could no longer preserve my silence.

"For Heaven's sake, my dear Madam," said I, "don't be alarmed,—you are in no danger—you are quite safe,—there is nothing but ———"

Here the chariot was stopped, by two men, in masks, who, at each side, put in their hands, as if for our purses. Madame Duval sunk to the bottom of the chariot, and implored their mercy. I shrieked involuntarily, although prepared for the attack: one of them held me fast, while the other tore poor Madame Duval out of the carriage, in spite of her cries, threats, and resistance.

I was really frightened, and trembled exceedingly. "My angel!" cried the man who held me, "you cannot surely be alarmed,—do you not know me?—I shall hold myself in eternal abhorrence, if I have really terrified you."

"Indeed, Sir Clement, you have," cried I,—"but, for Heaven's sake, where is Madame Duval?—why is she forced away?"

"She is perfectly safe; the Captain has her in charge: but suffer me now, my adored Miss Anville, to take the only opportunity that is allowed me, to speak upon another, a much dearer, much sweeter subject."

And then he hastily came into the chariot, and seated himself next to me. I would fain have disengaged myself from him, but he would not let me; "Deny me not, most charming of women," cried he, "deny me not this only moment that is lent me, to pour forth my soul into your gentle ears,—to tell you how much I suffer from your absence,—how much I dread your displeasure,—and how cruelly I am affected by your coldness!"

"O Sir, this is no time for such language,—pray leave me, pray go to the relief of Madame Duval,—I cannot bear that she should be treated with such indignity."

"And will you,—can you command my absence?—When may I speak to you, if not now?—does the Captain suffer me to breathe a moment out of his sight?—and are not a thousand impertinent[2] people for ever at your elbow?"

"Indeed, Sir Clement, you must change your style, or I will not hear you. The *impertinent people* you mean, are among my best friends; and you would not, if you really wished me well, speak of them so disrespectfully."

"Wish you well!—O Miss Anville, point but out to me how, in what manner I may convince you of the fervour of my passion,—tell me but what services you will accept from me,—and you shall find my life, my fortune, my whole soul at your devotion."

"I want *nothing*, Sir, that you can offer;—I beg you not to talk to me so—so strangely. Pray leave me, and pray assure yourself, you cannot

---

2. Irrelevant, not to the purpose.

take any method so successless to shew any regard for me, as entering into schemes so frightful to Madame Duval, and so disagreeable to myself."

"The scheme was the Captain's; I even opposed it: though, I own, I could not refuse myself the so-long-wished-for happiness, of speaking to you once more, without so many of—your *friends* to watch me. And I had flattered myself, that the note I charged the footman to give you, would have prevented the alarm you have received."

"Well, Sir, you have now, I hope, said enough; and, if you will not go yourself to see for Madame Duval, at least suffer *me* to enquire what is become of her."

"And when may I speak to you again?"

"No matter when,—I don't know,—perhaps—"

"Perhaps what, my angel?"

"Perhaps *never*, Sir, —— if you torment me thus."

"Never! O Miss Anville, how cruel, how piercing to my soul is that icy word!—Indeed, I cannot endure such displeasure."

"Then, Sir, you must not provoke it. Pray leave me directly."

"I will, Madam: but let me, at least, make a merit of my obedience,— allow me to hope that you will, in future, be less averse to trusting yourself for a few moments alone with me."

I was surprised at the freedom of this request; but, while I hesitated how to answer it, the other mask came up to the chariot-door, and, in a voice almost stifled with laughter, said, "I've done for her!—the old buck is safe;—but we must sheer off directly, or we shall be all aground."

Sir Clement instantly left me, mounted his horse, and rode off. The Captain, having given some directions to the servants, followed him.

I was both uneasy and impatient to know the fate of Madame Duval, and immediately got out of the chariot to seek her. I desired the footman to shew me which way she was gone; he pointed with his finger, by way of answer, and I saw that he dared not trust his voice to make any other. I walked on, a very quick pace, and soon, to my great consternation, perceived the poor lady, seated upright in a ditch. I flew to her, with unfeigned concern at her situation. She was sobbing, nay, almost roaring, and in the utmost agony of rage and terror. As soon as she saw me, she redoubled her cries, but her voice was so broken, I could not understand a word she said. I was so much shocked, that it was with difficulty I forebore exclaiming against the cruelty of the Captain, for thus wantonly ill-treating her; and I could not forgive myself for having passively suffered the deception. I used my utmost endeavours to comfort her, assuring her of our present safety, and begging her to rise, and return to the chariot.

Almost bursting with passion, she pointed to her feet, and with frightful violence, she actually beat the ground with her hands.

I then saw, that her feet were tied together with a strong rope, which was fastened to the upper branch of a tree, even with an hedge which ran along the ditch where she sat. I endeavoured to untie the knot, but soon found it was infinitely beyond my strength. I was, therefore, obliged to apply to the footman; but being very unwilling to add to his mirth, by the sight of Madame Duval's situation, I desired him to lend me a knife; I returned with it, and cut the rope. Her feet were soon disentangled, and then, though with great difficulty I assisted her to rise. But what was my astonishment, when, the moment she was up, she hit me a violent slap on the face! I retreated from her with precipitation and dread, and she then loaded me with reproaches, which, though almost untelligible, convinced me that she imagined I had voluntarily deserted her; but she seemed not to have the slightest suspicion that she had not been attacked by real robbers.

I was so much surprised and confounded at the blow, that, for some time, I suffered her to rave without making any answer; but her extreme agitation, and real suffering, soon dispelled my anger, which all turned into compassion. I then told her, that I had been forcibly detained from following her, and assured her of my real sorrow at her ill-usage.

She began to be somewhat appeased; and I again entreated her to return to the carriage, or give me leave to order that it should draw up to the place where we stood. She made no answer, till I told her, that the longer we remained still, the greater would be the danger of our ride home. Struck with this hint, she suddenly, and with hasty steps, moved forward.

Her dress was in such disorder, that I was quite sorry to have her figure exposed to the servants, who all of them, in imitation of their master, hold her in derision: however, the disgrace was unavoidable.

The ditch, happily, was almost quite dry, or she must have suffered still more seriously; yet, so forlorn, so miserable a figure, I never before saw. Her head-dress had fallen off; her linen was torn; her negligee had not a pin left in it; her petticoats she was obliged to hold on; and her shoes were perpetually slipping off. She was covered with dirt, weeds, and filth, and her face was really horrible, for the pomatum and powder from her head, and the dust from the road, were quite *pasted* on her skin by her tears, which, with her *rouge*, made so frightful a mixture, that she hardly looked human.

The servants were ready to die with laughter, the moment they saw her; but not all my remonstrances could prevail upon her to get into her carriage, till she had most vehemently reproached them both, for not rescuing her. The footman, fixing his eyes on the ground, as if fearful of again trusting himself to look at her, protested that the robbers had vowed they would shoot him, if he moved an inch, and that one of them had stayed to watch the chariot, while the other carried her off; adding, that the reason of their behaving so barbarously, was to revenge our having secured our purses. Notwithstanding her anger, she gave immediate credit to what he said, and really imagined that her want of money had irritated the pretended robbers to treat her with such cruelty. I determined, therefore, to be carefully upon my guard, not to betray the imposition, which could now answer no other purpose, than occasioning an irreparable breach between her and the Captain.

Just as we were seated in the chariot, she discovered the loss which her head had sustained, and called out, "My God! what is become of my hair?—why the villain has stole all my curls!"

She then ordered the man to run and see if he could find any of them in the ditch. He went, and presently returning, produced a great quantity of hair, in such a nasty condition, that I was amazed she would take it; and the man, as he delivered it to her, found it impossible to keep his countenance; which she no sooner observed, than all her stormy passions were again raised. She flung the battered curls in his face, saying, "Sirrah, what do you grin for? I wish you'd been served so yourself, and you would n't have found it no such joke: you are the impudentest fellow ever I see, and if I find you dare grin at me any more, I shall make no ceremony of boxing your ears."

Satisfied with the threat, the man hastily retired, and we drove on.

Her anger now subsiding into grief, she began most sorrowfully to lament her case. "I believe," she cried, "never nobody was so unlucky as I am! and so here, because I ha'nt had misfortunes enough already, that puppy has made me lose my curls!—Why, I can't see nobody without them:—only look at me,—I was never so bad off in my life before. *Pardi*, if I'd know'd as much, I'd have brought two or three sets with me: but I'd never a thought of such a thing as this."

Finding her now somewhat pacified, I ventured to ask an account of her adventure, which I will endeavour to write in her own words.

"Why, child, all this misfortune comes of that puppy's making us leave our money behind us; for as soon as the robber see I did not put nothing in his hands, he lugged me out of the chariot by main force, and I verily thought he'd have murdered me. He was as strong as a lion; I was no more in his hands than a child. But I believe never nobody was so abused before, for he dragged me down the road, pulling and hawling me all the way, as if I'd no more feeling than a horse. I'm sure I wish I could see that man cut up and quartered alive! however, he'll come to the gallows, that's one good thing. So, as soon as we'd got out of sight of the chariot, though he need n't have been afraid, for if he'd beat me to a mummy,[3] those cowardly fellows would n't have said nothing to it—So, when I was got there, what does he do, but, all of a sudden, he takes me by both the shoulders, and he gives me such a shake!—*Mon Dieu!* I shall never forget it, if I live to be an hundred. I'm sure I dare say I'm out of joint all over. And, though I made as much

3. "A pulpy substance or mass" (*OED*).

noise as I ever could, he took no more notice of it than nothing at all, but there he stood, shaking me in that manner, as if he was doing it for a wager. I'm determined, if it costs me all my fortune, I'll see that villain hanged. He shall be found out, if there's e'er a justice in England. So when he had shook me till he was tired, and I felt all over like a jelly, without saying never a word, he takes and pops me into the ditch! I'm sure I thought he'd have murdered me, as much as I ever thought any thing in my life, for he kept bumping me about, as if he thought nothing too bad for me. However, I'm resolved I'll never leave my purse behind me again, the longest day I have to live. So when he could n't stand over me no longer, he holds out his hands again for my money; but he was as cunning as could be, for he would n't speak a word, because I should n't swear to his voice; however, that sha'nt save him, for I'll swear to him any day in the year, if I can but catch him. So, when I told him I had no money, he fell to jerking me again, just as if he had but that moment begun! And, after that, he got me close by a tree, and out of his pocket he pulls a great cord!—It's a wonder I did not swoon away, for as sure as you're alive, he was going to hang me to that tree. I screamed like any thing mad, and told him if he would but spare my life, I'd never prosecute him, nor tell nobody what he'd done to me: so he stood some time, quite in a brown study, a thinking what he should do. And so, after that, he forced me to sit down in the ditch, and he tied my feet together, just as you see them, and then, as if he had not done enough, he twitched off my cap, and, without saying nothing, got on his horse, and left me in that condition, thinking, I suppose, that I might lie there and perish."

Though this narrative almost compelled me to laugh, yet I was really irritated with the Captain, for carrying his love of tormenting,—*sport*, he calls it,—to such barbarous and unjustifiable extremes. I consoled and soothed her as well as I was able, and told her that, since M. Du Bois had escaped, I hoped when she recovered from her fright, all would end well.

"Fright, child!" repeated she, "why that's not half;—I promise you, I wish it was; but here I'm bruised from top to toe, and it's well if ever I have the right use of my limbs again. However, I'm glad the villain got nothing but his trouble for his pains. But here the worst is to come, for I can't go out, because I've got no curls, and so he'll be escaped, before I can get to the Justice to stop him. I'm resolved I'll tell Lady Howard how her man served me, for if he had n't made me fling 'em away, I dare say I could have pinned them up well enough for the country."

"Perhaps Lady Howard may be able to lend you a cap that will wear without them."

"Lady Howard, indeed! why, do you think I'd wear one of her dowdies? No, I'll promise you, I sha'nt put on no such disguisement. It's the unluckiest thing in the world that I did not make the man pick up the curls again; but he put me in such a passion, I could not think of nothing. I know I can't get none at Howard Grove for love nor money, for of all the stupid places ever I see, that Howard Grove is the worst! there's never no getting nothing one wants."

This sort of conversation lasted till we arrived at our journey's end; and then, a new distress occurred; Madame Duval was eager to speak to Lady Howard and Mrs. Mirvan, and to relate her misfortunes, but she could not endure that Sir Clement or the Captain should see her in such disorder, for she said they were so ill-natured, that instead of pitying her, they would only make a jest of her disasters. She therefore sent me first into the house, to wait for an opportunity of their being out of the way, that she might steal up stairs unobserved. In this I succeeded, as the gentlemen thought it most prudent not to seem watching for her; though they both contrived to divert themselves with peeping at her as she passed.

She went immediately to bed, where she had her supper. Lady Howard and Mrs. Mirvan both of them very kindly sat with her, and listened to her tale with compassionate attention; while Miss Mirvan and I retired to our own room, where I was very glad to end the troubles of the day in a comfortable conversation.

The Captain's raptures, during supper, at the success of his plan, were boundless. I spoke, afterwards, to Mrs. Mirvan, with the openness which her kindness encourages, and begged her to remonstrate with him upon the cruelty of tormenting Madame Duval so causelessly. She promised to take the first opportunity of starting the subject, but said he was, at present, so much elated that he would not listen to her with any patience. However, should he make any new efforts to molest her, I can by no means consent to be passive. Had I imagined he would have been so violent, I would have risked his anger in her defence much sooner.

She has kept her bed all day, and declares she is almost bruised to death.

Adieu, dear Sir. What a long letter have I written! I could almost fancy I sent it you from London!

Letter III.

EVELINA IN CONTINUATION.

Howard Grove, May 15th.

This insatiable Captain, if left to himself, would not, I believe, rest, till he had tormented Madame Duval into a fever. He seems to have no delight but in terrifying or provoking her, and all his thoughts apparently turn upon inventing such methods as may do it most effectually.

She had her breakfast again in bed yesterday morning; but during ours, the Captain, with a very significant look at Sir Clement, gave us to understand, that he thought she had now rested long enough to bear the hardships of a fresh campaign.

His meaning was obvious, and, therefore, I resolved to endeavour immediately to put a stop to his intended exploits. When breakfast was over, I followed Mrs. Mirvan out of the parlour, and begged her to lose no time in pleading the cause of Madame Duval with the Captain. "My love," answered she, "I have already expostulated with him; but all I can say is fruitless, while his favourite Sir Clement contrives to urge him on."

"Then I will go and speak to Sir Clement," said I, "for I know he will desist, if I request him."

"Have a care, my dear!" said she, smiling, "it is sometimes dangerous to make requests to men, who are too desirous of receiving them."

"Well then, my dear Madam, will you give me leave to speak myself to the Captain?"

"Willingly; nay, I will accompany you to him."

I thanked her, and we went to seek him. He was walking in the garden with Sir Clement. Mrs. Mirvan most obligingly made an opening for my purpose, by saying, "Mr. Mirvan, I have brought a petitioner with me."

"Why what's the matter now?" cried he.

I was fearful of making him angry, and stammered very much, when I told him, I hoped he had no new plan for alarming Madame Duval.

"*New* plan!" cried he "why, you don't suppose the *old* one would do again, do you? Not but what it was a very good one, only I doubt she would n't bite."

"Indeed, Sir," said I, "she has already suffered too much, and I hope you will pardon me, if I take the liberty of telling you, that I think it my duty to do all in my power to prevent her being again so much terrified."

A sullen gloominess instantly clouded his face, and, turning short from me, he said, I might do as I pleased, but that I should much sooner repent than repair my officiousness.

I was too much disconcerted at this rebuff, to attempt making any answer, and, finding that Sir Clement warmly espoused my cause, I walked away, and left them to discuss the point together.

Mrs. Mirvan, who never speaks to the Captain when he is out of humour, was glad to follow me, and with her usual sweetness, made a thousand apologies for her husband's ill-manners.

When I left her, I went to Madame Duval, who was just risen, and employed in examining the cloaths she had on the day of her ill usage.

"Here's a sight!" cried she. "Come here, child,—only look—*Pardi*, so long as I've lived, I never see so much before! Why, all my things are spoilt, and, what's worse, my sacque [1] was as good as new. Here's the

---

1. A loose gown.

second *negligee* I've had used in this manner!—I am sure I was a fool to put it on, in such a lonesome place as this; however, if I stay here these ten years, I'll never put on another good gown, that I'm resolved."

"Will you let the maid try if she can iron it out, or clean it, Ma'am?"

"No, she'll only make bad worse.—But look here, now, here's a cloak! *Mon Dieu!* why, it looks like a dish-clout! Of all the unluckinesses, that ever I met, this is the worst! for, do you know, I bought it but the day before I left Paris?—Besides, into the bargain, my cap's quite gone; where the villain twitched it, I don't know, but I never see no more of it, from that time to this. Now you must know this was the becomingest cap I had in the world, for I've never another with pink ribbon in it; and, to tell you the truth, if I had n't thought to have seen M. Du Bois, I'd no more have put it on than I'd have flown; for as to what one wears in such a stupid place as this, it signifies no more than nothing at all."

She then told me, that she had been thinking all night of a contrivance to hinder the Captain from finding out her loss of curls; which was, having a large gauze handkerchief pinned on her head as a hood, and saying she had the tooth-ach.

"To tell you the truth," added she, "I believe that Captain is one of the worst men in the world; he's always making a joke of me; and as to his being a gentleman, he has no more manners than a bear, for he's always upon the grin when one's in distress; and, I declare, I'd rather be done anything to than laugh'd at, for, to my mind, it's one or other the disagreeablest thing in the world."

Mrs. Mirvan, I found, had been endeavouring to dissuade her from the design she had formed, of having recourse to the law, in order to find out the supposed robbers; for she dreads a discovery of the Captain, during Madame Duval's stay at Howard Grove, as it could not fail being productive of infinite commotion. She has, therefore, taken great pains to shew the inutility of applying to justice, unless she were more able to describe the offenders against whom she would appear; and has assured her, that as she neither heard their voices, nor saw their faces, she cannot possibly swear to their persons, or obtain any redress.

Madame Duval, in telling me this, extremely lamented her hard fate, that she was thus prevented from revenging her injuries; which, however, she vowed she would not be persuaded to *pocket tamely*,[2] "because," added she, "if such villains as these are let to have their own way, and nobody takes no notice of their impudence, they'll make no more ado than nothing at all of tying people in ditches, and such things as that: however, I shall consult with M. Du Bois, as soon as I can ferret out where he's hid himself. I'm sure I've a right to his advice, for it's all along of his gaping about at the Tower that I've met with these misfortunes."

2. To accept the insult meekly.

"M. Du Bois," said I, "will, I am sure, be very sorry when he hears what has happened."

"And what good will that do now?—that won't unspoil all my cloaths; I can tell him, I a'n't much obliged to him, though it's no fault of his;—yet it i'n't the less provokinger for that. I'm sure, if he had been there, to have seen me served in that manner, and put neck and heels into a ditch, he'd no more have thought it was me, than the Pope of Rome. I'll promise you, whatever you may think of it, I sha'nt have no rest, night nor day, till I find out that rogue."

"I have no doubt, Madam, but you will soon discover him."

"*Pardi*, if I do, I'll hang him, as sure as fate!—but what's the oddest, is that he should take such a' special spite against *me*, above all the rest! it was as much for nothing, as could be, for I don't know what I had done, so particular bad, to be used in that manner: I'm sure, I had n't given him no offence, as I know of, for I never see his face all the time; and as to screaming a little, I think it's very hard if one must n't do such a thing as that, when one's put in fear of one's life."

During this conversation, she endeavoured to adjust her head dress, but could not at all please herself. Indeed, had I not been present, I should have thought it impossible for a woman at her time of life to be so very difficult in regard to dress. What she may have in view, I cannot imagine, but the labour of the toilette seems the chief business of her life.

When I left her, in my way down stairs, I met Sir Clement, who, with great earnestness, said he must not be denied the honour of a moment's conversation with me; and then, without waiting for an answer, he led me to the garden, at the door of which, however, I absolutely insisted upon stopping.

He seemed very serious, and said, in a grave tone of voice, "At length, Miss Anville, I flatter myself I have hit upon an expedient that will oblige you, and therefore, though it is death to myself, I will put in practice."

I begged him to explain himself.

"I saw your desire of saving Madame Duval, and scarce could I refrain giving the brutal Captain my real opinion of his savage conduct; but I am unwilling to quarrel with him, lest I should be denied entrance into a house which you inhabit; I have been endeavouring to prevail with him to give up his absurd new scheme, but I find him impenetrable:—I have therefore determined to make a pretence for suddenly leaving this place, dear as it is to me, and containing all I most admire and adore;—and I will stay in town till the violence of this boobyish humour is abated."

He stopped; but I was silent, for I knew not what I ought to say. He took my hand, which he pressed to his lips, saying, "And must I, then,

Miss Anville, must I quit you—sacrifice voluntarily my greatest felicity,—and yet not be honoured with one word, one look of approbation?"

I withdrew my hand, and said, with a half laugh, "You know so well, Sir Clement, the value of the favours you confer, that it would be superfluous for me to point it out."

"Charming, charming girl! how does your wit, your understanding rise upon me daily! and must I, can I part with you?—will no other method —— "

"O Sir, do you so soon repent the good office you had planned for Madame Duval?"

"For Madame Duval!—cruel creature, and will you not even suffer me to place to your account the sacrifice I am about to make?"

"You must place it, Sir, to what account you please; but I am too much in haste now to stay here any longer."

And then I would have left him, but he held me, and, rather impatiently, said, "If, then, I cannot be so happy as to oblige *you*, Miss Anville, you must not be surprised, should I seek to oblige myself. If my scheme is not honoured with your approbation, for which alone it was formed, why should I, to my own infinite dissatisfaction, pursue it?"

We were then, for a few minutes, both silent; I was really unwilling he should give up a plan which would so effectually break into the Captain's designs, and, at the same time, save me the pain of disobliging him; and I should instantly and thankfully have accepted his offered civility, had not Mrs. Mirvan's caution made me fearful. However, when he pressed me to speak, I said, in an ironical voice, "I had thought, Sir, that the very strong sense you have yourself of the favour you propose to me, would sufficiently have repaid you, but, as I was mistaken, I must thank you myself." "And now," making a low court'sy, "I hope, Sir, you are satisfied."

"Loveliest of thy sex—" he began; but I forced myself from him, and ran upstairs.

Soon after, Miss Mirvan told me that Sir Clement had just received a letter, which obliged him instantly to leave the Grove, and that he had actually ordered a chaise. I then acquainted her with the real state of the affair. Indeed, I conceal nothing from her, she is so gentle and sweet-tempered, that it gives me great pleasure to place an entire confidence in her.

At dinner, I must own, we all missed him; for though the flightiness of his behaviour to me, when we are by ourselves, is very distressing, yet, in large companies, and general conversation, he is extremely entertaining and agreeable. As to the Captain, he has been so much chagrined at his departure, that he has scarce spoken a word since he went: but Madame Duval, who made her first public appearance since her accident, was quite in raptures that she escaped seeing him.

The money which we left at the farm-house, has been returned to us. What pains the Captain must have taken to arrange and manage the adventures which he chose we should meet with! Yet he must certainly be discovered, for Madame Duval is already very much perplexed, at having received a letter this morning from M. Du Bois, in which he makes no mention of his imprisonment. However, she has so little suspicion, that she imputes his silence upon the subject, to his fears that the letter might be intercepted.

Not one opportunity could I meet with, while Sir Clement was here, to enquire after his friend Lord Orville: but I think it was strange he should never mention him unasked. Indeed, I rather wonder that Mrs. Mirvan herself did not introduce the subject, for she always seemed particularly attentive to him.

And now, once more, all my thoughts involuntarily turn upon the letter I so soon expect from Paris. This visit of Sir Clement has, however, somewhat diverted my fears, and therefore I am very glad he made it at this time. Adieu, my dear Sir.

Letter IV.

SIR JOHN BELMONT TO LADY HOWARD.

Madam,   Paris, May 11.

I have this moment the honour of your Ladyship's letter, and I will not wait another, before I return an answer.

It seldom happens that a man, though extolled as a saint, is really without blemish; or that another, though reviled as a devil, is really without humanity. Perhaps the time is not very distant, when I may have the honour to convince your Ladyship of this truth, in regard to Mr. Villars and myself.

As to the young lady, whom Mr. Villars so obligingly proposes presenting to me, I wish her all the happiness to which, by your Ladyship's account, she seems entitled; and, if she has a third part of the merit of *her* to whom you compare her, I doubt not but Mr. Villars will be more successful in every other application he may make for her advantage, than he can ever be in any with which he may be pleased to favour me.

> I have the honour to be
> Madam,
> your Ladyship's most humble
> and most obedient servant
> JOHN BELMONT.

Letter V.

EVELINA TO THE REV. MR. VILLARS.

Howard Grove, May 18.

Well, my dear Sir, all is now over! the letter so anxiously expected, is at length arrived, and my doom is fixed. The various feelings which oppress me, I have not language to describe; nor need I,—you know my heart, you have yourself formed it,—and its sensations upon this occasion, you may but too readily imagine.

Outcast as I am, and rejected for ever by him to whom I of right belong,—shall I now implore *your* continued protection?—no, no,—I will not offend your generous heart, which, open to distress, has no wish but to relieve it, with an application that would seem to imply a doubt. I am more secure than ever of your kindness, since you now know upon that is my sole dependence.

I endeavour to bear this stroke with composure, and in such a manner as if I had already received your counsel and consolation. Yet, at times, my emotions are almost too much for me. O Sir, what a letter for a parent to write! must I not myself be deaf to the voice of Nature, if I could endure to be thus absolutely abandoned, without regret? I dare not even to you, nor would I, could I help it, to myself, acknowledge all that I think; for, indeed, I have sometimes sentiments upon this rejection, which my strongest sense of duty can scarcely correct. Yet, suffer me to ask,—might not this answer have been softened?—was it not enough to disclaim me for ever, without treating me with contempt, and wounding me with derision?

But, while I am thus thinking of myself, I forget how much more he is the object of sorrow, than I am! Alas, what amends can he make himself, for the anguish he is hoarding up for time to come! My heart bleeds for him, whenever this reflection occurs to me.

What is said of *you*, my protector, my friend, my benefactor!—I dare not trust myself to comment upon. Gracious Heaven! what a return for goodness so unparalleled!

I would fain endeavour to divert my thoughts from this subject, but even that is not in my power; for, afflicting as this letter is to me, I find that it will not be allowed to conclude the affair, though it does all my expectations: for Madame Duval has determined not to let it rest here. She heard the letter in great wrath, and protested she would not be so easily answered; she regretted her facility in having been prevailed upon to yield the direction of this affair to those who knew not how to manage it, and vowed she would herself undertake and conduct it in future.

It is in vain that I have pleaded against her resolution, and besought her to forbear an attack, where she has nothing to expect but resentment; especially as there seems to be a hint, that Lady Howard will one day be more openly dealt with: she will not hear me; she is furiously bent upon a project which is terrible to think of,—for she means to go herself to Paris, take me with her, and there, *face to face*, demand justice!

How to appease or to persuade her, I know not; but for the universe would I not be dragged, in such a manner, to an interview so awful, with a parent I have never yet beheld!

Lady Howard and Mrs. Mirvan are both of them infinitely shocked at the present situation of affairs, and they seem to be even more kind to me than ever; and my dear Maria, who is the friend of my heart, uses her utmost efforts to console me, and, when she fails in her design, with still greater kindness she sympathises in my sorrow.

I very much rejoice, however, that Sir Clement Willoughby had left us before this letter arrived. I am sure the general confusion of the house would, otherwise, have betrayed to him the whole of a tale which I now, more than ever, wish to have buried in oblivion.

Lady Howard thinks I ought not to disoblige Madame Duval, yet she acknowledges the impropriety of my accompanying her abroad upon such an enterprize. Indeed I would rather die, than force myself into his presence. But so vehement is Madame Duval, that she would instantly have compelled me to attend her to town, in her way to Paris, had not Lady Howard so far exerted herself, as to declare she could by no means consent to my quitting her house, till she gave me up to you, by whose permission I had entered it.

She was extremely angry at this denial; and the Captain, by his sneers and raillery, so much encreased her rage, that she has positively declared, should your next letter dispute her authority to guide me by her own pleasure, she will, without hesitation, make a journey to Berry Hill, and *teach you to know who she is*.

Should she put this threat in execution, nothing could give me greater uneasiness, for her violence and volubility would almost distract you.

Unable as I am to act for myself, or to judge what conduct I ought to pursue, how grateful do I feel myself, that I have such a guide and director to counsel and instruct me as yourself!

Adieu, my dearest Sir! Heaven, I trust, will never let me live to be repulsed and derided by *you*, to whom I may now sign myself

Wholly your
EVELINA.

Letter VI.

Berry Hill, May 21.

Let not my Evelina be depressed by a stroke of fortune for which she is not responsible. No breach of duty on your part, has incurred the unkindness which has been shewn you; nor have you, by any act of imprudence, provoked either censure or reproach. Let me entreat you, therefore, my dearest child, to support yourself with that courage which your innocency ought to inspire; and let all the affliction you allow yourself, be for him only, who, not having that support, must one day be but too severely sensible how much he wants it.

The hint thrown out concerning myself, is wholly unintelligible to me: my heart, I dare own, fully acquits me of vice, but *without blemish*, I have never ventured to pronounce myself. However, it seems his intention to be hereafter more explicit, and *then*,—should any thing appear, that has on *my* part, contributed to those misfortunes we lament, let me, at least, say, that the most partial of my friends cannot be so much astonished as I shall myself be, at such a discovery.

The mention, also, of any *future applications* I may make, is equally beyond my comprehension. But I will not dwell upon a subject which almost compels from me reflections that cannot but be wounding to a heart so formed for filial tenderness as my Evelina's. There is an air of mystery throughout the letter, the explanation of which I will await in silence.

The scheme of Madame Duval is such as might be reasonably expected from a woman so little inured to disappointment, and so totally incapable of considering the delicacy of your situation. Your averseness to her plan gives me pleasure, for it exactly corresponds with my own. Why will she not make the journey she projects by herself? She would not have even the wish of an opposition to encounter. And then, once more, might my child and myself be left to the quiet enjoyment of that peaceful happiness, which she alone has interrupted. As to her coming hither, I could, indeed, dispense with such a visit; but, if she will not be satisfied with my refusal by letter, I must submit to the task of giving it her in person.

My impatience for your return is encreased by your account of Sir Clement Willoughby's visit to Howard Grove. I am but little surprised at the perseverance of his assiduities to interest you in his favour; but I am very much hurt that you should be exposed to addresses, which, by their privacy, have an air that shocks me. You cannot, my love, be too circumspect; the slightest carelessness on your part, will be taken advantage of, by a man of his disposition. It is not sufficient for you to be reserved; his conduct even calls for your resentment: and should he again, as will doubtless be his endeavour, contrive to solicit your favour in private, let your disdain and displeasure be so marked, as to constrain a change in his behaviour. Though, indeed, should his visit be repeated while you remain at the Grove, Lady Howard must pardon me if I shorten your's.

Adieu, my child. You will always make my respects to the hospitable family to which we are so much obliged.

Letter VII.

MR. VILLARS TO LADY HOWARD.

Dear Madam,   Berry Hill, May 27.

I believe your Ladyship will not be surprised at hearing I have had a visit from Madame Duval, as I doubt not her having made known her intention before she left Howard Grove. I would gladly have excused myself this meeting, could I have avoided it decently; but, after so long a journey, it was not possible to refuse her admittance.

She told me, that she came to Berry Hill, in consequence of a letter I had sent to her grand-daughter, in which I had forbid her going to Paris. Very roughly she then called me to account for the authority which I assumed; and, had I been disposed to have argued with her, she would very angrily have disputed the right by which I used it. But I declined all debating. I therefore listened very quietly, till she had so much fatigued herself with talking, that she was glad, in her turn, to be silent. And then, I begged to know the purport of her visit.

She answered, that she came to make me relinquish the power I had usurped over her grand-daughter, and assured me she would not quit the place till she succeeded.

But I will not trouble your Ladyship with the particulars of this dis-agreeable conversation; nor should I, but on account of the result, have chosen so unpleasant a subject for your perusal. However, I will be as concise as I possibly can, that the better occupations of your Ladyship's time may be the less impeded.

When she found me inexorable in refusing Evelina's attending her to Paris, she peremptorily insisted, that she should, at least, live with her in London, till Sir John Belmont's return. I remonstrated against this scheme with all the energy in my power; but the contest was vain; she lost her patience, and I my time. She declared that if I was resolute in opposing her, she would instantly make a will, in which she would leave all her fortune to strangers, though, otherwise, she intended her grand-daughter for her sole heiress.

To me, I own, this threat seemed of little consequence; I have long accustomed myself to think, that, with a competency,[1] of which she is

---

1. A sufficient income.

sure, my child might be as happy as in the possession of millions: but the incertitude of her future fate, deters me from following implicitly the dictates of my present judgment. The connections she may hereafter form, the style of life for which she may be destined, and the future family to which she may belong, are considerations which give but too much weight to the menaces of Madame Duval. In short, Madam, after a discourse infinitely tedious, I was obliged, though very reluctantly, to compromise with this ungovernable woman, by consenting that Evelina should pass one month with her.

I never made a concession with so bad a grace, or so much regret. The violence and vulgarity of this woman, her total ignorance of propriety, the family to which she is related, and the company she is likely to keep, are objections so forcible to her having the charge of this dear child, that nothing less than my diffidence of the right I have of depriving her of so large a fortune, would have induced me to listen to her proposal. Indeed we parted, at last, equally discontented, she, at what I had refused, I, at what I had granted.

It now only remains for me to return your Ladyship my humble acknowledgments for the kindness which you have so liberally shewn to my ward: and to beg you would have the goodness to part with her, when Madame Duval thinks proper to claim the promise which she has extorted from me.

I am,
Dear Madam, &c.
ARTHUR VILLARS.

Letter VIII.

MR. VILLARS TO EVELINA.

Berry Hill, May 28.

With a reluctance which occasions me inexpressible uneasiness, I have been almost compelled to consent that my Evelina should quit the protection of the hospitable and respectable Lady Howard, and accompany Madame Duval to a city which I had hoped she would never again have entered. But alas, my dear child, we are the slaves of custom, the dupes of prejudice, and dare not stem the torrent of an opposing world, even though our judgments condemn our compliance! however, since the die is cast, we must endeavour to make the best of it.

You will have occasion, in the course of the month you are to pass with Madame Duval, for all the circumspection and prudence you can call to your aid: she will not, I know, propose any thing to you which she thinks wrong herself; but you must learn not only to *judge* but to *act* for yourself: if any schemes are started, any engagements made, which your understanding represents to you as improper, exert yourself resolutely in avoiding them, and do not, by a too passive facility, risk the censure of the world, or your own future regret.

You cannot too assiduously attend to Madame Duval herself; but I would wish you to mix as little as possible with her associates, who are not likely to be among those whose acquaintance would reflect credit upon you. Remember, my dear Evelina, nothing is so delicate as the reputation of a woman: it is, at once, the most beautiful and most brittle of all human things.

Adieu, my beloved child; I shall be but ill at ease till this month is elapsed.

A. V.

Letter IX.

EVELINA TO THE REV. MR. VILLARS.

London, June 6.

Once more, my dearest Sir, I write to you from this great city. Yesterday morning, with the truest concern, I quitted the dear inhabitants of Howard Grove, and most impatiently shall I count the days till I see them again. Lady Howard and Mrs. Mirvan took leave of me with the most flattering kindness; but indeed I knew not how to part with Maria, whose own apparent sorrow redoubled mine. She made me promise to send her a letter every post. And I shall write to her with the same freedom, and almost the same confidence, you allow me to make use of to yourself.

The Captain was very civil to me, but he wrangled with poor Madame Duval to the last moment; and, taking me aside, just before we got into the chaise, he said, "Hark'ee, Miss Anville, I've a favour for to ask of you, which is this; that you will write us word how the old gentlewoman finds herself, when she sees it was all a trick: and what the French lubber[1] says to it, and all about it."

I answered that I would obey him, though I was very little pleased with the commission, which, to me, was highly improper; but he will either treat me as an *informer*, or make me a party in his frolic.

As soon as we drove away, Madame Duval, with much satisfaction, exclaimed "*Dieu Merci*, we've got off at last! I'm sure I never desire to see that place again. It's a wonder I've got away alive; for I believe I've had the worst luck ever was known, from the time I set my foot upon the threshold. I know I wish I'd never a gone. Besides, into the bargain, it's the most dullest place in all Christendom: there's never no diversions, nor nothing at all."

Then she bewailed M. Du Bois, concerning whose adventures she continued to make various conjectures during the rest of our journey.

1. A big, clumsy, stupid fellow; a lout.

When I asked her what part of London she should reside in, she told me that Mr. Branghton was to meet us at an inn, and would conduct us to a lodging. Accordingly, we proceeded to a house in Bishopsgate-street,[2] and were led by a waiter into a room where we found Mr. Branghton.

He received us very civilly, but seemed rather surprized at seeing me, saying "Why I did n't think of your bringing Miss; however she's very welcome."

"I'll tell you how it was," said Madame Duval; "you must know I've a mind to take the girl to Paris, that she may see something of the world, and improve herself a little; besides, I've another reason, that you and I will talk more about; but do you know, that meddling old parson as I told you of, would not let her go: however, I'm resolved I'll be even with him, for I shall take her on with me, without saying never a word more to nobody."

I started at this intimation, which very much surprised me. But I am very glad she has discovered her intention, as I shall be carefully upon my guard not to venture from town with her.

Mr. Branghton then hoped we had passed our time agreeably in the country.

"O Lord, Cousin," cried she, "I've been the miserablest creature in the world! I'm sure all the horses in London sha'n't drag me into the country again of one while: why how do you think I've been served?— only guess."

"Indeed Cousin, I can't pretend to do that."

"Why then I'll tell you. Do you know, I've been robbed!—that is, the villain would have robbed me if he could, only I'd secured all my money."

"Why then, Cousin, I think your loss can't have been very great."

"O Lord, you don't know what you're a-saying; you're talking in the unthinkingest manner in the world: why it was all along of not having no money, that I met with that misfortune."

"How's that, Cousin? I don't see what great misfortune you can have met with, if you'd secured all your money."

"That's because you don't know nothing of the matter; for there the villain came to the chaise, and because we had n't got nothing to give him, though he'd no more right to our money than the man in the moon, yet, do you know, he fell into the greatest passion ever you see, and abused me in such a manner, and put me in a ditch, and got a rope, o' purpose to hang me,—and I'm sure, if that was n't misfortune enough, why I don't know what is."

"This is a hard case indeed, Cousin. But why don't you go to Justice Fielding?"

2. Named after one of the original city gates, Bishopsgate Street runs through the center of the City.

"O, as to that, I'm a going to him directly; but only I want first to see poor M. Du Bois, for the oddest thing of all is, that he has wrote to me, and never said nothing of where he is, nor what's become of him, nor nothing else."

"M. Du Bois! why he's at my house at this very time."

"M. Du Bois at your house! well, I declare this is the surprisingest part of all! however, I assure you, I think he might have comed for me, as well as you, considering what I have gone through on his account; for, to tell you the truth, it was all along of him that I met with that accident; so I don't take it very kind of him, I promise you."

"Well but, Cousin, tell me some of the particulars of this affair."

"As to the particulars, I'm sure they'd make your hair stand an end to hear them; however, the beginning of it all was through the fault of M. Du Bois: but I'll assure you, he may take care of himself in future, since he don't so much as come to see if I'm dead or alive;—but there I went for him to a justice of peace, and rode all out of the way, and did every thing in the world, and was used worser than a dog, and all for the sake of serving of him, and now, you see, he don't so much—well, I was a fool for my pains,—however, he may get somebody else to be treated so another time, for if he's taken up every day in the week, I'll never go after him no more."

This occasioned an explanation, in the course of which, Madame Duval, to her utter amazement, heard that M. Du Bois had never left London during her absence! nor did Mr. Branghton believe that he had ever been to the Tower, or met with any kind of accident.

Almost instantly, the whole truth of the transaction seemed to *rush upon her mind*, and her wrath was inconceivably violent. She asked me a thousand questions in a breath, but, fortunately, was too vehement to attend to my embarrassment, which must, otherwise, have betrayed my knowledge of the deceit. Revenge was her first wish, and she vowed she would go the next morning to Justice Fielding, and enquire what punishment she might lawfully inflict upon the Captain for his assault.

I believe we were an hour in Bishopsgate-street, before poor Madame Duval could allow any thing to be mentioned but her own story; at length, however, Mr. Branghton told her, that M. Du Bois, and all his own family, were waiting for her at his house. A hackney-coach was then called, and we proceeded to Snow-hill.

Mr. Branghton's house is small and inconvenient, though his shop, which takes in all the ground floor, is large and commodious. I believe I told you before that he is a silver-smith.

We were conducted up two pair of stairs; for the dining-room, Mr. Branghton told us, was *let*. His two daughters, their brother, M. Du Bois, and a young man, were at tea. They had waited some time for Madame Duval, but I found they had not any expectation that I should accompany her; and the young ladies, I believe, were rather more surprised than pleased when I made my appearance; for they seemed hurt that I should see their apartment. Indeed I would willingly have saved them that pain, had it been in my power.

The first person who saw me was M. Du Bois: "*Ah, mon Dieu!*" exclaimed he, "*voilà Mademoiselle!*"[3]

"Goodness," cried young Branghton, "if there is n't Miss!"

"Lord, so there is," said Miss Polly; "well, I'm sure I should never have dreamed of Miss's coming."

"Nor I neither, I'm sure," cried Miss Branghton, "or else I would not have been in this room to see her; I'm quite ashamed about it,—only not thinking of seeing any body but my aunt—however Tom, it's all your fault, for, you know very well I wanted to borrow Mr. Smith's room, only you were so *grumpy* you would not let me."

"Lord, what signifies?" said the brother, "I dare be sworn Miss has been up two pair of stairs before now;—Ha'nt you, Miss?"

I begged that I might not give them the least disturbance, and assured them that I had not any choice in regard to what room we sat in.

"Well," said Miss Polly, "when you come next, Miss, we'll have Mr. Smith's room; and it's a very pretty one, and only up one pair of stairs, and nicely furnished, and every thing."

"To say the truth," said Miss Branghton, "I thought that my cousin would not, upon any account, have come to town in the summer-time; for it's not at all the *fashion*,—so, to be sure, thinks I, she'll stay till September, when the play-houses open."

This was my reception, which I believe you will not call a very *cordial* one. Madame Duval, who, after having severely reprimanded M. Du Bois for his negligence, was just entering upon the story of her misfortunes, now wholly engaged the company.

M. Du Bois listened to her with a look of the utmost horror, repeatedly lifting up his eyes and hands, and exclaiming, "*O ciel! quel barbare!*"[4] The young ladies gave her the most earnest attention; but their brother, and the young man, kept a broad grin upon their faces during the whole recital. She was, however, too much engaged to observe them: but, when she mentioned having been tied in a ditch, young Branghton, no longer able to constrain himself, burst into a loud laugh, declaring that he had never heard any thing so *funny* in his life! His laugh was heartily re-echoed by his friend; the Miss Branghtons could not resist the example; and poor Madame Duval, to her extreme amazement, was absolutely overpowered and stopped by the violence of their mirth.

For some minutes the room seemed quite in an uproar; the rage of Madame Duval, the astonishment of M. Du Bois, and the angry interrogatories of Mr. Branghton, on one side; the convulsive tittering of the

3. "Oh, my God! . . . there's Miss!"
4. "Oh heavens! what a barbarian!"

sisters, and the loud laughs of the young men, on the other, occasioned such noise, passion, and confusion, that had any one stopped an instant on the stairs, he must have concluded himself in Bedlam. At length, however, the father brought them to order; and, half laughing, half frightened, they made Madame Duval some very awkward apologies. But she would not be prevailed upon to continue her narrative, till they had protested they were laughing at the Captain, and not at her. Appeased by this, she resumed her story; which, by the help of stuffing handkerchiefs into their mouths, the young people heard with tolerable decency.

Every body agreed, that the ill usage the Captain had given her was *actionable*, and Mr. Branghton said he was sure she might recover what damages she pleased, since she had been put in fear of her life.

She then, with great delight, declared, that she would lose no time in satisfying her revenge, and vowed she would not be contented with less than half his fortune: "For though," she said, "I don't put no value upon the money, because, *Dieu merci*,[5] I ha'n't no want of it, yet I don't wish for nothing so much as to punish that fellow; for, I'm sure, whatever's the cause of it, he owes me a great *grudge*,[6] and I know no more what it's for than you do, but he's always been doing me one spite or other ever since I knew him."

Soon after tea, Miss Branghton took an opportunity to tell me, in a whisper, that the young man I saw was a lover of her sister's, that his name was Brown, and that he was a haberdasher,[7] with many other particulars of his circumstances and family; and then she declared her utter aversion to the thoughts of such a match; but added, that her sister had no manner of spirit or ambition, though, for her part, she would ten times rather die an old maid, than marry any person but a gentleman. "And, for that matter," added she, "I believe Polly herself don't care much for him, only she's in such a hurry, because, I suppose, she's a mind to be married before me; however, she's very welcome, for, I'm sure, I don't care a pin's point whether I ever marry at all;—it's all one to me."

Some time after this, Miss Polly contrived to tell *her* story. She assured me, with much tittering, that her sister was in a great fright, lest she should be married first. "So I make her believe that I will," continued she, "for I love dearly to plague her a little; though, I declare, I don't intend to have Mr. Brown in reality; I'm sure I don't like him half well enough,—do you, Miss?"

"It is not possible for me to judge of his merits," said I, "as I am entirely a stranger to him."

"But, what do you think of him, Miss?"

5. "Thank God."
6. Has a great grudge against me.
7. A dealer in hats, caps, and small articles pertaining to dress, such as thread, tape, and ribbons.

"Why, really, I—I don't know—"

"But do you think him handsome? Some people reckon him to have a good pretty person,—but, I'm sure, for my part, I think he's monstrous ugly:—don't *you*, Miss?"

"I am no judge,—but I think his person is very—very well."

"*Very well!*—Why, pray, Miss," in a tone of vexation, "what fault can you find with it?"

"O, none at all!"

"I'm sure you must be very ill-natured if you could. Now there's Biddy says she thinks nothing of him,—but I know it's all out of spite. You must know, Miss, it makes her as mad as can be, that I should have a lover before her, but she's so proud that nobody will court her, and I often tell her she'll die an old maid. But, the thing is, she has taken it into her head, to have a liking for Mr. Smith, as lodges on the first floor; but, Lord, he'll never have her, for he's quite a fine gentleman; and besides, Mr. Brown heard him say, one day, that he'd never marry as long as he lived, for he'd no opinion of matrimony."

"And did you tell your sister this?"

"O, to be sure, I told her directly; but she did not mind me; however, if she will be a fool, she must."

This extreme want of affection, and good-nature increased the distaste I already felt for these unamiable sisters; and a confidence so entirely unsolicited and unnecessary, manifested equally their folly and their want of decency.

I was very glad when the time for our departing arrived. Mr. Branghton said our lodgings were in Holborn,[8] that we might be near his house, and neighbourly. He accompanied us to them himself.

Our rooms are large, and not inconvenient; our landlord is an hosier. I am sure I have a thousand reasons to rejoice that I am so little known; for my present situation is, in every respect, very unenviable; and I would not, for the world, be seen by any acquaintance of Mrs. Mirvan.

This morning Madame Duval, attended by all the Branghtons, actually went to a Justice in the neighbourhood, to report the Captain's ill usage of her. I had great difficulty in excusing myself from being of the party, which would have given me very serious concern. Indeed, I was extremely anxious, though at home, till I heard the result of the application; for I dread to think of the uneasiness which such an affair would occasion the amiable Mrs. Mirvan. But, fortunately, Madame Duval has received very little encouragement to proceed in her design, for she has been informed that, as she neither heard the voice, nor saw the face of the person suspected, she will find difficulty to cast[9] him upon *conjecture*, and will have but little probability of gaining her cause, unless she can procure witnesses of the transaction. Mr. Branghton, therefore, who

8. The borough to the north of the Strand in which Lincoln's Inn and Gray's Inn are located.
9. To find guilty or convict.

has considered all the circumstances of the affair, is of opinion, that the law-suit will not only be expensive, but tedious and hazardous, and has advised against it. Madame Duval, though very unwillingly, has acquiesced in his decision; but vows that if ever she is so affronted again, she will be revenged, even if she ruins herself. I am extremely glad that this ridiculous adventure seems now likely to end without more serious consequences.

Adieu, my dearest Sir. My direction is at Mr. Dawkin's, a hosier in High Holborn.[1]

Letter X.

EVELINA TO MISS MIRVAN.

June 7th.

I have no words, my sweet friend, to express the thankfulness I feel for the unbounded kindness which you, your dear mother, and the much-honoured Lady Howard, have shewn me; and still less can I find language to tell you with what reluctance I parted from such dear and generous friends, whose goodness reflects, at once, so much honour on their own hearts, and on her to whom it has been so liberally bestowed. But I will not repeat what I have already written to the kind Mrs. Mirvan; I will remember your admonitions, and confine to my own breast that gratitude with which you have filled it, and teach my pen to dwell upon subjects less painful to my generous correspondent.

O Maria, London now seems no longer the same place where I lately enjoyed so much happiness; every thing is new and strange to me; even the town itself has not the same aspect:—my situation so altered!—my home so different!—my companions so changed!—But you well know my averseness to this journey.

Indeed, to me, London now seems a desart; that gay and busy appearance it so lately wore, is now succeeded by a look of gloom, fatigue, and lassitude; the air seems stagnant, the heat is intense, the dust intolerable, and the inhabitants illiterate and under-bred. At least, such is the face of things in the part of the town where I at present reside.

Tell me, my dear Maria, do you never re-trace in your memory the time we passed here when together? to mine, it recurs for ever! And yet, I think I rather recollect a dream, or some visionary fancy, than a reality.—That I should ever have been known to Lord Orville,—that I should have spoken to—have danced with him,—seems now a romantic illusion: and that elegant politeness, that flattering attention, that high-bred delicacy, which so much distinguished him above all other men, and which struck us with such admiration, I now re-trace the remem-

1. A hosier is a maker or dealer in hose (socks and stockings). High Holborn, at the time, was the continuation of Holborn Street from Brook Street to Drury Lane.

brance of, rather as belonging to an object of ideal perfection, formed by my own imagination, than to a being of the same race and nature as those with whom I at present converse.

I have no news for you, my dear Miss Mirvan; for all that I could venture to say of Madame Duval, I have already written to your sweet mother; and as to adventures, I have none to record. Situated as I now am, I heartily hope I shall not meet with any; my wish is to remain quiet and unnoticed.

Adieu! excuse the gravity of this letter, and believe me,

Your most sincerely
affectionate and obliged
EVELINA ANVILLE.

Letter XI.

EVELINA TO THE REV. MR. VILLARS.

Holborn, June 9.

Yesterday morning, we received an invitation to dine and spend the day at Mr. Branghton's; and M. Du Bois, who was also invited, called to conduct us to Snow-hill.

Young Branghton received us at the door, and the first words he spoke were, "Do you know, sisters a'n't dressed yet."

Then, hurrying us into the house, he said to me, "Come, Miss, you shall go up stairs and catch 'em,—I dare say they're at the glass."

He would have taken my hand, but I declined this civility, and begged to follow Madame Duval.

Mr. Branghton then appeared, and led the way himself. We went, as before, up two pair of stairs; but the moment the father opened the door, the daughters both gave a loud scream. We all stopped, and then Miss Branghton called out, "Lord, Papa, what do you bring the company up here for? why, Polly and I a'n't half dressed."

"More shame for you," answered he, "here's your aunt, and cousin, and M. Du Bois, all waiting, and ne'er a room to take them to."

"Who'd have thought of their coming so soon?" cried she: "I'm sure for my part I thought Miss was used to nothing but quality hours."

"Why, I shan't be ready this half-hour yet," said Miss Polly; "can't they stay in the shop, till we're dressed?"

Mr. Branghton was very angry, and scolded them violently: however, we were obliged to descend, and stools were procured for us in the shop, where we found the brother, who was highly delighted, he said, that his sisters had been *catched*; and he thought proper to entertain me with a long account of their tediousness, and the many quarrels they all had together.

When, at length, these ladies were equipped to their satisfaction, they made their appearance; but before any conversation was suffered to pass between them and us, they had a long and most disagreeable dialogue with their father, to whose reprimands, though so justly incurred, they replied with the utmost pertness, and rudeness, while their brother, all the time, laughed aloud.

The moment they perceived this, they were so much provoked, that, instead of making any apologies to Madame Duval, they next began a quarrel with him. "Tom, what do you laugh for? I wonder what business you have to be always a laughing when Papa scolds us?"

"Then what business have you to be such a while getting on your cloaths? You're never ready, you know well enough."

"Lord, Sir, I wonder what that's to you! I wish you'd mind your own affairs, and not trouble yourself about ours. How should a boy like you know any thing?"

"A boy, indeed! not such a boy, neither; I'll warrant you'll be glad to be as young, when you come to be old maids."

This sort of dialogue we were amused with till dinner was ready, when we again mounted up two pair of stairs.

In our way, Miss Polly told me that her sister had asked Mr. Smith for his room to dine in, but he had refused to lend it; "because," she said, "one day it happened to be a little greased: however, we shall have it to drink tea in, and then, perhaps, you may see him, and I assure you he's quite like one of the quality, and dresses as fine, and goes to balls and dances, and every thing quite in taste;—and besides, Miss, he keeps a foot-boy of his own, too."

The dinner was ill-served, ill-cooked, and ill-managed. The maid who waited had so often to go down stairs for something that was forgotten, that the Branghtons were perpetually obliged to rise from table themselves, to get plates, knives and forks, bread or beer. Had they been without *pretensions*, all this would have seemed of no consequence; but they aimed at appearing to advantage, and even fancied they succeeded. However, the most disagreeable part of our fare was, that the whole family continually disputed whose turn it was to rise, and whose to be allowed to sit still.

When this meal was over, Madame Duval, ever eager to discourse upon *her travels*, entered into an argument with Mr. Branghton, and in broken English, M. Du Bois, concerning the French nation: and Miss Polly, then addressing herself to me, said, "Don't you think, Miss, it's very dull sitting up stairs here? we'd better go down *to shop*, and then we shall see the people go by."

"Lord, Poll," said the Brother, "you're always wanting to be staring and gaping; and I'm sure you need n't be so fond of shewing yourself, for you're ugly enough to frighten a horse."

"Ugly, indeed! I wonder which is best, you or me. But, I tell you what, Tom, you've no need to give yourself such airs, for if you do, I'll tell Miss of you know what ———"

"Who cares if you do? you may tell what you will; I don't mind ———"

"Indeed," cried I, "I do not desire to hear any secrets."

"O, but I'm resolved I'll tell you, because Tom's so very spiteful. You must know, Miss, t'other night ———"

"Poll," cried the brother, "if you tell of that, Miss shall know all about your meeting young Brown,—you know when!—So I'll be quits with you, one way or other."

Miss Polly coloured, and again proposed our going down stairs till Mr. Smith's room was ready for our reception.

"Aye, so we will," said Miss Branghton; "I'll assure you, Cousin, we have some very genteel people pass by our shop sometimes. Polly and I always go and sit there, when we've cleaned ourselves."

"Yes, Miss," cried the brother, "they do nothing else all day long, when father don't scold them. But the best fun is, when they've got all their dirty things on, and all their hair about their ears, sometimes I send young Brown up stairs to them; and then, there's such a fuss!—there they hide themselves, and run away, and squeal and squall like any thing mad: and so then I puts the two cats into the room, and I gives 'em a good whipping, and so that sets them a squalling too; so there's such a noise and such an uproar!—Lord, you can't think, Miss, what fun it is!"

This occasioned a fresh quarrel with the sisters; at the end of which, it was, at length, decided that we should go to the shop.

In our way down stairs, Miss Branghton said aloud, "I wonder when Mr. Smith's room will be ready."

"So do I," answered Polly; "I'm sure we should not do any harm to it now."

This hint had not the desired effect; for we were suffered to proceed very quietly.

As we entered the shop, I observed a young man, in deep mourning, leaning against the wall, with his arms folded, and his eyes fixed on the ground, apparently in profound and melancholy meditation: but the moment he perceived us, he started, and, making a passing bow, very abruptly retired. As I found he was permitted to go quite unnoticed, I could not forbear enquiring who he was.

"Lord!" answered Miss Branghton, "he's nothing but a poor Scotch poet."

"For my part," said Miss Polly, "I believe he's just starved, for I don't find he has any thing to live upon."

"Live upon!" cried the brother, "why he's a poet, you know, so he may live upon learning."

"Aye, and good enough for him, too," said Miss Branghton, "for he's as proud as he's poor."

"Like enough," replied the brother, "but, for all that, you won't find he will live without meat and drink: no, no, catch a Scotchman at that if you can! why, they only come here for what they can get."

"I'm sure," said Miss Branghton, "I wonder Papa 'll be such a fool as to let him stay in the house, for I dare say he'll never pay for his lodging."

"Why, no more he would if he could get another Lodger: you know the bill's been put up this fortnight. Miss, if you should hear of a person that wants a room, I assure you it is a very good one, for all it's up three pair of stairs."

I answered that as I had no acquaintance in London, I had not any chance of assisting them: but both my compassion and my curiosity were excited for this poor young man; and I asked them some further particulars concerning him.

They then acquainted me, that they had only known him three months. When he first lodged with them, he agreed to board also; but had lately told them, he would eat by himself, though they all believed he had hardly ever tasted a morsel of meat since he left their table. They said, that he had always appeared very low-spirited, but, for the last month, he had been *duller* than ever, and, all of a sudden, had put himself into mourning, though they knew not for whom, nor for what, but they supposed it was only for convenience, as no person had ever been to see or enquire for him since his residence amongst them: and they were sure he was very poor, as he had not paid for his lodgings the last three weeks: and finally, they concluded he was a poet, or else half-crazy, because they had, at different times, found scraps of poetry in his room.

They then produced some unfinished verses, written on small pieces of paper, unconnected, and of a most melancholy cast. Among them was the fragment of an ode, which, at my request, they lent me to copy; and, as you may perhaps like to see it, I will write it now.

> O LIFE! thou lingering dream of grief, of pain,
> And every ill that Nature can sustain,
>   Strange, mutable, and wild!
> Now flattering with Hope most fair,
> Depressing now with fell Despair,
>   The nurse of Guilt, the slave of Pride,
>   That, like a wayward child,
>   Who, to himself a foe,
> Sees joy alone in what's denied,
>   In what is granted, woe!
>
> O thou poor, feeble, fleeting pow'r,
> By Vice seduc'd, by Folly woo'd,

By Mis'ry, Shame, Remorse, pursu'd;
And as thy toilsome steps proceed,
Seeming to Youth the fairest flow'r,
Proving to Age the rankest weed,
    A gilded, but a bitter pill,
Of varied, great, and complicated ill!

These lines are harsh, but they indicate an internal wretchedness which, I own, affects me. Surely this young man must be involved in misfortunes of no common nature: but I cannot imagine what can induce him to remain with this unfeeling family, where he is, most unworthily, despised for being poor, and, most illiberally detested for being a Scotchman. He may indeed, have motives, which he cannot surmount, for submitting to such a situation. Whatever they are, I most heartily pity him, and cannot but wish it were in my power to afford him some relief.

During this conversation, Mr. Smith's foot-boy came to Miss Branghton, and informed her, that his master said she might have the room now when she liked it, for that he was presently going out.

This very genteel message, though it perfectly satisfied the Miss Branghtons, by no means added to my desire of being introduced to this gentleman: and upon their rising, with intention to accept his offer, I begged they would excuse my attending them, and said I would sit with Madame Duval till the tea was ready.

I therefore once more went up two pair of stairs, with young Branghton, who insisted upon accompanying me; and there we remained, till Mr. Smith's foot-boy summoned us to tea, when I followed Madame Duval into the dining-room.

The Miss Branghtons were seated at one window, and Mr. Smith was lolling indolently out of the other. They all approached us at our entrance, and Mr. Smith, probably to shew he was master of the department, most officiously handed me to a great chair, at the upper end of the room, without taking any notice of Madame Duval, till I rose, and offered her my own seat.

Leaving the rest of the company to entertain themselves, he, very abruptly, began to address himself to me, in a style of gallantry equally new and disagreeable to me. It is true, no man can possibly pay me greater compliments, or make more fine speeches, than Sir Clement Willoughby, yet his language, though too flowery, is always that of a gentleman, and his address and manners are so very superior to those of the inhabitants of this house, that to make any comparison between him and Mr. Smith would be extremely unjust. This latter seems very desirous of appearing a man of gaiety and spirit; but his vivacity is so low-bred, and his whole behaviour so forward and disagreeable, that I should prefer the company of *dullness* itself, even as that goddess is described by Pope,[1] to that of this *sprightly* young man.

He made many apologies that he had not lent his room for our dinner, which, he said, he should certainly have done, had he seen me first; and he assured me, that when I came again, he should be very glad to oblige me.

I told him, and with sincerity, that every part of the house was equally indifferent to me.

"Why, Ma'am, the truth is, Miss Biddy and Polly take no care of any thing, else, I'm sure, they should be always welcome to my room; for I'm never so happy as in obliging the ladies,—that's my character, Ma'am;—but, really, the last time they had it, every thing was made so greasy and so nasty, that, upon my word, to a man who wishes to have things a little genteel, it was quite cruel. Now, as to you, Ma'am, it's quite another thing; for I should not mind if every thing I had was spoilt, for the sake of having the pleasure to oblige you; and, I assure you, Ma'am, it makes me quite happy that I have a room good enough to receive you."

This elegant speech was followed by many others, so much in the same style, that to write them would be superfluous; and, as he did not allow me a moment to speak to any other person, the rest of the evening was consumed in a painful attention to this irksome young man, who seemed to intend appearing before me to the utmost advantage.

Adieu, my dear Sir. I fear you will be sick of reading about this family; yet I must write of them, or not of any, since I mix with no other. Happy shall I be, when I quit them all, and again return to Berry Hill.

Letter XII.

EVELINA IN CONTINUATION.

June 10th.

This morning, Mr. Smith called, *on purpose*, he said, to offer me a ticket for the next Hampstead assembly.[2] I thanked him, but desired to be excused accepting it: he would not, however, be denied, nor answered, and, in a manner both vehement and free, pressed and urged his offer till I was wearied to death: but, when he found me resolute, he seemed thunderstruck with amazement, and thought proper to desire I would tell him my reasons.

Obvious as they must, surely, have been to any other person, they

1. Her ample presence fills up all the place; / A veil of fogs dilates her awful face: / Great in her charms! as when on Shrieves and May'rs / She looks, and breathes herself into their airs (*Dunciad* 1: 261–64).
2. Hampstead, containing spas and pleasure gardens, is northwest of London. The Hampstead assemblies were held in a building known as the Long Room.

were such as I knew not how to repeat to him; and, when he found I hesitated, he said, "Indeed, Ma'am, you are too modest; I assure you the ticket is quite at your service, and I shall be very happy to dance with you; so pray don't be so coy."

"Indeed, Sir," returned I, "you are mistaken; I never supposed you would offer a ticket, without wishing it should be accepted; but it would answer no purpose to mention the reasons which make me decline it, since they cannot possibly be removed."

This speech seemed very much to mortify him, which I could not be concerned at, as I did not chuse to be treated by him with so much freedom. When he was, at last, convinced that his application to me was ineffectual, he addressed himself to Madame Duval, and begged she would interfere in his favour, offering, at the same time, to procure another ticket for herself.

"*Ma foi*, Sir," answered she, angrily, "you might as well have had the complaisance to ask me before, for, I assure you, I don't approve of no such rudeness: however, you may keep your tickets to yourself, for we don't want none of 'em."

This rebuke almost overset him; he made many apologies, and said that he should certainly have first applied to her, but that he had no notion the *young* lady would have refused him, and, on the contrary, had concluded that she would have assisted him to persuade Madame Duval herself.

This excuse appeased her; and he pleaded his cause so successfully, that, to my great chagrin, he gained it: and Madame Duval promised that she would go herself, and take me to the Hampstead assembly whenever he pleased.

Mr. Smith then, approaching me with an air of triumph, said, "Well, Ma'am, now, I think, you can't possibly keep to your denial."

I made no answer, and he soon took leave, though not till he had so wonderfully gained the favour of Madame Duval, that she declared, when he was gone, he was the prettiest young man she had seen since she came to England.

As soon as I could find an opportunity, I ventured, in the most humble manner, to entreat Madame Duval would not insist upon my attending her to this ball; and represented to her, as well as I was able, the impropriety of my accepting any present from a young man so entirely unknown to me: but she laughed at my scruples, called me a foolish, ignorant country-girl, and said she should make it her business to teach me something of the world.

This ball is to be next week. I am sure it is not more improper for, than unpleasant to me, and I will use every possible endeavour to avoid it. Perhaps I may apply to Miss Branghton for advice, as I believe she will be willing to assist me, from disliking, equally with myself, that I should dance with Mr. Smith.

June 11th.

O, my dear Sir! I have been shocked to death;—and yet, at the same time delighted beyond expression, in the hope that I have happily been the instrument of saving a human creature from destruction!

This morning, Madame Duval said she would invite the Branghton family to return our visit to-morrow; and, not chusing to rise herself,—for she generally spends the morning in bed,—she desired me to wait upon them with her message. M. Du Bois, who just then called, insisted upon attending me.

Mr. Branghton was in the shop, and told us that his son and daughters were out; but desired me to step up stairs, as he very soon expected them home. This I did, leaving M. Du Bois below. I went into the room where we had dined the day before, and, by a wonderful chance, I happened so to seat myself, that I had a view of the stairs, and yet could not be seen from them.

In about ten minutes time, I saw, passing by the door, with a look perturbed and affrighted, the same young man I mentioned in my last letter. Not heeding, as I suppose, how he went, in turning the corner of the stairs, which are narrow and winding, his foot slipped, and he fell, but almost instantly rising, I plainly perceived the end of a pistol, which started from his pocket, by hitting against the stairs.

I was inexpressibly shocked. All that I had heard of his misery occurring to my memory, made me conclude that he was, at that very moment, meditating suicide! Struck with the dreadful idea, all my strength seemed to fail me. He moved on slowly, yet I soon lost sight of him; I sat motionless with terror; all power of action forsook me; and I grew almost stiff with horror: till recollecting that it was yet possible to prevent the fatal deed, all my faculties seemed to return, with the hope of saving him.

My first thought was to fly to Mr. Branghton, but I feared, that an instant of time lost, might for ever be rued; and therefore, guided by the impulse of my apprehensions, as well as I was able, I followed him up stairs, stepping very softly, and obliged to support myself by the banisters.

When I came within a few stairs of the landing-place, I stopped, for I could then see into his room, as he had not yet shut the door.

He had put the pistol upon a table, and had his hand in his pocket, whence, in a few moments, he took out another: He then emptied something on the table from a small leather bag; after which, taking up both the pistols, one in each hand, he dropt hastily upon his knees, and called out "O God!—forgive me!"

In a moment, strength, and courage seemed lent to me as by inspiration: I started, and rushing precipitately into the room, just caught his arm, and then, overcome by my own fears, I fell down at his side, breathless and senseless. My recovery, however, was, I believe, almost instantaneous; and then the sight of this unhappy man, regarding me with a look of unutterable astonishment, mixed with concern, presently restored to me my recollection. I arose, though with difficulty; he did the same; the pistols, as I soon saw, were both on the floor.

Unwilling to leave them, and, indeed, too weak to move, I leant one hand on the table, and then stood perfectly still: while he, his eyes cast wildly towards me, seemed too infinitely amazed to be capable of either speech or action.

I believe we were some minutes in this extraordinary situation; but as my strength returned, I felt myself both ashamed and awkward, and moved towards the door. Pale, and motionless, he suffered me to pass, without changing his posture, or uttering a syllable; and, indeed,

He looked a bloodless image of despair. — [3]

When I reached the door, I turned round; I looked fearfully at the pistols, and, impelled by an emotion I could not repress, I hastily stepped back, with an intention of carrying them away: but their wretched owner, perceiving my design, and recovering from his astonishment, darting suddenly down, seized them both himself.

Wild with fright, and scarce knowing what I did, I caught, almost involuntarily hold of both his arms, and exclaimed, "O Sir! have mercy on yourself!"

The guilty pistols fell from his hands, which, disengaging from me, he fervently clasped, and cried, "Sweet Heaven! is this thy angel?"

Encouraged by such gentleness, I again attempted to take the pistols, but, with a look half frantic, he again prevented me, saying, "What would you do?"

"Awaken you," I cried, with a courage I now wonder at, "to worthier thoughts, and rescue you from perdition."

I then seized the pistols; he said not a word, — he made no effort to stop me; — I glided quick by him, and tottered down stairs, ere he had recovered from the extremest amazement.

The moment I reached again the room I had so fearfully left, I threw away the pistols, and flinging myself on the first chair, gave free vent to the feelings I had most painfully stifled, in a violent burst of tears, which, indeed, proved a happy relief to me.

In this situation I remained some time; but when, at length, I lifted up my head, the first object I saw was the poor man who had occasioned my terror, standing, as if petrified, at the door, and gazing at me with eyes of wild wonder.

I started from the chair, but trembled so excessively, that I almost instantly sunk again into it. He then, though without advancing, and in

3. Changed from "And looks" (Alexander Pope, *Iliad* 13: 365). Burney's original note says "Pope's Iliad." After reading *The Iliad* in 1768, Burney wrote in her journal: "I was never so charm'd with a poem in my life" (*The Early Journals and Letters of Fanny Burney*, ed. Lars E. Troide, vol. 1 [Oxford: Clarendon, 1988] 40).

a faultering voice, said, "Whoever or whatever you are, relieve me, I pray you, from the suspence under which my soul labours—and tell me if indeed I do not dream?"

To this address, so singular and so solemn, I had not then the presence of mind to frame any answer: but, as I presently perceived that his eyes turned from me to the pistols, and that he seemed to intend regaining them, I exerted all my strength, and saying "O for Heaven's sake forbear!" I rose and took them myself.

"Do my senses deceive me!" cried he, "do *I* live—? and do *you?*"

As he spoke, he advanced towards me! and I, still guarding the pistols, retreated, saying "No, no—you must not—must not have them!"

"Why—for what purpose, tell me!—do you withhold them?"—

"To give you time to *think*,—to save you from eternal misery,—and, I hope, to reserve you for mercy and forgiveness."

"Wonderful!" cried he, with uplifted hands and eyes, "most wonderful!"

For some time, he seemed wrapped in deep thought, till a sudden noise of tongues below announcing the approach of the Branghtons, made him start from his reverie: he sprung hastily forward,—dropt on one knee,——caught hold of my gown, which he pressed to his lips, and then, quick as lightning, he rose, and flew up stairs to his own room.

There was something in the whole of this extraordinary and shocking adventure, really too affecting to be borne; and so entirely had I spent my spirits and exhausted my courage, that, before the Branghtons reached me, I had sunk on the ground, without sense or motion.

I believe I must have been a very horrid sight to them, on their entrance into the room: for, to all appearance, I seemed to have suffered a violent death, either by my own rashness, or the cruelty of some murderer; as the pistols had fallen close by my side.

How soon I recovered, I know not, but, probably I was more indebted to the loudness of their cries, than to their assistance; for they all concluded that I was dead, and, for some time, did not make any effort to revive me.

Scarcely could I recollect *where*, or, indeed, *what* I was, ere they poured upon me such a torrent of questions and enquiries, that I was almost stunned with their vociferation. However, as soon and as well as I was able, I endeavoured to satisfy their curiosity, by recounting what had happened as clearly as was in my power. They all looked aghast at the recital, but, not being well enough to enter into any discussions, I begged to have a chair called, and to return instantly home.

Before I left them, I recommended, with great earnestness, a vigilant observance of their unhappy lodger, and that they would take care to keep from him, if possible, all means of self-destruction.

M. Du Bois, who seemed extremely concerned at my indisposition, walked by the side of the chair, and saw me safe to my own apartment.

The rashness and the misery of this ill-fated young man engross all my thoughts. If, indeed, he is bent upon destroying himself, all efforts to save him will be fruitless. How much do I wish it were in my power to discover the nature of the malady which thus maddens him, and to offer or to procure alleviation to his sufferings! I am sure, my dearest Sir, you will be much concerned for this poor man; and, were you here, I doubt not but you would find some method of awakening him from the error which blinds him, and of pouring the balm of peace and comfort into his afflicted soul!

Letter XIII.

EVELINA IN CONTINUATION.

Holborn, June 13th.

Yesterday all the Branghtons dined here.

Our conversation was almost wholly concerning the adventure of the day before. Mr. Branghton said, that his first thought was instantly to turn his lodger out of doors, "Lest," continued he, "his killing himself in my house, should bring me into any trouble; but then I was afraid I should never get the money he owes me; whereas, if he dies in my house, I have a right to all he leaves behind him, if he goes off in my debt. Indeed, I would put him in prison,—but what should I get by that? he could not earn any thing there to pay me. So I considered about it some time, and then I determined to ask him, point-blank, for my money out of hand. And so I did, but he told me he'd pay me next week: however, I gave him to understand, that, though I was no Scotchman, yet I did not like to be over-reached any more than he; so then he gave me a ring, which, to my certain knowledge, must be worth ten guineas, and told me he would not part with it for his life, and a good deal more such sort of stuff, but that I might keep it till he could pay me."

"It is ten to one, Father," said young Branghton, "if he came fairly by it."

"Very likely not," answered he, "but that will make no great difference; for I shall be able to prove my right to it all one."

What principles! I could hardly stay in the room.

"I'm determined," said the son, "I'll take some opportunity to affront him soon, now I know how poor he is, because of the airs he gave himself to me when he first came."

"And pray how was that, child?" said Madame Duval.

"Why you never knew such a fuss in your life as he made, because, one day at dinner, I only happened to say, that I supposed he had never got such a good meal in his life, before he came to England: there he fell in such a passion as you can't think; but, for my part, I took no notice of it, for to be sure, thinks I, he must needs be a gentleman, or he'd never go to be so angry about it. However, he won't put his tricks upon me again, in a hurry."

"Well," said Miss Polly, "he's grown quite another creature to what he was, and he does n't run away from us, nor hide himself, nor any thing; and he's as civil as can be, and he's always in the shop, and he saunters about the stairs, and he looks at every body as comes in."

"Why you may see what he's after plain enough," said Mr. Branghton; "he wants to see Miss again."

"Ha, ha, ha! Lord, how I should laugh," said the son, "if he should have fell in love with Miss!"

"I'm sure," said Miss Branghton, "Miss is welcome; but, for my part, I should be quite ashamed of such a beggarly conquest."

Such was the conversation till tea-time, when the appearance of Mr. Smith gave a new turn to the discourse.

Miss Branghton desired me to remark with what a *smart air* he entered the room, and asked me if he had not very much a *quality look?*

"Come," cried he, advancing to us, "you ladies must not sit together; wherever I go, I always make it a rule to part the ladies."

And then, handing Miss Branghton to the next chair, he seated himself between us.

"Well, now ladies, I think we sit very well. What say you? for my part, I think it was a very good motion."

"If my Cousin likes it," said Miss Branghton, "I'm sure I've no objection."

"O," cried he, "I always study what the ladies like,—that's my first thought. And, indeed, it is but natural that you should like best to sit by the gentlemen, for what can you find to say to one another?"

"Say?" cried young Branghton, "O, never you think of that, they'll find enough to say, I'll be sworn. You know the women are never tired of talking."

"Come, come, Tom," said Mr. Smith, "don't be severe upon the ladies; when I'm by, you know I always take their part."

Soon after, when Miss Branghton offered me some cake, this man of gallantry said, "Well, if I was that lady, I'd never take any thing from a woman."

"Why not, Sir?"

"Because I should be afraid of being poisoned for being so handsome."

"Who is severe upon the ladies *now?*" said I.

"Why, really, Ma'am, it was a slip of the tongue; I did-not intend to say such a thing; but one can't always be on one's guard."

Soon after, the conversation turning upon public places, young Branghton asked if I had ever been to *George's* at Hampstead?[1]

1. New Georgia, a two-story wooden cottage and grounds in Turner's Wood, Hampstead, built in 1737. "The chief attractions were the number of mechanical oddities set in motion in the

"Indeed, I never heard the place mentioned."

"Did n't you, Miss," cried he eagerly, "why then you've a deal of fun to come, I'll promise you; and, I tell you what, I'll treat you there some Sunday soon. So now, Bid and Poll, be sure you don't tell Miss about the chairs, and all that, for I've a mind to surprise her; and if I pay, I think I've a right to have it my own way."

"George's at Hampstead!" repeated Mr. Smith, contemptuously, "how came you to think the young lady would like to go to such a low place as that! But, pray Ma'am, have you ever been to Don Saltero's at Chelsea?"[2]

"No, Sir."

"No!—nay, then, I must insist on having the pleasure of conducting you there before long. I assure you, Ma'am, many genteel people go, or else, I give you my word, *I* should not recommend it."

"Pray, Cousin," said Mr. Branghton, "have you been at Sadler's Wells, yet?"[3]

"No, Sir."

"No! why then you've seen nothing!"

"Pray, Miss," said the Son, "how do you like the Tower of London?"

"I have never been to it, Sir."

"Goodness!" exclaimed he, "not seen the Tower!—why, may be you ha' n't been o' top of the Monument,[4] neither?"

"No, indeed, I have not."

"Why then you might as well not have come to London, for aught I see, for you've been no where."

"Pray, Miss," said Polly, "have you been all over Paul's Church, yet?"

"No, Ma'am."

"Well, but, Ma'am," said Mr. Smith, "how do you like Vauxhall and Marybone?"[5]

---

garden and in various little rooms into which the house was divided. London shopkeepers . . . often made their way to the place on Sunday afternoons" (W. W. Wroth, *The London Pleasure Gardens* [London, 1896] 187–88).

2. A coffee shop with an attached museum in Cheyne Walk, opened by James Salter (d. 1728), a barber and former servant of Sir Hans Sloane (1660–1753). In the *Tatler*, No. 34, Richard Steele writes: "When I came into the coffee-house, I had not time to salute the company, before my eye was diverted by ten thousand gimcracks round the room, and on the ceiling" (28 June 1709).

3. Thomas Sadler built a theater at a small spa in East London in 1683. It had a somewhat unsavory reputation, which was partly alleviated when the actor and dramatist Thomas King (1730–1805) took it over in 1772 and instituted changes to attract a more fashionable audience.

4. A 202-foot obelisk commemorating the Great Fire of London, designed by Christopher Wren and Robert Hooke (1635–1703) and erected in 1671–72.

5. Vauxhall Gardens, pleasure gardens that rivalled Ranelagh, were first opened as the New Spring Garden in 1661. They were open every day except Sundays from May until September. James Boswell described them as "peculiarly adapted to the taste of the English nation; there being a mixture of curious shew,—gay exhibition,—musick, vocal and instrumental, not too refined for the general ear;—for all which only a shilling is paid" (*Life of Johnson*, ed. G. B. Hill and L. F. Powell [Oxford, 1934] 3:309). Marylebone Gardens, pleasure gardens opened in 1650, at first offered dogfights, cockfights, bear baiting, and boxing matches. In 1738 an entrance fee made them more expensive and, hence, exclusive, and in 1739 assembly rooms

"I never saw either, Sir."

"No—God bless me!—you really surprise me,—why Vauxhall is the first pleasure in life!—I know nothing like it.—Well, Ma'am, you must have been with strange people, indeed, not to have taken you to Vauxhall. Why you have seen nothing of London yet.—However, we must try if *we* can't make you amends."

In the course of this *catechism*, many other places were mentioned, of which I have forgotten the names; but the looks of surprise and contempt that my repeated negatives incurred, were very diverting.

"Come," said Mr. Smith, after tea, "as this lady has been with such a queer set of people, let's shew her the difference; suppose we go somewhere to-night!—I love to do things with spirit!—Come, Ladies, where shall we go? For my part, I should like Foote's[6]—but the Ladies must chuse; I never speak myself."

"Well, Mr. Smith is always in such spirits!" said Miss Branghton.

"Why yes, Ma'am, yes, thank God, pretty good spirits;—I have not yet the cares of the world upon me,—I am not *married*,—ha, ha, ha,— you'll excuse me, Ladies,—but I can't help laughing!"

No objection being made, to my great relief, we all proceeded to the little theatre in the Haymarket, where I was extremely entertained by the performance of the Minor and the Commissary.[7]

They all returned hither to supper.

Letter XIV.

EVELINA IN CONTINUATION.

June 15th.

Yesterday morning, Madame Duval again sent me to Mr. Branghton's attended by M. Du Bois, to make some party for the evening; because she had had the vapours[1] the preceding day, from staying at home.

As I entered the shop, I perceived the unfortunate North Briton, seated in a corner, with a book in his hand. He cast his melancholy eyes up, as we came in, and, I believe, immediately recollected my face, for he started and changed colour. I delivered Madame Duval's message to Mr. Branghton; who told me I should find Polly up stairs, but that the others were gone out.

---

were built for balls and concerts. In Burney's time, they were renowned for the quality of both their music and their fireworks.

6. Originally a summer theater opened in 1721, it was known as the Little Theatre in the Haymarket to distinguish it from the Haymarket Opera House across the street. In July 1766, the then-manager, the playwright and actor Samuel Foote (1720–77), obtained a patent making it a royal theater. Purchasing the theater in 1767, he refurbished and remodelled it, adding an upper gallery. See *London Past and Present* 2:200–201.

7. Two of Samuel Foote's satirical comedies. *The Minor* opened at Drury Lane in 1760, and *The Commissary* opened at the Haymarket in 1765.

1. "Depression of spirits, hypochondria, hysteria, or other nervous disorder" (*OED*).

Up stairs, therefore, I went; and seated on a window, with Mr. Brown at her side, sat Miss Polly. I felt a little awkward at disturbing them, and much more so, at their behaviour afterwards: for, as soon as the common enquiries were over, Mr. Brown grew so fond, and so foolish, that I was extremely disgusted. Polly, all the time, only rebuked him with "La, now, Mr. Brown, do be quiet, can't you?—you should not behave so before company.—Why now, what will Miss think of me?"—while her looks plainly shewed not merely the pleasure, but the pride which she took in his caresses.

I did not, by any means, think it necessary to punish myself by witnessing their tenderness, and, therefore, telling them I would see if Miss Branghton were returned home, I soon left them, and again descended into the shop.

"So, Miss, you've come again," said Mr. Branghton, "what, I suppose, you've mind to sit a little in the shop, and see how the world goes, hay, Miss?"

I made no answer; and M. Du Bois instantly brought me a chair.

The unhappy stranger, who had risen at my entrance, again seated himself; and, though his head leant towards his book, I could not help observing, that his eyes were most intently and earnestly turned towards me.

M. Du Bois, as well as his broken English would allow him, endeavoured to entertain us, till the return of Miss Branghton and her brother.

"Lord, how tired I am!" cried the former, "I have not a foot to stand upon." And then, without any ceremony, she flung herself into the chair from which I had risen to receive her.

"You tired!" said the brother, "why then what must I be, that have walked twice as far?" And with equal politeness, he paid the same compliment to M. Du Bois which his sister had done to me.

Two chairs and three stools compleated the furniture of the shop, and Mr. Branghton, who chose to keep his own seat himself, desired M. Du Bois to take another; and then, seeing that I was without any, called out to the stranger, "Come, Mr. Macartney, lend us your stool."

Shocked at their rudeness, I declined the offer, and approaching Miss Branghton, said, "If you will be so good as to make room for me on your chair, there will be no occasion to disturb that gentleman."

"Lord, what signifies that?" cried the brother, "he has had his share of sitting, I'll be sworn.' "

"And if he has not," said the sister, "he has a chair up stairs; and the shop is our own, I hope."

This grossness so much disgusted me, that I took the stool, and carrying it back to Mr. Macartney myself, I returned him thanks, as civilly as I could, for his politeness, but said that I had rather stand.

He looked at me as if unaccustomed to such attention, bowed very respectfully, but neither spoke, nor yet made use of it.

I soon found that I was an object of derision to all present, except M. Du Bois, and, therefore, I begged Mr. Branghton would give me an answer for Madame Duval, as I was in haste to return.

"Well, then, Tom,—Biddy,—where have you a mind to go to-night? your Aunt and Miss want to be abroad and amongst them."

"Why then, Papa," said Miss Branghton, "we'll go to Don Saltero's. Mr. Smith likes that place, so may be he'll go along with us."

"No, no," said the son, "I'm for White-Conduit House[2] so let's go there."

"White-Conduit House, indeed?" cried his sister, "no Tom, that I won't."

"Why then let it alone; nobody wants your company;—we shall do as well without you, I'll be sworn, and better too."

"I'll tell you what Tom, if you don't hold your tongue, I'll make you repent it,—that I assure you."

Just then, Mr. Smith came into the shop, which he seemed to intend passing through; but when he saw me, he stopped and began a most courteous enquiry after my health, protesting that, had he known I was there, he should have come down sooner. "But, bless me, Ma'am," added he, "what is the reason you stand?" and then he flew to bring me the seat from which I had just parted.

"Mr. Smith, you are come in very good time," said Mr. Branghton, "to end a dispute between my son and daughter, about where they shall all go to-night."

"O fie, Tom,—dispute with a lady!" cried Mr. Smith, "Now, as for me, I'm for where you will, provided this young lady is of the party,— one place is the same as another to me, so that it be but agreeable to the ladies,—I would go any where with you, Ma'am," (to me) "unless, indeed, it were to *church*;—ha, ha, ha,—you'll excuse me, Ma'am, but, really, I never could conquer my fear of a parson;—ha, ha, ha,—really, ladies, I beg your pardon, for being so rude, but I can't help laughing for my life!"

"I was just saying, Mr. Smith," said Miss Branghton, "that I should like to go to Don Saltero's;—now pray where should *you* like to go?"

"Why really, Miss Biddy, you know I always let the ladies decide; I never fix any thing myself; but I should suppose it would be rather hot at the coffee-house,—however, pray, Ladies, settle it among your-selves,—I'm agreeable to whatever you chuse."

It was easy for me to discover, that this man, with all his parade of *conformity*, objects to every thing that is not proposed by himself: but he is so much admired, by this family, for his *gentility*, that he thinks him-self a complete fine gentleman!

"Come," said Mr. Branghton, "the best way will be to put it to the

2. A tavern near the White Conduit in Islington, opened in 1649 by Robert Bartholomew, which featured gardens, a pool, bowling greens, and a cricket field.

vote, and then every body will speak their minds. Biddy, call Poll down stairs. We'll start fair."

"Lord, Papa," said Miss Branghton, "why can't you as well send Tom?—you're always sending me of the errands."

A dispute then ensued, but Miss Branghton was obliged to yield.

When Mr. Brown and Miss Polly made their appearance, the latter uttered many complaints of having been called, saying she did not want to come, and was very well where she was.

"Now, Ladies, your votes;" cried Mr. Smith, "and so, Ma'am, (to me) we'll begin with you. What place shall you like best?" and then, in a whisper, he added, "I assure you, I shall say the same as you do, whether I like it or not."

I said, that as I was ignorant what choice was in my power, I must beg to hear their decisions first. This was reluctantly assented to; and then Miss Branghton voted for Saltero's Coffee-house; her sister, for a party to *Mother Red Cap's:* the brother, for White-Conduit House; Mr. Brown, for Bagnigge Wells;[3] Mr. Branghton for Sadler's Wells; and Mr. Smith for Vauxhall.

"Well now, Ma'am," said Mr. Smith, "we have all spoken, and so you must give the casting vote. Come, what will you fix upon?"

"Sir," answered I, "I was to speak *last.*"

"Well, so you will," said Miss Branghton, "for we've all spoke first."

"Pardon me," returned I, "the voting has not yet been quite general."

And I looked towards Mr. Macartney, to whom I wished extremely to shew that I was not of the same brutal nature with those by whom he was treated so grossly.

"Why pray," said Mr. Branghton, "who have we left out? would you have the cats and dogs vote?"

"No, Sir," cried I, with some spirit, "I would have *that gentleman* vote,—if, indeed, he is not superior to joining our party."

They all looked at me, as if they doubted whether or not they had heard me right: but, in a few moments, their surprise gave way to a rude burst of laughter.

Very much displeased, I told M. Du Bois that if he was not ready to go, I would have a coach called for myself.

O yes, he said, he was always ready to attend me.

Mr. Smith then advancing, attempted to take my hand, and begged me not to leave them till I had settled the evening's plan.

"I have nothing, Sir," said I, "to do with it, as it is my intention to stay at home; and therefore Mr. Branghton will be so good as to send

3. Mother Red-Cap's was a public house on the Great North Road in Lower Holloway; its sign portrayed a woman sporting a high hat. Samuel Pepys mentions it in his diary for 24 September 1661: "So we rode easily through and only drinking at Holloway at the sign of a woman with Cakes in one hand and a pot of ale in the other." Bagnigge Wells, opened in 1758, was a fashionable spa in what is now King's Cross Road; it contained tea gardens, a bowling green, a grotto, a fish pond, and formal walks and offered concerts.

Madame Duval word what place is fixed upon, when it is convenient to him."

And then, making a slight courtsie, I left them.

How much does my disgust for these people encrease my pity for poor Mr. Macartney! I will not see them when I can avoid so doing; but I am determined to take every opportunity in my power, to shew civility to this unhappy man, whose misfortunes with this family, only render him an object of scorn. I was, however, very well pleased with M. Du Bois, who, far from joining in their mirth, expressed himself extremely shocked at their ill-breeding.

We had not walked ten yards before we were followed by Mr. Smith, who came to make excuses, and to assure me they were *only joking*, and hoped I took nothing ill, for if I did, he would make a quarrel of it himself with the Branghtons, rather than I should receive any offence.

I begged him not to take any trouble about so immaterial an affair, and assured him I should not myself. He was so officious, that he would not be prevailed upon to return home, till he had walked with us to Mr. Dawkins's.

Madame Duval was very much displeased that I brought her so little satisfaction. White-Conduit House was, at last, fixed upon; and, notwithstanding my great dislike of such parties and such places, I was obliged to accompany them.

Very disagreeable, and much according to my expectations, the evening proved. There were many people all smart and gaudy, and so pert and low-bred, that I could hardly endure being amongst them; but the party to which, unfortunately, I belonged, seemed all *at home*.

Letter XV.

EVELINA IN CONTINUATION.

Holborn, June 17th.

Yesterday Mr. Smith carried his point, of making a party for Vauxhall, consisting of Madame Duval, M. Du Bois, all the Branghtons, Mr. Brown, himself,—and me!—for I find all endeavours vain to escape any thing which these people desire I should not.

There were twenty disputes previous to our setting out; first, as to the *time* of our going: Mr. Branghton, his son, and young Brown, were for six o'clock; and all the ladies and Mr. Smith were for eight;—the latter, however, conquered.

Then, as to the *way* we should go; some were for a boat, others for a coach, and Mr. Branghton himself was for walking: but the boat, at length, was decided upon. Indeed this was the only part of the expedition that was agreeable to me, for the Thames was delightfully pleasant.

The Garden is very pretty, but too formal; I should have been better pleased, had it consisted less of strait walks, where

Grove nods at grove, each alley has its brother.[1]

The trees, the numerous lights, and the company in the circle round the orchestra make a most brilliant and gay appearance; and had I been with a party less disagreeable to me, I should have thought it a place formed for animation and pleasure. There was a concert, in the course of which, a hautbois[2] concerto was so charmingly played, that I could have thought myself upon enchanted ground, had I had spirits more gentle to associate with. The hautboy in the open air is heavenly.

Mr. Smith endeavoured to attach himself to me, with such officious assiduity, and impertinent freedom, that he quite sickened me. Indeed, M. Du Bois was the only man of the party to whom, voluntarily, I ever addressed myself. He is civil and respectful, and I have found nobody else so since I left Howard Grove. His English is very bad, but I prefer it to speaking French myself, which I dare not venture to do. I converse with him frequently, both to disengage myself from others, and to oblige Madame Duval, who is always pleased when he is attended to.

As we were walking about the orchestra, I heard a bell ring, and, in a moment, Mr. Smith, flying up to me, caught my hand, and, with a motion too quick to be resisted, ran away with me many yards before I had breath to ask his meaning, though I struggled as well as I could, to get from him. At last, however, I insisted upon stopping; "Stopping, Ma'am!" cried he, "why, we must run on, or we shall lose the cascade!"[3]

And then again, he hurried me away, mixing with a crowd of people, all running with so much velocity, that I could not imagine what had raised such an alarm. We were soon followed by the rest of the party; and my surprise and ignorance proved a source of diversion to them all, which was not exhausted the whole evening. Young Branghton, in particular, laughed till he could hardly stand.

The scene of the cascade I thought extremely pretty, and the general effect striking and lively.

But this was not the only surprise which was to divert them at my expence; for they led me about the garden, purposely to enjoy my first sight of various other deceptions.

About ten o'clock, Mr. Smith having chosen a *box* in a very conspicuous place, we all went to supper. Much fault was found with every thing that was ordered, though not a morsel of any thing was left; and the dearness of the provisions, with conjectures upon what profit was made by them, supplied discourse during the whole meal.

1. Should be "a brother"; Pope, *Epistle to Burlington* 117.
2. Oboe.
3. Water works, which took place at 9:00 P.M.

When wine and cyder were brought, Mr. Smith said, "Now let's enjoy ourselves; now is the time, or never. Well, Ma'am, and how do you like Vauxhall?"

"Like it!" cried young Branghton, "why, how can she help liking it? she has never seen such a place before, that I'll answer for."

"For my part," said Miss Branghton, "I like it because it is not vulgar."

"This must have been a fine treat for you, Miss," said Mr. Branghton; "why, I suppose you was never so happy in all your life before?"

I endeavoured to express my satisfaction with some pleasure, yet I believe they were much amazed at my coldness.

"Miss ought to stay in town till the last night," said young Branghton, "and then, it's my belief, she'd say something to it. Why, Lord, it's the best night of any; there's always a riot,—and there the folks run about,—and then there's such squealing and squalling!—and there all the lamps are broke,—and the women run skimper scamper;—I declare I would not take five guineas to miss the last night!"

I was very glad when they all grew tired of sitting, and called for the waiter to pay the bill. The Miss Branghtons said they would walk on, while the gentlemen settled the account, and asked me to accompany them; which, however, I declined.

"You girls may do as you please," said Madame Duval, "but as to me, I promise you, I sha'n't go nowhere without the gentlemen."

"No more, I suppose, will my *Cousin*," said Miss Branghton, looking reproachfully towards Mr. Smith.

This reflection, which I feared would flatter his vanity, made me, most unfortunately, request Madame Duval's permission to attend them. She granted it, and away we went, having promised to meet in the room.[4]

To the room, therefore, I would immediately have gone: but the sisters agreed that they would first have a *little pleasure*, and they tittered and talked so loud, that they attracted universal notice.

"Lord, Polly," said the eldest, "suppose we were to take a turn in the dark walks!"[5]

"Ay, do," answered she, "and then we'll hide ourselves, and then Mr. Brown will think we are lost."

I remonstrated very warmly against this plan, telling them, that it would endanger our missing the rest of the party all the evening.

"O dear," cried Miss Branghton, "I thought how uneasy Miss would be, without a beau!"

This impertinence I did not think worth answering; and, quite by compulsion, I followed them down a long alley, in which there was hardly any light.

4. The large picture room to the east of the rotunda.
5. Unlighted alleyways, often used for assignations and frequented by prostitutes. They had been fenced off in 1763, but in the following year, a large band of young men tore up the railings.

By the time we came near the end, a large party of gentlemen, apparently very riotous, and who were hallowing, leaning on one another, and laughing immoderately, seemed to rush suddenly from behind some trees, and, meeting us face to face, put their arms at their sides, and formed a kind of circle, which first stopped our proceeding, and then our retreating, for we were presently entirely inclosed. The Miss Branghtons screamed aloud, and I was frightened exceedingly: our screams were answered with bursts of laughter, and, for some minutes, we were kept prisoners, till at last, one of them, rudely, seizing hold of me, said I was a pretty little creature.

Terrified to death, I struggled with such vehemence to disengage myself from him, that I succeeded, in spite of his efforts to detain me; and immediately, and with a swiftness which fear only could have given me, I flew rather than ran up the walk, hoping to secure my safety by returning to the lights and company we had so foolishly left: but, before I could possibly accomplish my purpose, I was met by another party of men, one of whom placed himself so directly in my way, calling out, "Whither so fast, my love?"—that I could only have proceeded, by running into his arms.

In a moment both my hands, by different persons, were caught hold of; and one of them, in a most familiar manner, desired, when I ran next, to accompany me in a race; while the rest of the party stood still and laughed.

I was almost distracted with terror, and so breathless with running, that I could not speak, till another advancing, said, I was as handsome as an angel, and desired to be of the party. I then just articulated, "For Heaven's sake, Gentlemen, let me pass!"

Another, then, rushing suddenly forward, exclaimed, "Heaven and earth! what voice is that?—"

"The voice of the prettiest little actress I have seen this age," answered one of my persecutors.

"No,—no,—no,—" I *panted* out, "I am no actress,—pray let me go,—pray let me pass—."

"By all that's sacred," cried the same voice, which I then knew for Sir Clement Willoughby's, "'tis herself!"

"Sir Clement Willoughby!" cried I. "O Sir, assist—assist me—or I shall die with terror!"

"Gentlemen," cried he, disengaging them all from me in an instant, "pray leave this lady to me."

Loud laughs proceeded from every mouth, and two or three said, *Willoughby has all the luck!* But one of them, in a passionate manner, vowed he would not give me up, for that he had the first right to me, and would support it.

"You are mistaken," said Sir Clement, "this lady is—I will explain myself to you another time; but, I assure you, you are all mistaken."

And then, taking my willing hand, he led me off, amidst the loud acclamations, laughter, and gross merriment of his impertinent companions.

As soon as we had escaped from them, Sir Clement, with a voice of surprise, exclaimed, "My dearest creature, what wonder, what strange revolution, has brought you to such a spot as this?"

Ashamed of my situation, and extremely mortified to be thus recognized by him, I was for some time silent, and when he repeated his question, only stammered out, "I have,—I hardly know how,—lost myself from my party.—"

He caught my hand, and eagerly pressing it, in a passionate voice, said, "O that I had sooner met with thee!"

Surprised at a freedom so unexpected, I angrily broke from him, saying, "Is this the protection you give me, Sir Clement?"

And then I saw, what the perturbation of my mind had prevented my sooner noticing, that he had led me, though I know not how, into another of the dark alleys, instead of the place whither I meant to go.

"Good God!" I cried, "where am I?—What way are you going?"

"Where," answered he, "we shall be least observed."

Astonished at this speech, I stopped short, and declared I would go no further.

"And why not, my angel?" again endeavouring to take my hand.

My heart beat with resentment; I pushed him away from me with all my strength, and demanded how he dared treat me with such insolence?

"Insolence!" repeated he.

"Yes, Sir Clement, *insolence*; from you, who know me, I had a claim for protection,—not to such treatment as this."

"By heaven," cried he with warmth, "you distract me,—why, tell me,—why do I see you here?—Is this a place for Miss Anville?—these dark walks!—no party!—no companion!—by all that's good, I can scarce believe my senses!"

Extremely offended at this speech, I turned angrily from him, and, not deigning to make any answer, walked on towards that part of the garden whence I perceived the lights and company.

He followed me; but we were both some time silent.

"So you will not explain to me your situation?" said he, at length.

"No, Sir," answered I, disdainfully.

"Nor yet—suffer me to make my own interpretation? ——"

I could not bear this strange manner of speaking; it made my very soul shudder,—and I burst into tears.

He flew to me, and actually flung himself at my feet, as if regardless who might see him, saying, "O Miss Anville—loveliest of women—forgive my—my—I beseech you forgive me;—if I have offended,—if I have hurt you—I could kill myself at the thought!—"

"No matter, Sir, no matter," cried I, "if I can but find my friends,—I will never speak to—never see you again!"

"Good God!—good Heaven!—my dearest life, what is it I have done?—what is it I have said?—"

"You best know, Sir, *what* and *why*;—but don't hold me here,—let *me* be gone; and do *you*!"

"Not till you forgive me!—I cannot part with you in anger."

"For shame, for shame, Sir!" cried I indignantly, "do you suppose I am to be thus compelled?—do you take advantage of the absence of my friends to affront me?"

"No, Madam," cried he, rising, "I would sooner forfeit my life than act so mean a part. But you have flung me into amazement unspeakable, and you will not condescend to listen to my request of giving me some explanation."

"The manner, Sir," said I, "in which you spoke that request, made, and will make me scorn to answer it."

"Scorn!—I will own to you, I expected not such displeasure from Miss Anville."

"Perhaps, Sir, if you had, you would less voluntarily have merited it."

"My dearest life, surely it must be known to you, that the man does not breathe, who adores you so passionately, so fervently, so tenderly as I do!—why then will you delight in perplexing me?—in keeping me in suspense—in torturing me with doubt?"

"I, Sir, delight in perplexing you!—you are much mistaken.—Your suspence, your doubts, your perplexities,—are of your own creating; and believe me, Sir, they may *offend*, but they can never *delight* me:—but, as you have yourself raised, you must yourself satisfy them."

"Good God!—that such haughtiness and such sweetness can inhabit the same mansion!"

I made no answer, but quickening my pace, I walked on silently and sullenly; till this most impetuous of men, snatching my hand, which he grasped with violence, besought me to forgive him, with such earnestness of supplication, that, merely to escape his importunities, I was forced to speak, and, in some measure, to grant the pardon he requested: though it was accorded with a very ill grace: but, indeed, I knew not how to resist the humility of his entreaties: yet never shall I recollect the occasion he gave me of displeasure, without feeling it renewed.

We now soon arrived in the midst of the general crowd, and my own safety being then insured, I grew extremely uneasy for the Miss Branghtons, whose danger, however imprudently incurred by their own folly, I too well knew how to tremble for. To this consideration all my pride of heart yielded, and I determined to seek my party with the utmost speed; though not without a sigh did I recollect the fruitless attempt I had made, after the opera, of concealing from this man my unfortunate connections, which I was now obliged to make known.

I hastened, therefore, to the room, with a view of sending young Branghton to the aid of his sisters. In a very short time, I perceived Madame Duval, and the rest, looking at one of the paintings.

I must own to you, honestly, my dear Sir, that an involuntary repugnance seized me, at presenting such a set to Sir Clement,—he who had been used to see me in parties so different!—My pace slackened as I approached them,—but they presently perceived me.

"*Ah, Mademoiselle!*" cried M. Du Bois, "*Que je suis charmé de vous voir!*"[6]

"Pray, Miss," cried Mr. Brown, "where's Miss Polly?"

"Why, Miss, you've been a long while gone," said Mr. Branghton; "we thought you'd been lost. But what have you done with your cousins?"

I hesitated,—for Sir Clement regarded me with a look of wonder.

"*Pardi,*" cried Madame Duval, "I sha'n't let you leave me again in a hurry. Why, here we've been in such a fright!—and, all the while, I suppose, you've been thinking nothing about the matter."

"Well," said young Branghton, "as long as Miss is come back, I don't mind, for as to Bid and Poll, they can take care of themselves. But the best joke is, Mr. Smith is gone all about a looking for you."

These speeches were made almost all in a breath: but when, at last, they waited for an answer, I told them, that in walking up one of the long alleys, we had been frightened and separated.

"The long alleys!" repeated Mr. Branghton, "and, pray, what had you to do in the long alleys? why, to be sure, you must all of you have had a mind to be affronted!"

This speech was not more impertinent to me, than surprising to Sir Clement, who regarded all the party with evident astonishment. However, I told young Branghton that no time ought to be lost, for that his sisters might require his immediate protection.

"But how will they get it?" cried this brutal brother; "if they've a mind to behave in such a manner as that, they ought to protect themselves; and so they may for me."

"Well," said the simple Mr. Brown, "whether you go or no, I think I may as well see after Miss Polly."

The father, then, interfering, insisted that his son should accompany him; and away they went.

It was now that Madame Duval first perceived Sir Clement; to whom turning with a look of great displeasure, she angrily said, "*Ma foi,* so you are comed here, of all the people in the world!—I wonder, child, you would let such a—such a *person* as that keep company with you."

"I am very sorry, Madam," said Sir Clement, in a tone of surprise, "if I have been so unfortunate as to offend you; but I believe you will not regret the honour I now have of attending Miss Anville, when you hear

6. "Oh, Miss, how charmed I am to see you!"

that I have been so happy as to do her some service."

Just as Madame Duval, with her usual *Ma foi*, was beginning to reply, the attention of Sir Clement was wholly drawn from her, by the appearance of Mr. Smith, who coming suddenly behind me, and freely putting his hands on my shoulders, cried, "O ho, my little runaway, have I found you at last? I have been scampering all over the gardens for you, for I was determined to find you, if you were above ground.—But how could you be so cruel as to leave us?"

I turned round to him, and looked with a degree of contempt that I hoped would have quieted him; but he had not the sense to understand me; and, attempting to take my hand, he added, "Such a demure looking lady as you are, who'd have thought of your leading one such a dance?—Come, now, don't be so coy,—only think what a trouble I have had in running after you!"

"The trouble, Sir," said I, "was of your own choice,—not mine." And I walked round to the other side of Madame Duval.

Perhaps I was too proud,—but I could not endure that Sir Clement, whose eyes followed him with looks of the most surprised curiosity, should witness his unwelcome familiarity.

Upon my removal, he came up to me, and, in a low voice, said, "You are not, then, with the Mirvans?"

"No, Sir."

"And pray—may I ask,—have you left them long?"

"No, Sir."

"How unfortunate I am!—but yesterday I sent to acquaint the Captain I should reach the Grove by to-morrow noon! However, I shall get away as fast as possible. Shall you be long in town?"

"I believe not, Sir."

"And then, when you leave it,—which way—will you allow me to ask, which way you shall travel?"

"Indeed,—I don't know."

"Not know!—But do you return to the Mirvans any more?"

"I—I can't tell, Sir."

And then, I addressed myself to Madame Duval, with such a pretended earnestness, that he was obliged to be silent.

As he cannot but observe the great change in my situation, which he knows not how to account for, there is something in all these questions, and this unrestrained curiosity, that I did not expect from a man, who when he pleases can be so well-bred as Sir Clement Willoughby. He seems disposed to think that the alteration in my companions authorises an alteration in his manners. It is true, he has always treated me with uncommon freedom, but never before with so disrespectful an abruptness. This observation, which he has given me cause to make, of his *changing with the tide,* has sunk him more in my opinion, than any other part of his conduct.

Yet I could almost have laughed, when I looked at Mr. Smith, who no sooner saw me addressed by Sir Clement, than, retreating aloof from the company, he seemed to lose at once all his happy self-sufficiency and conceit; looking now at the baronet, now at himself, surveying, with sorrowful eyes, his dress, struck with his air, his gestures, his easy gaiety; he gazed at him with envious admiration, and seemed himself, with conscious inferiority, to shrink into nothing.

Soon after, Mr. Brown, running up to us, called out, "La, what, i'n't Miss Polly come yet?"

"Come!" said Mr. Branghton, "why, I thought you went to fetch her yourself, did n't you?"

"Yes, but I could n't find her;—yet I daresay I've been over half the garden."

"Half! but why did not you go over it all?"

"Why, so I will: but only I thought I'd just come and see if she was here first?"

"But where's Tom?"

"Why, I don't know; for he would not stay with me, all as ever I could say; for we met some young gentlemen of his acquaintance, and so he bid me go and look by myself, for he said, says he, I can divert myself better another way, says he."

This account being given, away again went this silly young man! and Mr. Branghton, extremely incensed, said he would go and see after them himself.

"So, now," cried Madame Duval, "he's gone too! why, at this rate we shall have to wait for one or other of them all night!"

Observing that Sir Clement seemed disposed to renew his enquiries, I turned towards one of the paintings, and, pretending to be very much occupied in looking at it, asked M. Du Bois some questions concerning the figures.

"O! *Mon Dieu!*" cried Madame Duval, "don't ask him; your best way is to ask Mr. Smith, for he's been here the oftenest. Come, Mr. Smith, I dare say you can tell us all about them."

"Why, yes, Ma'am, yes," said Mr. Smith, who, brightening up at this application, advanced towards us, with an air of assumed importance, which, however, sat very uneasily upon him, and begged to know what he should explain first; "For I have attended," said he, "to all these paintings, and know every thing in them perfectly well; for I am rather fond of pictures, Ma'am; and, really, I must say, I think a pretty picture is a—a very—is really a very—is something very pretty.—"

"So do I too," said Madame Duval, "but pray now, Sir, tell us who that is meant for," pointing to a figure of Neptune.[7]

"That!—why that, Ma'am, is,—Lord bless me, I can't think how I

7. Austin Dobson identifies the painting as the "allegorical representation of Admiral Hawkes's defeat of the French at Quiberon Bay," by Francis Hayman (1708–76) (*Evelina*, 1903, xvii).

come to be so stupid, but really I have forgot his name,—and yet, I know it as well as my own, too,—however, he's a *General*, Ma'am they are all Generals."

I saw Sir Clement bite his lips; and, indeed, so did I mine.

"Well," said Madame Duval, "it's the oddest dress for a general ever I see!"

"He seems so capital a figure," said Sir Clement to Mr. Smith, "that I imagine he must be *Generalissimo* of the whole army."

"Yes, Sir, yes," answered Mr. Smith, respectfully bowing, and highly delighted at being thus referred to, "you are perfectly right,—but I cannot for my life think of his name;—perhaps, Sir, you may remember it?"

"No, really," replied Sir Clement, "my acquaintance among the generals is not so extensive."

The ironical tone of voice in which Sir Clement spoke, entirely disconcerted Mr. Smith; who again, retiring to an humble distance, seemed sensibly mortified at the failure of his attempt to recover his consequence.

Soon after, Mr. Branghton returned with his youngest daughter, whom he had rescued from a party of insolent young men; but he had not yet been able to find the eldest. Miss Polly was really frightened, and declared she would never go into the dark walks again. Her father, leaving her with us, went in quest of her sister.

While she was relating her adventures, to which nobody listened more attentively than Sir Clement, we saw Mr. Brown enter the room. "O la!" cried Miss Polly, "let me hide myself, and don't tell him I'm come."

She then placed herself behind Madame Duval, in such a manner that she could not be seen.

"So Miss Polly is not come yet!" said the simple swain; "well, I can't think where she can be! I've been a looking, and looking, and looking all about, and I can't find her, all I can do."

"Well but, Mr. Brown," said Mr. Smith, "sha'n't you go and look for the lady again?"

"Yes, Sir," said he, sitting down, "but I must rest me a little bit first. You can't think how tired I am."

"O fie, Mr. Brown, fie," cried Mr. Smith, winking at us, "tired of looking for a lady! Go, go, for shame!"

"So I will, Sir, presently; but you'd be tired too, if you'd walked so far: besides, I think she's gone out of the garden, or else I must have seen something or other of her."

A *he, he, he!* of the tittering Polly, now betrayed her, and so ended this ingenious little artifice.

At last appeared Mr. Branghton and Miss Biddy, who, with a face of mixed anger and confusion, addressing herself to me, said, "So Miss, so you ran away from me! Well, see if I don't do as much by you some day or other! But I thought how it would be, you'd no mind to leave the *gentlemen*, though you run away from *me*."

I was so much surprised at this attack, that I could not answer her for very amazement; and she proceeded to tell us how ill she had been used, and that two young men had been making her walk up and down the dark walks by absolute force, and as fast as ever they could tear her along; and many other particulars, which I will not tire you with relating. In conclusion, looking at Mr. Smith, she said, "But, to be sure, thought I, at least all the company will be looking for me; so I little expected to find you all here, talking as comfortably as ever you can. However, I know I may thank my cousin for it!"

"If you mean *me*, Madam," said I, very much shocked, "I am quite ignorant in what manner I can have been accessary to your distress."

"Why, by running away so. If you'd stayed with us, I'll answer for it, Mr. Smith, and M. Du Bois would have come to look for us; but I suppose they could not leave your ladyship."

The folly and unreasonableness of this speech would admit of no answer. But what a scene was this for Sir Clement! his surprise was evident; and I must acknowledge, my confusion was equally great.

We had now to wait for young Branghton, who did not appear for some time; and, during this interval, it was with difficulty that I avoided Sir Clement, who was on the rack of curiosity, and dying to speak to me.

When, at last, the hopeful youth returned, a long and frightful quarrel ensued between him and his father, in which his sisters occasionally joined, concerning his neglect; and he defended himself only by a brutal mirth, which he indulged at their expence.

Every one, now, seemed inclined to depart,—when, as usual, a dispute arose, upon the *way* of our going, whether in a coach or a boat. After much debating, it was determined that we should make two parties, one by the water and the other by land; for Madame Duval declared she would not, upon any account, go into a boat at night.

Sir Clement then said, that if she had no carriage in waiting, he should be happy to see her and me safe home, as his was in readiness.

Fury started into her eyes, and passion inflamed every feature, as she answered, "*Pardi*, no—you may take care of yourself, if you please; but as to me, I promise you I sha'n't trust myself with no such person."

He pretended not to comprehend her meaning, yet, to waive a discussion, acquiesced in her refusal. The coach party fixed upon consisted of Madame Duval, M. Du Bois, Miss Branghton, and myself.

I now began to rejoice, in private, that, at least, our lodgings would be neither seen nor known by Sir Clement. We soon met with an hackney-coach, into which he handed me, and then took leave.

Madame Duval, having already given the coachman her direction, he mounted the box, and we were just driving off, when Sir Clement exclaimed, "By Heaven, this is the very coach I had in waiting for myself!"

"This coach, your honour!" said the man, "no, that it i'n't."

Sir Clement, however, swore that it was, and, presently, the man, begging his pardon, said he had really forgotten that he was engaged.

I have no doubt but that this scheme occurred to him at the moment, and that he made some sign to the coachman, which induced him to support it: for there is not the least probability that the accident really happened, as it is most likely his own chariot was in waiting.

The man then opened the coach-door, and Sir Clement advancing to it, said, "I don't believe there is another carriage to be had, or I would not incommode you; but, as it may be disagreeable to you to wait here any longer, I beg you will not get out, for you shall be set down before I am carried home, if you will be so good as to make a little room."

And so saying, in he jumpt, and seated himself between M. Du Bois and me, while our astonishment at the whole transaction was too great for speech. He then ordered the coachman to drive on, according to the directions he had already received.

For the first ten minutes, no one uttered a word; and then, Madame Duval, no longer able to contain herself, exclaimed, "*Ma foi,* if this is n't one of the most impudentest things ever I see!"

Sir Clement, regardless of this rebuke, attended only to me; however, I answered nothing he said, when I could possibly avoid so doing. Miss Branghton made several attempts to attract his notice, but in vain, for he would not take the trouble of paying her any regard.

Madame Duval, during the rest of the ride, addressed herself to M. Du Bois in French, and in that language exclaimed with great vehemence against boldness and assurance.

I was extremely glad when I thought our journey must be nearly at an end, for my situation was very uneasy to me, as Sir Clement perpetually endeavoured to take my hand. I looked out of the coach-window, to see if we were near home; Sir Clement, stooping over me did the same, and then, in a voice of infinite wonder, called out, "Where the D——l is the man driving to? —— why we are in broad St. Giles's!"[8]

"O, he's very right," cried Madame Duval, "so never trouble your head about that, for I sha'n't go by no directions of yours, I promise you."

When, at last, we stopped, at *an hosier's* in *High Holborn*—Sir Clement said nothing, but his *eyes*, I saw, were very busily employed in viewing the place, and the situation of the house. The coach, he said, belonged to him, and therefore he insisted upon paying for it; and then he took leave. M. Du Bois walked home with Miss Branghton, and Madame Duval and I retired to our apartments.

How disagreeable an evening's adventure! not one of the party

8. That is, "we are well into the parish of St. Giles-in-the-Fields."

seemed satisfied, except Sir Clement, who was in high spirits: but Madame Duval, was enraged at meeting with him; Mr. Branghton, angry with his children; the frolic of the Miss Branghtons had exceeded their plan, and ended in their own distress; their brother was provoked that there had been no riot; Mr. Brown was tired; and Mr. Smith mortified. As to myself, I must acknowledge, nothing could be more disagreeable to me, than being seen by Sir Clement Willoughby with a party at once so vulgar in themselves, and so familiar to me.

And you, too, my dear Sir, will, I know, be sorry that I have met him; however, there is no apprehension of his visiting here, as Madame Duval is far too angry to admit him.

Letter XVI.

EVELINA IN CONTINUATION.

Holborn, June 18th.

Madame Duval rose very late this morning, and, at one o'clock, we had but just breakfasted, when Miss Branghton, her brother, Mr. Smith, and Monsieur Du Bois, called to enquire after our healths.

This civility in young Branghton, I much suspect, was merely the result of his father's commands; but his sister and Mr. Smith, I soon found, had motives of their own. Scarce had they spoken to Madame Duval, when, advancing eagerly to me, "Pray, Ma'am," said Mr. Smith, "Who was that gentleman?"

"Pray, Cousin," cried Miss Branghton, "was not he the same gentleman you ran away with that night at the opera?"

"Goodness! that he was," said young Branghton; "and, I declare, as soon as ever I saw him, I thought I knew his face."

"I'm sure I'll defy you to forget him," answered his sister, "if once you had seen him: he is the finest gentleman I ever saw in my life; don't you think so, Mr. Smith?"

"Why, you won't give the lady time to speak," said Mr. Smith.

—"Pray, Ma'am, what is the gentleman's name?"

"Willoughby, Sir."

"Willoughby! I think I have heard the name. Pray, Ma'am, is he married?"

"Lord, no, that he is not," cried Miss Branghton; "he looks too smart, by a great deal, for a married man. Pray, cousin, how did you get acquainted with him?"

"Pray, Miss," said young Branghton, in the same breath, "what's his business?"

"Indeed I don't know," answered I.

"Something very genteel, I dare say," added Miss Branghton, "because he dresses so fine."

"It ought to be something that brings in a good income," said Mr. Smith, "for I'm sure he did not get that suit of cloaths he had on under thirty or forty pounds; for I know the price of cloaths pretty well;—pray, Ma'am, can you tell me what he has a year?"

"Don't talk no more about him," cried Madame Duval, "for I don't like to hear his name; I believe he's one of the worst persons in the world; for though I never did him no manner of harm, nor so much as hurt a hair of his head, I know he was an accomplice with that fellow, Captain Mirvan, to take away my life."

Everybody, but myself, now crowding around her for an explanation, a violent rapping at the street-door was unheard; and, without any previous notice, in the midst of her narration, Sir Clement Willoughby entered the room. They all started, and, with looks of guilty confusion, as if they feared his resentment for having listened to Madame Duval, they scrambled for chairs, and, in a moment were all formally seated.

Sir Clement, after a general bow, singling out Madame Duval, said with his usual easiness, "I have done myself the honour of waiting on you, Madam, to enquire if you have any commands to Howard Grove, whither I am going to-morrow morning."

Then, seeing the storm that gathered in her eyes, before he allowed her time to answer, he addressed himself to me;—"And if you, Madam, have any with which you will honour me, I shall be happy to execute them."

"None at all, Sir."

"None!—not to Miss Mirvan!—no message! no letter!—"

"I wrote to Miss Mirvan yesterday by the post."

"My application should have been earlier, had I sooner known your address."

"*Ma foi*," cried Madame Duval, recovering from her surprise, "I believe never nobody saw the like of this!"

"Of what! Madam!" cried the undaunted Sir Clement, turning quick towards her, "I hope no one has offended you!"

"You don't hope no such a thing!" cried she, half choaked with passion, and rising from her chair. This motion was followed by the rest, and, in a moment, every body stood up.

Still Sir Clement was not abashed; affecting to make a bow of *acknowledgment* to the company in general, he said, "Pray—I beg— Ladies,—Gentlemen,—pray don't let me disturb you, pray keep your seats."

"Pray, Sir," said Miss Branghton, moving a chair towards him, "won't you sit down yourself?"

"You are extremely good, Ma'am:—rather than make any disturbance—"

And so saying, this strange man seated himself, as did, in an instant, every body else, even Madame Duval herself, who, overpowered by his boldness, seemed too full for utterance.

He then, and with as much composure as if he had been an expected guest, began to discourse on the weather,—its uncertainty,—the heat of the public places in summer,—the emptiness of the town,—and other such common topics.

Nobody, however, answered him; Mr. Smith seemed afraid, young Branghton ashamed, M. Du Bois amazed, Madame Duval enraged, and myself determined not to interfere. All that he could obtain, was the notice of Miss Branghton, whose nods, smiles, and attention, had some appearance of entering into conversation with him.

At length, growing tired, I suppose, of engaging every body's eyes, and nobody's tongue; addressing himself to Madame Duval and to me, he said, "I regard myself as peculiarly unfortunate, Ladies, in having fixed upon a time for my visit to Howard Grove, when you are absent from it."

"So I suppose, Sir, so I suppose," cried Madame Duval, hastily rising, and the next moment as hastily seating herself,—"you'll be a wanting of somebody to make your game of, and so you may think to get *me* there again;—but, I promise you, Sir, you won't find it so easy a matter to make me a fool: and besides that," raising her voice, "I've found you out, I assure you; so if ever you go to play your tricks upon me again, I'll make no more ado, but go directly to a justice of peace; so, Sir, if you can't think of nothing but making people ride about the country, at all hours of the night, just for your diversion, why you'll find I know some justices as well as Justice Tyrrell."

Sir Clement was evidently embarrassed at this attack; yet he affected a look of surprise, and protested he did not understand her meaning.

"Well," cried she, "if I don't wonder where people can get such impudence! if you'll say that, you'll say any thing; however, if you swear till you're black in the face, I sha'n't believe you; for nobody sha'n't persuade me out of my senses, that I'm resolved."

"Doubtless not, Madam," answered he with some hesitation, "and I hope you do not suspect I ever had such an intention; my respect for you—"

"O Sir, you're vastly polite all of a sudden! but I know what it's all for! it's only for what you can get!—you could treat me like nobody at Howard Grove—but now you see I've a house of my own you've a mind to wheedle yourself into it; but I sees your design, so you need n't trouble yourself to take no more trouble about that, for you shall never get nothing at my house,—not so much as a dish of tea:—so now, Sir, you see I can play you trick for trick."

There was something so extremely gross in this speech, that it even disconcerted Sir Clement, who was too much confounded to make any answer.

It was curious to observe the effect which his embarrassment, added to the freedom with which Madame Duval addressed him, had upon the rest of the company: every one, who, before, seemed at a loss how, or if at all, to occupy a chair, now filled it with the most easy composure: and Mr. Smith, whose countenance had exhibited the most striking picture of mortified envy, now began to recover his usual expression of satisfied conceit. Young Branghton, too, who had been apparently awed by the presence of so fine a gentleman, was again himself, rude and familiar; while his mouth was wide distended into a broad grin, at hearing *his aunt give the beau such a trimming*.[1]

Madame Duval encouraged by this success, looked around her with an air of triumph, and continued her harangue: "And so, Sir, I suppose you thought to have had it all your own way, and to have comed here as often as you pleased, and to have got me to Howard Grove again, on purpose to have served me as you did before; but you shall see I'm as cunning as you, so you may go and find somebody else to use in that manner, and to put your mask on, and to make a fool of; for as to me, if you go to tell me your stories about the Tower again, for a month together, I'll never believe 'em no more; and I'll promise you, Sir, if you think I like such jokes, you'll find I'm no such person."

"I assure you, Ma'am,—upon my honour—I really don't comprehend—I fancy there is some misunderstanding—"

"What, I suppose you'll tell me next you don't know nothing of the matter?"

"Not a word, upon my honour."

O Sir Clement! thought I, is it thus you prize your honour!

"*Pardi*," cried Madam Duval, "this is the most provokingest part of all! why you might as well tell me I don't know my own name."

"Here is certainly some mistake; for I assure you, Ma'am—"

"Don't assure me nothing," cried Madame Duval, raising her voice, "I know what I'm saying, and so do you too; for did not you tell me all that about the Tower, and about M. Du Bois?—why M. Du Bois was n't never there, nor nigh it, and so it was all your own invention."

"May there not be two persons of the same name? the mistake was but natural.—"

"Don't tell me of no mistake, for it was all on purpose; besides, did not you come, all in a mask, to the chariot-door, and help to get me put in that ditch?—I'll promise you, I've had the greatest mind in the world to take the law of you ever since, and if ever you do as much again, so I will, I assure you!"

Here Miss Branghton tittered; Mr. Smith smiled contemptuously, and young Branghton thrust his handkerchief into his mouth to stop his laughter.

---

1. A sharp censure.

The situation of Sir Clement, who saw all that passed, became now very awkward even to himself, and he stammered very much in saying, "Surely, Madam—surely you—you cannot do me the—the injustice to think—that I had any share in the—the—the misfortune which—"

"*Ma foi*, Sir," cried Madame Duval, with increasing passion, "you'd best not stand talking to me at that rate; I know it *was* you,—and if you stay there, a provoking me in such a manner, I'll send for a constable this minute."

Young Branghton, at these words, in spite of all his efforts, burst into a loud laugh; nor could either his sister, or Mr. Smith, though with more moderation, forbear joining in his mirth.

Sir Clement darted his eyes towards them, with looks of the most angry contempt, and then told Madame Duval, that he would not now detain her to make his vindication, but would wait on her some time when she was alone.

"O *Pardi*, Sir," cried she, "I don't desire none of your company; and if you was n't the most boldest person in the world, you would not dare look me in the face."

The ha, ha, ha's, and he, he, he's, grew more and more uncontroulable, as if the restraint from which they had burst, had added to their violence. Sir Clement could no longer endure being the object who excited them, and, having no answer ready for Madame Duval, he hastily stalked towards Mr. Smith and young Branghton, and sternly demanded what they laughed at?

Struck by the air of importance which he assumed, and alarmed at the angry tone of his voice, their merriment ceased, as instantaneously as if it had been directed by clock-work, and they stared foolishly, now at him, now at each other, without making any answer but a simple "*Nothing*, Sir."

"O *pour le coup*,"[2] cried Madame Duval, "this is too much! pray, Sir, what business have you to come here a ordering people that comes to see me? I suppose next, nobody must laugh but yourself!"

"With me, Madam," said Sir Clement, bowing, "a *lady* may do any thing, and, consequently, there is no liberty in which I shall not be happy to indulge *you*:—but it has never been my custom to give the same licence to *gentlemen*."

Then, advancing to me, who had sat very quietly, on a window, during this scene, he said, "Miss Anville, I may at least acquaint our friends at Howard Grove that I had the honour of leaving you in good health." And then, lowering his voice, he added, "For Heaven's sake, my dearest creature, who are these people? and how came you so strangely situated?"

2. "This time."

"I beg my respects to all the family, Sir," answered I, aloud, "and I hope you will find them well."

He looked at me reproachfully, but kissed my hand; and then, bowing to Madame Duval and Miss Branghton, passed hastily by the men, and made his exit.

I fancy he will not be very eager to repeat his visits, for I should imagine he has rarely, if ever, been before in a situation so awkward and disagreeable.

Madame Duval has been all spirits and exultation ever since he went, and only wishes Captain Mirvan would call, that she might *do the same by him*. Mr. Smith, upon hearing that he was a baronet, and seeing him drive off in a very beautiful chariot, declared that he would not have laughed upon any account, had he known his rank, and regretted extremely having missed such an opportunity of making so *genteel* an *acquaintance*. Young Branghton vowed, that, if he had known as much, he would have *asked for his custom*[3] and his sister has sung his praises ever since, protesting she thought, *all along*, he was a man of *quality* by his *look*.

Letter XVII.

EVELINA IN CONTINUATION.

June 21.

The last three evenings have passed tolerably quiet, for the Vauxhall adventures had given Madame Duval a surfeit of public places: home, however, soon growing tiresome, she determined to night, she said, to relieve her *ennui* by some amusement; and it was therefore settled that we should call upon the Branghtons, at their house, and thence proceed to Marybone Gardens.

But, before we reached Snow-Hill, we were caught in a shower of rain: we hurried into the shop, where the first object I saw was Mr. Macartney, with a book in his hand, seated in the same corner where I saw him last; but his looks were still more wretched than before, his face yet thinner, and his eyes sunk almost hollow into his head. He lifted them up as we entered, and I even thought that they emitted a gleam of joy: involuntarily, I made to him my first courtesie; he rose and bowed, with a precipitation that manifested surprise and confusion.

In a few minutes, we were joined by all the family, except Mr. Smith, who fortunately was engaged.

Had all the future prosperity of our lives depended upon the good or bad weather of this evening, it could not have been treated as a subject of greater importance. "Sure never anything was so unlucky!"—"Lord

---

3. Business patronage or support.

how provoking!"—"It might rain for ever, if it would hold up now!"—
These, and such expressions, with many anxious observations upon the
kennels,[1] filled up all the conversation till the shower was over.

And then a very warm debate arose, whether we should pursue our
plan, or defer it to some finer evening; Miss Branghtons were for the
former; their father was sure it would rain again; Madame Duval,
though she detested returning home, yet dreaded the dampness of the
gardens.

M. Du Bois then proposed going to the top of the house, to examine
whether the clouds looked threatening or peaceable; Miss Branghton,
starting at this proposal, said they might go to Mr. Macartney's room, if
they would, but not to hers.

This was enough for the brother; who, with a loud laugh, declared
he would have some *fun*, and immediately led the way, calling to us all
to follow. His sisters both ran after him, but no one else moved.

In a few minutes, young Branghton, coming half way down stairs,
called out, "Lord, why don't you all come? why here's Poll's things all
about the room!"

Mr. Branghton then went, and Madame Duval, who cannot bear to
be excluded from whatever is going forward, was handed up stairs by
M. Du Bois.

I hesitated a few moments whether or not to join them; but, soon
perceiving that Mr. Macartney had dropped his book, and that I
engrossed his whole attention, I prepared, from mere embarrassment,
to follow them.

As I went, I heard him move from his chair, and walk slowly after me.
Believing that he wished to speak to me, and earnestly desiring myself
to know if, by your means, I could possibly be of any service to him, I
first slackened my pace, and then turned back. But, though I thus met
him half-way, he seemed to want courage or resolution to address me;
for when he saw me returning, with a look extremely disordered, he
retreated hastily from me.

Not knowing what I ought to do, I went to the street-door, where I
stood some time, hoping he would be able to recover himself: but, on
the contrary, his agitation encreased every moment; he walked up and
down the room, in a quick, but unsteady pace, seeming equally distressed and irresolute: and, at length, with a deep sigh, he flung himself
into a chair.

I was so much affected by the appearance of such extreme anguish,
that I could remain no longer in the room; I therefore glided by him,
and went up stairs; but, ere I had gone five steps, he precipitately followed me, and, in a broken voice, called out, "Madam!—for Heaven's
sake—"

---

1. Open gutters in the centers of the streets.

He stopped, but I instantly descended, restraining, as well as I was able, the fullness of my own concern. I waited some time, in painful expectation, for his speaking: all that I had heard of his poverty, occurring to me, I was upon the point of presenting him my purse, but the fear of mistaking or offending him, deterred me. Finding, however, that he continued silent, I ventured to say, "Did you—Sir, wish to speak to me?"

"I did!" cried he with quickness, "but now—I cannot!"—

"Perhaps, Sir, another time,—perhaps if you recollect yourself—"

"Another time!" repeated he mournfully, "alas! I look not forward but to misery and despair!"

"O Sir," cried I, extremely shocked, "you must not talk thus!—if you forsake *yourself*, how can you expect—"

I stopped. "Tell me, tell me," cried he, with eagerness, "who you are?—whence you come?—and by what strange means you seem to be arbitress and ruler of the destiny of such a wretch as I am?"

"Would to Heaven," cried I, "I could serve you!"

"You can!"

"And how? pray tell me how?"

"To tell you—is death to me! yet I *will* tell you,—I have a *right* to your assistance,—you have deprived me of the only resource to which I could apply,—and therefore—"

"Pray, pray speak;" cried I, putting my hand into my pocket, "they will be down stairs in a moment!"

"I will, Madam.—Can you—will you—I think you will!—may I then—" he stopped and paused, "say, will you"—then suddenly turning from me, "Great Heaven! I cannot speak!" and he went back to the shop.

I now put my purse in my hand, and following him, said, "If indeed, Sir, I can assist you, why should you deny me so great a satisfaction? Will you permit me to—"

I dared not go on; but with a countenance very much softened, he approached me, and said, "Your voice, Madam, is the voice of compassion!—such a voice as these ears have long been strangers to!"

Just then, young Branghton called out vehemently to me, to come up stairs; I seized the opportunity of hastening away: and therefore saying, "Heaven, Sir, protect and comfort you!" I let fall my purse upon the ground, not daring to present it to him, and ran up stairs with the utmost swiftness.

Too well do I know you, my ever honoured Sir, to fear your displeasure for this action: I must, however, assure you I shall need no fresh supply during my stay in town, as I am at little expence, and hope soon to return to Howard Grove.

Soon, did I say! when not a fortnight is yet expired, of the long and tedious month I must linger out here!

I had many witticisms to endure from the Branghtons, upon account of my staying so long with the *Scotch mope*, as they call him; but I attended to them very little, for my whole heart was filled with pity and concern. I was very glad to find the Marybone scheme was deferred, another shower of rain having put a stop to the dissension upon this subject; the rest of the evening was employed in most violent quarrelling between Miss Polly and her brother, on account of the discovery made by the latter, of the state of her apartment.

We came home early; and I have stolen from Madame Duval and M. Du Bois, who is here for ever, to write to my best friend.

I am most sincerely rejoiced, that this opportunity has offered for my contributing what little relief was in my power, to this unhappy man; and I hope it will be sufficient to enable him to pay his debts to this pitiless family.

Letter XVIII.

MR. VILLARS TO EVELINA.

Berry Hill.

Displeasure? my Evelina!—you have but done your duty; you have but shewn that humanity without which I should blush to own my child. It is mine, however, to see that your generosity be not repressed by your suffering from indulging it; I remit to you, therefore, not merely a token of my approbation, but an acknowledgment of my desire to participate in your charity.

O my child, were my fortune equal to my confidence in thy benevolence, with what transport should I, through thy means, devote it to the relief of indigent virtue! yet let us not repine at the limitation of our power, for, while our bounty is proportioned to our ability, the difference of the greater or less donation, can weigh but little in the scale of justice.

In reading your account of the misguided man, whose misery has so largely excited your compassion, I am led to apprehend, that his unhappy situation is less the effect of misfortune, than of misconduct. If he is reduced to that state of poverty represented by the Branghtons, he should endeavour by activity and industry to retrieve his affairs, and not pass his time in idle reading in the very shop of his creditor.

The pistol scene made me shudder: the courage with which you pursued this desperate man, at once delighted and terrified me. Be ever thus, my dearest Evelina, dauntless in the cause of distress! let no weak fears, no timid doubts, deter you from the exertion of your duty, according to the fullest sense of it that Nature has implanted in your mind. Though gentleness and modesty are the peculiar attributes of your sex, yet fortitude and firmness, when occasion demands them, are virtues as noble and as becoming in women as in men: the right line of conduct is the same for both sexes, though the manner in which it is pursued, may somewhat vary, and be accommodated to the strength or weakness of the different travellers.

There is, however, something so mysterious in all you have yet seen or heard of this wretched man, that I am unwilling to stamp a bad impression of his character, upon so slight and partial a knowledge of it. Where any thing is doubtful, the ties of society, and the laws of humanity, claim a favourable interpretation; but remember, my dear child, that those of discretion have an equal claim to your regard.

As to Sir Clement Willoughby, I know not how to express my indignation at his conduct. Insolence so insufferable, and the implication of suspicions so shocking, irritate me to a degree of wrath, which I hardly thought my almost worn-out passions were capable of again experiencing. You must converse with him no more; he imagines, from the pliability of your temper, that he may offend you with impunity; but his behaviour justifies, nay, calls for, your avowed resentment: do not, therefore, hesitate in forbidding him your sight.

The Branghtons, Mr. Smith, and young Brown, however ill-bred, and disagreeable, are objects too contemptible for serious displeasure: yet I grieve much that my Evelina should be exposed to their rudeness and impertinence.

The very day that this tedious month expires, I shall send Mrs. Clinton to town, who will accompany you to Howard Grove. Your stay there will, I hope, be short, for I feel daily an encreasing impatience to fold my beloved child to my bosom!

Arthur Villars.

Letter XIX.

EVELINA TO THE REV. MR. VILLARS.

Holborn, June 27th.

I have just received, my dearest Sir, your kind present, and still kinder letter. Surely never had orphan so little to regret as your grateful Evelina! Though motherless, though worse than fatherless, bereft from infancy of the two first and greatest blessings of life, never has she had cause to deplore their loss; never has she felt the omission of a parent's tenderness, care or indulgence; never, but from sorrow for *them*, had reason to grieve at the separation! Most thankfully do I receive the token of your approbation, and most studiously will I endeavour so to dispose of it, as may merit your generous confidence in my conduct.

Your doubts concerning Mr. Macartney give me some uneasiness. Indeed, Sir, he has not the appearance of a man whose sorrows are the effect of guilt. But I hope, before I leave town, to be better acquainted with his situation, and enabled, with more certainty of his worth, to recommend him to your favour.

I am very willing to relinquish all acquaintance with Sir Clement Willoughby, as far as it may depend upon myself so to do; but indeed, I know not how I should be able to absolutely *forbid him my sight.*

Miss Mirvan, in her last letter, informs me that he is now at Howard Grove, where he continues in high favour with the Captain, and is the life and spirit of the house. My time, since I wrote last, has passed very quietly; Madame Duval having been kept at home by a bad cold, and the Branghtons by bad weather. The young man, indeed, has called two or three times, and his behaviour, though equally absurd, is more unaccountable than ever: he speaks very little, takes hardly any notice of Madame Duval, and never looks at me, without a broad grin. Sometimes he approaches me, as if with intention to communicate intelligence of importance, and then, suddenly stopping short, laughs rudely in my face.

O how happy shall I be, when the worthy Mrs. Clinton arrives!

June 29th.

Yesterday morning, Mr. Smith called, to acquaint us that the Hampstead assembly was to be held that evening; and then he presented Madame Duval with one ticket, and brought another to me. I thanked him for his intended civility, but told him I was surprised he had so soon forgotten my having already declined going to the ball.

"Lord, Ma'am," cried he, "how should I suppose you was in earnest? come, come, don't be cross; here's your Grand-mama ready to take care of you, so you can have no fair objection, for she'll see that I don't run away with you. Besides, Ma'am, I got the tickets on purpose."

"If you were determined, Sir," said I, "in making me this offer, to allow me no choice of refusal or acceptance, I must think myself less obliged to your intention, than I was willing to do."

"Dear Ma'am," cried he, "you're so smart, there is no speaking to you;—indeed, you are monstrous smart, Ma'am! but come, your Grand-mama shall ask you, and then I know you'll not be so cruel."

Madame Duval was very ready to interfere; she desired me to make no further opposition, said she should go herself, and insisted upon my accompanying her. It was in vain that I remonstrated; I only incurred her anger, and Mr. Smith, having given both the tickets to Madame Duval, with an air of triumph, said he should call early in the evening, and took leave.

I was much chagrined at being thus compelled to owe even the shadow of an obligation to so forward a young man; but I determined that nothing should prevail upon me to dance with him, however my refusal might give offence.

In the afternoon, when he returned, it was evident that he purposed to both charm and astonish me by his appearance; he was dressed in a very showy manner, but without any taste, and the inelegant smartness of his air and deportment, his visible struggle, against education, to put on the fine gentleman, added to his frequent conscious glances at a dress to which he was but little accustomed, very effectually destroyed his aim of *figuring*,[1] and rendered all his efforts useless.

During tea, entered Miss Branghton and her brother. I was sorry to observe the consternation of the former, when she perceived Mr. Smith. I had intended applying to her for advice upon this occasion, but been always deterred by her disagreeable abruptness. Having cast her eyes several times from Mr. Smith to me, with manifest displeasure, she seated herself sullenly in the window, scarce answering Madame Duval's enquiries, and when I spoke to her, turning absolutely away from me.

Mr. Smith delighted at this mark of his importance, sat indolently quiet on his chair, endeavouring by his looks rather to display, than to conceal, his inward satisfaction.

"Good gracious!" cried young Branghton, "why, you're all as fine as five-pence! Why, where are you going?"

"To the Hampstead ball," answered Mr. Smith.

"To a ball!" cried he, "Why, what, is Aunt going to a ball? Ha, ha, ha!"

"Yes, to be sure," cried Madame Duval; "I don't know nothing need hinder me."

"And pray, Aunt, will you dance too?"

"Perhaps I may; but I suppose, Sir, that's none of your business, whether I do or not."

"Lord! well, I should like to go! I should like to see Aunt dance of all things! But the joke is, I don't believe she'll get ever a partner."

"You're the most rudest boy ever I see," cried Madame Duval, angrily: "but, I promise you, I'll tell your father what you say, for I've no notion of such vulgarness."

"Why, Lord, Aunt, what are you so angry for? there's no speaking a word, but you fly into a passion: you're as bad as Biddy or Poll for that, for you're always a scolding."

"I desire, Tom," cried Miss Branghton, "you'd speak for yourself, and not make so free with my name."

"There, now, she's up! there's nothing but quarrelling with the women: it's my belief they like it better than victuals and drink."

"Fie, Tom," cried Mr. Smith, "you never remember your manners before the ladies: I'm sure you never heard *me* speak so rude to them."

"Why, Lord, *you* are a beau; but that's nothing to me. So, if you've a mind, you may be so polite as to dance with Aunt yourself." Then, with

1. Making a distinguished appearance.

a loud laugh, he declared it would be *good fun* to see them.

"Let it be never so good, or never so bad," cried Madame Duval, "you won't see nothing of it, I promise you; so pray don't let me hear no more of such vulgar pieces of fun; for, I assure you, I don't like it. And as to my dancing with Mr. Smith, you may see wonderfuller things than that any day in the week."

"Why, as to that, Ma'am," said Mr. Smith, looking much surprised, "I always thought you intended to play at cards, and so I thought to dance with the young lady."

I gladly seized this opportunity to make my declaration, that I should not dance at all.

"Not dance at all!" repeated Miss Branghton; "yes, that's a likely matter truly, when people go to balls."

"I wish she mayn't," said the brother; "'cause then Mr. Smith will have nobody but Aunt for a partner. Lord, how mad he'll be!"

"O, as to that," said Mr. Smith, "I don't at all fear prevailing with the young lady, if once I get her to the room."

"Indeed, Sir," cried I, much offended by his conceit, "you are mistaken; and therefore I beg leave to undeceive you, as you may be assured my resolution will not alter."

"Then pray, Miss, if it is not impertinent," cried Miss Branghton, sneeringly, "what do you go for?"

"Merely and solely," answered I, "to comply with the request of Madame Duval."

"Miss," cried young Branghton, "Bid only wishes it was she, for she has cast a sheep's eye[2] at Mr. Smith this long while."

"Tom," cried the sister, rising, "I've the greatest mind in the world to box your ears! How dare you say such a thing of me?"

"No, hang it, Tom, no, that's wrong," said Mr. Smith, simpering, "it is indeed, to tell the lady's secrets.—But never mind him, Miss Biddy, for I won't believe him."

"Why, I know Bid would give her ears to go," returned the brother; "but only Mr. Smith likes Miss best,—so does every body else."

While the sister gave him a very angry answer, Mr. Smith said to me, in a low voice, "Why now, Ma'am, how can you be so cruel as to be so much handsomer than your cousins? Nobody can look at them when you are by."

"Miss," cried young Branghton, "whatever he says to you, don't mind him, for he means no good; I'll give you my word for it, he'll never marry you, for he has told me again and again, he'll never marry as long as he lives; besides, if he'd any mind to be married, there's Bid would have had him long ago, and thanked him too."

2. "To look lovingly, longingly, or amorously at" (*OED*).

"Come, come, Tom, don't tell secrets; you'll make the ladies afraid of me: but I assure you," lowering his voice, "if I *did* marry, it should be your cousin."

Should be!——did you ever, my dear Sir, hear such unauthorised freedom? I looked at him with a contempt I did not wish to repress, and walked to the other end of the room.

Very soon after, Mr. Smith sent for a hackney-coach. When I would have taken leave of Miss Branghton, she turned angrily from me, without making any answer. She supposes, perhaps, that I have rather sought, than endeavoured to avoid, the notice and civilities of this conceited young man.

The ball was at the *long room* at Hampstead.[3]

This room seems very well named, for I believe it would be difficult to find any other epithet which might, with propriety, distinguish it, as it is without ornament, elegance, or any sort of singularity, and merely to be marked by its length.

I was saved from the importunities of Mr. Smith, the beginning of the evening, by Madame Duval's declaring her intention to dance the two first dances with him herself. Mr. Smith's chagrin was very evident, but as she paid no regard to it, he was necessitated to lead her out.

I was, however, by no means pleased, when she said she was determined to dance a minuet. Indeed, I was quite astonished, not having had the least idea she would have consented to, much less proposed, such an exhibition of her person. She had some trouble to make her intentions known, as Mr. Smith was rather averse to speaking to the Master of the ceremonies.

During this minuet, how much did I rejoice in being surrounded only with strangers! She danced in a style so uncommon; her age, her showy dress, and an unusual quantity of *rouge*, drew upon her the eyes, and, I fear, the derision of the whole company. Who she danced with, I know not; but Mr. Smith was so ill-bred as to laugh at her very openly, and to speak of her with as much ridicule as was in his power. But I would neither look at, nor listen to him; nor would I suffer him to proceed with a speech which he began, expressive of his vexation at being forced to dance with her. I told him, very gravely, that complaints upon such a subject might, with less impropriety, be made to every person in the room than to me.

When she returned to us, she distressed me very much, by asking what I thought of her minuet. I spoke as civilly as I could, but the coldness of my compliment evidently disappointed her. She then called upon Mr. Smith to secure a good place among the country-dancers; and away they went, though not before he had taken the liberty to say to me

3. See above, p. 148, n. 2.

in a low voice, "I protest to you, Ma'am, I shall be quite out of countenance, if any of my acquaintance should see me dancing with the old
lady!"

For a few moments I very much rejoiced at being relieved from this
troublesome man; but scarce had I time to congratulate myself, before
I was accosted by another, who *begged the favour of hopping a dance*
with me.

I told him that I should not dance at all; but he thought proper to
importune me, very freely, not to be so cruel; and I was obliged to
assume no little haughtiness before I could satisfy him I was serious.

After this, I was addressed, much in the same manner, by several
other young men, of whom the appearance and language were equally
inelegant and low-bred: so that I soon found my situation was both disagreeable and improper; since, as I was quite alone, I fear I must seem
rather to invite, than to forbid, the offers and notice I received. And yet,
so great was my apprehension of this interpretation, that I am sure, my
dear Sir, you would have laughed had you seen how proudly grave I
appeared.

I knew not whether to be glad or sorry, when Madame Duval and
Mr. Smith returned. The latter instantly renewed his tiresome entreaties, and Madame Duval said she would go to the card-table: and as soon
as she was accommodated, she desired us to join the dancers.

I will not trouble you with the arguments which followed. Mr. Smith
teazed me till I was weary of resistance; and I should at last have been
obliged to submit, had I not fortunately recollected the affair of Mr.
Lovel, and told my persecutor, that it was impossible I should dance
with him, even if I wished it, as I had refused several persons in his
absence.

He was not contented with being extremely chagrined, but took the
liberty, openly and warmly, to expostulate with me upon not having said
I was engaged.

The total disregard with which, involuntarily, I heard him, made him
soon change the subject. In truth, I had no power to attend to him, for
all my thoughts were occupied in re-tracing the transactions of the two
former balls at which I had been present. The party—the conversation—the company—O how great the contrast!

In a short time, however, he contrived to draw my attention to himself, by his extreme impertinence; for he chose to express what he called
his *admiration* of me, in terms so open and familiar, that he forced me
to express my displeasure with equal plainness.

But how was I surprised, when I found he had the temerity—what
else can I call it?—to impute my resentment to doubts of his honour;
for he said, "My dear Ma'am, you must be a little patient; I assure you I
have no bad designs, I have not upon my word; but, really, there is no
resolving upon such a thing as matrimony all at once; what with the loss

of one's liberty, and what with the ridicule of all one's acquaintance,—I assure you Ma'am, you are the first lady who ever made me even demur[4] upon this subject; for, after all, my dear Ma'am, marriage is the devil!"

"Your opinion, Sir," answered I, "of either the married or the single life, can be of no manner of consequence to me, and therefore I would by no means trouble you to discuss their different merits."

"Why, really, Ma'am, as to your being a little out of sorts, I must own. I can't wonder at it, for, to be sure, marriage is all in all with the ladies; but with us gentlemen it's quite another thing! Now only put yourself in my place,—suppose you had such a large acquaintance of gentlemen as I have,—and that you had always been used to appear a little—a little smart among them,—why now, how should you like to let yourself down all at once into a married man?"

I could not tell what to answer; so much conceit, and so much ignorance, both astonished and silenced me.

"I assure you, Ma'am," added he, "there is not only Miss Biddy, —— though I should have scorned to mention her, if her brother had not blab'd, for I'm quite particular in keeping ladies secrets,—but there are a great many other ladies that have been proposed to me, —— but I never thought twice of any of them,—that is, not in a *serious* way,—so you may very well be proud," offering to take my hand, "for I assure you, there is nobody so likely to catch me at last as yourself."

"Sir," cried I, drawing myself back as haughtily as I could, "you are totally mistaken, if you imagine you have given me any pride I felt not before, by this conversation; on the contrary, you must allow me to tell you, I find it too humiliating to bear with it any longer."

I then placed myself behind the chair of Madame Duval; who, when she heard of the partners I had refused, pitied my ignorance of the world, but no longer insisted upon my dancing.

Indeed, the extreme vanity of this man, makes me exert a spirit which I did not, till now, know that I possessed: but I cannot endure that he should think me at his disposal.

The rest of the evening passed very quietly, as Mr. Smith did not again attempt speaking to me; except, indeed, after we had left the room, and while Madame Duval was seating herself in the coach, he said, in a voice of *pique*, "Next time I take the trouble to get any tickets for a young lady, I'll make a bargain beforehand that she sha'n't turn me over to her grandmother."

We came home very safe; and thus ended this so long projected, and most disagreeable affair.

4. Hesitate, pause.

Letter XX.

I have just received a most affecting letter from Mr. Macartney. I will inclose it, my dear Sir, for your perusal. More than ever have I cause to rejoice that I was able to assist him.

Mr. Macartney to Miss Anville.

Madam,

IMPRESSED with the deepest, the most heart-felt sense of the exalted humanity with which you have rescued from destruction an unhappy stranger, allow me, with the humblest gratitude, to offer you my fervent acknowledgments, and to implore your pardon for the terror I have caused you.

You bid me, Madam, live: I have now, indeed, a motive for life, since I should not willingly quit the world, while I withhold from the needy and distressed any share of that charity which a disposition so noble would, otherwise bestow, upon them.

The benevolence with which you have interested yourself in my affairs, induces me to suppose you would wish to be acquainted with the cause of that desperation from which you snatched me, and the particulars of that misery of which you have, so wonderfully, been a witness. Yet, as this explanation will require that I should divulge secrets of a nature the most delicate, I must entreat you to regard them as sacred, even though I forbear to mention the names of the parties concerned.

I was brought up in Scotland, though my mother, who had the sole care of me, was an Englishwoman, and had not one relation in that country. She devoted to me her whole time. The retirement in which we lived, and the distance from our natural friends, she often told me, were the effect of an unconquerable melancholy with which she was seized, upon the sudden loss of my father, some time before I was born.

At Aberdeen, where I finished my education, I formed a friendship with a young man of fortune, which I considered as the chief happiness of my life;—but, when he quitted his studies, I considered it as my chief misfortune, for he immediately prepared, by direction of his friends, to make the tour of Europe. As I was designed for the church, and had no prospect even of maintenance but from my own industry, I scarce dared permit even a wish of accompanying him. It is true, he would joyfully have borne my expences; but my affection was as free from meanness as his own, and I made a determination the most solemn, never to lessen its dignity, by submitting to pecuniary obligations.

We corresponded with great regularity, and the most unbounded confidence, for the space of two years, when he arrived at Lyons in his way home.

He wrote me, thence, the most pressing invitation to meet him at Paris, where he intended to remain some time. My desire to comply with his request, and shorten our absence, was so earnest, that my mother, too indulgent to controul me, lent me what assistance was in her power, and, in an ill-fated moment, I set out for that capital.

My meeting with this dear friend was the happiest event of my life: he introduced me to all his acquaintance; and so quickly did time seem to pass at that delightful period, that the six weeks I had allotted for my stay were gone, ere I was sensible I had missed so many days. But I must now own, that the company of my friend was not the sole subject of my felicity: I became acquainted with a young lady, daughter of an Englishman of distinction, with whom I formed an attachment which I have a thousand times vowed, a thousand times sincerely thought would be lasting as my life. She had but just quitted a convent, in which she had been placed when a child, and though English by birth, she could scarcely speak her native language. Her person and disposition were equally engaging; but chiefly I adored her for the greatness of the expectations which, for my sake, she was willing to resign.

When the time for my residence in Paris expired, I was almost distracted at the idea of quitting her; yet I had not the courage to make our attachment known to her father, who might reasonably form for her such views as would make him reject, with a contempt which I could not bear to think of, such an offer as mine. Yet I had free access to the house, where she seemed to be left almost wholly to the guidance of an old servant, who was my fast friend.

But, to be brief, the sudden and unexpected return of her father, one fatal afternoon, proved the beginning of the misery which has ever since devoured me. I doubt not but he had listened to our conversation, for he darted into the room with the rage of a madman. Heavens! what a scene followed!—what abusive language did the shame of a clandestine affair, and the consciousness of acting ill, induce me to brook! At length, however, his fury exceeded my patience,—he called me a beggarly, cowardly Scotchman. Fired at the words, I drew my sword; he, with equal alertness, drew his; for he was not an old man, but, on the contrary, strong and able as myself. In vain his daughter pleaded;—in vain did I, repentant of my anger, retreat—his reproaches continued; myself, my country, were loaded with infamy, till, no longer constraining my rage,—we fought,—and he fell!

At that moment I could almost have destroyed myself! The young lady fainted with terror; the old servant, drawn to us by the noise of the scuffle, entreated me to escape, and promised to bring intelligence of what should pass to my apartment. The disturbance which I heard raised in the house obliged me to comply, and, in a state of mind inconceivably wretched, I tore myself away.

My friend, whom I found at home, soon discovered the whole affair.

It was near midnight before the woman came. She told me that her master was living, and her young mistress restored to her senses. The absolute necessity for my leaving Paris, while any danger remained, was forcibly urged by my friend: the servant promised to acquaint him of whatever passed, and he to transmit to me her information. Thus circumstanced, with the assistance of this dear friend, I effected my departure from Paris, and, not long after, I returned to Scotland. I would fain have stopped by the way, that I might have been nearer the scene of all my concerns, but the low state of my finances denied me that satisfaction.

The miserable situation of my mind was soon discovered by my mother; nor would she rest till I communicated the cause. She heard my whole story with an agitation which astonished me;—the *name* of the parties concerned seemed to strike her with horror;—but when I said, *We fought, and he fell*;—"My son," cried she, "you have then murdered your father!" and she sunk breathless at my feet. Comments, Madam, upon such a scene as this, would to you be superfluous, and to me agonizing: I cannot, for both our sakes, be too concise. When she recovered, she confessed all the particulars of a tale which she had hoped never to have revealed.—Alas! the loss she had sustained of my father was not by death!—bound to her by no ties but those of honour, he had voluntarily deserted her!—Her settling in Scotland was not the effect of choice,—she was banished thither by a family but too justly incensed;—pardon, Madam, that I cannot be more explicit!

My senses, in the greatness of my misery, actually forsook me, and for more than a week I was wholly delirious. My unfortunate mother was yet more to be pitied, for she pined with unmitigated sorrow, eternally reproaching herself for the danger to which her too strict silence had exposed me. When I recovered my reason, my impatience to hear from Paris almost deprived me of it again; and though the length of time I waited for letters might justly be attributed to contrary winds, I could not bear the delay, and was twenty times upon the point of returning thither at all hazards. At length, however, several letters arrived at once, and from the most insupportable of my afflictions I was then relieved, for they acquainted me that the horrors of parricide were not in reserve for me. They informed me also, that as soon as the wound was healed, a journey would be made to England, where my unhappy *sister* was to be received by an aunt with whom she was to live.

This intelligence somewhat quieted the violence of my sorrows. I instantly formed a plan of meeting them in London, and, by revealing the whole dreadful story, convincing this irritated parent that he had nothing more to apprehend from his daughter's unfortunate choice. My mother consented, and gave me a letter to prove the truth of my assertions. As I could but ill afford to make this journey, I travelled in the cheapest way that was possible. I took an obscure lodging, I need not,

Madam, tell you where,—and boarded with the people of the house.

Here I languished, week after week, vainly hoping for the arrival of my *family*; but my impetuosity had blinded me to the imprudence of which I was guilty in quitting Scotland so hastily. My wounded father, after his recovery, relapsed; and when I had waited in the most comfortless situation, for six weeks, my friend wrote me word, that the journey was yet deferred for some time longer.

My finances were then nearly exhausted, and I was obliged, though most unwillingly, to beg further assistance from my mother, that I might return to Scotland. Oh! Madam!—my answer was not from herself,—it was written by a lady who had long been her companion, and acquainted me that she had been taken suddenly ill of a fever,—and was no more!

The compassionate nature of which you have given such noble proofs, assures me I need not, if I could, paint to you the anguish of a mind overwhelmed with such accumulated sorrows.

Inclosed was a letter to a near relation, which she had, during her illness, with much difficulty, written, and in which, with the strongest maternal tenderness, she described my deplorable situation, and entreated his interest to procure me some preferment. Yet so sunk was I by misfortune, that a fortnight elapsed before I had the courage or spirit to attempt delivering this letter. I was then compelled to it by want. To make my appearance with some decency, I was necessitated, myself, to the melancholy task of changing my coloured cloaths for a suit of mourning;—and then I proceeded to seek my relation.

I was informed that he was not in town.

In this desperate situation, the pride of my heart, which hitherto had not bowed to adversity, gave way, and I determined to intreat the assistance of my friend, whose offered services I had a thousand times rejected. Yet, Madam, so hard is it to root from the mind its favourite principles, or prejudices, call them which you please, that I lingered another week ere I had the resolution to send away a letter which I regarded as the death of my independence.

At length, reduced to my last shilling, dunned insolently by the people of the house, and almost famished, I sealed this fatal letter, and, with a heavy heart, determined to take it to the post-office. But Mr. Branghton and his son suffered me not to pass through their shop with impunity; they insulted me grossly, and threatened me with imprisonment, if I did not immediately satisfy their demands. Stung to the soul, I bid them have but a day's patience, and flung from them, in a state of mind too terrible for description.

My letter, which I now found would be received too late to save me from disgrace, I tore into a thousand pieces, and scarce could I refrain from putting an instantaneous, an unlicensed period to my existence.

In this disorder of my senses, I formed the horrible plan of turning foot-pad;[1] for which purpose I returned to my lodging, and collected whatever of my apparel I could part with, which I immediately sold, and with the profits purchased a brace of pistols, powder and shot. I hope, however, you will believe me, when I most solemnly assure you, my sole intention was to *frighten* the passengers I should assault, with these dangerous weapons, which I had not loaded, but from a resolution,—a dreadful one, I own,—to save *myself* from an ignominious death if seized. And, indeed, I thought that if I could but procure money sufficient to pay Mr. Branghton, and make a journey to Scotland, I should soon be able, by the public papers, to discover whom I had injured, and to make private retribution.

But, Madam, new to every species of villainy, my perturbation was so great that I could with difficulty support myself; yet the Branghtons observed it not as I passed through the shop.

Here I stop: what followed is better known to yourself. But no time can ever efface from my memory that moment, when in the very action of preparing for my own destruction, or the lawless seizure of the property of others, you rushed into the room, and arrested my arm!—It was, indeed, an awful moment!—the hand of Providence seemed to intervene between me and eternity; I beheld you as an angel!—I thought you dropt from the clouds;—the earth, indeed, had never before presented to my view a form so celestial!—What wonder, then, that a spectacle so astonishing should, to a man disordered as I was, appear too beautiful to be human?

And now, Madam, that I have performed this painful task, the more grateful one remains of rewarding, as far as is in my power, your generous goodness, by assuring you it shall not be thrown away. You have awakened me to a sense of the false pride by which I have been actuated,—a pride which, while it scorned assistance from a friend, scrupled not to compel it from a stranger, though at the hazard of reducing that stranger to a situation as destitute as my own. Yet, Oh! how violent was the struggle which tore my conflicting soul ere I could persuade myself to profit by the benevolence which you were so evidently disposed to exert in my favour!

By means of a ring, the gift of my much-regretted mother, I have for the present satisfied Mr. Branghton; and by means of your compassion, I hope to support myself, either till I hear from my friend, to whom at length I have written, or till the relation of my mother returns to town.

To talk to you, Madam, of paying my debt, would be vain; I never can! the service you have done me exceeds all power of return; you have restored me to my senses, you have taught me to curb those passions which bereft me of them, and, since I cannot avoid calamity, to bear it as a man! An interposition so wonderfully circumstanced can never be

---

1. Mugger.

recollected without benefit. Yet allow me to say, the pecuniary part of my obligation must be settled by my first ability.

I am, Madam, with the most profound respect, and heart-felt gratitude,

Your obedient,
and devoted humble servant,
J. MACARTNEY.

Letter XXI.

EVELINA IN CONTINUATION.

Holborn, July 1. 5 o'clock in the morn.

O Sir, what an adventure have I to write!—all night it has occupied my thoughts, and I am now risen thus early to write it to you.

Yesterday it was settled that we should spend the evening in Marybone-gardens, where M. Torre,[1] a celebrated foreigner, was to exhibit some fireworks. The party consisted of Madame Duval, all the Branghtons, M. Du Bois, Mr. Smith, and Mr. Brown.

We were almost the first persons who entered the Gardens, Mr. Branghton having declared he would have *all he could get for his money*, which, at best, was only fooled away, at such silly and idle places.

We walked in parties, and very much detached from one another; Mr. Brown and Miss Polly led the way by themselves; Miss Branghton and Mr. Smith followed, and the latter seemed determined to be revenged for my behaviour at the ball, by transferring all his former attention for me, to Miss Branghton, who received it with an air of exultation: and very frequently they each of them, though from different motives, looked back, to discover whether I observed their good intelligence. Madame Duval walked with M. Du Bois; and Mr. Branghton by himself; but his son would willingly have attached himself wholly to me, saying frequently, "Come, Miss, let's you and I have a little fun together; you see they have all left us, so now let's leave them." But I begged to be excused, and went to the other side of Madame Duval.

This Garden, as it is called, is neither striking for magnificence nor for beauty; and we were all so dull and languid, that I was extremely glad when we were summoned to the orchestra, upon the opening of a concert; in the course of which, I had the pleasure of hearing a concerto on the violin by Mr. Barthelemon,[2] who, to me, seems a player of exquisite fancy, feeling, and variety.

1. Giovanni Battista Torré (d. 1780), director of fireworks at Marylebone Gardens. Burney, her father, and her sister Susanna (1755–1800) intended to see Torré's fireworks on 11 June 1773, but they were rained out (*Early Journals and Letters of Fanny Burney* 1: 267–68).
2. François-Hippolyte Barthélemon (1741–1808), French violinist and composer. Dr. Burney refers to Barthélemon's "powerful hand and truly vocal adagio" (*General History of Music* 2:

When notice was given us, that the fireworks were preparing, we hurried along to secure good places for the sight: but very soon, we were so encircled and incommoded by the crowd, that Mr. Smith proposed the *ladies* should make interest for a form to stand upon; this was soon effected, and the men then left us, to accommodate themselves better, saying they would return the moment the exhibition was over.

The firework was really beautiful, and told, with wonderful ingenuity, the story of Orpheus and Eurydice; but, at the moment of the fatal look, which separated them for ever,[3] there was such an explosion of fire, and so horrible a noise, that we all as of one accord, jumpt hastily from the form,[4] and ran away some paces, fearing that we were in danger of mischief, from the innumerable sparks of fire which glittered in the air.

For a moment or two, I neither knew nor considered whither I had run; but my recollection was soon awakened by a stranger's addressing me with, "Come along with me, my dear, and I'll take care of you."

I started, and then, to my great terror, perceived that I had out-run all my companions, and saw not one human being I knew! With all the speed in my power, and forgetful of my first fright, I hastened back to the place I had left;—but found the form occupied by a new set of people.

In vain, from side to side, I looked for some face I knew; I found myself in the midst of a crowd, yet without party, friend, or acquaintance. I walked, in disordered haste, from place to place, without knowing which way to turn, or whither I went. Every other moment, I was spoken to, by some bold and unfeeling man, to whom my distress, which, I think, must be very apparent, only furnished a pretence for impertinent witticisms, or free gallantry.

At last, a young officer, marching fiercely up to me, said, "You are a sweet pretty creature, and I enlist you in my service;" and then, with great violence, he seized my hand. I screamed aloud with fear, and, forcibly snatching it away, I ran hastily up to two ladies, and cried, "For Heaven's sake, dear ladies, afford me some protection!"

They heard me with a loud laugh, but very readily said, "Ay, let her walk between us;" and each of them took hold of an arm.

Then, in a drawling, ironical tone of voice, they asked *what had frightened my little Ladyship?* I told them my adventure very simply, and intreated they would have the goodness to assist me in finding my friends.

O yes, to be sure, they said, I should not want for friends, whilst I was with them. Mine, I said, would be very grateful for any civilities with

1021), and Burney herself attended a concert "at which he performed his part very delightfully" (*Early Journals and Letters of Fanny Burney* 1: 230).

3. Hades, because of the beauty of Orpheus's music, allowed Eurydice, Orpheus's wife, to return from the underworld on condition that Orpheus not look back during their journey. Orpheus looked back at the last moment and lost Eurydice forever.

4. A bench.

which they might favour me. But imagine, my dear Sir, how I must be confounded, when I observed, that every other word I spoke produced a loud laugh! However, I will not dwell upon a conversation, which soon, to my inexpressible horror, convinced me I had sought protection from insult, of those who were themselves most likely to offer it! You, my dearest Sir, I well know, will both feel for, and pity my terror, which I have no words to describe.

Had I been at liberty, I should have instantly run away from them, when I made the shocking discovery,[5] but, as they held me fast, that was utterly impossible: and such was my dread of their resentment or abuse, that I did not dare make any open attempt to escape.

They asked me a thousand questions, accompanied by as many hallows, of who I was, what I was, and whence I came. My answers were very incoherent,—but what, good Heaven, were my emotions, when, a few moments afterwards, I perceived advancing our way,—Lord Orville!

Never shall I forget what I felt at that instant: had I, indeed, been sunk to the guilty state, which such companions might lead him to suspect, I could scarce have had feelings more cruelly depressing.

However, to my infinite joy, he passed us without distinguishing me; though I saw that, in a careless manner, his eyes surveyed the party.

As soon as he was gone, one of these unhappy women said "Do you know that young fellow?"

Not thinking it possible she should mean Lord Orville by such a term, I readily answered, "No, Madam."

"Why then," answered she, "you have a monstrous good stare, for a little country Miss."

I now found I had mistaken her, but was glad to avoid an explanation.

A few minutes after, what was my delight, to hear the voice of Mr. Brown, who called out, "Lord, i'n't that Miss what's her name?"

"Thank God," cried I, suddenly springing from them both, "thank God, I have found my party."

Mr. Brown was, however, alone, and, without knowing what I did, I took hold of his arm.

"Lord, Miss," cried he, "we've had such a hunt you can't think! some of them thought you was gone home; but I says, says I, I don't think, says I, that she's like to go home all alone, says I."

"So that gentleman belongs to you, Miss, does he?" said one of the women.

"Yes, Madam," answered I, "and I now thank you for your civility; but, as I am safe, will not give you any further trouble."

I courtsied slightly, and would have walked away; but, most unfortunately, Madame Duval and the two Miss Branghtons just then joined us.

5. That the two women are prostitutes.

They all began to make a thousand enquiries, to which I briefly answered, that I had been obliged to these two ladies for walking with me, and would tell them more another time: for, though I felt great *comparative* courage, I was yet too much intimidated by their presence, to dare be explicit.

Nevertheless, I ventured, once more, to wish them good night, and proposed seeking Mr. Branghton. These unhappy women listened to all that was said with a kind of callous curiosity, and seemed determined not to take any hint. But my vexation was terribly augmented, when, after having whispered something to each other, they very cavalierly declared, that they intended joining our party! and then, one of them very boldly took hold of my arm, while the other, going round, seized that of Mr. Brown; and thus, almost forcibly, we were moved on between them, and followed by Madame Duval and the Miss Branghtons.

It would be very difficult to say which was greatest, my fright, or Mr. Brown's consternation; who ventured not to make the least resistance, though his uneasiness made him tremble almost as much as myself. I would instantly have withdrawn my arm; but it was held so tight, I could not move it; and poor Mr. Brown was circumstanced in the same manner on the other side; for I heard him say, "Lord, Ma'am, there's no need to squeeze one's arm so!"

And this was our situation,—for we had not taken three steps, when,—O Sir,—we again met Lord Orville!—but not again did he pass quietly by us,—unhappily I caught his eye;—both mine, immediately, were bent to the ground; but he approached me, and we all stopped.

I then looked up. He bowed. Good God, with what expressive eyes did he regard me! Never were surprise and concern so strongly marked,—yes, my dear Sir, he looked *greatly* concerned; and that, the remembrance of that, is the only consolation I feel for an evening the most painful of my life.

What he first said I know not; for, indeed, I seemed to have neither ears nor understanding; but I recollect that I only courtsied in silence. He paused for an instant, as if—I believe so,—as if unwilling to pass on; but then, finding the whole party detained, he again bowed, and took leave.

Indeed, my dear Sir, I thought I should have fainted, so great was my emotion from shame, vexation, and a thousand other feelings, for which I have no expressions. I absolutely tore myself from the woman's arm, and then, disengaging myself from that of Mr. Brown, I went to Madame Duval, and besought that she would not suffer me to be again parted from her.

I fancy—that Lord Orville saw what passed; for scarcely was I at liberty, ere he returned. Methought, my dear Sir, the pleasure, the surprise of that moment, recompensed me for all the chagrin I had before felt:

for do you not think, that this return manifests, from a character so quiet, so reserved as Lord Orville's, something like solicitude in my concerns?—such, at least, was the interpretation I involuntarily made upon again seeing him.

With a politeness to which I have been some time very little used, he apologized for returning; and then inquired after the health of Mrs. Mirvan, and the rest of the Howard Grove family. The flattering conjecture which I have just acknowledged, had so wonderfully restored my spirits, that I believe I never answered him so readily, and with so little constraint. Very short, however, was the duration of this conversation: for we were soon most disagreeably interrupted.

The Miss Branghtons, though they saw almost immediately the characters of the women to whom I had so unfortunately applied, were, nevertheless, so weak and foolish, as merely to *titter* at their behaviour. As to Madame Duval, she was for some time so strangely imposed upon, that she thought they were two real fine ladies. Indeed it is wonderful to see how easily and how frequently she is deceived. Our disturbance, however, arose from young Brown, who was now between the two women, by whom his arms were absolutely pinioned to his sides: for a few minutes, his complaints had been only murmured; but he now called out aloud, "Goodness, Ladies, you hurt me like any thing! why I can't walk at all, if you keep pinching my arms so!"

This speech raised a loud laugh in the women, and redoubled the tittering of the Miss Branghtons. For my own part, I was most cruelly confused; while the countenance of Lord Orville manifested a sort of indignant astonishment; and, from that moment, he spoke to me no more, till he took leave.

Madame Duval, who now began to suspect her company, proposed our taking the first box we saw empty, bespeaking a supper, and waiting till Mr. Branghton should find us.

Miss Polly mentioned one she had remarked, to which we all turned; Madame Duval instantly seated herself; and the two bold women, forcing the frightened Mr. Brown to go between them, followed her example.

Lord Orville, with an air of gravity that wounded my very soul, then wished me good night. I said not a word; but my face, if it had any connection with my heart, must have looked melancholy indeed: and so, I have some reason to believe, it did; for he added, with much more softness, though not less dignity, "Will Miss Anville allow me to ask her address, and to pay my respects to her before I leave town?"

O how I changed colour at this unexpected request!—yet what was the mortification I suffered, in answering, "My Lord, I am—in Holborn!"

He then bowed and left us.

What, what can he think of this adventure! how strangely, how cruelly have all appearances turned against me! Had I been blessed with any presence of mind, I should instantly have explained to him the accident which occasioned my being in such terrible company;—but I have none!

As to the rest of the evening, I cannot relate the particulars of what passed; for, to you, I only write of what I think, and I can think of nothing but this unfortunate, this disgraceful meeting. These two wretched women continued to torment us all, but especially poor Mr. Brown, who seemed to afford them uncommon diversion, till we were discovered by Mr. Branghton, who very soon found means to release us from their persecutions, by frightening them away. We stayed but a short time after they left us, which was all employed in explanations.

Whatever may be the construction which Lord Orville may put upon this affair, to me it cannot fail of being unfavourable; to be seen—gracious Heaven! to be seen in company with two women of such character!——How vainly, how proudly have I wished to avoid meeting him when only with the Branghtons and Madame Duval,—but now, how joyful should I be had he seen me to no greater disadvantage!—Holborn, too! what a direction! he who had always—but I will not torment you, my dearest Sir, with any more of my mortifying conjectures and apprehensions: perhaps he may call,—and then I shall have an opportunity of explaining to him all the most shocking part of the adventure. And yet, as I did not tell him at whose house I lived, he may not be able to discover me; I merely said *in Holborn*, and he, who I suppose saw my embarrassment, forbore to ask any other direction.

Well, I must take my chance!

Yet let me, in justice to Lord Orville, and in justice to the high opinion I have always entertained of his honour and delicacy,—let me observe the difference of his behaviour, when nearly in the same situation to that of Sir Clement Willoughby. He had at least equal cause to depreciate me in his opinion, and to mortify and sink me in my own: but far different was his conduct;——perplexed, indeed, he looked, and much surprised,—but it was benevolently, not with insolence. I am even inclined to think, that he could not see a young creature whom he had so lately known in a higher sphere, appear so suddenly, so strangely, so disgracefully altered in her situation, without some pity and concern. But, whatever might be his doubts and suspicions, far from suffering them to influence his behaviour, he spoke, he looked, with the same politeness and attention with which he had always honoured me when countenanced by Mrs. Mirvan.

Once again, let me drop this subject.

In every mortification, every disturbance, how grateful to my heart, how sweet to my recollection, is the certainty of your never-failing tenderness, sympathy, and protection! Oh Sir, could I, upon this subject, could I write as I feel,—how animated would be the language of

Your devoted
EVELINA!

Letter XXII.

EVELINA TO THE REV. MR. VILLARS.

Holborn, July 1.

Listless, uneasy, and without either spirit or courage to employ myself, from the time I had finished my last letter, I indolently seated myself at the window, where, while I waited Madame Duval's summons to breakfast, I perceived, among the carriages which passed by, a coronet coach,[1] and, in a few minutes, from the window of it, Lord Orville! I instantly retreated, but not, I believe, unseen; for the coach immediately drove up to our door.

Indeed, my dear Sir, I must own I was greatly agitated; the idea of receiving Lord Orville by myself,—the knowledge that his visit was entirely to *me*,—the wish of explaining the unfortunate adventure of yesterday,—and the mortification of my present circumstances,—all these thoughts, occurring to me nearly at the same time, occasioned me more anxiety, confusion, and perplexity, than I can possibly express.

I believe he meant to send up his name; but the maid, unused to such a ceremony, forgot it by the way, and only told me, that a great Lord was below, and desired to see me: and, the next moment, he appeared himself.

If formerly, when in the circle of high life, and accustomed to its manners, I so much admired and distinguished the grace, the elegance of Lord Orville, think, Sir, how they must strike me now,——now, when far removed from that splendid circle, I live with those to whom even civility is unknown, and decorum a stranger!

I am sure I received him very awkwardly; depressed by a situation so disagreeable, could I do otherwise? When his first enquiries were made, "I think myself very fortunate," he said, "in meeting with Miss Anville at home, and still more so, in finding her disengaged."

I only courtsied. He then talked of Mrs. Mirvan; asked how long I had been in town, and other such general questions, which, happily, gave me time to recover from my embarrassment. After which, he said, "If Miss Anville will allow me the honour of sitting by her a few minutes (for we were both standing) I will venture to tell her the motive which,

---

1. The coronet signals that the owner of the coach is a nobleman. Its form varies according to rank.

next to enquiring after her health, has prompted me to wait on her thus early."

We were then both seated, and, after a short pause, he said, "How to apologise for so great a liberty as I am upon the point of taking, I know not;—shall I, therefore, rely wholly upon your goodness, and not apologise at all?"

I only bowed.

"I should be extremely sorry to appear impertinent,—yet hardly know how to avoid it."

"Impertinent! O my Lord," cried I, eagerly, "that, I am sure, is impossible!"

"You are very good," answered he, "and encourage me to be ingenuous ——"

Again he stopped: but my expectation was too great for speech: at last, without looking at me, in a low voice and hesitating manner, he said, "Were those ladies with whom I saw you last night, ever in your company before?"

"No, my Lord," cried I, rising, and colouring violently, "nor will they ever be again."

He rose too, and, with an air of the most condescending concern, said, "Pardon, Madam, the abruptness of a question which I knew not how to introduce as I ought, and for which I have no excuse to offer, but my respect for Mrs. Mirvan, joined to the sincerest wishes for your happiness: yet I fear I have gone too far!"

"I am very sensible of the honour of your lordship's attention," said I, "but ——."

"Permit me to assure you," cried he, finding I hesitated, "that officiousness is not my characteristic, and that I would by no means have risked your displeasure, had I not been fully satisfied you were too generous to be offended, without a real cause of offence."

"Offended!" cried I, "no, my Lord, I am only grieved—grieved, indeed! to find myself in a situation so unfortunate, as to be obliged to make explanations which cannot but mortify and shock me."

"It is I alone," cried he, with some eagerness, "who am shocked, as it is I who deserve to be mortified. I seek no explanation, for I have no doubt; but, in mistaking me, Miss Anville injures herself: allow me, therefore, frankly and openly, to tell you the intention of my visit."

I bowed, and we both returned to our seats.

"I will own myself to have been greatly surprised," continued he, "when I met you yesterday evening, in company with two persons who I was sensible merited not the honour of your notice; nor was it easy for me to conjecture the cause of your being so situated; yet, believe me, my incertitude did not for a moment do you injury; I was satisfied that their characters must be unknown to you, and I thought with concern of the shock you would sustain, when you discovered their unworthiness. I should not, however, upon so short an acquaintance, have usurped the privilege of intimacy, in giving my unasked sentiments upon so delicate a subject, had I not known that credulity is the sister of innocence, and therefore feared you might be deceived. A something, which I could not resist, urged me to the freedom I have taken to caution you; but I shall not easily forgive myself, if I have been so unfortunate as to give you pain."

The pride which his first question had excited, now subsided into delight and gratitude, and I instantly related to him, as well as I could, the accident which had occasioned my joining the unhappy women with whom he had met me. He listened with an attention so flattering, seemed so much interested during the recital, and, when I had done, thanked me, in terms so polite, for what he was pleased to call my condescension, that I was almost ashamed either to look at, or hear him.

Soon after, the maid came to tell me, that Madame Duval desired to have breakfast made in her own room.

"I fear," cried Lord Orville, instantly rising, "that I have intruded upon your time,—yet who, so situated, could do other-wise?" Then, taking my hand, "Will Miss Anville allow me thus to seal my peace?" he pressed it to his lips, and took leave.

Generous, noble Lord Orville! how disinterested his conduct! how delicate his whole behaviour! willing to advise, yet afraid to wound me!—Can I ever, in future, regret the adventure I met with at Marybone, since it has been productive of a visit so flattering? Had my mortifications been still more humiliating, my terrors still more alarming, such a mark of esteem—may I not call it so?—from Lord Orville, would have made me ample amends.

And indeed, my dear Sir, I require some consolation in my present very disagreeable situation; for, since he went, two incidents have happened, that, had not my spirits been particularly elated, would greatly have disconcerted me.

During breakfast, Madame Duval, very abruptly, asked, if I should like to be married? and added, that Mr. Branghton had been proposing a match for me with his son. Surprised, and, I must own, provoked, I assured her, that in thinking of me, Mr. Branghton would very vainly lose his time.

"Why," cried she, "I have had greater views for you, myself, if once I could get you to Paris, and make you be owned; but, if I can't do that, and you can do no better, why, as you are both my relations, I think to leave my fortune between you, and then, if you marry, you never need want for nothing."

I begged her not to pursue the subject, as, I assured her, Mr. Branghton was totally disagreeable to me: but she continued her admonitions and reflections, with her usual disregard of whatever I could answer. She charged me, very peremptorily, neither wholly to discourage, nor yet to accept Mr. Branghton's offer, till she saw what could be done for me: the young man, she added, had often intended to speak to me himself, but not well knowing how to introduce the subject, he had desired her to pave the way for him.

I scrupled not, warmly and freely to declare my aversion to this proposal; but it was to no effect; she concluded, just as she had begun, by saying, that I should not *have him, if I could do better.*

Nothing, however, shall persuade me to listen to any other person concerning this odious affair.

My second cause of uneasiness arises, very unexpectedly, from M. Du Bois, who, to my infinite surprise, upon Madame Duval's quitting the room after dinner, put into my hand a note, and immediately left the house.

This note contains an open declaration of an attachment to me, which, he says, he should never have presumed to have acknowledged, had he not been informed that Madame Duval destined my hand to young Branghton,—a match which he cannot endure to think of. He beseeches me, earnestly to pardon his temerity, professes the most inviolable respect, and commits his fate to time, patience, and pity.

This conduct in M. Du Bois gives me real concern, as I was disposed to think very well of him. It will not, however, be difficult to discourage him, and therefore, I shall not acquaint Madame Duval of his letter, as I have reason to believe it would greatly displease her.

Letter XXIII.

EVELINA IN CONTINUATION.

July 3.

O Sir, how much uneasiness must I suffer, to counterbalance one short morning of happiness!

Yesterday, the Branghtons proposed a party to Kensington-gardens, and, as usual, Madame Duval insisted upon my attendance.

We went in a hackney-coach to Piccadilly, and then had a walk through Hyde Park, which, in any other company, would have been delightful. I was much pleased with Kensington-gardens,[1] and think them infinitely preferable to those of Vauxhall.

Young Branghton was extremely troublesome; he insisted upon walking by my side, and talked with me almost by compulsion: however, my reserve and coldness prevented his entering upon the hateful subject

1. Picadilly was one of the two ancient highways leading westward out of London. The name is derived from "picadil," a kind of stiff collar sold by a tailor, Robert Baker, who purchased lands to the north of what is now Picadilly Circus. It extended to Tyburn Lane, which marked the eastern boundary of Hyde Park, the largest of the London parks. Opened to the public in the early seventeenth century, the park became very fashionable. In the west, it merges with Kensington Gardens, which George II opened on Saturdays to "respectably dressed people" when the Court was at session at Richmond or Hampton Court. See *London Encyclopaedia.*

which Madame Duval had prepared me to apprehend. Once, indeed, when I was, accidentally, a few yards before the rest, he said, "I suppose, Miss, aunt has told you about you know what?—ha'n't she, Miss?"— But I turned from him without making any answer. Neither Mr. Smith nor Mr. Brown were of the party; and poor M. Du Bois, when he found that I avoided him, looked so melancholy, that I was really sorry for him.

While we were strolling round the garden, I perceived, walking with a party of ladies at some distance, Lord Orville! I instantly retreated behind Miss Branghton, and kept out of sight till we had passed him: for I dreaded being seen by him again, in a public walk, with a party of which I was ashamed.

Happily I succeeded in my design, and saw no more of him; for a sudden and violent shower of rain made us all hasten out of the gardens. We ran till we came to a small green-shop,[2] where we begged shelter. Here we found ourselves in company with two footmen, whom the rain had driven into the shop. Their livery, I thought, I had before seen; and upon looking from the window, I perceived the same upon a coachman belonging to a carriage, which I immediately recollected to be Lord Orville's.

Fearing to be known, I whispered Miss Branghton not to speak my name. Had I considered but a moment, I should have been sensible of the inutility of such a caution, since not one of the party call me by any other appellation than that of *Cousin* or of *Miss*; but I am perpetually involved in some distress or dilemma from my own heedlessness.

This request excited very strongly her curiosity; and she attacked me with such eagerness and bluntness of enquiry, that I could not avoid telling her the reason of my making it, and, consequently, that I was known to Lord Orville: an acknowledgment which proved the most unfortunate in the world; for she would not rest till she had drawn from me the circumstances attending my first making the acquaintance. Then, calling to her sister, she said, "Lord, Polly, only think! Miss has danced with a Lord!"

"Well," cried Polly, "that's a thing I should never have thought of! And pray Miss, what did he say to you?"

This question was much sooner asked than answered; and they both became so very inquisitive and earnest, that they soon drew the attention of Madame Duval and the rest of the party, to whom, in a very short time, they repeated all they had gathered from me.

"Goodness, then," cried young Branghton, "if I was Miss, if I would not make free with his Lordship's coach to take me to town."

"Why, ay," said the father, "there would be some sense in that; that would be making some use of a Lord's acquaintance, for it would save us coach-hire."

2. Greengrocer.

"Lord, Miss," cried Polly, "I wish you would, for I should like of all things to ride in a coronet coach."

"I promise you," said Madame Duval, "I'm glad you've thought of it, for I don't see no objection;—so let's have the coachman called."

"Not for the world," cried I, very much alarmed, "indeed it is utterly impossible."

"Why so?" demanded Mr. Branghton; "pray where's the good of your knowing a Lord, if you're never the better for him?"

"*Ma foi*, child," said Madame Duval, "you don't know no more of the world than if you was a baby. Pray, Sir, (to one of the footmen,) tell that coachman to draw up, for I wants to speak to him."

The man stared, but did not move. "Pray, pray, Madame," said I, "pray, Mr. Branghton, have the goodness to give up this plan; I know but very little of his Lordship, and cannot, upon any account, take so great a liberty."

"Don't say nothing about it," said Madame Duval, "for I shall have it my own way: so if *you* won't call the coachman, Sir, I'll promise you I'll call him myself."

The footman, very impertinently, laughed and turned upon his heel. Madame Duval, extremely irritated, ran out in the rain, and beckoned the coachman, who instantly obeyed her summons. Shocked beyond all expression, I flew after her, and entreated her with the utmost earnestness, to let us return in a hackney-coach:—but oh!—she is impenetrable to persuasion! She told the man she wanted him to carry her directly to town, and that she would answer for him to Lord Orville. The man, with a sneer, thanked her, but said he should answer for himself; and was driving off, when another footman came up to him, with information that his Lord was gone into Kensington Palace,[3] and would not want him for an hour or two.

"Why then, friend," said Mr. Branghton, (for we were followed by all the party) "where will be the great harm of your taking us to town?"

"Besides," said the son, "I'll promise you a pot of beer for my own share."

These speeches had no other answer from the coachman than a loud laugh, which was echoed by the insolent footmen. I rejoiced at their resistance, though I was certain that if their Lord had witnessed their impertinence, they would have been instantly dismissed his service.

"*Pardi*," cried Madame Duval, "if I don't think all the footmen are the most impudentest fellows in the kingdom! But I'll promise you I'll have your master told of your airs; so you'll get no good by 'em."

"Why, pray," said the coachman, rather alarmed, "did my Lord give you leave to use the coach?"

3. In 1689, William III purchased Nottingham House and had it reconstructed as a palace by Christopher Wren and Nicholas Hawksmoor (1661–1736). George III, who preferred Buckingham House, did not use it as a royal residence. See *London Encyclopaedia* 425–27.

"It's no matter for that," answered she; "I'm sure if he's a gentleman, he'd let us have it sooner than we should be wet to the skin: but I'll promise you he shall know how saucy you've been, for this young lady knows him very well."

"Ay, that she does," said Miss Polly; "and she's danced with him too."

Oh how I repented my foolish mismanagement! The men bit their lips, and looked at one another in some confusion. This was perceived by our party, who, taking advantage of it, protested they would write Lord Orville word of their ill behaviour without delay. This quite startled them, and one of the footmen offered to run to the palace, and ask his Lord's permission for our having the carriage.

This proposal really made me tremble; and the Branghtons all hung back upon it: but Madame Duval is never to be dissuaded from a scheme she has once formed. "Do so," cried she, "and give this child's compliments to your master, and tell him, as we ha'n't no coach here, we should be glad to go just as far as Holborn in his."

"No, no, no!" cried I; "don't go,—I know nothing of his Lordship,—I send no message,—I have nothing to say to him!"

The men, very much perplexed, could with difficulty restrain themselves from resuming their impertinent mirth. Madame Duval scolded me very angrily, and then desired them to go directly. "Pray, then," said the coachman, "what name is to be given to my Lord?"

"Anville," answered Madame Duval, "tell him Miss Anville wants the coach; the young lady he danced with once."

I was really in an agony; but the winds could not have been more deaf to me, than those to whom I pleaded! and therefore the footman, urged by the repeated threats of Madame Duval, and perhaps recollecting the name himself, actually went to the palace with this strange message!

He returned in a few minutes, and bowing to me with the greatest respect, said, "My Lord desires his compliments, and his carriage will be always at Miss Anville's service."

I was so much affected by this politeness, and chagrined at the whole affair, that I could scarce refrain from tears. Madame Duval and the Miss Branghtons eagerly jumped into the coach, and desired me to follow. I would rather have submitted to the severest punishment;—but all resistance was vain.

During the whole ride, I said not a word; however, the rest of the party were so talkative, that my silence was very immaterial. We stopped at our lodgings; but when Madame Duval and I alighted, the Branghtons asked if they could not be carried on to Snow Hill? The servants, now all civility, made no objection. Remonstrances from me, would, I too well knew, be fruitless; and therefore, with a heavy heart, I retired to my room, and left them to their own direction.

Seldom have I passed a night in greater uneasiness:—So lately to have cleared myself in the good opinion of Lord Orville,—so soon to forfeit it!—to give him reason to suppose I presumed to boast of his acquaintance,—to publish his having danced with me!—to take with him a liberty I should have blushed to have taken with the most intimate of my friends!—to treat with such impertinent freedom one who has honoured *me* with such distinguished respect!—indeed, Sir, I could have met with no accident that would so cruelly have tormented me!

If such were, then, my feelings, imagine,—for I cannot describe, what I suffered during the scene I am now going to write.

This morning, while I was alone in the dining-room, young Branghton called. He entered with a most important air, and strutting up to me, said, "Miss, *Lord Orville* sends his compliments to you."

"Lord Orville!" repeated I, much amazed.

"Yes, Miss, Lord Orville; for *I* know his Lordship now, as well as you.—And a very civil gentleman he is, for all he's a Lord."

"For Heaven's sake," cried I, "explain yourself."

"Why you must know, Miss, after we left you, we met with a little misfortune; but I don't mind it now, for it's all turned out for the best: but, just as we were a going up Snow Hill, plump we comes against a cart, with such a jogg it almost pulled the coach-wheel off; however, that i'n't the worst, for as I went to open the door in a hurry, a thinking the coach would be broke down, as ill-luck would have it, I never minded that the glass was up, and so I poked my head fairly through it.—Only see, Miss, how I've cut my forehead!"

A much worse accident to himself, would not, I believe, at that moment, have given me any concern for him: however, he proceeded with his account, for I was too much confounded to interrupt him.

"Goodness, Miss, we were in such a stew, us, and the servants, and all, as you can't think; for, besides the glass being broke, the coachman said how the coach would n't be safe to go back to Kensington. So we did n't know what to do; however, the footmen said they'd go and tell his Lordship what had happened. So then father grew quite uneasy, like, for fear of his Lordship's taking offence, and prejudicing us in our business: so he said I should go this morning and ask his pardon, 'cause of having broke the glass. So then I asked the footmen the direction, and they told me he lived in Berkeley-square;[4] so this morning I went,—and I soon found out the house."

"You did!" cried I, quite out of breath with apprehension.

"Yes, Miss, and a very fine house it is. Did you ever see it?"

"No."

"No!—why then, Miss, I know more of his Lordship than you do, for all you knew him first. So, when I came to the door, I was in a peck of troubles, a thinking what I should say to him; however, the servants had

---

4. A fashionable development to the north of Piccadilly, originally laid out in the 1730s.

no mind I should see him, for they told me he was busy, but I might leave my message. So I was just a coming away, when I bethought myself to say I come from you."

"From *me!*"

"Yes, Miss,—for you know why should I have such a long walk as that for nothing? So I says to the porter, says I, tell his Lordship, says I, one wants to speak to him as comes from one Miss Anville, says I."

"Good God," cried I, "and by what authority did you take such a liberty?"

"Goodness, Miss, don't be in such a hurry, for you'll be as glad as me when you hear how well it all turned out. So then they made way for me, and said his Lordship would see me directly; and there I was led through such a heap of servants, and so many rooms, that my heart quite misgave me; for I thought, thinks I, he'll be so proud he'll hardly let me speak; but he's no more proud than I am, and he was as civil as if I'd been a lord myself. So then I said, I hoped he would n't take it amiss about the glass, for it was quite an accident; but he bid me not mention it, for it did n't signify. And then he said he hoped you got safe home, and was n't frightened; and so I said yes, and I gave your duty to him."

"My duty to him!" exclaimed I,—"and who gave you leave?—who desired you?"

"O, I did it of my own head, just to make him think I came from you. But I should have told you before how the footman said he was going out of town to-morrow evening, and that his sister was soon to be married, and that he was a ordering a heap of things for that; so it come into my head, as he was so affable, that I'd ask him for his custom. So I says, says I, my Lord, says I, if your Lordship i'n't engaged particularly, my father is a silversmith, and he'd be very proud to serve you, says I; and Miss Anville, as danced with you, is his cousin, and she's my cousin too, and she'd be very much obliged to you, I'm sure."

"You'll drive me wild," (cried I, starting from my seat) "you have done me an irreparable injury;—but I will hear no more!"—and then I ran into my own room.

I was half frantic, I really raved; the good opinion of Lord Orville seemed now irretrievably lost: a faint hope, which in the morning I had vainly encouraged, that I might see him again, and explain the transaction, wholly vanished, now I found he was so soon to leave town: and I could not but conclude that, for the rest of my life, he would regard me as an object of utter contempt.

The very idea was a dagger to my heart!—I could not support it, and—but I blush to proceed—I fear your disapprobation, yet I should not be conscious of having merited it, but that the repugnance I feel to relate to you what I have done, makes me suspect I must have erred. Will you forgive me, if I own that I *first* wrote an account of this transaction to Miss Mirvan?—and that I even thought of *concealing* it from you?—Short-lived, however, was the ungrateful idea, and sooner will I risk the justice of your displeasure, than unworthily betray your generous confidence.

You are now probably prepared for what follows—which is a letter,— a hasty letter, that, in the height of my agitation, I wrote to Lord Orville.

"My Lord,

"I am so infinitely ashamed of the application made yesterday for your Lordship's carriage in my name, and so greatly shocked at hearing how much it was injured, that I cannot forbear writing a few lines, to clear myself from the imputation of an impertinence which I blush to be suspected of, and to acquaint you, that the request for your carriage was made against my consent, and the visit with which you were importuned this morning, without my knowledge.

"I am inexpressibly concerned at having been the instrument, however innocently, of so much trouble to your Lordship; but I beg you to believe, that reading these lines is the only part of it which I have given voluntarily.

"I am, my Lord,
"Your Lordship's most humble servant,
"EVELINA ANVILLE."

I applied to the maid of the house to get this note conveyed to Berkeley-square; but scarce had I parted with it, before I regretted having written at all, and I was flying down stairs to recover it, when the voice of Sir Clement Willoughby stopped me. As Madame Duval had ordered we should be denied to him, I was obliged to return up stairs; and after he was gone, my application was too late, as the maid had given it to a porter.

My time did not pass very serenely while he was gone; however, he brought me no answer, but that Lord Orville was not at home. Whether or not he will take the trouble to send any;—or whether he will condescend to call;—or whether the affair will rest as it is, I know not;—but, in being ignorant, am most cruelly anxious.

Letter XXIV.

July 4.

You may now, my dear Sir, send Mrs. Clinton for your Evelina with as much speed as she can conveniently make the journey, for no further opposition will be made to her leaving this town: happy had it perhaps been for her had she never entered it!

This morning Madame Duval desired me to go to Snow-hill, with an invitation to the Branghtons and Mr. Smith, to spend the evening with her: and she desired M. Du Bois, who breakfasted with us, to accompany me. I was very unwilling to obey her, as I neither wished to walk with M. Du Bois, nor yet to meet young Branghton. And, indeed, another, a yet more powerful reason, added to my reluctance,—for I thought it possible that Lord Orville might send some answer, or perhaps might call, during my absence; however, I did not dare dispute her commands.

Poor M. Du Bois spoke not a word during our walk, which was, I believe, equally unpleasant to us both. We found all the family assembled in the shop. Mr. Smith, the moment he perceived me, addressed himself to Miss Branghton, whom he entertained with all the gallantry in his power. I rejoice to find that my conduct at the Hampstead ball has had so good an effect. But young Branghton was extremely troublesome, he repeatedly laughed in my face, and looked so impertinently significant, that I was obliged to give up my reserve to M. Du Bois, and enter into conversation with him, merely to avoid such boldness.

"Miss," said Mr. Branghton, "I'm sorry to hear from my son that you was n't pleased with what we did about that Lord Orville; but I should like to know what it was you found fault with, for we did all for the best."

"Goodness!" cried the son, "why if you'd seen Miss, you'd have been surprised—she went out of the room quite in a huff, like."

"It is too late, now," said I, "to reason upon this subject; but, for the future, I must take the liberty to request, that my name may never be made use of without my knowledge. May I tell Madame Duval that you will do her the favour to accept her invitation?"

"As to me, Ma'am," said Mr. Smith, "I am much obliged to the old lady, but I have no mind to be taken in by her again; you'll excuse me, Ma'am."

All the rest promised to come, and I then took leave: but as I left the shop, I heard Mr. Branghton say, "Take courage, Tom, she's only coy." And, before I had walked ten yards, the youth followed.

I was so much offended that I would not look at him, but began to converse with M. Du Bois, who was now more lively than I had ever before seen him; for, most unfortunately, he misinterpreted the reason of my attention to him.

The first intelligence I received when I came home, was, that two gentlemen had called, and left cards. I eagerly enquired for them, and read the names of Lord Orville and Sir Clement Willoughby. I by no means regretted that I missed seeing the latter, but perhaps I may all my life regret that I missed the former, for probably he has now left town,— and I may see him no more!

"My goodness!" cried young Branghton, rudely looking over me, "only think of that Lord's coming all this way! It's my belief he'd got some order ready for father, and so he'd a mind to call and ask you if I'd told him the truth."

"Pray, Betty," cried I, "how long has he been gone?"

"Not two minutes, Ma'am."

"Why then I'll lay you any wager," said young Branghton, "he saw you and I a-walking up Holborn Hill."

"God forbid!" cried I, impatiently; and, too much chagrined to bear with any more of his remarks, I ran up stairs: but I heard him say to M. Du Bois, "Miss is so *uppish*[1] this morning, that I think I had better not speak to her again."

I wish M. Du Bois had taken the same resolution; but he chose to follow me into the dining-room, which he found empty.

"*Vous ne l'aimez donc pas, ce garçon, Mademoiselle!*"[2] cried he.

"Me!" cried I, "no, I detest him!" for I was sick at heart.

"*Ah, tu me rends la vie!*"[3] cried he, and flinging himself at my feet, he had just caught my hand, as the door was opened by Madame Duval.

Hastily, and with marks of guilty confusion in his face, he arose; but the rage of that lady quite amazed me! advancing to the retreating M. Du Bois, she began, in French, an attack which her extreme wrath and wonderful volubility almost rendered unintelligible; yet I understood but too much, since her reproaches convinced me she had herself proposed being the object of his affection.

He defended himself in a weak and evasive manner, and upon her commanding him from her sight, very readily withdrew: and then, with yet greater violence, she upbraided me with having *seduced* his heart, called me an ungrateful, designing girl, and protested she would neither take me to Paris, nor any more interest herself in my affairs, unless I would instantly agree to marry young Branghton.

Frightened as I had been at her vehemence, this proposal restored all my courage; and I frankly told her that in this point I never could obey her. More irritated than ever, she ordered me to quit the room.

Such is the present situation of affairs. I shall excuse myself from seeing the Branghtons this afternoon: indeed, I never wish to see them again. I am sorry, however innocently, that I have displeased Madame Duval, yet I shall be very glad to quit this town, for I believe it does not, now contain one person I ever wish to again meet. Had I but seen Lord Orville, I should regret nothing: I could then have more fully explained what I so hastily wrote; yet it will always be a pleasure to me to recollect that he called, since I flatter myself it was in consequence of his being satisfied with my letter.

Adieu, my dear Sir; the time now approaches when I hope once more to receive your blessing, and to owe all my joy, all my happiness to your kindness.

Stop Here

1. Peevish.
2. "You don't love that boy, then, Miss!"
3. "Oh, you give me life!"

Letter XXV.

MR. VILLARS TO EVELINA.

Berry Hill, July 7.

Welcome, thrice welcome, my darling Evelina, to the arms of the truest, the fondest of your friends! Mrs. Clinton, who shall hasten to you with these lines, will conduct you directly hither, for I can consent no longer to be parted from the child of my bosom!—the comfort of my age!—the sweet solace of all my infirmities! Your worthy friends at Howard Grove must pardon me that I rob them of the visit you proposed to make them before your return to Berry Hill, for I find my fortitude unequal to a longer separation.

I have much to say to you, many comments to make upon your late letters, some parts of which give me no little uneasiness; but I will reserve my remarks for our future conversations. Hasten, then, to the spot of thy nativity, the abode of thy youth, where never yet care or sorrow had power to annoy thee;—O that they might ever be banished this peaceful dwelling!

Adieu, my dearest Evelina! I pray but that thy satisfaction at our approaching meeting, may bear any comparison with mine!

ARTHUR VILLARS.

Letter XXVI.

EVELINA TO MISS MIRVAN.

Berry Hill, July 14.

My sweet Maria will be much surprised, and, I am willing to flatter myself, concerned, when, instead of her friend, she receives this letter;—this cold, this inanimate letter, which will but ill express the feelings of the heart which indites it.

When I wrote to you last Friday, I was in hourly expectation of seeing Mrs. Clinton, with whom I intended to have set out for Howard Grove; Mrs. Clinton came, but my plan was necessarily altered, for she brought me a letter,—the sweetest that ever was penned, from the best and kindest friend that ever orphan was blesst with, requiring my immediate attendance at Berry Hill.

I obeyed,—and pardon me if I own I obeyed without reluctance; after so long a separation, should I not else have been the most ungrateful of mortals?—And yet,—oh Maria? though I *wished* to leave London, the gratification of my wish afforded me no happiness! and though I felt an impatience inexpressible to return hither, no words, no language can explain the heaviness of heart with which I made the journey. I believe you would hardly have known me;—indeed, I hardly know myself. Perhaps had I first seen *you*, in your kind and sympathizing bosom I might have ventured to have reposed every secret of my soul; and then—but let me pursue my journal.

Mrs. Clinton delivered Madame Duval a letter from Mr. Villars, which requested her leave for my return, and, indeed, it was very readily accorded: yet, when she found, by my willingness to quit town, that M. Du Bois was really indifferent to me, she somewhat softened in my favour, and declared that, but for punishing his folly in thinking of such a child, she would not have consented to my being again buried in the country.

All the Branghtons called to take leave of me: but I will not write a word more about them; indeed I cannot with any patience think of that family, to whose forwardness and impertinence is owing all the uneasiness I at this moment suffer!

So great was the depression of my spirits upon the road, that it was with difficulty I could persuade the worthy Mrs. Clinton I was not ill: but alas, the situation of my mind was such as would have rendered any mere bodily pain, by comparison, even enviable!

And yet, when we arrived at Berry Hill,—when the chaise stopped at this place,—how did my heart throb with joy! and when, through the window, I beheld the dearest, the most venerable of men, with uplifted hands, returning, as I doubt not, thanks for my safe arrival,—good God! I thought it would have burst my bosom!—I opened the chaise-door myself, I flew,—for my feet did not seem to touch the ground,—into the parlour; he had risen to meet me, but the moment I appeared, he sunk into his chair, uttering, with a deep sigh, though his face *beamed* with delight, "My God, I thank thee!"

I sprung forward, and with a pleasure that bordered upon agony, I embraced his knees, I kissed his hands, I wept over them, but could not speak: while he, now raising his eyes in thankfulness towards heaven, now bowing down his reverend head, and folding me in his arms, could scarce articulate the blessings with which his kind and benevolent heart overflowed.

O Miss Mirvan, to be so beloved by the best of men,—should I not be happy?—Should I have one wish save that of meriting his goodness?—Yet think me not ungrateful; indeed I am not, although the internal sadness of my mind unfits me, at present, for enjoying as I ought the bounties of Providence.

I cannot journalize; cannot arrange my ideas into order.

How little has situation to do with happiness! I had flattered myself that, when restored to Berry Hill, I should be restored to tranquillity: far otherwise have I found it, for never yet had tranquillity and Evelina so little intercourse.

I blush for what I have written. Can you, Maria, forgive my gravity? but I restrain it so much and so painfully, in the presence of Mr. Villars, that I know not how to deny myself the consolation of indulging it to you.

Adieu, my dear Miss Mirvan.

Yet one thing I must add; do not let the seriousness of this letter deceive you; do not impute to a wrong cause the melancholy I confess, by supposing that the heart of your friend mourns a too great susceptibility; no, indeed! believe me it never was, never can be, more assuredly her own than at this moment. So witness in all truth,

Your affectionate
EVELINA.

You will make my excuses to the honoured Lady Howard, and to your dear mother.

Letter XXVII.

EVELINA IN CONTINUATION.

Berry Hill, July 21.

You accuse me of mystery, and charge me with reserve: I cannot doubt but I must have merited the accusation;—yet, to clear myself,—you know not how painful will be the task. But I cannot resist your kind entreaties,—indeed, I do not wish to resist them, for your friendship and affection will soothe my chagrin. Had it arisen from any other cause, not a moment would I have deferred the communication you ask;—but, as it is, I would, were it possible, not only conceal it from all the world, but endeavour to disbelieve it myself. Yet, since I *must* tell you, why trifle with your impatience?

I know not how to come to the point; twenty times have I attempted it in vain;—but I will *force* myself to proceed.

Oh, Miss Mirvan, could you ever have believed, that one who seemed formed as a pattern for his fellow-creatures, as a model of perfection,—one whose elegance surpassed all description,—whose sweetness of manners disgraced all comparison,—Oh, Miss Mirvan, could you ever have believed that *Lord Orville* would have treated me with indignity?

Never, never again will I trust to appearances,—never confide in my own weak judgment,—never believe that person to be good, who seems to be amiable! What cruel maxims are we taught by a knowledge of the world!—But while my own reflections absorb me, I forget you are still in suspence.

I had just finished the last letter which I wrote to you from London, when the maid of the house brought me a note. It was given to her, she said, by a footman, who told her he would call the next day for an answer.

This note,—but let it speak for itself.

"To Miss Anville.

"With transport, most charming of thy sex, did I read the letter with which you yesterday morning favoured me. I am sorry the affair of the carriage should have given you any concern, but I am highly flattered by the anxiety you express so kindly. Believe me, my lovely girl, I am truly sensible of the honour of your good opinion, and feel myself deeply penetrated with love and gratitude. The correspondence you have so sweetly commenced I shall be proud of continuing, and I hope the strong sense I have of the favour you do me, will prevent your withdrawing it. Assure yourself that I desire nothing more ardently than to pour forth my thanks at your feet, and to offer those vows which are so justly the tribute of your charms and accomplishments. In your next, I entreat you to acquaint me how long you shall remain in town. The servant whom I shall commission to call for an answer, has orders to ride post with it to me. My impatience for his arrival will be very great, though inferior to that with which I burn, to tell you, in person, how much I am, my sweet girl,

"Your grateful admirer,
"ORVILLE."

What a letter! how has my proud heart swelled every line I have copied! What I wrote to him you know; tell me then, my dear friend, do you think it merited such an answer?—and that I have deservedly incurred the liberty he has taken? I meant nothing but a simple apology, which I thought as much due to my own character as to his; yet by the construction he seems to have put upon it, should you not have imagined it contained the avowal of sentiments which might, indeed, have provoked his contempt?

The moment the letter was delivered to me, I retired to my own room to read it, and so eager was my first perusal, that,—I am ashamed to own—it gave me no sensation but of delight. Unsuspicious of any impropriety from Lord Orville, I perceived not immediately the impertinence it implied,—I only marked the expressions of his own regard; and I was so much surprised, that I was unable, for some time, to compose myself, or read it again,—I could only walk up and down the room, repeating to myself, "Good God, is it possible?—am I, then, loved by Lord Orville?"

But this dream was soon over, and I awoke to far different feelings; upon a second reading, I thought every word changed,—it did not seem the same letter,—I could not find one sentence that I could look at without blushing: my astonishment was extreme, and it was succeeded by the utmost indignation.

If, as I am very ready to acknowledge, I erred in writing to Lord

Orville, was it for *him* to punish the error? If he was offended, could he not have been silent? If he thought my letter ill-judged, should he not have pitied my ignorance? have considered my youth, and allowed for my inexperience?

Oh Maria, how have I been deceived in this man! Words have no power to tell the high opinion I had of him; to that was owing the unfortunate solicitude which prompted my writing,—a solicitude I must for ever repent!

Yet perhaps I have rather reason to rejoice than to grieve, since this affair has shewn me his real disposition, and removed that partiality, which, covering his every imperfection, left only his virtues and good qualities exposed to view. Had the deception continued much longer, had my mind received any additional prejudice in his favour, who knows whither my mistaken ideas might have led me? Indeed I fear I was in greater danger than I apprehended, or can now think of without trembling,—for oh, if this weak heart of mine had been penetrated with too deep an impression of his merit,—my peace and happiness had been lost for ever.

I would fain encourage more chearful thoughts, fain drive from my mind the melancholy that has taken possession of it,—but I cannot succeed; for, added to the humiliating feelings which so powerfully oppress me, I have yet another cause of concern;—alas, my dear Maria, I have broken the tranquillity of the best of men!

I have never had the courage to shew him this cruel letter: I could not bear so greatly to depreciate in his opinion, one whom I had, with infinite anxiety, raised in it myself. Indeed, my first determination was to confine my chagrin totally to my own bosom; but your friendly enquiries have drawn it from me; and now I wish I had made no concealment from the beginning, since I know not how to account for a gravity which not all my endeavours can entirely hide or repress.

My greatest apprehension is, lest he should imagine that my residence in London has given me a distaste to the country. Every body I see takes notice of my being altered, and looking pale and ill. I should be very indifferent to all such observations, did I not perceive that they draw upon me the eyes of Mr. Villars, which glisten with affectionate concern.

This morning, in speaking of my London expedition, he mentioned Lord Orville. I felt so much disturbed, that I would instantly have changed the subject; but he would not allow me, and, very unexpectedly, he began his panegyric, extolling in strong terms, his manly and honourable behaviour in regard to the Marybone adventure. My cheeks glowed with indignation every word he spoke;—so lately as I had myself fancied him the noblest of his sex, now that I was so well convinced of my mistake, I could not bear to hear his undeserved praises uttered by one so really good, so unsuspecting, so pure of heart!

What he thought of my silence and uneasiness I fear to know, but I hope he will mention the subject no more. I will not, however, with ungrateful indolence, give way to a sadness which I find infectious to him who merits the most chearful exertion of my spirits. I am thankful that he has forborne to probe my wound, and I will endeavour to heal it by the consciousness that I have not deserved the indignity I have received. Yet I cannot but lament to find myself in a world so deceitful, where we must suspect what we see, distrust what we hear, and doubt even what we feel!

Letter XXVIII.

EVELINA IN CONTINUATION.

Berry Hill, July 29.

I must own myself somewhat distressed how to answer your raillery: yet believe me, my dear Maria, your suggestions are those of *fancy*, not of *truth*. I am unconscious of the weakness you suspect; yet, to dispel your doubts, I will animate myself more than ever to conquer my chagrin, and to recover my spirits.

You wonder, you say, since my *heart* takes no part in this affair, why it should make me so unhappy? And can you, acquainted as you are with the high opinion I entertained of Lord Orville, can you wonder that so great a disappointment in his character should affect me? indeed, had so strange a letter been sent to me from *any* body, it could not have failed shocking me; how much more sensibly, then, must I feel such an affront, when received from the man in the world I had imagined least capable of giving it?

You are glad I made no reply; assure yourself, my dear friend, had this letter been the most respectful that could be written, the clandestine air given to it, by his proposal of sending his servant for my answer, instead of having it directed to his house, would effectually have prevented my writing. Indeed, I have an aversion the most sincere to all mysteries, all private actions; however foolishly and blameably, in regard to this letter, I have deviated from the open path which, from my earliest infancy, I was taught to tread.

He talks of my having *commenced a correspondence* with him; and could Lord Orville indeed believe I had such a design? believe me so forward, so bold, so strangely ridiculous? I know not if his man called or not, but I rejoice that I quitted London before he came, and without leaving any message for him. What, indeed, could I have said? it would have been a condescension very unmerited to have taken any, the least notice of such a letter.

Never shall I cease to wonder how he could write it. Oh, Maria, what, what could induce him so causelessly to wound and affront one who

would sooner have died than wilfully offended *him*? —— How mortifying a freedom of style! how cruel an implication conveyed by his
thanks, and expressions of gratitude! Is it not astonishing, that any man
can *appear* so modest, who is so vain?

Every hour I regret the secrecy I have observed with my beloved Mr.
Villars; I know not what bewitched me, but I felt at first, a repugnance
to publishing this affair that I could not surmount,—and now, I am
ashamed of confessing that I have any thing to confess! Yet I deserve to
be punished for the false delicacy which occasioned my silence; since,
if Lord Orville himself was contented to forfeit his character, was it for
me, almost at the expence of my own, to support it?

Yet I believe I should be very easy, now the first shock is over, and
now that I see the whole affair, with the resentment it merits, did not all
my good friends in this neighbourhood, who think me extremely
altered, teaze me about my gravity, and torment Mr. Villars with observations upon my dejection, and falling away.[1] The subject is no sooner
started, than a deep gloom overspreads his venerable countenance, and
he looks at me with a tenderness so melancholy, that I know not how to
endure the consciousness of exciting it.

Mrs. Selwyn, a lady of large fortune, who lives about three miles from
Berry Hill, and who has always honoured me with very distinguishing marks of regard, is going, in a short time, to Bristol, and has proposed to Mr. Villars to take me with her, for the recovery of my health.
He seemed very much distressed whether to consent or refuse; but I,
without any hesitation, warmly opposed the scheme, protesting my
health could no where be better than in this pure air. He had the goodness to thank me for this readiness to stay with him: but he is all goodness! Oh that it were in my power to be, indeed, what in the kindness
of his heart he has called me, the comfort of his age, and solace of his
infirmities!

Never do I wish to be again separated from him. If here I am grave,
elsewhere I should be unhappy. In his presence, with a very little exertion, all the chearfulness of my disposition seems ready to return; the
benevolence of his countenance reanimates, the harmony of his temper
composes, the purity of his character edifies me! I owe to him every
thing; and, far from finding my debt of gratitude a weight, the first pride,
first pleasure of my life, is the recollection of the obligations conferred
upon me by a goodness so unequalled.

Once, indeed, I thought there existed another,—who, when *time had
wintered o'er his locks*, would have shone forth among his fellow-creatures with the same brightness of worth which dignifies my honoured
Mr. Villars; a brightness, how superior in value to that which results
from mere quickness of parts, wit, or imagination! a brightness, which,

1. Losing weight.

not contented with merely diffusing smiles, and gaining admiration from the sallies of the spirits, reflects a real and a glorious lustre upon all mankind! Oh how great was my error! how ill did I judge! how cruelly have I been deceived!

I will not go to Bristol, though Mrs. Selwyn is very urgent with me;—but I desire not to see any more of the world; the few months I have already passed in it, have sufficed to give me a disgust even to its name.

I hope, too, I shall see Lord Orville no more; accustomed, from my first knowledge of him, to regard him as a *being superior to his race,* his presence, perhaps, might banish my resentment, and I might forget his ill conduct,—for oh, Maria!—I should not know how to see *Lord Orville*—and to think of displeasure!

As a sister I loved him,—I could have entrusted him with every thought of my heart, had he deigned to wish my confidence; so steady did I think his honour, so *feminine* his delicacy, and so amiable his nature! I have a thousand times imagined that the whole study of his life, and whole purport of his reflections, tended solely to the good and happiness of others:—but I will talk,—write,—think of him no more!

Adieu, my dear friend!

Letter XXIX.

EVELINA IN CONTINUATION.

Berry Hill, August 10.

You complain of my silence, my dear Miss Mirvan,—but what have I to write? Narrative does not offer, nor does a lively imagination supply the deficiency. I have, however, at present, sufficient matter for a letter, in relating a conversation I had yesterday with Mr. Villars.

Our breakfast had been the most chearful we have had since my return hither; and, when it was over, he did not, as usual, retire to his study, but continued to converse with me while I worked. We might, probably, have passed all the morning thus sociably, but for the entrance of a farmer, who came to solicit advice concerning some domestic affairs. They withdrew together into the study.

The moment I was alone, my spirits failed me; the exertion with which I had supported them, had fatigued my mind: I flung away my work, and, leaning my arms on the table, gave way to a train of disagreeable reflections, which, bursting from the restraint that had smothered them, filled me with unusual sadness.

This was my situation, when, looking towards the door, which was open, I perceived Mr. Villars, who was earnestly regarding me. "Is Farmer Smith gone, Sir?" cried I, hastily rising, and snatching up my work.[1]

---

1. Needle-work; sewing, embroidery, or the like.

"Don't let me disturb you," said he, gravely; "I will go again to my study."

"Will you, Sir?—I was in hopes you were coming to sit here."

"In hopes!—and why, Evelina, should you hope it?"

This question was so unexpected, that I knew not how to answer it; but, as I saw he was moving away, I followed, and begged him to return. "No, my dear, no," said he, with a forced smile, "I only interrupt your meditations."

Again I knew not what to say; and while I hesitated, he retired. My heart was with him, but I had not the courage to follow. The idea of an explanation, brought on in so serious a manner, frightened me. I recollected the inference *you* had drawn from my uneasiness, and I feared that he might make a similar interpretation.

Solitary and thoughtful, I passed the rest of the morning in my own room. At dinner I again attempted to be chearful; but Mr. Villars himself was grave, and I had not sufficient spirits to support a conversation merely by my own efforts. As soon as dinner was over, he took a book, and I walked to the window. I believe I remained near an hour in this situation. All my thoughts were directed to considering how I might dispel the doubts which I apprehended Mr. Villars had formed, without acknowledging a circumstance which I had suffered so much pain merely to conceal. But, while I was thus planning for the future, I forgot the present; and so intent was I upon the subject which occupied me, that the strange appearance of my unusual inactivity and extreme thoughtfulness, never occurred to me. But when, at last, I recollected myself, and turned round, I saw that Mr. Villars, who had parted with his book, was wholly engrossed in attending to me. I started from my reverie, and, hardly knowing what I said, asked if he had been reading?

He paused a moment, and then replied, "Yes, my child;—a book that both afflicts and perplexes me!"

He means *me*, thought I; and therefore I made no answer.

"What if we read it together?" continued he, "will you assist me to clear its obscurity?"

I knew not what to say, but I sighed, involuntarily, from the bottom of my heart. He rose, and, approaching me, said, with emotion, "My child, I can no longer be a silent witness of thy sorrow,—is not *thy* sorrow *my* sorrow?—and ought I to be a stranger to the cause, when I so deeply sympathise in the effect?"

"Cause, Sir!" cried I, greatly alarmed, "what cause?—I don't know,—I can't tell—I—"

"Fear not," said he, kindly, "to unbosom thyself to me, my dearest Evelina; open to me thy whole heart,—it can have no feelings for which I will not make allowance. Tell me, therefore, what it is that thus afflicts us both, and who knows but I may suggest some means of relief?"

"You are too, too good," cried I, greatly embarrassed; "but indeed I know not what you mean."

"I see," said he, "it is painful to you to speak: suppose then, I endeavour to save you by guessing?"

"Impossible! impossible!" cried I, eagerly, "no one living could ever guess, ever suppose—" I stopped abruptly; for I then recollected I was acknowledging something *was* to be guessed: however, he noticed not my mistake.

"At least let me try," answered he, mildly; "perhaps I may be a better diviner than you imagine: if I guess every thing that is probable, surely I must approach near the real reason. Be honest, then, my love, and speak without reserve,—does not the country, after so much gaiety, so much variety, does it not appear insipid and tiresome?"

"No, indeed! I love it more than ever, and more than ever do I wish I had never, never quitted it!"

"Oh, my child! that I had not permitted the journey! My judgment always opposed it, but my resolution was not proof against persuasion."

"I blush, indeed," cried I, "to recollect my earnestness;—but I have been my own punisher!"

"It is too late, now," answered he, "to reflect upon this subject; let us endeavour to avoid repentance for the time to come, and we shall not have erred without reaping some instruction." Then seating himself, and making me sit by him, he continued: "I must now guess again; perhaps you regret the loss of those friends you knew in town,—perhaps you miss their society, and fear you may see them no more?—perhaps Lord Orville——"

I could not keep my seat, but, rising hastily, said, "Dear Sir, ask me nothing more!—for I have nothing to own,—nothing to say;—my gravity has been merely accidental, and I can give no reason for it at all. Shall I fetch you another book?—or will you have this again?"

For some minutes he was totally silent, and I pretended to employ myself in looking for a book: at last, with a deep sigh, "I see," said he, "I see but too plainly, that though Evelina is returned,—I have lost my child!"

"No, Sir, no," cried I, inexpressibly shocked, "she is more your's than ever! Without you, the world would be a desart to her, and life a burthen;—forgive her, then, and,—if you can,—condescend to be, once more, the confidant of all her thoughts."

"How highly I value, how greatly I wish for her confidence," returned he, "she cannot but know;—yet to extort, to tear it from her,—my justice, my affection, both revolt at the idea. I am sorry that I was so earnest with you;—leave me, my dear, leave me and compose yourself;—we will meet again at tea."

"Do you then refuse to hear me?"

"No, but I abhor to compel you. I have long seen that your mind has been ill at ease, and mine has largely partaken of your concern: I forbore to question you; for I hoped that time, and absence from whatever excited your uneasiness, might best operate in silence: but alas! your affliction seems only to augment,—your health declines,—your look alters,—Oh Evelina, my aged heart bleeds to see the change!—bleeds to behold the darling it had cherished, the prop it had reared for its support, when bowed down by years and infirmities, sinking itself under the pressure of internal grief!—struggling to hide, what it should seek to participate![2]—But go, my dear, go to your own room,—we both want composure, and we will talk of this matter some other time."

"Oh Sir," cried I, penetrated to the soul, "bid me not leave you!—think me not so lost to feeling, to gratitude——"

"Not a word of that," interrupted he; "it pains me you should think upon that subject; pains me you should ever remember that you have not a natural, an hereditary right to every thing within my power. I meant not to affect you thus,—I hoped to have soothed you!—but my anxiety betrayed me to an urgency that has distressed you. Comfort yourself, my love, and doubt not but that time will stand your friend, and all will end well."

I burst into tears: with difficulty had I so long restrained them; for my heart, while it glowed with tenderness and gratitude, was oppressed with a sense of its own unworthiness. "You are all, all goodness!" cried I, in a voice scarce audible, "little as I deserve,—unable as I am to repay, such kindness,—yet my whole soul feels,—thanks you for it!"

"My dearest child," cried he, "I cannot bear to see thy tears;—for *my* sake dry them,—such a sight is too much for me: think of that, Evelina, and take comfort, I charge thee!"

"Say then," cried I, kneeling at his feet, "say then that you forgive me! that you pardon my reserve,—that you will again suffer me to tell you my most secret thoughts, and rely upon my promise never more to forfeit your confidence!——my father! my protector!—my ever-hon-oured—ever-loved—my best and only friend!—say you forgive your Evelina, and she will study better to deserve your goodness!"

He raised, he embraced me; he called me his sole joy, his only earthly hope, and the child of his bosom! He folded me to his heart, and, while I wept from the fulness of mine, with words of sweetest kindness and consolation, he soothed and tranquillised me.

Dear to my remembrance will ever be that moment, when, banishing the reserve I had so foolishly planned and so painfully supported, I was restored to the confidence of the best of men!

When, at length, we were again quietly and composedly seated by each other, and Mr. Villars waited for the explanation I had begged him to hear, I found myself extremely embarrassed how to introduce the

2. To share with others.

subject which must lead to it. He saw my distress, and, with a kind of benevolent pleasantry, asked me if I would let him *guess* any more? I assented in silence.

"Shall I, then, go back to where I left off?"

"If—if you please;—I believe so,—" said I, stammering.

"Well, then, my love, I think I was speaking of the regret it was natural you should feel upon quitting those from whom you had received civility and kindness, with so little certainty of ever seeing them again, or being able to return their good offices? These are circumstances that afford but melancholy reflections to young minds; and the affectionate disposition of my Evelina, open to all social feelings, must be hurt more than usual by such considerations.—You are silent, my dear?—Shall I name those whom I think most worthy the regret I speak of? We shall then see if our opinions coincide."

Still I said nothing, and he continued.

"In your London journal, nobody appears in a more amiable, a more respectable light, than Lord Orville, and perhaps ——— "

"I knew what you would say," cried I, hastily, "and I have long feared where your suspicions would fall; but indeed, Sir, you are mistaken: I hate Lord Orville,—he is the last man in the world in whose favour I should be prejudiced."

I stopped; for Mr. Villars looked at me with such infinite surprise, that my own warmth made me blush.

"You *hate* Lord Orville!" repeated he.

I could make no answer, but took from my pocket-book the letter, and giving it to him, "See, Sir," said I, "how differently the same man can *talk* and *write!*"

He read it three times before he spoke; and then said, "I am so much astonished, that I know not what I read. When had you this letter?"

I told him. Again he read it; and, after considering its contents some time, said, "I can form but one conjecture concerning this most extraordinary performance: he must certainly have been intoxicated when he wrote it."

"Lord Orville intoxicated!" repeated I; "once I thought him a stranger to all intemperance,—but it is very possible, for I can believe any thing now."

"That a man who had behaved with so strict a regard to delicacy," continued Mr. Villars, "and who, as far as occasion had allowed, manifested sentiments the most honourable, should thus insolently, thus wantonly insult a modest young woman, in his perfect senses, I cannot think possible. But, my dear, you should have inclosed this letter in an empty cover, and have returned it to him again: such a resentment would at once have become *your* character, and have given him an opportunity, in some measure, of clearing his own. He could not well have read this letter the next morning, without being sensible of the impropriety of having written it."

Oh Maria! why had not I this thought? I might then have received some apology; the mortification would then have been *his*, not *mine*. It is true, he could not have reinstated himself so highly in my opinion as I had once ignorantly placed him, since the conviction of such intemperance would have levelled him with the rest of his imperfect race; yet, my humbled pride might have been consoled by his acknowledgments.

But why should I allow myself to be humbled by a man who can suffer his reason to be thus abjectly debased, when I am exalted by one who knows no vice, and scarcely a failing,—but by hearsay? To think of his kindness, and reflect upon his praises, might animate and comfort me even in the midst of affliction. "Your indignation," said he, "is the result of virtue; you fancied Lord Orville was without fault—he had the appearance of infinite worthiness, and you supposed his character accorded with his appearance: guileless yourself, how could you prepare against the duplicity of another? Your disappointment has but been proportioned to your expectations, and you have chiefly owed its severity to the innocence which hid its approach."

I will bid these words dwell ever in my memory, and they shall cheer, comfort, and enliven me! This conversation, though extremely affecting to me at the time it passed, has relieved my mind from much anxiety. Concealment, my dear Maria, is the foe of tranquillity: however I may err in future, I will never be disingenuous in acknowledging my errors. To you, and to Mr. Villars, I vow an unremitting confidence.

And yet, though I am more at ease, I am far from well: I have been some time writing this letter; but I hope I shall send you, soon, a more chearful one.

Adieu, my sweet friend. I entreat you not to acquaint even your dear mother with this affair; Lord Orville is a favourite with her, and why should I publish that he deserves not that honour?

Letter XXX.

EVELINA IN CONTINUATION.

Bristol Hotwells,[1] August 28.

You will be again surprised, my dear Maria, at seeing whence I date my letter: but I have been very ill, and Mr. Villars was so much alarmed, that he not only insisted upon my accompanying Mrs. Selwyn hither, but earnestly desired she would hasten her intended journey.

We travelled very slowly, and I did not find myself so much fatigued

1. Also Hotwell, a summer resort at Clifton, a mile west of Bristol, featuring a hot spring, music, and public balls. The season at the Hotwell was May to September inclusive.

as I expected. We are situated upon a most delightful spot; the prospect is beautiful, the air pure, and the weather very favourable to invalids. I am already better, and I doubt not but I shall soon be well; as well, in regard to mere health, as I wish to be.

I cannot express the reluctance with which I parted from my revered Mr. Villars: it was not like that parting which, last April, preceded my journey to Howard Grove, when, all expectation and hope, though I wept, I rejoiced, and, though I sincerely grieved to leave him, I yet wished to be gone: the sorrow I now felt was unmixed with any livelier sensation; expectation was vanished, and hope I had none! All that I held most dear upon earth, I quitted, and that upon an errand to the success of which I was totally indifferent, the re-establishment of my health. Had it been to have seen my sweet Maria, or her dear mother, I should not have repined.

Mrs. Selwyn is very kind and attentive to me. She is extremely clever; her understanding, indeed, may be called *masculine*; but, unfortunately, her manners deserve the same epithet; for, in studying to acquire the knowledge of the other sex, she has lost all the softness of her own. In regard to myself, however, as I have neither courage nor inclination to argue with her, I have never been personally hurt at her want of gentleness; a virtue which, nevertheless, seems so essential a part of the female character, that I find myself more awkward, and less at ease, with a woman who wants it, than I do with a man. She is not a favourite with Mr. Villars, who has often been disgusted at her unmerciful propensity to satire: but his anxiety that I should try the effect of the Bristol waters, overcame his dislike of committing me to her care. Mrs. Clinton is also here; so that I shall be as well attended as his utmost partiality could desire.

I will continue to write to you, my dear Miss Mirvan, with as much constancy as if I had no other correspondent; though, during my absence from Berry Hill, my letters may, perhaps, be shortened on account of the minuteness of the journal which I must write to my beloved Mr. Villars: but you, who know his expectations, and how many ties bind me to fulfil them, will, I am sure, rather excuse any omission to yourself, than any negligence to him.

VOLUME THREE

Letter I.

EVELINA TO THE REV. MR. VILLARS.

Bristol Hotwells, Sept. 12.

The first fortnight that I passed here, was so quiet, so serene, that it gave me reason to expect a settled calm during my stay; but if I may now judge of the time to come, by the present state of my mind, the calm will be succeeded by a storm, of which I dread the violence!

This morning, in my way to the pump-room,[1] with Mrs. Selwyn, we were both very much incommoded by three gentlemen, who were sauntering by the side of the Avon, laughing, and talking very loud, and lounging so disagreeably, that we knew not how to pass them. They all three fixed their eyes very boldly upon me, alternately looking under my hat, and whispering one another. Mrs. Selwyn assumed an air of uncommon sternness, and said, "You will please, gentlemen, either to proceed yourselves, or to suffer us."

"Oh! Ma'am," cried one of them, "we will suffer *you* with the greatest pleasure in life."

"You will suffer us *both*," answered she, "or I am much mistaken: you had better, therefore, make way quietly, for I should be sorry to give my servant the trouble of teaching you better manners."

Her commanding air struck them, yet they all chose to laugh, and one of them wished the fellow would begin his lesson, that he might have the pleasure of rolling him into the Avon; while another advancing to me with a freedom which made me start, said, "By my soul I did not know you!—but I am sure I cannot be mistaken;—had not I the honour of seeing you once, at the Pantheon?"

I then recollected the nobleman who, at that place, had so much embarrassed me. I courtsied without speaking. They all bowed, and making, though in a very easy manner, an apology to Mrs. Selwyn, they suffered us to pass on, but chose to accompany us.

"And where," continued this Lord, "can you so long have hid yourself? do you know I have been in search of you this age? I could neither find you out, nor hear of you: not a creature could inform me what was become of you. I cannot imagine where you could be immured. I was at two or three public places every night, in hopes of meeting you. Pray did you leave town?"

"Yes, my Lord."

"So early in the season!—what could possibly induce you to go before the birth-day?"

"I had nothing, my Lord, to do with the birth-day."

"By my soul, all the women who *had*, may rejoice you were away. Have you been here any time?"

"Not above a fortnight, my Lord."

"A fortnight!—how unlucky that I did not meet you sooner! but I have had a run of ill luck ever since I came. How long shall you stay?"

"Indeed, my Lord, I don't know."

"Six weeks, I hope; for I shall wish the place at the devil when you go."

1. "A place at a spa where the medicinal water is dispensed for drinking" (*OED*).

"Do you, then, flatter yourself, my Lord," said Mrs. Selwyn, who had hitherto listened in silent contempt, "that you shall see such a beautiful spot as this, when you visit the dominions of the devil?"

"Ha, ha, ha! Faith, my Lord," said one of his companions, who still walked with us, though the other had taken leave; "the Lady is rather hard upon you."

"Not at all," answered Mrs. Selwyn; "for as I cannot doubt but his Lordship's rank and interest will secure him a place there, it would be reflecting on his understanding, to suppose he should not wish to enlarge and beautify his dwelling."

Much as I was disgusted with this Lord, I must own Mrs. Selwyn's severity rather surprised me: but you, who have so often observed it, will not wonder she took so fair an opportunity of indulging her humour.

"As to *places*," returned he, totally unmoved, "I am so indifferent to them, that the devil take me if I care which way I go! *objects*, indeed, I am not so easy about; and therefore I expect, that those angels with whose beauty I am so much enraptured in this world, will have the goodness to afford me some little consolation in the other."

"What, my Lord!" cried Mrs. Selwyn, "would you wish to degrade the habitation of your friend, by admitting into it the insipid company of the upper regions?"

"What do you do with yourself this evening?" said his Lordship, turning to me.

"I shall be at home, my Lord."

"O, *à-propos*,—where are you?"

"Young ladies, my Lord," said Mrs. Selwyn, "are *no where*."

"Prithee," whispered his Lordship, "is that queer woman your mother?"

Good Heavens, Sir, what words for such a question!

"No, my Lord."

"Your maiden aunt, then?"

"No."

"Whoever she is, I wish she would mind her own affairs: I don't know what the devil a woman lives for after thirty: she is only in other folk's way. Shall you be at the assembly?"

"I believe not, my Lord."

"No!—why then how in the world can you contrive to pass your time?"

"In a manner which your Lordship will think very extraordinary," cried Mrs. Selwyn; "for the young Lady *reads*."

"Ha, ha, ha! Egad, my Lord," cried the facetious companion, "you are got into bad hands."

"You had better, Madam," answered he, "attack Jack Coverley, here, for you will make nothing of me."

"Of *you*, my Lord!" cried she; "Heaven forbid I should ever entertain so idle an expectation! I only talk, like a silly woman, for the sake of talking; but I have by no means so low an opinion of your Lordship, as to suppose you vulnerable to censure."

"Do, pray, Ma'am," cried he, "turn to Jack Coverley; he's the very man for you;—he'd be a wit himself if he was not too modest."

"Prithee, my Lord, be quiet," returned the other; "if the lady is contented to bestow all her favours upon *you*, why should you make such a point of my going snacks?" [2]

"Don't be apprehensive, Gentlemen," said Mrs. Selwyn, drily, "I am not romantic,—I have not the least design of doing good to either of you."

"Have not you been ill since I saw you?" said his Lordship again, addressing himself to me.

"Yes, my Lord."

"I thought so; you are paler than you was, and I suppose that's the reason I did not recollect you sooner."

"Has not your Lordship too much gallantry," cried Mrs. Selwyn, "to discover a young lady's illness by her looks?"

"The devil a word can I speak for that woman," said he, in a low voice; "do, prithee, Jack, take her in hand."

"Excuse me, my Lord!" answered Mr. Coverley.

"When shall I see you again?" continued his Lordship; "do you go to the pump-room every morning?"

"No, my Lord."

"Do you ride out?"

"No, my Lord."

Just then we arrived at the pump-room, and an end was put to our conversation, if it is not an abuse of words to give such a term to a string of rude questions and free compliments.

He had not opportunity to say much more to me, as Mrs. Selwyn joined a large party, and I walked home between two ladies. He had, however, the curiosity to see us to the door.

Mrs. Selwyn was very eager to know how I had made acquaintance with this nobleman, whose manners so evidently announced the character of a confirmed libertine. I could give her very little satisfaction, as I was ignorant even of his name. But, in the afternoon, Mr. Ridgeway, the apothecary, gave us very ample information.

As his person was easily described, for he is remarkably tall, Mr. Ridgeway told us he was Lord Merton, a nobleman who is but lately come to his title, though he has already dissipated more than half his fortune: a professed admirer of beauty, but a man of most licentious character: that among men, his companions consisted chiefly of gamblers and jockeys, and among women he was rarely admitted.

"Well, Miss Anville," said Mrs. Selwyn, "I am glad I was not more

2. Having a share in something; dividing profits.

civil to him. You may depend upon *me* for keeping him at a distance."

"O, Madam," said Mr. Ridgeway, "he may now be admitted any where, for he is going to *reform*."

"Has he, under that notion, persuaded any fool to marry him?"

"Not yet, Madam, but a marriage is expected to take place shortly: it has been some time in agitation, but the friends of the Lady have obliged her to wait till she is of age: however, her brother, who has chiefly opposed the match, now that she is near being at her own disposal, is tolerably quiet. She is very pretty, and will have a large fortune. We expect her at the Wells every day."

"What is her name?" said Mrs. Selwyn.

"Larpent," answered he: "Lady Louisa Larpent, sister of Lord Orville."

"Lord Orville!" repeated I, all amazement.

"Yes, Ma'am; his Lordship is coming with her. I have had certain information. They are to be at the Honourable Mrs. Beaumont's.[3] She is a relation of my Lord's and has a very fine house upon Clifton Hill."[4]

His Lordship is coming with her!—Good God, what an emotion did those words give me! How strange, my dear Sir, that, just at this time, he should visit Bristol! It will be impossible for me to avoid seeing him, as Mrs. Selwyn is very well acquainted with Mrs. Beaumont. Indeed, I have had an escape in not being under the same roof with him, for Mrs. Beaumont invited us to her house immediately upon our arrival; but the inconveniency of being so distant from the pump-room made Mrs. Selwyn decline her civility.

Oh that the first meeting were over!—or that I could quit Bristol without seeing him!—inexpressibly do I dread an interview: should the same impertinent freedom be expressed by his looks, which dictated this cruel letter, I shall not know how to endure either him or myself. Had I but returned it, I should be easier, because my sentiments of it would then be known to him; but now, he can only gather them from my behaviour, and I tremble lest he should mistake my indignation for confusion!—lest he should misconstrue my reserve into embarrassment!—for how, my dearest Sir, how shall I be able totally to divest myself of the respect with which I have been used to think of him?—the pleasure with which I have been used to see him?

Surely he, as well as I, must recollect the letter at the moment of our meeting, and he will, probably, mean to gather my thoughts of it from my looks;—oh that they could but convey to him my real detestation of impertinence and vanity! then would he see how much he had mistaken my disposition when he imagined them my due.

There was a time when the very idea that such a man as Lord Merton should ever be connected with Lord Orville would have both surprised

---

3. The courtesy title "Honourable" is given to daughters of peers below the rank of Earl and to younger sons of peers below the rank of Marquis.
4. Clifton is situated on the sides and summit of lofty cliffs overhanging the River Avon.

and shocked me, and even yet I am pleased to hear of his repugnance to the marriage.

But how strange, that a man of so abandoned a character should be the choice of a sister of Lord Orville! and how strange that, almost at the moment of the union, he should be so importunate in gallantry to another woman! What a world is this we live in! how corrupt! how degenerate! well might I be contented to see no more of it! If I find that the *eyes* of Lord Orville agree with his *pen*,—I shall then think, that of all mankind, the only virtuous individual resides at Berry Hill.

Letter II.

EVELINA IN CONTINUATION.

Bristol Hotwells, Sept. 16.

Oh Sir, Lord Orville is still himself! still, what from the moment I beheld, I believed him to be—all that is amiable in man! and your happy Evelina, restored at once to spirits and tranquillity, is no longer sunk in her own opinion, nor discontented with the world;—no longer, with dejected eyes, sees the prospect of passing her future days in sadness, doubt, and suspicion!—with revived courage she now looks forward, and expects to meet with goodness, even among mankind:— though still she feels, as strongly as ever, the folly of hoping, in any *second* instance, to meet with *perfection*.

Your conjecture was certainly right; Lord Orville, when he wrote that letter, could not be in his senses. Oh that intemperance should have power to degrade so low, a man so noble!

This morning I accompanied Mrs. Selwyn to Clifton Hill, where, beautifully situated, is the house of Mrs. Beaumont. Most uncomfortable were my feelings during our walk, which was very slow, for the agitation of my mind made me more than usually sensible how weak I still continue. As we entered the house, I summoned all my resolution to my aid, determined rather to die than give Lord Orville reason to attribute my weakness to a wrong cause. I was happily relieved from my perturbation, when I saw Mrs. Beaumont was alone. We sat with her for, I believe, an hour without interruption, and then we saw a phaeton[1] drive up to the gate, and a lady and gentleman alight from it.

They entered the parlour with the ease of people who were at home. The gentleman, I soon saw, was Lord Merton; he came shuffling into the room with his boots on, and his whip in his hand; and, having made something like a bow to Mrs. Beaumont, he turned towards me. His surprise was very evident, but he took no manner of notice of me. He waited, I believe, to discover, first, what chance had brought me to that

1. "A species of four-wheeled open carriage, of light construction; ususally drawn by a pair of horses" (*OED*).

house, where he did not look much rejoiced at meeting me. He seated himself very quietly at the window, without speaking to any body.

Mean time, the lady, who seemed very young, hobbling rather than walking into the room, made a passing courtsie to Mrs. Beaumont, saying, "How are you, Ma'am?" and then, without noticing any body else, with an air of languor she flung herself upon a sofa, protesting, in a most affected voice, and speaking so softly she could hardly be heard, that she was fatigued to death. "Really, Ma'am, the roads are so monstrous dusty,—you can't imagine how troublesome the dust is to one's eyes!—and the sun, too, is monstrous disagreeable!—I dare say I shall be so tanned I shan't be fit to be seen this age. Indeed, my Lord, I won't go out with you any more, for you don't care where you take one."

"Upon my honour," said Lord Merton, "I took you the pleasantest ride in England; the fault was in the sun, not me."

"Your Lordship is in the right," said Mrs. Selwyn, "to transfer the fault to the *sun*, because it has so many excellencies to counterbalance partial inconveniences, that a *little* blame will not injure *that* in our estimation."

Lord Merton looked by no means delighted at this attack; which I believe she would not so readily have made, but to revenge his neglect of us.

"Did you meet your brother, Lady Louisa?" said Mrs. Beaumont.

"No Ma'am. Is he rode out this morning?"

I then found, what I had before suspected, that this lady was Lord Orville's sister: how strange, that such near relations should be so different to each other! There is, indeed, some resemblance in their features, but in their manners, not the least.

"Yes," answered Mrs. Beaumont, "and I believe he wished to see you."

"My Lord drove so monstrous fast," said Lady Louisa, "that perhaps we passed him. He frightened me out of my senses; I declare my head is quite giddy. Do you know, Ma'am, we have done nothing but quarrel all the morning?—You can't think how I've scolded; have not I, my Lord?" and she smiled expressively at Lord Merton.

"You have been, as you always are," said he, twisting his whip with his fingers, "all sweetness."

"O fie, my Lord," cried she, "I know you don't think so; I know you think me very ill-natured;—don't you, my Lord?"

"No, upon my honour;—how can your Ladyship ask such a question? Pray how goes time? my watch stands."[2]

"It is almost three," answered Mrs. Beaumont.

"Lord, Ma'am, you frighten me!" cried Lady Louisa; and then, turning to Lord Merton, "why now, you wicked creature, you, did you not tell me it was but one?"

---

2. That is, has stopped.

Mrs. Selwyn then rose to take leave; but Mrs. Beaumont asked if she would look at the shrubbery. "I should like it much," answered she, "but that I fear to fatigue Miss Anville."

Lady Louisa then, raising her head from her hand, on which it had leant, turned round to look at me, and, having fully satisfied her curiosity, without any regard to the confusion it gave me, turned about, and, again leaning on her hand, took no further notice of me.

I declared myself very able to walk, and begged that I might accompany them. "What say *you*, Lady Louisa," cried Mrs. Beaumont, "to a stroll in the garden?"

"Me, Ma'am!—I declare I can't stir a step; the heat is so excessive, it would kill me. I'm half dead with it already; besides, I shall have no time to dress. Will any body be here to-day, Ma'am?"

"I believe not, unless Lord Merton will favour us with his company."

"With great pleasure, Madam."

"Well, I declare you don't deserve to be asked," cried Lady Louisa, "you wicked creature, you!—I *must* tell you one thing, Ma'am,—you can't think how abominable he was! do you know we met Mr. Lovel in his new phaeton, and my Lord was so cruel as to drive against it?—we really flew. I declare I could not breathe. Upon my word, my Lord, I'll never trust myself with you again,—I won't indeed!"

We then went into the garden, leaving them to discuss the point at their leisure.

Do you remember a *pretty but affected young lady* I mentioned to have seen, in Lord Orville's party, at the Pantheon? How little did I then imagine her to be his sister! yet Lady Louisa Larpent is the very person. I can now account for the piqued manner of her speaking to Lord Merton that evening, and I can now account for the air of displeasure with which Lord Orville marked the undue attention of his future brother-in-law to me.

We had not walked long, ere, at a distance, I perceived Lord Orville, who seemed just dismounted from his horse, enter the garden. All my perturbation returned at the sight of him!—yet I endeavoured to repress every feeling but resentment. As he approached us, he bowed to the whole party; but I turned away my head, to avoid taking any share in his civility. Addressing himself immediately to Mrs. Beaumont, he was beginning to enquire after his sister, but upon seeing my face, he suddenly exclaimed "Miss Anville!—" and then he advanced, and made his compliments to me,—not with an air of vanity or impertinence, nor yet with a look of consciousness or shame,—but with a countenance open, manly, and charming!—with a smile that indicated pleasure, and eyes that sparkled with delight! on *my side* was all the consciousness, for by him, I really believe, the letter was, at that moment, entirely forgotten.

With what politeness did he address me! with what sweetness did he look at me! the very tone of his voice seemed flattering! he congratulated himself upon his good fortune in meeting with me,—hoped I should spend some time in Bristol, and enquired, even with anxiety enquired, if my health was the cause of my journey; in which case his satisfaction would be converted into apprehension.

Yet, struck as I was with his manner, and charmed to find him such as he was wont to be, imagine not, my dear Sir, that I forgot the resentment I owe him, or the cause he has given me of displeasure; no, my behaviour was such as, I hope, had you seen, you would not have disapproved: I was grave and distant, I scarce looked at him when he spoke, or answered him when he was silent.

As he must certainly observe this alteration in my conduct, I think it could not fail making him both recollect and repent the provocation he had so causelessly given me: for surely he was not so wholly lost to reason, as to be now ignorant he had ever offended me.

The moment that, without absolute rudeness, I was able, I turned entirely from him, and asked Mrs. Selwyn if we should not be late home? How Lord Orville looked I know not, for I avoided meeting his eyes, but he did not speak another word as we proceeded to the garden gate. Indeed I believe my abruptness surprised him, for he did not seem to expect I had so much spirit. And, to own the truth, convinced as I was of the propriety, nay, necessity of shewing my displeasure, I yet almost hated myself for receiving his politeness so ungraciously.

When we were taking leave, my eyes accidentally meeting his, I could not but observe that his gravity equalled my own, for it had entirely taken place of the smiles and good-humour with which he had met me.

"I am afraid this young Lady," said Mrs. Beaumont, "is too weak for another long walk till she is again rested."

"If the ladies will trust to my driving," said Lord Orville, "and are not afraid of a phaeton, mine shall be ready in a moment."

"You are very good, my Lord," said Mrs. Selwyn, "but my will is yet unsigned, and I don't chuse to venture in a phaeton with a young man while that is the case."

"O," cried Mrs. Beaumont, "you need not be afraid of my Lord Orville, for he is remarkably careful."

"Well, Miss Anville," answered she, "what say you?"

"Indeed," cried I, "I had much rather walk.—" But then, looking at Lord Orville, I perceived in his face a surprise so serious at my abrupt refusal, that I could not forbear adding, "for I should be sorry to occasion so much trouble."

Lord Orville brightening at these words, came forward, and pressed his offer in a manner not to be denied;—so the phaeton was ordered! And indeed, my dear Sir,—I know not how it was,—but, from that moment, my coldness and reserve insensibly wore away! You must not be angry,—it was my intention, nay, my endeavour, to support them with firmness; but when I formed the plan, I thought only of the letter,—not of Lord Orville!—and how is it possible for resentment to subsist without provocation? yet, believe me, my dearest Sir, had he sustained the part he began to act when he wrote the ever-to-be-regretted letter, your Evelina would have not forfeited her title to your esteem, by contentedly submitting to be treated with indignity.

We continued in the garden till the phaeton was ready. When we parted from Mrs. Beaumont, she repeated her invitation to Mrs. Selwyn to accept an apartment in her house, but the reason I have already mentioned made it be again declined.

Lord Orville drove very slow, and so cautiously, that, notwithstanding the height of the phaeton, fear would have been ridiculous. I supported no part in the conversation, but Mrs. Selwyn extremely well supplied the place of two. Lord Orville himself did not speak much, but the excellent sense and refined good-breeding which accompany every word he utters, give value and weight to whatever he says.

"I suppose, my Lord," said Mrs. Selwyn, when we stopped at our lodgings, "you would have been extremely confused had we met any gentlemen who have the honour of knowing you."

"If I had," answered he, gallantly, "it would have been from mere compassion at their envy."

"No, my Lord," answered she, "it would have been from mere shame, that, in an age so daring, you alone should be such a coward as to forbear to frighten women."

"O," cried he laughing, "when a man is in a fright for himself, the ladies cannot but be in security; for you have not had half the apprehension for the safety of your persons, that I have for that of my heart." He then alighted, handed us out, took leave, and again mounting the phaeton, was out of sight in a minute.

"Certainly," said Mrs. Selwyn, when he was gone, "there must have been some mistake in the birth of that young man; he was, undoubtedly, designed for the last age; for he is really polite!"

And now, my dear Sir, do not you think, according to the present situation of affairs, I may give up my resentment without imprudence or impropriety? I hope you will not blame me. Indeed, had you, like me, seen his respectful behaviour, you would have been convinced of the impracticability of supporting any further indignation.

Letter III.

EVELINA IN CONTINUATION.

Bristol Hotwells, Sept. 19.

Yesterday morning Mrs. Selwyn received a card from Mrs. Beaumont, to ask her to dine with her to-day; and another, to the same purpose, came to me. The invitation was accepted, and we are but just arrived from Clifton Hill.

We found Mrs. Beaumont alone in the parlour. I will write you the character of that lady, in the words of our satirical friend Mrs. Selwyn. "She is an absolute *Court Calendar*[1] bigot; for, chancing herself to be born of a noble and ancient family, she thinks proper to be of opinion, that *birth* and *virtue* are one and the same thing. She has some good qualities, but they rather originate from pride than principle, as she piques herself upon being too high born to be capable of an unworthy action, and thinks it incumbent upon her to support the dignity of her ancestry. Fortunately for the world in general, she has taken it into her head, that condescension is the most distinguishing virtue of high life; so that the same pride of family which renders others imperious, is with her the motive of affability. But her civility is too formal to be comfortable, and too mechanical to be flattering. That she does *me* the honour of so much notice, is merely owing to an accident which, I am sure, is very painful to her remembrance; for it so happened that I once did her some service, in regard to an apartment, at Southampton; and I have since been informed, that, at the time she accepted my assistance, she thought I was a woman of quality: and I make no doubt but she was miserable when she discovered me to be a mere country gentlewoman: however, her nice notions of decorum have made her load me with favours ever since. But I am not much flattered by her civilities, as I am convinced I owe them neither to attachment nor gratitude, but solely to a desire of cancelling an obligation which she cannot brook being under, to one whose name is no where to be found in the *Court Calendar.*"

You well know, my dear Sir, the delight this lady takes in giving way to her satirical humour.

Mrs. Beaumont received us very graciously, though she somewhat distressed me by the questions she asked concerning my family,—such as, Whether I was related to the Anvilles in the North?—Whether some of my name did not live in Lincolnshire? and many other enquiries, which much embarrassed me.

The conversation, next, turned upon the intended marriage in her family. She treated the subject with reserve, but it was evident she disapproved Lady Louisa's choice. She spoke in terms of the highest esteem of Lord Orville, calling him, in Marmontel's words, "*Un jeune homme comme il y en a peu.*"[2]

I did not think this conversation very agreeably interrupted by the entrance of Mr. Lovel. Indeed I am heartily sorry he is now at the Hotwells. He made his compliments with the most obsequious respect to

---

1. "An annual hand-book of royal families and their courts" (*OED*).
2. "A young man like whom there are few." The allusion is to the story "*La Femme comme il y en a peu,*" in the *Contes Moraux* (1761) of Jean-François Marmontel (1723–99).

Mrs. Beaumont, but took no sort of notice of any other person.

In a few minutes Lady Louisa Larpent made her appearance. The same manners prevailed; for courtsying, with "I hope you are well, Ma'am," to Mrs. Beaumont, she passed straight forward to her seat on the sofa, where, leaning her head on her hand, she cast her languishing eyes round the room, with a vacant stare, as if determined, though she looked, not to see who was in it.

Mr. Lovel, presently approaching her, with reverence the most profound, hoped her Ladyship was not indisposed.

"Mr. Lovel!" cried she, raising her head, "I declare I did not see you: Have you been here long?"

"By my *watch*, Madam," said he, "only five minutes,—but by your Ladyship's absence, as many hours."

"O! now I think of it," cried she, "I am very angry with you,—so go along, do, for I sha'n't speak to you all day."

"Heaven forbid your La'ship's displeasure should last so long! in such cruel circumstances, a day would seem an age. But in what have I been so unfortunate as to offend?"

"O, you half killed me, the other morning, with terror! I have not yet recovered from my fright. How could you be so cruel as to drive your phaeton against my Lord Merton's?"

"'Pon honour, Ma'am, your La'ship does me wrong; it was all owing to the horses,—there was no curbing them. I protest I suffered more than your Ladyship from the terror of alarming you."

Just then entered Lord Merton; stalking up to Mrs. Beaumont, to whom alone he bowed, he hoped he had not made her wait; and then advancing to Lady Louisa, said, in a careless manner, "How is your Ladyship this morning?"

"Not well at all," answered she; "I have been dying with the head-ach ever since I got up."

"Indeed!" cried he, with a countenance wholly unmoved, "I am very unhappy to hear it. But should not your Ladyship have some advice?"

"I am quite sick of advice," answered she; "Mr. Ridgeway has but just left me,—but he has done me no good. Nobody here knows what is the matter with me, yet they all see how indifferent[3] I am."

"Your Ladyship's constitution," said Mr. Lovel, "is infinitely delicate."

"Indeed it is," cried she, in a low voice "I am *nerve* all over!"

"I am glad, however," said Lord Merton, "that you did not take the air this morning, for Coverley has been driving against me as if he was mad: he has got two of the finest spirited horses I ever saw."

"Pray, my Lord," cried she, "why did not you bring Mr. Coverley with you? he's a droll creature; I like him monstrously."

3. Ailing.

"Why, he promised to be here as soon as me. I suppose he'll come before dinner's over."

In the midst of this trifling conversation, Lord Orville made his appearance. O how different was his address! how superior did he look and move, to all about him! Having paid his respects to Mrs. Beaumont, and then to Mrs. Selwyn, he came up to me, and said, "I hope Miss Anville has not suffered from the fatigue of Monday morning!" Then, turning to Lady Louisa, who seemed rather surprised at his speaking to me, he added, "Give me leave, Sister, to introduce Miss Anville to you."

Lady Louisa, half-rising, said, very coldly, that she should be glad of the honour of knowing me; and then, abruptly turning to Lord Merton and Mr. Lovel, continued, in a half-whisper, her conversation.

For my part, I had risen and courtsied, and now, feeling very foolish, I seated myself again; first I blushed at the unexpected politeness of Lord Orville, and immediately afterwards, at the contemptuous failure of it in his sister. How can that young lady see her brother so universally admired for his manners and deportment, and yet be so unamiably opposite to him in hers! But while *his* mind, enlarged and noble, rises superior to the little prejudices of rank, *hers*, feeble and unsteady, sinks beneath their influence.

Lord Orville, I am sure, was hurt and displeased: he bit his lips, and turning from her, addressed himself wholly to me, till we were summoned to dinner. Do you think I was not grateful for his attention? yes, indeed, and every angry idea I had entertained was totally obliterated.

As we were seating ourselves at the table, Mr. Coverley came into the room: he made a thousand apologies in a breath for being so late, but said he had been retarded by a little accident, for that he had overturned his phaeton, and broke it all to pieces. Lady Louisa screamed at this intelligence, and looking at Lord Merton, declared she would never go into a phaeton again.

"O," cried he, "never mind Jack Coverley, for he does not know how to drive."

"My Lord," cried Mr. Coverley, "I'll drive against *you* for a thousand pounds."

"Done!" returned the other; "name your day, and we'll each chuse a judge."

"The sooner the better," cried Mr. Coverley; "to-morrow, if the carriage can be repaired."

"These enterprises," said Mrs. Selwyn, "are very proper for men of rank, since 'tis a million to one but both parties will be incapacitated for any better employment."

"For Heaven's sake," cried Lady Louisa, changing colour, "don't talk so shockingly! Pray, my Lord, pray Mr. Coverley, don't alarm me in this manner."

"Compose yourself, Lady Louisa," said Mrs. Beaumont, "the gentle-

men will think better of the scheme; they are neither of them in earnest."

"The very mention of such a scheme," said Lady Louisa, taking out
her salts, "makes me tremble all over! Indeed, my Lord, you have frightened me to death! I sha'n't eat a morsel of dinner."

"Permit me," said Lord Orville, "to propose some other subject for
the present, and we will discuss this matter another time."

"Pray, Brother, excuse me; my Lord must give me his word to drop
this project,—for, I declare, it has made me sick as death."

"To compromise the matter," said Lord Orville, "suppose, if both parties are unwilling to give up the bet, that, to make the ladies easy, we
change its object to something less dangerous?"

This proposal was so strongly seconded by all the party, that both
Lord Merton and Mr. Coverley were obliged to comply with it: and it
was then agreed that the affair should be finally settled in the afternoon.

"I shall now be entirely out of conceit with phaetons again," said Mrs.
Selwyn, "though Lord Orville had almost reconciled me to them."

"My Lord Orville!" cried the witty Mr. Coverley, "why, my Lord
Orville is as careful,—egad, as careful as an old woman! Why, I'd drive
a one-horse cart against my Lord's phaeton for a hundred guineas!"

This sally occasioned much laughter; for Mr. Coverley, I find, is
regarded as a man of infinite humour.

"Perhaps, Sir," said Mrs. Selwyn, "you have not discovered the *reason*
my Lord Orville is so careful?"

"Why, no, Ma'am; I must own, I never heard any particular reason
for it."

"Why then, Sir, I'll tell it you; and I believe you will confess it to be
very particular; his Lordship's friends are not yet tired of him."

Lord Orville laughed and bowed. Mr. Coverley, a little confused,
turned to Lord Merton, and said, "No foul play, my Lord! I remember
your Lordship recommended me to the notice of this lady the other
morning, and, egad, I believe you have been doing me the same office
to-day."

"Give you joy, Jack!" cried Lord Merton, with a loud laugh.

After this, the conversation turned wholly upon eating, a subject
which was discussed with the utmost delight; and, had I not known they
were men of rank and fashion, I should have imagined that Lord Merton, Mr. Lovel, and Mr. Coverley, had all been professed cooks; for they
displayed so much knowledge of sauces and made dishes, and of the
various methods of dressing the same things, that I am persuaded they
must have given much time, and much study, to make themselves such
adepts in this *art*. It would be very difficult to determine, whether they
were most to be distinguished as *gluttons*, or *epicures*; for they were, at
once, dainty and voracious, understood the right and the wrong of every
dish, and alike emptied the one and the other. I should have been quite

sick of their remarks, had I not been entertained by seeing that Lord Orville, who, I am sure, was equally disgusted, not only read my sentiments, but, by his countenance, communicated to me his own.

When dinner was over, Mrs. Beaumont recommended the gentlemen to the care of Lord Orville, and then attended the ladies to the drawing-room.

The conversation, till tea-time, was extremely insipid; Mrs. Selwyn reserved herself for the gentlemen, Mrs. Beaumont was grave, and Lady Louisa languid.

But, at tea, every body revived; we were joined by the gentlemen, and gaiety took place of dullness.

Since I, as Mr. Lovel says, am *Nobody*, I seated myself quietly on a window, and not very near to any body: Lord Merton, Mr. Coverley, and Mr. Lovel, severally passed me without notice, and surrounded the chair of Lady Louisa Larpent. I must own, I was rather piqued at the behaviour of Mr. Lovel, as he had formerly known me. It is true, I most sincerely despise his foppery, yet I should be grieved to meet with *contempt* from any body. But I was by no means sorry to find, that Lord Merton was determined not to know me before Lady Louisa, as his neglect relieved me from much embarrassment. As to Mr. Coverley, his attention or disregard were equally indifferent to me. Yet, altogether, I feel extremely uncomfortable in finding myself considered in a light very inferior to the rest of the company.

But, when Lord Orville appeared, the scene changed: he came up stairs last, and seeing me sit alone, not only spoke to me directly, but drew a chair next mine, and honoured me with his entire attention.

He enquired very particularly after my health, and hoped I had already found benefit from the Bristol air. "How little did I imagine," added he, "when I had last the pleasure of seeing you in town, that ill health would, in so short a time, have brought you hither! I am ashamed of myself for the satisfaction I feel at seeing you,—yet, how can I help it?"

He then enquired after the Mirvan family, and spoke of Mrs. Mirvan in terms of most just praise. "She is gentle and amiable," said he, "a true feminine character."

"Yes, indeed," answered I, "and her sweet daughter, to say every thing of her at once, is just the daughter such a mother deserves."

"I am glad of it," said he, "for both their sakes, as such near relations must always reflect credit or disgrace on each other."

After this, he began to speak of the beauties of Clifton; but, in a few moments, he was interrupted by a call from the company, to discuss the affair of the wager. Lord Merton and Mr. Coverley, though they had been discoursing upon the subject some time, could not fix upon any thing that satisfied them both.

When they asked the assistance of Lord Orville, he proposed that every body present should vote something, and that the two gentlemen should draw lots which, from the several votes, should decide the bet.

"We must then begin with the ladies," said Lord Orville; and applied to Mrs. Selwyn.

"With all my heart," answered she, with her usual readiness; "and, since the gentlemen are not allowed to risk their *necks*, suppose we decide the bet by their *heads?*"

"By our heads?" cried Mr. Coverley; "Egad, I don't understand you."

"I will then explain myself more fully. As I doubt not but you are both excellent classics, suppose, for the good of your own memories, and the entertainment and surprise of the company, the thousand pounds should fall to the share of him who can repeat by heart the longest ode of Horace?"[4]

Nobody could help laughing, the two gentlemen applied to excepted; who seemed, each of them, rather at a loss in what manner to receive this unexpected proposal. At length Mr. Coverley, bowing low, said, "Will your Lordship please to begin?"

"Devil take me if I do!" answered he, turning on his heel, and stalking to the window.

"Come, gentlemen," said Mrs. Selwyn, "why do you hesitate? I am sure you cannot be afraid of a weak *woman?* Besides, if you should chance to be out, Mr. Lovel, I dare say, will have the goodness to assist you."

The laugh, now, turned against Mr. Lovel, whose change of countenance manifested no great pleasure at the transition.

"Me, Madam!" said he, colouring, "no, really I must beg to be excused."

"Why so, Sir?"

"Why so, Ma'am?—Why, really,—as to that,—'pon honour, Ma'am, you are rather—a little severe;—for how is it possible for a man who is in the House, to study the classics? I assure you, Ma'am," (with an affected shrug) "I find quite business enough for *my* poor head, in studying politics."

"But, did you study politics at school, and at the university?"

"At the university!" repeated he with an embarrassed look; "why, as to that, Ma'am,—no, I can't say I did; but then, what with riding,—and—and—and so forth,—really, one has not much time, even at the university, for mere reading."

"But, to be sure, Sir, you *have* read the classics?"

"O dear, yes, Ma'am!—very often,—but not very—not very lately."

"Which of the odes do you recommend to these gentlemen to begin with?"

"Which of the odes!—Really, Ma'am, as to that, I have no very partic-

---

4. Quintus Horatius Flaccus (65–8 B.C.), Roman poet.

ular choice,—for, to own the truth, that Horace was never a very great favourite with me."

"In truth I believe you!" said Mrs. Selwyn, very drily.

Lord Merton, again advancing into the circle, with a nod and a laugh, said, "Give you joy, Lovel!"

Lord Orville next applied to Mrs. Beaumont for her vote.

"It would very agreeably remind me of past times," said she, "when *bowing* was in fashion, if the bet was to depend upon the best-made bow."

"Egad, my Lord!" cried Mr. Coverley, "there I should beat you hollow, for your Lordship never bows at all."

"And, pray Sir, do *you?*" said Mrs. Selwyn.

"Do *I,* Ma'am?" cried he, "Why, only see!"

"I protest," cried she, "I should have taken *that* for a *shrug,* if you had not told me 'twas a bow."

"My lord," cried Mr. Coverley, "let's practise;" and then, most ridiculously, they pranced about the room, making bows.

"We must now," said Lord Orville, turning to me, "call upon Miss Anville."

"O no, my Lord," cried I, "indeed I have nothing to propose." He would not, however, be refused, but urged me so much to say *something,* that at last, not to make him wait any longer, I ventured to propose an extempore couplet upon some given subject. Mr. Coverley instantly made me a bow, or, according to Mrs. Selwyn, a *shrug,* crying, "Thank you, Ma'am; egad, that's my *fort!* [5] —Why, my Lord, the Fates seem against you."

Lady Louisa was then applied to; and every body seemed eager to hear her opinion. "I don't know what to say, I declare," cried she, affectedly; "can't you pass me?"

"By no means!" said Lord Merton.

"Is it possible your Ladyship can make so cruel a request?" said Mr. Lovel.

"Egad," cried Mr. Coverley, "if your Ladyship does not help us in this dilemma, we shall be forced to return to our phaetons."

"Oh," cried Lady Louisa, screaming, "you frightful creature, you, how can you be so abominable?"

I believe this trifling lasted near half an hour; when, at length, every body being tired, it was given up, and she said she would consider against another time.

Lord Orville now called upon Mr. Lovel, who, after about ten minutes' deliberation, proposed, with a most important face, to determine the wager by who should draw the longest straw!

I had much difficulty to forbear laughing at this unmeaning scheme;

5. Strength.

but saw, to my great surprise, not the least change of countenance in any other person: and, since we came home, Mrs. Selwyn has informed me, that to *draw straws* is a fashion of betting by no means uncommon! Good God! my dear Sir, does it not seem as if money were of no value or service, since those who possess, squander it away in a manner so infinitely absurd!

It now only remained for Lord Orville to speak; and the attention of the company shewed the expectations he had raised; yet, I believe, they by no means prevented his proposal from being heard with amazement; for it was no other, than that the money should be his due, who, according to the opinion of two judges, should bring the worthiest object with whom to share it!

They all stared, without speaking. Indeed, I believe every one, for a moment at least, experienced something like shame, from having either proposed or countenanced an extravagance so useless and frivolous. For my part, I was so much struck and affected by a rebuke so noble to these spendthrifts, that I felt my eyes filled with tears.

The short silence, and momentary reflection into which the company was surprised, Mr. Coverley was the first to dispel, by saying, "Egad, my Lord, your Lordship has a most remarkable odd way of taking things."

"Faith," said the incorrigible Lord Merton, "if this scheme takes, I shall fix upon my Swiss[6] to share with me; for I don't know a worthier fellow breathing."

After a few more of these attempts at wit, the two gentlemen agreed that they would settle the affair the next morning.

The conversation then took a different turn, but I did not give it sufficient attention to write any account of it. Not long after, Lord Orville resuming his seat next mine, said, "Why is Miss Anville so thoughtful?"

"I am sorry, my Lord," said I, "to consider myself among those who have so justly incurred your censure."

"My censure!—you amaze me!"

"Indeed, my Lord, you have made me quite ashamed of myself, for having given my vote so foolishly, when an opportunity offered, if, like your Lordship, I had had the sense to use it, of shewing some humanity."

"You treat this too seriously," said he smiling; "and I hardly know if you do not now mean a rebuke to *me*."

"To you, my Lord!"

"Nay, who are most deserving of it, those who adapt their conversation to the company, or, those who affect to be superior to it?"

"O, my Lord, who else would do you so little justice?"

"I flatter myself," answered he, "that, in fact, your opinion and mine, in this point, are the same, though you condescended to comply with the humour of the company. It is for me, therefore, to apologize for so

6. His Swiss servant.

unseasonable a gravity, which, but for the particular interest that I now take in the affairs of Lord Merton, I should not have been so officious to display."

Such a compliment as this could not fail to reconcile me to myself; and with revived spirits, I entered into a conversation, which he supported with me till Mrs. Selwyn's carriage was announced, and we returned home.

During our ride, Mrs. Selwyn very much surprised me, by asking if I thought my health would now permit me to give up my morning walks to the pump-room, for the purpose of spending a week at Clifton? "for this poor Mrs. Beaumont," added she, "is so eager to have a discharge in full of her debt to me, that, out of mere compassion, I am induced to listen to her. Besides, she has always a house full of people, and though they are chiefly fools and coxcombs, yet there is some pleasure in cutting them up."

I begged I might not, by any means, prevent her following her inclination, as my health was now very well established. And so, my dear Sir, to-morrow we are to be, actually, the guests of Mrs. Beaumont.

I am not much delighted at this scheme for, greatly as I am flattered by the attention of Lord Orville, it is not very comfortable to be neglected by every body else. Besides, as I am sure I owe the particularity of his civility to a generous feeling for my situation, I cannot expect him to support it so long as a week.

How often do I wish, since I am absent from you, that I was under the protection of Mrs. Mirvan! It is true, Mrs. Selwyn is very obliging, and, in every respect, treats me as an equal; but she is contented with behaving well herself, and does not, with a distinguishing politeness, raise and support me with others. Yet I mean not to blame her, for I know she is sincerely my friend; but the fact is, she is herself so much occupied in conversation, when in company, that she has neither leisure nor thought to attend to the silent.

Well, I must take my chance! But I knew not, till now, how requisite are birth and fortune to the attainment of respect and civility.

Letter IV.

Clifton, Sept. 20th.

Here I am, my dear Sir, under the same roof, and inmate of the same house, as Lord Orville! Indeed, if this were not the case, my situation would be very disagreeable, as you will easily believe, when I tell you the light in which I am generally considered.

"My dear," said Mrs. Selwyn, "did you ever before meet with that egregious fop, Lovel?"

I very readily satisfied her as to my acquaintance with him.

"O then," said she, "I am the less surprised at his ill-nature, since he has already injured you."

I begged her to explain herself; and then she told me, that while Lord Orville was speaking to me, Lady Louisa said to Mr. Lovel, "Do you know who that is?"

"Why, Ma'am, no, 'pon honour," answered he, "I can't absolutely say I do; I only know she is a kind of a toad-eater.[1] She made her first appearance in that capacity last Spring, when she attended Miss Mirvan, a young lady of Kent."

How cruel is it, my dear Sir, to be thus exposed to the impertinent suggestions of a man who is determined to do me ill offices! Lady Louisa may well despise a *toad-eater*; but, thank Heaven, her brother has not heard, or does not credit, the mortifying appellation. Mrs. Selwyn said, she would advise me to *pay my court* to this Mr. Lovel; "for," said she, "though he is malicious, he is fashionable, and may do you some harm in the great world." But I should disdain myself as much as I do him, were I capable of such duplicity, as to flatter a man whom I scorn and despise.

We were received by Mrs. Beaumont with great civility, and by Lord Orville with something more. As to Lady Louisa, she scarcely perceived that we were in the room.

There has been company here all day, part of which I have spent most happily; for after tea, when the ladies played at cards, Lord Orville, who does not, and I who cannot play, were consequently at our own disposal; and then his Lordship entered into a conversation with me, which lasted till supper-time.

Almost insensibly, I find the constraint, the reserve, I have been wont to feel in his presence, wear away; the politeness, the sweetness, with which he speaks to me, restore all my natural chearfulness, and make me almost as easy as he is himself; and the more so, as, if I may judge by his looks, I am rather raised, than sunk, of late in his opinion.

I asked him, how the bet was, at last, to be decided? He told me, that, to his great satisfaction, the parties had been prevailed upon to lower the sum from one thousand to one hundred pounds; and that they had agreed it should be determined, by a race between two old women, one of which was to be chosen by each side, and both were to be proved more than eighty years of age, though, in other respects, strong and healthy as possible.

When I expressed my surprise at this extraordinary method of spending so much money, "I am charmed," said he, "at the novelty of meeting with one so unhackneyed in the world, as not to be yet influenced by custom to forget the use of reason: for certain it is, that the prevalence

---

1. "A humble friend or dependant; specifically, a female companion or attendant" (*OED*).

of fashion makes the greatest absurdities pass uncensured, and the mind naturally accommodates itself, even to the most ridiculous improprieties, if they occur frequently."

"I should have hoped," said I, "that the humane proposal made yesterday by your Lordship, would have had more effect."

"O," cried he, laughing, "I was so far from expecting any success, that I shall think myself very fortunate if I escape the wit of Mr. Coverley in a lampoon! yet I spoke openly, because I do not wish to conceal that I am no friend to gaming."

After this, he took up the New Bath Guide,[2] and read it with me till supper-time. In our way down stairs, Lady Louisa said, "I thought, Brother, you were engaged this evening?"

"Yes, Sister," answered he, "and I *have* been engaged."[3] And he bowed to me with an air of gallantry that rather confused me.

September 23d.

Almost insensibly have three days glided on since I wrote last, and so serenely, that, but for your absence, I could not have formed a wish. My residence here is much happier than I had dared expect. The attention with which Lord Orville honours me is as uniform as it is flattering, and seems to result from a benevolence of heart that proves him as much a stranger to caprice as to pride; for, as his particular civilities arose from a generous resentment at seeing me neglected, so will they, I trust, continue, as long as I shall, in any degree, deserve them. I am now not merely easy, but even gay in his presence: such is the effect of true politeness, that it banishes all restraint and embarrassment. When we walk out, he condescends to be my companion, and keeps by my side all the way we go. When we read, he marks the passages most worthy to be noticed, draws out my sentiments, and favours me with his own. At table, where he always sits next to me, he obliges me by a thousand nameless attentions, while the distinguishing good-breeding with which he treats me, prevents my repining at the visibly-felt superiority of the rest of the company. A thousand occasional meetings could not have brought us to that degree of social freedom, which four days spent under the same roof have, insensibly, been productive of: and, as my only friend in this house, Mrs. Selwyn, is too much engrossed in perpetual conversation to attend much to me, Lord Orville seems to regard me as a helpless stranger, and, as such, to think me entitled to his good offices and protection. Indeed, my dear Sir, I have reason to hope, that the depreciating opinion he formerly entertained of me is succeeded by one infinitely more partial. — It may be that I flatter myself, but yet his looks, his attentions, his desire of drawing me into conversation, and his solici-

---

2. *The New Bath Guide: or Memoirs of the B-r-d Family. In a Series of Poetical Epistles* (1766), a comic poem by Christopher Anstey (1724–1805).

3. Lady Louisa means "engaged" in the sense of having made an appointment, while Lord Orville means "charmed" or "attracted."

tude to oblige me, all conspire to make me hope I do not. In short, my dearest Sir, these last four happy days would repay me for months of sorrow and pain!

Letter V.

Clifton, Sept. 24th.

This morning I came down stairs very early, and, supposing that the family would not assemble for some time, I strolled out, purposing to take a long walk, in the manner I was wont to do at Berry Hill, before breakfast. But I had scarce shut the garden-gate, before I was met by a gentleman, who, immediately bowing to me, I recollected to be the unhappy Mr. Macartney. Very much surprised, I courtsied, and stopped till he came up to me. He was still in mourning, but looked better than when I saw him last, though he had the same air of melancholy which so much struck me at first sight of him.

Addressing me with the utmost respect, "I am happy, Madam," said he, "to have met with you so soon. I came to Bristol but yesterday, and have had no small difficulty in tracing you to Clifton."

"Did you know, then, of my being here?"

"I did, Madam; the sole motive of my journey was to see you. I have been to Berry Hill, and there I had my intelligence, and, at the same time, the unwelcome information of your ill health."

"Good God! Sir,—and can you possibly have taken so much trouble?"

"Trouble! Oh, Madam, could there be any, to return you, the moment I had the power, my personal acknowledgments for your goodness?"

I then enquired after Madame Duval and the Snow-hill family. He told me, they were all well, and that Madame Duval proposed soon returning to Paris. When I congratulated him upon looking better, "It is yourself, Madam," said he, "you should congratulate, for to your humanity alone it may now be owing that I exist at all." He then told me, that his affairs were now in a less desperate situation, and that he hoped, by the assistance of time and reason, to accommodate his mind to a more chearful submission to his fate. "The interest you so generously took in my affliction," added he, "assures me you will not be displeased to hear of my better fortune: I was therefore eager to acquaint you with it." He then told me, that his friend, the moment he had received his letter, quitted Paris, and flew to give him his personal assistance and consolation. With a heavy heart, he acknowledged, he accepted it; "but yet," he added, "I *have* accepted it, and therefore, as bound equally by duty and honour, my first step was to hasten to the benefactress of my distress, and to return" (presenting me something in a paper) "the only part of my obligations that *can* be returned; for the rest, I have nothing but my gratitude to offer, and must always be contented to consider myself her debtor."

I congratulated him most sincerely upon his dawning prosperity, but begged he would not deprive me of the pleasure of being his friend, and declined receiving the money, till his affairs were more settled.

While this point was in agitation, I heard Lord Orville's voice, enquiring of the gardener if he had seen me? I immediately opened the garden-gate, and his Lordship, advancing to me with quickness, said, "Good God, Miss Anville, have you been out, alone? Breakfast has been ready some time, and I have been round the garden in search of you."

"Your Lordship has been very good," said I; "but I hope you have not waited."

"Not waited!" repeated he, smiling. "Do you think we could sit down quietly to breakfast, with the idea that you had run away from us? But come," (offering to hand me) "if we do not return, they will suppose *I* am run away too; and they very naturally may, as they know the attraction of the magnet that draws me."

"I will come, my Lord," said I, rather embarrassed, "in two minutes." Then, turning to Mr. Macartney, with yet more embarrassment, I wished him good morning.

He advanced towards the garden, with the paper still in his hand.

"No, no," cried I, "some other time."

"May I then, Madam, have the honour of seeing you again?"

I did not dare take the liberty of inviting any body to the house of Mrs. Beaumont, nor yet had I the presence of mind to make an excuse; and, therefore, not knowing how to refuse him, I said, "Perhaps you may be this way again to-morrow morning,—and I believe I shall walk out before breakfast."

He bowed, and went away; while I, turning again to Lord Orville, saw his countenance so much altered, that I was frightened at what I had so hastily said. He did not again offer me his hand, but walked, silent and slow, by my side. Good Heaven! thought I, what may he not suppose from this adventure? May he not, by my desire of meeting Mr. Macartney to-morrow, imagine it was by design I walked out to meet him to-day? Tormented by this apprehension, I determined to avail myself of the freedom which his behaviour since I came hither has encouraged; and, since he would not ask any questions, begin an explanation myself. I therefore slackened my pace, to gain time, and then said, "Was not your Lordship surprised to see me speaking with a stranger?"

"A stranger?" repeated he; "is it possible that gentleman can be a stranger to you?"

"No, my Lord,"—said I, stammering, "not to *me*,—but only it might look—he might seem—"

"No, believe me," said he, with a forced smile, "I could never suppose Miss Anville would make an appointment with a stranger."

"An appointment, my Lord?" repeated I, colouring violently.

"Pardon me, Madam," answered he, "but I thought I had heard one."

I was so much confounded, that I could not speak; yet, finding he walked quietly on, I could not endure he should make his own interpretation of my silence; and therefore, as soon as I recovered from my surprise, I said, "Indeed, my Lord, you are much mistaken,—Mr. Macartney had particular business with me,—and I could not,—I knew not how to refuse seeing him,—but indeed, my Lord—I had not,—he had not,—" I stammered so terribly that I could not go on.

"I am very sorry," said he, gravely, "that I have been so unfortunate as to distress you; but I should not have followed you had I not imagined you were merely walked out for the air."

"And so I was!" cried I, eagerly, "indeed, my Lord, I was! My meeting with Mr. Macartney was quite accidental; and if your Lordship thinks there is any impropriety in my seeing him to-morrow, I am ready to give up that intention."

"If *I* think!" said he, in a tone of surprise; "surely Miss Anville must best judge for herself! surely she cannot leave the arbitration of a point so delicate to one who is ignorant of all the circumstances which attend it?"

"If," said I, "it was worth your Lordship's time to hear them,—you should *not* be ignorant of the circumstances which attend it."

"The sweetness of Miss Anville's disposition," said he, in a softened voice, "I have long admired, and the offer of a communication which does me so much honour, is too grateful to me not to be eagerly caught at."

Just then, Mrs. Selwyn opened the parlour-window, and our conversation ended. I was rallied upon my passion for solitary walking, but no questions were asked me.

When breakfast was over, I hoped to have had some opportunity of speaking with Lord Orville; but Lord Merton and Mr. Coverley came in, and insisted upon his opinion of the spot they had fixed upon for the old women's race. The ladies declared they would be of the party, and accordingly, we all went.

The race is to be run in Mrs. Beaumont's garden; the two gentlemen are as anxious, as if their joint lives depended upon it. They have, at length, fixed upon objects, but have found great difficulty in persuading them to practise running, in order to try their strength. This grand affair is to be decided next Thursday.

When we returned to the house, the entrance of more company still prevented my having any conversation with Lord Orville. I was very much chagrined, as I knew he was engaged at the Hotwells in the afternoon. Seeing, therefore, no probability of speaking to him before the time of my meeting Mr. Macartney arrived, I determined that, rather than risk his ill opinion, I would leave Mr. Macartney to his own suggestions.

Yet, when I reflected upon his peculiar situation, his poverty, his sadness, and, more than all the rest, the idea I knew he entertained of what he calls his obligations to me, I could not resolve upon a breach of promise, which might be attributed to causes of all others the most offensive to one whom misfortune has made extremely suspicious of slights and contempt.

After the most uneasy consideration, I at length determined upon writing an excuse, which would, at once, save me from either meeting or affronting him. I therefore begged Mrs. Selwyn's leave to send her man to the Hotwells, which she instantly granted; and then I wrote the following note.

To Mr. Macartney.

SIR,

As it will not be in my power to walk out to-morrow morning, I would by no means give you the trouble of coming to Clifton.

I hope, however, to have the pleasure of seeing you before you quit Bristol. I am,

Sir,
Your obedient servant,
EVELINA ANVILLE

I desired the servant to enquire at the Pump-room where Mr. Macartney lived, and returned to the parlour.

As soon as the company dispersed, the ladies retired to dress. I then, unexpectedly, found myself alone with Lord Orville; who, the moment I rose to follow Mrs. Selwyn, advanced to me, and said, "Will Miss Anville pardon my impatience, if I remind her of the promise she was so good as to make me this morning?"

I stopped, and would have returned to my seat, but, before I had time, the servants came to lay the cloth. He retreated, and went towards the window; and, while I was considering in what manner to begin, I could not help asking myself what *right* I had to communicate the affairs of Mr. Macartney; and I doubted whether, to clear myself from one act of imprudence, I had not committed another.

Distressed by this reflection, I thought it best to quit the room, and give myself some time for consideration before I spoke; and therefore, only saying I must hasten to dress, I ran up stairs: rather abruptly, I own, and so, I fear, Lord Orville must think; yet what could I do? unused to the situations in which I find myself, and embarrassed by the slightest difficulties, I seldom, till too late, discover how I ought to act.

Just as we were all assembled to dinner, Mrs. Selwyn's man, coming into the parlour, presented to me a letter, and said, "I can't find out Mr. Macartney, Madam; but the post-office people will let you know if they hear of him."

I was extremely ashamed of this public message; and meeting the eyes of Lord Orville, which were earnestly fixed on me, my confusion redoubled, and I knew not which way to look. All dinner-time, he was as silent as myself, and the moment it was in my power, I left the table, and went to my own room. Mrs. Selwyn presently followed me, and her questions obliged me to own almost all the particulars of my acquaintance with Mr. Macartney, in order to excuse my writing to him. She said it was a most romantic affair, and spoke her sentiments with great severity, declaring that she had no doubt but he was an adventurer and an impostor.

And now, my dear Sir, I am totally at a loss what I ought to do: the more I reflect, the more sensible I am of the utter impropriety, nay, treachery, of revealing the story, and publishing the misfortunes and poverty of Mr. Macartney? who has an undoubted right to my secrecy and discretion, and whose letter charges me to regard his communication as sacred.—And yet, the appearance of mystery,—perhaps something worse, which this affair must have to Lord Orville,—his seriousness,—and the promise I have made him, are inducements scarce to be resisted for trusting him, with the openness he has reason to expect from me.

I am equally distressed, too, whether or not I should see Mr. Macartney to-morrow morning.

Oh, Sir, could I now be enlightened by your counsel, from what anxiety and perplexity should I be relieved!

But no,—I ought not to betray Mr. Macartney, and I will not forfeit a confidence which would never have been reposed in me, but from a reliance upon my honour which I should blush to find myself unworthy of. Desirous as I am of the good opinion of Lord Orville, I will endeavour to act as if I was guided by your advice, and, making it my sole aim to *deserve* it, leave to time and to fate my success or disappointment.

Since I have formed this resolution, my mind is more at ease; but I will not finish my letter till the affair is decided.

Sept. 25th.

I rose very early this morning, and, after a thousand different plans, not being able to resolve upon giving poor Mr. Macartney leave to suppose I neglected him, I thought it incumbent upon me to keep my word, since he had not received my letter; I therefore determined to make my own apologies, not to stay with him two minutes, and to excuse myself from meeting him any more.

Yet, uncertain whether I was wrong or right, it was with fear and trembling that I opened the garden-gate,—judge, then, of my feelings, when the first object I saw was Lord Orville!—he, too, looked extremely disconcerted, and said, in a hesitating manner, "Pardon me, Madam,—I did not intend,—I did not imagine you would have been here so soon—or,—or I would not have come."—And then, with a hasty bow, he passed me, and proceeded to the garden.

I was scarce able to stand, so greatly did I feel myself shocked; but, upon my saying, almost involuntarily, "Oh my Lord!"—he turned back, and, after a short pause, said, "Did you speak to *me*, Madam?"

I could not immediately answer; I seemed *choaked*, and was even forced to support myself by the garden-gate.

Lord Orville, soon recovering his dignity, said, "I know not how to apologize for being, just now, at this place;—and I cannot, immediately,—if *ever*,—clear myself from the imputation of impertinent curiosity, to which I fear you will attribute it: however, at present, I will only entreat your pardon, without detaining you any longer." Again he bowed, and left me.

For some moments, I remained fixed to the same spot, and in the same position, immoveably as if I had been transformed to stone. My first impulse was to call him back, and instantly tell him the whole affair; but I checked this desire, though I would have given the world to have indulged it; something like pride aided what I thought due to Mr. Macartney, and I determined not only to keep his secret, but to delay any sort of explanation till Lord Orville, should condescend to request it.

Slowly he walked, and before he entered the house, he looked back, but hastily withdrew his eyes, upon finding I observed him.

Indeed, my dear Sir, you cannot easily imagine a situation more uncomfortable than mine was at that time; to be suspected by Lord Orville of any clandestine actions, wounded my soul; I was too much discomposed to wait for Mr. Macartney, nor, in truth, could I endure to have the design of my staying so well known. Yet I was so extremely agitated, that I could hardly move, and, I have reason to believe, Lord Orville, from the parlour-window, saw me tottering along, for, before I had taken five steps, he came out, and hastening to meet me, said, "I fear you are not well; pray allow me, (offering his arm) to assist you."

"No, my Lord," said I, with all the resolution I could assume; yet I was affected by an attention, at that time so little expected, and forced to turn away my head to conceal my emotion.

"You *must*," said he, with earnestness, "indeed you must,—I am sure you are not well;—refuse me not the honour of assisting you;" and, almost forcibly, he took my hand, and drawing it under his arm, obliged me to lean upon him. That I submitted was partly the effect of surprise at an earnestness so uncommon in Lord Orville, and partly, that I did not, just then, dare trust my voice to make any objection.

When we came to the house, he led me into the parlour, and to a chair, and begged to know if I would not have a glass of water.

"No, my Lord, I thank you," said I, "I am perfectly recovered;" and, rising, I walked to the window, where, for some time, I pretended to be occupied in looking at the garden.

Determined as I was to act honourably by Mr. Macartney, I yet most anxiously wished to be restored to the good opinion of Lord Orville; but his silence, and the thoughtfulness of his air, discouraged me from speaking.

My situation soon grew disagreeable and embarrassing, and I resolved to return to my chamber till breakfast was ready. To remain longer, I feared, might seem *asking* for his enquiries; and I was sure it would ill become me to be more eager to speak, than he was to hear.

Just as I reached the door, turning to me hastily, he said, "Are you going, Miss Anville?"

"I am, my Lord," answered I, yet I stopped.

"Perhaps to return to—but I beg your pardon!" he spoke with a degree of agitation that made me readily comprehend he meant *to the Garden*, and I instantly said, "To my own room, my Lord." And again I would have gone; but, convinced by my answer that I understood him, I believe he was sorry for the insinuation; he approached me with a very serious air, though, at the same time, he forced a smile, and said, "I know not what evil genius pursues me this morning, but I seem destined to do or to say something I ought not: I am so much ashamed of myself, that I can scarce solicit your forgiveness."

"My forgiveness! my Lord?" cried I, abashed, rather than elated by his condescension, "surely you cannot—you are not serious?"

"Indeed never more so; yet, if I may be my own interpreter, Miss Anville's countenance pronounces my pardon."

"I know not, my Lord, how any one can *pardon*, who has never been offended."

"You are very good; yet I could expect no less from a sweetness of disposition which baffles all comparison: will you not think I am an encroacher, and that I take advantage of your goodness, should I once more remind you of the promise you vouchsafed me yesterday?"

"No, indeed; on the contrary, I shall be very happy to acquit myself in your Lordship's opinion."

"Acquittal you need not," said he, leading me again to the window, "yet I own my curiosity is strongly excited."

When I was seated, I found myself much at a loss what to say; yet, after a short silence, assuming all the courage in my power, "Will you not, my Lord," said I, "think me trifling and capricious, should I own I have repented the promise I made, and should I entreat your Lordship not to insist upon my strict performance of it?"—I spoke so hastily, that I did not, at the time, consider the impropriety of what I said.

As he was entirely silent, and profoundly attentive, I continued to speak without interruption.

"If your Lordship, by any other means, knew the circumstances attending my acquaintance with Mr. Macartney, I am most sure you would yourself disapprove my relating them. He is a gentleman, and has been very unfortunate,—but I am not,—I think,—at liberty to say more; yet I am sure, if he knew your Lordship wished to hear any particulars of his affairs, he would readily consent to my acknowledging them;— shall I, my Lord, ask his permission?"

"*His* affairs!" repeated Lord Orville; "by no means, I have not the least curiosity about them."

"I beg your Lordship's pardon,—but indeed I had understood the contrary."

"Is it possible, Madam, you could suppose the affairs of an utter stranger can excite my curiosity?"

The gravity and coldness with which he asked this question, very much abashed me; but Lord Orville is the most delicate of men, and, presently recollecting himself, he added, "I mean not to speak with indifference of any friend of yours,—far from it; any such will always command my good wishes: yet I own I am rather disappointed; and though I doubt not the justice of your reason, to which I implicitly submit, you must not wonder, that, when upon the point of being honoured with your confidence, I should feel the greatest regret at finding it withdrawn."

Do you think, my dear Sir, I did not, at that moment, require all my resolution to guard me from frankly telling him whatever he wished to hear? yet I rejoice that I did not; for added to the actual wrong I should have done, Lord Orville himself, when he had heard, would, I am sure, have blamed me. Fortunately, this thought occurred to me, and I said, "Your Lordship shall yourself be my judge; the promise I made, though voluntary, was rash and inconsiderate; yet, had it concerned myself, I would not have hesitated in fulfilling it; but the gentleman whose affairs I should be obliged to relate."

"Pardon me," cried he, "for interrupting you; yet allow me to assure you, I have not the slightest desire to be acquainted with his affairs, further than what belongs to the motives which induced you yesterday morning——" He stopped; but there was no occasion to say more.

"That, my Lord," cried I, "I will tell you honestly. Mr. Macartney had some particular business with me,—and I could not take the liberty to ask him hither."

"And why not?—Mrs. Beaumont, I am sure,—"

"I could not, my Lord, think of intruding upon Mrs. Beaumont's complaisance; and so, with the same hasty folly I promised your Lordship, I much *more* rashly, promised to meet him."

"And did you?"

"No, my Lord," said I, colouring, "I returned before he came."

Again, for some time, we were both silent; yet, unwilling to leave him to reflections which could not but be to my disadvantage, I summoned sufficient courage to say, "There is no young creature, my Lord, who so greatly wants, or so earnestly wishes for, the advice and assistance of her friends, as I do; I am new to the world, and unused to acting for myself;—my intentions are never wilfully blameable, yet I err perpetually!—I have, hitherto, been blest with the most affectionate of friends, and, indeed, the ablest of men, to guide and instruct me upon every occasion;—but he is too distant, now, to be applied to at the moment I want his aid;—and *here*,—there is not a human being whose counsel I can ask."

"Would to Heaven," cried he, with a countenance from which all coldness and gravity were banished, and succeeded by the mildest benevolence, "that *I* were worthy,—and capable,—of supplying the place of such a friend to Miss Anville!"

"You do me but too much honour," said I; "yet I hope your Lordship's candour,—perhaps I ought to say indulgence,—will make some allowance, on account of my inexperience, for behaviour, so inconsiderate:— May I, my Lord, hope that you will?"

"May *I*," cried he, "hope that you will pardon the ill-grace with which I have submitted to my disappointment? and that you will permit me, (kissing my hand) thus to seal my peace?"

"*Our* peace, my Lord," said I, with revived spirits.

"This, then," said he, again pressing it to his lips, "for *our* peace: and now,—are we not friends?"

Just then, the door opened, and I had only time to withdraw my hand, before the ladies came in to breakfast.

I have been, all day, the happiest of human beings!—to be thus reconciled to Lord Orville, and yet to adhere to my resolution,—what could I wish for more?—he, too, has been very chearful, and more attentive, more obliging to me than ever. Yet Heaven forbid I should again be in a similar situation, for I cannot express how much uneasiness I have suffered from the fear of incurring his ill opinion.

But what will poor Mr. Macartney think of me? Happy as I am, I much regret the necessity I have been under of disappointing him.

Adieu, my dearest Sir.

Letter VI.

MR. VILLARS TO EVELINA.

Berry Hill, Sept. 28.

Dead to the world, and equally insensible to its pleasures or its pains, I long since bid adieu to all joy, and defiance to all sorrow, but what should spring from my Evelina,—sole source, to me, of all earthly felicity. How strange, then, is it, that the letter in which she tells me she is the *happiest of human beings*, should give me most mortal inquietude!

Alas, my child!—that innocence, the first, best gift of Heaven, should, of all others, be the blindest to its own danger,—the most exposed to treachery,—and the least able to defend itself, in a world where it is little known, less valued, and perpetually deceived!

Would to Heaven you were here!—then, by degrees, and with gentleness, I might enter upon a subject too delicate for distant discussion. Yet is it too interesting, and the situation too critical, to allow of delay.—Oh my Evelina, your situation is critical indeed!—your peace of mind is at stake, and every chance for your future happiness may depend upon the conduct of the present moment.

Hitherto I have forborne to speak with you upon the most important of all concerns, the state of your heart:—alas, I need no information! I have been silent, indeed, but I have not been blind.

Long, and with the deepest regret, have I perceived the ascendancy which Lord Orville has gained upon your mind.—You will start at the mention of his name,—you will tremble every word you read;—I grieve to give pain to my gentle Evelina, but I dare not any longer spare her.

Your first meeting with Lord Orville was decisive. Lively, fearless, free from all other impressions, such a man as you describe him could not fail exciting your admiration, and the more dangerously, because he seemed as unconscious of his power as you of your weakness; and therefore you had no alarm, either from *his* vanity or *your own* prudence.

Young, animated, entirely off your guard, and thoughtless of consequences, *Imagination* took the reins, and *Reason*, slow-paced, though sure-footed, was unequal to a race with so eccentric and flighty a companion. How rapid was then my Evelina's progress through those regions of fancy and passion whither her new guide conducted her!— She saw Lord Orville at a ball,—and he was *the most amiable of men!*— She met him again at another,—and *he had every virtue under heaven!*

I mean not to depreciate the merit of Lord Orville, who, one mysterious instance alone excepted, seems to have deserved the idea you formed of his character; but it was not time, it was not the knowledge of his worth, obtained your regard; your new comrade had not patience to wait any trial; her glowing pencil,[1] dipt in the vivid colours of her creative ideas, painted to you, at the moment of your first acquaintance, all the excellencies, all the good and rare qualities, which a great length of time, and intimacy, could alone have really discovered.

You flattered yourself, that your partiality was the effect of esteem,

---

1. Paintbrush.

founded upon a general love of merit, and a principle of justice: and your heart, which fell the sacrifice of your error, was totally gone ere you suspected it was in danger.

A thousand times have I been upon the point of shewing you the perils of your situation; but the same inexperience which occasioned your mistake, I hoped, with the assistance of time and absence, would effect a cure: I was, indeed, most unwilling to destroy your illusion, while I dared hope it might itself contribute to the restoration of your tranquility; since your ignorance of the danger and force of your attachment, might possibly prevent that despondency with which young people, in similar circumstances, are apt to persuade themselves that what is only difficult, is absolutely impossible.

But now, since you have again met, and have become more intimate than ever, all my hope from silence and seeming ignorance is at an end. Awake, then, my dear, my deluded child, awake to the sense of your danger, and exert yourself to avoid the evils with which it threatens you,—evils which, to a mind like yours, are most to be dreaded, secret repining, and concealed, yet consuming regret! Make a noble effort for the recovery of your peace, which now, with sorrow I see it, depends wholly upon the presence of Lord Orville. This effort, may, indeed, be painful, but trust to my experience, when I assure you it is requisite.

You must quit him!—his sight is baneful to your repose, his society is death to your future tranquility! Believe me, my beloved child, my heart aches for your suffering, while it dictates its necessity.

Could I flatter myself that Lord Orville would, indeed, be sensible of your worth, and act with a nobleness of mind which should prove it congenial to his own, then would I leave my Evelina to the unmolested enjoyment of the chearful society and encreasing regard of a man she so greatly admires: but this is not an age in which we may trust to appearances, and imprudence is much sooner regretted than repaired. Your health, you tell me, is much mended,—can you then consent to leave Bristol?—not abruptly, that I do not desire, but in a few days from the time you receive this? I will write to Mrs. Selwyn, and tell her how much I wish your return; and Mrs. Clinton can take sufficient care of you.

I have meditated upon every possible expedient that might tend to your happiness, ere I fixed upon exacting from you a compliance which I am convinced will be most painful to you;—but I can satisfy myself in none. This will at least be safe, and as to success,—we must leave it to time.

I am very glad to hear of Mr. Macartney's welfare.

Adieu, my dearest child; Heaven preserve and strengthen you!

A.V.

Letter VII.

Clifton, Sept. 28.

Sweetly, most sweetly, have two days more passed since I wrote; but I have been too much engaged to be exact in my journal.

To-day has been less tranquil. It was destined for the decision of the important bet, and has been productive of general confusion throughout the house. It was settled that the race should be run at five o'clock in the afternoon. Lord Merton breakfasted here, and stayed till noon. He wanted to engage the Ladies to *bet on his side,* in the true spirit of gaming, without seeing the racers. But he could only prevail on Lady Louisa, as Mrs. Selwyn said she never laid a wager against her own wishes, and Mrs. Beaumont would not *take sides.* As for *me,* I was not applied to. It is impossible for negligence to be more pointed, than that of Lord Merton to me, in the presence of Lady Louisa.

But, just before dinner, I happened to be alone in the drawing-room, when his Lordship suddenly returned, and coming in with his usual familiarity, he was beginning, "You see, Lady Louisa,—" but stopping short, "Pray where's every body gone?"

"Indeed I don't know, my Lord."

He then shut the door, and, with a great alteration in his face and manner, advanced eagerly towards me, and said, "How glad I am, my sweet girl, to meet you, at last, alone! By my soul, I began to think there was a plot against me, for I've never been able to have you a minute to myself." And, very freely, he seized my hand.

I was so much surprised at this address, after having been so long totally neglected, that I could make no other answer than staring at him with unfeigned astonishment.

"Why now," continued he, "if you was not the cruellest little angel in the world, you would have helped me to some expedient: for you see how I am watched here; Lady Louisa's eyes are never off me. She gives me a charming foretaste of the pleasures of a wife! however, it won't last long."

Disgusted to the greatest degree, I attempted to draw away my hand, but I believe I should not have succeeded, if Mrs. Beaumont had not made her appearance. He turned from me with the greatest assurance, and said, "How are you, Ma'am?—how is Lady Louisa?—you see I can't live a moment out of the house."

Could you, my dearest Sir, have believed it possible for such effrontery to be in man?

Before dinner, came Mr. Coverley, and before five o'clock, Mr. Lovel and some other company. The place marked out for the race, was a gravel-walk in Mrs. Beaumont's garden, and the length of the ground twenty yards. When we were summoned to the *course*, the two poor old women made their appearance. Though they seemed very healthy for their time of life, they yet looked so weak, so infirm, so feeble, that I could feel no sensation but that of pity at the sight. However, this was not the general sense of the company, for they no sooner came forward, than they were greeted with a laugh from every beholder, Lord Orville excepted, who looked very grave during the whole transaction. Doubtless he must be greatly discontented at the dissipated conduct and extravagance, of a man with whom he is, soon, to be so nearly connected.

For some time, the scene was truly ridiculous; the agitation of the parties concerned, and the bets that were laid upon the old women, were absurd beyond measure. *Who are you for?* and *whose side are you of?* was echoed from mouth to mouth by the whole company. Lord Merton and Mr. Coverley were both so excessively gay and noisy, that I soon found they had been too free in drinking to their success. They handed, with loud shouts, the old women to the race-ground, and encouraged them, by liberal promises, to exert themselves.

When the signal was given for them to set off, the poor creatures, feeble and frightened, ran against each other, and neither of them able to support the shock, they both fell on the ground.

Lord Merton and Mr. Coverley flew to their assistance. Seats were brought for them, and they each drank a glass of wine. They complained of being much bruised; for, heavy and helpless, they had not been able to save themselves, but fell, with their whole weight upon the gravel. However, as they seemed equal sufferers, both parties were too eager to have the affair deferred.

Again, therefore, they set off, and hobbled along, nearly even with each other, for some time, yet frequently, and to the inexpressible diversion of the company, they stumbled and tottered; and the confused hallowing of *"Now Coverley!"* *"Now Merton!"* rung from side to side during the whole affair.

Not long after, a foot of one of the poor women slipt, and, with great force, she came again to the ground. Involuntarily, I sprung forward to assist her, but Lord Merton, to whom she did not belong, stopped me, calling out, *"No foul play! no foul play!"*

Mr. Coverley, then, repeating the same words, went himself to help her, and insisted that the other should stop. A debate ensued; but the poor creature was too much hurt to move, and declared her utter inability to make another attempt. Mr. Coverley was quite brutal; he swore at her with unmanly rage, and seemed scarce able to refrain even from striking her.

Lord Merton then, in great rapture, said it was a *hollow*[1] *thing*; but

---

1. Complete.

Mr. Coverley contended that the fall was accidental, and time should be allowed for the woman to recover. However, all the company being against him, he was pronounced the loser.

We then went to the drawing-room, to tea. After which, the evening being remarkably warm we all walked in the garden. Lord Merton was quite riotous, and Lady Louisa in high spirits; but Mr. Coverley endeavoured in vain to conceal his chagrin.

As Lord Orville was thoughtful, and walked by himself, I expected that, as usual, I should pass unnoticed, and be left to my own meditations; but this was not the case; for Lord Merton, entirely off his guard, giddy equally from wine and success, was very troublesome to me; and, regardless of the presence of Lady Louisa, which, hitherto, has restrained him even from common civility, he attached himself to me, during the walk, with a freedom of gallantry that put me extremely out of countenance. He paid me the most high-flown compliments, and frequently and forcibly seized my hand, though I repeatedly, and with undissembled anger, drew it back. Lord Orville, I saw, watched us with earnestness, and Lady Louisa's smiles were converted into looks of disdain.

I could not bear to be thus situated, and complaining I was tired, I quickened my pace, with intention to return to the house; but Lord Merton, hastily following, caught my hand, and saying the *day was his own*, vowed he would not let me go.

"You *must*, my Lord," cried I, extremely flurried.

"You are the most charming girl in the world," said he, "and never looked better than at this moment."

"My Lord," cried Mrs. Selwyn, advancing to us, "you don't consider, that the better Miss Anville looks, the more striking is the contrast with your Lordship; therefore, for your own sake, I would advise you not to hold her."

"Egad, my Lord," cried Mr. Coverley, "I don't see what right you have to the best *old*, and the best *young* woman too, in the same day."

"*Best young woman!*" repeated Mr. Lovel; "'pon honour, Jack, you have made a most unfortunate speech; however, if Lady Louisa can pardon you,—and her Ladyship is all goodness,—I am sure nobody else can, for you have committed an outrageous solecism in good manners."

"And pray, Sir," said Mrs. Selwyn, "under what denomination may your own speech pass?"

Mr. Lovel, turning another way, affected not to hear her: and Mr. Coverley, bowing to Lady Louisa, said, "Her Ladyship is well acquainted with my devotion,—but egad, I don't know how it is,—I had always an unlucky turn at an epigram, and never could resist a smart play upon words in my life."

"Pray, my Lord," cried I, "let go my hand! pray, Mrs. Selwyn, speak for me."

"My Lord," said Mrs. Selwyn, "in detaining Miss Anville any longer, you only lose time, for we are already as well convinced of your valour and your strength as if you were to hold her an age."

"My lord," said Mrs. Beaumont, "I must beg leave to interfere; I know not if Lady Louisa can pardon you, but, as this young lady is at my house, I do not chuse to have her made uneasy."

"*I* pardon him!" cried Lady Louisa, "I declare I am monstrous glad to get rid of him."

"Egad, my Lord," cried Mr. Coverley, "while you are grasping at a shadow, you'll lose a substance; you'd best make your peace while you can."

"Pray, Mr. Coverley, be quiet," said Lady Louisa, peevishly, "for I declare I won't speak to him. Brother," (taking hold of Lord Orville's arm) "will you walk in with me?"

"Would to Heaven," cried I, frightened to see how much Lord Merton was in liquor, "that I, too, had a brother!—and then I should not be exposed to such treatment."

Lord Orville, instantly quitting Lady Louisa, said, "Will Miss Anville allow *me* the honour of taking that title?" and then, without waiting for any answer, he disengaged me from Lord Merton, and, handing me to Lady Louisa, "Let me," added he, "take equal care of *both* my sisters;" and then, desiring her to take hold of one arm, and begging me to make use of the other, we reached the house in a moment. Lord Merton, disordered as he was, attempted not to stop us.

As soon as we entered the house I withdrew my arm, and courtsied my thanks, for my heart was too full for speech. Lady Louisa, evidently hurt at her brother's condescension, and piqued extremely by Lord Merton's behaviour, silently drew away her's, and biting her lips, with a look of infinite vexation, walked sullenly up the hall.

Lord Orville asked her if she would not go into the parlour?

"No," answered she, haughtily; "I leave you and your new sister together;" and then she walked up stairs.

I was quite confounded at the pride and rudeness of this speech. Lord Orville himself seemed thunderstruck, I turned from him, and went into the parlour; he followed me, saying, "Must I, now, apologize to Miss Anville for the liberty of my interference?—or ought I to apologize, that I did not, as I wished, interfere sooner?"

"O my Lord," cried I, with an emotion I could not repress, "it is from you alone I meet with any respect,—all others treat me with impertinence or contempt!"

I am sorry I had not more command of myself, as he had reason, just then, to suppose I particularly meant his sister; which, I am sure, must very much hurt him.

"Good Heaven," cried he, "that so much sweetness and merit can fail to excite the love and admiration so justly their due! I cannot,—I dare not express to you half the indignation I feel at this moment!"

"I am sorry, my Lord," said I, more calmly, "to have raised it; but yet,—in a situation that calls for protection, to meet only with mortifications,—indeed, but I am ill formed to bear them!"

"My *dear* Miss Anville," cried he, warmly, "allow *me* to be your friend; think of me as if I were indeed your brother, and let me entreat you to accept my best services, if there is any thing in which I can be so happy as to shew my regard,—my respect for you!"

Before I had time to speak, the rest of the party entered the parlour, and, as I did not wish to see any thing more of Lord Merton, at least before he had slept, I determined to leave it. Lord Orville, seeing my design, said, as I passed him, "Will you go?" "Had not I best, my Lord?" said I. "I am afraid," said he, smiling, "since I must now speak as your *brother*, I am afraid you *had*;—you see you may trust me, since I can advise against my own interest."

I then left the room, and have been writing ever since. And methinks I can never lament the rudeness of Lord Merton, as it has more than ever confirmed to me the esteem of Lord Orville.

Letter VIII.

EVELINA IN CONTINUATION.

Sept. 30.

Oh Sir, what a strange incident have I to recite! what a field of conjecture to open!

Yesterday evening, we all went to an assembly. Lord Orville presented tickets to the whole family, and did me the honour, to the no small surprise of all here, I believe, to dance with me. But every day abounds in fresh instances of his condescending politeness, and he now takes every opportunity of calling me his *friend*, and his *sister*.

Lord Merton offered a ticket to Lady Louisa; but she was so much incensed against him, that she refused it with the utmost disdain; neither could he prevail upon her to dance with him; she sat still the whole evening, and deigned not to look at; or speak to him. To me her behaviour is almost the same, for she is cold, distant, and haughty, and her eyes express the greatest contempt. But for Lord Orville, how miserable would my residence here make me!

We were joined, in the ball-room, by Mr. Coverley, Mr. Lovel, and Lord Merton, who looked as if he was doing penance, and sat all the evening next to Lady Louisa, vainly endeavouring to appease her anger.

Lord Orville began the minuets: he danced with a young Lady who seemed to engage the general attention, as she had not been seen here before. She is pretty, and looks mild and good-humoured.

"Pray, Mr. Lovel," said Lady Louisa, "who is that?"

"Miss Belmont," answered he, "the young heiress; she came to the Wells yesterday."

Struck with the name, I involuntarily repeated it, but nobody heard me.

"What is her family?" said Mrs. Beaumont.

"Have you not heard of her, Ma'am?" cried he, "she is only daughter and heiress of Sir John Belmont."

Good Heaven, how did I start! the name struck my ear like a thunder-bolt. Mrs. Selwyn, who immediately looked at me, said, "Be calm, my dear, and we will learn the truth of all this."

Till then, I had never imagined her to be acquainted with my story; but she has since told me, that she knew my unhappy mother, and was well informed of the whole affair.

She asked Mr. Lovel a multitude of questions, and I gathered from his answers, that this young Lady was just come from abroad, with Sir John Belmont, who was now in London; that she was under the care of his sister, Mrs. Paterson; and that she would inherit a considerable estate.

I cannot express the strange feelings with which I was agitated during this recital. What, my dearest Sir, can it possibly mean? Did you ever hear of any after-marriage?[1] —or must I suppose, that, while the lawful child is rejected, another is adopted?—I know not what to think! I am bewildered with a contrariety of ideas!

When we came home, Mrs. Selwyn passed more than an hour in my room, conversing upon this subject. She says that I ought instantly to go to town, find out my father, and have the affair cleared up. She assures me I have too strong a resemblance to my dear, though unknown mother, to allow of the least hesitation in my being owned, when once I am seen. For my part, I have no wish but to act by your direction.

I cannot give any account of the evening; so disturbed, so occupied am I by this subject, that I can think of no other. I have entreated Mrs. Selwyn to observe the strictest secrecy, and she has promised that she will. Indeed, she has too much sense to be idly communicative.

Lord Orville took notice of my being absent and silent, but I ventured not to entrust him with the cause. Fortunately, he was not of the party at the time Mr. Lovel made the discovery.

Mrs. Selwyn says that if you approve my going to town, she will herself accompany me. I had a thousand times rather ask the protection of Mrs. Mirvan, but, after this offer, that will not be possible.

Adieu, my dearest Sir. I am sure you will write immediately, and I shall be all impatience till your letter arrives.

---

1. Second marriage.

Letter IX.

Oct. 1st.

Good God, my dear Sir, what a wonderful tale have I again to relate! even yet, I am not recovered from my extreme surprise.

Yesterday morning, as soon as I had finished my hasty letter, I was summoned to attend a walking party to the Hotwells. It consisted only of Mrs. Selwyn and Lord Orville. The latter walked by my side all the way, and his conversation dissipated my uneasiness, and insensibly restored my serenity.

At the pump-room, I saw Mr. Macartney; I courtsied to him twice ere he would speak to me. When he did, I began to apologize for having disappointed him; but I did not find it very easy to excuse myself, as Lord Orville's eyes, with an expression of anxiety that distressed me, turned from him to me, and me to him, every word I spoke. Convinced, however, that I had really trifled with Mr. Macartney, I scrupled not to beg his pardon. He was then, not merely appeased, but even grateful.

He requested me to see him to-morrow: but I had not the folly to be again guilty of an indiscretion which had, already, caused me so much uneasiness; and therefore, I told him frankly, that it was not in my power, at present, to see him but by accident; and, to prevent his being offended, I hinted to him the reason I could not receive him as I wished to do.

When I had satisfied both him and myself upon this subject, I turned to Lord Orville, and saw, with concern, the gravity of his countenance. I would have spoken to him, but knew not how; I believe, however, he read my thoughts, for, in a little time, with a sort of serious smile, he said, "Does not Mr. Macartney complain of his disappointment?"

"Not much, my Lord."

"And how have you appeased him?" Finding I hesitated what to answer, "Am I not your brother," continued he, "and must I not enquire into your affairs?"

"Certainly, my Lord," said I, laughing. "I only wish it were better worth your Lordship's while."

"Let me, then, make immediate use of my privilege. When shall you see Mr. Macartney again?"

"Indeed, my Lord, I can't tell."

"But,—do you know that I shall not suffer *my sister* to make a private appointment?"

"Pray, my Lord," cried I, earnestly, "use that word no more! Indeed you shock me extremely."

"That would I not do for the world," cried he; "yet you know not how warmly, how deeply I am interested, not only in all your concerns, but in all your actions."

This speech,—the most particular one Lord Orville had ever made to me, ended our conversation at that time; for I was too much struck by it to make any answer.

Soon after, Mr. Macartney, in a low voice, entreated me not to deny him the gratification of returning the money. While he was speaking, the young Lady I saw yesterday at the assembly, with the large party, entered the pump-room. Mr. Macartney turned as pale as death, his voice faltered, and he seemed not to know what he said. I was myself almost equally disturbed, by the croud of confused ideas that occurred to me. Good Heaven, thought I, why should he be thus agitated?—is it possible this can be the young Lady he loved?—

In a few minutes, we quitted the pump-room, and, though I twice wished Mr. Macartney good morning, he was so absent he did not hear me.

We did not immediately return to Clifton, as Mrs. Selwyn had business at a pamphlet-shop. While she was looking at some new poems, Lord Orville again asked me when I should see Mr. Macartney?

"Indeed, my Lord," cried I, "I know not, but I would give the universe for a few moments' conversation with him!" I spoke this with a simple sincerity, and was not aware of the force of my own words.

"The universe!" repeated he, "Good God, Miss Anville, do you say this to *me*?"

"I would say it," returned I, "to any body, my Lord."

"I beg your pardon," said he, in a voice that shewed him ill pleased, "I am answered."

"My Lord," cried I, "you must not judge hardly of me. I spoke inadvertently; but if you knew the painful suspense I suffer at this moment, you would not be surprised at what I have said."

"And would a meeting with Mr. Macartney relieve you from that suspense?"

"Yes, my Lord, two words might be sufficient."

"Would to Heaven," cried he, after a short pause, "that I were worthy to know their import!"

"Worthy, my Lord!—O, if that were all, your Lordship could ask nothing I should not be ready to answer! If I were but a liberty to speak, I should be *proud* of your Lordship's enquiries; but indeed I am not, I have not any right to communicate the affairs of Mr. Macartney,—your Lordship cannot suppose I have."

"I will own to you," answered he, "I know not *what* to suppose; yet there seems a frankness even in your mystery—and such an air of openness in your countenance, that I am willing to hope—" He stopped a moment, and then added, "This meeting, you say, is essential to your repose?"

"I did not say *that*, my Lord; but yet I have the most important reasons for wishing to speak to him."

He paused a few minutes, and then said, with warmth, "Yes, you *shall* speak to him!—I will myself assist you!—Miss Anville, I am sure, cannot form a wish against propriety, I will ask no questions, I will rely upon her own purity, and uninformed, blindfold as I am, I will serve her with all my power!" And then he went into the shop, leaving me so strangely affected by his generous behaviour, that I almost wished to follow him with my thanks.

When Mrs. Selwyn had transacted her affairs, we returned home.

The moment dinner was over, Lord Orville went out, and did not come back till just as we were summoned to supper. This is the longest time he has spent from the house since I have been at Clifton, and you cannot imagine, my dear Sir, how much I missed him. I scarce knew before how infinitely I am indebted to him alone for the happiness I have enjoyed since I have been at Mrs. Beaumont's.

As I generally go down stairs last, he came to me the moment the ladies had passed by, and said, "Shall you be at home to-morrow morning?"

"I believe so, my Lord."

"And will you, then, receive a visitor for me?"

"For you, my Lord?"

"Yes;—I have made acquaintance with Mr. Macartney, and he has promised to call upon me to-morrow about three o'clock."

And then, taking my hand, he led me down stairs.

O, Sir!—was there ever such another man as Lord Orville?—Yes, *one* other now resides at Berry Hill!

This morning there has been a great deal of company here, but at the time appointed by Lord Orville, doubtless with that consideration, the parlour is almost always empty, as every body is dressing.

Mrs. Beaumont, however, was not gone up stairs, when Mr. Macartney sent in his name.

Lord Orville immediately said, "Beg the favour of him to walk in. You see, Madam, that I consider myself as at home."

"I hope so," answered Mrs. Beaumont, "or I should be very uneasy."

Mr. Macartney then entered. I believe we both felt very conscious to whom the visit was paid: but Lord Orville received him as his own guest, and not merely entertained him as such while Mrs. Beaumont remained in the room, but for some time after she had left it: a delicacy that saved me from the embarrassment I should have felt, had he immediately quitted us.

In a few minutes, however, he gave Mr. Macartney a book,—for I, too, by way of pretence for continuing in the room, pretended to be reading,—and begged he would be so good as to look it over, while he answered a note, which he would dispatch in a few minutes, and return to him.

When he was gone, we both parted with our books, and Mr. Macartney, again producing the paper with the money, besought me to accept it.

"Pray," said I, still declining it, "did you know the young lady who came into the pump-room yesterday morning?"

"Know her!" repeated he, changing colour, "Oh, but too well!"

"Indeed!"

"Why, Madam, do you ask?"

"I must beseech you to satisfy me further upon this subject; pray tell me who she is."

"Inviolably as I meant to keep my secret, I can refuse you, Madam, nothing;—that lady—is the daughter of Sir John Belmont!—of my father!"

"Gracious Heaven!" cried I, involuntarily laying my hand on his arm, "you are then—," *my brother*, I would have said, but my voice failed me, and I burst into tears.

"Oh, Madam," cried he, "what does this mean?—What can thus distress you?"

I could not answer, but held out my hand to him. He seemed greatly surprised, and talked in high terms of my condescension.

"Spare yourself," cried I, wiping my eyes, "spare yourself this mistake,—you have a *right* to all I can do for you; the similarity of our circumstances—"

We were then interrupted by the entrance of Mrs. Selwyn; and Mr. Macartney, finding no probability of our being left alone, was obliged to take leave, though I believe, very reluctantly, while in such suspence.

Mrs. Selwyn then, by dint of interrogatories, drew from me the state of this affair. She is so penetrating, that there is no possibility of evading to give her satisfaction.

Is not this a strange event? Good Heaven, how little did I think that the visits I so unwillingly paid at Mr. Branghton's would have introduced me to so near a relation! I will never again regret the time I spent in town this summer: a circumstance so fortunate will always make me think of it with pleasure.

*   *   *   *

I have just received your letter,—and it has almost broken my heart!—Oh, Sir! the illusion is over, indeed!—How vainly have I flattered, how miserably deceived myself! Long since, doubtful of the situation of my heart, I dreaded a scrutiny,—but now, now that I have so long escaped, I began, indeed, to think my safety insured, to hope that my fears were causeless, and to believe that my good opinion and esteem of Lord Orville might be owned without suspicion, and felt without danger:—miserably deceived, indeed!

His sight is baneful to my repose,—his society is death to my future tranquillity! Oh, Lord Orville! could I have believed that a friendship so grateful to my heart, so soothing to my distresses,—a friendship which, in every respect, did me so much honour, would only serve to embitter all my future moments!—What a strange, what an unhappy circumstance, that my gratitude, though so justly excited, should be so fatal to my peace!

Yes, Sir, I *will* quit him;—would to Heaven I could at this moment! without seeing him again,—without trusting to my now conscious emotion!—Oh, Lord Orville, how little do you know the evils I owe to you! how little suppose that, when most dignified by your attention, I was most to be pitied,—and when most exalted by your notice, you were most my enemy!

You, Sir, relied upon my ignorance;—I, alas, upon your experience; and, whenever I doubted the weakness of my heart, the idea that *you* did not suspect it, reassured me,—restored my courage, and confirmed my error!—Yet am I most sensible of the kindness of your silence.

Oh, Sir! why have I ever quitted you! why been exposed to dangers to which I am so unequal?

But I will leave this place,—leave Lord Orville,—leave him, perhaps, for ever!—no matter; your counsel, your goodness, may teach me how to recover the peace and the serenity of which my unguarded folly has beguiled me. To you alone do I trust,—in you alone confide for every future hope I may form.

The more I consider of parting with Lord Orville, the less fortitude do I feel to bear the separation;—the friendship he has shewn me,—his politeness,—his sweetness of manners,—his concern in my affairs,—his solicitude to oblige me,—all, all to be given up!—

No, I cannot tell him I am going,—I dare not trust myself to take leave of him,—I will run away without seeing him:—implicitly will I follow your advice, avoid his sight, and shun his society!

To-morrow morning I will set off for Berry Hill. Mrs. Selwyn and Mrs. Beaumont shall alone know my intention. And to-day—I will spend in my own room. The readiness of my obedience is the only atonement I can offer, for the weakness which calls for its exertion.

Can you, will you, most honoured, most dear Sir! sole prop by which the poor Evelina is supported,—can you, without reproach, without displeasure, receive the child you have so carefully reared,—from whose education better fruit might have been expected, and who, blushing for her unworthiness, fears to meet the eye by which she has been cherished?—Oh yes, I am sure you will! Your Evelina's errors are those of the judgment,—and you, I well know, pardon all but those of the heart!

Letter X.

EVELINA IN CONTINUATION.

Clifton, October 1st.

I have only time, my dearest Sir, for three words, to overtake my last letter, and prevent your expecting me immediately; for, when I communicated my intention to Mrs. Selwyn, she would not hear of it, and declared it would be highly ridiculous for me to go before I received an answer to my intelligence concerning the journey from Paris. She has, therefore, insisted upon my waiting till your next letter arrives. I hope you will not be displeased at my compliance, though it is rather against my own judgment; but Mrs. Selwyn quite overpowered me with the force of her arguments. I will, however, see very little of Lord Orville; I will never come down stairs before breakfast; give up all my walks in the garden,—seat myself next to Mrs. Selwyn, and not merely avoid his conversation, but shun his presence. I will exert all the prudence and all the resolution in my power, to prevent this short delay from giving you any further uneasiness.

Adieu, my dearest Sir. I shall not now leave Clifton till I have your directions.

Letter XI.

EVELINA IN CONTINUATION.

October 2d.

Yesterday, from the time I received your kind, though heart-piercing letter, I kept my room,—for I was equally unable and unwilling to see Lord Orville: but this morning, finding I seemed destined to pass a few days longer here, I endeavoured to calm my spirits, and to appear as usual; though I determined to avoid him to the utmost of my power. Indeed, as I entered the parlour, when called to breakfast, my thoughts were so much occupied with your letter, that I felt as much confusion at his sight, as if he had himself been informed of its contents.

Mrs. Beaumont made me a slight compliment upon my recovery, for I had pleaded illness to excuse keeping my room: Lady Louisa spoke not a word: but Lord Orville, little imagining himself the cause of my indisposition, enquired concerning my health with the most distinguishing politeness. I hardly made any answer; and, for the first time since I have been here, contrived to sit at some distance from him.

I could not help observing that my reserve surprised him; yet he persisted in his civilities, and seemed to wish to remove it. But I paid him very little attention; and the moment breakfast was over, instead of taking a book, or walking in the garden, I retired to my own room.

Soon after, Mrs. Selwyn came to tell me that Lord Orville had been proposing I should take an airing, and persuading her to let him drive us both in his phaeton. She delivered the message with an archness that made me blush; and added, that an airing, in *my Lord Orville's carriage*, could not fail to revive my spirits. There is no possibility of escaping her discernment; she has frequently rallied me upon his Lordship's attention,—and, alas!—upon the pleasure with which I have received it! However, I absolutely refused the offer.

"Well," said she, laughing, "I cannot just now indulge you with any solicitation; for, to tell you the truth, I have business to transact at the Wells, and am glad to be excused myself. I would ask you to walk with *me*,—but, since *Lord Orville* is refused, I have not the presumption to hope for success."

"Indeed," cried I, "you are mistaken; I will attend you with pleasure."

"O rare coquetry!" cried she, "surely it must be inherent in our sex, or it could not have been imbibed at Berry Hill."

I had not spirits to answer her, and therefore put on my hat and cloak in silence.

"I presume," continued she, drily, "his Lordship may walk with us."

"If so, Madam," said I, "you will have a companion, and I will stay at home."

"My dear child," cried she, "did you bring the certificate of your birth with you?"

"Dear Madam, no!"

"Why then, we shall never be known again at Berry Hill."

I felt too conscious to enjoy her pleasantry; but I believe she was determined to torment me; for she asked if she should inform Lord Orville that I desired him not to be of the party?

"By no means, Madam;—but, indeed, I had rather not walk myself."

"My dear," cried she, "I really do not know you this morning,—you have certainly been taking a lesson of Lady Louisa."

She then went down stairs; but presently returning, told me she had acquainted Lord Orville that I did not choose to go out in the phaeton, but preferred a walk, *tête-à-tête* with her, by way of *variety*.

I said nothing, but was really vexed. She bad me go down stairs, and said she would follow immediately.

Lord Orville met me in the hall. "I fear," said he, "Miss Anville is not yet quite well?" and he would have taken my hand, but I turned from him, and courtsying slightly, went into the parlour.

Mrs. Beaumont and Lady Louisa were at work: Lord Merton was talking with the latter; for he has now made his peace, and is again received into favour.

I seated myself, as usual, by the window. Lord Orville, in a few minutes, came to me, and said, "Why is Miss Anville so grave?"

"Not grave, my Lord," said I, "only stupid;"[1] and I took up a book.

"You will go," said he, after a short pause, "to the assembly to-night?"

"No, my Lord, certainly not."

"Neither, then, will I; for I should be sorry to sully the remembrance I have of the happiness I enjoyed at the last."

Mrs. Selwyn then coming in, general enquiries were made, to all but me, of who would go to the assembly? Lord Orville instantly declared he had letters to write at home; but every one else settled to go.

I then hastened Mrs. Selwyn away, though not before she had said to Lord Orville, "Pray, has your Lordship obtained Miss Anville's leave to favour us with your company?"

"I have not, Madam," answered he, "had the vanity to ask it."

During our walk, Mrs. Selwyn tormented me unmercifully. She told me, that since I declined any addition to our party, I must, doubtless, be conscious of my own powers of entertainment; and begged me, therefore, to exert them freely. I repented a thousand times having consented to walk alone with her: for though I made the most painful efforts to appear in spirits, her raillery quite overpowered me.

We went first to the pump-room. It was full of company! and the moment we entered, I heard a murmuring of, *"That's she!"* and, to my great confusion, I saw every eye turned towards me. I pulled my hat over my face, and, by the assistance of Mrs. Selwyn, endeavoured to screen myself from observation: nevertheless, I found I was so much the object of general attention, that I entreated her to hasten away. But unfortunately, she had entered into conversation, very earnestly, with a gentleman of her acquaintance, and would not listen to me, but said, that if I was tired of waiting, I might walk on to the milliner's with the Miss Watkins, two young ladies I had seen at Mrs. Beaumont's, who were going thither.

I accepted the offer very readily, and away we went. But we had not gone three yards, before we were followed by a party of young men, who took every possible opportunity of looking at us, and, as they walked behind, talked aloud, in a manner at once unintelligible and absurd.

"Yes," cried one, "'tis certainly she!—mark but her *blushing cheek!*"

"And then her *eye*—her *downcast eye!*" cried another.

"True, oh most true," said a third, "*every beauty is her own!*"

"But then," said the first, "her *mind*,—now the difficulty is, to find out the truth of *that*, for she will not say a word."

"She is *timid*," answered another; "mark but her *timid air.*"

During this conversation, we walked on silent and quick; as we knew not to whom it was particularly addressed, we were all equally ashamed, and equally desirous to avoid such unaccountable observations.

---

1. Dull, out-of-sorts.

Soon after, we were caught in a shower of rain. We hurried on, and these gentlemen, following us, offered their services in the most pressing manner, begging us to make use of their arms; and while I almost ran, in order to avoid their impertinence, I was suddenly met by Sir Clement Willoughby!

We both started; "Good God!" he exclaimed, "Miss Anville!" and then, regarding my tormentors with an air of displeasure, he earnestly enquired, if any thing had alarmed me?

"No, no," cried I, for I found no difficulty now to disengage myself from these youths, who, probably, concluding from the commanding air of Sir Clement, that he had a right to protect me, quietly gave way to him, and entirely quitted us.

With his usual impetuosity, he then began a thousand enquiries, accompanied with as many compliments; and he told me, that he arrived at Bristol but this morning, which he had entirely devoted to endeavours to discover where I lodged.

"Did you know then," said I, "that I was at Bristol?"

"Would to Heaven," cried he, "that I *could* remain in ignorance of your proceedings with the same contentment you do of mine! then should I not for ever journey upon the wings of hope, to meet my own despair! *You* cannot even judge of the cruelty of my fate, for the ease and serenity of your mind incapacitates you from feeling for the agitation of mine!"

The ease and serenity of *my* mind! alas, how little do I merit those words!

"But," added he, "had *accident* brought me hither, had I not known of your journey, the voice of fame would have proclaimed it to me instantly upon my arrival."

"The voice of fame!" repeated I.

"Yes, for your's was the first name I heard at the pump-room. But had I *not* heard your name, such a description could have painted no one else."

"Indeed," said I, "I do not understand you." But, just then arriving at the milliner's, our conversation ended; for Miss Watkins called me to look at caps and ribbons.

Sir Clement, however, has the art of being always *at home*; he was very soon engaged, as busily as ourselves, in looking at lace ruffles. Yet he took an opportunity of saying to me in a low voice, "How charmed I am to see you look so well! I was told you were ill;—but I never saw you in better health,—never more infinitely lovely!"

I turned away, to examine the ribbons, and soon after Mrs. Selwyn made her appearance. I found that she was acquainted with Sir Clement, and her manner of speaking to him convinced me that he was a favourite with her.

When their mutual compliments were over, she turned to me, and said, "Pray, Miss Anville, how long can you live without nourishment?"

"Indeed, Ma'am," said I, laughing, "I have never tried."

"Because so long, and no longer," answered she, "you may remain at Bristol."

"Why, what is the matter, Ma'am?"

"The matter!—why, all the ladies are at open war with you,—the whole pump-room is in confusion; and you, innocent as you pretend to look, are the cause. However, if you take my advice, you will be very careful how you eat and drink during your stay."

I begged her to explain herself: and she then told me, that a copy of verses had been dropt in the pump-room, and read there aloud: "The Beauties of the Wells," said she, "are all mentioned, but *you* are the Venus to whom the prize is given."[2]

"Is it then possible," cried Sir Clement, "that you have not seen these verses?"

"I hardly know," answered I, "whether *any* body has."

"I assure you," said Mrs. Selwyn, "if you give *me* the invention of them, you do me an honour I by no means deserve."

"I wrote down in my tablets," said Sir Clement, "the stanzas which concern Miss Anville, this morning at the pump-room; and I will do myself the honour of copying them for her this evening."

"But why the part that concerns *Miss Anville?*" said Mrs. Selwyn; "Did you ever see her before this morning?"

"O yes," answered he, "I have had that happiness frequently at Captain Mirvan's. Too, too frequently!" added he, in a low voice, as Mrs. Selwyn turned to the milliner: and, as soon as she was occupied in examining some trimmings, he came to me, and, almost whether I would or not, entered into conversation with me.

"I have a thousand things," cried he, "to say to you. Pray where are you?"

"With Mrs. Selwyn, Sir."

"Indeed—then, for once, Chance is my friend. And how long have you been here?"

"About three weeks."

"Good Heaven! what an anxious search have I had, to discover your abode, since you so suddenly left town! The termagant Madame Duval, refused me all intelligence. Oh, Miss Anville, did you know what I have endured! the sleepless, restless state of suspence I have been tortured with, you could not, all cruel as you are, you could not have received me with such frigid indifference?"

"*Received* you, Sir!"

"Why, is not my visit to *you?* Do you think I should have made this journey, but for the happiness of again seeing you?"

2. The Trojan warrior Paris, asked to judge among the beauty of three goddesses, Hera, Aphrodite, and Athena, awarded the prize to Aphrodite (or Venus).

"Indeed it is possible I might,—since so many others do."

"Cruel, cruel girl! you *know* that I adore you! you *know* you are the mistress of my soul, and arbitress of my fate!"

Mrs. Selwyn then advancing to us, he assumed a more disengaged air, and asked if he should not have the pleasure of seeing her, in the evening, at the assembly?

"Oh, yes," cried she, "we shall certainly be there; so you may bring the verses with you, if Miss Anville can wait for them so long."

"I hope then," returned he, "that you will do me the honour to dance with me?"

I thanked him, but said I should not be at the assembly.

"Not be at the assembly!" cried Mrs. Selwyn, "Why, have *you*, too, letters to write?"

She looked at me with a significant archness that made me colour; and I hastily answered, "No, indeed, Ma'am!"

"You have not!" cried she, yet more drily, "then pray, my dear, do you stay at home to *help*,—or to *hinder* others?"

"To do neither, Ma'am," answered I, in much confusion; "so, if you please, I will *not* stay at home."

"You allow me, then," said Sir Clement, "to hope for the honour of your hand?"

I only bowed,—for the dread of Mrs. Selwyn's raillery made me not dare refuse him.

Soon after this we walked home, Sir Clement accompanied us, and the conversation that passed between Mrs. Selwyn and him was supported in so lively a manner that I should have been much entertained, had my mind been more at ease: but alas! I could think of nothing but the capricious, the unmeaning appearance which the alteration in my conduct must make in the eyes of Lord Orville? And much as I wish to avoid him, greatly as I desire to save myself from having my weakness known to him,—yet I cannot endure to incur his ill opinion,—and, unacquainted as he is with the reasons by which I am actuated, how can he fail contemning a change to him so unaccountable?

As we entered the garden, he was the first object we saw. He advanced to meet us, and I could not help observing, that at sight of each other both he and Sir Clement changed colour.

We went into the parlour, where we found the same party we had left. Mrs. Selwyn presented Sir Clement to Mrs. Beaumont; Lady Louisa and Lord Merton he seemed well acquainted with already.

The conversation was upon the general subjects, of the weather, the company at the Wells, and the news of the day. But Sir Clement, drawing his chair next to mine, took every opportunity of addressing himself to me in particular.

I could not but remark the striking difference of *his* attention, and that of Lord Orville: the latter has such gentleness of manners, such delicacy of conduct, and an air so respectful, that, when he flatters most, he never distresses, and when he most confers honour, appears to receive it! The former *obtrudes* his attention, and *forces* mine; it is so pointed, that it always confuses me, and so public, that it attracts general notice. Indeed I have sometimes thought that he would rather *wish*, than dislike to have his partiality for me known, as he takes great care to prevent my being spoken to by any body but himself.

When, at length, he went away, Lord Orville took his seat, and said with a half-smile, "Shall *I* call Sir Clement,—or will *you* call me an usurper for taking this place?—You make me no answer?—Must I then suppose that Sir Clement—"

"It is little worth your Lordship's while," said I, "to suppose any thing upon so insignificant an occasion."

"Pardon me," cried he,—"to *me* nothing is insignificant in which you are concerned."

To this I made no answer, neither did he say any thing more, till the ladies retired to dress: and then, when I would have followed them, he stopped me, saying, "One moment, I entreat you!"

I turned back, and he went on, "I greatly fear that I have been so unfortunate as to offend you; yet so repugnant to my very soul is the idea, that I know not how to suppose it possible I can unwittingly have done the thing in the world that, designedly, I would most wish to avoid."

"No, indeed, my Lord, you have not!" said I.

"You sigh!" cried he, taking my hand, "would to Heaven I were the sharer of your uneasiness whencesoever it springs! with what earnestness would I not struggle to alleviate it!—Tell me, my dear Miss Anville,—my new-adopted sister, my sweet and most amiable friend!—tell me, I beseech you, if I can afford you any assistance?"

"None, none, my Lord!" cried I, withdrawing my hand, and moving towards the door.

"Is it then impossible I can serve you?—perhaps you wish to see Mr. Macartney again?"

"No, my Lord." And I held the door open.

"I am not, I own, sorry for that. Yet, oh, Miss Anville, there *is* a question,—there is a conjecture,—I know not how to mention, because I dread the result!—But I see you are in haste;—perhaps in the evening I may have the honour of a longer conversation.—Yet one thing will you have the goodness to allow me to ask?—Did you, this morning when you went to the Wells,—did you *know* who you should meet there?"

"Who, my Lord?"

"I beg your pardon a thousand times for a curiosity so unlicensed,—but I will say no more at present."

He bowed, expecting me to go,—and then, with quick steps, but a heavy heart, I came to my own room. His question, I am sure, meant

Sir Clement Willoughby; and, had I not imposed upon myself the severe task of avoiding, flying Lord Orville with all my power, I would instantly have satisfied him of my ignorance of Sir Clement's journey. And yet more did I long to say something of the assembly, since I found he depended upon my spending the evening at home.

I did not go down stairs again till the family was assembled to dinner. My dress, I saw, struck Lord Orville with astonishment; and I was myself so much ashamed of appearing whimsical and unsteady, that I could not look up.

"I understood," said Mrs. Beaumont, "that Miss Anville did not go out this evening."

"Her intention in the morning," said Mrs. Selwyn, "was to stay at home; but there is a fascinating power in an *assembly*, which, upon second thoughts, is not to be resisted."

"The assembly!" cried Lord Orville, "are you then going to the assembly?"

I made no answer; and we all took our places at table.

It was not without difficulty that I contrived to give up my usual seat; but I was determined to adhere to the promise in my yesterday's letter, though I saw that Lord Orville seemed quite confounded at my visible endeavours to avoid him.

After dinner, we all went into the drawing-room together, as there were no gentlemen to detain his Lordship; and then, before I could place myself out of his way, he said, "You are then really going to the assembly?——May I ask if you shall dance?"

"I believe not,—my Lord."

"If I did not fear," continued he, "that you would be tired of the same partner at two following assemblies, I would give up my letter-writing till to-morrow, and solicit the honour of your hand."

"If I *do* dance," said I, in great confusion, "I believe I am engaged."

"Engaged!" cried he, with earnestness, "May I ask to whom?"

"To—Sir Clement Willoughby, my Lord."

He said nothing, but looked very little pleased, and did not address himself to me any more all the afternoon. Oh, Sir!—thus situated, how comfortless were the feelings of your Evelina!

Early in the evening, with his accustomed assiduity, Sir Clement came to conduct us to the assembly. He soon contrived to seat himself next me, and, in a low voice, paid me so many compliments, that I knew not which way to look.

Lord Orville hardly spoke a word, and his countenance was grave and thoughtful; yet, whenever I raised my eyes, his, I perceived, were directed towards me, though instantly, upon meeting mine, he looked another way.

In a short time, Sir Clement, taking from his pocket a folded paper, said, almost in a whisper, "Here, loveliest of women, you will see a faint, an unsuccessful attempt to paint the object of all my adoration! yet, weak as are the lines for the purpose, I envy beyond expression the happy mortal who has dared make the effort."

"I will look at them," said I, "some other time." For, conscious that I was observed by Lord Orville, I could not bear he should see me take a written paper, so privately offered, from Sir Clement. But Sir Clement is an impracticable man, and I never succeeded in any attempt to frustrate whatever he had planned.

"No," said he, still in a whisper, "you must take them now, while Lady Louisa is away;" for she and Mrs. Selwyn were gone up stairs to finish their dress, "as she must by no means see them."

"Indeed," said I, "I have no intention to shew them."

"But the only way," answered he, "to avoid suspicion, is to take them in her absence. I would have read them aloud myself, but that they are not proper to be seen by any body in this house, yourself and Mrs. Selwyn excepted."

Then again he presented me the paper, which I now was obliged to take, as I found declining it was vain. But I was sorry that this action should be seen, and the whispering remarked, though the purport of the conversation was left to conjecture.

As I held it in my hand, Sir Clement teazed me to look at it immediately; and told me, the reason he could not produce the lines publicly, was, that, among the ladies who were mentioned, and supposed to be rejected, was Lady Louisa Larpent. I am much concerned at this circumstance, as I cannot doubt but that it will render me more disagreeable to her than ever, if she should hear of it.

I will now copy the verses, which Sir Clement would not let me rest till I had read.

> SEE last advance, with bashful grace,
>   Downcast eye, and blushing cheek,
> Timid air, and beauteous face,
>   Anville,—whom the Graces[3] seek,
>
> Though ev'ry beauty is her own,
>   And though her mind each virtue fills,
> Anville,—to her power unknown,
>   Artless strikes,—unconscious kills!

I am sure, my dear Sir, you will not wonder that a panegyric such as this, should, in reading, give me the greatest confusion; and, unfortunately, before I had finished it, the ladies returned.

"What have you there, my dear?" said Mrs. Selwyn.

"Nothing, Ma'am," said I, hastily folding, and putting it in my pocket.

3. Or Charites, goddesses personifying charm, grace, and beauty. Their names reveal their qualities: Aglaia, the Radiant; Auxo, the Grower; Euphrosyme, Joy; Kale, the Beautiful; Thalia, the Flowering, etc.

"And has *nothing*," cried she, "the power of *rouge?*"

I made no answer; a deep sigh which escaped Lord Orville at that moment, reached my ears, and gave me sensations—which I dare not mention!

Lord Merton then handed Lady Louisa and Mrs. Beaumont to the latter's carriage. Mrs. Selwyn led the way to Sir Clement's, who handed me in after her.

During the ride, I did not once speak; but when I came to the assembly-room, Sir Clement took care that I should not preserve my silence. He asked me immediately to dance; I begged him to excuse me, and seek some other partner. But on the contrary, he told me he was very glad I would sit still, as he had a million of things to say to me.

He then began to tell me how much he had suffered from absence; how greatly he was alarmed when he heard I had left town, and how cruelly difficult he had found it to trace me; which, at last, he could only do by sacrificing another week to Captain Mirvan.

"And Howard Grove," continued he, "which, at my first visit, I thought the most delightful spot upon earth, now appeared to me the most dismal; the face of the country seemed altered: the walks which I had thought most pleasant, were now most stupid: Lady Howard, who had appeared a chearful and respectable old lady, now appeared in the common John Trot[4] style of other aged dames: Mrs. Mirvan, whom I had esteemed as an amiable piece of still-life, now became so insipid, that I could hardly keep awake in her company: the daughter too, whom I had regarded as a good-humoured, pretty sort of girl, now seemed too insignificant for notice: and as to the Captain, I had always thought him a booby,—but now he appeared a savage!"

"Indeed, Sir Clement," cried I, angrily, "I will not hear you talk thus of my best friends."

"I beg your pardon," said he, "but the contrast of my two visits was too striking, not to be mentioned."

He then asked what I thought of the verses?

"Either," said I, "they are written ironically, or by some madman."

Such a profusion of compliments ensued, that I was obliged to propose dancing, in my own defence. When we stood up, "I intended," said he, "to have discovered the author by his looks; but I find you so much the general loadstone of attention, that my suspicions change their object every moment. Surely you must yourself have some knowledge who he is?"

I told him, no. Yet, my dear Sir, I must own to you, I have no doubt but that Mr. Macartney must be the author; no one else would speak of me so partially; and, indeed, his poetical turn puts it, with me, beyond dispute.

---

4. Slow, uncultured.

He asked me a thousand questions concerning Lord Orville; how long he had been at Bristol?—what time I had spent at Clifton?—whether he rode out every morning?—whether I ever trusted myself in a phaeton? and a multitude of other enquiries, all tending to discover if I was honoured with much of his Lordship's attention, and all made with his usual freedom and impetuosity.

Fortunately, as I much wished to retire early, Lady Louisa makes a point of being the first who quit the rooms, and therefore we got home in very tolerable time.

Lord Orville's reception of us was grave and cold: far from distinguishing me, as usual, by particular civilities, Lady Louisa herself could not have seen me enter the room with more frigid unconcern, nor have more scrupulously avoided honouring me with any notice. But chiefly I was struck to see, that he suffered Sir Clement, who stayed supper, to sit between us, without any effort to prevent him, though till then, he had seemed to be even tenacious of a seat next mine.

This little circumstance affected me more than I can express: yet I endeavoured to *rejoice* at it, since neglect and indifference from him may be my best friends.—But, alas!—so suddenly, so abruptly to forfeit his attention!—to lose his friendship!—Oh Sir, these thoughts pierced my soul!—scarce could I keep my seat; for not all my efforts could restrain the tears from trickling down my cheeks: however, as Lord Orville saw them not, for Sir Clement's head was constantly between us, I tried to collect my spirits, and succeeded so far as to keep my place with decency, till Sir Clement took leave: and then, not daring to trust my eyes to meet those of Lord Orville, I retired.

I have been writing ever since; for, certain that I could not sleep, I would not go to bed. Tell me, my dearest Sir, if you possibly can, tell me that you approve my change of conduct,—tell me that my altered behaviour to Lord Orville is right,—that my flying his society, and avoiding his civilities, are actions which *you* would have dictated.—Tell me this, and the sacrifices I have made will comfort me in the midst of my regret,—for never, never can I cease to regret that I have lost the friendship of Lord Orville!—Oh Sir, I have slighted, have rejected,—have thrown it away!—No matter, it was an honour I merited not to preserve, and I now see,—that my mind was unequal to sustaining it without danger.

Yet so strong is the desire you have implanted in me to act with uprightness and propriety, that, however the weakness of my heart may distress and afflict me, it will never, I humbly trust, render me wilfully culpable. The wish of doing well governs every other, as far as concerns my conduct,—for am I not *your* child?—the creature of your own forming?—Yet, Oh Sir, friend, parent of my heart!—my feelings are all at war with my duties; and, while I most struggle to acquire self-approbation, my peace, my happiness, my hopes,—are lost!

'Tis you alone can compose a mind so cruelly agitated; you, I well know, can feel pity for the weakness to which you are a stranger; and, though you blame the affliction, soothe and comfort the afflicted.

Letter XXII.

Berry Hill, Oct. 3.

Your last communication, my dearest child, is indeed astonishing; that an acknowledged daughter and heiress of Sir John Belmont should be at Bristol, and still my Evelina bear the name of Anville, is to me inexplicable: yet the mystery of the letter to Lady Howard prepared me to expect something extraordinary upon Sir John Belmont's return to England.

Whoever this young lady may be, it is certain she now takes a place to which you have a right indisputable. An *after-marriage* I never heard of; yet, supposing such a one to have happened, Miss Evelyn was certainly the first wife, and therefore her daughter must, at least, be entitled to the name of Belmont.

Either there are circumstances in this affair at present utterly incomprehensible, or else some strange and most atrocious fraud has been practised; which of these two is the case, it now behoves us to enquire.

My reluctance to this step gives way to my conviction of its propriety, since the reputation of your dear and much-injured mother must now either be fully cleared from blemish, or receive its final and indelible wound.

The public appearance of a daughter of Sir John Belmont will revive the remembrance of Miss Evelyn's story in all who have heard it,—who the *mother* was, will be universally demanded,—and if any other Lady Belmont should be named,—the birth of my Evelina will receive a stigma, against which honour, truth, and innocence may appeal in vain! a stigma which will eternally blast the fair fame of her virtuous mother, and cast upon her blameless self the odium of a title[1] which not all her purity can rescue from established shame and dishonour!

No, my dear child, no; I will not quietly suffer the ashes of your mother to be treated with ignominy! her spotless character shall be justified to the world—her marriage shall be acknowledged, and her child shall bear the name to which she is lawfully entitled.

It is true, that Mrs. Mirvan would conduct this affair with more delicacy than Mrs. Selwyn; yet, perhaps, to save time is, of all considerations, the most important, since the longer this mystery is suffered to continue, the more difficult may be rendered its explanation. The

---

1. That is, a bastard.

sooner, therefore, you can set out for town, the less formidable will be your task.

Let not your timidity, my dear love, depress your spirits: I shall, indeed, tremble for you at a meeting so singular, and so affecting, yet there can be no doubt of the success of your application: I enclose a letter from your unhappy mother, written, and reserved purposely for this occasion: Mrs. Clinton too, who attended her in her last illness, must accompany you to town.—But, without any other certificate of your birth, that which you carry in your countenance, as it could not be effected by artifice, so it cannot admit of a doubt.

And now, my Evelina, committed, at length, to the care of your real parent, receive the fervent prayers, wishes, and blessings, of him who so fondly adopted you!

May'st thou, oh child of my bosom! may'st thou, in this change of situation, experience no change of disposition! but receive with humility, and support with meekness, the elevation to which thou art rising! May thy manners, language, and deportment, all evince that modest equanimity, and chearful gratitude, which not merely deserve, but dignify prosperity! May'st thou, to the last moments of an unblemished life, retain thy genuine simplicity, thy singleness of heart, thy guileless sincerity! And may'st thou, stranger to ostentation, and superior to insolence, with true greatness of soul, shine forth conspicuous only in beneficence!

ARTHUR VILLARS.

Letter XIII.
[Inclosed in the preceding Letter.]

LADY BELMONT TO SIR JOHN BELMONT.

In the firm hope that the moment of anguish which approaches will prove the period of my sufferings, once more I address myself to Sir John Belmont, in behalf of the child, who, if it survives its mother, will hereafter be the bearer of this letter.

Yet in what terms,—oh most cruel of men!—can the lost Caroline address you, and not address you in vain? Oh deaf to the voice of compassion—deaf to the sting of truth,—deaf to every tie of honour—say, in what terms may the lost Caroline address you, and not address you in vain?

Shall I call you by the loved, the respected title of husband?—No, you disclaim it!—the father of my infant?—No, you doom it to infamy!—the lover who rescued me from a forced marriage?—No, you have yourself betrayed me!—the friend from whom I hoped succour and protection?—No, you have consigned me to misery and destruction!

Oh hardened against every plea of justice, remorse, or pity! how, and in what manner, may I hope to move thee? Is there one method I have left untried? remains there one resource unessayed? No! I have exhausted all the bitterness of reproach, and drained every sluice of compassion!

Hopeless, and almost desperate, twenty times have I flung away my pen;—but the feelings of a mother, a mother agonizing for the fate of her child, again animating my courage, as often I have resumed it.

Perhaps when I am no more, when the measure of my woes is compleated, and the still, silent, unreproaching dust has received my sad remains,—then, perhaps when accusation is no longer to be feared, nor detection to be dreaded, the voice of equity, and the cry of nature may be heard.

Listen, oh Belmont, to their dictates! reprobate not your child, though you have reprobated its mother. The evils that are past, perhaps, when too late, you may wish to recall; the young creature you have persecuted, perhaps, when too late, you may regret that you have destroyed;—you may think with horror of the deceptions you have practiced, and the pangs of remorse may follow me to the tomb:—oh Belmont, all my resentment softens into pity at the thought! what will become of thee, good Heaven, when with the eye of penitence, thou reviewest thy past conduct!

Hear, then, the solemn, the last address with which the unhappy Caroline will importune thee.

If when the time of thy contrition arrives,—for arrive it must!—when the sense of thy treachery shall rob thee of almost every other, if then thy tortured heart shall sigh to expiate thy guilt,—mark the conditions upon which I leave thee my forgiveness.

Thou know'st I am thy wife!—clear, then, to the world the reputation thou hast sullied, and receive as thy lawful successor, the child who will present thee this my dying request!

The worthiest, the most benevolent, the best of men, to whose consoling kindness I owe the little tranquillity I have been able to preserve, has plighted me his faith that, upon no other conditions, he will part with his helpless charge.

Should'st thou, in the features of this deserted innocent, trace the resemblance of the wretched Caroline,—should its face bear the marks of its birth, and revive in thy memory the image of its mother, wilt thou not, Belmont, wilt thou not therefore renounce it?—Oh babe of my fondest affection! for whom already I experience all the tenderness of maternal pity!—look not like thy unfortunate mother,—lest the parent whom the hand of death may spare, shall be snatched from thee by the more cruel means of unnatural antipathy!

I can write no more. The small share of serenity I have painfully acquired, will not bear the shock of the dreadful ideas that crowd upon me.

Adieu,—for ever!—

Yet oh!—shall I not, in this last farewell, which thou wilt not read till every stormy passion is extinct,—and the kind grave has embosomed all my sorrows,—shall I not offer to the man once so dear to me, a ray of consolation to those afflictions he has in reserve? Suffer me, then, to tell thee, that my pity far exceeds my indignation,—that I will pray for thee in my last moments—and that the recollection of the love I once bore thee, shall swallow up every other!

Once more, adieu!

CAROLINE BELMONT.

Letter XIV.

EVELINA TO THE REV. MR. VILLARS.

Clifton, Oct. 3rd.

This morning I saw from my window, that Lord Orville was walking in the garden; but I would not go down stairs till breakfast was ready: and then, he paid me his compliments almost as coldly as Lady Louisa paid her's.

I took my usual place, and Mrs. Beaumont, Lady Louisa, and Mrs. Selwyn, entered into their usual conversation.—Not so your Evelina: disregarded, silent, and melancholy, she sat like a cypher, whom to nobody belonging, by nobody was noticed.

Ill brooking such a situation, and unable to support the neglect of Lord Orville, the moment breakfast was over I left the room; and was going up stairs, when, very unpleasantly, I was stopped by Sir Clement Willoughby, who, flying into the hall, prevented my proceeding.

He enquired very particularly after my health, and entreated me to return into the parlour. Unwillingly I consented, but thought any thing preferable to continuing alone with him; and he would neither leave me, nor suffer me to pass on. Yet, in returning, I felt not a little ashamed of appearing thus to take the visit of Sir Clement to myself. And, indeed, he endeavoured, by his manner of addressing me, to give it that air.

He stayed, I believe, an hour; nor would he, perhaps, even then have gone, had not Mrs. Beaumont broken up the party, by proposing an airing in her coach. Lady Louisa consented to accompany her: but Mrs. Selwyn, when applied to, said, "If my Lord, or Sir Clement, will join us, I shall be happy to make one;—but really, a trio of females will be nervous to the last degree."

Sir Clement readily agreed to attend them; indeed, he makes it his evident study to court the favour of Mrs. Beaumont. Lord Orville excused himself from going out; and I retired to my own room. What he did with himself I know not, for I would not go down stairs till dinner was ready: his coldness, though my own change of behaviour has occasioned it, so cruelly depresses my spirits, that I know not how to support myself in his presence.

At dinner, I found Sir Clement again of the party. Indeed he manages every thing his own way; for Mrs. Beaumont, though by no means easy to please, seems quite at his disposal.

The dinner, the afternoon, and the evening, were to me the most irksome imaginable: I was tormented by the assiduity of Sir Clement, who not only *took*, but *made* opportunities of speaking to me,—and I was hurt,—oh how inexpressibly hurt!—that Lord Orville not only forbore, as hitherto, *seeking*, he even *neglected* all occasions of talking with me!

I begin to think, my dear Sir, that the sudden alteration in my behaviour was ill-judged and improper; for, as I had received no offence, as the cause of the change was upon *my* account, not *his*, I should not have assumed, so abruptly, a reserve for which I dared assign no reason,—nor have shunned his presence so obviously, without considering the strange appearance of such a conduct.

Alas, my dearest Sir, that my reflections should always be too late to serve me! dearly, indeed, do I purchase experience! and much I fear I shall suffer yet more severely, from the heedless indiscretion of my temper, ere I attain that prudence and consideration, which, by foreseeing distant consequences, may rule and direct in present exigencies.

Oct. 4th.

Yesterday morning, every body rode out, except Mrs. Selwyn and myself: and we two sat for some time together in her room; but, as soon as I could, I quitted her, to saunter in the garden; for she diverts herself so unmercifully with rallying me, either upon my gravity,—or concerning Lord Orville,—that I dread having any conversation with her.

Here I believe I spent an hour by myself; when, hearing the garden-gate open, I went into an arbour at the end of a long walk, where, ruminating, very unpleasantly, upon my future prospects, I remained quietly seated but a few minutes, before I was interrupted by the appearance of Sir Clement Willoughby.

I started; and would have left the arbour, but he prevented me. Indeed I am almost certain he had heard in the house where I was, as it is not, otherwise, probable he would have strolled down the garden alone.

"Stop, stop," cried he, "loveliest and most beloved of women, stop and hear me!"

Then, making me keep my place, he sat down by me, and would have taken my hand; but I drew it back, and said I could not stay.

"Can you, then," cried he, "refuse me the smallest gratification, though, but yesterday, I almost suffered martyrdom for the pleasure of seeing you?"

"Martyrdom! Sir Clement."

"Yes, beauteous insensible! *martyrdom:* for did I not compel myself to be immured in a carriage, the tedious length of a whole morning, with the three most fatiguing women in England?"

"Upon my word the Ladies are extremely obliged to you."

"O," returned he, "they have, every one of them, so copious a share of their own personal esteem, that they have no right to repine at the failure of it in the world; and, indeed, they will themselves be the last to discover it."

"How little," cried I, "are those Ladies aware of such severity from *you!*"

"They are guarded," answered he, "so happily and so securely by their own conceit, that they are not aware of it from any body. Oh Miss Anville, to be torn away from *you*, in order to be shut up with *them*,—is there a human being, except your cruel self, could forbear to pity me?"

"I believe, Sir Clement, however hardly you may choose to judge of them, your situation, by the world in general, would rather have been envied, than pitied."

"The world in general," answered he, "has the same opinion of them that I have myself: Mrs. Beaumont is every where laughed at, Lady Louisa ridiculed, and Mrs. Selwyn hated."

"Good God, Sir Clement, what cruel strength of words do you use!"

"It is you, my angel, are to blame, since your perfections have rendered their faults so glaring. I protest to you, during our whole ride, I thought the carriage drawn by snails. The absurd pride of Mrs. Beaumont, and the respect she exacts, are at once insufferable and stupifying; had I never before been in her company, I should have concluded that this had been her first airing from the herald's office,[2]—and wished her nothing worse than that it might also be the last. I assure you, that but for gaining the freedom of her house, I would fly her as I would plague, pestilence, and famine. Mrs. Selwyn, indeed, afforded some relief from this formality, but the unbounded licence of her tongue—"

"O Sir Clement, do *you* object to that?"

"Yes, my sweet reproacher, in a *woman*, I do; in a *woman* I think it intolerable. She has wit, I acknowledge, and more understanding than half her sex put together; but she keeps alive a perpetual expectation of satire, that spreads a general uneasiness among all who are in her presence; and she talks so much, that even the best things she says weary the attention. As to the little Louisa, 'tis such a pretty piece of languor,

2. The office of the Herald's College, "a royal corporation . . . recording proved pedigrees and granting armorial bearings" (*OED*); a reference to Mrs. Beaumont's excessive pride in her rank.

that 'tis almost cruel to speak rationally about her,—else I should say, she is a mere compound of affectation, impertinence, and airs."

"I am quite amazed," said I, "that, with such opinions, you can behave to them all with so much attention and civility."

"Civility! my angel,—why I could worship, could adore them, only to procure myself a moment of your conversation? Have you not seen me pay my court to the gross Captain Mirvan, and the virago Madame Duval? Were it possible that a creature so horrid could be formed, as to partake of the worst qualities of all these characters,—a creature who should have the haughtiness of Mrs. Beaumont, the brutality of Captain Mirvan, the self-conceit of Mrs. Selwyn, the affectation of Lady Louisa, and the vulgarity of Madame Duval,—even to such a monster as that, I would pay homage, and pour forth adulation, only to obtain one word, one look from my adored Miss Anville!"

"Sir Clement," said I, "you are greatly mistaken if you suppose such duplicity of character recommends you to my good opinion. But I must take this opportunity of begging you never more to talk to me in this strain."

"Oh Miss Anville, your reproofs, your coldness, pierce me to the soul! look upon me with less rigour, and make me what you please;—you shall govern and direct all my actions,—you shall new-form, new-model me:—I will not have even a wish but of your suggestion;—only deign to look upon me with pity,—if not with favour!"

"Suffer me, Sir," said I very gravely, "to make use of this occasion to put a final conclusion to such expressions. I entreat you never again to address me in a language so flighty and so unwelcome. You have already given me great uneasiness; and I must frankly assure you, that if you do not desire to banish me from wherever you are, you will adopt a very different style and conduct in future."

I then rose, and was going, but he flung himself at my feet to prevent me, exclaiming, in a most passionate manner, "Good God! Miss Anville, what do you say?—is it, can it be possible, that so unmoved, that with such petrifying indifference, you can tear from me even the remotest hope!"

"I know not, Sir," said I, endeavouring to disengage myself from him, "what hope you mean, but I am sure that I never intended to give you any."

"You distract me," cried he, "I cannot endure such scorn;—I beseech you to have some moderation in your cruelty, lest you make me desperate:—say, then, that you pity me,—O fairest inexorable! loveliest tyrant!—say, tell me, at least, that you pity me!"

Just then, who should come in sight, as if intending to pass by the arbour, but Lord Orville! Good Heaven, how did I start! and he the moment he saw me, turned pale, and was hastily retiring;—but I called out "Lord Orville!—Sir Clement, release me,—let go my hand!"

Sir Clement, in some confusion, suddenly rose, but still grasped my hand. Lord Orville, who had turned back, was again walking away; but, still struggling to disengage myself, I called out "Pray, pray, my Lord, don't go!—Sir Clement, I *insist* upon your releasing me!"

Lord Orville then, hastily approaching us, said, with great spirit, "Sir Clement, you cannot wish to detain Miss Anville by force!"

"Neither, my Lord," cried Sir Clement, proudly, "do I request the honour of your Lordship's interference."

However, he let go my hand, and I immediately ran into the house.

I was now frightened to death lest Sir Clement's mortified pride should provoke him to affront Lord Orville: I therefore ran hastily to Mrs. Selwyn, and entreated her, in a manner hardly to be understood, to walk towards the arbour. She asked no questions, for she is quick as lightning in taking a hint, but instantly hastened into the garden.

Imagine, my dear Sir, how wretched I must be till I saw her return! scarce could I restrain myself from running back: however, I checked my impatience, and waited, though in agonies, till she came.

And, now, my dear Sir, I have a conversation to write, the most interesting to me, that I ever heard. The comments and questions with which Mrs. Selwyn interrupted her account, I shall not mention; for they are such as you may very easily suppose.

Lord Orville and Sir Clement were both seated very quietly in the arbour: and Mrs. Selwyn, standing still, as soon as she was within a few yards of them, heard Sir Clement say, "Your question, my Lord, alarms me, and I can by no means answer it, unless you will allow me to propose another?"

"Undoubtedly, Sir."

"You ask me, my Lord, what are my intentions?—I should be very happy to be satisfied as to your Lordship's."

"I have never, Sir, professed *any*."

Here they were both, for a few moments, silent; and then Sir Clement said, "To what, my Lord, must I, then, impute your desire of knowing mine?"

"To an unaffected interest in Miss Anville's welfare."

"Such an interest," said Sir Clement, drily, "is, indeed, very generous: but, except in a father,—a brother,—or a lover—"

"Sir Clement," interrupted his Lordship, "I know your inference: and I acknowledge I have not the right of enquiry which any of those three titles bestow, and yet I confess the warmest wishes to serve her, and to see her happy. Will you, then, excuse me, if I take the liberty to repeat my question?"

"Yes, if your Lordship will excuse my repeating that I think it a rather extraordinary one."

"It may be so," said Lord Orville; "but this young lady seems to be peculiarly situated; she is very young, very inexperienced, yet appears to be left totally to her own direction. She does not, I believe, see the dangers to which she is exposed, and I will own to you, I feel a strong desire to point them out."

"I don't rightly understand your Lordship,—but I think you cannot mean to prejudice her against me?"

"Her sentiments of *you*, Sir, are as much unknown to me as your intentions towards *her*. Perhaps, were I acquainted with either, my officiousness might be at an end: but I presume not to ask upon what terms—"

Here he stopped; and Sir Clement said, "You know, my Lord, I am not given to despair; I am by no means such a puppy as to tell you I am upon *sure ground*, however, perseverance—"

"You are, then, determined to persevere?"

"I am, my Lord."

"Pardon me, then, Sir Clement, if I speak to you with freedom. This young lady, though she seems alone, and, in some measure, unprotected, is not entirely without friends; she has been extremely well educated, and accustomed to good company; she has a natural love of virtue, and a mind that might adorn *any* station, however exalted: is such a young lady, Sir Clement, a proper object to trifle with?—for your principles, excuse me, Sir, are well known."

"As to that, my Lord, let Miss Anville look to herself; she has an excellent understanding, and needs no counsellor."

"Her understanding is, indeed, excellent; but she is too young for suspicion, and has an artlessness of disposition that I never saw equalled."

"My Lord," cried Sir Clement, warmly, "your praises make me doubt your disinterestedness, and there exists not the man who I would so unwillingly have for a rival as yourself. But you must give me leave to say, you have greatly deceived me in regard to this affair."

"How so, Sir?" cried Lord Orville, with equal warmth.

"You were pleased, my Lord," answered Sir Clement, "upon our first conversation concerning this young lady, to speak of her in terms by no means suited to your present encomiums; you said she was a *poor, weak, ignorant girl*, and I had great reason to believe you had a most contemptuous opinion of her."

"It is very true," said Lord Orville," "that I did not, at our first acquaintance, do justice to the merit of Miss Anville; but I knew not, then, how new she was to the world; at present, however, I am convinced, that whatever might appear strange in her behaviour, was simply the effect of inexperience, timidity, and a retired education, for I find her informed, sensible, and intelligent. She is not, indeed, like most modern young ladies; to be known in half an hour; her modest worth, and fearful excellence, require both time and encouragement to shew themselves. She does not, beautiful as she is, seize the soul by surprise, but, with more dangerous fascination, she steals it almost imperceptibly."

"Enough, my Lord," cried Sir Clement, "your solicitude for her welfare is now sufficiently explained."

"My friendship and esteem," returned Lord Orville, "I do not wish to disguise; but assure yourself, Sir Clement, I should not have troubled *you* upon this subject, had Miss Anville and I ever conversed but as friends. However, since you do not chuse to avow your intentions, we must drop the subject."

"My intentions," cried he, "I will frankly own, are hardly known to myself. I think Miss Anville the loveliest of her sex, and, were I a *marrying man*, she, of all the women I have seen, I would fix upon for a wife: but I believe that not even the philosophy of your Lordship would recommend to me a connection of that sort, with a girl of obscure birth, whose only dowry is her beauty, and who is evidently in a state of dependency."

"Sir Clement," cried Lord Orville, with some heat, "we will discuss this point no further; we are both free agents, and must act for ourselves."

Here Mrs. Selwyn, fearing a surprise, and finding my apprehensions of danger were groundless, retired hastily into another walk, and soon after came to give me this account.

Good Heaven, what a man is this Sir Clement! so designing, though so easy; so deliberately artful, though so flighty! Greatly, however, is he mistaken, all confident as he seems; for the girl, obscure, poor, dependent as she is, far from wishing the honour of his alliance, would not only *now*, but *always* have rejected it.

As to Lord Orville,—but I will not trust my pen to mention him,— tell me, my dear Sir, what *you* think of him?—tell me if he is not the noblest of men?—and if you can either wonder at, or blame my admiration?

The idea of being seen by either party, immediately after so singular a conversation, was both awkward and distressing to me; but I was obliged to appear at dinner. Sir Clement, I saw, was absent and uneasy; he watched me, he watched Lord Orville, and was evidently disturbed in his mind. Whenever he spoke to me, I turned from him with undisguised disdain, for I am too much irritated against him, to bear with his ill-meant assiduities any longer.

But, not once,—not a moment, did I dare meet the eyes of Lord Orville! All consciousness myself, I dreaded his penetration, and directed mine every way—but towards his. The rest of the day I never quitted Mrs. Selwyn.

Adieu, my dear Sir: to-morrow I expect your directions whether I am to return to Berry Hill, or once more to visit London.

Letter XV.

EVELINA IN CONTINUATION.

Oct. 6th.

And now, my dearest Sir, if the perturbation of my spirits will allow me, I will finish my last letter from Clifton Hill.

This morning, though I did not go down stairs early, Lord Orville was the only person in the parlour when I entered it. I felt no small confusion at seeing him alone, after having so long and successfully avoided such a meeting. As soon as the usual compliments were over, I would have left the room, but he stopped me by saying, "If I disturb you, Miss Anville, I am gone."

"My Lord," said I, rather embarrassed, "I did not mean to stay."

"I flattered myself," cried he, "I should have had a moment's conversation with you."

I then turned back; and he seemed himself in some perplexity: but after a short pause, "You are very good" said he, "to indulge my request; I have, indeed, for some time past, most ardently desired an opportunity of speaking to you."

Again he paused; but I said nothing, so he went on.

"You allowed me, Madam, a few days since, you allowed me to lay claim to your friendship,—to interest myself in your affairs,—to call you by the affectionate title of sister;—and the honour you did me, no man could have been more sensible of; I am ignorant, therefore, how I have been so unfortunate as to forfeit it:—but, at present, all is changed! you fly me,—your averted eye shuns to meet mine, and you sedulously avoid my conversation."

I was extremely disconcerted at this grave, and but too just accusation, and I am sure I must look very simple;—but I made no answer.

"You will not, I hope," continued he, "condemn me unheard; if there is any thing I have done,—or any thing I have neglected, tell me, I beseech you, *what*, and it shall be the whole study of my thoughts how to deserve your pardon."

"Oh my Lord," cried I, penetrated at once with shame and gratitude, "your too, too great politeness oppresses me!—you have done nothing,—I have never dreamt of offence;—if there is any pardon to be asked, it is rather for *me*, than for *you*, to ask it."

"You are all sweetness and condescension!" cried he, "and I flatter myself you will again allow me to claim those titles which I find myself so unable to forego. Yet, occupied as I am with an idea that gives me the greatest uneasiness, I hope you will not think me impertinent, if I still solicit, still entreat, nay implore you to tell me, to what cause your late sudden, and to me most painful, reserve was owing?"

"Indeed, my Lord," said I, stammering, "I don't,—I can't,—indeed, my Lord,—"

"I am sorry to distress you," said he, "and ashamed to be so urgent,— yet I know not how to be satisfied while in ignorance,—and the *time* when the change happened, makes me apprehend—may I, Miss Anville, tell you *what* it makes me apprehend?"

"Certainly, my Lord."

"Tell me, then,—and pardon a question most essentially important to me;—Had, or had not, Sir Clement Willoughby, any share in causing your inquietude?"

"No, my Lord," answered I, with firmness, "none in the world."

"A thousand, thousand thanks!" cried he: "you have relieved me from a weight of conjecture which I supported very painfully. But one thing more; is it, in any measure, to Sir Clement that I may attribute the alteration in your behaviour to myself, which I could not but observe, began the very day of his arrival at the Hotwells?"

"To Sir Clement, my Lord," said I, "attribute nothing. He is the last man in the world who would have any influence over my conduct."

"And will you, then, restore to me that share of confidence and favour with which you honoured me before he came?"

Just then, to my great relief,—for I knew not what to say,—Mrs. Beaumont opened the door, and in a few minutes, we went to breakfast.

Lord Orville was all gaiety; never did I see him more lively or more agreeable. Very soon after, Sir Clement Willoughby called, to pay his respects, he said, to Mrs. Beaumont. I then came to my own room, where, indulging my reflections, which now soothed, and now alarmed me, I remained very quietly, till I received your most kind letter.

Oh Sir, how sweet are the prayers you offer for your Evelina! how grateful to her are the blessings you pour upon her head!—You *commit me to my real parent*,—Ah, Guardian, Friend, Protector of my youth!— by whom my helpless infancy was cherished, my mind formed, my very life preserved,—*you* are the Parent my heart acknowledges, and to you do I vow eternal duty, gratitude, and affection!

I look forward to the approaching interview with more fear than hope; but important as is this subject, I am just now, wholly engrossed with another, which I must hasten to communicate.

I immediately acquainted Mrs. Selwyn with the purport of your letter. She was charmed to find your opinion agreed with her own, and settled that we should go to town to-morrow morning. And a chaise is actually ordered to be here by one o'clock.

She then desired me to pack up my cloaths; and said she must go, herself, to *make speeches*, and *tell lies* to Mrs. Beaumont.

When I went down stairs to dinner, Lord Orville, who was still in excellent spirits, reproached me for secluding myself so much from the company. He sat next me,—he *would* sit next me,—at table; and he might, I am sure, repeat what he once said of me before, *that he almost exhausted himself in fruitless endeavours to entertain me*;—for, indeed, I was not to be entertained: I was totally spiritless and dejected; the idea of the approaching meeting,—and oh Sir, the idea of the approaching parting,—gave a heaviness to my heart, that I could neither conquer nor repress. I even regretted the half explanation that had passed, and wished Lord Orville had supported his own reserve, and suffered me to support mine.

However, when, during dinner, Mrs. Beaumont spoke of our journey, my gravity was no longer singular; a cloud instantly overspread the countenance of Lord Orville, and he became nearly as thoughtful and as silent as myself.

We all went together to the drawing-room. After a short and unentertaining conversation, Mrs. Selwyn said she must prepare for her journey, and begged me to see for some books she had left in the parlour.

And here, while I was looking for them, I was followed by Lord Orville. He shut the door after he came in, and approaching me with a look of great anxiety, said, "Is this true, Miss Anville, are you going?"

"I believe so, my Lord," said I, still looking for the books.

"So suddenly, so unexpectedly, must I lose you?"

"No great loss, my Lord," cried I, endeavouring to speak chearfully.

"Is it possible," said he, gravely, "Miss Anville can doubt my sincerity?"

"I can't imagine," cried I, "what Mrs. Selwyn has done with these books."

"Would to Heaven," continued he, "I might flatter myself you would allow me to prove it!"

"I must run up stairs," cried I, greatly confused, "and ask what she has done with them."

"You are going, then," cried he, taking my hand, "and you give me not the smallest hope of your return!—will you not, then, my too lovely friend!—will you not, at least, teach me, with fortitude like your own, to support your absence?"

"My Lord," cried I, endeavouring to disengage my hand, "pray let me go!"

"I will;" cried he, to my inexpressible confusion, dropping on one knee, "if you wish to leave me!"

"Oh my Lord," exclaimed I, "rise, I beseech you, rise!—such a posture to me!—surely your Lordship is not so cruel as to mock me!"

"Mock you!" repeated he earnestly, "no, I revere you! I esteem and I admire you above all human beings! you are the friend to whom my soul is attached as to its better half! you are the most amiable, the most perfect of women! and you are dearer to me than language has the power of telling!"

I attempt not to describe my sensations at that moment; I scarce breathed; I doubted if I existed,—the blood forsook my cheeks, and my feet refused to sustain me: Lord Orville, hastily rising, supported me to a chair, upon which I sunk, almost lifeless.

For a few minutes, we neither of us spoke; and then, seeing me recover, Lord Orville, though in terms hardly articulate, entreated my pardon for his abruptness. The moment my strength returned, I attempted to rise, but he would not permit me.

I cannot write the scene that followed, though every word is engraven on my heart: but his protestations, his expressions, were too flattering for repetition: nor would he, in spite of my repeated efforts to leave him, suffer me to escape;—in short, my dear Sir, I was not proof against his solicitations—and he drew from me the most sacred secret of my heart!

I know not how long we were together, but Lord Orville was upon his knees, when the door was opened by Mrs. Selwyn!—To tell you, Sir, the shame with which I was overwhelmed, would be impossible;—I snatched my hand from Lord Orville.—he, too, started and rose, and Mrs. Selwyn, for some instants, stood facing us both in silence.

At last, "My Lord," said she, sarcastically, "have you been so good as to help Miss Anville to look for my books?"

"Yes, Madam," answered he, attempting to rally, "and I hope we shall soon be able to find them."

"Your Lordship is extremely kind," said she, drily, "but I can by no means consent to take up any more of your time." Then, looking on the window-seat, she presently found the books, and added, "Come, here are just three, and so, like the servants in the Drummer,[1] this important affair may give employment to us all." She then presented one of them to Lord Orville, another to me, and taking a third herself, with a most provoking look, she left the room.

I would instantly have followed her; but Lord Orville, who could not help laughing, begged me to stay a minute, as he had many important matters to discuss.

"No, indeed, my Lord, I cannot,—perhaps I have already stayed too long."

"Does Miss Anville so soon repent her goodness?"

"I scarce know what I do, my Lord,—I am quite bewildered!"

"One hour's conversation," cried he, "will I hope compose your spirits, and confirm my happiness. When, then, may I hope to see you alone?—shall you walk in the garden to-morrow before breakfast?"

"No, no, my Lord; you must not, a second time, reproach me with making an *appointment*."

"Do you then," said he, laughing, "reserve that honour only for Mr. Macartney?"

1. *The Drummer; or, The Haunted House,* a comedy by Joseph Addison (1672–1719), first produced at Drury Lane in 1716 and revived in 1771.

"Mr. Macartney," said I, "is poor, and thinks himself obliged to me; otherwise—"

"Poverty," cried he, "I will not plead; but if being *obliged* to you has any weight, who shall dispute *my* title to an appointment?"

"My Lord, I can stay no longer,—Mrs. Selwyn will lose all patience."

"Deprive her not of the pleasure of her *conjectures*;—but tell me, are you under Mrs. Selwyn's care?"

"Only for the present, my Lord."

"Not a few are the questions I have to ask Miss Anville: among them, the most important is, whether she depends wholly on herself, or whether there is any other person for whose interest I must solicit?"

"I hardly know, my Lord, I hardly know myself to whom I most belong."

"Suffer, suffer me, then," cried he, with warmth, "to hasten the time when that shall no longer admit a doubt!—when your grateful Orville may call you all his own!"

At length, but with difficulty, I broke from him. I went, however, to my own room, for I was too much agitated to follow Mrs. Selwyn. Good God, my dear Sir, what a scene! surely the meeting for which I shall prepare to-morrow, cannot so greatly affect me! To be loved by Lord Orville,—to be the honoured choice of his noble heart,—my happiness seemed too infinite to be borne, and I wept, even bitterly I wept, from the excess of joy which overpowered me.

In this state of almost painful felicity, I continued, till I was summoned to tea. When I re-entered the drawing-room, I rejoiced much to find it full of company, as the confusion with which I met Lord Orville was rendered the less observable.

Immediately after tea, most of the company played at cards,—and then—and till supper-time, Lord Orville devoted himself wholly to me.

He saw that my eyes were red, and would not let me rest till he had made me confess the cause; and when, though most reluctantly, I had acknowledged my weakness, I could with difficulty refrain from weeping again at the gratitude he expressed.

He earnestly desired to know if my journey could not be postponed; and when I said no, entreated permission to attend me to town.

"Oh, my Lord," cried I, "what a request!"

"The sooner," answered he, "I make my devotion to you public, the sooner I may expect, from your delicacy, you will convince the world you encourage no mere *danglers*."[2]

"You teach me, then, my Lord, the inference I might expect, if I complied."

"And can you wonder I should seek to hasten the happy time, when no scruples, no discretion will demand our separation? and when the

2. Dallying followers.

most punctilious delicacy will rather promote, than oppose, my happiness in attending you?"

To this I was silent, and he re-urged his request.

"My Lord," said I, "you ask what I have no power to grant. This journey will deprive me of all right to act for myself."

"What does Miss Anville mean?"

"I cannot now explain myself; indeed, if I could, the task would be both painful and tedious."

"O Miss Anville," cried he, "when may I hope to date the period of this mystery? when flatter myself that my promised friend will indeed honour me with her confidence?"

"My Lord," said I, "I mean not to affect any mystery,—but my affairs are so circumstanced, that a long and most unhappy story, can alone explain them. However, if a short suspense will give your Lordship any uneasiness,—"

"My beloved Miss Anville," cried he, eagerly, "pardon my impatience!—You shall tell me nothing you would wish to conceal,—I will wait your own time for information, and trust to your goodness for its speed."

"There is *nothing*, my Lord, I wish to conceal,—to *postpone* an explanation is all I desire."

He then requested, that, since I would not allow him to accompany me to town, I would permit him to write to me, and promise to answer his letters.

A sudden recollection of the two letters which had already passed between us occurring to me, I hastily answered, "No indeed, my Lord!—"

"I am extremely sorry," said he, gravely, "that you think me too presumptuous. I must own I had flattered myself that to soften the inquietude of an absence which seems attended by so many inexplicable circumstances, would not have been to incur your displeasure."

This seriousness hurt me; and I could not forbear saying, "Can you indeed desire, my Lord, that I should, a second time, expose myself, by an unguarded readiness to write to you?"

"A *second time! unguarded readiness!*" repeated he; "you amaze me!"

"Has your Lordship then quite forgot the foolish letter I was so imprudent as to send you when in town?"

"I have not the least idea," cried he, "of what you mean."

"Why then, my Lord," said I, "we had better let the subject drop."

"Impossible!" cried he, "I cannot rest without an explanation!"

And then, he obliged me to speak very openly of both the letters; but, my dear Sir, imagine my surprise, when he assured me, in the most solemn manner, that far from having ever written me a single line, he had never received, seen, or heard of my letter!

This subject, which caused mutual astonishment and perplexity to us both, entirely engrossed us for the rest of the evening; and he made me promise to shew him the letter I had received in his name to-morrow morning, that he might endeavour to discover the author.

After supper, the conversation became general.

And now, my dearest Sir, may I not call for your congratulations upon the events of this day? a day never to be recollected by me but with the most grateful joy! I know how much you are inclined to think well of Lord Orville, I cannot, therefore, apprehend that my frankness to him will displease you. Perhaps the time is not very distant when your Evelina's choice may receive the sanction of her best friend's judgment and approbation,—which seems now all she has to wish!

In regard to the change in my situation which must first take place, surely I cannot be blamed for what has passed! the partiality of Lord Orville must not only reflect honour upon me, but upon all to whom I do, or may belong.

Adieu, most dear Sir. I will write again when I arrive at London.

Letter XVI.

EVELINA IN CONTINUATION.

Clifton, Oct. 7th.

You will see, my dear Sir, that I was mistaken in supposing I should write no more from this place, where my residence, now, seems more uncertain than ever.

This morning, during breakfast, Lord Orville took an opportunity to beg me, in a low voice, to allow him a moment's conversation before I left Clifton; "May I hope," added he, "that you will stroll into the garden after breakfast?"

I made no answer, but I believe my looks gave no denial; for, indeed I much wished to be satisfied concerning the letter. The moment, therefore, that I could quit the parlour I ran up stairs for my calash;[1] but before I reached my room, Mrs. Selwyn called after me, "If you are going to walk, Miss Anville, be so good as to bid Jenny bring down my hat, and I'll accompany you."

Very much disconcerted, I turned into the drawing-room, without making any answer, and there I hoped to wait unseen, till she had otherwise disposed of herself. But, in a few minutes, the door opened, and Sir Clement Willoughby entered.

Starting at the sight of him, in rising hastily, I let drop the letter which I had brought for Lord Orville's inspection, and, before I could recover it, Sir Clement, springing forward, had it in his hand. He was just presenting it to me, and, at the same time, enquiring after my health, when

---

1. "A woman's hood made of silk, supported with whalebone or cane hoops, and projecting beyond the face" (*OED*).

the signature caught his eye, and he read aloud "Orville."

I endeavoured, eagerly, to snatch it from him, but he would not permit me, and, holding it fast, in a passionate manner exclaimed, "Good God, Miss Anville, is it possible you can value such a letter as this?"

The question surprised and confounded me, and I was too much ashamed to answer him; but, finding he made an attempt to secure it, I prevented him, and vehemently demanded him to return it.

"Tell me first," said he, holding it above my reach, "tell me if you have, since, received any more letters from the same person?"

"No, indeed," cried I, "never!"

"And will you also, sweetest of women, promise that you never will receive any more? Say that, and you will make me the happiest of men."

"Sir Clement," cried I, greatly confused, "pray give me the letter."

"And will you not first satisfy my doubts?—will you not relieve me from the torture of the most distracting suspence?—tell me but that the detested Orville has written to you no more!"

"Sir Clement," cried I, angrily, "you have no right to make any conditions,—so pray give me the letter directly."

"Why such solicitude about this hateful letter? can it possibly deserve your eagerness? tell me, with truth, with sincerity tell me; Does it really merit the least anxiety?"

"No matter, Sir," cried I, in great perplexity, "the letter is mine, and therefore—"

"I must conclude, then," said he, "that the letter deserves your utmost contempt,—but that the name of Orville is sufficient to make you prize it."

"Sir Clement," cried I, colouring, "you are quite—you are very much—the letter is not—"

"O Miss Anville," cried he, "you blush!—you stammer!—Great Heaven! it is then all as I feared!"

"I know not," cried I, half frightened, "what you mean; but I beseech you to give me the letter, and to compose yourself."

"The letter," cried he, gnashing his teeth, "you shall never see more! You ought to have burnt it the moment you had read it!" And in an instant, he tore it into a thousand pieces.

Alarmed at a fury so indecently outrageous, I would have run out of the room; but he caught hold of my gown, and cried, "Not yet, not yet must you go! I am but half-mad yet, and you must stay to finish your work. Tell me, therefore, does Orville know your fatal partiality?—Say yes," added he, trembling with passion, "and I will fly you for ever!"

"For Heaven's sake, Sir Clement," cried I, "release me!—if you do not, you will force me to call for help."

"Call then," cried he, "inexorable and most unfeeling girl; call, if you please, and bid all the world witness your triumph;—but could ten worlds obey your call, I would not part from you till you had answered me. Tell me, then, does Orville know you love him?"

At any other time, an enquiry so gross would have given me inexpressible confusion; but now, the wildness of his manner terrified me, and I only said, "Whatever you wish to know, Sir Clement, I will tell you another time; but for the present, I entreat you to let me go!"

"Enough," cried he, "I understand you!—the art of Orville has prevailed;—cold, inanimate, phlegmatic as he is, you have rendered him the most envied of men!—One thing more, and I have done:—Will he marry you?"

What a question! my cheeks glowed with indignation, and I felt too proud to make any answer.

"I see, I see how it is," cried he, after a short pause, "and I find I am undone for ever!" Then, letting loose my gown, he put his hand to his forehead, and walked up and down the room in a hasty and agitated manner.

Though now at liberty to go, I had not the courage to leave him: for his evident distress excited all my compassion. And this was our situation, when Lady Louisa, Mr. Coverley, and Mrs. Beaumont entered the room.

"Sir Clement Willoughby," said the latter, "I beg pardon for making you wait so long, but—"

She had not time for another word; Sir Clement, too much disordered to know or care what he did, snatched up his hat, and, brushing hastily past her, flew down stairs, and out of the house.

And with him went my sincerest pity, though I earnestly hope I shall see him no more. But what, my dear Sir, am I to conclude from his strange speeches concerning the letter? Does it not seem as if he was himself the author of it? How else should he be so well acquainted with the contempt it merits? Neither do I know another human being who could serve any interest by such a deception. I remember, too, that just as I had given my own letter to the maid, Sir Clement came into the shop; probably he prevailed upon her, by some bribery, to give it to him, and afterwards, by the same means, to deliver to me an answer of his own writing. Indeed I can in no other manner account for this affair. Oh Sir Clement, were you not yourself unhappy, I know not how I could pardon an artifice that has caused me so much uneasiness!

His abrupt departure occasioned a kind of general consternation.

"Very extraordinary behaviour this!" cried Mrs. Beaumont.

"Egad," said Mr. Coverley, "the baronet has a mind to tip us a touch of the heroicks this morning!"

"I declare," cried Lady Louisa, "I never saw any thing so monstrous in my life! it's quite abominable,—I fancy the man's mad;—I'm sure he has given me a shocking fright!"

Soon after, Mrs. Selwyn came up stairs, with Lord Merton. The for-

mer, advancing hastily to me, said, "Miss Anville, have you an almanack?"

"Me!—no, Madam."

"Who has one, then?"

"Egad," cried Mr. Coverley, "I never bought one in my life; it would
make me quite melancholy to have such a time-keeper in my pocket. I
would as soon walk all day before an hour-glass."

"You are in the right," said Mrs. Selwyn, "not to *watch time*, lest you
should be betrayed, unawares, into reflecting how you employ it."

"Egad, Ma'am," cried he, "if Time thought no more of me than I do
of Time, I believe I should bid defiance, for one while, to old age and
wrinkles,—for deuce take me if ever I think about it at all."

"Pray, Mr. Coverley," said Mrs. Selwyn, "why do you think it necessary to tell me this so often?"

"Often!" repeated he; "Egad, Madam, I don't know why I said it
now,—but I'm sure I can't recollect that ever I owned as much before."

"Owned it before!" cried she, "why, my dear Sir, you own it all day
long; for every word, every look, every action proclaims it."

I know not if he understood the full severity of her satire, but he only
turned off with a laugh: and she then applied to Mr. Lovel, and asked if
he had an almanack?

Mr. Lovel, who always looks alarmed when she addresses him, with
some hesitation answered, "I assure you, Ma'am, I have no manner of
antipathy to an almanack,—none in the least,—I assure you;—I dare
say I have four or five."

"Four or five!—pray may I ask what use you make of so many?"

"Use!—really, Ma'am, as to that,—I don't make any particular use of
them,—but one must have them, to tell one the day of the month,—
I'm sure, else I should never keep it in my head."

"And does your time pass so smoothly unmarked, that, without an
almanack, you could not distinguish one day from another?"

"Really, Ma'am," cried he, colouring, "I don't see any thing so very
particular in having a few almanacks; other people have them, I believe,
as well as me."

"Don't be offended," cried she, "I have but made a little digression.
All I want to know, is the state of the moon,—for if it is at the *full* I shall
be saved a world of conjectures, and know at once to what cause to
attribute the inconsistencies I have witnessed this morning. In the first
place, I heard Lord Orville excuse himself from going out, because he
had business of importance to transact at home,—yet have I seen him
sauntering alone in the garden this half hour. Miss Anville, on the other
hand, I invited to walk out with me; and, after seeking her every where
round the house, I find her quietly seated in the drawing-room. And but
a few minutes since, Sir Clement Willoughby, with even more than his
usual politeness, told me he was come to spend the morning here,—

when, just now, I met him flying down stairs, as if pursued by the Furies;[2] and, far from repeating his compliments, or making any excuse, he did not even answer a question I asked him, but rushed past me, with the rapidity of a thief from a bailiff!"

"I protest," said Mrs. Beaumont, "I can't think what he meant; such rudeness from a man of any family is quite incomprehensible."

"My Lord," cried Lady Louisa to Lord Merton, "do you know he did the same by *me?*—I was just going to ask him what was the matter, but he ran past me so quick, that I declare he quite dazzled my eyes. You can't think, my Lord, how he frightened me; I dare say I look as pale—don't I look very pale, my Lord?"

"Your Ladyship," said Mr. Lovel, "so well becomes the lilies, that the roses might blush to see themselves so excelled."

"Pray, Mr. Lovel," said Mrs. Selwyn, "if the roses should blush, how would you find it out?"

"Egad," cried Mr. Coverley, "I suppose they must blush, as the saying is, like a blue dog,[3]—for they are *red* already."

"Prithee, Jack," said Lord Merton, "don't you pretend to talk about blushes, that never knew what they were in your life."

"My Lord," said Mrs. Selwyn, "if experience alone can justify mentioning them, what an admirable treatise upon the subject may we not expect from your Lordship!"

"O, pray, Ma'am," answered he, "stick to Jack Coverley,—he's your only man; for my part, I confess I have a mortal aversion to arguments."

"O fie, my Lord," cried Mrs. Selwyn, "a senator of the nation! a member of the noblest parliament[4] in the world!—and yet neglect the art of oratory!"

"Why, faith, my Lord," said Mr. Lovel, "I think, in general, your House is not much addicted to study; we of the lower House have indubitably most application; and, if I did not speak before a superior power," bowing low to Lord Merton, "I should presume to add, we have likewise the most able speakers."

"Mr. Lovel," said Mrs. Selwyn, "you deserve immortality for that discovery! But for this observation, and the confession of Lord Merton, I protest I should have supposed that a peer of the realm, and an able logician, were synonymous terms."

Lord Merton, turning upon his heel, asked Lady Louisa if she should *take the air* before dinner?

"Really," answered she, "I don't know;—I'm afraid it's monstrous hot; besides," (putting her hand to her forehead) "I a'n't half well; it's quite

---

2. The Furies or Erinyes, spirits of punishment avenging wrongs done to kindred, were three in number: Tisiphone, the Avenger of blood; Alecto, the Implacable; and Magaera, the Jealous one.
3. Not to blush at all (*Brewer's Dictionary of Phrase and Fable*, rev. ed. (New York: Harper, 1970) 128.
4. Because he is a nobleman, Lord Merton is a member of the House of Lords.

horrid to have such weak nerves!—the least thing in the world discomposes me: I declare, that man's oddness has given me such a shock,—I don't know when I shall recover from it. But I'm a sad weak creature,—don't you think I am, my Lord?"

"O, by no means," answered he, "your Ladyship is merely delicate,—and devil take me if ever I had the least passion for an Amazon."

"I have the honour to be quite of your Lordship's opinion," said Mr. Lovel, looking maliciously at Mrs. Selwyn, "for I have an insuperable aversion to strength, either of body or mind, in a female."

"Faith, and so have I," said Mr. Coverley; "for egad I'd as soon see a woman chop wood, as hear her chop logic."

"So would every man in his senses," said Lord Merton; "for a woman wants nothing to recommend her but beauty and good-nature; in every thing else she is either impertinent or unnatural. For my part, deuce take me if ever I wish to hear a word of sense from a woman as long as I live!"

"It has always been agreed," said Mrs. Selwyn, looking round her with the utmost contempt, "that no man ought to be connected with a woman whose understanding is superior to his own. Now I very much fear, that to accommodate all this good company, according to such a rule, would be utterly impracticable, unless we should chuse subjects from Swift's hospital of idiots."[5]

How many enemies, my dear Sir, does this unbounded severity excite! Lord Merton, however, only whistled; Mr. Coverley sang; and Mr. Lovel, after biting his lips some time, said, "'Pon honour, that lady—if she was *not* a lady,—I should be half tempted to observe,—that there is something,—in such severity,—that is rather, I must say,—rather—*oddish*."

Just then, a servant brought Lady Louisa a note upon a *waiter*,[6] which is a ceremony always used to her Ladyship; and I took the opportunity of this interruption to the conversation, to steal out of the room.

I went immediately to the parlour, which I found quite empty; for I did not dare walk in the garden after what Mrs. Selwyn had said.

In a few minutes, a servant announced Mr. Macartney, saying, as he entered the room, that he would acquaint Lord Orville he was there.

Mr. Macartney rejoiced much at finding me alone. He told me he had taken the liberty to enquire for Lord Orville, by way of pretext for coming to the house.

I then very eagerly enquired if he had seen his father.

"I have, Madam," said he; "and the generous compassion you have shewn made me hasten to acquaint you, that upon reading my unhappy mother's letter, he did not hesitate to acknowledge me."

5. Saint Patrick's Hospital in Dublin (opened 1757), which was endowed by the will of Jonathan Swift (1667–1745).
6. "A salver, small tray" (*OED*).

"Good God," cried I, with no little emotion, "how similar are our circumstances! And did he receive you kindly?"

"I could not, Madam, expect that he would: the cruel transaction which obliged me to fly Paris, was too recent in his memory."

"And,—have you seen the young lady?"

"No, Madam," said he mournfully, "I was forbid her sight."

"Forbid her sight!—and why?"

"Partly, perhaps, from prudence,—and partly from the remains of a resentment which will not easily subside. I only requested leave to acquaint her with my relationship, and be allowed to call her sister;—but it was denied me! 'You have no sister,' said Sir John, 'you must forget her existence.' Hard, and vain command!"

"You have—you have a sister!" cried I, from an impulse of pity which I could not, repress, "a sister who is most warmly interested in your welfare, and who only wants opportunity to manifest her friendship and regard."

"Gracious Heaven!" cried he, "what does Miss Anville mean?"

"Anville," said I, "is not my real name; Sir John Belmont is my father,—he is your's,—and I am your sister!—You see, therefore, the claim we mutually have to each other's regard; we are not merely bound by the ties of friendship, but by those of blood. I feel for you, already, all the affection of a sister,—I felt it, indeed, before I knew I was one.—Why, my dear brother, do you not speak?—do you hesitate to acknowledge me?"

"I am so lost in astonishment," cried he, "that I know not if I hear right!"—

"I have then found a brother," cried I, holding out my hand, "and he will not own me!"

"Own you!—Oh, Madam," cried he, accepting my offered hand, "is it, indeed, possible you can own me?—a poor, wretched adventurer! who so lately had no support but from your generosity?—whom your benevolence snatched from utter destruction?—Can you,—Oh Madam, can you indeed, and without a blush, condescend to own such an outcast for a brother?"

"Oh, forbear, forbear," cried I, "is this language proper for a sister? are we not reciprocally bound to each other?——Will you not suffer me to expect from you all the good offices in your power?—But tell me, where is our father at present?"

"At the Hotwell, Madam; he arrived there yesterday morning."

I would have proceeded with further questions, but the entrance of Lord Orville prevented me. The moment he saw us, he started, and would have retreated; but drawing my hand from Mr. Macartney's, I begged him to come in.

For a few moments we were all silent, and, I believe, all in equal confusion. Mr. Macartney, however, recollecting himself, said, "I hope your Lordship will forgive the liberty I have taken in making use of your name."

Lord Orville, rather coldly, bowed, but, said nothing.

Again we were all silent, and then Mr. Macartney took leave.

"I fancy," said Lord Orville, when he was gone, "I have shortened Mr. Macartney's visit?"

"No, my Lord, not at all."

"I had presumed," said he, with some hesitation, "I should have seen Miss Anville in the garden;—but I knew not she was so much better engaged."

Before I could answer, a servant came to tell me the chaise was ready, and that Mrs. Selwyn was enquiring for me.

"I will wait on her immediately," cried I, and away I was running; but Lord Orville, stopping me, said, with great emotion, "Is it thus, Miss Anville, you leave me?"

"My Lord," cried I, "how can I help it?—perhaps, soon, some better opportunity may offer—"

"Good Heaven!" cried he, "do you indeed take me for a Stoic?[7] What better opportunity may I hope for?—is not the chaise come?—are you not going? have you even deigned to tell me whither?"

"My journey, my Lord, will now be deferred. Mr. Macartney has brought me intelligence which renders it, at present, unnecessary."

"Mr. Macartney," said he, gravely, "seems to have great influence,—yet he is a very young counsellor."

"Is it possible, my Lord, Mr. Macartney can give you the least uneasiness?"

"My dearest Miss Anville," said he, taking my hand, "I see, and I adore the purity of your mind, superior as it is to all little arts, and all apprehensions of suspicion; and I should do myself, as well as you, injustice, if I were capable of harbouring the smallest doubts of that goodness which makes you mine for ever: nevertheless, pardon me, if I own myself surprised,—nay, alarmed, at these frequent meetings with so young a man as Mr. Macartney."

"My Lord," cried I, eager to clear myself, "Mr. Macartney is my brother!"

"Your brother! you amaze me!—What strange mystery, then, makes his relationship a secret?"

Just then, Mrs. Selwyn opened the door. "O, you are here!" cried she; "Pray is my Lord so kind as to assist you in *preparing* for your journey,—or in *retarding* it?"

"I should be most happy," said Lord Orville, smiling, "if it were in my power to do the *latter*."

---

7. "One who practises repression of emotion, indifference to pleasure or pain, and patient endurance" (OED); the term is derived from a school of Greek philosophers, founded by Zeno (flourished circa 300 B.C.).

I then acquainted her with Mr. Macartney's communication.

She immediately ordered the chaise away, and then took me into her own room, to consider what should be done.

A few minutes sufficed to determine her, and she wrote the following note.

To Sir John Belmont, Bart.[8]

Mrs. Selwyn presents her compliments to Sir John Belmont, and, if he is at leisure, will be glad to wait on him this morning, upon business of importance.

She then ordered her man to enquire at the pump room for a direction; and went herself to Mrs. Beaumont to apologise for deferring her journey.

An answer was presently returned, that he would be glad to see her.

She would have had me immediately accompany her to the Hotwells; but I entreated her to spare me the distress of so abrupt an introduction, and to pave the way for my reception. She consented rather reluctantly, and, attended only by her servant, walked to the Wells.

She was not absent two hours, yet so miserably did time seem to linger, that I thought a thousand accidents had happened, and feared she would never return. I passed the whole time in my own room, for I was too much agitated even to converse with Lord Orville.

The instant that, from my window, I saw her returning, I flew down stairs, and met her in the garden.

We both walked to the arbour.

Her looks, in which disappointment and anger were expressed, presently announced to me the failure of her embassy. Finding that she did not speak, I asked her, in a faultering voice, whether or not I had a father?

"You have *not*, my dear!" said she abruptly.

"Very well, Madam," said I, with tolerable calmness, "let the chaise, then, be ordered again,—I will go to Berry Hill,—and there, I trust, I shall still find one!"

It was some time ere she could give, or I could hear, the account of her visit; and then she related it in a hasty manner; yet I believe I can recollect every word.

"I found Sir John alone. He received me with the utmost politeness. I did not keep him a moment in suspence as to the purport of my visit. But I had no sooner made it known, than, with a supercilious smile, he said, 'And have you, Madam, been prevailed upon to revive that ridiculous old story?' Ridiculous, I told him, was a term which he would find no one else do him the favour to make use of, in speaking of the horrible actions belonging to the *old story* he made so light of; 'actions,' continued I, 'which would dye still deeper the black annals of Nero or Calig-

8. Baronet.

ula.'[9] He attempted in vain to rally, for I pursued him with all the severity in my power, and ceased not painting the enormity of his crime, till I stung him to the quick, and in a voice of passion and impatience, he said, 'No more, Madam,—this is not a subject upon which I need a monitor.' 'Make then,' cried I, 'the only reparation in your power.—Your daughter is now at Clifton; send for her hither, and, in the face of the world, proclaim the legitimacy of her birth, and clear the reputation of your injured wife.' 'Madam,' said he, 'you are much mistaken, if you suppose I waited for the honour of this visit, before I did what little justice now depends upon me, to the memory of that unfortunate woman: her daughter has been my care from her infancy; I have taken her into my house; she bears my name, and she will be my sole heiress.' For some time this assertion appeared so absurd, that I only laughed at it; but, at last, he assured me, I had myself been imposed upon, for that the very woman who attended Lady Belmont in her last illness, conveyed the child to him while he was in London, before she was a year old. 'Unwilling,' he added, 'at that time to confirm the rumour of my being married, I sent the woman with the child to France; as soon as she was old enough, I put her into a convent, where she has been properly educated; and now I have taken her home. I have acknowledged her for my lawful child, and paid, at length, to the memory of her unhappy mother, a tribute of fame, which has made me wish to hide myself hereafter from all the world.' This whole story sounded so improbable, that I did not scruple to tell him I discredited every word. He then rung his bell, and enquiring if his hair-dresser was come, said he was sorry to leave me, but that, if I would favour him with my company to-morrow, he would do himself the honour of introducing Miss Belmont to *me*, instead of troubling me to introduce her to *him*. I rose in great indignation, and assuring him I would make his conduct as public as it was infamous—I left the house."

Good Heaven, how strange the recital! how incomprehensible an affair! The Miss Belmont, then, who is actually at Bristol, passes for the daughter of my unhappy mother!—passes, in short, for your Evelina! Who she can be, or what this tale can mean, I have not any idea.

Mrs. Selwyn soon after left me to my own reflections. Indeed they were not very pleasant. Quietly as I had borne her relation, the moment I was alone I felt most bitterly both the disgrace and the sorrow of a rejection so cruelly inexplicable.

I know not how long I might have continued in this situation, had I not been awakened from my melancholy reverie by the voice of Lord Orville. "May I come in," cried he, "or shall I interrupt you?"

I was silent, and he seated himself next me.

"I fear," he continued, "Miss Anville will think I persecute her; yet so

---

9. The Roman emperors Nero (A.D. 37–68) and Caligula (A.D. 12–41) were infamous for their cruelty and bloodthirstiness.

much as I have to say, and so much as I wish to hear, with so few opportunities for either, she cannot wonder,—and I hope she will not be offended,—that I seize with such avidity every moment in my power to converse with her. You are grave," added he, taking my hand; "I hope you do not regret the delay of your journey?—I hope the pleasure it gives to *me*, will not be a subject of pain to *you?*—You are silent?—Something, I am sure, has afflicted you:—would to Heaven I were able to console you!—Would to Heaven I were worthy to participate in your sorrows!"

My heart was too full to bear this kindness, and I could only answer by my tears. "Good Heaven," cried he, "how you alarm me!—My love, my sweet Miss Anville, deny me no longer to be the sharer of your griefs!—tell me, at least, that you have not withdrawn your esteem!—that you do not repent the goodness you have shewn me!—that you still think me the same grateful Orville whose heart you have deigned to accept!"

"Oh, my Lord," cried I, "your generosity overpowers me!" And I wept like an infant. For now that all my hopes of being acknowledged seemed finally crushed, I felt the nobleness of his disinterested regard so forcibly, that I could scarce breathe under the weight of gratitude which oppressed me.

He seemed greatly shocked, and in terms the most flattering, the most respectfully tender, he at once soothed my distress, and urged me to tell him its cause.

"My Lord," said I, when I was able to speak, "you little know what an outcast you have honoured with your choice!—a child of bounty,—an orphan from infancy,—dependent, even for subsistence dependent, upon the kindness of compassion!—Rejected by my natural friends,[1]—disowned for ever by my nearest relation,—Oh, my Lord, so circumstanced, can I deserve the distinction with which you honour me? No, no, I feel the inequality too painfully;—you must leave me, my Lord, you must suffer me to return to obscurity,—and there, in the bosom of my first, best, my only friend,—I will pour forth all the grief of my heart!—while you, my Lord, must seek elsewhere—"

I could not proceed; my whole soul recoiled against the charge I would have given, and my voice refused to utter it.

"Never!" cried he, warmly; "my heart is yours, and I swear to you an attachment eternal!—You prepare me, indeed, for a tale of horror, and I am almost breathless with expectation,—but so firm is my conviction, that, whatever are your misfortunes, to have merited them is not of the number, that I feel myself more strongly, more invincibly devoted to you than ever!—Tell me but where I may find this noble friend, whose virtues you have already taught me to reverence,—and I will fly to

1. Kinfolk or near relations.

obtain his consent and intercession, that henceforward our fates may be indissolubly united,—and then shall it be the sole study of my life to endeavour to soften your past,—and guard you from future misfortunes!"

I had just raised my eyes, to answer this most generous of men, when the first object they met was Mrs. Selwyn.

"So, my dear," cried she, "what, still courting the rural shades!—I thought ere now you would have been satiated with this retired seat, and I have been seeking you all over the house. But I find the only way to meet with *you*,—is to enquire for *Lord Orville*. However, don't let me disturb your meditations; you are possibly planning some pastoral dialogue."

And, with this provoking speech, she walked on.

In the greatest confusion, I was quitting the arbour, when Lord Orville said, "Permit *me* to follow Mrs. Selwyn,—it is time to put an end to all impertinent conjectures; will you allow me to speak to her openly?"

I assented in silence, and he left me.

I then went to my own room, where I continued till I was summoned to dinner; after which, Mrs. Selwyn invited me to hers.

The moment she had shut the door, "Your Ladyship," said she, "will, I hope, be seated."

"Ma'am!" cried I, staring.

"O the sweet innocent! So you don't know what I mean?—but, my dear, my sole view is to accustom you a little to your dignity elect, lest, when you are addressed by your title, you should look another way, from an apprehension of listening to a discourse not meant for you to hear."

Having in this manner, diverted herself with my confusion, till her raillery was almost exhausted, she congratulated me very seriously upon the partiality of Lord Orville, and painted to me, in the strongest terms, his disinterested desire of being married to me immediately. She had told him, she said, my whole story; and yet he was willing, nay eager, that our union should take place of any further application to my family. "Now, my dear," continued she, "I advise you by all means to marry him directly; nothing can be more precarious than our success with Sir John; and the young men of this age are not to be trusted with too much time for deliberation, where their interests are concerned."

"Good God, Madam," cried I, "do, you think I would *hurry* Lord Orville?"

"Well, do as you will," said she, "luckily you have an excellent subject for Quixotism;—otherwise, this delay might prove your ruin: but Lord Orville is almost as romantic as if he had been born and bred at Berry Hill."

She then proposed, as no better expedient seemed likely to be suggested, that I should accompany her at once in her visit to the Hotwells to-morrow morning.

The very idea made me tremble; yet she represented so strongly the necessity of pursuing this unhappy affair with spirit, or giving it totally up, that, wanting her force of argument, I was almost obliged to yield to her proposal.

In the evening, we all walked in the garden: and Lord Orville, who never quitted my side, told me he had been listening to a tale, which, though it had removed the perplexities that had so long tormented him, had penetrated him with sorrow and compassion. I acquainted him with Mrs. Selwyn's plan for to-morrow, and confessed the extreme terror it gave me. He then, in a manner almost unanswerable, besought me to leave to him the conduct of the affair, by consenting to be his before an interview took place.

I could not but acknowledge my sense of his generosity; but I told him I was wholly dependent upon you, and that I was certain your opinion would be the same as mine, which was, that it would be highly improper I should dispose of myself for ever, so very near the time which must finally decide by whose authority I ought to be guided. The subject of this dreaded meeting, with the thousand conjectures and apprehensions to which it gives birth, employed all our conversation then, as it has all my thoughts since.

Heaven only knows how I shall support myself, when the long-expected,—the wished,—yet terrible moment arrives, that will prostrate me at the feet of the nearest, the most reverenced of all relations, whom my heart yearns to know, and longs to love!

Letter XVII.

EVELINA IN CONTINUATION.

Oct. 9.

I could not write yesterday, so violent was the agitation of my mind,—but I will not, now, lose a moment till I have hastened to my best friend an account of the transactions of a day I can never recollect without emotion.

Mrs. Selwyn, determined upon sending no message, "Lest," said she, "Sir John, fatigued with the very idea of my reproaches, should endeavour to avoid a meeting: all we have to do, is to take him by surprise. He cannot but see who you are, whether he will do you justice or not."

We went early, and in Mrs. Beaumont's chariot; into which, Lord Orville, uttering words of the kindest encouragement, handed us both. My uneasiness, during the ride, was excessive, but, when we stopped at the door, I was almost senseless with terror! the meeting, at last, was not so dreadful as that moment! I believe I was carried into the house;

but I scarce recollect what was done with me: however, I know we remained some time in the parlour, before Mrs. Selwyn could send any message up stairs.

When I was somewhat recovered, I entreated her to let me return home, assuring her I felt myself quite unequal to supporting the interview.

"No," said she; "you must stay now; your fears will but gain strength by delay, and we must not have such a shock as this repeated." Then, turning to the servant, she sent up her name.

An answer was brought, that he was going out in great haste, but would attend her immediately. I turned so sick, that Mrs. Selwyn was apprehensive I should have fainted; and opening a door which led to an inner apartment, she begged me to wait there till I was somewhat composed, and till she had prepared for my reception.

Glad of every moment's reprieve, I willingly agreed to the proposal, and Mrs. Selwyn had but just time to shut me in, before her presence was necessary.

The voice of a *father*—Oh dear and revered name!—which then, for the first time, struck my ears, affected me in a manner I cannot describe, though it was only employed in giving orders to a servant as he came down stairs.

Then, entering the parlour, I heard him say, "I am sorry, Madam, I made you wait, but I have an engagement which now calls me away: however, if you have any commands for me, I shall be glad of the honour of your company some other time."

"I am come, Sir," said Mrs. Selwyn, "to introduce your daughter to you."

"I am infinitely obliged to you," answered he, "but I have just had the satisfaction of breakfasting with her. Ma'am, your most obedient."

"You refuse, then, to see her?"

"I am much indebted to you, Madam, for this desire of encreasing my family, but you must excuse me if I decline taking advantage of it. I have already a daughter, to whom I owe every thing; and it is not three days since that I had the pleasure of discovering a son; how many more sons and daughters may be brought to me, I am yet to learn, but I am, already, perfectly satisfied with the size of my family."

"Had you a thousand children, Sir John," said Mrs. Selwyn, warmly, "this only one, of which Lady Belmont was the mother, ought to be most distinguished; and, far from avoiding her sight, you should thank your stars, in humble gratitude, that there yet remains in your power the smallest opportunity of doing the injured wife you have destroyed, the poor justice of acknowledging her child!"

"I am very unwilling, Madam," answered he, "to enter into any discussion of this point; but you are determined to compel me to speak. There lives not at this time, the human being who should talk to *me* of the regret due to the memory of that ill-fated woman; no one can feel it so severely as myself: but let me, nevertheless, assure you I have already done all that remained in my power to prove the respect she merited from me; her child I have educated and owned for my lawful heiress; if, Madam, you can suggest to me any other means by which I may more fully do her justice, and more clearly manifest her innocence, name them to me, and though they should wound my character still deeper, I will perform them readily."

"All this sounds vastly well," returned Mrs. Selwyn, "but I must own it is rather too enigmatical for *my* faculties of comprehension. You can, however, have no objection to seeing this young lady."

"None in the world."

"Come forth, then, my dear," cried she, opening the door, "come forth, and see your father!" Then, taking my trembling hand, she led me forward. I would have withdrawn it, and retreated, but as he advanced instantly towards me, I found myself already before him.

What a moment for your Evelina!—an involuntary scream escaped me, and covering my face with my hands, I sunk on the floor.

He had, however, seen me first; for in a voice scarce articulate, he exclaimed, "My God! does Caroline Evelyn still live!"

Mrs. Selwyn said something, but I could not listen to her; and, in a few minutes, he added, "Lift up thy head,—if my sight has not blasted thee,—lift up thy head, thou image of my long-lost Caroline!"

Affected beyond measure, I half arose, and embraced his knees, while yet on my own.

"Yes, yes," cried he, looking earnestly in my face, "I see, I see thou art her child! she lives—she breathes—she is present to my view;—Oh God, that she indeed lived!—Go, child, go" added he, wildly starting, and pushing me from him, "take her away, Madam,—I cannot bear to look at her!" And then, breaking hastily from me, he rushed out of the room.

Speechless, motionless myself, I attempted not to stop him: but Mrs. Selwyn, hastening after him, caught hold of his arm. "Leave me, Madam," cried he, with quickness, "and take care of the poor child;—bid her not think me unkind, tell her I would at this moment plunge a dagger in my heart to serve her,—but she has set my brain on fire, and I can see her no more!" Then, with a violence almost frantic, he ran up stairs.

Oh Sir, had I not indeed cause to dread this interview?—an interview so unspeakably painful and afflicting to us both! Mrs. Selwyn would have immediately returned to Clifton; but I entreated her to wait some time, in the hope that my unhappy father, when his first emotion was over, would again bear me in his sight. However, he soon after sent his servant to enquire how I did, and to tell Mrs. Selwyn he was much indisposed, but would hope for the honour of seeing her to-morrow, at any time she would please to appoint.

She fixed upon ten o'clock in the morning; and then, with a heavy heart, I got into the chariot. Those afflicting words, *I can see her no more*, were never a moment absent from my mind.

Yet the sight of Lord Orville, who handed us from the carriage, gave some relief to the sadness of my thoughts. I could not, however, enter upon the painful subject, but begging Mrs. Selwyn to satisfy him, I went to my own room.

As soon as I communicated to the good Mrs. Clinton the present situation of my affairs, an idea occurred to her, which seemed to clear up all the mystery of my having been so long disowned.

The woman, she says, who attended my ever-to-be-regretted mother in her last illness, and who nursed me the first four months of my life, soon after being discharged from your house, left Berry Hill entirely, with her baby, who was but six weeks older than myself. Mrs. Clinton remembers, that her quitting the place appeared, at the time, very extraordinary to the neighbours, but, as she was never heard of afterwards, she was, by degrees, quite forgotten.

The moment this was mentioned, it struck Mrs. Selwyn, as well as Mrs. Clinton herself, that my father had been imposed upon, and that the nurse who said she had brought his child to him, had, in fact, carried her own.

The name by which I was known, the secrecy observed in regard to my family, and the retirement in which I lived, all conspired to render this scheme, however daring and fraudulent, by no means impracticable, and, in short, the idea was no sooner started, than conviction seemed to follow it.

Mrs. Selwyn determined immediately to discover the truth or mistake of this conjecture; therefore, the moment she had dined, she walked to the Hotwells, attended by Mrs. Clinton.

I waited in my room till her return, and then heard the following account of her visit:

She found my poor father in great agitation. She immediately informed him of the occasion of her so speedy return, and of her suspicions of the woman who had pretended to convey to him his child. Interrupting her with quickness, he said he had just sent her from his presence: that the certainty I carried in my countenance, of my real birth, made him, the moment he had recovered from a surprise which had almost deprived him of reason, suspect, himself, the imposition she mentioned. He had, therefore, sent for the woman, and questioned her with the utmost austerity: she turned pale, and was extremely embarrassed, but still she persisted in affirming, that she had really brought him the daughter of Lady Belmont. His perplexity, he said, almost distracted him; he had *always* observed that his daughter bore no resemblance to either of her parents, but, as he had never doubted the veracity of the nurse, this circumstance did not give birth to any suspicion.

At Mrs. Selwyn's desire, the woman was again called, and interrogated with equal art and severity; her confusion was evident, and her answers often contradictory, yet she still declared she was no impostor. "We will see that in a minute," said Mrs. Selwyn, and then desired Mrs. Clinton might be called up stairs. The poor wretch, changing colour, would have escaped out of the room, but, being prevented, dropt on her knees, and implored forgiveness. A confession of the whole affair was then extorted from her.

Doubtless, my dear Sir, you must remember *Dame Green*, who was my first nurse. The deceit she has practised, was suggested, she says, by a conversation she overheard, in which my unhappy mother besought you, that, if her child survived her, you would take the sole care of its education; and, in particular, if it should be a female, you would by no means part with her early in life. You not only consented, she says, but assured her you would even retire abroad with me yourself, if my father should importunately demand me. Her own child, she said, was then in her arms, and she could not forbear wishing it were possible to give *her* the fortune which seemed so little valued for me. This wish once raised, was not easily suppressed; on the contrary, what at first appeared a mere idle desire, in a short time seemed a feasible scheme. Her husband was dead, and she had little regard for any body but her child; and, in short, having saved money for the journey, she contrived to enquire a direction to my father, and telling her neighbours she was going to settle in Devonshire, she set out on her expedition.

When Mrs. Selwyn asked her, how she dared perpetrate such a fraud, she protested she had no ill designs, but that, as *Miss* would be never the worse for it, she thought it pity *nobody* should be the better.

Her success we are already acquainted with. Indeed everything seemed to contribute towards it: my father had no correspondent at Berry Hill, the child was instantly sent to France, where being brought up in as much retirement as myself, nothing but accident could discover the fraud.

And here, let me indulge myself in observing, and rejoicing to observe, that the total neglect I thought I met with, was not the effect of insensibility or unkindness, but of imposition and error; and that at the very time, we concluded I was unnaturally rejected, my deluded father meant to shew me most favour and protection.

He acknowledges that Lady Howard's letter flung him into some perplexity; he immediately communicated it to Dame Green, who confessed it was the greatest shock she had ever received in her life; yet she had the art and boldness to assert, that Lady Howard must herself have been deceived: and as she had, from the beginning of her enterprize, declared she had stolen away the child without your knowledge, he concluded that some deceit was *then* intended him; and this thought occasioned his abrupt answer.

Dame Green owned, that from the moment the journey to England was settled, she gave herself up for lost. All her hope was to have had her daughter married before it took place, for which reason she had so much promoted Mr. Macartney's addresses: for though such a match was inadequate to the pretensions of *Miss Belmont*, she well knew it was far superior to those *her daughter* could form, after the discovery of her birth.

My first enquiry was, if this innocent daughter was yet acquainted with the affair? "No," Mrs. Selwyn said, nor was any plan settled how to divulge it to her. Poor unfortunate girl! how hard is her fate! She is entitled to my kindest offices, and I shall always consider her as my sister.

I then asked whether my father would again allow me to see him!

"Why no, my dear, not yet," answered she; "he declares the sight of you is too much for him: however, we are to settle everything concerning you to-morrow, for this woman took up all our time to-day."

This morning, therefore, she is again gone to the Hotwell. I am waiting in all impatience for her return; but as I know you will be anxious for the account this letter contains, I will not delay sending it.

Letter XVIII.

EVELINA IN CONTINUATION.

Oct. 9.

How agitated, my dear Sir, is the present life of your Evelina! every day seems important, and one event only a prelude to another.

Mrs. Selwyn, upon her return this morning from the Hotwell, entering my room very abruptly, said, "Oh my dear, I have terrible news for you!"

"For me, Ma'am!—Good God! what now?"

"Arm yourself," cried she, "with all your Berry Hill philosophy;—con over every lesson of fortitude or resignation you ever learnt in your life,—for know,—you are next week to be married to Lord Orville!"

Doubt, astonishment, and a kind of perturbation I cannot describe, made this abrupt communication alarm me extremely, and, almost breathless, I could only exclaim, "Good God, Madam, what do you tell me?"

"You may well be frightened, my dear," said she, ironically, "for really there is something mighty terrific, in becoming at once, the wife of the man you adore,—and a Countess!"[1]

1. Lord Orville is an Earl, the English equivalent of the continental Count.

I entreated her to spare her raillery, and tell me her real meaning. She could not prevail with herself to grant the *first* request, though she readily complied with the second.

My poor father, she said, was still in the utmost uneasiness. He entered upon his affairs with great openness, and told her he was equally disturbed how to dispose either of the daughter he had discovered, or the daughter he was now to give up; the former he dreaded to trust himself with again beholding, and the latter he knew not how to shock with the intelligence of her disgrace. Mrs. Selwyn then acquainted him with my situation in regard to Lord Orville; this delighted him extremely, and, when he heard of his Lordship's eagerness, he said he was himself of opinion, the sooner the union took place the better: and in return, he informed her of the affair of Mr. Macartney. "And, after a very long conversation," continued Mrs. Selwyn, "we agreed, that the most eligible scheme for all parties would be to have both the real and the fictitious daughter married without delay. Therefore, if either of you have any inclination to pull caps for the title of Miss Belmont, you must do it with all speed, as next week will take from both of you all pretensions to it."

"Next week!—dear Madam, what a strange plan!—without my being consulted—without applying to Mr. Villars,—without even the concurrence of Lord Orville!"

"As to consulting *you*, my dear, it was out of all question, because, you know, young ladies' hearts and hands are always to be given with reluctance;—as to Mr. Villars, it is sufficient we know him for your friend;—and as for Lord Orville, he is a party concerned."

"A party concerned!—you amaze me!"

"Why, yes; for as I found our consultation likely to redound to his advantage, I persuaded Sir John to send for him."

"Send for him!—Good God!"

"Yes, and Sir John agreed. I told the servant, that if he could not hear of his Lordship in the house, he might be pretty certain of encountering him in the arbour.—Why do you colour, my dear?—Well, he was with us in a moment; I introduced him to Sir John, and we proceeded to business."

"I am very, very sorry for it!—Lord Orville must, himself, think this conduct strangely precipitate."

"No, my dear, you are mistaken, Lord Orville has too much good sense. Everything was then discussed in a rational manner. You are to be married privately, though not secretly, and then go to one of his Lordship's country seats: and poor little Miss Green and your brother, who have no house of their own, must go to one of Sir John's."

"But why, my dear Madam, why all this haste? why may we not be allowed a little longer time."

"I could give you a thousand reasons," answered she, "but that I am tolerably certain *two* or *three* will be more than you can controvert, even with all the logic of genuine coquetry. In the first place, you doubtless wish to quit the house of Mrs. Beaumont,—to whose, then, can you with such propriety remove, as to Lord Orville's?"

"Surely, Madam," cried I, "I am not more destitute now, than when I thought myself an orphan."

"Your father, my dear," answered she, "is willing to save the little impostor as much of the mortification of her disgrace as is in his power: now if you immediately take her place, according to your right, as Miss Belmont, why not all that either of you can do for her, will prevent her being eternally stigmatized, as the bantling[2] of Dame Green, washwoman and wet nurse of Berry Hill, Dorsetshire. Now such a genealogy will not be very flattering, even to Mr. Macartney, who, all-dismal as he is, you will find by no means wanting in pride and self-consequence."

"For the universe," interrupted I, "I would not be accessary to the degradation you mention; but, surely, Madam, I may return to Berry Hill?"

"By no means," said she; "for though compassion may make us wish to save the poor girl the confusion of an immediate and public fall, yet justice demands you should appear, henceforward, in no other light than that of Sir John Belmont's daughter. Besides, between friends, I, who know the world, can see that half this prodigious delicacy for the little usurper, is the mere result of self-interest; for while *her* affairs are hushed up, Sir John's, you know, are kept from being brought further to light. Now the double marriage we have projected, obviates all rational objections. Sir John will give you, immediately, £30,000; all settlements,[3] and so forth, will be made for you in the name of Evelina Belmont;—Mr. Macartney will, at the same time, take poor Polly Green,—and yet, at first, it will only be generally known, that *a daughter of Sir John Belmont's is married.*"

In this manner, though she did not convince me, yet the quickness of her arguments silenced and perplexed me. I enquired, however, if I might not be permitted to again see my father, or whether I must regard myself as banished his presence for ever?

"My dear," said she, "he does not know you; he concludes that you have been brought up to detest him, and therefore he is rather prepared to dread, than to love you."

This answer made me very unhappy; I wished, most impatiently, to remove his prejudice, and endeavour, by dutiful assiduity, to engage his kindness, yet knew not how to propose seeing him, while conscious he wished to avoid me.

This evening, as soon as the company was engaged with cards, Lord Orville exerted his utmost eloquence to reconcile me to this hasty plan:

2. "A young or small child, a brat" (*OED*); formerly used as a synonym for "bastard."
3. Money and property to be settled on the wife and sometimes the children.

but how was I startled, when he told me that next *Tuesday* was the day appointed by my father to be the most important of my life!

"Next Tuesday!" repeated I, quite out of breath, "Oh my Lord!—"

"My sweet Evelina," said he, "the day which will make me the happiest of mortals, would probably appear awful to you, were it to be deferred a twelvemonth: Mrs. Selwyn has, doubtless, acquainted you with the many motives which, independent of my eagerness, require it to be speedy; suffer, therefore, its acceleration, and generously complete my felicity, by endeavouring to suffer it without repugnance."

"Indeed, my Lord, I would not wilfully raise objections, nor do I desire to appear insensible of the honour of your good opinion;—but there is something in this plan, so very hasty,—so unreasonably precipitate,—besides, I shall have no time to hear from Berry Hill,—and believe me, my Lord, I should be for ever miserable, were I in an affair so important, to act without the sanction of Mr. Villars' advice."

He offered to wait on you himself, but I told him I had rather write to you. And then he proposed, that, instead of my immediately accompanying him to Lincolnshire, we should, first, pass a month *at my native Berry Hill.*

This was, indeed, a grateful proposal to me, and I listened to it with undisguised pleasure. And,—in short, I was obliged to consent to a compromise, in merely deferring the day till Thursday! He readily undertook to engage my father's concurrence in this little delay, and I besought him, at the same time, to make use of his influence to obtain me a second interview, and to represent the deep concern I felt in being thus banished his sight.

He would then have spoken of *settlements,* but I assured him, I was almost ignorant of the word.

And now, my dearest Sir, what is your opinion of these hasty proceedings? believe me, I half regret the simple facility with which I have suffered myself to be hurried into compliance, and, should you start but the smallest objection, I will yet insist upon being allowed more time.

I must now write a concise account of the state of my affairs to Howard Grove, and to Madame Duval.

Adieu, dearest and most honoured Sir! everything, at present, depends upon your single decision, to which, though I yield in trembling, I yield implicitly.

Letter XIX.

EVELINA IN CONTINUATION.

Oct. 11.

Yesterday morning, as soon as breakfast was over, Lord Orville went to the Hotwells, to wait upon my father with my double petition.

Mrs. Beaumont then, in general terms, proposed a walk in the garden. Mrs. Selwyn said she had letters to write, but Lady Louisa arose to accompany her.

I had had some reason to imagine, from the notice with which her Ladyship had honoured me during breakfast, that her brother had acquainted her with my present situation: and her behaviour now confirmed my conjecture; for, when I would have gone up stairs, instead of suffering me, as usual, to pass disregarded, she called after me with an affected surprise, "Miss Anville, don't you walk with us?"

There seemed something so little-minded in this sudden change of conduct, that, from an involuntary motion of contempt, I thanked her, with a coldness like her own, and declined her offer. Yet, observing that she blushed extremely at my refusal, and recollecting she was sister to Lord Orville, my indignation subsided, and upon Mrs. Beaumont repeating the invitation, I accepted it.

Our walk proved extremely dull; Mrs. Beaumont, who never says much, was more silent than usual; Lady Louisa strove in vain to lay aside the restraint and distance she has hitherto preserved; and as to me, I was too conscious of the circumstances to which I owed their attention, to feel either pride or pleasure from receiving it.

Lord Orville was not long absent; he joined us in the garden with a look of gaiety and good-humour that revived us all. "You are just the party," said he, "I wished to see together. Will you, Madam, taking my hand, allow me the honour of introducing you, by your real name, to two of my nearest relations? Mrs. Beaumont, give me leave to present to you the daughter of Sir John Belmont; a young lady who, I am sure, must long since have engaged your esteem and admiration, though you were a stranger to her birth."

"My Lord," said Mrs. Beaumont, graciously saluting[1] me, "the young lady's rank in life,—your Lordship's recommendation,—or her own merit, would any one of them, have been sufficient to have entitled her to my regard; and I hope she has always met with that respect in my house which is so much her due; though, had I been sooner made acquainted with her family, I should, doubtless, have better known how to have secured it."

"Miss Belmont," said Lord Orville, "can receive no lustre from family, whatever she may give to it. Louisa, you will, I am sure, be happy to make yourself an interest in the friendship of Miss Belmont, whom I hope shortly, kissing my hand, and joining it with her Ladyship's, to have the happiness of presenting to you by yet another name, and by the most endearing of all titles."

I believe it would be difficult to say whose cheeks were, at that moment, of the deepest dye, Lady Louisa's or my own; for the conscious

---

1. Kissing (by way of salutation).

pride with which she has hitherto slighted me, gave to her an embarrassment which equalled the confusion that an introduction so unexpected gave to me. She saluted me, however, and, with a faint smile, said, "I shall esteem myself very happy to profit by the honour of Miss Belmont's acquaintance."

I only courtsied, and we walked on; but it was evident, from the little surprise they expressed, that they had been already informed of the state of the affair.

We were, soon after, joined by more company: and Lord Orville then, in a low voice, took an opportunity to tell me the success of his visit. In the first place, Thursday was agreed to; and, in the second, my father, he said, was much concerned to hear of my uneasiness, sent me his blessing, and complied with my request of seeing him, with the same readiness he should agree to any other I could make. Lord Orville, therefore, settled that I should wait upon him in the evening, and, at his particular request, unaccompanied by Mrs. Selwyn.

This kind message, and the prospect of so soon seeing him, gave me sensations of mixed pleasure and pain, which wholly occupied my mind till the time of my going to the Hotwells.

Mrs. Beaumont lent me her chariot, and Lord Orville absolutely insisted upon attending me. "If you go alone," said he, "Mrs. Selwyn will certainly be offended; but, if you allow me to conduct you, though she may give the freer scope to her raillery, she cannot possibly be affronted: and we had much better suffer her laughter, than provoke her satire."

Indeed, I must own I had no reason to regret being so accompanied; for his conversation supported my spirits from drooping, and made the ride seem so short, that we actually stopt at my father's door, before I knew we had proceeded ten yards.

He handed me from the carriage, and conducted me to the parlour, at the door of which I was met by Mr. Macartney. "Ah, my dear brother," cried I, "how happy am I to see you here!"

He bowed and thanked me. Lord Orville, then, holding out his hand, said, "Mr. Macartney, I hope we shall be better acquainted; I promise myself much pleasure from cultivating your friendship."

"Your Lordship does me but too much honour," answered Mr. Macartney.

"But where," cried I, "is my sister? for so I must already call, and always consider her:—I am afraid she avoids me;—you must endeavour, my dear brother, to prepossess her in my favour, and reconcile her to owning me."

"Oh Madam," cried he, "you are all goodness and benevolence! but at present, I hope you will excuse her, for I fear she has hardly fortitude sufficient to see you: in a short time, perhaps—"

"In a *very* short time, then," said Lord Orville, "I hope you will yourself introduce her, and that we shall have the pleasure of wishing you both joy: allow me, my Evelina, to say *we,* and permit me, in your name as well as my own, to entreat that the first guests we shall have the happiness of receiving, may be Mr. and Mrs. Macartney."

A servant then came to beg I would walk up stairs.

I besought Lord Orville to accompany me; but he feared the displeasure of Sir John, who had desired to see me alone. He led me, however, to the foot of the stairs, and made the kindest efforts to give me courage; but indeed he did not succeed, for the interview appeared to me in all its terrors, and left me no feeling but apprehension.

The moment I reached the landing place, the drawing-room door was opened, and my father, with a voice of kindness, called out, "My child, is it you?"

"Yes, Sir," cried I, springing forward, and kneeling at his feet, "it is your child, if you will own her!"

He knelt by my side, and folding me in his arms, "Own thee," repeated he, "yes, my poor girl, and Heaven knows with what bitter contrition!" Then raising both himself and me, he brought me into the drawing-room, shut the door, and took me to the window, where, looking at me with great earnestness, "Poor unhappy Caroline!" cried he, and, to my inexpressible concern, he burst into tears. Need I tell you, my dear Sir, how mine flowed at the sight?

I would again have embraced his knees; but, hurrying from me, he flung himself upon a sopha, and leaning his face on his arms, seemed, for some time, absorbed in bitterness of grief.

I ventured not to interrupt a sorrow I so much respected, but waited in silence, and at a distance, till he recovered from his violence. But then it seemed, in a moment, to give way to a kind of frantic fury; for, starting suddenly, with a sternness which at once surprised and frightened me. "Child," cried he, "hast thou yet sufficiently humbled thy father?—if thou hast, be contented with this proof of my weakness, and no longer force thyself into my presence!"

Thunderstruck by a command so unexpected, I stood still and speechless, and doubted whether my own ears did not deceive me.

"Oh go, go!" cried he, passionately, "in pity—in compassion,—if thou valuest my senses, leave me,—and for ever!"

"I will, I will," cried I, greatly terrified; and I moved hastily towards the door: yet stopping when I reached it, and, almost involuntarily, dropping on my knees, "Vouchsafe," cried I, "oh, Sir, vouchsafe but once to bless your daughter, and her sight shall never more offend you!"

"Alas," cried he, in a softened voice, "I am not worthy to bless thee!— I am not worthy to call thee daughter!—I am not worthy that the fair light of Heaven should visit my eyes!—Oh God! that I could but call back the time ere thou wast born,—or else bury its remembrance in eternal oblivion!"

"Would to Heaven," cried I, "that the sight of me were less terrible to you! that, instead of irritating, I could soothe your sorrows!—Oh Sir, how thankfully would I then prove my duty, even at the hazard of my life!"

"Are you so kind?" cried he, gently; "come hither, child,—rise, Evelina;—alas, it is for *me* to kneel, not you—and I *would* kneel,—I would crawl upon the earth;—I would kiss the dust,—could I by such submission, obtain the forgiveness of the representative of the most injured of women!"

"Oh, Sir," exclaimed I, "that you could but read my heart!—that you could but see the filial tenderness and concern with which it overflows!—you would not then talk thus,—you would not then banish me your presence, and exclude me from your affection!"

"Good God," cried he, "is it then possible that you do not hate me?—Can the child of the wronged Caroline look at,—and not execrate me? Wast thou not born to abhor, and bred to curse me? Did not thy mother bequeath thee her blessing, on condition that thou shouldst detest and avoid me?"

"Oh no, no, no!" cried I, "think not so unkindly of her, nor so hardly of me." I then took from my pocket-book her last letter, and, pressing it to my lips, with a trembling hand, and still upon my knees, I held it out to him.

Hastily snatching it from me, "Great Heaven!" cried he, "'tis her writing—Whence comes this?—who gave it you?—why had I it not sooner?"

I made no answer; his vehemence intimidated me, and I ventured not to move from the suppliant posture in which I had put myself.

He went from me to the window, where his eyes were for some time rivetted upon the direction of the letter, though his hand shook so violently he could hardly hold it. Then, bringing it to me, "Open it,"—cried he,—"for I cannot!"

I had, myself, hardly strength to obey him but, when I had, he took it back, and walked hastily up and down the room, as if dreading to read it. At length, turning to me, "Do you know," cried he, "its contents?"

"No, Sir," answered I, "it has never been unsealed."

He then again went to the window, and began reading. Having hastily run it over, he cast up his eyes with a look of desperation; the letter fell from his hand, and he exclaimed, "Yes! thou art sainted!—thou art blessed!—and I am cursed for ever!" He continued some time fixed in this melancholy position; after which, casting himself with violence upon the ground, "Oh wretch," cried he, "unworthy life and light, in what dungeon canst thou hide thy head?"

I could restrain myself no longer; I rose and went to him; I did not dare speak, but with pity and concern unutterable, I wept and hung over him.

Soon after, starting up, he again seized the letter, exclaiming, "Acknowledge thee, Caroline!—yes, with my heart's best blood would I acknowledge thee!—Oh that thou couldst witness the agony of my soul!—Ten thousand daggers could not have wounded me like this letter!"

Then, after again reading it, "Evelina," he cried, "she charges me to receive thee;—wilt thou, in obedience to her will, own for thy father the destroyer of thy mother?"

What a dreadful question! I shuddered, but could not speak.

"To clear her fame, and receive her child," continued he, looking stedfastly at the letter, "are the conditions upon which she leaves me her forgiveness: her fame, I have already cleared;—and oh how willingly would I take her child to my bosom,—fold her to my heart,—call upon her to mitigate my anguish, and pour the balm of comfort on my wounds, were I not conscious I deserve not to receive it, and that all my affliction is the result of my own guilt!"

It was in vain I attempted to speak; horror and grief took from me all power of utterance.

He then read aloud from the letter, "*Look not like thy unfortunate mother!*—Sweet soul, with what bitterness of spirit hast thou written?— Come hither, Evelina: Gracious Heaven!" looking earnestly at me "never was likeness more striking!—the eye,—the face,—the form,— Oh my child, my child!" Imagine, Sir,—for I can never describe my feelings, when I saw him sink upon his knees before me! "Oh dear resemblance of thy murdered mother!—Oh all that remains of the most injured of women! behold thy father at thy feet!—bending thus lowly to implore you would not hate him;—Oh then, thou representative of my departed wife, speak to me in her name, and say that the remorse which tears my soul, tortures me not in vain!"

"Oh rise, rise, my beloved father," cried I, attempting to assist him, "I cannot bear to see you thus;—reverse not the law of nature, rise yourself, and bless your kneeling daughter!"

"May Heaven bless thee, my child!—" cried he, "for I dare not." He then rose, and embracing me most affectionately, added, "I see, I see that thou art all kindness, softness, and tenderness; I need not have feared thee, thou art all the fondest father could wish, and I will try to frame my mind to less painful sensations at thy sight. Perhaps the time may come when I may know the comfort of such a daughter,—at present, I am only fit to be alone: dreadful as are my reflections, they ought merely to torment myself.—Adieu, my child;—be not angry,—I cannot stay with thee,—Oh Evelina! thy countenance is a dagger to my heart!—just so, thy mother looked,—just so—"

Tears and sighs seemed to choak him!—and waving his hand, he would have left me,—but, clinging to him, "Oh, Sir," cried I, "will you so soon abandon me?—am I again an orphan?—oh my dear, my long-lost father, leave me not, I beseech you! take pity on your child, and rob her not of the parent she so fondly hoped would cherish her!"

"You know not what you ask," cried he; "the emotions which now rend my soul are more than my reason can endure; suffer me, then, to leave you,—impute it not to unkindness, but think of me as well as thou canst.—Lord Orville has behaved nobly;—I believe he will make thee happy." Then, again embracing me, "God bless thee, my dear child," cried he, "God bless thee, my Evelina!—endeavour to love,—at least not to hate me,—and to make me an interest in thy filial bosom by thinking of me as thy father."

I could not speak; I kissed his hands on my knees; and then, with yet more emotion, he again blessed me, and hurried out of the room,—leaving me almost drowned in tears.

Oh Sir, all goodness as you are, how much will you feel for your Evelina, during a scene of such agitation! I pray Heaven to accept the tribute of his remorse, and restore him to tranquillity!

When I was sufficiently composed to return to the parlour, I found Lord Orville waiting for me with the utmost anxiety:—and then, a new scene of emotion, though of a far different nature, awaited me; for I learnt by Mr. Macartney, that this noblest of men had insisted the so-long supposed Miss Belmont should be considered *indeed* as my sister, and as the co-heiress of my father though not in *law*, in *justice*, he says, she ought ever to be treated as the daughter of Sir John Belmont.

Oh Lord Orville!—it shall be the sole study of my happy life, to express, better than by words, the sense I have of your exalted benevolence, and greatness of mind!

Letter XX.

EVELINA IN CONTINUATION.

Clifton, Oct. 12.

This morning, early, I received the following letter from Sir Clement Willoughby.

To Miss Anville.

I have this moment received intelligence that preparations are actually making for your marriage with Lord Orville.

Imagine not that I write with the imbecile idea of rendering those preparations abortive. No, I am not so mad. My sole view is to explain the motive of my conduct in a particular instance, and to obviate the accusation of treachery which may be laid to my charge.

My unguarded behaviour when I last saw you, has, probably, already acquainted you, that the letter I then saw you reading was written by myself. For your further satisfaction, let me have the honour of informing you, that the letter you had designed for Lord Orville, had fallen into my hands.

However I may have been urged on by a passion the most violent that ever warmed the heart of man, I can by no means calmly submit to be stigmatized for an action seemingly so dishonourable; and it is for this reason that I trouble you with my justification.

Lord Orville,—the happy Orville, whom you are so ready to bless,—had made me believe he loved you not,—nay, that he held you in contempt.

Such were my thoughts of his sentiments of you, when I got possession of the letter you meant to send him; I pretend not to vindicate either the means I used to obtain it, or the action of breaking the seal;—but I was impelled by an impetuous curiosity to discover the terms upon which you wrote to him.

The letter, however, was wholly unintelligible to me, and the perusal of it only added to my perplexity.

A tame suspense I was not born to endure, and I determined to clear my doubts at all hazards and events.

I answered it, therefore, in Orville's name.

The views which I am now going to acknowledge, must, infallibly, incur your displeasure,—yet I scorn all palliation.

Briefly, then,—I concealed your letter to prevent a discovery of your capacity,—and I wrote you an answer which I hoped would prevent your wishing for any other.

I am well aware of every thing which can be said upon this subject. Lord Orville will, possibly, think himself ill used;—but I am extremely indifferent as to his opinion, nor do I now write by way of offering any apology to him, but merely to make known to yourself the reasons by which I have been governed.

I intend to set off next week for the Continent. Should his Lordship have any commands for me in the mean time, I shall be glad to receive them. I say not this by way of defiance,—I should blush to be suspected of so doing through an indirect channel,—but simply that, if you shew him this letter, he may know I dare defend, as well as excuse my conduct.

Clement Willoughby.

What a strange letter! how proud and how piqued does its writer appear! To what alternate *meanness* and *rashness* do the passions lead, when reason and self-denial do not oppose them! Sir Clement is conscious he has acted dishonourably, yet the same unbridled vehemence which urged him to gratify a blameable curiosity, will sooner prompt him to risk his life, than confess his misconduct. The rudeness of his manner of writing to me springs from the same cause: the proof he has received of my indifference to him, has stung him to the soul, and he has neither the delicacy nor forbearance to disguise his displeasure.

I determined not to shew this letter to Lord Orville, and thought it most prudent to let Sir Clement know I should not. I therefore wrote the following note.

To Sir Clement Willoughby.

Sir,

THE letter you have been pleased to address to me, is so little calculated to afford Lord Orville any satisfaction, that you may depend upon my carefully keeping it from his sight. I will bear you no resentment for what is past; but I most earnestly entreat, nay implore, that you will not write again, while in your present frame of mind, by *any* channel, direct or indirect.

I hope you will have much pleasure in your purposed expedition, and I beg leave to assure you of my good wishes.

Not knowing by what name to sign, I was obliged to send it without any.

The *preparations* which Sir Clement mentions, go on just as if your consent were arrived: it is in vain that I expostulate; Lord Orville says, should any objections be raised, all shall be given up, but that, as his hopes forbid him to expect any, he must proceed as if already assured of your concurrence.

We have had, this afternoon, a most interesting conversation, in which we have traced our sentiments of each other from our first acquaintance. I have made him confess how ill he thought of me, upon my foolish giddiness at Mrs. Stanley's ball; but he flatters me with assurances, that every succeeding time he saw me, I appeared to something less and less disadvantage.

When I expressed my amazement that he could honour with his choice a girl who seemed so infinitely, in *every* respect, beneath his alliance, he frankly owned, that he had fully intended making more minute enquiries into my family and connections, and particularly concerning *those people* he saw me with at Marybone, before he acknowledged his prepossession in my favour: but the suddenness of my intended journey, and the uncertainty of seeing me again, put him quite off his guard, and "divesting him of prudence, left him nothing but love." These were his words; and yet, he has repeatedly assured me, that his partiality has known no bounds from the time of my residing at Clifton.

*   *   *   *   *

Mr. Macartney has just been with me, on an embassy from my father. He has sent me his kindest love, and assurances of favour, and desired to know if I am happy in the prospect of changing my situation, and if there is any thing I can name which he can do for me. And, at the same time, Mr. Macartney delivered to me a draught on my father's banker for a thousand pounds, which he insisted that I should receive entirely for my own use, and expend in equipping myself properly for the new rank of life to which I seem destined.

I am sure I need not say how much I was penetrated by this goodness; I wrote my thanks, and acknowledged, frankly, that if I could see *him* restored to tranquillity, my heart would be without a wish.

Letter XXI.

EVELINA IN CONTINUATION.

Clifton, October 13.

The time approaches now, when I hope we shall meet,—yet I cannot sleep,—great joy is as restless as sorrow,—and therefore I will continue my journal.

As I had never had an opportunity of seeing Bath, a party was formed last night for shewing me that celebrated city; and this morning, after breakfast, we set out in three phaetons. Lady Louisa and Mrs. Beaumont with Lord Merton; Mr. Coverley with Mr. Lovel; and Mrs. Selwyn and myself with Lord Orville.

We had hardly proceeded half a mile, when a gentleman from a post-chaise, which came galloping after us, called out to the servants, "Holla, my Lads,—pray is one Miss Anville in any of them *thing-em-bobs?*"

I immediately recollected the voice of Captain Mirvan, and Lord Orville stopt the phaeton. He was out of the chaise, and with us in a moment. "So, Miss Anville," cried he, "how do you do? so I hear you're Miss Belmont now;—pray how does old Madame French do?"

"Madame Duval," said I, "is, I believe, very well."

"I hope she's in *good case*," said he, winking significantly, "and won't flinch at seeing service: she has laid by long enough to refit and be made tight.[1] And pray how does poor *Monseer* Doleful do? is he as lank-jawed as ever?"

"They are neither of them," said I, "in Bristol."

"No!" cried he, with a look of disappointment, "but surely the old dowager intends coming to the wedding! 'twill be a most excellent opportunity to shew off her best Lyons silk. Besides I purpose to dance a new-fashioned jig with her. Don't you know when she'll come?"

"I have no reason to expect her at all."

"No!—'Fore George, this here's the worst news I'd wish to hear!—

1. In good physical condition ("in good case"), like a ship that has been refitted in dry dock, rendered watertight, and made ready for further service.

why I've thought of nothing all the way but what trick I should serve her."

"You have been very obliging!" said I, laughing.

"O, I promise you," cried he, "our Moll would never have wheedled me into this jaunt, if I'd known she was not here; for, to let you into the secret, I fully intended to have treated the old buck with another frolic."

"Did Miss Mirvan, then, persuade you to this journey?"

"Yes, and we've been travelling all night."

"We!" cried I: "Is Miss Mirvan, then, with you?"

"What, Molly?—yes, she's in that there chaise."

"Good God, Sir, why did not you tell me sooner?" cried I; and immediately, with Lord Orville's assistance, I jumpt out of the phaeton, and ran to the dear girl. Lord Orville opened the chaise door, and I am sure I need not tell you what unfeigned joy accompanied our meeting.

We both begged we might not be parted during the ride, and Lord Orville was so good as to invite Captain Mirvan into his phaeton.

I think I was hardly ever more rejoiced than at this so seasonable visit from my dear Maria; who had no sooner heard the situation of my affairs, than with the assistance of Lady Howard and her kind mother, she besought her father with such earnestness to consent to the journey, that he had not been able to withstand their united entreaties; though she owned that, had he not expected to have met with Madame Duval, she believes he would not so readily have yielded. They arrived at Mrs. Beaumont's but a few minutes after we were out of sight, and overtook us without much difficulty.

I say nothing of our conversation, because you may so well suppose both the subjects we chose, and our manner of discussing them.

We all stopped at a great hotel, where we were obliged to enquire for a room, as Lady Louisa, *fatigued to death*, desired to *take something* before we began our rambles.

As soon as the party was assembled, the Captain, abruptly saluting me, said, "So, Miss Belmont, I wish you joy; so I hear you've quarrelled with your new name already?"

"Me!—no, indeed, Sir."

"Then please for to tell me the reason you're in such a hurry to change it?"

"Miss Belmont!" cried Mr. Lovel, looking around him with the utmost astonishment, "I beg pardon,—but, if it is not impertinent,—I must beg leave to say, I always understood that lady's name was Anville."

"'Fore George," cried the Captain, "it runs in my head, I've seen you somewhere before! and now I think on't, pray a'n't you the person I saw at the play one night, and who did n't know, all the time, whether it was a tragedy or a comedy, or a concert of fiddlers?"

"I believe, Sir," said Mr. Lovel, stammering, "I had once,—I think— the pleasure of seeing you last spring."

"Aye, and if I live an hundred springs," answered he, "I shall never forget it; by Jingo, it has served me for a most excellent good joke ever since. Well, howsomever, I'm glad to see you still in the land of the living," shaking him roughly by the hand; "pray, if a body may be so bold, how much a night may you give at present to keep the undertakers aloof?"

"Me, Sir!" said Mr. Lovel, very much discomposed; "I protest I never thought myself in such imminent danger as to—really, Sir, I don't understand you."

"O, you don't!—why then I'll make free for to explain myself. Gentlemen and Ladies, I'll tell you what; do you know this here gentleman, simple as he sits there, pays five shillings a night to let his friends know he's alive!"

"And very cheap too," said Mrs. Selwyn, "if we consider the value of the intelligence."

Lady Louisa, being now refreshed, we proceeded upon our expedition.

The charming city of Bath[2] answered all my expectations. The Crescent, the prospect from it, and the elegant symmetry of the Circus, delighted me. The Parades, I own, rather disappointed me; one of them is scarce preferable to some of the best paved streets in London; and the other, though it affords a beautiful prospect, a charming view of Prior Park and of the Avon, yet wanted something in *itself* of more striking elegance than a mere broad pavement, to satisfy the ideas I had formed of it.

At the pump-room, I was amazed at the public exhibition of the ladies in the bath: it is true, their heads are covered with bonnets, but the very idea of being seen, in such a situation, by whoever pleases to look, is indelicate.

"Fore George," said the Captain, looking into the bath, "this would be a most excellent place for old Madame French to dance a fandango in! By Jingo, I woud n't wish for better sport than to swing her round this here pond!"

"She would be very much obliged to you," said Lord Orville, "for so extraordinary a mark of your favour."

"Why, to let you know," answered the Captain, "she hit my fancy mightily; I never took so much to an old tabby[3] before."

---

2. England's most fashionable spa, located on the River Avon, eleven and three-quarters miles southeast of Bristol, on the site of a former Roman town called Aquae Sulis ("Waters of Sul"). The Royal Crescent, designed by John Wood the Younger (d. 1782), begun in 1767 and completed in 1774, is a semicircle of town houses with a superb view of the city. The King's Circus, begun by John Wood the Elder (1705?–1754) the year of his death and completed by his son in 1758, is a circle of townhouses. The North and South Parades front a square of terraced houses bordered on the west by Pierrepont Street and on the east by Duke Street. Prior Park, the country estate of Ralph Allen (1694–1764) with its magnificent mansion built by John Wood the Elder, is about one mile southeast of Bath.
3. "An old or elderly maiden lady" (*OED*).

"Really, now," cried Mr. Lovel, looking also into the bath, "I must confess it is, to me, very incomprehensible why the ladies chuse that frightful unbecoming dress to bathe in! I have often pondered very seriously upon the subject, but could never hit upon the reason."

"Well, I declare," said Lady Louisa, "I should like of all things to set something new a going; I always hated bathing, because one can get no pretty dress for it; now do, there's a good creature, try to help me to something."

"Who, me!—O dear Ma'am," said he, simpering, "I can't pretend to assist a person of your Ladyship's taste; besides, I have not the least head for fashions.—I really don't think I ever invented above three in my life! but I never had the least turn for dress,—never any notion of fancy or elegance."

"O fie, Mr. Lovel! how can you talk so?—don't we all know that you lead the *ton* in the *beau monde?*[4] I declare, I think you dress better than any body."

"O dear Ma'am, you confuse me to the last degree! *I* dress well!—I protest I don't think I'm ever fit to be seen! I'm often shocked to death to think what a figure I go. If your Ladyship will believe me, I was full half an hour this morning thinking what I should put on!"

"Odds my life," cried the Captain, "I wish I'd been near you! I warrant I'd have quickened your motions a little! Half an hour thinking what you'd put on? and who the deuce do you think cares the snuff of a candle whether you've any thing on or not?"

"O pray, Captain," cried Mrs. Selwyn, "don't be angry with the gentleman for *thinking*, whatever be the cause, for I assure you he makes no common practice of offending in that way."

"Really, Ma'am, you're prodigiously kind!" said Mr. Lovel, angrily.

"Pray now," said the Captain, "did you ever get a ducking in that there place yourself?"

"A ducking, Sir!" repeated Mr. Lovel; "I protest I think that's rather an odd term!—but if you mean a *bathing*, it is an honour I have had many times."

"And pray, if a body may be so bold, what do you do with that frizlefrize top of your own? Why I'll lay you what you will, there is fat and grease enough on your crown, to buoy you up, if you were to go in head downwards."[5]

"And I don't know," cried Mrs. Selwyn, "but that might be the easiest way, for I'm sure it would be the lightest."

"For the matter of that there," said the Captain, "you must make him a soldier, before you can tell which is lightest, head or heels. Howsomever, I'd lay ten pounds to a shilling, I could whisk him so dexterously

---

4. The "ton" is "the fashion, the vogue, the mode" (*OED*); the "beau monde" is the fashionable world.
5. The captain is mocking Lovel's dressed hair.

over into the pool, that he should light plump upon his foretop, and turn round like a tetotum."[6]

"Done!" cried Lord Merton; "I take your odds."

"Will you?" returned he; "why then, 'fore George, I'd do it as soon as say Jack Robinson."

"He, he!" faintly laughed Mr. Lovel, as he moved abruptly from the window, "'pon honour, this is pleasant enough; but I don't see what right any body has to lay wagers about one, without one's consent."

"There, Lovel, you are out;" cried Mr. Coverley; "any man may lay what wager about you he will; your consent is nothing to the purpose: he may lay that your nose is a sky-blue, if he pleases."

"Ay," said Mrs. Selwyn, "or that your mind is more adorned than your person;—or any absurdity whatsoever."

"I protest," said Mr. Lovel, "I think it's a very disagreeable privilege, and I must beg that nobody may take such a liberty with *me*."

"Like enough you may," cried the Captain; "but what's that to the purpose? Suppose I've a mind to lay that you've never a tooth in your head?—pray, how will you hinder me?"

"You'll allow me, at least, Sir, to take the liberty of asking how you'll *prove* it?"

"How?—why, by knocking them all down your throat."

"Knocking them all down my throat, Sir!" repeated Mr. Lovel, with a look of horror, "I protest I never heard any thing so shocking in my life; and I must beg leave to observe, that no wager, in my opinion, could justify such a barbarous action."

Here Lord Orville interfered, and hurried us to our carriages.

We returned in the same order we came. Mrs. Beaumont invited all the party to dinner, and has been so obliging as to beg Miss Mirvan may continue at her house during her stay. The Captain will lodge at the Wells.

The first half-hour after our return, was devoted to hearing Mr. Lovel's apologies for dining in his riding-dress.

Mrs. Beaumont then, addressing herself to Miss Mirvan and me, enquired how we liked Bath?

"I hope," said Mr. Lovel, "the Ladies do not call this seeing Bath."

"No!—what should ail 'em?" cried the Captain; "do you suppose they put their eyes in their pockets?"

"No, Sir; but I fancy you will find no person,—that is,—no person of any condition,—call going about a few places in a morning *seeing Bath*."

"Mayhap, then" said the literal Captain, "you think we should see it better by going about at midnight?"

6. Or "teetotum," "a small four-sided disk or die having an initial letter inscribed on each of its sides, and a spindle passing down through it by which it could be twirled or spun with the fingers like a small top, the letter which lay uppermost, when it fell, deciding the fortune of the player" (*OED*).

"No, Sir, no," said Mr. Lovel, with a supercilious smile, "I perceive you don't understand me,—*we* should never call it *seeing Bath*, without going at the right season."

"Why, what a plague, then," demanded he, "can you only see at one season of the year?"

Mr. Lovel again smiled; but seemed superior to making any answer.

"The Bath amusements," said Lord Orville, "have a sameness in them, which, after a short time, renders them rather insipid: but the greatest objection that can be made to the place, is the encouragement it gives to gamesters."

"Why I hope, my Lord, you would not think of abolishing *gaming*," cried Lord Merton; "'tis the very *zest* of life! Devil take me if I could live without it."

"I am sorry for it," said Lord Orville, gravely, and looking at Lady Louisa.

"Your Lordship is no judge of this subject," continued the other;— "but if once we could get you to a gaming-table, you'd never be happy away from it."

"I hope, my Lord," cried Lady Louisa, "that nobody *here* ever occasions your quitting it."

"Your Ladyship," said Lord Merton, recollecting himself, "has power to make me quit any thing."

"Except *herself*," said Mr. Coverley. "Egad, my Lord, I think I've helpt you out there!"

"You men of wit, Jack," answered his Lordship, "are always ready;— for my part, I don't pretend to any talents that way."

"Really, my Lord?" asked the sarcastic Mrs. Selwyn; "well, that is wonderful, considering success would be so much in your power."

"Pray, Ma'am," said Mr. Lovel to Lady Louisa, "has your Ladyship heard the news?"

"News!—what news?"

"Why the report circulating at the Wells concerning a certain person."

"O Lord, no; pray tell me what it is?"

"O no, Ma'am, I beg your La'ship will excuse me; 'tis a profound secret, and I would not have mentioned it, if I had not thought you knew it."

"Lord, now, how can you be so monstrous?—I declare, now, you're a provoking creature! But come, I know you'll tell me;—won't you, now?"

"Your La'ship knows I am but too happy to obey you; but, 'pon honour, I can't speak a word, if you won't all promise me the most inviolable secrecy."

"I wish you'd wait for that from me," said the Captain, "and I'll give you my word you'd be dumb for one while. Secrecy, quoth a!—'Fore George, I wonder you a'n't ashamed to mention such a word, when you talk of telling it to a woman. Though for the matter of that, I'd as lieve blab it to the whole sex at once, as to go for to tell it to such a thing as you."

"Such a thing as me, Sir!" said Mr. Lovel, letting fall his knife and fork, and looking very important: "I really have not the honour to understand your expression."

"It's all one for that," said the Captain; "you may have it explained whenever you like it."

"'Pon honour, Sir," returned Mr. Lovel, "I must take the liberty to tell you, that I should be extremely offended, but that I suppose it to be some sea-phrase and therefore I'll let it pass without further notice."

Lord Orville, then, to change the discourse, asked Miss Mirvan if she should spend the ensuing winter in London?

"No, to be sure," said the Captain, "what should she for? she saw all that was to be seen before."

"Is London, then," said Mr. Lovel, smiling at Lady Louisa, "only to be regarded as a *sight*?"

"Why pray, Mr. Wiseacre, how are you pleased for to regard it yourself?—Answer me to that."

"O Sir, *my* opinion I fancy, you would hardly find intelligible. I don't understand *sea-phrases* enough to define it to your comprehension. Doesn't your La'ship think the task would be rather difficult?"

"O Lard, yes," cried Lady Louisa; "I declare I'd as soon teach my parrot to talk Welsh."

"Ha! ha! ha! admirable!—'Pon honour your La'ship's quite in luck to day; but that, indeed, your La'ship is every day. Though—to be sure, it is but candid to acknowledge, that the gentlemen of the ocean have a set of ideas, as well as a dialect, so opposite to *ours*, that it is by no means surprising *they* should regard London as a mere *shew*, that may be seen by being *looked at*. Ha! ha! ha!"

"Ha! ha!" echoed Lady Louisa: "Well, I declare you are the drollest creature."

"He! he! 'pon honour I can't help laughing at the conceit of *seeing London* in a few weeks!"

"And what a plague should hinder you?" cried the Captain; "do you want to spend a day in every street?"

Here again Lady Louisa and Mr. Lovel interchanged smiles.

"Why, I warrant you, if I had the shewing it, I'd haul you from St. James's to Wapping [7] the very first morning."

The smiles were now, with added contempt, repeated; which the Captain observing, looked very fiercely at Mr. Lovel, and said, "Hark'ee, my spark, none of your grinning!—'tis a lingo I don't understand; and if you give me any more of it, I shall go near to lend you a box o' the ear."

7. From the West End of London to the East End.

"I protest, Sir," said Mr. Lovel, turning extremely pale, "I think it's taking a very particular liberty with a person, to talk to one in such a style as this!"

"It's like you may," returned the Captain; "but give a good gulp and I'll warrant you'll swallow it." Then, calling for a glass of ale, with a very provoking and significant nod, he drank to his easy digestion.

Mr. Lovel made no answer, but looked extremely sullen: and soon after, we left the gentlemen to themselves.

I had then two letters delivered to me; one from Lady Howard and Mrs. Mirvan, which contained the kindest congratulations; and the other from Madame Duval,—but not a word from you,—to my no small surprise and concern.

Madame Duval seems greatly rejoiced at my late intelligence: a violent cold, she says, prevents her coming to Bristol. The Branghtons she tells me, are all well; Miss Polly is soon to be married to Mr. Brown, but Mr. Smith has changed his lodgings, "which," she adds, "has made the house extremely dull. However, that's not the worst news; *pardi*, I wish it was! but I've been used like nobody,—for Monsieur Du Bois has had the baseness to go back to France without me." In conclusion, she assures me as you prognosticated she would, that I shall be sole heiress of all she is worth, when Lady Orville.

At tea-time, we were joined by all the gentlemen but Captain Mirvan, who went to the hotel where he was to sleep, and made his daughter accompany him, to separate her *trumpery*, as he called it, from his cloaths.

As soon as they were gone, Mr. Lovel, who still appeared extremely sulky, said, "I protest, I never saw such a vulgar, abusive fellow in my life, as that Captain: 'pon honour, I believe he came here for no purpose in the world but to pick a quarrel; however, for my part, I vow I won't humour him."

"I declare," cried Lady Louisa, "he put me in a monstrous fright,—I never heard any body talk so shocking in my life!"

"I think," said Mrs. Selwyn, with great solemnity, "he threatened to box your ears, Mr. Lovel,—did not he?"

"Really, Ma'am," said Mr. Lovel, colouring, "if one was to mind every thing those low kind of people say,—one should never be at rest for one impertinence or other,—so I think the best way is to be above taking any notice of them."

"What," said Mrs. Selwyn, with the same gravity, "and so receive the blow in silence!"

During this discourse, I heard the Captain's chaise stop at the door, and ran downstairs to meet Maria. She was alone, and told me that her father, who, she was sure, had some scheme in agitation against Mr. Lovel, had sent her on before him. We continued in the parlour till his return, and were joined by Lord Orville, who begged me not to insist on a patience so unnatural, as submitting to be excluded our society. And let me, my dear Sir, with a grateful heart let me own, I never before passed half an hour in such perfect felicity.

I believe we were all sorry when the Captain returned; yet his inward satisfaction, from however different a cause, did not seem inferior to what ours had been. He chucked Maria under the chin, rubbed his hands, and was scarce able to contain the fullness of his glee. We all attended him to the drawing-room, where, having composed his countenance, without any previous attention to Mrs. Beaumont, he marched up to Mr. Lovel, and abruptly said, "Pray have you e'er a brother in these here parts?"

"Me, Sir?—no, thank Heaven, I'm free from all encumbrances of that sort."

"Well," cried the Captain, "I met a person just now, so like you, I could have sworn he had been your twin-brother."

"It would have been a most singular pleasure to me," said Mr. Lovel, "if I also could have seen him; for, really, I have not the least notion what sort of a person I am, and I have a prodigious curiosity to know."

Just then, the Captain's servant opening the door, said, "A little gentleman below desires to see one Mr. Lovel."

"Beg him to walk up stairs," said Mrs. Beaumont. "But pray what is the reason William is out of the way?"

The man shut the door without any answer.

"I can't imagine who it is," said Mr. Lovel; "I recollect no little gentleman of my acquaintance now at Bristol,—except, indeed, the Marquis of Charlton,—but I don't much fancy it can be him. Let me see, who else is there so very little?"—

A confused noise among the servants now drew all eyes towards the door; the impatient Captain hastened to open it, and then, clapping his hands, called out, "'Fore George, 'tis the same person I took for your relation!"

And then, to the utter astonishment of every body but himself, he hauled into the room a monkey, full dressed, and extravagantly à-la-mode!

The dismay of the company was almost general. Poor Mr. Lovel seemed thunderstruck with indignation and surprise; Lady Louisa began a scream, which for some time was incessant; Miss Mirvan and I jumped involuntarily upon the seats of our chairs: Mrs. Beaumont herself followed our example; Lord Orville placed himself before me as a guard; and Mrs. Selwyn, Lord Merton, and Mr. Coverley, burst into a loud, immoderate, ungovernable fit of laughter, in which they were joined by the Captain, till, unable to support himself, he rolled on the floor.

The first voice which made its way through this general noise, was that of Lady Louisa, which her fright and screaming rendered extremely shrill. "Take it away!" cried she, "take the monster away,—I shall faint, I shall faint if you don't!"

Mr. Lovel, irritated beyond endurance, angrily demanded of the Captain what he meant?

"Mean?" cried the Captain, as soon as he was able to speak, "why only to shew you in your proper colours." Then rising, and pointing to the monkey, "Why now, Ladies and Gentlemen, I'll be judged by you all!—Did you ever see any thing more like? Odds my life, if it was n't for this here tail, you would n't know one from t'other."

"Sir," cried Mr. Lovel, stamping, "I shall take a time to make you feel my wrath."

"Come, now," continued the regardless Captain, "just for the fun's sake, duff your coat and waistcoat, and swop with *Monsieur Grinagain* here, and I'll warrant you'll not know yourself which is which."

"Not know myself from a monkey?—I assure you, Sir, I'm not to be used in this manner, and I won't bear it,—curse me if I will!"

"Why hey day," cried the Captain, "what, is Master in a passion?— well, don't be angry,—come, he sha'n't hurt you;—here, shake a paw with him,—why he'll do you no harm, man!—come, kiss and friends!"—

"Who I?" cried Mr. Lovel, almost mad with vexation, "as I'm a living creature, I would not touch him for a thousand worlds!"

"Send him a challenge," cried Mr. Coverley, "and I'll be your second."

"Ay, do," said the Captain, "and I'll be second to my friend, Monsieur Clapperclaw[8] here. Come, to it at once!—tooth and nail!"

"God forbid!" cried Mr. Lovel, retreating, "I would sooner trust my person with a mad bull!"

"I don't like the looks of him myself," said Lord Merton, "for he grins most horribly."

"Oh I'm frightened out of my senses!" cried Lady Louisa, "take him away, or I shall die!"

"Captain," said Lord Orville, "the ladies are alarmed, and I must beg you would send the monkey away."

"Why, where can be the mighty harm of one monkey more than another?" answered the Captain; "howsomever, if it's agreeable to the ladies, suppose we turn them out together?"

"What do you mean by that, Sir?" cried Mr. Lovel, lifting up his cane.

"What do *you* mean?" cried the Captain, fiercely: "be so good as to down with your cane."

Poor Mr. Lovel, too much intimidated to stand his ground, yet too much enraged to submit, turned hastily round, and, forgetful of consequences, vented his passion by giving a furious blow to the monkey.

---

8. Beat or drub; figuratively, revile, abuse (*OED*).

The creature darting forwards, sprung instantly upon him, and cling-ing round his neck, fastened his teeth to one of his ears.

I was really sorry for the poor man, who, though an egregious fop, had committed no offence that merited such chastisement.

It was impossible, now, to distinguish whose screams were loudest, those of Mr. Lovel, or of the terrified Lady Louisa, who, I believe thought her own turn was approaching: but the unrelenting Captain roared with joy.

Not so Lord Orville: ever humane, generous, and benevolent, he quitted his charge, who he saw was wholly out of danger, and seizing the monkey by the collar, made him loosen the ear, and then, with a sudden swing, flung him out of the room, and shut the door.

Poor Mr. Lovel, almost fainting with terror, sunk upon the floor, cry-ing out, "Oh I shall die, I shall die!—Oh I'm bit to death!"

"Captain Mirvan," said Mrs. Beaumont, with no little indignation, "I must own I don't perceive the wit of this action; and I am sorry to have such cruelty practised in my house."

"Why, Lord, Ma'am," said the Captain, when his rapture abated suf-ficiently for speech, "how could I tell they'd fall out so?—by Jingo, I brought him to be a messmate for t'other."

"Egad," said Mr. Coverley, "I would not have been served so for a thousand pounds."

"Why then there's the odds of it," said the Captain, "for you see he is served so for nothing. But come," (turning to Mr. Lovel) "be of good heart, all may end well yet, and you and *Monseer* Longtail be as good friends as ever."

"I'm surprised, Mrs. Beaumont," cried Mr. Lovel, starting up, "that you can suffer a person under your roof to be treated so inhumanly."

"What argufies so many words?" said the unfeeling Captain, "it is but a slit of the ear; it only looks as if you had been in the pillory." [9]

"Very true," added Mrs. Selwyn, "and who knows but it may acquire you the credit of being an anti-ministerial writer?" [1]

"I protest," cried Mr. Lovel, looking ruefully at his dress, "my new riding-suit's all over blood!"

"Ha, ha, ha!" cried the Captain; "see what comes of studying for an hour what you shall put on!"

Mr. Lovel then walked to the glass, and looking at the place, exclaimed, "Oh Heaven, what a monstrous wound! my ear will never be fit to be seen again!"

"Why then," said the Captain, "you must hide it;—'tis but wearing a wig."

9. "A wooden framework erected on a post or pillar . . . leav[ing] holes through which the head and hands of an offender were thrust" (*OED*). In Burney's day, it was rare for anyone to have his or her ears or nostrils slit as a punishment.
1. Writing against the government or "ministry" could earn one a turn in the pillory for seditious libel.

"A wig!" repeated the affrighted Mr. Lovel, "I wear a wig? — [2] no, not if you would give me a thousand pounds an hour!"

"I declare," said Lady Louisa, "I never heard such a shocking proposal in my life!"

Lord Orville then, seeing no prospect that the altercation would cease, proposed to the Captain to walk. He assented; and having given Mr. Lovel, a nod of exultation, accompanied his Lordship down stairs.

"'Pon honour," said Mr. Lovel, the moment the door was shut, "that fellow is the greatest brute in nature! he ought not to be admitted into a civilized society."

"Lovel," said Mr. Coverley, affecting to whisper, "you must certainly pink[3] him: you must not put up with such an affront."

"Sir," said Mr. Lovel, "with any common person, I should not deliberate an instant; but, really, with a fellow who has done nothing but fight all his life, 'pon honour, Sir, I can't think of it!"

"Lovel," said Lord Merton, in the same voice, "you *must* call him to account."

"Every man," said he, pettishly, "is the best judge of his own affairs, and I don't ask the honour of any person's advice."

"Egad, Lovel," said Mr. Coverley, "you're in for it! — you can't possibly be off!"

"Sir," cried he, very impatiently, "upon any proper occasion I should be as ready to shew my courage as any body; — but as to fighting for such a trifle as this, — I protest I should blush to think of it!"

"A trifle!" cried Mrs. Selwyn, "good Heaven! and have you made this astonishing riot about a *trifle?*"

"Ma'am," answered the poor wretch, in great confusion, "I did not know at first but that my cheek might have been bit: — but as 'tis no worse, why it does not a great deal signify. Mrs. Beaumont, I have the honour to wish you good evening; I'm sure my carriage must be waiting." And then, very abruptly, he left the room.

What a commotion has this mischief-loving Captain raised! Were I to remain here long, even the society of my dear Maria could scarce compensate for the disturbances which he excites.

When he returned, and heard of the quiet exit of Mr. Lovel, his triumph was intolerable. "I think, I think," cried he, "I have peppered him well! I'll warrant he won't give an hour to-morrow morning to settling what he shall put on; why his coat," turning to me, "would be a most excellent match for old Madame Furbelow's[4] best Lyons silk! 'Fore George, I'd desire no better sport, than to have that there old cat here, to go her snacks!"

---

2. Wigs were going out of style at this time.
3. "Pierce, prick, or stab with any pointed weapon or instrument" (*OED*).
4. "Furbelow" — "a contemptuous term for showy ornaments or trimmings, esp. in a lady's dress" (*OED*).

All the company then, Lord Orville, Miss Mirvan, and myself excepted, played at cards, and *we*—oh how much better did we pass our time!

While we were engaged in a most delightful conversation, a servant brought me a letter, which he told me had, by some accident, been mislaid. Judge of my feelings, when I saw, my dearest Sir, your revered hand-writing! My emotions soon betrayed to Lord Orville whom the letter was from; the importance of the contents he well knew, and, assuring me I should not be seen by the card-players, he besought me to open it without delay.

Open it, indeed I did,—but read it I could not;—the willing, yet awful consent you have granted,—the tenderness of your expressions,—the certainty that no obstacle remained to my eternal union with the loved owner of my heart, gave me sensations too various, and though joyful, too little placid for observation. Finding myself unable to proceed, and blinded by the tears of gratitude and delight, which started into my eyes, I gave over the attempt of reading, till I retired to my own room: and, having no voice to answer the enquiries of Lord Orville, I put the letter into his hands, and left it to speak both for me and itself.

Lord Orville was himself affected by your kindness; he kissed the letter as he returned it, and, pressing my hand affectionately to his heart, "You are now," (said he, in a low voice) "all my own! Oh my Evelina, how will my soul find room for its happiness?—it seems already bursting!" I could make no reply; indeed I hardly spoke another word the rest of the evening; so little talkative is the fullness of contentment.

O my dearest Sir, the thankfulness of my heart I must pour forth at our meeting, when, at your feet, my happiness receives its confirmation from your blessing, and when my noble-minded, my beloved Lord Orville, presents to you the highly-honoured and thrice-happy Evelina.

A few lines I will endeavour to write on Thursday, which shall be sent off express, to give you, should nothing intervene, yet more certain assurance of our meeting.

Now then, therefore, for the first—and probably the last time I shall ever own the name, permit me to sign myself,

Most dear Sir,
Your gratefully affectionate,
Evelina Belmont.

Lady Louisa, at her own particular desire, will be present at the ceremony, as well as Miss Mirvan and Mrs. Selwyn: Mr. Macartney will, the same morning, be united to my foster-sister, and my father himself will give us both away.

Letter XXII.

MR. VILLARS TO EVELINA.

Every wish of my soul is now fulfilled—for the felicity of my Evelina is equal to her worthiness!

Yes, my child, thy happiness is engraved, in golden characters, upon the tablets of my heart! and their impression is indelible; for, should the rude and deep-searching hand of Misfortune attempt to pluck them from their repository, the fleeting fabric of life would give way, and in tearing from my vitals the nourishment by which they are supported, she would but grasp at a shadow insensible to her touch.

Give thee my consent?—Oh thou joy, comfort, and pride of my life, how cold is that word to express the fervency of my approbation! Yes, I do indeed give thee my consent, and so thankfully, that, with the humblest gratitude to Providence, I would seal it with the remnant of my days.

Hasten, then, my love, to bless me with thy presence, and to receive the blessings with which my fond heart overflows!—And, oh my Evelina, hear and assist in one only, humble, but ardent prayer which yet animates my devotions: that the height of bliss to which thou art rising may not render thee giddy, but that the purity of thy mind may form the brightest splendour of thy prosperity!—and that the weak and aged frame of thy almost idolizing parent, nearly worn out by time, past afflictions, and infirmities, may yet be able to sustain a meeting with all its better part holds dear; and then, that all the wounds which the former severity of fortune inflicted, may be healed and purified by the ultimate consolation of pouring forth my dying words in blessings on my child!—closing these joy-streaming eyes in her presence, and breathing my last faint sighs in her loved arms!

Grieve not, oh child of my care, grieve not at the inevitable moment! but may thy own end be equally propitious! Oh may'st thou, when full of days, and full of honour, sink down as gently to rest,—be loved as kindly, watched as tenderly as thy happy father! And may'st thou, when thy glass is run, be sweetly but not bitterly mourned, by some remaining darling of thy affections,—some yet surviving Evelina!

ARTHUR VILLARS.

Letter XXIII.

EVELINA TO THE REV. MR. VILLARS.

All is over, my dearest Sir, and the fate of your Evelina is decided! This morning, with fearful joy, and trembling gratitude, she united herself for ever with the object of her dearest, her eternal affection.

I have time for no more; the chaise now waits which is to conduct me to dear Berry Hill, and to the arms of the best of men.

EVELINA.

FINIS.

CONTEXTS AND CONTEMPORARY REACTIONS

CONDUCT BOOKS

Modesty

One of the chief beauties in a female character, is that modest reserve, that retiring delicacy, which avoids the public eye, and is disconcerted even at the gaze of admiration.—I do not wish you to be insensible to applause. If you were, you must become, if not worse, at least less amiable women. But you may be dazzled by that admiration, which yet rejoices your hearts.

*   *   *

This modesty, which I think so essential in your sex, will naturally dispose you to be rather silent in company, especially in a large one.— People of sense and discernment will never mistake such silence for dulness. One may take a share in conversation without uttering a syllable. The expression in the countenance shews it; and this never escapes an observing eye.†

If to your natural softness you join that Christian meekness, which I now preach; both together will not fail, with the assistance of proper reflexion and friendly advice, to accomplish you in the best and truest kind of breeding. You will not be in danger of putting yourselves forward in company, of contradicting bluntly, of asserting positively, of debating obstinately, of affecting a superiority to any present, or engrossing the discourse, of listening to yourselves with apparent satisfaction, of neglecting what is advanced by others, or of interrupting them without necessity.*

Passivity

The same degree of active courage is not to be expected in woman as in man; and, not belonging to her nature, it is not agreeable in her; but passive courage, patience, and fortitude under sufferings—presence of mind, and calm resignation in danger, are surely desirable in every rational creature; especially in one professing to believe in an over-ruling Providence.‡

Wit

Wit is the most dangerous talent you can possess. It must be guarded with great discretion and good nature, otherwise it will create you many

---

† From John Gregory, A *Father's Legacy to His Daughters* (1774; London, 1795) 37, 39.
* From James Fordyce, *Sermons to Young Women*, 5th ed., vol. 2 (London, 1766) 218.
‡ From Hester Chapone, *Letters on the Improvement of the Mind, Addressed to a Young Lady* (1778; Wellington, 1809) 50, letter 4.

enemies. Wit is perfectly consistent with softness and delicacy; yet they are seldom found united. Wit is so flattering to vanity, that they who possess it become intoxicated, and lose all self-command.§

Learning

Be even cautious of displaying your good sense. It will be thought you assume a superiority over the rest of the company—But if you happen to have any learning, keep it a profound secret, especially from the men, who generally look with a jealous and malignant eye on a woman of great parts, and a cultivated understanding.†

Aging

* * * Let every seven years make some alteration in you towards the *Graver* side, and not be like the *Girls* of Fifty, who resolve to be always *Young*, whatever *Time* with his Iron Teeth hath determined to the contrary. Unnatural things carry a *Deformity* in them never to be *Disguised*; the *Liveliness* of *Youth* in a riper Age, looketh like a *new patch* upon an *old Gown*; so that a *Gay Matron*, a cheerful *old Fool* may be reasonably put into the List of the *Tamer* kind of *Monsters*. There is a certain Creature call'd a *Grave Hobby-Horse*, a kind of a she *Numps*, that pretendeth to be pulled to a Play, and must needs go to *Bartholomew Fair*, to look after the young Folks, whom she only seemeth to make her care, in reality she taketh them for her excuse. Such an old *Butterfly* is of all *Creatures* the most ridiculous, and the soonest found out.*

Dangerous Connections

* * * Avoid Dangerous Connections. The man that behaves with open rudeness, the man that avowedly laughs at virtue, the man that impudently pleads for vice; such a man is to be shunned like a rattle snake.

Of artful men the approaches will be silent and slow; all will be soft insinuation: or else they will put on a blunt face of seeming good humour, the appearance of honest frankness, drawing you to every scene of dissipation with a kind of obliging violence, should violence of any kind be necessary. If withal they are agreeable in their person, or lively in their conversation; above all, if they wear the air of gentlemen, which, unfortunately for your sex, is too often the case; then indeed your danger is extreme. Thus far the trap is concealed. You apprehend nothing: your unsuspecting hearts begin to slide: they are gone, gone before you are aware. The men I am speaking of perceive their advan-

§ From Gregory 41–42.
† From Gregory 42–43.
* From George Saville, Lord Halifax, *The Lady's New-Year's Gift or: Advice to a Daughter* (1700; Stamford, CT: Overbrook, 1934) 72–73.

tage the moment it appears. I have supposed them destitute of worth. If they are also unchecked by fear, what can preserve you? A sense of reputation? the dread of ruin? They have often, no doubt, come in to prevent the last excess. And, but for such restraints, what would become of many a woman who is not under that best one, religious Principle? The experiment, however, you will own is hazardous. Multitudes have trusted to it, and have been undone.‡

Inequality

You must first lay it down for a Foundation in general, That there is *Inequality* in the *Sexes*, and that for the better Oeconomy of the World, the *Men*, who were to be the Law-givers, had the larger share of *Reason* bestow'd upon them; by which means your Sex is the better prepar'd for the *Compliance* that is necessary for the better performance of those *Duties* which seem to be most properly assign'd to it.§

Love

When you observe in a gentleman's behaviour these marks I have described [the effects of love], reflect seriously what you are to do. If his attachment is agreeable to you, I leave you to do as nature, good sense, and delicacy shall direct you. If you love him, let me advise you never to discover to him the full extent of your love, no not although you marry him. That sufficiently shews your preference, which is all he is entitled to know.†

Do not give way to a sudden sally of passion, and dignify it with the name of love.—Genuine love is not founded in caprice; it is founded in nature, on honourable views, on virtue, on familiarity of tastes and sympathy of souls.*

Whatever romantic notions you may hear, or read of, depend upon it those matches are the happiest which are made on rational grounds—on suitableness of character, degree, and fortune—on mutual esteem, and the prospect of a real and permanent friendship. Far be it from me, to advise you to marry where you do not love;—a mercenary marriage is a detestable prostitution:—but, on the other hand, an union formed upon mere personal liking, without the requisite foundation of esteem—without the sanction of parental approbation—and, consequently, without the blessing of God, can be productive of nothing but misery and shame.‡

‡ From Fordyce 1: 49–50.
§ From Halifax 16.
† From Gregory 97–98.
* From Gregory 137.
‡ From Chapone 77, letter 5.

Amusements

Some amusements are conducive to health, as various kinds of exercise: some are connected with qualities really useful, as different kinds of women's work, and all the domestic concerns of a family: some are elegant accomplishments, as dress, dancing, music, and drawing. Such books as improve your understanding, enlarge your knowledge, and cultivate your taste, may be considered in a higher point of view than mere amusements. There are a variety of others, which are neither useful nor ornamental, such as play of different kinds.

*   *   *

The intention of your being taught needle-work, knitting, and such like, is not on account of the intrinsic value of all you can do with your hands, which is trifling, but to enable you to judge more perfectly of that kind of work, and to direct the execution of it in others. Another principal end is to enable you to fill up, in a tolerably agreeable way, some of the many solitary hours you must necessarily pass at home. — It is a great article in the happiness of life, to have your pleasures as independent of others as possible. By continually gadding abroad in search of amusement, you lose the respect of all your acquaintances, whom you oppress with those visits, which, by a more discreet management, might have been courted.

The domestic economy of a family, is entirely a woman's province, and furnishes a variety of subjects for the exertion both of good sense and good taste. If you ever come to have the charge of a family, it ought to engage much of your time and attention; nor can you be excused from this by any extent of fortune, tho' with a narrow one the ruin that follows the neglect of it may be more immediate.§

Theatre

I know no entertainment that gives such pleasure to any person of sentiment or humour, as the theatre. — But I am sorry to say, there are few English comedies a lady can see, without a shock to delicacy. You will not readily suspect the comments gentlemen make on your behaviour on such occasions. * * * A virtuous girl often hears very indelicate things with a countenance no wise embarrassed, because, in truth she does not understand them. Yet this is, most ungenerously, ascribed to that command of features, and that ready presence of mind, which you are thought to possess in a degree far beyond us; or, by still more malignant observers, it is ascribed to hardened effrontery.

Sometimes a girl laughs will all the simplicity of unsuspecting innocence, for no other reason but being infected with other people's laugh-

§   From Gregory 58–59, 62–64.

ing: she is then believed to know more than she should do—If she does happen to understand an improper thing, she suffers a very complicated distress: she feels her modesty hurt in the most sensible manner, and at the same time is ashamed of appearing conscious of the injury. The only way to avoid these inconveniences, is never to go to a play that is particularly offensive to delicacy.—Tragedy subjects you to no such distress—Its sorrows will soften and ennoble your hearts.†

Dancing

In dancing, the principal points you are to attend to are ease and grace. I would have you to dance with spirit; but never allow yourselves to be so far transported with mirth, as to forget the delicacy of your sex.— Many a girl, dancing in the gaiety and innocence of her heart, is thought to discover a spirit she little dreams of.*

To *Dance* sometimes will not be imputed to you as a fault; but remember that the end of your *Learning* it, was, that you might the better know how to move *gracefully*. It is only an *advantage* so far. When it goeth beyound it, one may call it *excelling* in a Mistake, which is no very great Commendation. It is better for a *Woman* never to *Dance*, because she hath no skill in it, than to do it too often, because she doth it well. The easiest as well as the safest *Method* of doing it, is in *private Companies*, amongst *particular Friends*, and then carelessly, like a *Diversion*, rather than with *Solemnity*, as if it was a business, or had any thing in it to deserve a *Month's preparation* by serious Conference with a *Dancing-Master*.‡

MADAME D'ARBLAY [FRANCES BURNEY]

Publication of *Evelina*†

Frances, the second daughter of Dr. Burney, was during her childhood the most backward of all his family in the faculty of receiving instruction. At eight years of age she was ignorant of the letters of the alphabet; though at ten, she began scribbling, almost incessantly, little works of invention; but always in private; and in scrawling characters, illegible, save to herself.

---

† From Gregory 69–71.
* From Gregory 68–69.
‡ From Halifax 106.
† From Madame d'Arblay [Frances Burney], *Memoirs of Doctor Burney, Arranged from His Own Manuscripts, from Family Papers, and from Personal Recollections*, vol. 2 (London, 1832) 123–49.

One of her most remote remembrances, previously to this writing mania, is that of hearing a neighbouring lady recommend to Mrs. Burney, her mother, to quicken the indolence, or stupidity, whichever it might be, of the little dunce, by the chastening ordinances of Solomon. The alarm, however, of that little dunce, at a suggestion so wide from the maternal measures that had been practised in her childhood, was instantly superseded by a joy of gratitude and surprise that still rests upon her recollection, when she heard gently murmured in reply, "No, no,—I am not uneasy about her!"

But, alas! the soft music of those encouraging accents had already ceased to vibrate on human ears, before these scrambling pot-hooks had begun their operation of converting into Elegies, Odes, Plays, Songs, Stories, Farces,—nay, Tragedies and Epic Poems, every scrap of white paper that could be seized upon without question or notice; for she grew up, probably through the vanity-annihilating circumstances of this conscious intellectual disgrace, with so affrighted a persuasion that what she scribbled, if seen, would but expose her to ridicule, that her pen, though her greatest, was only her clandestine delight.

To one confidant, indeed, all was open; but the fond partiality of the juvenile Susanna[1] made her opinion of little weight; though the affection of her praise rendered the stolen moments of their secret readings the happiest of their adolescent lives.

From the time, however, that she attained her fifteenth year, she considered it her duty to combat this writing passion as illaudable, because fruitless. Seizing, therefore, an opportunity, when Dr. Burney was at Chesington, and the then Mrs. Burney, her mother-in-law,[2] was in Norfolk, she made over to a bonfire, in a paved play-court, her whole stock of prose goods and chattels; with the sincere intention to extinguish for ever in their ashes her scribbling propensity. But Hudibras too well says—

> "He who complies against his will,
> Is of his own opinion still."

This grand feat, therefore, which consumed her productions, extirpated neither the invention nor the inclination that had given them birth; and, in defiance of all the projected heroism of the sacrifice, the last of the little works that was immolated, which was the History of Caroline Evelyn, the Mother of Evelina, left, upon the mind of the writer, so animated an impression of the singular situations to which that Caroline's infant daughter,—from the unequal birth by which she hung suspended between the elegant connexions of her mother, and the vulgar ones of her grandmother,—might be exposed; and presented contrasts and mixtures of society so unusual, yet, thus circumstanced, so natural,

1. Susanna Elizabeth Burney (1755–1800), Burney's sister and closest friend. [*Editor*]
2. Stepmother. [*Editor*]

that irresistibly and almost unconsciously, the whole of A *Young Lady's Entrance into the World*, was pent up in the inventor's memory, ere a paragraph was committed to paper.

Writing, indeed, was far more difficult to her than composing; for that demanded what she rarely found attainable—secret opportunity: while composition, in that hey-day of imagination, called only for volition.

When the little narrative, however slowly, from the impediments that always annoy what requires secrecy, began to assume a "questionable shape"; a wish—as vague, at first, as it was fantastic—crossed the brain of the writer, to "see her work in print."

She communicated, under promise of inviolable silence, this idea to her sisters; who entered into it with much more amusement than surprise, as they well knew her taste for quaint sports; and were equally aware of the sensitive affright with which she shrunk from all personal remark.

She now copied the manuscript in a feigned hand; for as she was the Doctor's principal amanuensis, she feared her common writing might accidentally be seen by some compositor of the History of Music, and lead to detection.

She grew weary, however, ere long, of an exercise so merely manual; and had no sooner completed a copy of the first and second volumes, than she wrote a letter, without any signature, to offer the unfinished work to a bookseller; with a desire to have the two volumes immediately printed, if approved; and a promise to send the sequel in the following year.

This was forwarded by the London post, with a desire that the answer should be directed to a coffee-house.

Her younger brother—the elder, Captain James, was 'over the hills and far away,'—her younger brother, afterwards the celebrated Greek scholar,[3] gaily, and without reading a word of the work, accepted a share in so whimsical a frolic; and joyously undertook to be her agent at the coffee-house with her letters, and to the bookseller with the manuscript.

After some consultation upon the choice of a bookseller, Mr. Dodsley was fixed upon; for Dodsley, from his father's,—or perhaps grandfather's,—well chosen collection of fugitive poetry, stood foremost in the estimation of the juvenile set.

Mr. Dodsley, in answer to the proposition, declined looking at any thing that was anonymous.

The party, half-amused, half-provoked, sat in full committee upon this lofty reply; and came to a resolution to forego the *eclat* of the west end of the town, and to try their fortune with the urbanity of the city.

3. James Burney (1750–1821), captain (1782), Royal Navy, and Charles Burney, Jr. (1757–1817), D. Div. (1812). [*Editor*]

Chance fixed them upon the name of Mr. Lowndes.

The city of London here proved more courtly than that of Westminster; and, to their no small delight, Mr. Lowndes desired to see the manuscript.

And what added a certain pride to the author's satisfaction in this assent, was, that the answer opened by

"Sir," —

which gave her an elevation to manly consequence, that had not been accorded to her by Mr. Dodsley, whose reply began

"Sir, or Madam."

The young agent was muffled up now by the laughing committee, in an old great coat, and a large old hat, to give him a somewhat antique as well as vulgar disguise; and was sent forth in the dark of the evening with the two first volumes to Fleet-street, where he left them to their fate.

In trances of impatience the party awaited the issue of the examination.

But they were all let down into the very 'Slough of Despond,'[4] when the next coffee-house letter coolly declared, that Mr. Lowndes could not think of publishing an unfinished book; though he liked the work, and should be 'ready to purchase and print it when it should be finished.'

There was nothing in this unreasonable; yet the disappointed author, tired of what she deemed such priggish punctilio, gave up, for awhile, and in dudgeon, all thought of the scheme.

Nevertheless, to be thwarted on the score of our inclination acts more frequently as a spur than as a bridle; the third volume, therefore, which finished *The young lady's entrance into the world,* was, ere another year could pass away, almost involuntarily completed and copied.

But while the scribe was yet wavering whether to abandon or to prosecute her enterprise, the chasm caused by this suspense to the workings of her imagination, left an opening from their vagaries to a mental interrogatory, whether it were right to allow herself such an amusement, with whatever precautions she might keep it from the world, unknown to her father?

She had never taken any step without the sanction of his permission; and had now refrained from requesting it, only through the confusion of acknowledging her authorship; and the apprehension, or, rather, the horror of his desiring to see her performance.

Nevertheless, reflection no sooner took place of action, than she found, in this case at least, the poet's maxim reversed, and that

'The female who deliberates — is sav'd,'

4. A deep bog through which Christian had to pass in *Pilgrim's Progress* (1678), by John Bunyan (1628–88); proverbial for doubts and fears. [*Editor*]

for she saw in its genuine light what was her duty; and seized, therefore, upon a happy moment of a kind *tête à tête* with her father, to avow, with more blushes than words, her secret little work; and her odd inclination to see it in print; hastily adding, while he looked at her, incredulous of what he heard, that her brother Charles would transact the business with a distant bookseller, who should never know her name. She only, therefore, entreated that he would not himself ask to see the manuscript.

His amazement was without parallel; yet it seemed surpassed by his amusement; and his laugh was so gay, that, revived by its cheering sound, she lost all her fears and embarrassment, and heartily joined in it; though somewhat at the expence of her new author-like dignity.

She was the last person, perhaps, in the world from whom Dr. Burney could have expected a similar scheme. He thought her project, however, as innocent as it was whimsical, and offered not the smallest objection; but, kindly embracing her, and calling himself *le pere confident*, he enjoined her to be watchful that Charles was discreet; and to be invariably strict in guarding her own incognita: and then, having tacitly granted her personal petition, he dropt the subject.

With fresh eagerness, now, and heightened spirits, the incipient author rolled up her packet for the bookseller; which was carried to him by a newly trusted agent,[5] her brother being then in the country.

The suspense was short; in a very few days Mr. Lowndes sent his approbation of the work, with an offer of 20£ for the manuscript—an offer which was accepted with alacrity, and boundless surprise at its magnificence!!

The receipt for this settlement, signed simply by *"the Editor of Evelina,"* was conveyed by the new agent to Fleet-street.

In the ensuing January, 1778, the work was published; a fact which only became known to its writer, who had dropped all correspondence with Mr. Lowndes, from hearing the following advertisement read, accidentally, aloud at breakfast-time, by Mrs. Burney, her mother-in-law.

This day was published,
EVELINA,
OR, A YOUNG LADY'S ENTRANCE INTO THE WORLD.
Printed for T. LOWNDES, Fleet-street.

Mrs. Burney, who read this unsuspectingly, went on immediately to other articles; but, had she lifted her eyes from the paper, something more than suspicion must have met them, from the conscious colouring of the scribbler, and the irresistible smiles of the two sisters, Susanna and Charlotte,[6] who were present.

5. Her cousin, Edward Francesco Burney (1760–1848). [*Editor*]
6. Charlotte Ann Burney (1761–1838). [*Editor*]

Dr. Burney probably read the same advertisement the same morning; but as he knew neither the name of the book, nor of the bookseller, nor the time of publication, he must have read it without comment, or thought.

*   *   *

Evelina had now been published four or five months, though Dr. Burney still knew nothing of its existence; and the author herself had learnt it only by the chance-read advertisement already mentioned. Yet had that little book found its way abroad; fallen into general reading; gone through three editions, and been named with favour in sundry Reviews; till, at length, a sort of cry was excited amongst its readers for discovering its author.

*   *   *

June came; and a sixth month was elapsing in the same silent con-cealment, when early one morning the Doctor, with great eagerness and hurry, began a search amongst the pamphlets in his study for a Monthly Review, which he demanded of his daughter Charlotte, who alone was in the room. After finding it, he earnestly examined its con-tents, and then looked out hastily for an article which he read with a countenance of so much emotion, that Charlotte stole softly behind him, to peep over his shoulder; and then saw, with surprise and joy, that he was perusing an account, which she knew to be most favourable, of Evelina, beginning, 'A great variety of natural characters—'

When he had finished the article, he put down the Review, and sat motionless, without raising his eyes, and looking in deep—but charmed astonishment. Suddenly, then, he again snatched the Review, and again ran over the article, with an air yet more intensely occupied. Placing it afterwards on the chimney-piece, he walked about the room, as if to recover breath, and recollect himself; though always with looks of the most vivid pleasure.

Some minutes later, holding the Review in his hand, while inspecting the table of contents, he beckoned to Charlotte to approach; and point-ing to "Evelina," 'you know,' he said, in a whisper, 'that book? Send William for it to Lowndes', as if for yourself; and give it to me when we are alone.'

Charlotte obeyed; and, joyous in sanguine expectation, delivered to him the little volumes, tied up in brown paper, in his study, when, late at night, he came home from some engagement.

He locked them up in his bureau, without speaking, and retired to his chamber.

The kindly impatient Charlotte was in his study the next morning with the lark, waiting the descent of the Doctor from his room.

He, also, was early, and went straight to his desk, whence, taking out and untying the parcel, he opened the first volume upon the little ode to himself,—"Oh author of my being! far more dear," &c.

He ejaculated a 'Good God!' and his eyes were suffused with tears.

Twice he read it, and then re-committed the book to his writing desk, as if his mind were too full for further perusal; and dressed, and went out, without uttering a syllable.

All this the affectionate Charlotte wrote to her sister;[7] who read it with a perturbation inexpressible. It was clear that the Doctor had discovered the name of her book; and learned, also, that Charlotte was one of her cabal: but how, was inexplicable;[8] though what would be his opinion of the work absorbed now all the thoughts and surmises of the clandestine author.

From this time, he frequently, though privately and confidentially, spoke with all the sisters upon the subject; and with the kindliest approbation.

* * *

* * * Dr. Burney now, from his numerous occupations, stole a few hours for a flying visit to Chesington;[9] where his meeting with his daughter, just rescued from the grave, and still barely convalescent, at a period of such peculiar interest to his paternal, and to her filial heart, was of the tenderest description. Yet, earnestly as she coveted his sight, she felt almost afraid, and quite ashamed, to be alone with him, from her doubts how he might accept her versified dedication.

She held back, therefore, from any *tête à tête* till he sent for her to his little gallery cabinet; or in Mr. Crisp's words, conjuring closet.[1] But there, when he had shut the door, with a significant smile, that told her what was coming, and gave a glow to her very forehead from anxious confusion, he gently said, 'I have read your book, Fanny!—but you need not blush at it—it is full of merit—it is, really,—extraordinary!'

She fell upon his neck with heart-throbbing emotion; and he folded her in his arms so tenderly, that she sobbed upon his shoulder; so moved was she by his precious approbation.

* * *

* * * This was conveyed in a packet from Susanna, containing the ensuing letter from Mrs. Thrale to Dr. Burney; written two days after

---

7. Burney, at this time, was residing at Chessington Hall, in Chessington, Surrey, a country boarding-place or rest-home, recuperating from a long and dangerous illness, the result of overwork and mental stress. Charlotte's letter is missing. [*Editor*]
8. Susanna had told him, as he revealed in a fragmentary memoir written between 1792 and 1806. [*Editor*]
9. He arrived at Chessington on June 23. [*Editor*]
1. One of the tenants of Chessington Hall, Samuel Crisp (*c.* 1707–83), an old friend of Dr. Burney and practically a second father to Frances. "Cabinet" and "closet" refer to a private study or small inner chamber. [*Editor*]

she had put the first volume of Evelina into her coach, as Dr. Johnson
was quitting Streatham for a day's residence in Bolt Court.[2]

" 'Dear Doctor Burney,

" 'Doctor Johnson returned home last night full of the praises of the
book I had lent him; protesting there were passages in it that might do
honour to Richardson. We talk of it for ever; and he, Doctor Johnson,
feels ardent after the denouement. *He could not get rid of the Rogue!* he
said. I then lent him the second volume, which he instantly read; and
he is, even now, busy with the third.

" 'You must be more a philosopher, and less a father than I wish you,
not to be pleased with this letter; and the giving such pleasure yields to
nothing but receiving it. Long, my dear Sir, may you live to enjoy the
just praises of your children! And long may they live to deserve and
delight such a parent!' "

This packet was accompanied by intelligence, that Sir Joshua Reynolds had been fed while reading the little work, from refusing to quit it
at table! and that Edmund Burke[3] had sat up a whole night to finish
it!!! It was accompanied, also, by a letter from Dr. Burney, that almost
dissolved the happy scribbler with touching delight, by its avowal of his
increased approbation upon a second reading: "Thou hast made," he
says, "thy old father laugh and cry at thy pleasure. . . . I never yet heard
of a novel writer's statue;—yet who knows?—above all things, then, take
care of thy head, for if that should be at all turned out of its place by all
this intoxicating success, what sort of figure wouldst thou cut upon a
pedestal? *Prens y bien garde!'*

This playful goodness, with the wondrous news that Doctor Johnson
himself had deigned to read the little book, so struck, so nearly bewildered the author, that, seized with a fit of wild spirits, * * * she darted
out of the room in which she had read the tidings by his side, to a
small lawn before the window, where she danced, lightly, blithely, gaily,
around a large old mulberry tree, as impulsively and airily as she had
often done in her days of adolescence: * * *

❋   ❋   ❋

---

2. Hester Lynch Thrale Salusbury (1741–1821), m. (1763) Henry Thrale (?1729–81, brewer and
   MP). Dr. Burney had been paying weekly visits to the Thrales' estate, Streatham Park, since
   12 December 1776 to give music lessons to their eldest daughter Hester Maria ("Queeney")
   (1764–1857). Samuel Johnson (1709–84), eminent fiction writer, poet, critic, dramatist, and
   lexicographer. Johnson, who been an intimate friend of the Thrales since 1765, had his own
   room at Streatham and at the Thrales's town house in Southwark although his own residence
   was at Bolt Court, Fleet Street. [*Editor*]
3. Sir Joshua Reynolds (1723–92), the most celebrated portrait painter of the century, and
   Edmund Burke (1729–97), the famous politician and writer, author of *A Philosophical Enquiry
   into the Origin of Our Ideas of the Sublime and Beautiful* (1757). [*Editor*]

FRANCES BURNEY

Extracts from the Journals and Letters†

June 18, 1778

✳   ✳   ✳

✳ ✳ ✳ Susan begged to have, then, my Father's *real* & *final* opinion;—& it is such as I almost blush to write, even for my own private reading;—but yet is such as I can by no means suffer to pass unrecorded, as my whole Journal contains nothing so grateful to me.—I will copy his own words, according to Susan's solemn declaration of their authenticity.

'Upon my soul I think it the best Novel I know excepting Fieldings,—&, in some respects, *better* than his! I have been *excessively* pleased with it; there are, perhaps, a few things that might have been otherwise,—Mirvan's trick upon Lovel is, I think, carried too far, there is something even disgusting in it: however, this Instance excepted, I protest I think it will *scarce bear an Improvement.* I wish I may die, if I do not believe it to be *the very best Novel in the Language,* except Fielding's! for Smollets, with all their Wit, are quite too gross. The *Language* is as good as *any body* need write, I declare as good as I would *wish* to read. Lord Orville's Character is just what it should be, perfectly benevolent & upright; & there is a *boldness* in it that struck me mightily, for he is a man not *ashamed* of being better than the rest of mankind. Evelina is in a new style too, so perfectly innocent & Natural; & the scene between her & her Father, Sir John Belmont, is a scene for a *Tragedy!* I *blubbered* at it, & Lady Hales & Miss Coussmaker[1] are not yet recovered from hearing it; it made them quite ill; it is, indeed, wrought up in a most extraordinary manner!'

✳   ✳   ✳

July 20, 1778

Nothing but Laurels do I receive; & about nothing else can I write! very hard!—I had, yesterday, a Letter from my mother herself, written in consequence of my Father's Discovering me to her, as soon as they had finished Evelina. She has written purposely 'to Congratulate me,' she says, 'on the merit & success of my 1st publication.' She declares it has given her more pleasure than any Book she has read of a *long, long*

---

† From Lars E. Troide and Stewart J. Cooke, eds., *The Early Journals and Letters of Fanny Burney,* vol. 3 (Oxford: Clarendon, 1994) 28–29, 55–56, 88–90, 109–10, 141–42, 149, 234–35. Reprinted by permission of Lars E. Troide. The authors' notes have been edited for brevity.
1. Mary, Lady Hales, née Hayward (c. 1741–1803), a friend of Dr. Burney, and her daughter Catherine Coussmaker (flourished 1764–1803), by Lady Hales's first husband, Evert George Coussmaker, Esq. Miss Coussmaker was a particular friend of Susanna Burney.

while, & that it has *revived* in her both pleasure & sensation, by alternate
Tears & Laughter: she owns she had a *whimsical* idea of the Writer, or
writers, ere she saw the Book, but protests that every Letter in it tended
to remove it,—she then adds 'throughout the serious part, I traced your
feelings, but wondered at your powers of delineation. In the sportive
way of holding up Ignorance, Conceit & Folly to ridicule, I thought I
discovered Your attentive Ear, & observing Eye; but there is a knowledge
of the ill manners & absurd conduct of Bon Ton in domestic Life, that
almost puzzled me,—till a Leaf I had over looked at the beginning,[2]
brought me back, & gave it *all* to you.' She adds many yet more flattering things, promises me her secresy if I wish it, but concludes with
saying no one need Blush to be the acknowledged Author.

*   *   *

August 21, 1778

*   *   *

Dr. Johnson, as usual, came last into the Library: he was quite in high
spirits, & full of mirth & sport. I had the Honour of sitting next to
him: & now, all at once, he flung aside his reserve, thinking, perhaps,
that it was Time *I* should fling aside mine!

*   *   *

* * * Then, suddenly he snatched my Hand, & kissing it;—*true 'pon
Honour!* he added, 'Ah! they will little think what a *Tartar*[3] you carry to
them!'
 'No, that they won't! cried Mrs. Thrale; Miss Burney looks so
meek, & so quiet,—nobody would suspect what a comical Girl she is:—
but I believe she has a great deal of *malice* at Heart.'
 'Oh she's a Toad!—cried the Doctor, Laughing,—a sly Young Rogue!
with her Smiths & her Branghtons!

*   *   *

* * * A few minutes after, he put his Hand on my arm, & shaking his
Head, exclaimed 'O, You are a sly little Rogue!—What a *Holbourn
Beau*[4] have you drawn!'
 'Ay, Miss Burney, said Mrs. Thrale, the *Holbourn Beau* is Mr. John-
son's favourite;—& we have *all* your Characters by Heart, from Mr.
Smith up to Lady Louisa.'
 'O, Mr. Smith, Mr. Smith is the Man! cried he, Laughing violently,
Harry[5] Fielding *never* drew so good a Character!—such a fine *varnish*

---

2. The "Leaf" contained Burney's dedicatory verses to her father.
3. A vixen or shrew.
4. That is, Mr. Smith.
5. A nickname for "Henry."

of low politeness!—such a *struggle* to appear a Gentleman!—Madam, there is *no* Character better drawn *any* where—in *any* Book, or by *any* Author.'

＊　＊　＊

August 23, 1778

＊　＊　＊

I then rose to look for a Book which we had been talking of, & Dr. Johnson said most civil things of me *the while*,—but I did not distinctly hear them. However, when I returned to my seat, he said he wished Richardson had been alive, 'And then, he added, you should have been Introduced to him,—though, I don't know, niether;—Richardson would have been afraid of her!'

'O yes!—that's a likely matter!' quoth I.

'It's very true, continued he; Richardson would have been really *afraid* of her;—there is merit in Evelina which he could not have borne.—No, it would not have done!—unless, indeed, she would have flattered him prodigiously.—Harry Fielding, too, would have been afraid of her,—there is nothing so delicately finished in *all* Harry Fielding's Works, as in Evelina;—(Then, shaking his Head at me, he exclaimed) O, you little *Character-monger*, you!'

Mrs. Thrale then returned to her charge, & again urged me about a Comedy,—& again I tried to silence her,—& we had a *fine fight* together;—till she called upon Dr. Johnson to *back* her,—'Why, Madam, said he, Laughing,—she *is* Writing one!—What a rout is here, indeed!—She is writing one up stairs all the Time.—Who ever knew when she began Evelina?'

Post September 15, 1778

＊　＊　＊

'A Gentleman whom we know very well, said Miss Palmer,[6] when he could learn nothing at the *Printers*, took the trouble to go all about *Snow Hill*, to see if he could find any *silversmith's*.

'Well, *he was* a Cunning Creature! said Mrs. Thrale. But Mr. Johnson's favourite is Mr. Smith.'

'So he is of every body, answered she; he & all that Family; every body says such a Family never was Drawn before. But Mrs. Cholmondely's[7] favourite is Madame Duval; she *acts* her from morning to night, & *ma-fois* every body she sees. But though we all want so much to know the Author, both Mrs. Cholmondeley, & my uncle himself, say they should be frightened to Death to be in her Company, because she must be

6. Mary Palmer, later Lady Inchiquin (*c.* 1750–1820), niece of Sir Joshua Reynolds. [*Editor*]
7. Mary Cholmondeley, née Woffington (*c.* 1729–1811), society hostess. [*Editor*]

such a very nice observer, that there would be no escaping her with safety.'

Good God, my dear Susy,—what strange ideas are taken from mere *Book-reading!*—But what follows gave me the highest delight I can feel.

'Mr. Burke, she continued, *doats* on it: he began it one morning at 7 o'clock, & could not leave it a moment, he sat up *all* night reading it. He says he has not seen such a Book he can't tell when.'

*   *   *

Post September 16–21, 1778

*   *   *

A little while after, he[8] asked Mrs. Thrale who had Read Evelina in his absence?

'Who? cried she;—why *Burke!*—Burke sat up all night to finish it;—& Sir Joshua Reynolds is *mad* about it, & said he would give 50 pounds to know the Author. * * *

*   *   *

She then told him that Mrs. Cholmondeley was *acting* Madame Duval all over the Town.

'Mrs. Cholmondeley, said he, was the first I ever heard mention the Book; she used to talk to me forever of Evelina & Evelina,—but I never heeded her,—I had no intention to read it, till I fell upon it that Day in the Coach;—& a delightful thing it is!'—

January 11, 1779

*   *   *

Some Time after, Sir Joshua, returning to his *standing* place, entered into *confab.* with Miss Linley & your slave upon various matters;— during which, Mr. Sheridan,[9] joining us, said 'Sir Joshua I have been telling Miss Burney that she must not suffer her Pen to lie idle;—*ought* she?'

Sir Joshua. No, indeed, ought she not.

Mr. Sheridan.—Do *you*, then, Sir Joshua, persuade her.—But perhaps you *have* begun some thing?—may we *ask?*—Will you answer a Question candidly?'

F.B.—I don't know,—but *as* candidly as *Mrs. Candour*[1] I think I certainly shall!

Mr. Sheridan. What, then, are you about now?

8. Dr. Johnson. [*Editor*]
9. Mary Linley, later Mrs. Tickell (1758–87), singer, and Richard Brinsley Sheridan (1751–1816), dramatist, theater manager. "Your slave" refers to Burney herself. [*Editor*]
1. That is, not at all candidly. Mrs. Candour is an ironically named character in Sheridan's celebrated play *School for Scandal* (1777). [*Editor*]

F.B.—Why—twirling my Fan, I think!'

Mr. Sheridan. No, no,—but what are you about *at Home?*—however,—it is not a fair Question, so I won't press it.

Yet he *looked* very inquisitive; but I was glad to get off without any *downright* answer.

Sir Joshua. Any thing in the *Dialogue* way, I think, she *must* succeed in,—& I am sure *invention* will not be wanting,—

Mr. Sheridan. No, indeed;—I think, & say, she should write a *Comedy.*

Lord, Susy, I could not believe my own Ears! *This* from Mr. *Sheridan!*

Sir Joshua. I am sure *I* think so; & I hope she *will.*

I could only answer by *incredulous* exclamations.

'Consider, continued Sir Joshua, you have already had all the applause & fame you *can* have given you in the *Clozet,*—but the Acclamation of a *Theatre* will be *new* to you.'

And then he put down his Trumpet, & began a violent clapping of his Hands.

I actually shook from Head to foot! I felt myself already in Drury Lane, amidst the *Hub bub* of a first Night.

'O no! cried I, there *may* be a *Noise,*—but it will be just the *reverse,*—' And I returned his salute with a Hissing.

Mr. Sheridan joined Sir Joshua very warmly.

'O Sir! cried I, *you* should not run on so,—you don't know what mischief you may do!'

Mr. Sheridan. I wish I *may,*—I shall be very glad to be accessory.

Sir Joshua. She has, certainly, something of a knack at Characters;—*where* she got it, I don't know,—&*how* she got it, I can't imagine,—but she certainly *has* it. And to throw it away is ———

Mr. Sheridan. O she *won't,*—she will write a Comedy,—she has promised me she will!

F.B. O Good God!—if you both run on in this manner, I shall ———

I was going to say *get under the Chair,* but Mr. Sheridan, interrupting me with a Laugh, said 'Set about one?—very well, that's right!'

'Ay, cried Sir Joshua, that's *very* right.—And *you,* (to Mr. Sheridan,) would *take* any thing of *Her's,*—would you not?—*Unsight unseen?*'

What a *point blank* Question! Who but Sir Joshua would have ventured it!

'*Yes;* answered Mr. Sheridan, with quickness,—& make her a Bow & my best Thanks into the Bargain!'

Now, my dear Susy, tell me, did you ever hear the *fellow* to such a speech as this!—it was all I could do to sit it.

'Good God, Mr. Sheridan, I exclaimed, are you not mocking me?'

'No, upon my Honour! this is what I have *meditated* to say to you the first Time I should have the pleasure of seeing you.'

To be sure, as Mrs. Thrale says, if folks *are* to be spoilt,—there is nothing in the World so *pleasant* as spoiling! But I *never* was so much

Astonished, & *seldom* have been so much delighted as by this attack of Mr. Sheridan. Afterwards he took my Father aside, & formally repeated his opinion that I should write for the stage, & his desire to see my Play,—with encomiums the most flattering of Evelina.

MADAME D' ARBLAY [FRANCES BURNEY]

Dedication to *The Wanderer*†

*   *   *

The power of prejudice annexed to nomenclature is universal: the same being who, unnamed, passes unnoticed, if preceded by the title of a hero, or a potentate, catches every eye, and is pursued with clamorous praise, or,—its common reverberator!—abuse: but in nothing is the force of denomination more striking than in the term Novel; a species of writing which, though never mentioned, even by its supporter, but with a look that fears contempt, is not more rigidly excommunicated, from its appellation, in theory, than sought and fostered, from its attractions, in practice.

So early was I impressed myself with ideas that fastened degradation to this class of composition, that at the age of adolescence, I struggled against the propensity which, even in childhood, even from the moment I could hold a pen, had impelled me into its toils; and on my fifteenth birth-day, I made so resolute a conquest over an inclination at which I blushed, and that I had always kept secret, that I committed to the flames whatever, up to that moment, I had committed to paper. And so enormous was the pile, that I thought it prudent to consume it in the garden.

*   *   *

Reviews

From the London Review *

The history of a young lady exposed to very critical situations. There is much more merit, as well respecting stile, character and incident, than is usually to be met with among our modern novels.

---

† From "To Doctor Burney," *The Wanderer; or, Female Difficulties*, vol. 1 (London, 1814): xix–xxi.
* From William Kenrick, *London Review* 7 (Feb. 1778): 151.

From the Monthly Review ‡

This novel has given us so much pleasure in the perusal, that we do not hesitate to pronounce it one of the most sprightly, entertaining, and agreeable productions of this kind, which has of late fallen under our notice. A great variety of natural incidents, some of the comic stamp, render the narrative extremely interesting. The characters, which are agreeably diversified, are conceived and drawn with propriety, and supported with spirit. The whole is written with great ease and command of language. From this commendation, however, we must except the character of a son of Neptune, whose manners are rather those of a rough, uneducated country squire, than those of a genuine sea-captain.

From the Westminster Magazine §

May prove equally useful and entertaining to the younger part of our *male* as well as *female* Readers; to the latter of whom we particularly recommend it, as conveying many practical lessons both on morals and manners.

From the Critical Review †

This performance deserves no common praise, whether we consider it in a moral or literary light. It would have disgraced neither the head nor the heart of Richardson.—The father of a family, observing the knowledge of the world and the lessons of experience which it contains, will recommend it to his daughters; they will weep and (what is not so commonly the effect of novels) will laugh, and grow wiser, as they read; the experienced mother will derive pleasure and happiness from being present at its reading; even the sons of the family will forego the diversions of the town or the field to pursue the entertainment of Evelina's acquaintance, who will imperceptibly lead them, as well as their sisters, to improvement and to virtue.

If the author of this amusing and instructive novel posses any of Richardson's merits, he labours also under one of his principal faults. The gold is in some places beat out considerably too fine. The second volume deserves few of the solid praises which we with pleasure bestow on the first and the third. The Roman sibyl, after she had burnt part of her work, still persisted in demanding the same price for what remained; we should set a higher value upon this performance had the writer made it shorter—but perhaps, as Swift said of a long letter, he had not time.

The outline of Evelina's story is this.—The child of a mother who gave her existence at the expence of her own life: and of a brutal father

‡ From the *Monthly Review* 58 (April 1778): 316.
§ From the *Westminster Magazine* 6 (June 1778): 325.
† From the *Critical Review* 46 (September 1778): 202–04.

who occasioned that mother's death, and refused, as it was supposed, to acknowledge her daughter; she is educated under the paternal care of Mr. Villars, a worthy clergyman. The novel opens when Evelina is of the age at which young ladies are, as the phrase is, introduced into the world. Mr. Villars trusts his accomplished ward with a family of fashion and fortune, that she may be brought upon the public stage in that great theatre of the world, London. Her simplicity, good sense, and inexperience, are productive of useful humour and diverting satire. The characters of her newly-discovered grandmother Madame Du Val, and of a captain Mirvan, the latter an honest English sailor, the former a frenchified English waiting-woman, whose good stars had made her the widow of a man of rank and fortune, are well supported, finely drawn, and in a great measure original. During the few months which Evelina spends at a distance from Mr. Villars, she commences an acquaintance, that ripens into love, with lord Orville. His lordship's rivals are painted from nature, the progress of the amour is traced by the hand of an artist. The winding up of the story is obvious—Evelina gets a husband, and discovers a father.—We could wish her husband had not been a lord, and that her father had been less rich. Lords and ladies cannot afford to spend their *precious* time reading novels; and, if they could, they bear no proportion on the commonality of the literary world. The purchasers of novels, the subscribers to circulating libraries, are seldom in more elevated situations than the middle ranks of life.—The subjects of novels are, with a dangerous uniformity, almost always taken from superior life.—The satirists complain with injustice of the want of virtue in our modern nobility; when the hero and the heroine of every novel hardly ever fail, sooner or later, to turn out a lady or a lord. What effect has this upon the readers? They are convinced that happiness is not to be found in the chilling climate of low life, nor even, where one of our poets so truly fixed it, in the temperate zone of middle life—Rank alone contains this unknown good, wealth alone can bestow this coveted joy—The title of Sir Charles Grandison, the fortune of Miss Byron,[1] are the least with which our young novel readers are determined to sit down satisfied. What is the consequence? Their fates have perhaps destined them to be a petty attorney or a silversmith's daughter, a grocer's son or a clergyman's heiress; fortune *positively* refuses to realize any of their romantic dreams; and a quarter of an hour's perusal of an unnatural novel has embittered all their lives.

We have heard of an advertisement for a house with a N. B. that it must not be within a mile of a lord: we wish, to see one novel in which there is no lord.

To the well written performance now before us is prefixed this poetical and affectionate dedication.

1. Sir Charles Grandison, baronet, and Harriet Byron, characters in Samuel Richardson's novel *The History of Sir Charles Grandison* (1754).

Oh author of my being! — far more dear
　　To me than light, than nourishment, or rest,
Hygeia's blessings, Rapture's burning tear,
　　Or the life blood that mantles in my breast!

If in my heart the love of virtue glows,
　　'T was planted there by an unerring rule;
From thy example the pure flame arose,
　　Thy life, my precept — thy good works, my school.

Could my weak pow'rs thy num'rous virtues trace,
　　By filial love each fear should be repress'd;
The blush of incapacity I'd chace,
　　And stand, recorder of thy worth, confess'd:

But since my niggard stars that gift refuse,
　　Concealment is the only boon I claim;
Obscure be still th' unsuccessful muse,
　　Who cannot raise, but would not risk, your fame.

Oh! of my life at once the source and joy!
　　If e'er thy eyes these feeble lines survey,
Let not their folly their intent destroy;
　　Accept the tribute — but forget the lay.

From the Gentleman's Magazine *

"To draw characters from nature, tho' not from life, and to mark the manners of the times, is the attempted plan of the following letters. For this purpose, a young female, educated in the most secluded retirement, makes, at the age of seventeen, her first appearance upon the great and busy stage of life: with a virtuous mind, a cultivated understanding, and a feeling heart, her ignorance of the forms, and inexperience of the manners of the world, occasion all the little incidents which these volumes record, and which form the natural progression of the life of a young woman of obscure birth, but conspicuous beauty, for the first six months after her *Entrance into the World.*" — Such is the just account given of this work by the author; to which we shall only add, that these volumes will afford a pleasing, innocent amusement, exhibiting, in an easy style, many such characters as occur in the world, not raised so high as to be extravagant, nor sunk so low as to be disgusting.

---

* From the *Gentleman's Magazine* 48 (September 1778): 425.

CRITICISM

ANNA LETITIA BARBAULD

Miss Burney†

Scarcely any name, if any, stands higher in the list of novel-writers than that of Miss Burney, now Mrs. D'Arblay, daughter of the ingenious Dr. Burney. She has given to the world three productions of this kind; *Evelina*, in three vols., *Cecilia*, in five vols., and, after a long interval, in which, however honourable her employment might be deemed, she was completely lost to the literary world, *Camilla*, also in five vols. * * *

*   *   *

* * * Miss Burney composed her *Evelina* when she was in the early bloom of youth, about seventeen. She wrote it without the knowledge of any of her friends. With the modesty of a young woman, and the diffidence of a young author, she contrived to throw it into the press anonymously, and, when published, laid the volumes in the way of her friends, whose impartial plaudits soon encouraged her to confess to whom they were obliged for their entertainment. There is perhaps no purer or higher pleasure than the young mind enjoys in the first burst of praise and admiration which attends a successful performance. To be lifted up at once into the favourite of the public; to be sensible that the name, hitherto pronounced only in the circle of family connexions, is become familiar to all that read, through every province of a large kingdom; to feel in the glow of genius and freshness of invention powers to continue that admiration to future years;—to feel all this, and at the same time to be happily ignorant of all the chills and mortifications, the impossibility not to flag in a long work, the ridicule and censure which fasten on vulnerable parts, and the apathy or diffidence which generally seizes an author before his literary race is run;—this is happiness for youth, and youth alone.

Evelina became at once a fashionable novel: there are even those who still prefer it to *Cecilia*, though that preference is probably owing to the partiality inspired by a first performance. Evelina is a young lady, amiable and inexperienced, who is continually getting into difficulties from not knowing or not observing the established etiquettes of society, and from being unluckily connected with a number of vulgar characters, by whom she is involved in a series of adventures both ludicrous and mortifying. Some of these are certainly carried to a very extravagant excess, particularly the tricks played upon the poor Frenchwoman; but the fondness for humour, and low humour, which Miss Burney discovered in this piece, runs through all her subsequent works, and strongly characterizes, sometimes perhaps blemishes, her genius. Lord Orville is

† From Anna Letitia Barbauld, *The British Novelists*, vol. 38 (London, 1810) i–iii.

a generous and pleasing lover; and the conclusion is so wrought, as to leave upon the mind that glow of happiness which is not found in her subsequent works. The meeting between Evelina and her father is pathetic. The agonizing remorse and perturbation of the man who is about to see, for the first time, his child whom he had deserted, and whose mother had fallen a sacrifice to his unkindness; the struggles between the affection which impels him towards her, and the dread he feels of seeing in her the image of his injured wife; are described with many touches of nature and strong effect.—Other characters in the piece are, Mrs. Selwyn, a wit and an oddity; a gay insolent baronet; a group of vulgar cits;[1] a number of young bucks, whose coldness, carelessness, rudeness, and impertinent gallantry, serve as a foil to the delicate attentions of Lord Orville. * * *

* * *

WILLIAM HAZLITT

[The Spirit of Cockneyism] †

* * *

Mr. Smith and the Brangtons, in 'Evelina,' are the finest possible examples of the spirit of *Cockneyism.* I once knew a linen-draper in the City, who owned to me he did not quite like this part of Miss Burney's novel. He said, 'I myself lodge in a first floor, where there are young ladies in the house: they sometimes have company, and if I am out, they ask me to lend them the use of my apartment, which I readily do out of politeness, or if it is an agreeable party, I perhaps join them. All this is so like what passes in the novel, that I fancy myself a sort of second Mr. Smith, and am not quite easy at it!' This was mentioned to the fair Authoress, and she was delighted to find that her characters were so true, that an actual person fancied himself to be one of them. The resemblance, however, was only in the externals; and the real modesty of the individual stumbled on the likeness to a city coxcomb!

* * *

---

1. Short for "citizens"; usually applied somewhat contemptuously to townsmen or to tradesmen or shopkeepers.
† From William Hazlitt, "On Londoners and Country People," *The Collected Works of William Hazlitt,* ed. A. R. Waller and Arnold Glover, vol. 7 (London: Dent, 1903) 72–73.

WILLIAM HAZLITT

[On Burney's Characters] †

It is not to be wondered at, if amidst the tumult of events crowded into this period, our literature has partaken of the disorder of the time; if our prose has run mad, and our poetry grown childish. Among those persons who 'have kept the even tenor of their way,' the author of Evelina, Cecilia, and Camilla, must be allowed to hold a distinguished place. Mrs. Radcliffe's 'enchantments drear,' and mouldering castles, derived part of their interest, no doubt, from the supposed tottering state of all old structures at the time; and Mrs. Inchbald's 'Nature and Art' would scarcely have had the same popularity, but that it fell in (as to its two main characters) with the prevailing prejudice of the moment, that judges and bishops were not invariably pure abstractions of justice and piety. Miss Edgeworth's Tales again (with the exception of Castle Rackrent,[1] which is a genuine, unsophisticated, national portrait) are a kind of pedantic, pragmatical common sense, tinctured with the pertness and pretensions of the paradoxes to which they are so self-complacently opposed. Madame D'Arblay is, on the contrary, quite of the old school, a mere common observer of manners, and also a very woman. It is this last circumstance which forms the peculiarity of her writings, and distinguishes them from those masterpieces which I have before mentioned. She is a quick, lively, and accurate observer of persons and things; but she always looks at them with a consciousness of her sex, and in that point of view in which it is the particular business and interest of women to observe them. There is little in her works of passion or character, or even manners, in the most extended sense of the word, as implying the sum-total of our habits and pursuits; her *forts* is in describing the absurdities and affectations of external behaviour, or *the manners of people in company*. Her characters, which are ingenious caricatures, are, no doubt, distinctly marked, and well kept up; but they are slightly shaded, and exceedingly uniform. Her heroes and heroines, almost all of them, depend on the stock of a single phrase or sentiment, and have certain mottoes or devices by which they may always be known. They form such characters as people might be supposed to assume for a night at a masquerade. She presents, not the whole-length figure, nor even the face, but some prominent feature. In one of her novels, for example, a lady appears regularly every ten pages, to get a lesson in music for nothing. She never appears for any other purpose; this is all you know

† From William Hazlitt, "On the English Novelists," *The Collected Works of William Hazlitt*, ed. A. R. Waller and Arnold Glover, vol. 8 (London: Dent, 1903) 123–25.

1. Ann Radcliffe (1764–1823), popular gothic novelist; Elizabeth Inchbald (1753–1821), novelist and playwright, author of *Nature and Art* (1796); Maria Edgeworth (1768–1849), novelist and educational writer, author of *Castle Rackrent* (1800).

of her; and in this the whole wit and humour of the character consists. Meadows[2] is the same, who has always the cue of being tired, without any other idea. It has been said of Shakespeare, that you may always assign his speeches to the proper characters;—and you may infallibly do the same thing with Madame D'Arblay's, for they always say the same thing. The Branghtons are the best. Mr. Smith is an exquisite city portrait. Evelina is also her best novel, because it is the shortest; that is, it has all the liveliness in the sketches of character, and smartness of common dialogue and repartee, without the tediousness of the story, and endless affectation of sentiment which disfigures the others.

*   *   *

There is little other power in Miss Burney's novels, than that of immediate observation: her characters, whether of refinement or vulgarity, are equally superficial and confined. The whole is a question of form, whether that form is adhered to or infringed upon. It is this circumstance which takes away dignity and interest from her story and sentiments, and makes the one so teazing and tedious, and the other so insipid. The difficulties in which she involves her heroines are too much 'Female Difficulties'; they are difficulties created out of nothing. The author appears to have no other idea of refinement than that it is the reverse of vulgarity; but the reverse of vulgarity is fastidiousness and affectation. There is a true and a false delicacy. Because a vulgar country Miss would answer 'yes' to a proposal of marriage in the first page, Madame D'Arblay makes it a proof of an excess of refinement, and an indispensable point of etiquette in her young ladies, to postpone the answer to the end of five volumes, without the smallest reason for their doing so, and with every reason to the contrary. The reader is led every moment to expect a *denouement*, and is as often disappointed on some trifling pretext. The whole artifice of her fable consists in coming to no conclusion. Her ladies 'stand so upon the order of their going,' that they do not go at all. They will not abate an ace of their punctilio in any circumstances, or on any emergency. They would consider it as quite indecorous to run down stairs though the house were in flames, or to move an inch off the pavement though a scaffolding was falling. She has formed to herself an abstract idea of perfection in common behaviour, which is quite as romantic and impracticable as any other idea of the sort: and the consequence has naturally been, that she makes her heroines commit the greatest improprieties and absurdities in order to avoid the smallest. In opposition to a maxim in philosophy, they constantly act from the weakest motive, or rather from pure contradiction. The whole tissue of the fable is, in general, more wild and chimerical than any thing in Don Quixote, without the poetical truth or elevation.

---

2. Mr. Meadows is a bored young man in Burney's second novel *Cecilia* (1782).

Madame D'Arblay has woven a web of difficulties for her heroines, something like the green silken threads in which the shepherdesses entangled the steed of Cervantes's hero, who swore, in his fine enthusiastic way, that he would sooner cut his passage to another world than disturb the least of those beautiful meshes. * * *

*   *   *

JOHN WILSON CROKER

[Review of *The Wanderer*] †

None of our female novelists (not even Miss Edgeworth) ever attained so early and so high a reputation as Miss Burney, or, as we must now call her, Madame D'Arblay. Her Evelina, published at the age of seventeen, was a most extraordinary instance of early talent, and excited an expectation of excellence which her Cecilia almost fulfilled, and which her Camilla did not altogether disappoint; but we regret to say, that the Wanderer, which might be expected to finish and crown her literary labours, is not only inferior to its sister-works, but cannot in our judgment, claim any very decided superiority over the thousand-and-one volumes with which the Minerva Press inundates the shelves of circulating libraries, and increases, instead of diverting the ennui of the loungers at watering-places.

If we had not been assured in the title-page that this work had been produced by the same pen as Cecilia, we should have pronounced Madame D'Arblay to be a feeble imitator of the style and manner of Miss Burney—we should have admitted the flat fidelity of her copy, but we should have lamented the total want of vigour, vivacity, and originality; and, conceding to the fair author (as we should have been inclined to do) some discrimination of character, and some power of writing, we should have strenuously advised her to avoid, in future, the dull mediocrity of a copyist, and to try the flight of her own genius in some work, that should not recall to us in every page the mortifying recollection of excellence which, though she had the good sense to admire it, she never would have the power to rival.

Such being the opinion which we should have felt ourselves obliged to pronounce on an imitator, it follows that we have a still more severe judgment to pass on Madame D'Arblay herself. We are afraid that she is self-convicted of being what the painters technically call a *mannerist*; that is, she has given over painting from the life, and has employed

† From John Wilson Croker, Review of *The Wanderer*, by Frances Burney, *Quarterly Review* 11 (Apr. 1814): 123–24.

herself in copying from her own copies, till, instead of a power of natural delineation, she has acquired a certain trick and habitual style of portraiture:—but the Wanderer is not only the work of a mannerist, but of a mannerist who is *épuisée*, whose manner is the worst, and who convinces us that, during the last thirty years which have elapsed since the publication of Cecilia, she has been gradually descending from the elevation which the vigour of her youth had attained.

* * *

THOMAS BABINGTON MACAULAY

[On Burney's Art] †

* * *Madame D'Arblay has left us scarcely anything but humours. Almost every one of her men and women has some one propensity developed to a morbid degree.

* * *

We are, therefore, forced to refuse Madame D' Arblay a place in the highest rank of art; but we cannot deny that, in the rank to which she belonged, she had few equals, and scarcely any superior. The variety of humours which is to be found in her novels is immense; and though the talk of each person separately is monotonous, the general effect is not monotony, but a very lively and agreeable diversity. Her plots are rudely constructed and improbable, if we consider them in themselves. But they are admirably framed for the purpose of exhibiting striking groups of eccentric characters, each governed by his own peculiar whim, each talking his own peculiar jargon, and each bringing out by opposition the peculiar oddities of all the rest.

THOMAS BABINGTON MACAULAY

[On Burney's Morality] *

* * *

* * * It is not only on account of the intrinsic merit of Madame D'Arblay's early works that she is entitled to honourable mention. Her

---

† From Thomas Babington Macaulay, "Madame d'Arblay," *Critical and Miscellaneous Essays,* vol. 5 (New York, 1863) 59.

* From Thomas Babington Macaulay, "Madame d'Arblay," *Critical and Miscellaneous Essays,* vol. 5 (New York, 1863) 66–67.

appearance is an important epoch in our literary history. Evelina was the first tale written by a woman, and purporting to be a picture of life and manners, that lived or deserved to live. The Female Quixote[1] is no exception. That work has undoubtedly great merit when considered as a wild satirical harlequinade; but, if we consider it as a picture of life and manners, we must pronounce it more absurd than any of the romances which it was designed to ridicule.

Indeed, most of the popular novels which preceded Evelina were such as no lady would have written; and many of them were such as no lady could without confusion own that she had read. The very name of the novel was held in horror among religious people. In decent families which did not profess extraordinary sanctity, there was a strong feeling against all such works. Sir Anthony Absolute, two or three years before Evelina appeared, spoke the sense of the great body of sober fathers and husbands, when he pronounced the circulating library an evergreen tree of diabolical knowledge. This feeling, on the part of the grave and reflecting, increased the evil from which it had sprung. The novelist, having little character to lose, and having few readers among serious people, took without scruple liberties which in our generation seem almost incredible.

Miss Burney did for the English novel what Jeremy Collier did for the English drama;[2] and she did it in a better way. She first showed that a tale might be written in which both the fashionable and the vulgar life of London might be exhibited with great force, and with broad comic humour, and which yet should not contain a single line inconsistent with rigid morality, or even with virgin delicacy. She took away the reproach which lay on a most useful and delightful species of composition. She vindicated the right of her sex to an equal share in a fair and noble province of letters. Several accomplished women have followed in her track. At present, the novels which we owe to English ladies form no small part of the literary glory of our country. No class of works is more honourably distinguished by fine observation, by grace, by delicate wit, by pure moral feeling. Several among the successors of Madame D'Arblay have equalled her; two, we think, have surpassed her. But the fact that she has been surpassed gives her an additional claim to our respect and gratitude; for in truth we owe to her, not only Evelina, Cecilia, and Camilla, but also Mansfield Park and the Absentee.[3]

1. Charlotte Lennox (?1729–1804), *The Female Quixote; or the Adventures of Arabella* (1752), whose heroine, like Don Quixote, is bedazzled by reading romances.
2. Collier's pamphlet, *A Short View of the Immorality and Profaneness of the English Stage* (1698), which castigates the licentiousness of Restoration drama, initiated a reform of the English stage.
3. Novels by Jane Austen (1775–1817) and Maria Edgeworth (1768–1849), published in 1814 and 1812 respectively.

VIRGINIA WOOLF

[The Mother of English Fiction] †

* * * What, * * * was the origin of the extraordinary outburst in the eighteenth century of novel writing by women? Why did it begin then, and not in the time of the Elizabethan renaissance? Was the motive which finally determined them to write a desire to correct the current view of their sex expressed in so many volumes and for so many ages by male writers? If so, their art is at once possessed of an element which should be absent from the work of all previous writers. It is clear enough, however, that the work of Miss Burney, the mother of English fiction, was not inspired by any single wish to redress a grievance: the richness of the human scene as Dr Burney's daughter had the chance of observing it provided a sufficient stimulus; but however strong the impulse to write had become, it had at the outset to meet opposition not only of circumstance but of opinion. Her first manuscripts were burnt by her stepmother's orders, and needlework was inflicted as a penance, much as, a few years later, Jane Austen would slip her writing beneath a book if anyone came in, and Charlotte Brontë stopped in the middle of her work to pare the potatoes. But the domestic problem, being overcome or compromised with, there remained the moral one. Miss Burney had showed that it was 'possible for a woman to write novels and be respectable', but the burden of proof still rested anew upon each authoress. Even so late as the mid-Victorian days George Eliot was accused of 'coarseness and immorality' in her attempt 'to familiarise the minds of our young women in the middle and higher ranks with matters on which their fathers and brothers would never venture to speak in their presence'.

JOYCE HEMLOW

[The Composition of *Evelina*] *

I never yet heard of a novel writer's statue;—yet who knows?—above all things, then, take care of thy head, for if that should be at all turned

† From Virginia Woolf, "Women Novelists," *The Essays of Virginia Woolf, 1912–1918*, ed. Andrew McNeillie, vol. 2 (London: Hogarth, 1987) 314–15. Copyright © 1987 by Quentin Bell and Angelica Garnett. Reprinted by permission of the Estate of Virginia Woolf, the Hogarth Press, and Harcourt Brace & Company.

* From Joyce Hemlow, *The History of Fanny Burney* (Oxford: Clarendon, 1958) 78–104. Reprinted by permission of Oxford University Press. The author's notes have been edited for brevity.

out of its place by all this intoxicating success, what sort of figure
wouldst thou cut upon a pedestal?

Prens y bien garde!
—Dr. Burney to Fanny[1]

The composition of the first draft of *Evelina* had not been difficult. The
episodes in Evelina's world had taken form readily in Fanny's imagination, and she had only to write them down graphically and naturally in
the unbowdlerized idiom of the early journals—the familiar style that
had always pleased her sisters and Mr. Crisp well enough. In 1776,
however, after she had begun to think of an audience much wider than
the family group, and at the beginning of 1777, when Mr. Lowndes had
approved her work for publication and when she thought that it would
be read at least by misses in boarding schools, she grew dissatisfied with
the first informal drafts. She perceived for one thing that her novel,
written with such speed and secrecy and designed merely for her own
enjoyment and that of her sisters, was colloquial in style and therefore
lacked elegance.

A manuscript of one of the early drafts of *Evelina* is still extant, a
priceless possession in itself, and of peculiar interest in showing various
stages in composition. As this manuscript indicates, the speech
employed in the first drafts was often that of everyday life at Lynn Regis
or Poland Street, broken by picturesque dialectal expressions and tags
picked up in the theatre and the City, which the Burneys incorporated
in their own speech—odd words or the idiom of foreigners learning
English, or phrases from plays they knew well. Thus they amused one
another; but this would never do in print. As the revisions of the extant
manuscript show, Miss Burney eliminated such expressions from the
conversation of Evelina, Lord Orville, and the other 'gentles', and con-
centrated the vulgar idiom in the speech of the lower classes. With these
strokes she brought out contrasts in birth and character, and avoided the
monotony of the sentimental novel of the day; she raised her work above
the level of *Betsy Thoughtless* and its kind, and added to it refinement
of manner along with refinement of expression—in brief, *elegance*, a
quality by no means lost on her young contemporaries. 'So much wit,
so much *sport*, such humour, such *Life!*' 'So much Elegance in it too! I
know not how to say enough of it!'[2] The elegance, however, was not
lightly attained. The first text, produced characteristically at headlong
speed, was the spontaneous ebullition of a fun-loving spirit and probably
read much as the Burneys spoke. 'The sudden sallies of imagination,
clap'd down on paper, just as they arise, are worth folios', Mr. Crisp had
said, and though this advice might apply very well to 'familiar epistolary

1. *Memoirs of Dr. Burney*, vol. 2 (London, 1832) 148.
2. *The Early Diary of Frances Burney, 1768–1778*, ed. Annie Raine Ellis, vol. 2 (London, 1913)
221.

writing', to letters and journals to be circulated only among friends,
Fanny judged that a book would require more care. Thoughts of the
criticism her work must brave, of notices or reviews with the usual contemptuous remarks about 'the commonplace trash that novels abound
in' and about their vulgarity, spurred her to fresh efforts, or, more specifically, to revisions in the diction. A new critical faculty emerged. It
was almost as if the stern but delicate, spidery, and informing hand of a
professor in stylistics had gone over the girlish text. Thus the colloquial
and somewhat broken style of

> Home early. I cannot but be hurt at the opinion this man enter-
> tains of me—though I deserve no better—yet he is himself, the
> most agreeable, & seemingly the most amiable man in the world—
> well! I can't help it—but I think I have done assemblies!—This
> morning was set apart for *seeing sights*—such as the Tower—the
> abbey . . .[3]

is changed to—

> I cannot but be hurt at the opinion he entertains of me. It is true,
> my own behaviour incurred it—yet he is himself the most agree-
> able and, seemingly, the most amiable man in the world, and there-
> fore it is, that I am grieved to be thought ill of by him: for of whose
> esteem ought we to be ambitious, if not of those who most merit
> our own?—But it is too late to reflect upon this now. Well, I can't
> help it;—However, I think I have done with assemblies!
>   This morning was destined for *seeing sights*, auctions, curious
> shops . . .

A comparison of the original section with the printed text will show
the trend of the improvements: the clarifying of occasional ambiguous
phrases, pruning of unimportant or superfluous details, tightening of
the sentence structure, replacing of direct, artless, and informal effect by
one of greater finish, dignity, and elegance. The manuscript text reads:

>   Feb. 11, London Tuesday
> My dear Sir,
>   We came Home from the Ridotto so late, or rather so early, that
> I c[d] hardly persuade myself to go to Bed, Indeed we did not go—
> you will be frightened to hear it—till past Eleven—but nobody
> does—a terrible reverse of the Order of Nature! We sleep with the
> sun, & Live with the moon—the Captain went with us. The Room
> was magnificent the decorations brilliant & the company splen-
> did—Though I should have told you, I objected to going very
> much—but Maria Laughed me out of any scruples—& so, once
> again, unfortunately for me I went to an assembly!

3. Vol. 1, letter 12. This collation and those to follow are made between the manuscript of
Evelina (Berg) and a first edition of *Evelina* (of which the Berg Collection, New York Public
Library, has three copies).

Miss Mirvan danced a minuet—who with I know not.—In our walks—we saw Ld. Orville—he was quite alone—but did not observe us. As he seemed of no Party, I thought it was not impossible he might join us—& though I did not wish to Dance at all— yet as I knew more of him than of any body else in the Room— why I thought it would be preferable to me to Dance again with him than with an entire stranger. To be sure, after all that had passed, my thoughts had no probability to strengthen them—but I am obliged to mention them, on acct. of what followed. Maria was soon engaged—& presently after, a Gentleman, much dressed, who seemed about 30—came & asked *me* to dance—Now Maria's partner was of Mrs. Mirvan's acquaintance—for she had told us that at a Public assembly no girls should dance with strangers. I blush to tell it you—but I told him I was engaged.—For then, I th^t I was still at liberty to Dance in case of accident.

For the letter that was to be printed, however, Evelina managed a much more polished account.

Tuesday, April 12.

My dear Sir,

We came home from the ridotto so late, or rather, so early, that it was not possible for me to write. Indeed we did not *go*, you will be frightened to hear it,—till past eleven o'clock: but nobody does. A terrible reverse of the order of nature! We sleep with the sun, and wake with the moon.

The room was very magnificent, the lights and decorations were brilliant, and the company gay and splendid. But I should have told you, that I made many objections to being of the party, according to the resolution I had formed. However, Maria laughed me out of my scruples, and so, once again—I went to an assembly.

Miss Mirvan danced a minuet, but I had not the courage to follow her example. In our walks I saw Lord Orville. He was quite alone, but did not observe us. Yet, as he seemed of no party, I thought it was not impossible that he might join us; and tho' I did not wish much to dance at all,—yet, as I was more acquainted with him than with any other person in the room, I must own I could not help thinking it would be infinitely more desirable to dance again with him, than with an entire stranger. To be sure, after all that had passed, it was very ridiculous to suppose it even probable, that Lord Orville would again honour me with his choice; yet I am compelled to confess my absurdity, by way of explaining what follows.

Miss Mirvan was soon engaged; and, presently after, a very fashionable gay-looking man, who seemed about 30 years of age, addressed himself to me, and begged to have the honour of dancing with me. Now Maria's partner was a gentleman of Mrs. Mirvan's acquaintance; for she had told us it was highly improper for

> young women to dance with strangers, at any public assembly.
> Indeed it was by no means my wish so to do; yet I did not like to
> confine myself from dancing at all; neither did I dare refuse this
> gentleman, as I had done Mr. Lovel, and then, if any acquaintance
> should offer, accept him: and so, all these reasons combining,
> induced me to tell him—yet I blush to write it to you!—that I was
> *already engaged*; by which I meant to keep myself at liberty to
> dance or not, as matters should fall out.

Additions to the original manuscripts include reflections or sentiments,
such embellishments as 'Can you, *like patience on a monument* smile
in the midst of disappointment?', and, as time went on, comments on
current plays or operas, including praise of Pacchierotti as Evelina's
experience expanded in the wake of Fanny's own. Finally she amplified
the manuscript by character-sketches, which through long practice in
her journal-letters she had learned to fashion as brief introductions to
personages whom she was shortly to exhibit in action. The compact
character-sketch preceding specimens of comic dialogue became a characteristic of the later diaries, and may be seen in the series of pen pictures that in Letter XVII (Vol.I) introduces the Branghtons, and in the
sketch that in Letter XI (Vol.I) describes Lord Orville.

> His conversation was sensible and spirited; his air and address were
> open and noble; his manners gentle, attentive, and infinitely
> engaging; his person is all elegance, and his countenance, the most
> animated and expressive I have ever seen.

Some care had to be taken with Lord Orville's language lest by a rough
accent he should disturb this picture; and his utterances are, like himself, the last word in elegance though rather pontifical for modern taste:

> 'My dearest Miss Anville,' said he, taking my hand, 'I see, and I
> adore the purity of your mind, superior as it is to all little arts, and
> all apprehensions of suspicion; and I should do myself, as well as
> you, injustice, if I were capable of harbouring the smallest doubts
> of that goodness which makes you mine for ever: nevertheless, par-
> don me, if I own myself surprised, nay, alarmed, at these frequent
> meetings with so young a man as Mr. Macartney.'[4]

A comparison of passages in manuscript with their printed counterparts
will show that undignified expletives like 'Faith' are removed from Lord
Orville's utterances, and that he no longer 'wears himself out', but
'fatigues himself'. Sir Clement Willoughby's speeches are also repaired,
relieved of abruptness, and augmented as he assumes importance as the
villain of the piece. (' "The letter," cried he, gnashing his teeth, "you
shall never see more!" ') The conversation of the fop, Mr. Lovel, already
close to the language of the stage, is further rounded out with catch-

4. 3: 16.

words, mild oaths, and ejaculations. Such revisions helped to individual-
ize character. And always by the removal of awkward narrative detail or
naïve observation, Evelina becomes something above the schoolgirl,
and the novel is rendered pleasing to mature readers.

In the vulgar scenes too the dialogue sometimes seemed to demand
more cautious or judicious phrasing than that of the first draft. 'Mr.
Brown pulling Polly towards him sd. she must sit on his Lap' is deco-
rously changed to 'seated on a window, with Mr. Brown at her side, sat
Miss Polly'.[5] The manuscript states that in the Marylebone Gardens
Evelina is to be seen — 'gracious Heaven! . . . in company with 2 women
of the Town!' In the printed text she is 'with two women of such character!' By the insertion of additional speeches the scenes from low life
were often run to the length of acts in a play: ' "Miss must try if she
can't get a good husband," said Mr. Branghton, "and then she may stay
and live here." ' And later, the subject of the opera being introduced:
' "Miss will think us very vulgar," said Miss Branghton, "to live in London, and never have been to an Opera; but it's no fault of mine, I assure
you, Miss, only Papa don't like to go." '[6]

Great care had to be taken with Evelina's speech, comments, and
sentiments, not only because she was the heroine, but because the plan
of the epistolary novel caused other characters, situations, and events to
be known chiefly through her pen. She set the tone, therefore, for most
of the work. In the final draft of Evelina's letters the artless and feckless
remarks of the schoolgirl were in some measure restrained. The earlier
text reads:

> I am always to do wrong! Mrs. Mirvan & Maria have been all the
> Town over — & *so* entertain'd! — while I, like a Fool, was moping at
> Home. And at an auction in Pall Mall — who shd. they meet, but
> Lord Orville! Well he sat next to Mrs. Mirvan, & talked a great
> deal to her — but she gave me no account of their conversation — &
> either he did not recollect with whom he had seen her or did not
> think or — I suppose, care about it — but he never enquired after
> me — & Maria, who sat on the other side of her mother, he did not
> seem to know.
> But I shall never again have an opportunity of seeing London —
> how could I be such a Fool! — but, I was rightly served for indulging
> my ill-humour — Well — I do think I never will again — I shall cer-
> tainly be the happier for always combating my spleen —
>
> Thursday night.
> Just returned from the play — & within a few Boxes of us, sat
> Lord Orville — but he did not see us the whole evening. Well —
> adieu — it is too late to write more.

5. 2: 14.
6. 1: 17.

In Evelina's mind the success of the evening depended on a meeting
with Lord Orville, but in the printed text there is less peering about for
his lordship than in the manuscript and more attention to the entertainment in hand.

> I thought I had done wrong! Mrs. Mirvan and Maria have been
> half the town over, and so entertained!—while I, like a fool, stayed
> at home to do nothing. And, at an auction in Pall-mall, who should
> they meet but Lord Orville! He sat next to Mrs. Mirvan, and they
> talked a great deal together: but she gave me no account of their
> conversation.
>
> I may never have such another opportunity of seeing London; I
> am quite sorry that I was not of the party; but I deserve this mortifi-
> cation, for having indulged my ill-humour.
>
> Thursday night.
> We are just returned from the play, which was King Lear, and
> has made me very sad. We did not see any body we knew.

Some of the charm that won for *Evelina* the indulgence of aged eighteenth-century critics like the Dowager Duchess of Portland or Mrs.
Delany was perhaps owing to this revision in diction. Before her work
went to press, in her determination to make Evelina genteel and well-
bred, just such a young lady as the matchless Lord Orville could
approve, Fanny Burney turned Pygmalion. Evelina speaks no more of
Horse-Laughs, therefore, but of *loud laughter*; refers not to the *parlour*
but to the *drawing room*; not to *every fright* in it but to *whoever was old
or ugly*; not of *home strokes* but of *sarcasms*. She decided to say that Lord
Orville *made choice* of her rather than that he *fixed* upon her, and she
gave over some of the colloquialisms of the day, 'Monstrous provoking!',
and 'Lord, how *horrid slow* the man drives!' There is a difference
between the Evelina who said 'I was so mad at this sneering speech that
I had hardly patience to make any reply', and the one who wrote more
carefully 'I was so much disconcerted at this sneering speech that I said
not a word.' Like most people who grow up in places where dialectal
expressions are preserved, Fanny Burney had at least two levels of
speech at her command; and one of her tasks before sending *Evelina* to
the printer was, as we have seen, to make a greater differentiation
between the idioms of the upper and of the lower classes. She transposed the speech of the 'gentles' (and especially of Evelina) from the
levels she had acquired at Lynn Regis, Poland Street, or even at St.
Martin's Street, where people from different strata of society met, to that
which she imagined was spoken in London drawing-rooms, which she
did not yet know very well. Nothing surprised her contemporary readers
more than the *range* of life depicted in *Evelina* unless it was the realism
or verisimilitude of many of the characters. Her success in both
depended in large part on her attentive ear and the pains she took to

provide her personages with their characteristic speech.

Some of these revisions were made, no doubt, in transcribing the fair copy in the feigned hand. Two volumes were ready for the press at the end of December, 1776, while the visit to Chessington in March, 1777, must have taken Fanny far along in the third volume, though she was again delayed by the three months' visit to Worcester. Late summer and autumn of 1777 in deserted St. Martin's Street and at Chessington probably sufficed to complete the first draft of the third volume. Since, however, she wrote rapidly and in a colloquial style, scribbling from what may be termed an auditory memory of scenes and dialogue 'long pent in her head', there was much work still left in revising and copying. The latter presented special difficulties since it must be done at night when she could work unobserved. The October nights were getting cool; Susan with the incipient trouble in her lungs could never have stood these nights of writing added to the tasks and demands of the day, but Fanny had her father's constitution and his ability to recover from physical and mental exhaustion. Some of the phrases that she penned in her Memoir of him were equally applicable to herself: 'His Fancy was his dictator; his Spirit was his spur; and whatever the first started, the second pursued to the goal.'[7] Now she worked with her near-sighted eyes close to the paper, her slight body stooped and cramped with the cold. 'That murtherous stooping . . . will be your bane', said Mr. Crisp. She was thinking of a Preface.

Many authors, she knew, wrote resounding prefaces, and novelists especially thought it necessary to write *apologias* for their art. Since her preface was to appear with her book anonymously, she might venture to touch on a most pertinent matter, the disrepute of Novels and Novelists. No one 'is so much disdained by his brethren of the quill, as the humble Novelist'; but 'perhaps not one can be named of which the votaries are more numerous'. Thus the general situation; now the injustice of it and a vindication of herself for following her great precursors, Rousseau, Johnson, Marivaux, Fielding, Richardson, and Smollett. 'No man need blush at starting from the same post, though many, nay, most men, may sigh at finding themselves distanced.' And then the hopelessness of the attempt to condemn the new species of writing, and the good use to which it might be put:

> Perhaps were it possible to effect the total extirpation of novels, our young ladies in general, and boarding-school damsels in particular, might profit from their annihilation: but since the distemper they have spread seems incurable, since their contagion bids defiance to the medicine of advice or reprehension, and since they are found to baffle all the mental art of physic . . . surely all attempts to contribute to the number of those which may be read, if not

7. *Memoirs* 1: 233.

with advantage, at least without injury, ought rather to be encouraged than contemned.

The work here presented, she goes on to say in effect, is not a Gothic
novel depicting fantastic regions, not one of the current sentimental
pieces in which *Imagination* luxuriates and *Reason is an outcast.* All her
effort will be to copy what is. 'To draw characters from nature, though
not from life, and to mark the manners of the times, is the attempted
plan of the following letters.'

> For this purpose, a young female, educated in the most secluded
> retirement, makes, at the age of seventeen, her first appearance
> upon the great and busy stage of life; with a virtuous mind, a culti-
> vated understanding, and a feeling heart, her ignorance of the
> forms, and inexperience in the manners, of the world, occasion all
> the little incidents which these volumes record, and which form
> the natural progression of the life of a young woman of obscure
> birth, but conspicuous beauty, for the first six months after her
> Entrance into the world.

There is then a Dedication to the Authors of the Monthly and Critical
Reviews, 'Magistrates of the press, and Censors for the public', who are
asked to be just and, if not lenient, at least mindful that they too were
'all young writers once'. Then comes the dedicatory ode to the Author
of her being. The verses to this Author

far more dear
To me than light, than nourishment, or rest,

had come into her head in the 'Dead of the night' at Barborne Lodge
on the first night of her long visit there, when she thought of her father's
affectionate farewell and his kindness about the literary secret confided
to him that day.

> Obscure be still the unsuccessful Muse,
>   Who cannot raise, but would not sink, thy fame.
>
> If in my heart the love of Virtue glows,
>   'Twas planted there by an unerring rule;
> From thy example the pure flame arose,
>   Thy life, my precept—thy good works, my
> school.

There was a crookedly printed title-page: *Evelina or a Young Lady's
Entrance into Life,* afterwards revised to *Evelina, or, the History of a
Young Lady's entrance into the World.* The loss of the diary for 1777,
and contradictions between the story as recollected by Madame d'Arblay
in the *Memoirs* and extant drafts of letters written to Mr. Lowndes, but
perhaps never sent, make it difficult to say when the packet was finally

carried to the bookseller. The suspense was short. Very promptly (within a few days, as Madame d'Arblay remembered) Mr. Lowndes made his famous offer:

> Sir,
>
> I've read this 3^d Vol & think it better than 1 & 2^d. If you please I'll give you Twenty Guineas for the Manuscript and without loss of time put it to Press.
>
> Y^r Obed^t Servt
Thos Lowndes
>
> Fleetstreet,
Nov. 11,
1777

According to the *Memoirs* of 1832 the sum was accepted with no less alacrity and with 'boundless surprise at its magnificence'. These seem to be the roses of memory, for a somewhat thorny letter drafted at the time indicates that the author was by no means satisfied with the terms. Apparently Fanny had put a price of thirty guineas on her labours. 'I should not have taken the pains to copy & correct it for the Press, had I imagined that 10 Guineas a volume would have been more than its worth.' She had planned to submit the manuscript to a referee, possibly Mr. Crisp, but the dire news from Cambridge or some other family vicissitude may have prevented the plan. The letter, perhaps, was never sent. Lowndes had the novel for twenty guineas, and by the middle of January it was in print—in three volumes that he now wished to have read for a list of errata before binding. Fanny could not have the printed sheets appear in St. Martin's Street, but she had taken the precaution to tell her aunts about *Evelina* ('They will, I am sure, be discreet,—indeed, I exacted a vow from them of strict secresy'),[8] and the old ladies allowed her to use their address as a place less exposed to perilous accident.

In January a parcel addressed to Mr. Grafton arrived at the new address. Inside Fanny found the following letter:

> Mr Grafton
>> Sir
>
> I take the Liberty to send you a Novel wch a Gent. your acquaintance said you w^d hand to him I beg with expedition as 'tis time it should be published & 'tis requisite he should revise it or the Reviewers may find a flaw
>
> I am
Y^r obed^t serv^t
Thos Lowndes
>
> Fleetstreet
Jany 7, 1778

The aunts insisted that she read aloud as she looked for errors. 'Of course, they were all prodigiously charmed with it', but Fanny felt she

8. *Early Diary* 2: 213–19.

could place no reliance on critical faculties so biased by kindness and partiality for the author. Lowndes, having got the manuscript, was rushing it into print, scarcely waiting, as the author feared, for the corrections. Moreover, he had sent her a faulty copy.

> Sir,
>
> I am extremely sorry to have kept the press waiting, but I did not receive yours of the 10th till this Instant. I hope you have not gone on with the 2^d volume, without the corrections:—
>
> I will send you the conclusions before the End of the week: but I must beg you to let me have a waste sheet of the last of the 3^d volume as the set from which I correct is incomplete. You will be so good as to give it to the bearer.
>
> I am,
sr,
yr. ob^d serv^t.
>
> Pray let the sheet you send be put in a cover, & wafered, & without any direction.

When the list of errata was completed, the 'newly trusted agent' carried it to Mr. Lowndes.

The next dramatic scene was probably the breakfast table at St. Martin's Street when Mrs. Burney, securely in possession of the morning paper, favoured the family with items of interest, among them a notice inserted by Lowndes about a new novel, *Evelina*. Accustomed as she was to Treason, she did not seem to observe the extraordinary effect of the announcement—the crimson face of the authoress and the meaningful glances of Susan and Charlotte. The joke went on through February and March, when the aunts read the book to Richard Burney without giving away the secret of its authorship and, unknown to him, the authoress listened to his comments and criticisms.

The winter of 1777–8 was not a happy one. On February 22 Dr. Burney wrote to Mrs. Thrale that he had a cold, that he had been 'snivelling & sulking at Home all the Morning'. Presently, as the *Memoirs* record, he was dangerously ill with acute fever. Fanny shared 'the assiduous attendance upon the invaluable invalid', and one has only to turn from the language of the *Memoirs* and edited *Diaries* to the private correspondence, the letters of Maria Rishton, for example, to learn of the rages, jealousies, sulkiness, and malignity that such attentions provoked in 'the Lady'.

No sooner had Dr. Jebb pronounced the Doctor out of danger than he was called to attend Fanny. 'Severe mental suffering from a Family calamity', mental excitement, overwork, all added to the 'eternal avocations of this house', had combined to bring on one of the feverish illnesses to which she was from this time subject. At the end of March she began to recover from an indisposition 'long and dangerous'. 'Susy,

Charlotte, Hetty, & my Aunts vied in good offices,—& my beloved Father was hardly himself till my recovery was out of doubt.' For a long time she was unable to walk, read, write, or dress herself. Chessington was the place fixed on for change of air; and in May, Susan and her Cousin Edward accompanied her there, supporting her one on each side in a post-chaise all the way, and applying smelling salts when she seemed in danger of fainting. The tendency to faint continued for weeks; her eyes were still weak, and she could neither read, work, nor write for twenty minutes together. After a while she could 'stump' out into the garden by herself, though she could not keep pace at first even with Daddy Crisp. At the end of June, however, when her father visited Chessington, she was almost restored and quite able to enjoy the praise of *Evelina*, which had been making its way during this interval, though, as she adds, 'the length of my illness, joined to severe mental suffering from a Family calamity which had occurred at that period, had really made me too weak for a joy mixt with such excess of amazement'.

All this while the two confederates, Susan and Charlotte, kept faithful watch at St. Martin's Street, excitedly reporting to Chessington the perils, escapes, and vicissitudes of *Evelina* and finally the discovery of the secret. Sometimes the accomplices carried on hoaxes of their own. Without divulging the secret, Susan sent a copy of *Evelina* to Miss Coussmaker, whose comment is still extant.

> Good God! My Dearest Susy I hope Evelina will not have such an effect on you as it has on me . . . I cannot tell you how it has affected me but I have never been well since, some part of the discovery is so tragical that I declare it worked me as much as the death of Desdemona or Belvidera though the subject is totally different—and how mortifying it is to think that so few nay I hardly know any Lord Orvilles or Evelinas to be found & so many Sir C Willoughbys—I prefer their characters by far to either St. Preux or Julie though they seem more natural. . . . I cannot hear any body talking of not having read it with any patience & yet 'Twas pitiful, 'twas wondrous pitiful. . . . Not any one character in La Nouvelle Heloise gave me half the Idea of nobleness, generosity, & goodness this book has.

This reaction to *Evelina* seems typical of the novel-readers of the age. Later, when Miss Coussmaker had learned the name of the *incognita*, she rejoiced that she had come off with such flying colours in her criticisms. She praised the work ('infinitely beyond my Ideas of a Novel') on three counts:

> There is not only *true wit* & humour in it, But the *true* pathetic! Many parts of it excites all the tender feelings that a good tragedy wd. do. And the letters of the worthy good old clergyman too would have done honour even to the pen of a Johnson.

The three components here listed may explain the phenomenal success of *Evelina* in its age. It succeeded for its *wit and humour* (still tolerated), the *true pathetic* (now frequently called the *false pathetic*), and moral *observations* (now likely to be disdained). In a discarded preface Fanny Burney had asked pertinent questions. 'Will maxims of conduct have any weight, where their Inditer is unknown?' 'Will opinions of right & wrong be heeded, where their promulgator has no party?' The answer, of course, is 'No', but not for the reasons suggested. A third query, scribbled by quill and candlelight, 'Will the World value the notions of Those of other Times?', has a more winsome interest and may gain some hospitality or toleration even for old 'maxims of conduct' and 'opinions of right & wrong'. But whatever weight the 'maxims' and 'opinions' may carry now, they impressed eighteenth-century readers, many of whom thought the serious part of the book as good as the comic and realized that the cream of the seriousness was in Mr. Villars's letters.

These monitory letters from the worthy old gentleman at Berry Hill, if read in sequence, will soon be recognized as a compact courtesy-book covering a surprisingly full list of the stereotyped topics treated in such works, many of which were also epistolary in form. *Affectation, artifice, coquetry, imprudence* receive due emphasis. Thus at a public assembly when Evelina did not know how to dismiss a persistent follower, she pretended that she was engaged to Lord Orville for the next dance. When her graceless pursuer, destined, as she said, to be the scourge of her artifice, had the cunning to mention the alleged engagement to Lord Orville himself, 'the fair artificer' was ready to 'sink for shame' and, to the consternation of all, did indeed burst into tears. Nor did Mr. Villars in his role of moral commentator fail to point out how much more deserved this mortification was than others incurred more innocently through ignorance of the world.[9]

Like the authors of the courtesy-books and writers from Jean de Meun onwards who took some notice of the conduct of the young lady, Mr. Villars found it necessary to descant upon Prudence. Evelina often had cause to lament her lack of thought and foresight: 'Alas, my dearest Sir, that my reflections should always be too late to serve me! dearly, indeed, do I purchase experience!' And she went on to express a concern shared by Mr. Villars: 'Much I fear I shall suffer yet more severely, from the heedless indiscretion of my temper, ere I attain that prudence and consideration, which, by foreseeing distant consequences, may rule and direct in present exigencies.' Mr. Villars as well as Lord Orville worried over her private though well-intentioned meetings with so young a man as Mr. Macartney, and they had again to deplore her indiscretion, when, having been separated from her chaperons at an opera, she allowed the designing Sir Clement to entice her into his carriage. Her adventures

9. 1: 13, 15.

there taught her to repent 'heedless imprudence' and to beware of snares. Evelina's mother, Mr. Villars said, had been 'led to destruction by her own imprudence, the hardness of heart of Madame Duval, and the villainy of Sir John Belmont'. When Sir Clement's villainy began to appear, the aged monitor cautioned circumspection: 'The slightest carelessness on your part, will be taken advantage of, by a man of his disposition.' The old gentleman was filled with misgivings as he was persuaded to consent that Evelina 'quit the protection of the hospitable and respectable Lady Howard' and accompany her noisy old grandmother to London. His counsel might have come straight from the courtesy-books: 'Do not, by a too passive facility, risk the censure of the world, or your own future regret.' Finally the monitor advised her to be prudent in the choice of friends, and, adopting the sentiment and almost the words of the courtesy-books, he concluded:

> Remember, my dear Evelina, nothing is so delicate as the reputation of a woman: it is, at once, the most beautiful and most brittle of all human things.[1]

The monitor finally descanted on the dangers of the unbridled imagination. Evelina's painful disappointments could always be traced to the beguiling pictures suggested by that untrustworthy painter, the Imagination. 'Her glowing pencil, dipt in the vivid colours of her creative ideas', painted tender and thrilling possibilities in Lord Orville and in addition, said Mr. Villars, 'all the good and rare qualities, which a great length of time, and intimacy, could alone have really discovered'. '*Imagination* took the reins, and *Reason* slow-paced, though sure-footed, was unequal to a race with so eccentric and flighty a companion. How rapid was then my Evelina's progress through those regions of fancy and passion whither her new guide conducted her!'[2] The old gentleman concluded his counsel with a prayer for the kind of girl he wished Evelina to be.

> May thy manners, language, and deportment all evince that modest equanimity and chearful gratitude, which not merely deserve, but dignify prosperity! May'st thou, to the last moments of an unblemished life, retain thy genuine simplicity, thy singleness of heart, thy guileless sincerity! And may'st thou, stranger to ostentation, and superior to insolence, with true greatness of soul, shine forth conspicuous only in beneficence![3]

'*That man is* ALWAYS *right*,' said Dr. Burney, 'in his advice and judgement of things.'[4] Yet the moral burden of *Evelina* was by no means confined to the conduct of the young lady; it included also a model of gentlemanly conduct and one that brought about at least one known

1. 2: 8.
2. 3: 6.
3. 3: 12.
4. *Early Diary* 2: 242–43.

instance of reform. When the coxcombical Richard Burney, one of the Worcester cousins, was recovering from an illness at Brompton, his aunts had read him *Evelina* without divulging the enormous secret of its authorship. All through this illness he had 'penetrated us by his patient & most amiable behaviour'; but the greater wonder was that 'since his recovery he has *more* than kept his Ground, by having wholly discarded all the foibles that formerly tinged his manners, though they *never*', the loyal chroniclers affirmed, 'affected his Heart'. And all this reform was based on the example of Fanny's hero! There was something in the character and manners of Lord Orville 'so *refined*, and so polite', and something in his compliments so *new* as well as so *elegant*, which Richard had never seen in any book before. 'I think I can't read it too often,' he told the giggling Susan and Fanny, 'for you are to know that I think it very edifying.' Only he wished very much to know who the author could be — 'such amazing knowledge of characters, — such an acquaintance with *high* and *low* life, — such universal and extensive knowledge of the world'. Richard knew of no one who could have written such a book except his uncle Dr. Burney. Aunt Ann then told Fanny that she must tell him the secret. Well then, he must *kneel* and make a vow that 'he will never tell *any* body in the world'. When he protested, by all that he held sacred on Earth or in Heaven, that he would not tell, she gave him a slip of paper on which were penned the cryptic words NO MAN. Though he studied the message, it was the odd expression on Fanny's face that at length revealed how the affair stood. He blushed violently. Fanny thought it 'utterly impossible for astonishment to be greater than his was at that moment'. 'I believe I must now kneel indeed!' he said. She made him rise instantly; but the involuntary homage paid by the lively and foppish Richard to his cousin, as he knelt to her before the fire, is as charming and dramatic a scene as might have occurred in the book itself had Lord Orville been less stiff. Lord Orville, whose character, Richard said, he studied 'every day of his life', was a new model; and his unbiased judgement (formed before he knew his cousin had written the book) remains valid for the young generation of the seventies.

Launcelot and Gawain, however, are dead, and with them their 'olde courtesye', and with that also the eighteenth-century courtesy-books and many of the principles and tenets on which they were based. One may pass over the *models of behaviour* and the *maxims of conduct* and 'the notions of other Times, and choose another Tale'. There is still much left, for the 'opinions of right & wrong' encroach very little on the lively and lifelike episodes that remain perennially fresh and young and gay. The realistic delineation of comic character and situation was a contribution to the comedy of manners or to the novel of manners and is perhaps the part of Fanny Burney's achievement that now wins widest acclaim. Hear the 'Holborn beau' condescending to fall in love with Evelina:

> 'My dear Ma'am, you must be a little patient; I assure you I have no bad designs, I have not upon my word; but, really there is no resolving upon such a thing as matrimony all at once; what with the loss of one's liberty, and what with the ridicule of all one's acquaintance,—I assure you, Ma'am, you are the first lady who ever made me even demur upon this subject; for, after all, my dear Ma'am, marriage is the devil!' . . .
>
> 'Why, really, Ma'am, as to your being a little out of sorts, I must own I can't wonder at it, for, to be sure, marriage is all in all with the ladies; but with us gentlemen it's quite another thing! Now only put yourself in my place,—suppose you had such a large acquaintance of gentlemen as I have,—and that you had always been used to appear a little—a little smart among them,—why now, how should you like to let yourself down all at once into a married man?'
>
> I could not tell what to answer; so much conceit, and so much ignorance, both astonished and silenced me.
>
> 'I assure you, Ma'am,' added he, 'there is not only Miss Biddy,— though I should have scorned to mention her, if her brother had not blab'd, for I'm quite particular in keeping ladies secrets,—but there are a great many other ladies that have been proposed to me,—but I never thought twice of any of them, that is, not in a *serious* way,—so you may very well be proud,' offering to take my hand, 'for I assure you, there is nobody so likely to catch me at last as yourself.'
>
> 'Sir,' cried I, drawing myself back as haughtily as I could, 'you are totally mistaken, if you imagine you have given me any pride I felt not before, by this conversation. . . .'
>
> While Madame Duval was seating herself in the coach, he said in a voice of *pique*, 'Next time I take the trouble to get any tickets for a young lady, I'll make a bargain beforehand that she sha'n't turn me over to her grandmother.'[5]

Many of Evelina's journal-letters, it will be observed, are cast like acts in a lively comedy of manners. Both Arthur Murphy and Richard Brinsley Sheridan later thought that the author who could write such scenes ought to attempt comedy; and before 1786 producers in Paris had adapted the novel as both a play and an opera. Fanny Burney had set many of the scenes in pleasure-grounds like Ranelagh or the Marylebone Gardens, and filled her stage with a cross-section of the eighteenth-century types. Thus she could show a wide variety of contrasting characters in action and draw on an additional source of laugh-

5. 2: 19.

ter in their impact on one another. With her apt ear for idiomatic speech she was able to set them talking in natural, convincing dialogue. These scenes, lively as they were, had not been designed solely to amuse, but were everywhere tinged with satire. There was much fun in them, but they served also to castigate what she disliked in the manners of high and low alike. The self-revelatory dialogue exposed the pride, vanity, vapidity, conceit, and affectation she discerned in the upper classes; the vulgarity, squabbles, litigiousness, parsimony, violence, loud laughter, ignorance, and lack of feeling that she associated with low life. 'In the sportive way of holding up Ignorance, Conceit & Folly to ridicule, I thought I discovered your attentive Ear, & observing Eye', Mrs. Burney later said, and at Streatham also it was said that she 'hit off the City Manners wonderfully'. 'No writer so young and inexperienced had ever seen so deeply into character', said Dr. Johnson, 'or copied the manners of the time with more accuracy.' What seemed to impress her contemporaries was the realism of her sketches, their variety, their sportiveness, fun, and humour. For all this, and for the boisterousness of which Mrs. Montagu complained, her critics, including Lord David Cecil, have been tempted to compare her to Fielding.[6] The rough action of the scenes in which Captain Mirvan appears and the occasional use of caricature point to Smollett. Fanny had said in the Preface to *Evelina* that her great precursors had 'culled all the flowers' before her; yet in the minute and exact delineation of what goes on in the mind and heart of a young lady 'at her first entrance into the world' they had left a fair flower for her. 'One excellence is, that it is not *copied*', wrote Mr. Twining; 'it is fairly an *original* novel, both as to characters, & manner of writing.' As Dr. Burney noted 'Evelina is in a new style too— so perfectly natural and innocent.'[7] By associating with youth errors and shortcomings natural to youth, Fanny Burney created a character at once convincing and sympathetic; and in depicting a heroine lifelike in her imperfection the new realist surpassed even her four great predecessors, who tended to draw paragons for that role.

As we have seen, Fanny Burney pleased her eighteenth-century readers in a third respect by adding tears to their laughter. Men as well as women blubbered over the reunion of father and daughter. Mr. Twining thought the 'cit family' excellent, but 'the *serious & pathetic* part' struck him most. 'The account of the meeting between Evelina & her father has great force, strong *male* painting, & has some strokes of nature.' Everyone must feel them strongly and own them to *be* nature. At the risk of making Miss Burney ill and pale, he wished the Doctor to tell her how he had *cried* over the closing scenes, 'tho' I believe', he added, 'it will make her laugh'. Sir John Belmont's agonized remorse over the

---

6. "Fanny Burney's Novels," *Essays on the Eighteenth Century, presented to David Nichol Smith in Honour of His Seventieth Birthday* (Oxford, 1945) 212–24.
7. *Early Diary* 2: 231.

'injured Caroline', the scenes of 'filial tenderness' and reconciliation, had moved readers almost as much as the death of Desdemona or of Belvidera; and the eighteenth-century reader had no higher praise than this to bestow. 'Thou hast made thy old Father Laugh & Cry at thy pleasure', wrote Dr. Burney. Everybody had been brought to 'Laugh & Cry!' Lady Hales told Susan how she had 'been reading Evelina to Madame de Ferre, the Governess, & the children, & that the meeting with the Father made them all *sob* so much, she was obliged to leave it off'. This was the age of sensibility. The lordly librarians in the full-powdered wigs knew that misses preferred 'crying volumes'. 'Misses must cry or it's nothing.' A crying volume, Sir, 'brings me more money in six months than a heavy merry thing will do in six years'. 'Write for the white handkerchief, dear Webb, an' you love me.'[8] Fanny Burney also knew what the eighteenth century required in a novel, and the *Critical Review* marked the three principal components in *Evelina* with approval: Readers '*will weep* and (what is not so commonly the effect of novels) *will laugh*, and *grow wiser*, as they read'.[9]

The playful comedy and the monitory morals were the warp and woof of *Evelina*; the tears of sensibility are the time-marks in its texture, and are as inerasable as the ruffles, snuff-boxes, and the high head-dress of the drawing-rooms on royal birthdays. These three elements are woven inextricably through all Fanny Burney's works, though in each work they appear in different proportions. Happily in *Evelina* comedy pre-dominated. Though it may be said that the comedy of manners is the great asset of this novel and the main cause of its permanent attraction, Fanny had one other gift—one most necessary to novelists and story-tellers—the ability to tell a story. The central story of her novel was the love between Lord Orville and Evelina, from its inception through its tentative unfolding, growth, and resolution. In the third volume Fanny had no need to resort to comic scenes, *sententiae*, or extraneous sources of interest to depict the tension between the two lovers or to keep the reader interested in the outcome. *Evelina* is a period piece filled with lively dramatic scenes, but not only that: despite its stereotyped plot-devices, in the delicate tension of the scenes between Lord Orville and Evelina it constitutes a love story of persistent and enduring strength.

The welcome accorded *Evelina* by the literary world, the Wits, and the Great is a romance in itself and one of the most cherished of the Burney legends. The anonymous work, which had appeared at the end of January, by June had won great popularity. It was being read by every-one and had been favourably described in the *London Review* and the *Monthly Review*. Fanny's confidants kept with increasing difficulty the uneasy secret of its authorship. It quivered a dozen times a day at the

8. See Samuel Jackson Pratt, *Family Secrets*, vol. 1 (London, 1797) 384–90; and Thomas Bridges, *The Adventures of a Banknote*, vol. 3 (London, 1771) 3–4.
9. 46 (Sept. 1778): 202–04. The italics are mine.

tips of their tongues; and at Chessington Fanny herself, recovering from her long illness, awoke to read reviving letters from Susan and Charlotte about the outstanding success of their frolic. When in July she learned from her sisters that her father had discovered that *Evelina* was her work, she began to worry over his reception of the dedicatory ode.

> My dearest Sir,
>   I have just received from Susan an account of a little *Embarrass* you have been in, upon the affair of my *schtoff*; and I know not how to thank you for the kind manner in which you guard my secret: indeed from every soul, but yourself, who is acquainted with it, I have taken a solemn promise never to reveal it, without my consent.

As she had said in the Ode, she had power to *sink,* but not to raise, his fame; and, for that reason among others, she wished to remain incognita. She hoped the *sincerity* of the stanzas would recommend them to him, 'for I may truly say they *flowed from the Heart,* since I wrote them, in the very fullness of it, in the Dead of the very Night that I owned to you my secret'. In his Memoirs the Doctor said that it was Susan who confessed to him 'with a trembling voice, that the book was written by her sister Fanny, with a determination never to own the sin she had committed'. It was, however, Charlotte who had watched him read the account in the *Monthly Review* and been asked to procure the work from the bookseller's, and who had seen him, when it came, quell the tears that arose at the dedication to himself. 'I opened the first Vol. with fear & trembling', he wrote long afterwards in his Memoirs,

> not supposing she w^d disgrace her parentage; but not having the least idea, that without the use of the press, or knowledge of the world, she c^d write a book worth reading.

He was at once 'struck & astounded' by the 'good sense & good writing in the letters of Mr Villars', and before he had read half-way through the first volume all his fears had given way to delight. By June 23 he had reached the conclusion that Lowndes had had '*a devilish good Bargain* of it—for the book will *sell*—it has real merit, and the Review alone would sell it'.[1]

Fanny knew nothing of these changes of opinion and she trembled at the thought of her father's arrival at Chessington (June 23). 'I thought she w^d have fainted,' he wrote later,

> but I hastened to take her by the hand & tell her that I had read part of her book with such pleasure, that instead of being angry, I congratulated her on being able to write so well. this kindness affected her so much that she threw herself in my arms, & cried *à chaudes larmes,* till she sobbed.

---

1. *Early Diary* 2: 222–24.

'I have read your book, Fanny,' he said gently, 'but you need not blush at it—it is full of merit—it is, really,—extraordinary!' Her tears then gave way to 'a gayer pleasure—a pleasure more like his own' and 'the poor humble author I believe never was happier in her life'. Fanny reviewed the episode: 'I had written my little Book simply for my amusement, I printed it, by the means first of my brother Charles, next of my cousin Edward Burney, merely for a frolic, to see how a production of my own would figure in that Author like form.' She had hardly dared to hope that anyone except her sisters, to whom alone she had read her compositions, could be partial enough to like them. In a letter to Miss Coussmaker she confessed to having thought that Evelina's 'only admirers wd be among school girls'. She had 'destined her to no nobler habitation than a circulating library'.

Despite the rumours about persons great and humble who were sitting up all night to finish *Evelina*, she still wished to remain unknown. She feared the odium attached to the term 'novelist'. Yet, as she said, '*every body* longs to tell *one* body!', so that the 'Blabbation' of her scribbling went on apace. Dr. Burney's pride in her performance was not tinged with Fanny's delicate notions. 'Poor Fan's *such* a prude.' *Evelina* was a work no one need blush at—and therefore he did not scruple to tell Mrs. Thrale, Miss Coussmaker, Lady Hales, and many others, that it was his daughter, Fanny, who had written *Evelina*, and that this was the more remarkable because, unlike her sisters, she had not been given the advantages of a formal education or of travel abroad. Mrs. Thrale came second, but soon took first place as a publicity agent; and Fanny was not long in realizing that her hope for secrecy was desperate. And she protested: she herself had never told anybody outside her own family, 'nor half the bodies in it'. 'I really thought myself as safe, and meant to be as private, when the book was at Mr. Lowndes's, as when it was in my own bureau.' Such over-delicacy, Mrs. Thrale said, might make her unhappy all her life. 'Poor Miss Burney! so you thought just to have played and sported with your sisters and cousins, and had it all your own way; but now you are in for it! But if you will be an author and a wit, you must take the consequences!'[2] When Fanny saw that she was to be known as an Authoress, a Scribbler, or perhaps a Wit like her own Mrs. Selwyn, whom everybody disliked for her masculinity, she was ill all night and could not sleep. Nor did the painful feelings depart as Mr. Crisp said they ought 'when the salts of general applause [were] held continually under their nose'. 'I part with this, my dear, long loved, long cherished *snugship* with more regret than any body will believe, except my dear sisters who *Live with* me, & know me too well & too closely to doubt me.'

Before the close of 1779 *Evelina* went through four editions, 'travers-

2. *The Diary and Letters of Madame d'Arblay (1778–1840)*, ed. Austin Dobson, vol. 1 (London, 1904–5) 96–100, 137–39.

ing all London amongst the literary and the fashionable alike'. In the review of *Evelina* (the *Critical Review*, September, 1778) it was asserted that 'the purchasers of novels, the subscribers to circulating libraries, are seldom in more elevated situations than the middle ranks of life'. Yet by July, 1778, according to a letter from Mr. Lowndes, the Great World was sending to him for *Evelina*. Polite ladies feared being quite 'unfashionable for not having read it'. The booksellers at Bath, Brighton, and Reigate were also embarrassed by the demand for *Evelina*, which could not be kept upon the shelves. Other dealers found great faults in Mr. Lowndes. Thus Mr. Bowen, the bookseller at Brighton, to Mrs. Thrale: — 'O ma'am, what a Book thrown away was that! — all the Trade cry shame on Lowndes, not, ma'am, that I *expected* he could have known its worth, because that's out of the question, — but when its *profits* told him what it was, it's quite scandalous that he should have done nothing! — quite ungentleman like indeed!'[3]

Everyone had read *Evelina*: Mr. Jessop, a schoolmaster 'living in a remote part of Ireland' — 'a man of the finest taste, — a man of great profundity, — an extraordinary scholar'; the anatomy professor at Cambridge, who 'never read novels', but who for all that insisted that his friends read this one; Mr. Bewley's friend Mr. Everard, 'who could never be induced to read these novels in his life', but who was found 'nailed to his chair' at sunrise with Volume III of *Evelina* in his hand; Dr. Barnard, the Provost of Eton, who sang its praises; Lady Radnor and other representatives of the Great World, who had secured copies; Miss Hales, 'a formal old maid', who thought it 'destruction for a girl to read a novel'; Mrs. Horneck, who thought novels 'generally, so bad, that they are not to be read', but who had seen 'nothing like this since Fielding'; Mr. Sheridan, who declared publicly at the club that it was '*superior* to Fielding'; Mr. Edmund Burke, who had sat up all night to read it; and finally Dr. Johnson, a name in literary criticism to end all lists. When at Chessington Fanny heard that he had said there were 'things and characters in her book *more* than worthy of Fielding!', she danced a jig around the mulberry tree.

'I often think, when I am counting my laurels,' she wrote sportively to Susan, 'what a pity it would have been had I popped off in my last illness, without knowing what a person of consequence I was! — and I sometimes think that, were I now to have a relapse, I could never go off with so much *éclat!*' 'It's wonderful,' Mr. Crisp said, 'wonderful!' 'With all his powers of speech, his choice of language, and his general variety of expression', he could think of no other comment when at last he was informed by Dr. Burney that Fanny was the author of *Evelina*, the novel that she and Hetty had been roguishly reading to him and that was being read all over London for the preceding five months.

3. *Diary and Letters* 2:48.

Hetty had wished above all things to read the novel to Mr. Crisp, but Fanny, unable to resist the opportunity to observe his reaction and to obtain his unbiased opinion of it, sent excuses to her sister, and herself began on the first two volumes. Though she was breathless and tremulous with embarrassment and therefore *mauled* the book in the reading, she could see that, though Mr. Crisp 'by no means treated it with the praise so lavishly bestowed upon it from other quarters', he was 'even greedily eager to go on with it'. His 'ill humour' on being told (rather inaccurately) that he must wait for Hetty to bring the third volume was the 'delightful' proof of his interest.

Fanny had shown in *Evelina* how artifice will bring its own punishment in mortification. Just so at Chessington the ruse about the third volume led its authors into a *scrape*, as they would have called it, one day when their stepmother appeared for a short visit,

> for Mr. Crisp., before my mother, very innocently said to Susan, 'Oh, pray Susette, do send me the third volume of *Evelina*; Fanny brought me the two first on purpose, I believe, to tantalise me.'
>
> I felt myself in a ferment; and Susan, too, looked foolish, and knew not what to answer. As I sat on the same sofa with him, I gave him a gentle shove, as a token, which he could not but understand, that he had said something wrong—though I believe he could not imagine *what*. Indeed, how should he?
>
> My mother instantly darted forward, and repeated, '*Evelina*—what's that, pray?'
>
> Again I *jolted* Mr. Crisp, who, very much perplexed, said, in a boggling manner, that is was a novel—he supposed from the circulating library—'only a trumpery novel.'
>
> Ah, my dear daddy! thought I, you would have devised some other sort of speech, if you knew all!—but he was really, as he well might be, quite at a loss for what I *wanted* him to say.
>
> 'You have had it here, then, have you?' continued my mother.
>
> 'Yes—two of the volumes,' said Mr. Crisp.
>
> 'What! had you them from the library?' asked my mother.
>
> 'No, ma'am,' answered I horribly frightened, 'from my sister.'
>
> The truth is, the books are Susan's, who bought them the first day of publication; but I did not dare own that, as it would have been almost an acknowledgment of all the rest.
>
> She asked some further questions, to which we made the same sort of answers, and then the matter dropped. Whether it rests upon her mind or not I cannot tell.[4]

Susan and Fanny had then to devise replies to Mr. Crisp, who later wished to know why he could not mention *Evelina* without being joggled. At last he learned the true reason:

4. *Diary and Letters* 1: 52.

'Why you little hussy,—you young devil!—an't you ashamed to
look me in the face, you *Evelina*, you! Why, what a dance have
you led me about it! . . . Oh you little hussy, what tricks have you
served me!' [5]

He perhaps never realized his own part in the production of the famous
novel, and his amazement seemed to equal that of the age. How had
she found time to write so much unsuspected? Where and how had she
picked up such varied materials? 'It's wonderful!'

MARTHA G. BROWN

Fanny Burney's "Feminism": Gender or Genre? [†]

Reading older literature with modern glasses is a pervasive tendency.
In the nineteenth century, this approach resulted in a propensity to
judge eighteenth-century poetry by Romantic standards and to find it
wanting. The novel, too, has suffered from this sort of self-congratulatory
measurement in the twentieth century, in which the yardstick was Jame-
sian realism. In the past few years, a different manifestation of this
approach has been gaining in popularity as critics sift through the fiction of the eighteenth- and nineteenth-century women novelists, looking for evidence of latent feminism. Recent interpretations of Fanny
Burney's novels, in which feminist readings are becoming fashionable,
reflect this tendency. Critics point to the trials the heroine in each
endures, including her loss of fortune, and to the marriage at the end as
expressions, however repressed or even unconscious, of the frustrations
and resentment Burney felt in her role as a woman in a male-dominated
society. Each heroine does suffer a series of trials in which she falls prey
to an assortment of villainous males who attack her virtue, her heart, or
her purse; each novel is also concluded with a marriage. This is, however, a matter of genre, rather than gender, since these plot features,
which some critics trace to feminism, are instead debts to the romance
tradition, from which Burney drew heavily for plot, theme, and character.
    All feminist readings of Burney's fiction center around one recurring
theme—dependence. All stress three central plot features that these critics see as evidence that Burney visualized women as dependent—eco-
nomically, physically, and psychologically—on men. The first of these
arguments for Burney's feminism is that the heroine in each novel is

5. *Diary and Letters* 1: 52.
† From Martha G. Brown, "Fanny Burney's 'Feminism': Gender or Genre?" *Fetter'd or Free?*
   British Women Novelists, 1670–1815, ed. Mary Anne Schofield and Cecilia Macheski (Athens:
   Ohio UP, 1986) 29–39. Reprinted with the permission of Ohio University Press / Swallow
   Press, Athens. The author's notes have been edited for brevity.

denied her proper rank and fortune—at least until the end, a fact which
they interpret as a feminist resentment of women's financial dependence on men. Rose Marie Cutting argues that "all are cut off from
their rightful inheritance—a situation that serves as a good metaphor
for the historic poverty and economic dependence of women."[1]

The first part of this statement is undeniably true. Evelina, the unacknowledged but legitimate daughter of a nobleman, has been abandoned by her father, a libertine who burned the marriage certificate.
Aware of her questionable parentage, Evelina calls herself an "orphan,"
"motherless," and "worse than fatherless." Throughout the novel, as she
is forced to live in the vulgar world of Madame Duval and her Branghton relatives, the possibility that she may be accepted by her true
father seems remote, as Villars recognizes when he asks, "only child of
a wealthy baronet, whose person she has never seen, whose character
she has reason to abhor, and whose name she is forbidden to claim;
entitled as she is to lawfully inherit his fortune and estate, is there any
probability that he will properly own her?"[2]

* * *

Although inheritance is an important focus in all four novels, the
assertion that this "serves as a good metaphor for the historic poverty and
economic dependency of women" is unconvincing. Fielding's Joseph
Andrews and Tom Jones are both cut off from their rightful inheritance;
so is Smollett's Humphrey Clinker. Are we, therefore, to assume that
Fielding and Smollett meant this as a "metaphor" for men's "economic
dependence"? Of course not. The inheritance theme in so many eighteenth-century novels is clearly traceable to the romance tradition, a
tradition whose influence on the novel has recently been recognized by
several critics.

The typical romance plot, beginning with the Greek prose romances
of Heliodorus, Longus, and Tatius, centers on an infant who is abandoned, or "exposed," by his parents, rescued and reared by a kindly
shepherd. After the child reaches maturity, he falls in love, a romance
that is blocked, often by the mystery surrounding the hero's birth. After
a series of trials, the lovers are finally united when their true identities
are revealed, their inheritance is restored, and they are married. Varia-
tions on this story have supplied the plot for prose and verse romances
for many centuries; they continued to do so in the eighteenth-century
novel.

In Burney's novels, as in romance in general, the denial of the hero's
birthright has important implications for plot and theme. At the super-

1. Rose Marie Cutting, "Defiant Women: The Growth of Feminism in Fanny Burney's Novels,"
   Studies in English Literature, 1500–1900 17 (1977): 521.
2. Fanny Burney, *Evelina: or the History of a Young Lady's Entrance into the World* (London:
   Oxford UP, 1970) 19. Page numbers for Burney's works are supplied in parentheses in the text.
   [Bracketed page numbers refer to this Norton Critical Edition. *Editor*]

ficial level of plot, the hero's mysterious origin and lack of both rank and fortune make possible the adventures so necessary for romance. Evelina and Juliet[3] are forced on their journeys or quests by the dubious circumstances of their birth and by their rights to inherit. The economic plights of all four heroines make them vulnerable, which is necessary to set them up for the trials and tests that they must endure. Mr. Villars says of Evelina's vulnerability, "The supposed obscurity of your birth and situation makes you liable to a thousand disagreeable adventures" (p. 116) [97]. * * *

The disinheritance of the heroines also has important thematic implications, and these are moral and psychological, rather than economic. The quest for identity ending in the self-recognition so central in romance is really, as Northrop Frye suggests, "attaining one's original identity."[4] This attainment is especially apparent in *Evelina* and *The Wanderer*. Because Evelina has been stripped of her fortune and her name she must seek to discover who she is before she can claim her place in society. She must also seek to discover where and to whom she belongs. Her position makes her all *potentia*. Because she is nobody and belongs to nobody, she may be anybody and belong to anybody. Her quest for identity involves a series of moral tests and moral choices through which she proves herself worthy of the inheritance and name she has been denied. * * * A heroine who is secure in both her identity and her inheritance would simply not be an effective heroine of romance, where the quest is essential to both plot and meaning. Romance demands instead a heroine who is poised at the threshold of initiation into experience, who is ready to undergo the symbolic *rite de passage*, which involves testing and self-discovery. The lack of name and fortune are necessary plot devices embodying central thematic concerns.

*   *   *

A second argument for Burney's feminism—closely related to the first—is that the heroines in the novels suffer abuse because they exist in a world where women are powerless and oppressed. Cutting sees the cruelty in Burney's novels "as a manifestation of feminine sensibility: she was, after all, describing a world in which women had little power."[5] It is true that each heroine suffers abuse at the hands of a malicious man. Evelina is at the mercy of her chief tormentor, Sir Clement Willoughby, throughout and occasionally falls prey to a cast of minor villains who accost her physically in the alleys of Vauxhall and Marylebone gardens. * * *

Feminist readings of the cruelty in Burney's novels have two main

3. The heroine of *The Wanderer; or, Female Difficulties* (1814), Burney's fourth novel. [*Editor*]
4. Northrop Frye, *The Secular Scripture: A Study of the Structure of Romance*, Charles Eliot Norton Lectures, 1974–75 (Cambridge: Harvard UP, 1976) 152.
5. Cutting, 520.

weaknesses. First, the heroines are victimized by women as often as by men. Evelina's wicked "stepmother," Madame Duval, uses and abuses her as often and as maliciously as Sir Clement. * * *

If the malice is general, we must seek a source other than feminism; that source is the romance tradition, where the hero's mettle is tested by a series of trials. In the Greek romance, the heroine undergoes a bizarre series of adventures in which she is shipwrecked, kidnapped, tortured by pirates and savages—who are, by the way, males. Does this suggest that Heliodorus, Longus, and Tatius were avant-garde feminists? The idea is too absurd to entertain. But it is no more reasonable to attribute the trials of Burney's heroines to feminism when they are so clearly a feature of the genre in which she was working. As Frye explains, the quest in romance has three stages: "the stage of the perilous journey and the preliminary minor adventures, the crucial struggle . . . and the exaltation of the hero."[6] Burney's novels, all of which fall roughly into three parts analogous to these three stages, concern the "perilous journey" of the heroine. The "preliminary minor adventures" are typically social skirmishes, while the "crucial struggles" are moral and spiritual.

The quest is necessary for the heroine's moral growth because each is, at the beginning, virtuous but untried. All four heroines have been reared in seclusion and are of just that age when their innocence must be tested by experience. The theme of the initiation or *rite de passage* is implied in the title *Evelina: or, The History of a Young Lady's Entrance into the World*, and it is made explicit by the narrator who says in the first chapter of *Camilla*:

> The experience which teaches the lesson of truth, and the blessings of tranquillity, comes not in the shape of warning nor of wisdom; from such they turn aside, defying or disbelieving. 'Tis in the bitterness of personal proof alone, in suffering and in feeling, in erring and repenting, that experience comes home with conviction, or impresses to any use.[7]

Each heroine, then, must be thrust out of the rural world of innocence into the urban world of experience so that her virtue can be tried and perfected. On one level the tests involve manners, as the heroine is placed in social situations in which her choices are invested with symbolic and ritualistic significance. In speaking of the perilous journey of romance, Kathleen Williams says, "the hero's fate depends upon whether he takes a certain seat, asks or answers a certain question."[8]

On another level, the tests are moral. Basically virtuous, each heroine has only to add good judgment to a good heart. *Prudentia*, involving the ability to make moral choices leading to virtuous action, is what each

6. Frye, *Anatomy of Criticism* (Princeton: Princeton UP, 1957) 187.
7. Fanny Burney, *Camilla, or a Picture of Youth* (London: Oxford UP, 1972) 8.
8. Kathleen Williams, "Romance Tradition in *The Faerie Queene*," *Research Studies* 32 (1964); rpt. in *Edmund Spenser's Poetry*, ed. Hugh McClean (New York: Norton, 1968) 561.

heroine must acquire. And she can acquire this only through a series of tests in which her failure to judge well and to act wisely brings her perilously near disaster again and again. The more serious assaults on the heroine are a necessary part of the ritual initiation in which the quester must meet and slay the dragon. Frye explains that in romance, "the hero travels perilously through a dark labyrinthine underworld full of monsters" and that this often becomes "a structural principle of fiction."[9] In Burney's fiction the obligatory dragons and monsters of romance are transformed into a gallery of fops and rakes; the labyrinth becomes the dark alleys of Marylebone and Vauxhall.

The centrality of the quest to romance also provides the refutation for the third feminist argument, which is that the marriage at the end of each novel suggests a surrender to male power. Judith Newton calls Evelina's entrance into the world an "entrance into the marriage market" and argues that by marrying she abdicates adult responsibility and power.[1] * * * And Patricia Meyer Spacks argues that in Burney novels, the heroine's " 'growth' leads her back toward childhood" and that "the 'happy endings' of Burney novels reassert the charm and irresponsibility of the child as the greatest achievement to be hoped for by adolescents."[2] These are odd criticisms to make of Burney, indeed, they would be odd criticisms to make of any eighteenth-century novel, since, with the exception of *Clarissa*, all major novels of the period end in just this way—happily, and with marriage, or better yet, a set of marriages. In the romance tradition in all its different incarnations, including the eighteenth-century novel, marriage signifies in two essential ways. First of all, marriage and treasure are the two standard rewards awaiting the hero at the end of the successful quest. With the exception of Juliet, who is perfect from the beginning, each of the heroines is unfit at the onset of the quest to manage either marriage or money; these are rights that must be won. The marriage is also a way of placing the hero's individual moral maturation into a social and communal context, making it more symbolic than personal. As Henry Knight Miller suggests, "romance and comedy traditionally conclude with the celebration of a marriage, not because that marks the end but precisely because it celebrates a new beginning, the sacramental emblem of a new world of maturity and hope, the assertion of life and continuity as against the 'reality' of isolation and death."[3] Marriage, then, is not a matter of giving up, but of growing up.

And Burney is no more fettered by the tradition in which she was working than her heroines are fettered by the tradition of marriage that

9. Frye, *Anatomy* 190.
1. Judith Newton, "*Evelina*: Or, the History of a Young Lady's Entrance into the Marriage Market," *Modern Language Studies* 6 (1976): 53.
2. Patricia Meyer Spacks, *The Female Imagination* (New York: Knopf, 1975) 129.
3. Henry Knight Miller, *Henry Fielding's* Tom Jones *and the Romance Tradition*, English Literary Monograph Series, no. 6 (Victoria: U of Victoria P, 1976) 40.

they all enter. In fact, working within a tradition is freeing for an artist in a very real sense. Because the romance tradition supplies plot and character types, Burney was freed from these decisions, which enabled her to concentrate on other narrative areas, such as dialogue and setting. Of course another way a writer may use tradition is to react against it openly or, more subtly, to turn it to his or her own purposes. So that if one accepts the contention that these plot features—the heroine's lack of her rightful rank and fortune, her trials, and finally her marriage—are drawn straight from romance, it is possible to argue that Burney took these stock features of romance and put them to feminist uses. There is, however, no evidence, at least in the first three novels, to support this; there is instead ample evidence to refute it.

In the first place, as I suggested earlier, the numbers of villainous men and women are roughly equivalent. The moral types, too, are as often men as women. Each heroine has her chivalrous knight to protect her. Evelina is guarded and guided by Orville, who is a paragon of courtesy and morality. * * * In addition, there are several wise, kindly, father figures—the Reverend Villars in *Evelina* * * * —and a variety of decent men who befriend the heroines—Mr. Macartney in *Evelina*. * * *

In addition, in each novel, Burney creates one more-or-less liberated lady and clearly disapproves of her. Mrs. Selwyn in *Evelina* is such a character. Although she serves the positive function of occasionally protecting Evelina, she is too aggressively outspoken to suit Burney. Evelina says of this intelligent, independent, and sharp-tongued woman, "her understanding, indeed, may be called *masculine*, but, unfortunately, her manners deserve the same epithet; for in studying to acquire the knowledge of the other sex, she has lost all the softness of her own" (p. 269) [224].

* * * Although [*The Wanderer*] is clearly influenced, * * * by the romance in plot, character, style, and theme, there is a new note of anxiety and dissatisfaction with women's lot in life and a new focus on problems that are particularly female. This new concern is evidenced from the beginning by the subtitle. "Female Difficulties," which seems to have gynecological connotations, as well as social implications.

* * *

If there is indeed such a change, however subtle, in Burney's attitude and intentions in *The Wanderer*, there are two possible causes for it. The first is that in the years between the writing of *Camilla* and *The Wanderer*, Burney suffered many personal defeats and disappointments that may have seemed to her especially womanly ones. For one thing, she watched her favorite sister Susan abused by a cruel husband. She also experienced pain and humiliation when her brother James abandoned his wife and children to run away with his half-sister, Sally. Burney herself had been crushed by economic hardships, by a painful separation from her family, and by poor health. In 1811 she underwent a mastectomy, performed with no anesthetic; this was a female difficulty which may have scarred Burney emotionally as well as physically.[4] A second explanation may be found in a shifting social consciousness and intellectual climate typified by the publication—twenty-two years before *The Wanderer* was written—of Mary Wollstonecraft's A *Vindication of the Rights of Woman*.

Perhaps this apparent "feminism" in *The Wanderer* has led some critics into reading these tendencies, if they actually exist, back into the earlier novels. Because the novels are so similar on the surface in basic plot, characterization, and even in theme, it is tempting to lump them together and to generalize about them almost as though they were one novel. To do so, however, is reductive and slights the richness, the complexity, and the diversity of Burney's work. The young girl who wrote *Evelina* was different in many and important ways from the mature woman who wrote *The Wanderer*, which embodies new concerns and new attitudes.

KENNETH W. GRAHAM

Cinderella or Bluebeard: The Double Plot of *Evelina* †

A number of exciting and perceptive recent examinations of eighteenth-century woman are encouraging reassessment of traditional interpretations of literature. Of special note are Mary Poovey's account of the strains and anxieties entailed in living up to the eighteenth-century standard of a 'Proper Lady';[1] Nancy K. Miller's discussion of euphoric and disphoric plots as eighteenth-century heroines experience integration or alienation on entering society;[2] and Mary Jacobus's richly incoherent account of woman traditionally torn between suffering and desire in the introductory chapter of *Women Writing and Writing about Women*. Mary Jacobus includes that seething reference to the 'prison of sensibility created by patriarchy to contain women.'[3] In much of this writing, eighteenth-century woman is presented in terms of polarities: euphoric-disphoric, integration-alienation, desire-suffering, freedom-submission.

4. Joyce Hemlow, *The History of Fanny Burney* (Oxford: Clarendon, 1958).

† From Kenneth W. Graham, "Cinderella or Bluebeard: The Double Plot of *Evelina*," *Man and Nature/L'Homme et la Nature* 5 (1986): 85–98. Reprinted by permission of Academic Printing and Publishing. The author's notes have been edited for brevity.

1. Mary Poovey uses *Evelina* to help establish the context of her exploration in *The Proper Lady and the Woman Writer* (Chicago: U of Chicago P, 1984) 24–26.

2. Nancy K. Miller, *The Heroine's Text* (New York: Columbia UP, 1980).

3. Mary Jacobus, "The Difference of View," *Women Writing and Writing About Women*, ed. Mary Jacobus (New York: Barnes, 1979) 15.

A binary shape informs the interpretation of *Evelina* presented in this essay. The paradigm that best expresses the patterns of obligation and entrapment that regulated the lives of eighteenth-century ladies is the double hook (with homage to Sheilagh Watson). The two central virtues expected of ladies were modesty and delicacy, and each virtue spawned a series of double hooks: an approved manifestation of the virtue as well as a necessary subversive or destructive concomitant. Thus a manifestation of delicacy is innocence, but its destructive concomitant is ignorance, or at least credulity.[4] An approved characteristic of modesty is silence, but an accompanying condition is stifled or frustrated utterance. Delicacy involves a becoming dependency on parents and husbands, but the double hook of dependency is vulnerability, vulnerability to adventurers, rakes, and inadequate parents. The double hook paradigm represents also the counterpoint of text and subtext as proper lady writers acknowledge overtly the claims of social convention but covertly the related dangers. Fanny Burney's account of Evelina and her mother expresses the double hook of woman's entrapment in the conventional virtues of a cruel age when woman's service to the requirements of sensibility too often entails the destruction of self.

A startling view of the relations between the sexes in the late eighteenth century is offered in the influential courtesy book by John Gregory, *A Father's Legacy to His Daughters*, a book of guidance with which, according to Joyce Hemlow, Fanny Burney was familiar in 1778.[5] In an introductory passage Gregory observes of his book

> . . . you will hear, at least for once in your lives, the genuine sentiments of a man who has no interest in flattering and deceiving you.[6]

That 'at least for once in your lives' is Gregory's view of the state of communications between sexes. A widower, he feels obliged to prepare his daughters for life in a world where the frequent and, indeed, customary motives for men's attentions to women are flattery and deception. He regrets this lack of sincerity, but he accepts it as customary in man-woman relationships. His opinion is shared by two contrasting yet perceptive social commentators of the time. To Mary Wollstonecraft's ears, the passage rings with 'mournful truth,' and she castigates 'the cold unmeaning intercourse of gallantry'[7] and the various heartless devices employed by men to render women wretched. From an opposed con-

---

4. Burney's Lord Orville acknowledges that "credulity is the sister of innocence." Fanny Burney, *Evelina or The History of a Young Lady's Entrance into the World* (Oxford: Oxford UP, 1982) 240. All references are to this the most accessible edition. Subsequent citations will be placed in parentheses in the text. [Bracketed page numbers refer to this Norton Critical Edition. *Editor*]
5. Joyce Hemlow, "Fanny Burney and the Courtesy Books," *PMLA* 65 (1950) 738.
6. John Gregory, *A Father's Legacy to his Daughters* (Edinburgh, 1788) 102.
7. Mary Wollstonecraft, *A Vindication of the Rights of Woman with Strictures on Political and Moral Subjects* (London, 1792; rpt. 1970) 216.

ception of the nature of woman, Lord Chesterfield recommends the very deception that Wollstonecraft attacks.

> It is . . . absolutely necessary to manage, please and flatter them; and never to discover the least marks of contempt . . . A man of sense only trifles with them, plays with them, humours and flatters them . . . he neither consults them about, nor trusts them with, serious matters. . . .[8]

From their differing perspectives, the comments of Wollstonecraft and Chesterfield acknowledge as normal a contempt for women that makes them trifles and playthings and denies them full humanity. Dr. Gregory has in mind this alarming male attitude as he seeks to guide his daughters through the labyrinths of social living. He returns repeatedly to their need to maintain womanly delicacy and modesty in a list of hazards that includes the 'uncontrouled licence of men,' and 'the dissipation in . . . present manners.'[9] Recognizing that men and manners constitute a considerable threat to women, that delicacy and modesty are often difficult to maintain amidst strong counter-encouragements, and that even when maintained they do not offer always adequate defences, Dr. Gregory encourages 'a compassionate sympathy to unfortunate women, especially to those who are rendered so by the villainy of men.'[1] Ruined women are sad expectations in Dr. Gregory's world.

Fanny Burney's first published novel has the full title, *Evelina or the History of a Young Lady's Entrance into the World*. That 'World' is Dr. Gregory's world, a place of active and latent threat to women. Of active threat are the economic and glandular imperatives of men that make women objects of desire at the same time that they are objects of contempt. Of latent threat is the weight of social expectation that defines ladies in terms of passive virtues like Gregory's repeated favourites, modesty and delicacy, a definition that leaves women little scope for contending with the threats around them. To underline liabilities in a woman's life, Fanny Burney presents two stories of violence and betrayal centred on two young ladies entering a corrupt and vicious world for which their social conditionings have not equipped them.

This interpretation may not be the familiar one that treats *Evelina* as a comedy of manners and as a sensitive portrayal (before Jane Austen) of the intensitites of female mortification. The tendency to treat Burney

---

8. *Lord Chesterfield's Letters to his Son*, ed. R. K. Root (London: Dent, 1929; rpt. 1963) 66–67. Fanny Burney read Chesterfield's letters soon after their publication and recognized immediately their import where women are concerned. She saw them as "inculcating immorality, countenancing all *gentleman-like* vices, advising deceit and exhorting to inconstancy" (*The Early Diary of Frances Burney*, ed. A. R. Ellis [London: G. Bell, 1913] 1:314).
9. Gregory 105–11.
1. Gregory 124.

as a precursor of Austen has blinded readers and commentators to the fact that Burney's fictional world is much harsher than Austen's. The exclusively comic interpretation is not the fault of Burney who provided her novel with an artful double plot that expresses some serious realities beneath comic surfaces. The narrative recounts the similar histories of the entrance into the world of Evelina and her mother. The encounter with the world results in disaster and death for the mother and to success and triumph for the daughter. The contrasting fates of mother and daughter reveal the vulnerability of a young lady in an environment superficially well-regulated but at core a social and moral wilderness. Evelina's story is patterned on the outline of her mother's to demonstrate a young woman's perils in a society that esteems manners but slights morals.

The story of Caroline, the mother, frames the narrative of Evelina. The Caroline plot is introduced in the first two letters of this epistolary novel and concludes with a deathbed letter recounted near the end when Evelina is about to achieve recognition, wealth, and married happiness—everything that was denied to her mother. The history of Caroline begins in pastoral security under the guardianship of Mr. Villars and well removed from her coarse and vulgar mother living in Paris and married to a Monsieur Duval. When Caroline is eighteen, Mme. Duval calls her to Paris where she employs threats and violence to coerce Caroline into marrying one of her second husband's nephews. The intensity of Caroline's plight is reflected in the rashness of her attempted solution. Friendless, in an environment doubly alien by being both urban and foreign, subject to the tyrannies of an ignorant mother, Caroline turns to the only solution that her delicacy and modesty permit and gambles on marriage to escape an intolerable situation. Unfortunately she changes only the terms of her subjection and places herself in the power of a man apparently ready to use to his advantage her desperate isolation. Sir John Belmont marries her in an unwitnessed ceremony, and, when Caroline is disinherited by her vindictive mother, in an act of astonishing wickedness he burns the marriage certificate and repudiates the match. Caroline returns to Mr. Villars but does not survive the birth of her daughter, Evelina. The mother is victim of two forms of violence. Mme. Duval's is the violence of a parental authority whose purposes, because of differences in class and sensibility, are inimical to the daughter. Sir John Belmont manifests a male callousness that regards women as sources of income and as sexual playthings. Caroline's vulnerability to the most common sources of violence experienced by young women, parental and spousal, precipitates the beginning and the end of her catastrophe. The mother creates the vulnerability and Sir John capitalizes on it.

The thematic coherence of this account of a young woman's life as bracketed by violence demonstrates the care that Fanny Burney took in structuring her subplot. Indeed, the narrative art devoted to the presentation of Caroline's experience of the world suggests its importance in the central narrative of Evelina, and reminds us that 'The History of Caroline Evelyn' had an independent narrative life before *Evelina* was written. It was one of a number of works created by Fanny Burney during her early adolescence and burnt by her on her fifteenth birthday. Thus the history of Evelina was born from a fully and richly conceived history of Caroline. Much of the narrative and thematic complexity of *Evelina* results from the intertwining of two plots, both developed in considerable detail and both addressing the problem of woman's defences in a violent age.

When Evelina makes her entrance into the world, she too experiences the perplexity and violence that destroyed her mother. At the age of seventeen Evelina leaves the indulgent care of Mr. Villars and is plunged into a fashionable city life for which her upbringing has not well prepared her. Like her mother, Evelina becomes subject to Mme. Duval and must endure her match-making, her violent temper, her threats, and her authority as her closest living acknowledged relative. She is threatened as well by male aggression in a variety of forms. The fate of the mother forms a silent commentary on Evelina's choices and the dangers to her happiness. At a particular point their fates differ, in part because Evelina has the prudence to employ more active defences than delicacy and modesty to protect herself in a vicious world and in part because she has the luck to capture the affections of a worthy man.

The contrast between Evelina's active disposition and her mother's passive one may express a subtle criticism of notions of woman that Dr. Gregory's authoritative book of advice represents. Gregory's *Legacy* inculcates a narrow concept of womanliness in which the qualities of modesty and delicacy are paramount. For Gregory, modesty involves reserve and silence in public behavior and a 'native dignity . . . which is your natural protection from the familiarities of men.'[2] Delicacy is related to modesty in Gregory's book of advice although it seems to signal a context of sexuality. Delicacy reveals itself in blushes, in uneasiness 'even at the gaze of admiration.' Delicacy is threatened by too strong a sense of humour, by untoward mirth when dancing, by risqué conversations, and by most English comedies. With an insidious persuasiveness that repeatedly holds up their dead mother as a sterling example of the qualities he is seeking to foster, Gregory recommends to his daughters the guidance of the imagination and 'a warm, open and ingenuous heart' but does not encourage intellectual pursuits and learning: 'keep it a profound secret, especially from the men.' In many ways a puzzling work, it imposes a Hobbesian realism on its assessment of men but leaves women with no more than the most passive defences

2. Gregory 43 *et passim*.

against male wolfishness. Indeed, its use of the example of a dead mother conscripts the cooperation of guilt and anxiety to enforce the book's lessons.

Fanny Burney never recorded an opinion of Gregory's book, but the evidence of *Evelina* suggests that, for the most part, she accepted his strictures. Evelina behaves with the delicacy and modesty that Gregory commends. She is shy about her own beauty and maintains a quiet dignity which may at times protect her from male familiarity. Evelina reflects Gregory in her discomfort at a performance of Congreve's *Love for Love*: 'it was so extremely indelicate that Miss Mirvan and I were perpetually out of countenance' (78) [65]. Gregory had written: 'there are few English comedies a lady can see, without a shock to delicacy.'[3] An important similarity between the two works introduces at the same time an important difference. Both works have frequent recourse to the example of a dead mother, but with Gregory, the mother's example is to be followed, while in *Evelina* it must be rejected if the daughter is not to share the mother's fate and become a passive victim of male arrogance.

One of Evelina's adventures on an evening at the opera exemplifies the closeness of the parallel between mother and daughter, and demonstrates the liabilities of Gregory's standards of womanly conduct and the need for an active disposition. Evelina has planned to accompany the Mirvans and has dressed accordingly for the fashionable stalls (or pit) of the opera house. While dressing she has to refuse the unexpected invitation of the Branghton girls who are clearly attired for a less formal part of the house. Her grandmother appears and in a violent rage demands that Evelina accompany her cousins. The result for Evelina is a series of humiliations. The Branghtons are ignorant of opera decorums: they take seats in an unfashionable balcony of the theatre for which Evelina is wildly overdressed; they complain about costs; they make jejune comments during the performance. When at the end she is approached by Sir Clement Willoughby, she is anxious to avoid his making the acquaintance of her low connections. She intercepts him, and with the excuse that it will reduce crowding in the coach, she agrees to let him conduct her to the Mirvans to return home with them. Of course the Mirvans have already departed and Sir Clement conducts her to his coach instead.

Thus Caroline's history seems about to be repeated by Evelina. To avoid Mme. Duval's tactless authority, Evelina imprudently makes herself subject to the attentions of a rake. Sir Clement arranges for his coach to take them to an unknown part of the city while he flirts with the ideas of seduction and abduction, prepared to take his cue from the reactions of his passenger. Had Evelina offered even the encouragement

3. Gregory 58.

of passiveness and relied solely on delicacy and modesty to protect her, Sir Clement might have been more forceful in his attentions. But she replies to his overtures with direct and angry rejection, and when she sees that he has taken her out of her way, she tries to throw herself out of the moving coach. When a horrified Sir Clement prevents her, she makes ready to shout for help to the first passerby that appears. Her very vehemence frightens him and he orders his coach to proceed directly to Evelina's lodgings.

Sir Clement is the second plot's parallel to Sir John Belmont, the destroyer of Caroline. Both are examples of male opportunism, although Sir Clement appears to lack the calculated savagery of Sir John Belmont. I say 'appears' because Evelina never gives him the opportunity to do his worst. At their first encounter at the ridotto, his persistent badgering when she will not dance with him, a stranger, reduces her to tears. As her experience of the world increases, she becomes more self-possessed in her dealings with him. He continues to force himself upon her but the coach incident represents a turning-point in their relationship and never again does she lose control of herself or of Sir Clement. His every attempt to take advantage of her is repulsed with forthright eloquence that holds up to view the contrast between his pretensions to chivalry and his true behaviour. As the novel progresses, her self-respect and fluent candour gain her ascendency over him. By the time of his final exit from the novel, the erstwhile self-confident Sir Clement, his emotions confused by admiration for Evelina and jealousy for Lord Orville, is reduced to distress and agitation. It is a remarkable victory attained against odds from a position of weakness.

Sir Clement is a representative of a world of privilege and insensitivity to which Evelina was born vulnerable. Throughout her dealings with Sir Clement she has had to conceal a real uncertainty and anxiety beneath an apparent self-possession. What makes Sir Clement an especial threat to her is not only an impudent confidence based on his masculinity, but a self-assurance based on class that Evelina does not have and must strenuously feign. Legally, without the acknowledgment of Sir John Belmont, Evelina is a bastard. What has been interpreted by unkind critics as snobbishness is Evelina's meticulous maintenance of a genteel status. It is not only that her associations and education from birth make becoming the city wife of a Branghton or a Smith repugnant to her, but that any loss of status would make her more vulnerable to men like Sir Clement. To be reduced to one of Dr. Gregory's 'unfortunate women,' to decline into uncertain dependency as Sir Clement's mistress, is a dreadful possibility for Evelina in this environment.

By entering his carriage after the opera, Evelina is being prudently imprudent. She is desperate to deter any further contact between Madame Duval and Sir Clement who has already seen Evelina subject to the old lady's authority. The obvious contrast in behaviour and sensibility between the older and younger woman must make him curious of their relationship and of Evelina's birth. His suspicions would be heightened on hearing the indiscreetly ambiguous phrasing of Madame Duval's earlier introduction of Evelina to the Branghtons: '. . . my poor daughter Caroline had this child after she ran away from me' (68) [57]. Evelina confesses also that she drew Sir Clement away because she did not wish him 'to hear Miss Branghton call me cousin' (94) [79]. In her perceptive article, Toby Olshin discusses the importance of birth and family in *Evelina* but she does not lay sufficient stress on the sources and consequences of Evelina's equivocal birth. It is a subject of recurring anxiety to Evelina for good reason. Evelina is well aware that her obscure birth resulted from a form of male violence perpetrated upon a near-helpless woman and may certainly result in further violence directed at Evelina herself who, lacking the protection of legitimacy, is even more vulnerable than her mother. Professor Olshin accuses Evelina of moral shallowness in her lack of charity towards her grandmother, yet her coolness to Madame Duval, like her tart snobbishness towards the Branghtons and Mr. Smith, are consistent with her attitudes towards anyone who would endanger her status by revealing its ambiguities.

That acute anxieties based on class consciousness are the source of her dislike of her low relatives is suggested in the contrasting example of her attitudes to her father. Evelina has every cause to hate Sir John Belmont whose villainy destroyed her mother's 'peace, reputation, and life' (126) [106] and blighted her own young life with the taint of an irregular birth. Yet, barring one interesting exception, Evelina exhibits a most unexpected devotion towards him. When Lady Howard dispatches a letter that may result in his acknowledgment of Evelina, she refers to her father as the man 'who has the natural claim to that dear title; a title, which to write, mention, or think of, fills my whole soul with filial tenderness' (130) [109]. One might argue that Evelina's passionate piety is directed towards the *title* rather than the man, yet we have every reason to believe that, injustice to the mother forgotten, both the title and the man will enjoy the warm overflow of daughterly affection. Here we find none of the cold dutifulness and restrained embarrassment that characterizes Evelina's deportment towards her only other close relative, her grandmother. The reason for the contrast seems clear: with more reason to dislike the father than the grandmother, Evelina rejects the grandmother as a threat to her status, and embraces the father as her only source of legitimacy.

The link between Evelina's filial tenderness and her undiscriminating hunger for legitimacy is developed in two consequent episodes. When Sir John Belmont responds to Lady Howard's overture with a witty and derisive rejection of Evelina's pretensions to relationship, while not quite happily consigning him to help, Evelina is prepared to contemplate 'the anguish he is hoarding up for time to come' (159) [131]. When recognition is withheld, so is filial tenderness. This lapse from exemplary piety is forgotten towards the end of the novel when Sir John agrees to see her and she longs for the moment when she can prostrate herself 'at the feet of the nearest, the most reverenced of all relations, whom my heart yearns to know, and longs to love!' (370) [306]. The superlatives place her father above even her mother in her order of regard, but if her sense of justice may be awry her assessment of advantage cannot be faulted.

Evelina lives in a world where benefits are gained only if woman has the wit to distinguish a profitable submission from an unprofitable one. If she is to sacrifice herself to the uncertainties of marriage, it will be on the most advantageous terms. With sensitivities vulnerable to violence and vehemence, Evelina had been overwhelmed by her grandmother's authority in the first half of the novel. Yet once the grandmother insists on a marriage to young Branghton with its myriad disadvantages, Evelina, with firmness unshakeable, refuses. She will not submit her life to her grandmother's authority. Vehement self-respect and the determined maintenance of status are necessary in a social world in which men's customary attitudes to women are wolfish and contemptuous. Mr. Branghton encourages misogyny in his son in comments on women's irrationality (90) [76]. At a higher social level Lord Merton is capable of this brutal comment: 'I don't know what the devil a woman lives for after thirty: she is only in other folks way.' The most misogynistic men are the most in favour of passive virtues in women. Captain Mirvan rudely silences his daughter when she is invited to present an independent opinion (109) [91]. Mr. Lovel expresses 'an insuperable aversion to strength, either of body or mind, in a female,' and Lord Merton echoes his sentiments: 'a woman wants nothing to recommend her but her beauty and good nature; in every thing else she is either impertinent or unnatural' (361) [299]. Those most in favour of woman's weakness are those most likely to take advantage of it. Perceptive to such attitudes, Evelina will not display weakness that would make her vulnerable to the callousness surrounding her.

The novel demonstrates that delicacy and modesty are not adequate defences where young women, particularly those without the protections of male relatives and class position, are regarded as legitimate prey. With Mr. Lovel, the first man Evelina meets in London while perplexed by the intricacies of urban social life, the tactics for asserting male dominance extend to a malicious browbeating. He is eager to humiliate a clearly inexperienced seventeen-year-old at her first ball because she has innocently refused his complacent offer to dance and then unknowingly broken decorum by dancing with someone else. He is prepared thereafter to take every opportunity to remind Evelina, and those with her, of her ignorance of sophisticated city manners. Fanny Burney arranges her narrative so that, of the first three men Evelina meets in the city, two seek advantages from her inexperience that could lead to misfortune and even ruin. Sir Clement would seduce her and Lovel would see her publicly humiliated. Only Lord Orville seeks to protect her. The odds are against her. Male wolfishness, in combination with Evelina's inexperience of city life, seems destined to conquer her determined self-respect.

Evelina's experiences with men are examples of a wide-spread violence in Burney's setting, a violence significantly centred on conflict between the sexes in which male rapaciousness is an assumed norm. Intersexual turbulence is exemplified and exaggerated by Capt. Mirvan and Mme. Duval, whose dissensions take physical forms. On their second meeting Mme. Duval knocks a candle out of the captain's hand and spits in his face. He in turn takes her by the shoulders and shakes her. On another occasion he masquerades as a highway robber to tie her and fling her into a ditch. The broils of the captain and Mme. Duval are portrayed as rough farce, but their boisterous behaviour calls attention to a more general social disorder that darkens Burney's setting. Characters are pushed into mud, Lovel is attacked by a monkey, two old ladies are matched in a near-fatal footrace and all such scenes are portrayed with a sense of the grotesque that makes the events not only ludicrous but distressing. A disturbing proportion of the characters in *Evelina* are prepared to take advantage of superior wealth, superior status and superior skill at arms to inflict humiliations on others. We are reminded of the socially-sanctioned terminus of violence on at least four occasions when disputes threaten to result in duels. By underlining such reminders with references to Caroline's fate, the narrative undercuts the ludicrous to draw attention to the fact this society's lack of humanity can ultimately lead to death.

While Evelina learns to deal with some of the more obvious and innocuous male attempts on her, she is genuinely afraid of overt male compulsion for which she has little defence. Too often male sexual passions operate in concert with her society's tolerance of violence to threaten both her physical and her social well-being. A variety of men physically seize her, and she is rightly terrified when such encounters take place in private, as in Sir Clement's coach, or in darkness, as at Marylebone Gardens when she falls into the hands of a young officer, or at Vauxhall when her way is blocked by a party of riotous young men and, fleeing from them, she has her hand caught by a group of men of a higher class who take her, ominously, for an actress. On that occasion she is rescued by Sir Clement who, in turn, catches her hand and draws her into a dark alley of the park to take advantage of her fear, distraction and gratitude for his assistance. When she recovers her presence of mind she has to push him physically away from her and chastize him for his unchivalric behaviour of offering insolence when she had claimed protection. Her directness and her assumption of a genteel status keep Sir Clement off balance. At Mrs. Beaumont's however, she cannot avoid the drunken attentions of Lord Merton and, seeing Lord Orville about to conduct his sister away from Lord Merton's company, Evelina, with a *cri de coeur* exclaims the vulnerability of a woman and orphan and sums up her experience with the male sex:

> "Would to Heaven," cried I, frightened to see how much Lord Merton was in liquor, "that I too had a brother!—and then I should not be exposed to such treatment!"

She pronounces the death of chivalry:

> ". . . in a situation that calls for protection, to meet only with mortifications. . ." (315) [260]

So general is her experience of gentlemen who use courtliness as an aid but never a restraint to seduction that when Lord Orville kneels to propose to her, she thinks at first that he is mocking her.

If Evelina succeeds in overcoming the latent liability of society's conception of women, she can never rest secure of the active liability of male attitudes and behaviour. The world projected by the nervous sensibilities of the twenty-four year old Fanny Burney is certainly a man's world. Daddy Crisp had warned her that men are 'design'd to be—Animals of Prey . . . violent, and uncontroulable.'[4] All of Evelina's experiences of the delights of the superficial world of balls, plays, excursions and entertainments are touched by anxiety with her recognition of the underground world where male passions seethe and bubble, ever on the point of exploding in destructive violence. Her parentage and birth are constant reminders of that dark reality. Frustrated of a satisfactory marriage-settlement, her father had angrily destroyed his marriage and ultimately his wife. To contend with that world without father, mother or even the assurance of legitimacy, Evelina has to control those tender sensibilities that the culture encourages in its young women and assert her wit and understanding. One of the few men to appreciate these qualities in a woman, Lord Orville finds her 'informed, sensible, and intelligent' (347) [286]. In addition, the reader discovers in Evelina a growing toughness and resiliency whenever her status or morals are threatened. While her intelligence and strength of will distinguish her from her mother, they are not enough to separate her from her mother's fate. In a world where any private place might face her with the irreversible attentions of an uninhibited philanderer, Evelina is lucky to avoid all the snares and to love and be loved by a man as sensitive and virtuous as Lord Orville. The real source of the difference between Evelina's fate and her mother's is the difference between Lord Orville and Sir John Belmont.

4. *Early Diary* 1: 280.

In her perceptive study, *Romantics, Rebels, and Reactionaries*, Marilyn Butler reflects received opinion when she casually includes *Evelina* in a list of novels that base their plots on the Cinderella myth.[5] Superficially the observation is just: in the course of her narrative Evelina acquires independent wealth, legitimacy as the recognized daughter of a baronet, and a soaring social elevation with marriage to an earl. What the observation ignores is the significant second plot that counters the fairy-tale simplifications of the Cinderella story and directs attention to violent and vicious social realities. While Evelina defends herself actively from seductions and improves on her mother's example by resisting social encouragements to be passive, the double perspective of the novel reminds us that the comic outcome of Evelina's story may be conventional, but it is unrealistic. The second plot offers a counter-myth based on the novel's perception of relations between the sexes in a social setting characterized by an underlying violence. The novel pairs men and women in courtship and marriage, but apart from Evelina's, the sad reality is that there are no happy or potentially happy marriages in the novel. Capt. Mirvan's returns from the sea bring rudeness, domineering, insensitivity, vulgarity and humiliation to his wife. Evelina's grandfather's marriage brought him shame, bitterness and an early death. Her father abandoned her mother to disgrace and death. The two relationships likely to lead to marriage in the novel hold out no promise for future happiness. Mr. Brown is an indifferent suitor to Polly Branghton as is Lord Merton, whose real passions are for drinking, wenching and gambling, to Lady Louisa. It is the experience of Evelina's mother and of most married people to awake one morning to find themselves married to a monster. The double plot suggests that the appropriate myth is not Cinderella but Bluebeard.

KRISTINA STRAUB

Evelina: Marriage as the Dangerous Die†

If the vista of a middle-class young woman's future was composed, in Burney's day, of "gulphs, pits, and precipices," a happy marriage, according to the conventions of sentimental fiction, might well be expected to take her to another country, a timeless realm in which her problematic maturity could be subsumed into the promise of happy-ever-after. And this displacement of loss by gain, powerlessness by secu-

---

5. Marilyn Butler, *Romantics, Rebels and Reactionaries* (Oxford: Oxford UP, 1981) 105.
† From Kristina Straub, *Divided Fictions: Fanny Burney and Feminine Strategy* (Lexington: UP of Kentucky, 1987) 53–77. Copyright © 1987 by The University of Kentucky Press. Reprinted by permission of The University Press of Kentucky. The author's notes have been edited for brevity.

rity, is, of course, the psychic and social change dramatically expressed by Evelina's marriage and her removal to Berry Hill at the end of the novel, the retreat from the world to a sort of domestic utopia. *Evelina* is not, however, committed to the *probability* of happy marriage as a way out, however convinced it seems of the desirability of such an escape. Nor, apparently, was Fanny Burney, who wrote in her diaries prior to *Evelina* that she needed *"particular inducements"* to unite herself "for life with one who must have full power to make me miserable, and perhaps none to make me happy—for it is such chance!" (*ED* 2:88)[1] Marriage was, in Burney's view, a risk with potentially catastrophic results that was probably better avoided than taken. Judith Newton reads Evelina's marriage as Burney's reaction to her own traumatic experience as an unwilling prospective bride on the marriage market just two years before writing the main portion of *Evelina*: Burney, Newton argues, sought in the conventions of sentimental fiction ideological alternatives to the degradation she felt in her own experience as a marriageable young woman.[2] However ambivalent, even pessimistic, Burney's feelings about marriage seem to have been in life, fictional marriage could give both the author and her readers the illusion of culturally sanctioned personal empowerment for women. And Evelina's marriage is, in fact, just such an illusion, a fairy-tale drawing down of the curtain on the fair prospect of Evelina's future happiness.

But even in fiction, Burney does not fully endorse the romance of happily-ever-after. *Evelina*, the most happily and blithely romantic of Burney's novels, exposes the jarring contradictions between Burney's two ideologically determined perspectives on marriage—as both the means of escape from female maturity's hardships and as an institution that formalizes and justifies those hardships. The melodramatic story of the Evelyn family, related in one of Villars' first letters to Lady Howard, becomes the background against which both readers and characters in the novel see and understand Evelina's circumstances as a sexually desirable young woman, a history that sets up the premise that marriage for women means powerlessness and loss of integrity, perhaps even personal destruction. The Evelyns' history is distanced by time (it is a fictional "history," not an event), form (the stuff of romance, the remote doings of undefined, undeveloped characters), and placement in the novel (early—before readers can come to care much about the heroine's family), but it hints at the danger to female peace of mind posed by marriage—the primary institution defining the course of female life. This danger is transposed to the less tragic but more immediate portrayal of the Mirvans' marriage. Evelina does not explicitly apply the

1. *The Early Diary of Frances Burney, 1768–1778*, ed. Annie Raine Ellis, 2 vols. (London, 1913). [*Editor*]
2. Judith Lowder Newton, *Women, Power, and Subversion: Social Strategies in British Fiction, 1778–1860* (Athens: U of Georgia P, 1981) 23–28.

warnings of this marital portrait to herself, yet she records, in her letters to Villars, the helplessness and discomfort of the Mirvan women. And her own experiences as a young woman with "too much beauty to escape notice," and "too little wealth to be sought with propriety by men of the fashionable world" (18) [14]³ bear out the implications of the Evelyns' marital history and the unhappy circumstances of the Mirvan women: whether the young woman marries or remains single, her well-being, health, and sanity are more probably endangered than redeemed by the social institution of love and marriage, the main business of women's lives. This pessimistic vision of marriage's role in the female maturing process remains in unresolved and, I would argue, significant contradiction to the novel's conventional happy ending.

The novel evidences not only the conventional assumption that marriage is the shortest route to female happiness, but also the equally conventional notion that marriage is one of life's major snares, a trap in which people (especially women) are destroyed or at best given a life sentence of discomfort. The theme of disastrous marital connections opens in Villars' account to Lady Howard of Evelina's family history, starting with her grandfather's "ill-judged marriage" with Madame Duval. In this union, the husband is the victim, but the plot, as Villars relates it, emphasizes that Evelyn made his own marital bed before he died in it:

> His unhappy marriage . . . with Madame Duval, then a waiting-girl at a tavern, contrary to the advice and entreaties of all his friends, among whom I was myself the most urgent to dissuade him, induced him to abandon his native land, and fix his abode in France. Thither he was followed by shame and repentance; feelings which his heart was not framed to support: for, notwithstanding he had been too weak to resist the allurements of beauty, which nature, though a niggard to her of every other boon, had with a lavish hand bestowed on his wife; yet he was a young man of excellent character, and, till thus unaccountably infatuated, of unblemished conduct. He survived this ill-judged marriage but two years. (13–14) [10]

Burney makes Evelyn sympathetic—he is, after all, her heroine's grandfather and the charge of the admirable Mr. Villars—but she also makes it clear that Evelyn is responsible for his own destruction through the male privilege of free choice, however misused. His daughter's union with Sir John Belmont is quite a different matter. She wrongly trusts her husband in consenting to an "ill-judged" private marriage, but she does so under the duress of being pressured into another, even worse.

3. Frances Burney, *Evelina; or, the History of a Young Lady's Entrance into the World*, ed. Edward A. Bloom and Lillian D. Bloom (Oxford: Oxford UP, 1982) 164. Subsequent references are to this edition and are indicated parenthetically in the text. [Bracketed page numbers refer to this Norton Critical Edition. *Editor*]

"Madame Duval, at the instigation of her husband, earnestly, or rather tyrannically, endeavoured to effect an union between Miss Evelyn and one of his nephews. And, when she found her power inadequate to her attempt, enraged at her non-compliance, she treated her with the grossest unkindness, and threatened her with poverty and ruin" (14–15) [11]. Evelyn's tragedy stems from a marriage made in the weakness and misjudgment of a bad choice; Caroline Evelyn's destructive marriage is made through a total lack of options. Her victimization at the hands of her stepfather, husband, and mother results, ironically, from her father's bad choices—first, in his marriage and, second, in trusting to his conventional assumptions about his wife's maternal instincts. He leaves his daughter in her mother's financial power because it "never occurred to him that the mother, on her part, could fail in affection or justice" (14) [10]. Evelina's family history is an object lesson on the riskiness of "illjudged" marriages for both men and women, but it seems to stress women's lack of recourse or control in the matter. Even the actions of Madame Duval suggest that women haven't much power once sexual maturity has ushered them into the institution of marriage. Her tyrannies themselves arise from a chaotic rage against powerlessness, and she initially acts "at the instigation of her husband," not from any choice of her own. Although Evelyn suffers from marriage, such suffering arises from his own choices, however poorly conceived or misled; the suffering that awaits his daughter proceeds from masculine prerogative.

The theme of bad marriages and what they do to women's lives assumes more immediacy in the marriage of Mrs. Mirvan, Evelina's female mentor and protector in the first phase of her "entrance into the world." Evelyn and his daughter suggest melodramatic possibilities for resolving the "chance" of marriage-disgrace, humiliation, and, finally, death. The Mirvan women, eighteenth-century foremothers of the Victorian "Angel in the House," act within another set of ideological assumptions characteristic of nonfiction conceptions of femininity in the eighteenth century, the assumptions of many sermons, essays, and various forms of advice to "young ladies" written in the service of women's education: the domestic courage and strength of women maintaining their respectability—at a considerable personal cost in comfort and ease—in women's "sphere," the institution of marriage. The Evelyns' history belongs to the conventions of the sentimental novel or even the romance—the melodramatic romantic disasters so characteristic of the novels of Delariviere Manley and Eliza Haywood, for instances. But Mrs. Mirvan, her daughter, and her mother seem formed on the conventions of female virtue recommended by writers like James Fordyce, Thomas Gisborne, and George Saville, Earl of Halifax. And although these models for female conduct do not directly challenge the masculinist conventions that inspire them—female obedience and subservience to the male—they read as a double message. The Mirvan women are sympathetic, even, to some extent, animated patterns for how a male-dominated culture would have women behave, but their portrayal reveals what such behavior costs a woman in time, trouble, and peace of mind. They give readers an ambiguous message about the role of women in marriage—as both models of conventional correctness in whom Evelina and, by implication, Burney clearly invest their approval, and as walking wounded, illustrations of the personal cost of being such models. Thus they reflect both Burney's need to define femininity in socially conventional terms and her implicit fears about what those terms mean to the quality of female experience.

Mrs. Mirvan's life, especially, is seen by Evelina and the reader as a respectable hell of pained silences and strained, polite smiles that must have been recognized by married women in an age that offered them few recourses to an unhappy marriage beyond putting a decorous face on the matter. Mrs. Mirvan is one of the novel's few, feeble champions of politeness and social sanity and is Evelina's most determined, though inadequate, protector. "This dear lady seems eternally studying my happiness and advantage" (103) [87], writes Evelina, telling Villars that Mirvan is "so infinitely kind to me, that one would think she was your daughter" (73) [61]. Her sympathetic qualities have not been rewarded, however, as Evelina's may be, and Villars' apparently were, by a happy and fulfilling domestic life. Mrs. Mirvan seems to have made one of the marriages that eighteenth-century sermons and educational treatises warn women about. Matrimony is not, for Mrs. Mirvan, a happy-ever-after reward, but a lifelong trial of her forbearance. Whether or not readers find Captain Mirvan entertaining, few could call him a desirable husband, and most would agree with Evelina that "the kind and sweet-tempered woman . . . deserved a better lot. I am amazed she would marry him." Evelina finds the captain "surly, vulgar, and disagreeable," and "cannot imagine why the family was so rejoiced at his return. If he had spent his whole life abroad, I should have supposed they might rather have been thankful than sorrowful. However, I hope they do not think so ill of him as I do. At least, I am sure they have too much prudence to make it known" (38) [31]. Evelina, like the young Burney, has difficulty accepting the idea of marriage "for life with one who must have full power to make me miserable, and perhaps none to make me happy." But Mrs. Mirvan's marriage is testimony to the fact that not all virtuous and sympathetic women feel free to reject dismal offers if they mean economic security and social dignity. Like Charlotte Lucas's marriage in *Pride and Prejudice*, Mrs. Mirvan's suggests that the fairy-tale union of hero and heroine is not necessarily the fate of all good women.

Mrs. Mirvan seems a pattern for how to make the best out of a bad husband, an object lesson in how to survive marital discomfort. As Evelina comments, Mrs. Mirvan's "principal study seems to be healing those wounds which her husband inflicts" (53) [44]. Evelina relates, in her letters to Villars, Mirvan's attempts (usually unsuccessful) to subvert her husband's disagreeable quarrelings by "starting new subjects," or proposing walks after tea, conciliatory and diversionary skills that Burney characterizes as exemplary conduct under fire, making Mirvan a fictional embodiment of courtesy-book patience. But Burney also reveals—even stresses—Mirvan's frustration and discomfort:

> Mrs. Mirvan endeavoured to divert the Captain's ill-humour, by starting new subjects; but he left to her all the trouble of supporting them, and leant back in his chair in gloomy silence, except when any opportunity offered of uttering some sarcasm upon the French. Finding her efforts to render the evening agreeable were fruitless, Mrs Mirvan proposed a party to Ranelagh. (56) [47]

> Mrs. Mirvan, dreading such violent antagonists [the Captain and Madame Duval,] attempted frequently to change the subject. (57) [48]

> . . . every dispute in which her undeserving husband engages, is productive of pain, and uneasiness to herself. (73) [61]

Mrs. Mirvan's life with the Captain dramatizes the discomfort and powerlessness that so much literature (courtesy books, sermons, and educational tracts) warns are commonly the lot of women once they submit to the will of a husband. And if she serves as a model of female patience and forbearance worthy of the pages of Dr. Gregory or Thomas Gisborne, she also lives a fictionally realized life of quiet suffering that gives vivid expression to the psychological cost of model female behavior. Burney is not unusual in suggesting that female duty in marriage may be costly to a woman's mental and physical health—many eighteenth-century writers of nonfiction about the female role in marriage suggest this pessimistic view of the wife's lot. But the suggestion darkens in contrast to the novel's sentimental ideology of women's deserved happiness lying in married love. *Evelina*, I would argue, attempts to sustain this contradictory message about marriage: able to see the pain that the institution inflicts on women and unable to see her way to any alternative, Burney honestly presents us with the moral contradiction between the rightness of Mrs. Mirvan's behavior and the wrongness of its return. The contradiction itself creates an ideological disturbance in the novel, an incompletely articulated expression of uneasiness with the terms of women's lives.

The source of Mrs. Mirvan's discomfort is her husband, Captain Mirvan, whose broad comic humor may or may not blind readers to the role he plays as bully and manipulator—especially of women. Mirvan is, of course, a comic type whose most immediate ancestor is found, perhaps, in the works of Tobias Smollett. A prankster and rough "humorist," Mirvan acts as the satiric vehicle familiar enough in English drama and fiction. But he also illustrates, from Evelina's female perspective, the absolute power of the male in marriage, even over a woman who is superior to him in intellect, morals, and social standing. Mrs. Mirvan is not the only victim of his tyranny; it extends over his daughter, mother-in-law, and Evelina as long as she is "under his protection." When the Captain's practical jokes on Madame Duval make life too embarrassing and uncomfortable for his family to remain silent (their usual defensive response to his whims), his reaction is that of a ship's captain to a potentially mutinous crew: "As to all you, I expect obedience and submission to orders; I am now upon a hazardous expedition, having undertaken to convoy a crazy vessel to the shore of Mortification; so, d'ye see, if any of you have any thing to propose, that will forward the enterprize,—why speak and welcome; but if any of you, that are of my chosen crew, capitulate, or enter into any treaty with the enemy,—I shall look upon you as mutinying, and turn you adrift" (139) [114]. The analogy between the male head of a household and a ship's captain is strained and made comic by the Captain's sea-jargon (shades of Peregrine Pickle's sea-going uncle), but it accurately expresses the male's economic and social power over the women of his family (who apparently take his threats seriously enough not to cross him in his plans).

Mrs. Mirvan's only recourse in dealing with her husband's displeasure is avoidance and smoothing over the damage he so readily inflicts: "Mrs. Mirvan, who never speaks to the Captain when he is out of humour, was glad to follow me, and, with her usual sweetness, made a thousand apologies for her husband's ill-manners" (153) [126]. Similarly, Lady Howard (Mrs. Mirvan's mother), despite her title, house, and the personal strength apparent in her letters to Villars, can only avoid an unpleasant or demeaning contest with her son-in-law through a pretense of ignorance: "I believe that Lady Howard, from the beginning of the transaction, suspected some contrivance of the Captain, and this letter, I am sure, must confirm her suspicion: however, though she is not at all pleased with his frolick, yet she would not hazard the consequence of discovering his designs. . . . Indeed there seems to be a sort of tacit agreement between her and the Captain, that she should not appear to be acquainted with his schemes; by which means she at once avoids quarrels, and supports her dignity" (141–42) [117]. Neither Mrs. Mirvan's matronly status nor her mother's matriarchal position in the family is a match for the willfulness of husband and son-in-law. These women in Evelina's world are models of female powerlessness in the institution of marriage, as well as models of what their society defines as "good conduct"; they embody the everyday, garden-variety pathos of attempting to defend familial serenity and sanity against a culturally

powerful male's disruptive behavior. Burney insinuates into her sentimental love plot the suggestion that marriage is not an automatic escape
from female difficulties: marriage delivers Evelina from unhappiness,
but it also determines a life of powerlessness and discomfort for the
deserving Mrs. Mirvan.

Evelina seems to juggle two apparently contradictory ideas of marriage: the panacea that cures the ills of Evelina's life as opposed to "realistic," even grim notions of marriage. The happier view follows the
expectations raised by comic fiction, of course, whereas the darker
vision of marriage seems to proceed from implications in didactic and
polemical literature about female life, as well as the melodramatic disasters of early eighteenth-century romance fiction. *Evelina*'s mixed
generic heritage determines, to some extent, its mixed views on marriage. But this apparent contradiction may also be the result of Burney's
need to remain honest about both her negative impression of marriage
and her conservative endorsement of traditional female roles. Marriage
is, in Burney's words, "such chance," yet it is also women's *only* chance
at what convention defined as a full life, and the novelist can hardly be
blamed for stacking the deck so that her heroine wins the gamble. Such
"fixing" of the marital game is, in a sense, the fictional correlative of
some rather extraordinary exertions of will to which Burney resorted, in
real life, to ensure her own personal security and happiness. Her fictional resolution of her heroine's problems is an easy, perhaps wishful
version of the forcefulness of her own insistence on marrying only for
reasons of affection and compatibility. Evelina's match is, of course, a
sentimental convention, but it also represents an ideal of feminine happiness in married love that Burney used to defend herself from the
"chance" of less-than-likely-looking marriages—without, however, necessarily expecting the ideal to come true.

Marriage, for Burney as for many young middle-class women in mid-
eighteenth-century England, sustained a double and contradictory ideological value in determining female futurity: although its aspect in
much sentimental fiction offered them escape from the "gulphs, pits,
and precipices" of maturity, other conceptions of marriage in romantic
fiction and, especially, nonfiction didactic and polemical literature for
women codified and institutionalized that maturity's powerlessness. The
stasis and/or regression common to so many literary images of female
life may be a projection of the male-dominated literary mainstream's
fears: what if the linear continuity of consciousness failed? The worst
possibilities are projected as characteristics of women and are therefore
isolated as aspects of consciousness which do not threaten male personal
or social power. Pope can afford to explore the "mystick Mazes" of the
sylphs in *The Rape of the Lock* even though they may imply a chaos
too disturbing to include in the "Mighty Maze" of *Essay on Man:* the

regression and circularity of female life and consciousness can be absorbed by the (ostensible, at least) order of society as part of a reassuring whole. And the institution of marriage is crucial to that absorption.

Cultural assumptions about women's roles in that institution or their relationship to it rationalize the nonprogressive aspect of female life and consciousness as that which contributes to the good of society. As professional or business vocations codify men's lives in terms of progress toward a goal, the vocation of marriage reinforces and justifies the static, nonprogressive vision of female life. Besides serving as ideological packaging for the grimmer aspects of married life, fictional depictions of marriage traditionally signify both personal fulfillment and the social order, as in the endings of dramatic comedies. But late seventeenth- and eighteenth-century conduct literature, educational treatises, and similar forms of advice to "young ladies" anatomize the female role in the institution in a manner poorly calculated to excite anticipation of happiness; the young woman is asked to accept a career that brings early loss of personal gratification and little possibility of worldly reward. These mixed, indeed, contradictory signals created, I will argue, profoundly ambiguous feelings toward marriage in the young Fanny Burney. On the one hand, marriage offered romantic fulfillment, but, on the other, it codified the expectation of almost certain loss as a condition of female maturity by giving the inevitability of loss the importance and form of a cultural institution.

George Saville, Earl of Halifax, for example, in his *Advice to His Daughters*, instructs his young readers "to forget the great *Indulgence* you have found at home. . . . The tenderness we have had for you, *My Dear*, is of another nature, peculiar to kind Parents, and differing from that which you will meet with first in any Family into which you shall be transplanted." Future in-laws will not be the only source of trouble, however; Halifax warns the young women most emphatically about their future husbands. The *"Causes of Dissatisfaction* between Man and Wife" are composed of hardships borne more or less well by women and perpetuated by men. Adultery, drunkenness, emotional and physical violence, sullenness, avariciousness, and stupidity are defects in husbands with which women must learn to live.[4] Halifax does not rule out the possibility of a happy marriage, but he emphasizes the ways in which marriage inevitably makes life worse for women in order to prepare his daughters for the transition from the privileges and power granted them in the nursery to the relative hardship and powerlessness of marriage. Obviously, this approach to female indoctrination into the conjugal role is not designed to engender a progressive concept of life.

Even when love is admitted into the picture of marriage, the literature often sees it as a significant help to getting through a socially neces-

---

4. George Saville, Marquis of Halifax, *Miscellanies by the Right Noble Lord, the Late Lord Marquess of Halifax* (London, 1700; rpt. New York: Kelly, 1970) 19, 10–17.

sary but personally bad business, not as a prize that women can work for: "The state of matrimony is necessary to the support, order, and comfort of society. But it is a state, that subjects the women to a great variety of solicitude and pain. Nothing could carry them through it with any tolerable satisfaction or spirit, but very strong and almost unconquerable attachments." And the chances for this relief are poor, according to writers such as Sarah Pennington: "Happy is her Lot, who in an Husband, finds this invaluable Friend! yet, so great is the Hazard, so disproportioned the Chances, that I could almost wish the dangerous Die was never thrown for any of you!"[5] The unreliability of a husband's love is another constant theme, and writers often follow Halifax's lead in not mincing words about the "conjugal vexations" of the woman subject to the rule of an unloving husband.[6] One has not far to look for Burney's vision of marriage as "chance," a dangerous gamble carrying very bad odds.

Women cannot, however, avoid danger merely by refusing the bet: even if a woman does not marry, the institution of marriage as woman's vocation deforms and embitters her life. As depressingly as marriage is often depicted, it is the organizing principle, the raison d'être of female life. The prospect of failing at this vocation produces anxiety, and the actuality of spinsterhood brings a spiritual degradation grounded in negative social attitudes toward single women and in the real possibility of economic insecurity. Mary Hays describes the young lady groomed for the marriage market: "in dreams [of marriage] her youth passed away; every rising beauty became her rival; and every charm, as it faded, gave a pang to her heart, which was alternatively harrowed by jealousy, by envy, by disappointed hope, and unavailing regret." Finally, disappointed in her life's main goal, the acquisition of a husband, she finds relief in death, deliverance "from the dreadful vacuity of having nothing to do, to hope, or to fear."[7] Hays' condemnation of the role that marriage plays in shaping women's goals and, hence, their lives is hardly mainstream eighteenth-century thought on the subject, but her analysis of marriage's impact on female life, both in and out of the actual state, differs from more conservative ideas mainly in that she rejects the spiritual gratification of doing one's duty and the prospect of postmortem rewards as adequate compensations for the pain of disappointment, maltreatment, and boredom. The importance of religion as a compensatory avocation of women and the strength of social sanction should not be underestimated. Also, many happy marriages, obviously, did exist (Bur-

5. James Fordyce, *Sermons to Young Women*, vol. 1 (London, 1766) 167; Sarah Pennington, *An Unfortunate Mother's Advice to her Absent Daughters; in a letter to Miss Pennington* (London, 1761) 49–50.
6. Samuel Johnson, *The Rambler*, ed. W. J. Bate and Albrecht B. Strauss, vol. 1 (New Haven: Yale UP, 1969) 213.
7. *Letters and Essays, Moral and Miscellaneous* (London, 1793; rpt. New York: Garland, 1974) 84–85.

ney's was one), and much literature (especially novels) puffed mutually satisfying marriage as the most significant worldly engagement of human emotion. But the negative prospect of marriage probably shaped female consciousness as much as rosier visions of conjugal bliss. In Burney's case, the nightmare of hardship, disappointment, or vacuity seems as much a part of her marital expectations as dreams of romantic marriage.

In the *Early Diary*, Burney's reflections on a wedding she witnesses focus on what a poor business it is for the bride—"O how short a time does it take to put an eternal end to a woman's liberty!" (*ED*, 1:17)— and in a later passage she returns to the same theme: "'Tis preparing one to lead a long journey, and to know the path is not altogether strew'd with roses. . . . she [the bride] may not find the road it leads her to very short; be that as it may, she must trudge on, she can only return with her wishes, be she ever so wearied" (*ED*, 1:49). The *Early Diary's* account of Burney's responses to the proposals of one rather innocuous Mr. Barlow gives the impression that Burney saw marriage unsweetened by romantic love as psychic self-annihilation. Burney's record of a conversation with her father at the time of Mr. Barlow's suit suggests that, for Burney, nonromantic bourgeois marriage for economic security was a poor bargain: she would be risking her father's love and protection for an unknown and terrifying state in which she could not fully imagine living, let alone being happy:

> "Oh, Sir," cried I, "*I* wish for nothing! only let me live with you."
> "My life!" cried he, kissing me kindly, "Thou shalt live with me for ever, if thee wilt! Thou canst not think I meant to get rid of thee?"
> "I could not Sir; I could not!" cried I; "I could not outlive such a thought!"
>
> • • •
>
> Thus relieved, restored to future hopes, I went to bed, light, happy, and thankful, as if escaped from destruction. (*ED*, 2:70)

Marriage without love meant, literally, an end to Burney's "future hopes." It was better for her, she seems to have felt, to cling to the known safety and potential future happiness of remaining a "young lady" without definite prospects than to risk a marriage that she sees in terms of personal dissolution. Burney's desire to remain "for ever" with an indulgent father reflects what seems a likely, though probably unintentional effect of instructional propaganda on the female mind: if childhood and early youth are usually compared favorably with the trials of maturity and marriage, one can hardly wonder at a young woman's desire to extend the pleasanter state as long as possible.

In fact, such a desire seems as much an intelligent choice as Freudian regression, and, it would seem from the evidence of courtesy and educa-

tional literature, not an uncommon one. Once women's educators had
thoroughly warned their readers of the difficulties inherent in marriage,
they were apparently faced with the problem of getting young women
to marry anyway. The prevalence of social sanctions against women of
marriageable age who dragged their feet to the altar suggests that Burney
may not have been alone in her resistance to the pressure to marry
young enough to insure economic security. The *Spectator* sends out
warnings to the "demurrer"—she who is "for spinning out the Time of
Courtship to an immoderate Length"—on "what a strange Figure she
will make" when her beauty is gone and marriage is her only economic
and social haven.[8] The *Rambler* approves the parental management of
marriage because leaving women to their own devices allows them to
"trifle away youth and lose their bloom in a succession of diversions"
instead of performing their social duty.[9] Writers frequently warn young
readers about the ridiculousness of the unmarried older woman who
would like to ignore the passage of time—pushing women toward the
very object that they have taught them to dread.

The economic sanctions against women's remaining single are powerful arguments for marriage of which Burney was certainly aware. Samuel Richardson, Mary Astell, and Samuel Johnson discuss the financial
vulnerability of the unmarried woman, and it becomes, of course, a
major feminist issue in the nineties. Burney lived with the reality of a
father who could do very little for her financial security after his death,
and in middle age she took a position at court (much against her own
wishes) with this fact in mind.[1] Economic arguments apparently had
little effect on Burney in the matter of marriage, however. In 1775,
Samuel Crisp urged her to accept Mr. Barlow in order to avoid "the
situation of an unprotected, unprovided woman" (*ED*, 2:54), but Burney was unmoved in her determination to refuse a suitor who did little
worse than bore her, but whom she felt she could not love. Although
the economic motive must have been important enough to Burney's
friends and family to make them push the match, it was not strong
enough to carry all before it, and Burney would not have been without
moral reinforcement in refusing to give in to marriage on the sole
grounds of economic necessity. The heroines of romance—from Haywood's disinterested female characters, who fall in love for every reason
but monetary gain, to Maria Edgeworth's Helen at the end of the century, who specifically comments on women's foolishness in marrying for
money—would have offered Burney fictional precedent for rejecting
the primacy of economic motivation in marriage. And in this case, at
least, fiction is in accord with ideas pervasive in nonfictional writing for

8. *Spectator*, ed. Donald F. Bond, vol. 1 (Oxford: Clarendon, 1965) 377.
9. *Rambler* 1: 214.
1. *Diary and Letters of Madame d'Arblay (1778–1840)*, ed. Austin Dobson, vol. 2 (London, 1904–
05) 361–67.

women. Purely mercenary marriages are the object of Johnson's disgust at midcentury, and Hestor Chapone, at about the time of *Evelina*, advises young women not to risk an unhappy marriage for the prospect of financial security.[2] The Protestant nunnery scheme formulated by Mary Astell in the late seventeenth century and reiterated in the eighteenth by Richardson and Reeve suggests that Burney was probably not without support in imagining a single life as an option; as strong as the economic argument for marriage was, it was probably less overwhelming than the meanings (almost mythologies) that society built around the spinster.

Although the unmarried woman might choose to trade economic security for a pardon from the hardships of married life, she seems inevitably to have been handed a role that defined her as peevish, unattractive, ridiculous, or in some way an incomplete and sorry specimen of femininity. John Gregory warns his readers about "the chagrin and peevishness which are apt to infect their [spinsters'] tempers," and the "great difficulty of making a transition with dignity and cheerfulness, from the period of youth, beauty, admiration, and respect, into the calm, silent, unnoticed retreat of declining years." John Bennett assumes that married women are "generally more pleasing, than such, as never formed the connection"; Edward Moore sees spinsterhood as a "living death," and William Kendrick says that virginity is "unbecoming" in an old woman.[3] The century is not without awareness that such charges are rather cruelly directed at women whose worst fault was living in a society that provided them with few useful and productive roles, but its voice is usually defensive, speaking against a strong and influential opponent: "Those who believe themselves possessed of wit, use it to turn them [spinsters] to contempt and ridicule; not because they are unworthy, but because they are unfortunate. There are few modern Comedies that do not give irrefragable proofs of this—The Aunt Deborah's, and Mrs. Malprop's, are the standing jest of the Modern writers; and even Mr. Cumberland, though a chaste and refined writer, has lent his hand to throw a stone at sisters and aunts who are unmarried, what-

---

2. Johnson exposes the plight of a daughter "tricked out for sale" by a mercenary father (*Idler* 2: 131–34) and lampoons the young women who themselves participate in the "prostitution of the modern marriage market" (*Rambler* 1: 192). Hester Chapone writes: "The calamities of an unhappy marriage are so much greater than can befall a single person, that, the unmarried woman may find abundant argument to be contented with her condition, when pointed out to her by Providence (*Letters on the Improvement of the Mind Addressed to a Young Lady*, vol. 1 [London, 1778] 200).

3. John Gregory, *A Father's Legacy to his Daughters* (London, 1774; rpt. New York: Garland, 1974) 105; Bennett, *Letters* 2: 96 (see also 2: 94–95): A "*single* woman is, particularly, defenceless. She cannot move beyond the precincts of her house without apprehensions. . . . She is surrounded with many, real dangers, and fancy conjures up *more* spectres of its own. . . . As she goes down the *hill* of life, her friends *gradually* drop away from her, like the leaves in the autumn, and leave her a pining, *solitary* creature . . . she wanders through a wide, bustling world, uncomfortable in herself, uninteresting to others, *frequently* the sport of wanton ridicule, or a proverb of reproach"; Moore, *Fables* 79; William Kenrick, *The Whole Duty of Woman* (Boston, 1761) 38.

ever merit they may have, or whatever misfortunes they may have endured." The "stone" so commonly thrown at mature and aged spinsters in eighteenth-century comedy struck sparks from Clara Reeve's normally sedate pen. Society denies the mature, unmarried woman a dignified or even worthy part to play, and then adds to the injury by assuming that the moral deficiency lies with its victim. Reeve writes testily, "Every woman in this situation must be an old maid; or she must be something worse. What then; do you think the latter state the most honorable?"[4]

Thus, if marriage threatened to end a young woman's period of social pleasure and power, it at least saved her from becoming a pariah without even the consolation of her own self-respect. Spinsterhood brings an even more poignant loss of social value than marriage; Samuel Crisp urged the young Burney to accept the lesser deprivation before age left her without the power to do so: "The opportunity [of marriage] is never to be recover'd; the tide is lost, and you are left in shallows, fast aground, and struggling in vain for the remainder of your life to get on,—doom'd to pass it in obscurity and regret. Look round you Fan; look at your aunts! *Fanny Burney* won't always be what she is now!" (*ED*, 2:54). Yet if spinsterhood threatened "obscurity and regret," marriage without romantic love apparently did not seem a significantly better "opportunity" to Burney: her pessimism about women's role in the institution must have been validated later in her life by her sister Susan's grim marriage and early death, brought on, in Burney's view, by her husband's cruelty.[5] Burney's stepsister, Maria Allen Rishton, was also married unhappily, and Burney was her sometimes unwilling confidante during the long process of alienation that ended in separation—against Burney's advice.[6] Once a woman had placed her neck within the noose,

4. Clara Reeve, *Plans of Education, with Remarks on the Systems of Other Writers in a Series of Letters between Mrs. Damford and Her Friends* (London, 1792; rpt. New York: Garland, 1974) 122–23, 125.

5. See Frances Burney, *The Journals and Letters of Fanny Burney (Madame d'Arblay)*, ed. Joyce Hemlow, vol. 4 (Oxford: Clarendon, 1973), for the record of Burney's last correspondence with her sister, and her attempts to promote Susan's return to England and to gain information about her failing health without provoking the wrath of Molesworth Phillips, her sister's sometimes brutal, philandering husband. Susan's death was, perhaps, the severest blow that Burney sustained in her long life, and it cast a shadow over subsequent years as she regularly mourned the anniversary of Susan Burney Phillips' last day alive. In January of 1800, she wrote to Frederica Locke, "She was the soul of my soul—& tis wonderful to me my dearest Fredy that the first shock did not join them immediately by the flight of mine—but that over—that dreadful—harrowing—never to be forgotten moment of horrour that made me wish to be mad—over—the ties that after that first endearing period have shared with her my Heart came to my aid—Yet I was long incredulous—& still sometimes I think it is not—& that she will come—" (386). Unable to cry at the first news of Susan's death, Burney could only vent her pain by screaming (387). Subsequent references are indicated parenthetically in the text with the abbreviation *JL*.

6. Burney wrote to Susan Phillips: "Mrs. Rishton's history is long; but it's catastrophe is brief & briefly therefore I will relate it. When I was with her at Thornham, after quitting my Court service, she first opened to me her heart, & her misery; relating that she had never known real happiness with Mr. Rishton for more than a few weeks, though occasionally, & even frequently, she had had gleams of sunshine upon her discontent. Nevertheless, she had found his character austere, haughty, irascible, & impracticable . . . she conceived a hope of effecting a

Burney seems to have felt that she owed an absolute duty to her husband, whoever he was or whatever he did. Burney's ambiguous attitude toward her stepsister's increasingly unbearable marriage may seem distastefully priggish to us today: her sympathy with Rishton's plight is always mixed with admonitions to duty, and at times Burney almost seems to be hiding from her stepsister, as if she could not bear the combination of emotional empathy and conventional strictness herself. Burney could not see past the conventional limits for acceptable female behavior in the institution of marriage, although she could see quite clearly the suffering that took place within these limits. I suspect that she avoided confronting the implied contradiction in these two perspectives on marriage by holding as firmly as she could to what power she had in minimizing the unpleasanter of the two in her own personal life-prospect. She was, in fact, remarkably strong-minded—and careful—about making her own choice, finally marrying, at forty, the penniless French immigrant, Alexandre d'Arblay—to her own personal satisfaction and against both the wishes of her beloved father and all economic sanity.

One of d'Arblay's attractions for Burney seems to have been his personal and moral dependability; if marriage was, in her words, "such chance," then the only way to guarantee one's safety in the institution was to trust one's self to the right despot, as Burney reflects in a letter to her sister, Susan, just before her marriage to d'Arblay: "if it should, indeed, be my lot to fall into the hands of one so scrupulous in integrity, how thankfully shall I hail my Fate!" (*JL* 2:117). While Burney seems to have accepted the institutions and attitudes that darkened her prospects as a young woman, her response to them was to make as intelligently as possible the choices left open to her. Although she might dread the future, she did not passively accept the hardships and personal degradation implied in contemporary discussions of marriage, and her life, as well as her fiction, bears out the necessity of choosing carefully and knowledgeably among the options presented by female experience.

Burney controls her heroine's destiny as she controlled her own matrimonial course, guiding her through danger to a marriage that enables her to resist the destructive potential inherent in the institution. In her personal life, Burney resisted not only admonitions of writers on female duty, but probably a great deal of pressure, diffused through many areas of eighteenth-century life and letters, to avoid becoming an old maid, a

total separation from Mr. Rishton, & obtaining from my Father an honourable asylum under his roof, with such an allowance from her husband as her own fortune gave her a right to claim . . . she wrote to me almost incessantly, & came to me twice, to consult & counsel. I was always clearly of opinion that whatever were her wishes she had forfeited, by her marriage vow, the right of positively quitting him, if she could not obtain consent" (*JL* 4: 75). Maria's letters to Burney recounting her marital difficulties can be read in the Barrett Collection of the British Museum, and Virginia Woolf writes an account of Maria Rishton's story in "Fanny Burney's Half-Sister."

social pariah and an economic burden. Her novel gave her more choices than her life, or at least gave them to her sooner, and she resolves Evelina's problems more quickly and easily than she did her own; but Burney's fiction and her autobiographical writings seem to agree on a desire to reject the sacrifice of life and happiness to the institutions she both accepted and feared. Fiction could cheerfully and easily uphold Burney's desire not to go gentle into a bad marriage, but it also anticipates her refusal to do so in real life under circumstances often neither cheerful nor easy. Writing allowed her to manipulate the conventional stuff of fictional wish-fulfillment in a way that must have satisfied an understandable desire to escape the difficulty of avoiding real institutionalized dangers to her life and happiness. Yet her novel does not totally deny the dangers: it maintains the integrity of her personal life-choices by placing Evelina's extraordinary marriage in a social context that suggests just how extraordinary it really is. Survival, for Burney, meant sustaining the clarity of her double vision, for giving in to resolution meant either blinding herself to real, present dangers or encountering the new terrors of uncharted regions outside the conventional boundaries of feminine possibility.

While *Evelina* gratifies the desire for a happy ending, to see the heroine one has come to care about richly and happily settled, it may also have gratified eighteenth-century female readers on a different level, that which confirmed their experience of coming to terms with how society defined their lives. Evelina's "entrance into the world" is an entrance into sexual maturity and an introduction to the rituals and institutions that will define the quality of her experiences as a woman. Burney intertwines the discourse of Evelina's innocence and her sexual unselfconsciousness—the story of a passive Cinderella who will be duly rewarded with the prince—with an implied discourse that charts her transition from a protected, idyllic girlhood into the exposed and treacherous territory of young womanhood. Evelina's full consciousness of the dangers she faces, the "gulphs, pits, and precipices" of her future, comes late in the novel with Villars' warning to fly the disappointment and regret that an unrequited love for Orville threatens; the reader who lived with the social realities of eighteenth-century female life, however, may see, as Evelina does not, the deadly serious initiation into female sexual adulthood that places her unselfconscious narration in a socially determined context of imminent pain and loss. The text cues the reader's thoughts to the cultural pattern of marriage and spinsterhood as the forked path of young women's future expectations. Evelina's unselfconsciously experienced initiation into the social institution of female sexual maturity ultimately expresses hope for escape from the unpleasant prospects it implies, but her narrative also unselfconsciously dramatizes the imminence of such sinister prospects.

Villars' second letter to Lady Howard raises the theme of Evelina's "expectations." Villars fears that a trip from Berry Hill into London will cause her to hope for more from life than her social and economic position can offer: "Destined, in all probability, to possess a very moderate fortune, I wished to contract her views to something within it." Evelina's "views" are, Villars goes on to hint, inextricably connected to her expectations from marriage; her economic and social future is indivisible from her sexual future. His concern is specifically for the effects of Evelina's initiation into sexual consciousness and the cruelty and disappointment she must experience in discovering how little the world values her except as a sexual commodity: "The town-acquaintance of Mrs. Mirvan are all in the circle of high life; this artless young creature, with too much beauty to escape notice, has too much sensibility to be indifferent to it; but she has too little wealth to be sought with propriety by men of the fashionable world." Evelina's departure from Berry Hill is, in a sense, leaving behind sexual unconsciousness and the relative security of childhood's idyll; Villars, like the writers of sermons and courtesy literature he so resembles, envisions the probability of pain and loss in that transition. Also like such writers, he sees a season in town as inflammatory to the young's innate tendency to expect too much: "A youthful mind is seldom totally free from ambition; to curb that, is the first step to contentment, since to diminish expectation, is to increase enjoyment" (18) [14]. He fears that she will come to hope for more than life will probably give her. Whatever Evelina's expectations may be, the reader is cued to the low ceiling of possibility and the probable disappointments that characterize her specifically feminine future prospects.

When Evelina takes over the narration, Burney continues to remind readers of the social circumstances that narrow her heroine's chances of a peaceful, happy life through the running account of her relations with Lord Orville. Although she is not, of course, aware of her love for him until Villars' warning letter, her response to Orville expresses the vulnerability of the woman in courtship from the first moment of their meeting, appropriately, at a ball. Evelina's experience in dancing with Lord Orville is a nearly perfect analogue for the terrifying helplessness of a woman faced with the prospect of marriage. She "colours" when asked to dance (which she does not do when Lovel asks her earlier), and is frightened at being isolated among strangers, paired, even "worse, *with a stranger*" (29) [23]. Her terror turns to chagrin and disappointment, however, when she discovers Lord Orville's first impression of her as "*A poor weak girl*": "I would not live here for the world. I don't care how soon we leave town"(36) [29–30]. Evelina unselfconsciously wishes to reject the society in which she seems devalued: Orville's dismissive words reflect what little consequence she has in the eyes of a single, attractive male and, by implication, in the eyes of the social world that empowers him. Without being conscious of the fact, she is proving, so far, the truth of Villars' prediction that she cannot "be sought with propriety by men of the fashionable world." The first assembly is curiously emblematic of a young woman's entrapment in the assumption that marriage is her "career." Being paired off with a virtual stranger is frightening, but being rejected by that stranger increases her vulnerability by spitting her out of the system that is her best means of protection and social acceptance. Although Evelina apparently remains unconscious of any such implications, the reader is reminded of the dependency and precariousness of her social position as a marriageable young woman of no great means.

Similarly, although Evelina never evinces a conscious wish to marry Orville, her generalized admiration of him begins to offer her an important, though unfocused sense of hope for her future happiness. The qualities that attract her to Orville are precisely those that make Villars such a satisfactory protector, thus bridging the gap between the security and happiness of her childhood at Berry Hill and her undetermined future:

> I sometimes imagine, that, when [Orville's] youth is flown, his vivacity abated, and his life is devoted to retirement, he will, perhaps, resemble him whom I love and honour. His present sweetness, politeness, and diffidence, seem to promise *in future* the same benevolence, dignity, and goodness. (72, my emphasis) [60–61]

> I thought there existed another,—who, when *time had wintered o'er his locks*, would have shone forth among his fellow-creatures, with the same brightness of worth which dignifies my honoured Mr. Villars; a brightness, how superior in value to that which results from mere quickness of parts, wit, or imagination! a brightness, which, not contented with merely diffusing smiles, and gaining admiration from the sallies of the spirits, reflects a real and glorious lustre upon all mankind! (261, Burney's emphasis) [217–18]

Orville seems to offer Evelina the hope that there exists among "mankind" a protector as dependable as Mr. Villars. Instead of labeling her feelings as Oedipal and having done with them as tell-tale indications of Burney's repressed desire for her own vital and attractive father, it seems reasonable that Evelina is drawn to Lord Orville—as Burney was to her husband M. d'Arblay—out of an instinct for survival.[7] Villars and Orville are the only two men who seem likely to extend Evelina's personal consequence beyond the courtship stage of her worth as sexual

---

7. Burney wrote to Susan Phillips of d'Arblay, "except in my beloved Father and Mr. Lock, I have never seen such a man in this world, though I have drawn such in my imagination" (*JL* 1:42).

commodity; if Villars gives comfort and order to Evelina's youth, Lord Orville holds out the hope that a man exists who can do the same for her maturity and old age.

Evelina suggests, however, how fragile this hope may be. When Sir Clement's forgery causes Evelina a temporary disillusionment with Orville, her hope and expectation are converted to a pointed unwillingness to look ahead, a sense that happiness lies behind, not ahead of her: "I cannot express the reluctance with which I parted from my revered Mr. Villars: it was not like that parting which, last April, preceded my journey to Howard Grove, when, all expectation and hope, tho' I wept, I rejoiced, and though I sincerely grieved to leave him, I yet wished to be gone: the sorrow I now felt was unmixed with any livelier sensation; expectation was vanished, and hope I had none!" (268) [224]. Even if one is tempted to interpret Evelina's physical illness at this time as green-sickness, the eighteenth century's medical formulation for the ailment supposedly caused in virgins by frustrated sexual desire,[8] the heroine's sexual frustration encompasses a dimension beyond the disappointment of mere lust. Evelina's present sense of her future has come, not coincidentally, I would argue, to depend on her relations with Orville, the means of her romantic escape from a maturity culturally defined in terms of loss. Her letters to Maria Mirvan after her return from London to Berry Hill express confusion over her present circumstances and depression over her future prospects, a state that she attributes to disappointment in Orville and her own mortification. Her pain is, of course, what a heroine of "sensibility" should feel, but it also suggests her physical and emotional vulnerability to what Villars later calls "secret repining, and concealed, yet consuming regret" (309) [255]—a future of lost hopes. The impertinent letter that Evelina thinks is from Lord Orville ostensibly dissolves her confidence in disinterested male behavior—one buffer against the hopelessnes of female expectations. But beyond the limits of Evelina's consciousness, it also implies a damning flaw in the "prince" who is so necessary to the traditional protection afforded to women by romantic love.

Tellingly, Evelina's renewed confidence in Orville after meeting him at Bristol Wells restores her present complaisance and her expectation for the future: "Oh, Sir, Lord Orville is still himself! still, what from the moment I beheld, I believed him to be, all that is amiable in man! and your happy Evelina, restored at once to spirits and tranquillity, is no longer sunk in her own opinion, nor discontented with the world;—no longer with dejected eyes, sees the prospect of passing her future days in sadness, doubt, and suspicion!—with revived courage she now looks forward, and expects to meet with goodness, even among mankind" (278) [229]. Obviously, Evelina is in love, but her words reveal more

8. Dolores Peters, "The Pregnant Pamela: Characterization and Popular Medical Attitudes in the Eighteenth Century," *Eighteenth-Century Studies* 14 (1981): 432–51.

than a seventeen-year-old's crush. To build one's expectations of happiness on the sensitivity and kindness of one man may indeed be love, but it also implies that the young woman's ability to look forward to her life depends on the narrow chance of her future worth's validation by a single representative of masculine social power. Evelina's unselfconscious effusions express starry-eyed infatuation, of course, but they also imply a sense of the power men have over women, the "chance" of finding the lover who will justify female faith in "goodness, even among mankind."

Orville is Evelina's one possibility for lifting the darkness that seems to cover her prospect. The one eligible male in the novel who, in Villars' words, "may be sensible of her worth" (15) [11], he makes it possible for the future to mirror the happiness and security she has known at Berry Hill. Therefore, when Mr. Villars awakens Evelina to her dependency on Orville, and the tenuousness of his protection, Evelina realizes the grim potential of her "friendship" with Orville, the probability that he will not be willing or able to become her friend in the only way that can insure his protection converts her pleasure in his company to dread of the future: "Oh, Lord Orville! could I have believed that a friendship so grateful to my heart, so soothing to my distresses,—. . . would only serve to embitter all my future moments!" Terrified, Evelina re-entrusts her hopes to Villars: "To you alone do I trust,—in you alone confide for every future hope I may form" (322) [266]. She is rather in the position of a trapeze artist who lets go of one pair of hands only to realize in midair that no one waits to catch her—and there is no net.

Evelina's happy ending should not blind us to the implied, though ultimately incomplete, plot of the heroine's negative progress toward emotional deprivation, the barren realms of institutionalized failure. Marriage, or at least the expectation of it, shapes the course of Evelina's coming to maturity, and it is, in Burney's words, "such chance"; the institutions of marriage as woman's vocation and spinsterhood as woman's failure in that vocation form the course of female life into a gloomy prospect, which can be redeemed only by chance or by the woman writer's ability to create better alternatives through conventional sentimentality. The heroine's courtship, although ultimately successful, suggests the pattern that often ends in failure, "secret repining, and concealed, yet consuming regret"—a suggestion that contradicts and disturbs the resolution of Evelina's fears in the fairy-tale-like marriage that guarantees the happiness of her "futurity."

GINA CAMPBELL

How to Read Like a Gentleman: Burney's Instructions to Her Critics in *Evelina*†

In *Evelina*'s dedication, "To the Authors of the Monthly and Critical Reviews," Frances Burney courts her prospective critics' attention or, more precisely, their protection. What is peculiar about this dedication is its tone of instruction:

> The extensive plan of your critical observations,—which, not confined to works of utility or ingenuity, is equally open to those of frivolous amusement,—and, yet worse than frivolous, dullness,—encourages me to seek for your protection, since,—perhaps for my sins!—it entitles me to your annotations. To resent, therefore, this offering, however insignificant, would ill become the universality of your undertaking; though not to despise it may, alas! be out of your power.[4][1]

The extraordinary convolutions of her prose here testify to Burney's embarrassment at her own daring. She demands her critics' protection although she clearly knows that addressing them at all may backfire. Implicit in Burney's address is a criticism of the then-current critical climate for women's novels: she acknowledges that she needs a benign or at least impartial reception and recognizes that it won't be granted as a matter of course. I will argue that Burney includes a model of reading within *Evelina* that resembles conduct literature in its emphasis on propriety and that is meant to serve Burney's literary ambitions by teaching her critics how they *ought to read* her work.

The anxiety that prompts her dedication springs from the critical climate surrounding the publication of novels in general and novels by women in particular. The contemporaneous anonymous reviewer of *Woodbury or, the Memoirs of William Marchmont, Esq; and Miss Walbrook* prefaces the substance of his brief notice with a telling general lament: "Surely the youthful part of the fair sex have as keen a relish for novels, as they have for green apples, green gooseberries, or other such kind of crude trash, otherwise it would not be found worth while to cultivate these literary weeds, which spring up, plenteously, every month, even under the scythe of criticism."[2] The critic's duty, the

---

† From Gina Campbell, "How to Read Like a Gentleman: Burney's Instructions to Her Critics in *Evelina*." *ELH* 57 (1990): 557–84. Reprinted by permission of The Johns Hopkins University Press. The author's notes have been edited for brevity.

1. Frances Burney, *Evelina; or, the History of a Young Lady's Entrance into the World* (New York: Norton, 1965), unpaginated front matter. Both the Preface and the Dedication are unpaginated. All further references are to this edition and will be incorporated into the text. [Bracketed page numbers refer to this Norton Critical Edition. *Editor*]

2. Article 34, *Monthly Review*, May 1773.

reviewer suggests, is to discourage the writing of novels as much as possible in order that cultivated flowers, such as only formal education can produce, may grow. Since women were excluded from formal education, they should, according to the reviewer's notions, also be excluded from publishing.

Even benign attitudes towards women's writing presented problems. As Jane Spencer has noted, the terms of critical acceptance for women's novels were twofold: "When women writers were accepted it was on the basis of their femininity; and the kind of praise they received varied with their readers' conceptions of that quality, so that to some people feminine writing implied eroticism, to others, purity."[3] The two schools of feminine writing were well enough established by the early 1770s that an anonymous publication did not guarantee immunity from *ad feminam* criticism, as this review of *The History of Miss Dorinda Catsby and Miss Emilia Faulkner* makes clear: "Some romance writing female (as we guess from the style) with her head full of love-scenes,—shady groves, and purling streams, honourable passion and wicked purposes,—has here put together a flimsy series of such adventures and descriptions as we usually meet with in the amorous trash of the times."[4] Literary taste-makers were not the only ones to object to the impure strain of women's novels. The popular eighteenth-century moralist James Fordyce warns his female readers against novels in general not only because they "carry on their very forehead the mark of the beast" but also because they convey no instruction.[5] His reaction against novels differs from the critics' dismissal of "amorous trash" chiefly in its emphasis on the shocking effects of novels rather than on their formal failings. Defining herself entirely in the tradition of feminine purity, Fanny Burney in the preface to *Evelina* very carefully distinguishes *her* novel from those that undermine virtue:

> Let me, therefore, prepare for disappointment those who, in the perusal of these sheets, entertain the gentle expectation of being transported to the fantastic regions of Romance, where Fiction is coloured by all the gay tints of luxurious Imagination, where Reason is an outcast, and where the sublimity of the *Marvellous* rejects all aid from sober Probability.

Imagination, as Patricia Meyer Spacks has convincingly argued, was believed by Burney and her contemporaries to be the "*source* of sexual feeling."[6] (In *Evelina* itself, Villars objects to the way Evelina has let Imagination take the reins and lead her ideas about Lord Orville into

3. Jane Spencer, *The Rise of the Woman Novelist: From Aphra Behn to Jane Austen* (Oxford: Blackwell, 1986).
4. Article 30, *Monthly Review*, Aug. 1772.
5. James Fordyce, *Sermons for Young Women*, 2 vols., 2nd ed. (London, 1766) 1: 75.
6. Patricia Meyer Spacks, "Ev'ry Woman is at Heart a Rake," *Eighteenth-Century Studies* 8 (1974): 38.

regions of "fancy and passion"(290) [254].) The only novelist whom critics consistently proposed as a model for women writers, and whom Fordyce exempts from his condemnation of the genre as a whole, is Richardson.

An adoption of Richardson's domestic subject and of his focus on feminine virtue would therefore presumably offer a female novelist some promise of success were it not for the immodesty of publication itself. A woman novelist, such as Burney, who defined herself against the erotic feminine tradition would have to come to terms with a catch-22 built into the virtuous tradition. The eighteenth-century definition of feminine virtue, with its emphasis on modesty, forbade courting attention of any kind:

> This modesty, which I think so essential in your sex, will naturally dispose you to be rather silent in company, especially in a large one. People of sense and discernment will never mistake such a silence for dullness. One may take a share in conversation without uttering a syllable. The expression in the countenance shows it, and this never escapes the observing eye.[7]

Since eighteenth-century notions of modesty required women to be reticent or even silent, for a woman to publish was to define herself as immodest. If only a demonstration of her own probity gives a novelist the hope of escaping the hostile critical reception I have outlined, then the very act of publication ought to jeopardize her reception because it undermines her moral authority. This pitfall haunts Burney. Recognizing it compelled her to try to use the text of *Evelina* to redefine the relationship between male critic and female novelist in a way that permits women to publish and yet to be taken seriously. To this end Burney criticizes the code of feminine virtue for silencing women, invents the ideal critic in Lord Orville and proposes an ideal principle of reading.

In *Evelina; or the History of a Young Lady's Entrance into the World*, Burney emphasizes the parallels between a woman's social reception and a work's critical reception to allow the narrative of Evelina's social success to stand as a trope for *Evelina's* (and thus her own) literary recognition. In the social arena of the eighteenth-century novel of manners, a woman's reputation is established through the reading and/or decoding of her deportment by the doyens of "society," whose guidelines are defined and codified in conduct literature. Conduct books thus serve as an interpretive tool for reading women's behavior, and they constitute women as texts. But this interpretive tool produces simplistic readings: the conduct books' obsession with women's chastity narrows the range of questions asked about women and also narrows the infer-

7. John Gregory, *A Father's Legacy to his Daughters* (1774), *Eighteenth-Century Women: An Anthology*, ed. Bridget Hill (London: Allen, 1984), 19.

ences that one can draw from their behavior. The ways in which a woman's reputation is conventionally damaged in literature—one might think of Daisy Miller, Lily Bart, Cecilia, Cressida—make it clear not only that her reputation ultimately is based on a consensus about her chastity but also that appearance, or the evidence available to the public, is more important than fact or motive. Women in the eighteenth century were read according to interpretive principles that dismiss authorial intent and privilege critical consensus over exegesis.

To succeed with patriarchal critics Burney knew both she and her heroine had to appear to be conventionally good. Thus Burney had first of all to establish Evelina's virtue. But how does one immunize a portrayal of feminine virtue from the kind of derision *Shamela* aims at *Pamela?* Fielding's parody criticizes Richardson's portrait on two levels—he attacks the character Pamela for using her virtue as a commodity, and he attacks the book *Pamela* for titillating its readers. To succeed in her portrait Burney knew she had to make the source of readerly pleasure very chaste. Evelina, therefore, does not report hands groping in her bosom or under her skirts. The more difficult task Burney faced was to create an indisputably virtuous heroine, particularly in an epistolary novel. A character's hypocrisy or villainy is conventionally established by showing a disparity between motive and action. On the stage soliloquies and in novels psycho-narration, quoted monologue, and narrated monologue can establish the nature of a character's motives in moments of unselfconsciousness.[8] But the epistolary novel does not offer these resources because consciousness of an audience is built into the form. Given the inherent selfconciousness of letter-writing, a character's repeated reference to her own virtue does not in itself convince us of that virtue. Indeed it may have the opposite effect, as Fielding's response to *Pamela* makes clear.

Bald self-advertisement will not do, then, but neither will the kind of good deeds within Evelina's powers. Her gender and circumstances preclude her from impressing us with the heroics of a Tom Jones or the philanthropy of a Cecilia. Her range of allowable heroism is restricted by the miniature moral scale of assemblies and houseparties; but good behavior in this arena will not attract particular admiration, since perfect etiquette may well be the product of unthinking conformity. Paradoxically, Evelina proves her virtue by her nonconformity: her ignorance of the forms of etiquette testifies to her pastoral origin, and her tearful explanations of the motives behind her trespasses attest to her superior internalization of the morality on which the rules of etiquette are based. Her *faux pas* give her the opportunity to explain herself, while her embarrassment proves her to have been acting unselfconsciously.

8. I take my terms from Dorrit Cohn's *Transparent Minds: Narrative Modes for Presenting Consciousness in Fiction* (Princeton: Princeton UP, 1978).

The entire case for Evelina's virtue thus rests on moments of self-vindication. Putting aside the embarrassment and remorse she feels over her trivial crimes against form in the first two of *Evelina's* three volumes, I will focus instead on two complex and serious misapprehensions of her motives and one deliberate misreading. The misapprehensions are explicitly presented as problems of readerly interpretation. Evelina's social reception is centered around her gradual conquest of Lord Orville's heart, a conquest that suffers numerous reversals along the way. During one of these setbacks, Orville apparently misreads a note she sends to him. In her ensuing unhappiness, Evelina becomes a book for Villars to read; and later she is made into a poem whose deceptive provenance leads Orville to doubt her character and her regard for him. Both Villars's and Orville's receptions are influenced by Willoughby's willful and self-serving *prior* misreadings of Evelina. To save her reputation with Orville, Evelina must confront Willoughby, as she does in Mrs. Beaumont's arbor. Burney emphasizes the need for a focus on intentionality or interiority by presenting each setback in Evelina's romance twice: once in a social context, where public behavior is the focus of attention, and again in a private context, where motives may be explained. These juxtapositions throw discontinuities between public persona and private self into sharp relief and by extension criticize modes of reading that discount such discontinuities. Furthermore, a demonstration of such discontinuities implicitly recommends a reading or writing process that concerns itself with the relationship between the private self and public mask, and modes of writing, such as the epistolary novel for example, that make the private public. Cumulatively, these juxtapositions establish the purity of Evelina's motives, her virtue, and they validate women's literary accomplishment. Since virtue is an inner state, it cannot contribute to a reputation until it is announced, virtue must publish itself. And by extension, publication and the self-assertion involved in publication is also exonerated. There are situations in which publication is valuable and functions in the cause of virtue.

"Orville" as a Bad Reader

The nadir of Evelina's reception is marked by what appears to be Orville's extremely unflattering evaluation of her decision to write at all. Evelina writes Orville a letter of apology for the way her vulgar cousins have treated his coach. As she herself willingly admits, taking the initiative to write to Lord Orville is not strictly proper, but she excuses herself (to Maria Mirvan) on the grounds that his opinion of her would otherwise be permanently and unjustly damaged by the impudence of the Branghtons, who had shanghaied his coach in her name and damaged it.

Just as Burney in the preface to *Evelina* seeks to clear her novel of the notoriety attached to outlandishly imaginative novels (what the reviewer in the *Monthly Review* would presumably designate "amorous trash"), *Evelina* writes to clear herself of the vulgarity of her associates. The apology to Orville is thus an internal counterpart to Burney's prayer to her critics in her dedication. Both addresses give her interpreters an opening to impugn her motives. In the dedication Evelina is acutely aware that *any* address to critics may be interpreted as an attempt to compromise their integrity: "thus situated, to extol your judgment, would seem the effect of art, and to celebrate your impartiality, be attributed to suspecting it." The ulterior motive Burney disowns is sexualized in the novel; instead of wanting to buy her critics' favor with manipulative praises, Evelina uses her apology to insinuate herself into Orville's favor—at least, that is what the note signed in Orville's name suggests:

> Believe me, my lovely girl, I am truly sensible to the honour of your good opinion, and feel myself deeply penetrated with love and gratitude. The correspondence you have so sweetly commenced, I shall be proud of continuing; and I hope the strong sense I have of the favour you do me will prevent you withdrawing it. Assure yourself, that I desire nothing more ardently than to pour forth my thanks at your feet, and to offer those vows which are so justly the tribute of your charms and accomplishments. (242) [214]

The answering note, which has been forged by Willoughby, Orville's rival, who has intercepted Evelina's letter, reads her letter as an invitation to a clandestine correspondence. Entering into any kind of private exchange with a man before marriage was seen at the time as extremely disreputable in part because it afforded the correspondents an opportunity to set up a tryst. Orville's choice of the word "ardently" suggests that he himself takes Evelina's initiative to have sexual implications. His stated wish to thank her in person invites her to make a private assignation. In this context the promised "vows" do not appear in a respectable light—they may be vows merely of devotion and admiration but, given that suspicious word "ardently," it seems more likely that they would be vows of secrecy in a liaison. Initially exhilarated by what she takes as a declaration of love, Evelina herself on rereading inclines to a less flattering interpretation: "Upon a second reading I thought every word changed,—it did not seem the same letter,—I could not find one sentence that I could look at without blushing: my astonishment was extreme, and was succeeded by the utmost indignation." Her indignation is revived by having to copy the offending letter: "What a letter! how has my proud heart swelled every line I have copied!" (242) [214] Her self-defense requires her not only to relive the insult but to reproduce it.

The insult is not merely sexual. As Judith Newton convincingly argues, when Evelina is commodified by the two Holborn swains, Mr.

Smith and Tom Branghton, her moral worth is discounted. Their treatment of her reduces her to her marriage-market value and, in Newton's
term, denies her idea of herself as "treasure"; it denies the importance
of her virtue and intelligence.[9] The freedom of Orville's letter also com-
modifies her, only more disgracefully. Where the two bourgeois beaux
would marry Evelina, Orville is interested in a clandestine relationship
only; in other words, he excludes her from the marriage market within
his class. His use of the word "justly" in his expressed desire to "offer
those vows which are so justly the tribute of your charms and accomplishments" perhaps stings the most because it slights rather than
rewards the virtue and intelligence that, in a meritocracy like Villars's
pastoral world, would earn love. Evelina's virtue and intelligence are
translated in the letter to "charms and accomplishments," in this context
clearly sexual accessories that define Evelina more securely as sexual
commodity, thus trapping her in a social and economic underworld.

To bring the exchange back into the realm of her own values, Evelina
in turn evaluates Orville's response in a series of rhetorical questions:

> If, as I am very ready to acknowledge, I erred in writing to Lord
> Orville, was it for *him* to punish the error? If he was offended,
> could he not have been silent? If he thought my letter ill-judged,
> should he not have pitied my ignorance? have considered my
> youth, and allowed for my inexperience? (242) [214–15]

In their emphasis on Orville's failure to adopt a protective stance, these
questions recall one of James Fordyce's sermons on shamefacedness in
women, in which Nature speaks:

> "Behold these smiling innocents, whom I have graced with my
> fairest gifts, and committed to your protection? Behold them with
> tenderness and honour. They are timid, and want to be defended.
> They are frail; O do not take advantage of their weakness. Let their
> fears and blushes endear them. Let their confidence in you never
> be abused—But is it possible, that any of you can be such barbar-
> ians, so supremely wicked, as to abuse it? . . . Curst be the impious
> hand that would dare to violate the unblemished form of Chas-
> tity!"[1]

Fordyce's sermon identifies men's responsibility within a code that
requires female chastity—if women are to be innocent, men must be
protective. Fordyce is an external moral authority for Evelina's particular
defense against the aspersions the note casts on her virtue. In a similar
fashion, when Burney addresses her critics, she explicitly brings men's
assigned role as protectors into the relationship between critic and
author, so the rhetorical questions Evelina indirectly poses to Lord

---

9. Judith Lowder Newton, *Women, Power, and Subversion: Social Strategies in British Fiction,
1778–1860* (Athens: U of Georgia P, 1981) 31–32.
1. Fordyce 1: 99.

Orville recapitulate the reading instructions Burney offers the critics in her dedication. Without revealing her sex, Burney, like Evelina, there claims protection on the basis of other attributes she shares with her heroine—youth, ignorance, and inexperience:

> The extensive plan of your critical observations,—which, not confined to works of utility or ingenuity, is equally open to those of frivolous amusement,—and, yet worse than frivolous, dullness,—encourages me to seek for your protection, since,—perhaps for my sins!—it intitles me to your annotations. To resent, therefore, this offering, however insignificant, would ill become the universality of your undertaking; though not to despise it may, alas! be out of your power.
>
> • • •
>
> Let not the anxious solicitude with which I recommend myself to your notice expose me to your derision. Remember, Gentlemen, you were all young writers once, and the most experienced veteran of your corps may, by recollecting his first publication, renovate his first terrors, and learn to allow for mine.

Both in the text of the novel and in her introductory material, then, Burney insists that male readers adopt a protective stance to women and their writing. If they do not, she implies, they themselves breach the code of gentility by which they judge. "Orville" as a bad reader is guilty of just such a breach.

Villars as Bad Reader

Evelina's self-justification to her friend Maria Mirvan, however, does not by itself succeed in comforting her; she needs to be vindicated by a moral authority. Exiled by Madame Duval to Berry Hill, Evelina suffers physically from the misunderstanding. When she does not immediately reveal to Villars the cause of her evident unhappiness, he determines to *read* Evelina:

> But when, at last, I recollected myself, and turned round, I saw that Mr. Villars, who had parted with his book, was wholly engrossed in attending to me. I started from my reverie, and, hardly knowing what I said, asked if he had been reading?
>
> He paused a moment, and then replied, "Yes, my child;—a book that both afflicts and perplexes me."
>
> He means *me*, thought I; and therefore I made no answer.
>
> "What if we read it together?" continued he, "will you assist me to clear its obscurity?" (248) [219]

Villars's mistakes in reading Evelina are facilitated by the habitual textualization of women in good society, where the arbiters of that society (both men and women) read them as though their behavior corresponded immediately to their moral essence. However, as a sympathetic reader, Villars is unwilling to judge Evelina too quickly. He therefore enlists her help in construing her behavior; but his first mistake is to assume that *she* is the problem text. Motivated by modesty, Evelina is slow to testify to Orville's apparent depravity and perhaps reluctant to acknowledge herself as its object. Thus when Villars tries to encourage her to share the secrets of her heart with him as she was wont to do in childhood, she continues to evade him, until she sees that he is misreading her evasions:

> "I must now guess again: perhaps you regret the loss of those friends you knew in town;—perhaps you miss their society, and fear you may see them no more?—perhaps Lord Orville—"
> I could not keep my seat: but, rising hastily, said, "Dear sir, ask me nothing more!—for I have nothing to own,—nothing to say:—my gravity has been merely accidental, and I can give no reason for it at all.—Shall I fetch you another book?—or will you have this again?"
> For some minutes he was totally silent, and I pretended to employ myself in looking for a book. At last, with a deep sigh, "I see," said he, "I see but too plainly, that though Evelina is returned,—I have lost my child!"
> "No, Sir, no," cried I, inexpressibly shocked, "she is more your's than ever!" (249) [220]

Villar's mistake is complex and multilayered. His regret here has shocking implications indeed. "I have lost my child" as a response merely to Evelina's unwillingness to share the contents of her heart seems hyperbolic, since Villars associates "child" with innocence throughout the novel. Evelina's shock at the charge suggests how serious it is. While Villars does not exclude Evelina's person in his prayers for her, he is at least as anxious that she retain her purity of mind. Although he initially reads her exterior for signs of virtue, he knows that true virtue is not continuous with its outward signs. Early in the novel he sends her heaven's blessings with the prayer, "O may it guard, watch over you, defend you from danger, save you from distress, and keep vice as distant from your person as from your heart!" (14) [19]. And in his penultimate letter he prays that she may retain her "singleness of heart" and "guileless sincerity" (320) [279] in her new situation as Orville's bride. But how does one establish the purity of someone's heart? Villars's test for an immaculate conscience is the absence of secrets. He is not ready to come to the conclusion that Evelina has lost her purity of mind until her reserve prompts him to it.

When he is "reading" Evelina, Villars's interpretive method thus brings to the personal, private sphere the rules of conduct that apply to young women in the world, namely that anything secret or clandestine is incriminating. However, as the reading unfolds, the application of this rule for reading conduct broadens. Where publication of private thought had, in Evelina's case, been a means for establishing her feminine innocence, in "Orville's" case it becomes a means for exposing male hypocrisy. Villars's exoneration of Evelina puts the blame squarely on Orville as respondent/critic:

> Your indignation . . . is the result of virtue; you fancied Lord Orville was without fault—he had the appearance of infinite worthiness, and you supposed his character accorded with his appearance: guileless yourself, how could you prepare against the duplicity of another? Your disappointment has but been proportioned to your expectations, and you have chiefly owed its severity to the innocence which hid its approach. (252–53) [223]

Villars's reasoning opposes two terms, innocence and duplicity. If readability attests to innocence, illegibility indicates duplicity. Villars is talking about two styles of morality, hypocrisy versus directness, but his initial textualization of Evelina and his phrasing in this vindication, which emphasizes the innocent reader's (Evelina's) expectation that interiority or "character" is continuous with appearance, encourage one to think of the establishment of virtue and vice as a problem of reading, with special application to the novel of manners. Just as readability of character depends on a consonance between private and public selves, so a dissonance between these selves produces illegibility. Thus Orville's public good manners hide his essential badness, but his private writing reveals that essence. Evelina refers to this disparity when she hands Villars the letter: "See, Sir, how differently the same man can *talk* and *write*" (252) [222]. Similarly, by opening her heart to Villars, which entails showing him a hitherto clandestine correspondence, Evelina proves that she is still Villars's good child, still obedient to the laws of proper conduct, and still pure of mind. The publication of private writing, then, is as much a test of virtue as is the confiding of private thoughts to a moral authority. Throughout the novel the publishability of Evelina's private communication with men proves her innocence and worth just as the publishability of the epistolary, and therefore ostensibly private, contents of *Evelina* proves Burney's innocence of the scandal attached both to novels and to the female authors of novels. Innocent herself, Burney becomes eligible for consideration as a serious writer.

The effect of Villars's misinterpretation, then, is to establish Evelina's and Burney's probity while calling into question the private motives informing the reception of Evelina's note and, by extension, of women's writing in general. Villars's mistakes emphasize the shortcomings of an interpretive approach that fails to take into account the dynamics of critical reception, particularly the misleading effects of reception anxiety. When in response to Villars's hint about Orville Evelina suggests that he take up another book, that is, other than herself, she is also suggesting that the problem lies not in herself as a text but in the hostile response to her letter, Orville's note, which she hands to Villars with the claim that she "*hate*[*s*] Lord Orville" (251) [222]. Villars's misreading of Evelina is based on the effects of "Orville's" prior misreading of her rather than on the essential Evelina—Orville's letter has so shocked her modesty that Evelina's bearing suggests a troubled conscience, and Villars, responding to that bearing, thinks she has compromised her modesty in some way. To correct Villars's mistake Burney simultaneously vindicates Evelina's character (her text) and invalidates Orville as a critic by exposing (publishing) Evelina's note and Orville's improper response to it. By analogy Villars's vindication of Evelina once again puts external critics on their mettle, for Evelina's confidence in Orville's disposition to read her note fairly finds a parallel in Burney's confidence in the critics' fair reception of her novel. In terms of literary reception Willoughby's rationale for intercepting Evelina's letter and forging Orville's response suggests a motive for the suppression of women's writing by *ad feminam* criticism: "Briefly, then, I concealed your letter to prevent a discovery of your capacity; and I wrote you an answer, which I hoped would prevent you from wishing any other" (370) [321]. The suppression of Evelina's "capacity" serves Willoughby's design because it prevents Evelina, who is accessible to him only as sexual commodity, from being recognized as a moral subject. The publication of *Evelina*, similarly, reveals the moral basis of both novels and female novelists.

Orville as Bad Reader

The ramifications of Evelina's first metaphorical textualization as a book casts light on Burney's anxiety about both *Evelina's* critical reception and the riskiness of addressing her critics directly in the preface. With Evelina's second sustained textualization, during which she is turned into a blazon, Burney shows the interdependence of private, critical, and public receptions. Orville allows his private opinion of Evelina to be influenced by the literary reception, evaluative and public, that Willoughby exploits. Orville's misunderstanding of Evelina's motives highlights the ease with which women's reputations may be manipulated as long as women keep silent. When Evelina, according to Villars's instructions, begins to shun Orville as part of her program to suppress her own partiality for him, Willoughby appears and distinguishes her with his attentions. To Orville, Evelina's sudden reserve towards himself, although actuated by modesty and prudence (Villars convinces her that, given her circumstances, Orville cannot be intending to marry her), looks like partiality to Willoughby; and Willoughby does all in his power to encourage such a view. At the same time, a blazon of Evelina is circulated anonymously in the most public room in Bristol, the pump-room. While the publication of this eulogy damages Evelina's reputation, her dutifully assumed reserve towards Orville paradoxically prevents her from clearing herself easily. Although conduct literature of the time associates modesty with reticence, Burney demonstrates that silence in women leaves them and their reputations vulnerable to manipulation. In this way she justifies women's writing without directly attacking the feminine ideal of modesty.

The scene in the pump-room follows closely a revelation that shocks Evelina. At the beginning of the novel it is established that Evelina's mother, *née* Caroline Evelyn, dies in or shortly after childbirth, having been abandoned by her husband, Sir John Belmont. Belmont had eloped with her but, when the dowry was withheld, had burned the marriage certificate, thus leaving her no legal proof of her marital status or of the legitimacy of her child. Gradually Evelina's surrogate parent and moral mentor, Villars, is persuaded that Evelina should seek her father's recognition (and a retroactive clearing of her mother's good name). Villars absolutely refuses to consider a lawsuit on the grounds that it would attract unwanted attention, wounding Evelina's modesty. Shortly before Evelina enters the pump-room, she discovers that her father is travelling with a Miss Belmont, who is being introduced as his daughter and heir. Since the novel builds up to a recognition scene between Lord Belmont and Evelina, the way in which the young men compare Evelina's person to her blazon just when Belmont's eventual recognition of her seems most doubtful may be meant as a perverse or parodic recognition scene, one that, equally public, is as offensive to her modesty as the lawsuit proposed by Madame Duval would have been. The blazon directs attention to Evelina's body but does not, because it cannot, reveal anything about her mind:

> We went first to the pump-room. It was full of company; and the moment we entered, I heard a murmuring of, "That's she!" and, to my great confusion, I saw every eye turned towards me. I pulled my hat over my face, and, by the assistance of Mrs. Selwyn, endeavoured to screen myself from observation, nevertheless, I found I was so much the object of general attention, that I entreated her to hasten away. But unfortunately she had entered into conversation, very earnestly, with a gentleman of her acquaintance, and would not listen to me; but said, that if I was tired of waiting, I might walk on to the milliner's with the Miss Watkins, two young ladies I had seen at Mrs. Beaumont's, who were going thither.
>
> But we had not gone three yards, before we were followed by a party of young men, who took every possible opportunity of looking at us, and, as they walked behind, talked aloud, in a manner at once unintelligible and absurd. "Yes," cried one, "'tis certainly she! — mark but her *blushing cheek!*"

"And then her *eye*—her *downcast eye!*"—cried another.

"True, oh most true," said a third, "every beauty is her own!"

"But then," said the first, "her *mind*,—now the difficulty is, to find out the truth of *that*, for she will not say a word."

"She is *timid*," answered another; "mark but her *timid air*."

During this conversation, we walked on silent and quick: as we knew not to whom it was particularly addressed, we were all equally ashamed, and equally desirous to avoid unaccountable observations. (308) [269]

It is important to note that at the beginning of her report Evelina says every eye was on *her*, but at the end she says none of them knew who was the object of the persecution. The most obvious explanation for this inconsistency in Evelina's report is that she is unwilling to appear conceited to Villars—her modesty keeps her from saying but not from knowing that she alone is attracting all this attention.

Similarly, Evelina's conjecture about the identity of the poem's author serves her modesty more than likelihood. According to her, Mr. Macartney must be the author, and gratitude his motive—a much more becoming speculation than the more likely option that Willoughby is the author, and desire his motive. Yet the last two lines of the poem, "Anville,—to her power unknown, / Artless strikes,—unconscious kills" (315) [275], express not gratitude but desire. True, it is the kind of formulaic expression that a poet might resort to without passionate conviction, but its very conventionality within the courtly tradition suggests Willoughby as its author. He affects courtliness whenever he pursues Evelina, as Newton remarks: "What distinguishes Sir Clement . . . is the persistence with which he imposes upon his control of Evelina the courtly fiction that she *is* Cinderella. . . . Sir Clement's courtly language marks a farcical counterpoint to his behavior. . . . he sustains a running and sometimes hilarious pose as the powerless lover of an unreachable mistress."[2] The sentimental Macartney's characteristic style is more melodramatic and less courtly.

The minor adjustment in Evelina's story thus directs our attention to Villars's importance as addressee. Writing for him constrains Evelina from telling an immodest truth immodestly. As we become aware of Evelina's constraint before Villars, we are simultaneously made aware of how the immodesty of the pursuing swains silences the young women completely. And although the explanation Evelina offers for why they are all abashed is disingenuous, it still seems likely that the persecution she describes, in which a woman's person and mind are judged against the text of a blazon, would have the effect of striking dumb not just its particular victim, but all modest women, for the requirements of female

---

2. Newton 37.

modesty under normal social circumstances dictate reticence. In his recommendation that women be "rather silent" in company, Gregory assures them that "one may take a share in conversation without uttering a syllable. The expression in the countenance shows it, and this never escapes the observing eye."[3] Although Gregory does not gender the eye, in *Evelina* it is male readership, whether Villars's, Orville's, or the swains', that makes women into texts. Being objectified in this way automatically robs women of the subjectivity necessary to authorship. Whether the blazon is Willoughby's or not, it, like his forgery of Orville's note, serves his pursuit of Evelina, for while the publishability of Evelina's heart and behavior attests to her virtue, the publication of her external attributes wounds her modesty, effectually silences her, and thus prevents her from salvaging her reputation directly. Consequently she becomes first the prey of the young men, then of Willoughby himself, who takes advantage of the stir the poem has caused to become her self-appointed protector.

As with Villars's misreading, Orville's misreading involves two texts, in this case Evelina and the blazon of Evelina, and two separate but interdependent scenes of reception. We are presented first with the young men's public reading of Willoughby's version of Evelina and their comparison of the two texts (poem and heroine) before we see her own reaction to the poem. When Evelina gets to read the blazon, it wounds her modesty as much as the swains' reception of her does. Not only is it embarrassingly flattering, but Willoughby makes sure that the circumstances under which she receives it hurt her reputation with Orville: he passes the poem to Evelina in Orville's sight, knowing full well that its nature will prevent her from circulating it and thus defusing the appearance such private note-passing gives. To protect her reputation for modesty Evelina, paradoxically, must do that immodest thing, speak up for herself.

But a direct self-vindication, aside from being immodest, would not be as effective as Orville's accidental witnessing of Evelina's struggle against Willoughby is. Evelina's ongoing battle of wits with the rake reaches a crisis in Mrs. Beaumont's arbor, and Orville's happening on them there gives the same credibility to Evelina's self-defense as might be obtained from an accidental reading of a private form of writing. In other words, the accidental nature of Orville's witnessing guarantees the artlessness of the self-defense. As usual, Evelina opposes Willoughby's seductive rattle with the language of virtue, so that while they are contending over Evelina's chastity, they are also disputing the grounds of social discourse, and Evelina is convincing her patriarchal readers of her virtue.

Willoughby uses the language of courtly love, which accommodates

3. Gregory, in Hill 19.

a wide range of relationships, from platonic admiration, through married love, to adultery, and which is therefore inherently ambiguous.[4] Although Evelina has suspected Willoughby of being a rake all along, in the privacy of the arbor he lowers his usual mask of polite if pointed attention and allows his language to become clearly risqué. About midway through the scene, he offers to allow Evelina to reform him:

> Oh, Miss Anville, your reproofs, your coldness, pierce me to the soul! look upon me with less rigour, and make me what you please;—you shall govern and direct all my actions,—you shall new-form, new-model me;—I will not have even a wish but of your suggestion; only deign to look on me with pity—if not with favour! (326) [284]

Although the reformation of rakes was a conventional feminine temptation, it was notoriously dangerous. (Not every woman is a Pamela.) To look on Willoughby with favor would be to favor him with intimacies, presumably kisses, garters, and, eventually, her maidenhead. Merely to pity him would be to allow him to hope for these favors in the future. The prospect of reforming a rake here clearly comes with a price. According to Willoughby, before Evelina is to gain any influence she must give up her "rigor," that is, her morality. Since he has always valued Evelina exclusively for her prettiness, he predictably seeks to make her into an object by reducing her to her good looks, as the blazon does. Could he elicit looks of passion or at least of interest, those too would be welcome. However, he is indifferent to her regard, which would be an expression of her moral being. In fact he would like to purge moral principles from looks and speech because those principles define her as a moral subject rather than a sexual object, and are also the main deterrent to her seduction.

By insistently using the language of courtly love and responding to Evelina as though she too were using it, Willoughby seeks to pervert Evelina's own moral language. He reads in the spirit of Roland Barthes's *The Pleasure of the Text*. Barthes declares: "The text is a fetish object, and *this fetish desires me*." Barthes analyzes the pleasure gained by perverse readings: "The more a story is told in a proper, well-spoken, straightforward way, in an even tone, the easier it is to reverse it, to blacken it, to read it inside out (Mme de Segur read by Sade). This reversal, being a pure production, wonderfully develops the pleasure of the text."[5] Willoughby's willful misreading of Evelina is sadistic in this way, but Evelina interrupts his pleasure by rigorously insisting on clarity. Willoughby knows he cannot allow himself to be bluntly sexual, but he

4. Thomas A. Kirby, *Princeton Encyclopedia of Poetry and Poetics*, enlarged ed., ed. Alex Preminger (Princeton: Princeton UP, 1974).
5. Roland Barthes, *The Pleasures of the Text*, trans. Richard Miller (New York: Farrar, 1975) 27, 26.

depends on Evelina's propriety to allow his innuendo to pass as long as it presents itself as polite and conventional chitchat. His rhetoric depends on a discontinuity between polite form and wicked intent. By pretending she does not understand his polite language, Evelina leaves him the choice of abandoning his seduction or propositioning her openly:

> "Suffer me, Sir," said I, very gravely, "to make use of this occasion to put a final conclusion to such expressions. I entreat you never again to address me in a language so flighty and so unwelcome. You have already given me great uneasiness; and I must frankly assure you, that if you do not desire to banish me from wherever you are, you will adopt a very different style and conduct in the future."
>
> I then rose, and was going, but he flung himself at my feet to prevent me, exclaiming, in a most passionate manner, "Good God! Miss Anville, what do you say?—is it, can it be possible, that, so unmoved, that with such petrifying indifference, you can tear from me even the remotest hope!"
>
> "I know not, Sir," said I, endeavouring to disengage myself from him, "what hope you mean, but I am sure that I never intended to give you any." (326) [284]

Here it seems pertinent to make a distinction between Barthes's principles and Willoughby's. The reading process Barthes describes is masturbatory, but since it is applied to literary texts, its perversity (if it is perverse) is harmless. Willoughby is reading a woman, however, and his principles in the arbor scene seek to dominate Evelina and do threaten real violence:

> "You distract me," cried he, "I cannot endure such scorn;—I beseech you to have some moderation in your cruelty, lest you make me desperate;—say, then, that you pity me,—O fairest inexorable! loveliest tyrant!—say, tell me, at least that you pity me!" (326) [284]

The phrase, "lest you make me desperate," warns Evelina that her resistance to Willoughby's discourse and logic will provoke him, but to what is not clear.

As both Susan Staves and Judith Newton observe, the threat of violence permeates *Evelina*.[6] Whether the violence is his own or some other man's, the threat of violence gives Willoughby power over Evelina: he exploits the threat of the Captain's violent practical jokes on Madame Duval to indebt Evelina to him; he exploits her predicament at Vauxhall where some drunken men seem convinced of her sexual

---

6. Susan Staves, "*Evelina:* or, Female Difficulties," *Modern Philology* 73 (1976): 368–81; and Newton 23–54.

availability, and attempts to turn the ostensible rescue into a seduction for his own benefit; again, he exploits her anxiety at being followed and harassed by the three youths from the pump-room, whose willing transgression against decorum threatens something worse, to court her himself; and, he himself physically detains her in his coach, in the arbor, and in Mrs. Beaumont's drawing room.

All this pervasive danger requires that Evelina be protected, and Willoughby gains access to Evelina only when she is separated from her rightful guardians. So, in the pump-room, Mrs. Selwyn is too absorbed in conversation to accompany Evelina out of the room, although Evelina's distress would be obvious to anyone with "feminine delicacy." Mrs. Selwyn's indelicacy, specifically her teasing about Lord Orville, also drives Evelina into the garden for the arbor scene with Willoughby. But Orville himself most explicitly neglects his guardianship of Evelina almost immediately after he has pledged his protection as a brother. Evelina's description of his behavior during the blazon debacle suggests that not only her own silence but his inattention to her allows Willoughby to tarnish her reputation with him:

> Lord Orville's reception of us was grave and cold: far from distinguishing me, as usual, by particular civilities, Lady Louisa herself could not have seen me enter the room with more frigid unconcern, nor have more scrupulously avoided honouring me with any notice. But chiefly I was struck to see, that he suffered Sir Clement, who stayed supper, to sit between us, without any effort to prevent him, though till then, he had seemed to be tenacious of a seat next mine. (317) [277]

In the very next paragraph Orville's neglect at the dinner table prevents him from seeing Evelina's tears. Social reception and literary reception are collapsed into one—the circulation (publication) of the blazon attaches notoriety to Evelina's name and person, and, as we have seen, Willoughby cultivates an appearance of indecency in her by making her appear to receive the poem surreptitiously in Orville's sight. When, at the dinner table, Evelina cries over Orville's sudden, pointed neglect of her, Willoughby leans forward to physically block Evelina's tears from Orville's sight. Willoughby's manipulation of Orville's regard for Evelina thus becomes a metaphor for the way *ad feminam* criticism of women's writing screens the real worth of their achievements from serious, principled critics. Evelina regains Orville's attention and protection only after she defends her virtue at length to Villars and the external reader and briefly but urgently to Orville. To persuade Orville to reassume his protection of her, to intercede, Evelina must convince him that her compromising situation in the arbor is not of her choosing by calling to him twice and saying to Willoughby: "Sir Clement, *I insist* upon your releasing me!" (326) [285]. Ultimately her discourse, then, while in itself incapable of protecting her, is a prerequisite for Orville's protection. She must speak her innocence in order to save not only her physical purity (i.e., her chastity) but Orville's estimation of her as innocent.

Willoughby's machinations succeed in making Orville lose interest in Evelina, withdraw his protection from her, and thus deliver her to Willoughby. While Orville's "delicacy" has kept him from invading Evelina's privacy, it has also, as he now can see, kept him from understanding her danger. In this way his delicacy has contributed to Evelina's endangerment as much as has her own modest reticence. Previously, when Evelina recounts how Orville called on the Mirvans on the night of the attempted abduction, Villars praises Orville's freedom from false delicacy. By creating the appearance of indecency in Evelina, Willoughby has now betrayed Orville into just such an error.

Orville As Redeemed Reader

Almost immediately after Willoughby tries to seduce Evelina through *his* ambiguous and illicit discourse in the arbor, a discourse that ultimately rests on male force and the threat of violence, Orville's declaration of his love for Evelina offers a representation of alternate, ideal sexual relations based on a *denial* of male force. Both his interview with Willoughby in the arbor and his actual declaration make it clear that Orville's love is based on his estimation of Evelina as at least his equal. When Orville first asks Willoughby what the rake's intentions toward Evelina are, Willoughby's answering question elicits a reply that establishes Orville outside of any of the normal power relations that subjugate women:

> . . . and then Sir Clement said, "To what, my Lord, must I then impute your desire of knowing [my intentions]?"
> "To an unaffected interest in Miss Anville's welfare."
> "Such an interest," said Sir Clement, drily, "is indeed very generous; but, except in a father,—a brother,—or a lover—"
> "Sir Clement," interrupted his Lordship, "I know your inference and I acknowledge I have not the right of enquiry which any of those three titles bestow; and yet I confess the warmest wishes to serve her and to see her happy." (327) [285]

At issue here is the right to protect. Sir Clement would restrict that right to those to whom a woman "belongs" because that would leave Evelina, who appears to belong to nobody, available to him. However, a father's or brother's protection is not by definition disinterested, as Clarissa's sufferings demonstrate, nor are a lover's.

The disinterestedness that ideally motivates gentlemanly protection removes the threat of male violence from gender relations and thus would seem to permit an escape from patriarchal hierarchy. When pressed, Orville identifies the grounds of his concern in his esteem for Evelina and fear for her innocence. In other words, he is her friend:

> Pardon me, then, Sir Clement, if I speak to you with freedom. This young lady, though she seems alone, and, in some measure, unprotected, is not entirely without friends; she has been extremely well educated, and accustomed to good company; she has a natural love of virtue, and a mind that might adorn *any* station, however exalted: is such a young lady, Sir Clement, a proper object to trifle with?—for your principles, excuse me, Sir, are well known. (328) [286]

From this description it is clearly the value he puts on Evelina's mind and character that permits Orville to imagine a purely friendly relationship to a woman. By contrast, in its careful consideration of the ratio of beauty to booty, Willoughby's assessment of Evelina returns gender relations to an explicitly sexual and financial marketplace:

> I think Miss Anville the loveliest of her sex; and, were I a *marrying man*, she, of all the women I have seen, I would fix upon for a wife: But I believe that not even the philosophy of your Lordship would recommend me to a connection of that sort, with a girl of obscure birth, whose only dowry is her beauty, and who is evidently in a state of dependency. (329) [287]

The difference in the rivals' estimation of Evelina as friend or prey is underwritten by the difference in their attitude towards the use of force. Thus Willoughby's threat of force in the arbor scene is emphasized by Orville's interceding exclamation, "Sir Clement, you cannot wish to detain Miss Anville by force!" (326) [285]. Orville, on the other hand, explicitly rejects force in his declaration:

> "You are going, then," cried he, taking my hand, "and you give me not the smallest hope of your return!—will you not, then, my too lovely friend!—will you not, at least, teach me, with fortitude like your own, to support your absence?"
>
> "My Lord," cried I, endeavouring to disengage my hand, "pray let me go!"
>
> "I will," cried he, to my inexpressible confusion, dropping on one knee, "if you wish to leave me!" (333) [290]

By imagining this new category, "friendship," grounded on mutual esteem, Burney would seem to have found a basis for gender relations that does not of itself define women as inferior. Indeed, Orville's request that Evelina "teach" him makes her his superior. By contrast, Willoughby's request for "pity" is part of the courtly context he imposes on his conversation with Evelina, thus part of his willful misreading of her.

Despite the implications of making a petition, which would suggest
Evelina is in a position of power, the nature of Willoughby's petition
insists on the system of meaning he is trying to impose on their conversation. It thus reinforces Willoughby's power over Evelina as text. Orville's
request that Evelina "teach" him, which comes after he is convinced of
the ineptitude of his former attempts to read her, locates authority in
Evelina. Moreover, since Evelina is to teach him "fortitude," it recognizes her moral authority. The request, then, locates authority in Evelina and bases it on her superior moral nature. In making the request
and granting Evelina authority, Orville redeems himself as a reader.

Ideological Contradictions and Aporia

Each of Evelina's readers locates authority differently. Villars gives the
governing code of feminine propriety authority over Evelina and over
the reading process. For Villars, reading amounts to judging whether
the woman/text conforms to standards of feminine virtue. As judge and
moralist, he shares authority with the moral code by which he judges.
Willoughby retains authority for himself and seeks to impose his reading
on Evelina; reading for him is an act of domination. Orville initially
reads like Villars, but his mistakes lead him to question his own principles so that for him reading finally becomes an act of submission to the
greater authority of the text. Of the three, only Orville's reformed
approach to reading grants women authorial subjectivity and allows
women's writing, including *Evelina*, a respectful reception. Orville's reformation is effected by a subtle definition of male protection, which
according to conduct books is in any case a gentleman's duty towards a
lady. Burney would thus seem to have found a way to succeed as a writer
on patriarchy's own terms. However, Orville's declaration of love is
marked by an aporia that signals the ideological contradictions in Burney's achievement.

Orville's declaration serves a double function: as part of the allegory
of literary reception his recognition of her makes Evelina a peer's peer
and thus represents Burney's parallel wish to be recognized as the critics'
equal. However, as part of a love plot it provides the climax, and as such
it is unsatisfactory. Evelina reports no desire at all; instead her love is
expressed in silence, paradoxically by the collapse of her body:

> I attempted not to describe my sensations at that moment; I
> scarce breathed; I doubted if I existed,—the blood forsook my
> cheeks, and my feet refused to sustain me: Lord Orville, hastily
> rising, supported me to a chair, upon which I sunk, almost lifeless.
>
> For a few minutes, we neither of us spoke; and then, seeing me
> recover, Lord Orville, though in terms hardly articulate, intreated
> my pardon for his abruptness. The moment my strength returned,
> I attempted to rise, but he would not permit me.

> I cannot write the scene that followed, though every word is
> engraven on my heart; but his protestations, his expressions, were
> too flattering for repetition: nor would he, in spite of my repeated
> efforts to leave him, suffer me to escape:—in short, my dear Sir, I
> was not proof against his solicitations—and he drew from me the
> most sacred secret of my heart! (334)[291]

The aporia in Evelina's report of her own feelings during Orville's declaration dramatizes the denial of the body that the rules of propriety
require of chaste women. Evelina merely alludes to that organ of sentiment, the heart, as the locus of the passionate text; she cannot voice her
desire because she is not supposed to feel any.

For different reasons Orville too does not express sexual desire.
Because kneeling is so conventional for the male in love scenes, the
gesture hardly registers its meaning anymore, but Orville's posture
asserts Evelina's power over him in body-language at the same time that
he speaks his submission to her will. In other words, he reverses the
power-structure operating not only in the arbor scene, but in gender
relations generally. Passion is not admitted into Lord Orville's declaration:

> "Mock you!" repeated he earnestly, "no I revere you! I esteem and
> I admire you above all human beings! you are the friend to whom
> my soul is attached as to its better half! you are the most amiable,
> the most perfect of women! and you are dearer to me than lan-
> guage has the power of telling." (334) [290]

This is the entire available text of Orville's declaration, but what is he
declaring? In his esteem for Evelina, Orville does not even permit himself to use the word "love." Instead of a declaration of love Orville's
apostrophe may be seen as a declaration of equality paradoxically based
on inequality, for by calling Evelina his "better half," he suggests that
she is simultaneously his superior and his equal. This paradox reflects
Burney's acknowledgement of the inequity produced by superior
strength in men. Along similar lines, Burney goes to some length to
establish Orville's non-violence before the proposal scene. In the scene
itself she has him insisting on Evelina's moral superiority in an effort to
compensate for his physical advantage: by subordinating his will to her
superior will he neutralizes his ability to detain her by force and
removes the threat of force that Willoughby relies on for his access to
her. However, language fails him just when he is about to say how
"dear" she is to him. All Burney is able to do, then, is to distinguish the
basis of Orville's desire from the basis of Willoughby's; Orville cannot
articulate the desire itself lest it upset the balance of their equality. The
declaration scene's function as a scene between lovers is incompatible
with its other function as proleptic trope for Burney's recognition by her
critics because the first requires some show of desire, but, in *Evelina*,

sexual desire introduces gender inequality via the ubiquitous threat of male violence, including, at least implicitly, rape. Burney does not want to admit *any* inequality into the relationship between male critic and female writer.

While it may be difficult to avoid reproducing existing hierarchies in any text, Burney handicaps her project of winning authority for women at the outset by deciding to write from within the patriarchal code of feminine propriety. The way *Evelina* reinscribes the literary patriarchy is most clearly illustrated by the importance Burney gives to male protectorship. Just as a gentleman's protection ostensibly shields a woman from rape and preserves her reputation, a critic's protection shields a woman writer from misreadings that violate her text and her literary reputation. Now although this protection is available to innocence, the determination of innocence requires an act of reading: a man, potential protector or rapist, gauges (reads) the woman's relationship to sexuality and acts according to or in despite of *his* interpretation, which is not guided by a woman's simple "no" because within the code of modesty that trammels her she has no "yes." Thus, as Ellen Willis has pointed out, male protection, insofar as it depends on a woman's innocence, denies her desire and will, her autonomy as a sexual subject, and reinforces her objectification.[7] Burney's insistence that men, to be gentlemen, must be protective of feminine innocence potentially turns every gentleman critic into an interfering moral mentor and keeps the critical eye trained on women writers' personal probity.[8] Insofar as a focus on their personal behavior turns women into texts, the critical stance Burney implicitly recommends, in which gentlemanly attention is given only to innocent writers and their innocent texts, thus paradoxically has the effect of fixing both women writers and their texts as the objects of the interpretive, evaluative male gaze.

Whether as writer or as addressee, Villars, representing the ideology of conduct literature, constructs for Evelina an ego-ideal she continuously struggles to approximate even while her struggle implicitly criticises some aspects of it. As the emphasis in conduct literature on female chastity and feminine modesty suggests, this ego-ideal is based on a denial of female desire. So, while Burney can afford to have Evelina transgress against minor laws of etiquette in order to demonstrate her thorough probity, she cannot have Evelina and she cannot herself transgress against this major tenet of conduct literature, nor is there any indication that she might want to: hence the emphasis on Evelina's modesty, and on *Evelina*'s chastity as a text. Having accepted chastity as a require-

---

7. Ellen Willis, "Feminism, Moralism, and Pornography," *Powers of Desire: The Politics of Sexuality*, ed. Ann Snitow, Christine Stansell, and Sharon Thompson (New York: Monthly Review Press, 1983) 460–67.
8. Martin Price in conversation.

ment for morality in women, Burney cannot have her heroine express an autonomous sexual desire. But in the absence of female sexual autonomy, which depends on the recognition of female desire and the absence of male force, any male desire is threatening, hence she also cannot allow her otherwise innocuous hero to express *his* sexual desire. Orville's incongruous, slightly ridiculous declaration of equality or, rather, subordination to Evelina takes the place of a true equality, which the values of conduct literature that Burney accepts precludes. *Evelina's* aporia in the declaration scene, then, hides the fundamental contradiction of trying to assert gender equality within a patriarchal paradigm. While Burney recognizes that the silence the feminine ideal of modesty imposes on women can be a tool for reducing women to sexual objects, her unwillingness to renounce chastity means that in representing desire between equals she emasculates the hero, obliterates the heroine's body, and fails to report any passion. The proposal scene thus reasserts the silence of modesty that Burney combats in her account of Evelina's textualization.

Evelina is a book for Villars, a blazon for the swains; her heart is the engraved text of Orville's avowals, as, later, it holds the text of filial tenderness towards Belmont.[9] Not just during the declaration but during all these textualizations Evelina is curiously speechless. Burney would thus seem to privilege the authority of the (private) text over the authority of (public) speech, as Evelina does when she denounces what appears to be Orville's hypocritical note: "See, Sir, . . . how differently the same man can *talk* and *write!*" (252) [222]. As I have already suggested, since the virtuous text that substitutes for Evelina's speech is so often located in her heart, textualizing Evelina is a strategy for unequivocally publishing her virtue as well as valorizing publication in the literary sphere. Throughout her novel Burney discredits speech, and substitutes writing as the only medium of truth in the novel. In the declaration scene it is no surprise, therefore, to find that the truth of Evelina's feelings cannot be spoken; however, for the first time it also cannot be written in the letter to Villars, and it cannot be read. The emotion that is too strong for utterance we must assume to be sexual desire in Evelina; in Burney the parallel unutterable desire is her ambition to succeed with her critics. Disguising her writerly desire is the cost of her pact with the critics, in which she agrees that in the expectation of being read by gentlemen, she writes like a lady.

9. During her second interview with Belmont, Evelina exclaims: "Oh, Sir . . . that you could but read my heart!" (366) [318].

SUSAN FRAIMAN

Getting Waylaid in *Evelina*†

Evelina or The History of a Young Lady's Entrance into the World
(1778), Frances Burney's first published work of fiction, has long been
her most acclaimed, its seeming lightness and familiarity making it generally more acceptable than the darker books to come. *Evelina's* theme
of innocence abroad and epistolary form sit easily with traditional conceptions of the eighteenth-century novel; its domestic realism and satirical wit may be seen to anticipate if not directly to influence Jane
Austen's shaping of the novel for the subsequent century. Much of *Evelina* is legible in terms of our expectations for comedies of manners. Yet
for all that is reassuringly known, elements of Burney's first novel remain
strange and disturbing to students of *Pamela* and *Emma*. There are,
in this text (as elsewhere in Burney), repeated episodes of unabashed
brutality—victimizing most of the female characters and villainizing
most of the men—innocently registered by its heroine in letters to her
guardian. In addition, there is what looks like a *Bildungsroman* or narrative of education, leading at last to greater wisdom and appropriate part-
nering, which appears at the same time to advertise its insufficiency. For
while *Evelina's* subtitle describes a girl moving forward, its story leaves
us doubting whether she has in fact succeeded in doing so.

I want to take up the observation that Evelina's "entrance" rapidly
dead-ends, that her "formation" leaves her nonetheless immature, and
tie this to an ideological debate ongoing in Burney's text and in the
contemporary discourse about female formation. This novel, I will
argue, stages a conflict between two views of courtship from a growing
girl's perspective: in one view it passes for successful education, a female
approximation of male *Bildung* (which typically involves more formal
training and step-by-step maturation); in the other, on the contrary,
courtship is construed as antithetical to a girl's growing up. *Evelina*, in
my reading, is thus a work revealingly at odds with itself, continuing to
invoke and value some "masculine" notion of progressive, linear development, even as another geometry of obstructed female development
emerges. My project here is to map the less obvious and far less optimis-
tic developmental narrative in tension with the linear—what we might
call Burney's antiromantic account of female formation ending with
marriage. I do this by focusing on the violence against women that, as I
have noted, is so remarkably pervasive in *Evelina*.

Local sites of violence may be taken, I suggest, as figures for the over-

† From Susan Fraiman, *Unbecoming Women: British Women Writers and the Novel of Development* (New York: Columbia UP, 1993) 32–58. Copyright © 1993 by Columbia University
Press. Reprinted by permission of Columbia University Press. The author has removed some
of the original notes and rewritten the original text slightly.

all violence of the antiromantic narrative, identifying as rude arrest the marital conclusion so often seen as happy quiescence. Again and again the women in this novel are forcibly kept from doing what they would and made to do what they would not—Madame Duval dragged, dropped, and roped to a tree; elderly ladies raced and bet on like horses; Evelina herself so often ungently constrained—and the sum of these small imprisonings is a general, distinctly gendered, logic of impediment. Reading the end of *Evelina* through its many instances of women hindered or coerced, the heroine's nuptial knot (tying off her education) may be seen as the culmination of this logic, continuous with all previous obstruction and restraint. In this context it represents the ultimate waylaying of Evelina's destiny, at one with the waylaying of Madame Duval's coach. At the same time there is, as I say, a more overt and reassuring narrative, in which Evelina does appear to grow wiser as well as happier: the romantic story of a girl for whom true love is knowledge and marriage signifies completion. Yet this progressive apprenticeship is understood to be only problematically available to the heroine. Its purposes, I suggest, are several. First, it disguises the less acceptable tale of blockage and frustration, providing a consoling cover story. Second, wishful as well as fraudulent, it registers the appeal of a soaring trajectory. And finally, it indicates the currency of such a trajectory in the late eighteenth century as a female version of *Bildung*.[1] My object is to show how in *Evelina* this steadily climbing narrative is drastically undercut—its developmental myth placed at an ironic remove—by the circling counterstory that leaves Evelina back where she began.

I want first to evince more specifically what I am calling the logic of impediment and to show how it drives the plot whose dizzying circularity this chapter will trace. Its principal effect is a satiric and sadistic rewriting of the fairy tale, so that the very man who saves the heroine from distress takes advantage of her trust and gratitude to assault her in turn. As prince turns repeatedly into dragon, rescue into recapture, and relief into trepidation, Evelina begins to doubt not only the world but also her own ability to interpret it. More than simply blocked, she is worn down almost, as she says, to death. This holding pattern is familiar from nightmares and gothic novels, and its presence in Burney causes Margaret Doody to place her in a quasigothic tradition. In a full-fledged gothic novel such female terror is everywhere, while in Burney's later novels *Cecilia* (1782) and *Camilla* (1796) it is relegated, Doody

---

1. *Evelina* (1778) precedes by seventeen years the work conventionally regarded as the original *Bildungsroman*, Goethe's *Wilhelm Meisters Lehrjahre* (1795), and *Bildung* per se would not emerge fully as a concept until the twentieth century. Nevertheless, *Wilhelm Meister* was clearly indicative as well as constitutive of a generally progressive graphing of middle-class male development in the last half of the eighteenth century. Like Kristina Straub, I am arguing both that female development at this time was conceived along different, less triumphant lines and that the "male" model was, however, partially available to women, if only as the romantic myth of courtship as educational process (*Divided Fictions* [Athens: U of Georgia P, 1987] 4, 36–38).

explains, to fits of madness from which the heroine recovers or bad dreams from which she finally awakes. What interests me about *Evelina*, by contrast, is the sane, waking terror it deals in. Like Austen's *Northanger Abbey*, Burney's first novel locates danger to women neither in a peculiar state of consciousness nor in some dreary, implausible dungeon but on the street and in the carriages, ballrooms, and domestic settings of the realist novel.[2]

II

I will offer three examples of the logic of impediment at work in *Evelina*, observing that this logic is no sooner shown than disowned, for just as the telling of female obstruction intensifies, the text habitually reverts to the nicer story of gratification and growth. In the first case Evelina and the Branghton sisters, having strayed into a dark alley at Vauxhall, are ambushed and encircled by a "riotous" party of drunks. As Evelina recounts, "Our screams were answered with bursts of laughter, and for some minutes we were kept prisoners, till at last one of them, rudely seizing hold of me, said I was a pretty little creature."[3] Struggling furiously, she manages to free herself only to be blocked by a new gang of gentlemen. One of them, she writes, "placed himself so directly in my way, calling out, 'Whither so fast, my love?'—that I could only have proceeded by running into his arms" (181) [163]. Her captors leer and tease until suddenly the aristocratic rake Sir Clement Willoughby, recognizing Evelina's cries, rushes forward to her rescue. As his friends applaud enviously—"Willoughby has all the luck!"—Sir Clement conducts the ingenuous heroine to a still darker alley where he offers the "protection" of his more private advances (180–84) [162–65]. One effect of this passage is to code the flattering language of courtship—phrases of endearment and possession such as "pretty little creature" or "my love"—as a vocabulary of assault. Another is to depict in vignette the "progress" of courtship as the barring of Evelina's way, forcing her into imprisoning arms. Here in small, then, is the very repetition of constraint, the same systematic interception of Evelina's impulse forward, which in my view characterizes this narrative as a whole.

But once displayed, such logic is, as I say, quickly covered over. Finding his victim unyielding, Sir Clement exacts her pardon with surprising ease, and even her anger toward him abates more quickly than seems right. The reason for this involves not only Evelina's vulnerable female-

---

2. In her preface, Burney makes a point of distinguishing *Evelina*'s setting from those "fantastic regions of Romance, where Fiction is coloured by all the gay tints of luxurious Imagination, where Reason is an outcast, and where the sublimity of the *Marvellous* rejects all aid from sober Probability."

3. Frances Burney, *Evelina; or, The History of a Young Lady's Entrance into the World* (New York: Norton, 1965) 181 [163]. Subsequent references are to this edition and are indicated parenthetically in the text, with references to this Norton Critical Edition following in brackets. [*Editor*]

ness but also her precarious class position. Unacknowledged by her patrician father (Sir John Belmont), adopted by an obscure though gentlemanly cleric (Villars), and much ashamed of her "vulgar" maternal grandmother (Madame Duval), the heroine's social standing is conspicuously ambiguous. Thus when she and the noble Sir Clement rejoin her lowly relatives and the blatantly bourgeois Mr. Smith, Evelina's smarting sense of gender disadvantage is compounded by anxiety about class; it is no wonder that she takes advantage of a vacillating status to position herself, this time, on the side of power. Closing ranks with the man who has just deceived and assailed her, Evelina now joins Sir Clement in sneering at Mr. Smith. This alliance with nobility compensates Evelina for recent events, but only at the cost of denying their brutality. Identified with Sir Clement, Evelina leaves his indictment to Madame Duval, and even that brash grandmother, refusing to call Clement a gentleman, has difficulty voicing her suspicions: "I wonder, child, you would let such a—such a *person* as that keep company with you" (185) [166]. (Here she fulfills precisely that maternal duty she is alleged to shirk, as I explain later.) Sir Clement answers with a well-turned lie: "I believe you will not regret the honour I now have of attending Miss Anville, when you hear that I have been so happy as to do her some service" (185) [166–67].

Evelina says nothing, and in this she allows him to revise their encounter, letting the record of her harassment give way to a more decorous version. She bows to this version to the extent of deciding, by the end of a letter that began with the attack at Vauxhall: "*Nothing* could be more disagreeable to me, than being seen by Sir Clement Willoughby with a party at once so vulgar in themselves and so familiar to me" (my emphasis; 192) [172]. Of course, Madame Duval and her noisy kin are easier targets because less privileged than Sir Clement. Further, Evelina's vulnerability in the alley had actually to do both with her femaleness and with assumptions about what class of female she is— "the prettiest little actress I have seen in this age" (181) [163], one man says. It makes sense that Evelina should take shelter in snobbery. But if we are made to see this, we are also, and more forcefully, shown its effect: to obscure the routine abuse of lower-class women by ruling-class men behind the myth of chivalry and the fact of class prejudice. Nor does *Evelina* let hostility toward Sir Clement dissipate entirely, for even as the heroine's anger is displaced onto her middle-class cousins, it is stammeringly revived by Madame Duval, who proceeds to keep up a tirade against that "person" for the rest of this letter. As Evelina remarks in closing, "There is no apprehension of his visiting here, as Madame Duval is far too angry to admit him" (192) [172]. Though seeming to speak about her grandmother, the Evelina who succeeded in rebuffing Sir Clement continues to insist that a woman's outrage can keep a man from entering. Throughout *Evelina*, a leakage of female anger from the furious story of women deterred will keep this narrative, however receded, in partial view.

In my second example, as in the first, the pattern of impediment is inflected by hierarchical class as well as by gender relations, although here the heroine's snobbery works to occasion instead of to conceal the incident. Evelina is sitting in the cheap seats, suffering terribly from her cousins' concern with money and indifference to opera. Sir Clement's arrival promises escape, and she is desperate enough to ignore his ominous eagerness. Abandoning Madame Duval and believing the gentleman takes her to Mrs. Mirvan's more fashionable set, she ends up alone with him in his coach—taking the long way home. Once again, apparent liberation twists into a new captivity. Here, too, the "good" man slips unnervingly into "bad." And, in the deliberately misdirected coach, we are offered an additional image of female destiny gone awry; like the larger antiromantic narrative, it takes the heroine in circles, carrying her on and on, and always to the wrong address. Evelina's account of what follows is necessarily euphemistic. Her sexual innocence prevents her from articulating the precise danger posed by Sir Clement, and this, paradoxically, jeopardizes that innocence.[4]

> He caught hold of me, exclaiming, "For Heaven's sake, what is the matter?"
> "I—I don't know," cried I (quite out of breath). . . ."
> "You amaze me," answered he (still holding me), "I cannot imagine what you apprehend." (87) [83]

Later on Sir Clement makes Evelina promise not to tell. As before in the alley, so now in the coach they agree to overlook his indelicacy— although even before promising, Evelina, knowing something is up, can scarcely say what. Yet while the girl in the carriage cannot pronounce "seduction," her letter manages to describe it in nonetheless vivid detail. She writes that Sir Clement had seized and was passionately kissing her hand, when she cried out in terror, "If you do not intend to murder me . . . for mercy's, for pity's sake, let me get out!" (87) [83]. Susan Staves sees this cry as further euphemism: "Her vocabulary can hardly include terms directly descriptive of sexual assault and rape."[5] To me it operates on two levels: as euphemism and, at the same time, hyperbole. Though Evelina never does identify the threat, her fear is perfectly, even extremely, conveyed. As in my first example, the account of Evelina's persecution is elided only partially, for through the polite version both the full extent of Sir Clement's villainy and the process of its disavowal

---

4. Richardson's Pamela neatly inverts this paradox: if Evelina almost loses her status as virgin by being so obliviously much one, Pamela protects that status by being, in terms of her sexual awareness, hardly one at all. The result is that, while Evelina's innocence is constantly threatened, Pamela's is constantly suspected.
5. Susan Staves, "Evelina: or, Female Difficulties," Modern Philology 73 (1976): 371.

can be quite readily perceived. In these two scenes involving Sir Clement, *Evelina* not only dramatizes female anger provoked and then muted; it also, returning to the scene of the crime and telling what the heroine promised not to tell, recovers that anger and the story behind it.

This second case of rescuer-turned-assailant is structurally identical to its earliest and paradigmatic instance in *Evelina*, which I take as my third example: the tragic story of Caroline Evelyn, mother of the heroine raised by Villars and briefly recovered by her mother (Madame Duval) before being married and disowned by the profligate Sir John Belmont.[6] The obvious culprit here is Sir John, his rescue/betrayal of Caroline the original sin that generates Evelina and *Evelina* in the first place: the heroine and the heroine's quest for her father's recognition. But here the logic of impediment puts an interesting spin on the standard seduction plot. Usually marriage is the safe harbor reached by a Pamela Andrews or Lydia Bennet[7] after weathering the storm of seduction or its threat. But this time, by some sleight of hand, marriage is not the haven it appeared to be but is itself another danger. Sir John's deception reveals that even marriage may be a form of entrapment, and this insight will necessarily shade the meaning of the book's final union. As I have suggested, Sir John's place in this schema is the same as Sir Clement's in the last. Like Sir Clement, he is a highborn man offering a girl escape from her lowborn mother or grandmother (Madame Duval), and his intentions turn out to be dishonorable. One implication of this paradigm is a warning against snobbery and a loyalty to maternal as opposed to paternal figures that Burney critics have largely neglected. But what interests me most is the light it sheds on Villars's still earlier "rescue" of the daughter from her mother, since in this his position in the paradigm strongly resembles Sir John's and Sir Clement's.

Could the kindly, aging, clerical Villars possibly belong to the category of "redeemers" with ulterior motives? Does he, too, introduce the daughter to a species of captivity? At first glance this affectionate father appears irreproachable, as critics unanimously agree—yet given that *Evelina's* pattern of abuse depends precisely on the slide from saint to devil, even the holiest of male figures may be suspect. I am going to argue that Villars is indeed implicated by this pattern, defined by Sir

---

6. *Evelina* is actually derived from an earlier manuscript entitled "Caroline Evelyn," so that the story of Evelina is generated by the mother story both inside and outside the novel. The burning of "Caroline Evelyn" in a fit of guilt and remorse (on Frances Burney's fifteenth birthday, June 13, 1767) is one of the more sensational moments in a career vexed by ambivalence toward female authorship. The reincarnation of this older, completed text as *Evelina's* prehistory accounts for its unusual fullness. It has the effect, in keeping with my argument, of marking Evelina's entire life as *repetition*, her story but a doubling of her mother's. Thus the recurrence of constraint that organizes Evelina's single life also operates across women's lives, from one generation to the next.

7. Characters from Samuel Richardson's *Pamela; or, Virtue Rewarded* (1740) and Jane Austen's *Pride and Prejudice* (1813) respectively.

John and Sir Clement, in which the man abducting a daughter from her mother proves to be a scoundrel in spite of claiming to save her. In fact the novel's first sin may be not Sir John's refusal to acknowledge his relation to either mother or daughter, but Villars's much-replicated refusal to acknowledge and respect the mother-daughter tie.[8] Above all, I would stress that to view Evelina's guardian as in some sense her jailer and her mother's jailer, to see his direction as misdirected, is effectively to recast—as downcast—the narrative that begins and ends in his arms. I want to turn now from these mini-tales of obstruction to the masterplot they indicate: the overall courtship narrative that kills Evelina's linear momentum by circulating her between Villars and (his surrogate) Orville, so that even in this largest movement of her life she is passed from one spurious redeemer to another. However exemplary they may seem, both Villars and Orville further *Evelina's* logic of impediment by participating in local instances of hindrance such as those detailed above and, even more, by tracing out between them the regressive path of Evelina's destiny.

To elaborate on this characterization of Villars I want to return to the issue of female anger in *Evelina*, which as we have seen is closely tied to its antiromantic narrative. In fact, the novel begins with a woman's rage in two respects. The earliest letter we get in terms of the novel's fictional chronology is Caroline's dying outcry—"most cruel of men!"—against Sir John. In the context of Burney's text, however, this letter does not appear until chapter 74. Instead the novel starts with Madame Duval's explosion at Villars, conveyed to him in a letter from Lady Howard:

> Her letter is violent, sometimes abusive, and that of *you!*—*you*, to whom she is under obligations which are greater even than her faults, but to whose advice she wickedly imputes all the sufferings of her much injured daughter, the late Lady Belmont. (1) [8]

Mediated (and later echoed) by Lady Howard, Madame Duval's fury at Villars engrosses *Evelina's* opening page. Such a placement of female wrath serves, first, to sound it as one of the book's important motifs. In addition, by situating Madame Duval's maternal curse at the abducting surrogate father *before* the more obvious anger of the abandoned woman, it offers an unexpected etiology of seduction. One might say it starts the story of betrayal earlier, beginning not with the daughter's entrance into the world, but with her seclusion from the world by her father. It traces Sir John's cruelty and Caroline's cry back to Caroline's "ill-advised" (1) [8] upbringing by Villars, judging him complicitous in the crime against her.

8. If this is the original wrong the narrative strives (and, I believe, fails) to repair, then its underlying agenda may be not the misleading and redundant search for the father but the search (more integrally tied to female identity) for the mother. Perhaps Evelina does not advance in part because she misconstrues her quest.

Yet given that at some level the novel seems to credit Villars as father and discredit the Frenchwoman as mother, why should anyone believe her claim to the contrary? For one thing, Madame Duval's maternity is quietly but carefully authenticated by her extreme grief at Caroline's death (5) [11], her undeniable joy at recovering Evelina, and her despair when Evelina almost faints—"Let me not lose my poor daughter a second time!" (42) [44]. Though Villars accuses her of expressing no interest in Evelina, we are specifically informed she was prevented from doing so by a despotic husband (42) [44]. It was also this husband, and not Madame Duval, who instigated plans to marry Caroline against her will (4) [11]. Similarly it is Branghton, Senior, who invents (though Madame Duval would implement) the parallel plan to unite the unwilling Evelina with the acne-aged Branghton, Junior. A close reading of these instances suggests that Madame Duval is not merely a tyrant, but also tyranny's servant and further—what her continual abuse by Captain Mirvan serves to stress—its victim. She is also an unexampled mother in one decisive regard. If a warning against seduction is critical to eighteenth-century maternal discourse, Madame Duval enters this discourse more persuasively than anyone else. Mother figures Mrs. Mirvan, Mrs. Selwyn, as well as Villars, caution Evelina against Sir Clement, and her actual mother offers a warning by example. But only Madame Duval—by scorning male approval, spurning female modesty, and roaring with indignation at her own molestation—actually practices the self-defense they preach.

Villars, on the other hand, conveys at best a mixed message, bled by qualification, and this contributes not a little to his ward's developmental bind. In tones reminiscent of eighteenth-century conduct books by James Fordyce and John Gregory, he exhorts Evelina in terms that waver indecisively:

> Though gentleness and modesty are the peculiar attributes of your sex, yet fortitude and firmness, when occasion demands them, are virtues as noble and as becoming in women as in men: the right line of conduct is the same for both sexes, though the manner in which it is pursued may somewhat vary, and be accommodated to the strength or weakness of the different travellers. (202) [180–81]

Women, according to Villars, are gentle in contrast to men, but no less firm than men, at least when the occasion demands; women's right line of conduct is the same as that for men, but they pursue it differently because they are weaker. When it comes to resistance, in short, a disabling double standard is briefly questioned before being nervously reasserted. Further, the abstraction of Villars's advice from the sexist practices of her culture leaves Evelina dangerously unprepared to cope with them. Her first days in London teach her that female modesty means deference to men. She learns to squelch her dislike for Lovel,

hide her preference for Orville, and accept both these men's objecti-
fying views of her. Captain Mirvan, she finds, can mock his daughter
with impunity—"He began some rude jests upon the bad shape of her
nose, and called her a tall ill-formed thing"—while the women "have
too much prudence" to retaliate in kind (27) [31]. And Evelina is all
the more educable in acquiescence because of the inexperience Villars
has cultivated. Her rusticity calls attention to her as a curiosity and easy
target, while rendering her, for fear of committing a faux pas, all but
unresisting. The illegibility to her of high society, because it puts her
continually in the wrong, makes confidence unlikely and indignation
impossible. Along with her contemporary, Mary Wollstonecraft, Burney
seems to equate the "innocence" so prized in women with a bumbling
ignorance that only abets their exploitation.[9] Patricia Spacks tells us this
equation occurred to not a few women novelists of the eighteenth century, "whose hidden anger at the implications of the idea finds expression in the train of misfortunes they devise for their innocent heroines."[1]

Not only did Villars twice nurse (in mother as in daughter) such
highly exploitable innocence, there are numerous hints he did so for
selfish reasons. His paternal feelings are, Evelina implies, over-tender;
indeed he measures his love for Caroline by conjugal standards: "To me
she became so dear, that her loss was little less afflicting than that which
I have since sustained of Mrs. Villars herself" (4) [10–11]. Likewise,
regarding Evelina he seeks a husband who appears, in this ambiguous
sentence, to be himself: "My fondest wish is now circumscribed by the
desire of bestowing her on one who may be sensible of her worth, and
then sinking to eternal rest in her arms" (5) [11]. Little wonder, therefore, that Villars explains the cloistering of his ward in terms that are
defensive, apologetic, and even confessional. In his letter to Lady Howard, he comes close to admitting that the mother's demerit was trumped
up to indulge the father's desire: "Even had Madame Duval merited the
charge she claims, I fear my fortitude would have been unequal to the
parting" (5) [12]. "Such, Madame, is my tenderness," he pleads, "and
such my weakness!" (6) [12]. All this in his very first letter, followed by
one that begins: "I blush to incur the imputation of selfishness. In
detaining my young charge thus long with myself in the country, I consulted not solely my own inclination" (7) [13]. The blush, indicating
passion under pressure; the detention, implying an application of force;
the admission that he did indeed consult his own inclination while
appearing to consult her interest—all of these liken the virtuous Villars
to the scandalous Sir John and Sir Clement more than one might initially have thought.

9. In A Vindication of the Rights of Woman (1792), Wollstonecraft demands: "If then women are
   not a swarm of ephemeron triflers, why should they be kept in ignorance under the specious
   name of innocence?" (19).
1. Patricia Meyer Spacks, "Ev'ry Woman Is at Heart a Rake," Eighteenth-Century Studies 8
   (1974): 30.

They support, at least, Sir John's contention, and my own, that the "good" father is not so simply opposed to the "bad":

> It seldom happens that a man, though extolled as a saint, is really without blemish; or that another, though reviled as a devil, is really without humanity. Perhaps the time is not very distant, when I may have the honour to convince your Ladyship of this truth, in regard to Mr. Villars and myself. (143) [130]

Sir John never does pinpoint Villars's blemish, but he does raise a question about Villars's complexion that the text in general supports. As I have tried to show, Villars's rescue/confinement of Caroline/Evelina may differ in degree but not essentially in kind from Sir John's more notorious betrayal. Both men take advantage of female dependency to satisfy themselves. Both possess a young woman (whether briefly or permanently) in a way that impairs her self-possession. Both, finally, are aroused by an enfeebling female innocence, and the roles they play in relation to this are complementary: Villars fetishizes the intactness that makes its violation by Sir John a thrill. He overprotects the chastity that, Nancy K. Miller notes, in eighteenth-century fiction "attracts rape as the sacred invites sacrilege."[2] In practical terms, he teaches the docility and imbecility that make Sir John's scheme plausible. The significance of this blurring between chaperon and ravisher, between good father and bad—linked to a slippage between right suitor and wrong—cannot be underestimated. Its effect is to shift the blame for violence against women from the anomalous rogue to *paternalism per se*. It suggests that patriarchy itself is the villain.

I have been trying to argue that the similarity between "Villars" and "villain" may signify. It is a likeness that sets off a whole train of speculations about names involving "ville," popular in French novels and curiously ubiquitous in this English one. It serves, for one thing, to link "Villars" to "Orville"—adored by Evelina and universally admired by critics, who chide him for nothing worse than woodenness—and to associate "Orville" in turn with "villainy." The etymological case against Orville is clearer when we consider that, by *Cecilia*, the leading man's name has modulated to "Mortimer Del*vile*." In this second of Burney's novels, Orville's devilish successor does not defile, but does defraud the heroine before finally marrying her (nor is his first name consistent with a wholly comic outcome). The other reference in "ville" is, of course, to "city": the place Evelina seeks, like many a would-be *Bildungsheld*, to find the world and her place in it. She goes by the name of "Anville," a homonym for "*en ville*" or "in the city." What can we make of the fact that Orville is a homonym for "*hors ville*" ("outside the city") except that he is somehow opposed to her "entrance into the world?" Indeed, if we

---

2. Nancy K. Miller, *The Heroine's Text: Readings in the French and English Novel, 1722–1782* (New York: Columbia UP, 1980): 217.

look at Evelina's "progress" in terms of her name, we see only a retreat from worldliness, a flight from urbanity: the Miss *Anville* who begs to go to London leaves the city by way of the pastoral *Belmont* and ends up decidedly *Orville*. Her marriage, then, would seem to be semantically at odds with her desire for knowledge and her impulse to enter a less sheltered space.

I want to preface my discussion of Orville—in what sense he could possibly be, like Villars, a villain barricading Evelina's way—by recalling one of her early social blunders. To avoid dancing with Sir Clement, Evelina pretends to be preengaged. Sir Clement dogs and pesters her, faking indignation at his mystery rival: "I long to kick the fellow round the room!—unless, indeed,—(hesitating and looking earnestly at me,) unless, indeed,—it is a partner of your own *creating?*" (30) [34]. Tired and disconcerted, Evelina finally names Lord Orville, who profits from the confusion to engage her on the spot (for the rest of the book, as it turns out). Orville, is to be sure, portrayed in appealing contrast to his fellows, and it is easy enough to share Evelina's admiration for his almost feminine delicacy. Yet this question of Sir Clement's remains in the air, suggesting to me that the gallant hero who saves Evelina from the wicked rake may well be a convenient fiction—made up by Evelina in her effort to resolve the difficulties of courtship and useful to that narrative strain satisfied with marriage as the capstone of female development.

This comic strain is, as I have argued, contested by a less euphoric one, and here Orville and his relation to Evelina's quest are portrayed in more ambiguous terms. In fact, Lord Orville's dishonorable rival, Sir Clement (like Sir John in relation to Villars), occasionally seems less this lord's foil than his darker alter ego; at times the two men's actions or words are disturbingly continuous, complicitous, and even temporarily confused. The confusion of Clement with Orville follows the commandeering of Orville's coach by Evelina's pushy relatives. Evelina sends the coach owner a polite apology and gets back an insultingly passionate reply, signed "Orville." The pen turns out to have been Sir Clement's, but in the meantime Evelina and the reader are asked to believe that Orville is capable of a rakish turn. Evelina's first impression upon reading the letter is delight; it is only on a *second reading* (242) [214] that she recognizes the disrespect underlying its elaborate praises. We are invited by this, I propose, both to suspect Lord Orville's chivalry and to subject chivalry itself, its encomium to women, to a second reading; Evelina's double take on this letter models, it might be said, just that mode of double reading in which we are presently engaged.

Evelina provides many examples of an ugly, gang-banging kind of male bonding. Sir Clement helps Captain Mirvan torture Madame Duval, just as Captain Mirvan helps Sir Clement get his hands on Evelina. In the alley scene I have already described, Sir Clement's cohorts stand by smirking as he carries off their prize. It is by precisely this kind of misogynist complicity that Orville, too, seems compromised. As Evelina disappears into the gaping jaws of Sir Clement's coach, for example, Lord Orville stands by and watches resignedly (85) [81]. His attempt to intervene is perfunctory (Evelina wonders at how little he insists), and one senses at work a gentlemen's agreement concerning territorial rights. Even Evelina guesses that Orville "had a suspicion of Sir Clement's design" (89) [85], and the reader knows that Orville, man of the world, could hardly have mistaken his friend's intent. So what is intended by the curious "half smile" (85) [81], with which he bids Evelina good night? Is Orville trying to smile encouragingly, in spite of his fears for her? Or is he trying *not* to smile, in spite of his knowingness and the vicarious pleasure this induces? How different, finally, is Orville's expression from the smirks of Clement's other cohorts under similar circumstances?

This is not the only occasion on which Orville fails—by appearing to tolerate if not condone what *Evelina* defines as immoral male behavior—to be a credible redeemer. There is also his unpardonable good humor about Lord Merton's and Mr. Coverley's racing of elderly women for sport. The episode opens with Merton and Coverley determined, out of boredom, to drive their phaetons against each other for one thousand pounds. The ladies are alarmed, prompting gentle Orville to suggest they change the bet "to something less dangerous" (269) [237]. What began as a contest in machismo (Merton versus Coverley), now becomes a contest between two modes of masculinity (Merton/Coverly versus Orville): though both aim to bolster male esteem, the first dogmatically ignores or offends women, while the second assumes an attitude of deference toward them. When Orville's proposal passes, deference triumphs, and it seems to be from sour grapes that Coverley, reverting to his own terms, compares Orville's driving to an old lady's. Evelina tells us that "this sally occasioned much laughter" (270) [237], apparently injuring Orville, since later he half-jokes about escaping Coverley's wit (277) [244]. But clearly it is Orville who carries the day, for his ostentatiously humane suggestion—"The money should be his due, who, according to the opinion of the judges, should bring the worthiest object with whom to share it!" (274) [241]—succeeds in enchanting Evelina.

How unprepared one is, then, for Orville's announcement on the following day that

> to his great satisfaction, the parties had been prevailed upon to lower the sum from one thousand to one hundred pounds; and that they had agreed it should be determined by a race between

two old women, one of whom was to be chosen by each side, and both were to be proved more than eighty years of age, though, in other respects strong and healthy as possible. (277) [243]

While the gist of Orville's achievement is to lower the stakes, his "great satisfaction" appears to include the whipping on of two women in what must be, for them, a life-threatening activity. Could this be Orville's answer—I'll show you who the *real* old ladies are—to Coverley's quip?

Can this be the same man who, out of respect for womankind, seemed to offer a moral alternative? Now this prince-turned-dragon laughs off Evelina's surprise, admires the quaintness of her qualms, and admits that he never expected his humane proposal to be effected. As Orville matter-of-factly takes up the New Bath Guide, the distinction between competing masculinities collapses, noble courtier falling in upon vulgar boor. Of course these modes have distinct class connotations, which *Evelina* has already dismantled by picturing Lord Merton et al. as skirt-chasers and gluttons, inattentive at the theater, ignorant of the classics, and surpassing their social inferiors only in ribaldry.[3] Here, by portraying the *chevalier par excellence* blithely content to bruise old ladies, Burney once again tarnishes the tale of the knight in shining armor.

The point is driven home by the actual race, depicted in shocking detail. At a spot Orville has helped to choose, the men watch and cheer as the frightened contestants stumble repeatedly. Grandmothers run aground, they "complained of being much bruised; for, heavy and helpless, they had not been able to save themselves, but fell with their whole weight upon the gravel" (293) [257]. At this, their backers rush up with chairs and wine, reviving the women only to set them back on track. When Coverley finds his help unavailing—"the poor creature was too much hurt to move" (294) [257]—he suddenly becomes "quite brutal: he swore at her with unmanly rage, and seemed scarce able to refrain even from striking her" (294) [257]. Men who "help" the frailer sex, *Evelina* continually implies, usually have their own interests at heart, and when these are foiled, the force underlying their relation to women is soon enough explicit.

The race is followed by another case in point. Resuming his ongoing harassment of Evelina, Lord Merton drunkenly belies his "high-flown compliments" by resorting to violence, much to the company's distress and Evelina's terror. But the brutality of a Coverley or Merton is hardly surprising; the reader is more intrigued by the behavior of an Orville, and throughout these events Burney's hero is notably inactive. Never

---

3. Thus Burney participates in what Terry Eagleton describes as a general critique of aristocratic culture by the eighteenth-century middle class: "pitting the values of thrift, peace and chastity against a violent and profligate nobility (*The Rape of Clarissa* [Oxford: Blackwell, 1982] 6). In Burney's hands, as in Richardson's, the eighteenth-century novel helped to formulate this critique.

once during the race does he register the faintest disapproval, though Evelina imagines he looks "grave." Later he appears "thoughtful," and when Evelina is actually under attack his expression becomes, strangely enough, one of "earnestness" (294) [258]. He watches thus, biding his time until virtually everyone else has tried and failed to loosen Merton's grip, before at last disengaging her. We feel he is right to apologize for not interfering sooner, and can only remember the blamable earnestness of his gaze. Instead of sharing Evelina's "undissembled anger," Orville seems again to anticipate her molestation with mixed emotions, going almost so far as to participate in it as voyeur.

At moments like these, Orville slips from a boys-will-be-boys complacency into being, himself, one of the boys. He is arguably also of the fraternity in two telling conversations about female beauty. In the first, Orville joins Lovel in an extended meditation, in her presence, on Evelina's blush. Where Lovel means to insult, Orville intends to admire, but they likewise ensure that Evelina will continue to exhibit the phenomenon in question. Sir Clement and Captain Mirvan join in, and as the exchange concludes on a self-congratulatory note—Sir Clement pronouncing Orville "a *connoisseur* in beauty," Orville terming him "an enthusiast" (68) [67]—Burney's message emerges: though Orville savors Evelina instead of gulping her with Clement's gusto, he is equally guilty of appraising her as if she were a wine or a cheese.

The topic of the second conversation is still girl-watching, and Orville is droning on about nature and art and female beauty, much as he did in the earlier scene. Captain Mirvan begs to differ:

> "I should be glad to know what you can see in e'er a face among them that's worth half-a-guinea for a sight."
> "Half-a-guinea!" exclaimed [Orville], "I would give half I am worth for a sight of only *one*, provided I make my own choice." (96) [90]

Though meaning to disagree, Orville actually proves himself simply a more extravagant version of Mirvan, no less willing to estimate female value in monetary terms. Accepting the Captain's commodification of women, he finds himself once more sharing metaphorical ground with someone he thought to disdain. Complaining of Lord Merton's unmatched rudeness (Clement seems gracious by comparison), Evelina has earlier remarked that the "*audible whisper* . . . is a mode of speech very distressing and disagreeable to by-standers" (94–95) [89]. This is clearly the register of both conversations above, since they force Evelina to hear herself discussed in tones neglectful of her presence. I suggest that the whisper of masculinist discourse in a woman's ear may also approximate the register I would audit in this chapter.

Usually Orville's underlying condescension to women is so genteelly phrased as to pass unremarked. It is discernible, as I have tried to show, only in relation to Sir Clement's leer and Captain Mirvan's sneer, at which point its distant kinship to these becomes apparent. Orville is repeatedly guilty by association: with Sir Clement and Lord Merton, rabid womanizers; with Captain Mirvan, unapologetic woman-hater; and with Lovel, whose failure to be the first has made him the second. I want, however, to close my discussion of Orville by considering a case of more direct and independent willingness to regard women as objects for his purchase and use. Whereas Clement and Merton immediately place the illegitimate Evelina in the class of molestable not marriage-able women, Orville is distinguished chiefly by his more ennobled view of the heroine, even before her real aristocratic status is disclosed. As he says to Sir Clement:

> This young lady, though she seems alone, and, in some measure, unprotected, is not entirely without friends; she has been extremely well educated, and accustomed to good company; she has a natural love of virtue, and a mind that might adorn *any* station, however exalted: is such a young lady, Sir Clement, a proper object to trifle with? (328) [286]

Several pages later he proposes. Yet Orville does not question the prac-tice of trifling with unprotected ladies, only the choice of Evelina instead of a more "proper object." Orville reclasses Evelina, perceiving the imminent aristocrat in her, but he accepts, as unthinkingly as Sir Clement or Lord Merton, the dichotomization of women along class lines and the marking of lower-class women as fair game. Mrs. Beau-mont weakly claims, upon learning that Evelina is of noble birth and affianced to a nobleman, "The young lady's rank in life, your Lordship's recommendation, or her own merit, would, any one of them, have been sufficient to have entitled her to my regard" (363) [315]. In fact the whole book has gone to show the insufficiency of Evelina's own merit, in the absence of elevated rank, to secure her from insult. Her indefinite class status means that she is treated like a goddess one minute and taken for a prostitute the next. Balancing her bastard heroine on the thin line between male reverence and derision, Burney offers an inci-sive analysis of her culture's unstable, contradictory, and class-bound images of women.

Burney notes, moreover, that upper-class women also suffer, their pedestals the props of a chimerical chivalry. Lord Merton, she makes clear, treats his fiancée with only slightly more veiled disregard than he does Evelina. Nor is the loftiest woman ever secure, for as Maria Edgeworth's Belinda is warned: "Even a coronet cannot protect a woman, you see, from disgrace: if she falls, she and it, and all together, are trampled under foot" (181). With a bitterness shared by most women writers of the period, Burney uses Evelina and Caroline to show that a woman's position essentially depends on whether men call her madonna or whore. Though Evelina angrily objects to just this shifting, double view of women when she discovers it in Sir Clement—"he seems disposed to think that the alteration in my companions authorises an alteration in his manners" (186) [167]—she manages to overlook a comparable alteration in her beloved Orville. It occurs when Evelina flees an advancing officer and begs two women to protect her. Walking uncomfortably between, as she soon realizes, two prostitutes, Evelina is aghast to spy Lord Orville. "However," she relates, "to my infinite joy, he passed us without distinguishing me; though I saw that in a careless manner, his eyes surveyed the party" (219) [195]. Indeed it is Orville, not Evelina, who is disclosed by this unguarded moment. He has kept his distance as *Evelina's* patrician villains bully women; he has held his own as the same men posture at women's expense; now, faced with underclass women, he frankly discards his chivalrous attitude for the careless one of a Merton or Clement; and if Evelina misses the point, the reader finds it difficult to do so.

Surveying these women's wares, Orville *sees* Evelina but fails to *recognize* her, and in this he further refigures the marital and paternal crimes of that arch-villain Sir John Belmont, who sees but refuses legally to recognize his wife or daughter. By continually assimilating the "right" kind of partner to the disastrously "wrong," *Evelina* echoes the fears of conduct writers such as Pennington and Chapone who warn that marriage is a "dangerous die." I want to conclude and in some sense summarize this section by observing that—in contrast to many eighteenth-century protagonists of enigmatic origins, from Marivaux's Marianne to Fielding's Joseph Andrews—Evelina herself knows who she is from the outset. The issue, I have said, is getting Sir John not to see she exists but to identify her as his daughter, and the effect of rephrasing the problem in this way is to stress the dependence of women on ruling-class men to say who they are and what they may become. While Wilhelm Meister comes to recognize his true nature, the developing heroine becomes recognizable in terms of received female types. Against the fiction of individual self-making, *Evelina* poses a different, overdetermined story of deindividuation and conventionalization.

III

I have been trying to fathom the narrative level at which Villars and Orville are bound to a disreputable brotherhood, one whose predatory view of Evelina (and of women generally) stalks, snares, ambushes her formation. As we have seen, the thwarting of this formation is argued anecdotally by the accumulation of episodes in which Evelina's sense of mobility and potentiality is impaired. It is also argued in larger terms by a plot that runs against the grain of a *Bildungsroman*, shaped instead to suggest circularity, belatedness, and futility. Hardly a critic has failed to notice the resemblance between Villars and Orville, which Evelina describes and their names so strenuously imply. They are, more precisely, inversions of each other, and together their names map the circularity of Evelina's course as she moves from one father figure to another—a circularity literalized by her return to Villars and Berry Hill, hard upon her wedding, with vertiginous haste.

Toward the end of the novel Evelina seems to accomplish two things: first her engagement to Orville, then her recognition by Belmont. But if her marriage, as I argue, is actually regressive, her patrimony turns out to be irrelevant, for she is already Lady Orville by the time she becomes Miss Belmont, legitimate daughter of nobility. Orville's willingness to second-guess her status drains all the urgency from Evelina's quest for her rightful title. Practically speaking, Evelina's reunion with Belmont is belated and therefore useless, and it proves to be further redundant in psychological terms. Bearing her mother's face and letter, Evelina comes to Sir John for emotional as well as material restitution. Caroline's letter imagines her errant husband wracked by guilt and requires him to clear her name and receive their child. In fact, though Sir John writhes through renewed pangs of remorse, he has long since repented his desertion and adopted the girl he believes to be his daughter. As Evelina explains, "At the very time we concluded I was unnaturally rejected, my deluded father meant to show me most favour and protection" (357) [310]. All this yearning after the father to gain a pedigree and apology that are already hers; all this desire for the world only to return to rural seclusion; all this straining away from an overzealous guardian only to marry his mirror image, another man who cherishes the girlish in Evelina and chastens the adult. Surely a sense of futility is intrinsic to such a narrative, as it is to so many of the minor events that beset the women of this book.

I have already referred to the runoff of anger produced by this narrative, too great for the comic story to absorb. Female rage in *Evelina* is most theatrically expressed by Madame Duval and most subtly by Lady Howard, who turns out to be Madame Duval's unlikely ambassador and ally. It is, for example, Lady Howard who takes up the grandmother's suit against Villars, pressing him to release Evelina. "It is time that she should see something of the world" (7) [13], she argues. And later more accusingly: "She is a little angel! I cannot wonder that you sought to monopolize her: neither ought you, at finding it impossible" (10) [16]. Though proper as Mrs. Chapone herself, Lady Howard also joins Madame Duval in urging a lawsuit against Sir John, and when Villars objects, she once again takes up her pen on behalf of murdered mother, disinherited daughter, and irate, neglected grandmother.[4] The blue-

---

4. "A child appear against the father!" (116) Villars exclaims in response to the prospect of a suit against Sir John. Taking the nobleman's side against the women he has wronged, Villars is once again identified with the immoral father. I am arguing, of course, that *Evelina* puts

stocking, Mrs. Selwyn (whose insurgent with has been sufficiently discussed by other critics, notably Rose Marie Cutting), succeeds Lady Howard in this activity of confronting Sir John. Suffice it to say that Madame Duval is but the book's most obviously untamed shrew. Her ranting is reinforced by several less openly obstreperous figures, from Caroline and Evelina to the learned Mrs. Sewlyn and respectable Lady Howard. One purpose of my reading is to situate this ranting in the context of a narrative, to give it a reason and a shape. Throughout much of *Evelina*, however, feminist anger is deflected from its target and redirected against other women. When Captain Mirvan binds Madame Duval's feet and tethers her to a tree, Evelina cuts her grandmother loose, only to be slapped across the face. The slap is partly deserved punishment for Evelina's cooperation with the prank, but it also shows the powerless reduced to brawling among themselves, one mark of those with power being their inaccessibility. Just as Madame Duval's anger at Mirvan falls on Evelina, nearest and weakest, so I have already detailed the diversion of Evelina's anger at Sir Clement onto Madame Duval and her family. Even Mrs. Selwyn, whose satire does skewer a few noblemen, takes out much of her anger on her own sex. Her feminist strategy amounts to a kind of male impersonation, which, though empowering for Mrs. Selwyn herself, reproduces men's scorn for women as a class.

Attention to the way female anger in *Evelina* turns back at women and into self-hatred can help to clarify an otherwise obscure incident: the attempted suicide of Evelina's half-brother, Mr. Macartney. Dressed in black, afflicted by family problems, this latter-day Hamlet would seem odd and extraneous were it not that he serves to dramatize Evelina's inner life. Beth Kowaleski-Wallace has noted the similarity of their circumstances, explaining that, "As her double he embodies the instincts and desires not consonant with Evelina's ideal image of herself, instincts and desires she is not allowed to acknowledge explicitly to herself." [5] Chief among these is hostility toward their father (Sir John) and, in a completion of the oedipal pattern, desire for the mother. Stabbing his father out of incestuous love (for another apparent half-sister), Macartney acts out these feelings all too unsymbolically. As Evelina's double, Macartney externalizes her anger toward her real father, Sir John, as well as father figures Villars and Orville, and invokes a mythic structure supporting my contention that the underlying ambition in *Evelina* is for the mother and not the father. The ultimate superfluity of Evelina's rapprochement with Sir John, the circularity of her passage from Villars to Orville, the barely covert patricidal anger toward these

Villars as well as Belmont on trial for paternal crimes, offering its heroine's double-voiced letters as testimony for both sides, at once defending and accusing the male guardian.
5. Beth Kowaleski-Wallace, *"Evelina," Refiguring the Father*, ed. Beth Kowaleski-Wallace and Patricia Yaeger (Carbondale: Southern Illinois University, 1989) 11.

three figures, all combine to undercut the quest-for-the-father plot. But if Macartney enacts Evelina's rage toward paternal figures, he also enacts the introversion of this rage to a self-destructive degree. The episode of his suicide attempt is clearly a coded portrayal of Evelina's own death.

Macartney expresses his dejection in a fragment of poetry deploring life as a "lingering dream of grief, of pain." His ode strikes a chord in Evelina, who muses ambiguously, "These lines are harsh, but they indicate an internal wretchedness, which I own, affects me" (162) [147]. In this mood, Evelina sees his pistol and thinks immediately of suicide, and the very thought has a deathlike effect on her. "All power of action forsook me," she remembers, "and I grew almost stiff with horror" (166) [150]. Recovering enough to tail him upstairs, the fascinated heroine watches as he takes a pistol in each hand and calls on God to forgive him. Just when he seems about to shoot, Evelina leaps forward, grabs his arm, and—as if she had taken his place—falls down "breathless and senseless" (167) [150]. She awakens in time to wrest away his guns, leaving him wondering what angel has been sent to save him: "Do my senses deceive me! . . . do *I* live—? and do *you?*" (168) [152]. The Branghtons think not, for by the time they arrive Evelina has swooned again. "I seemed to have suffered a violent death," she writes, "either by my own rashness, or the cruelty of some murderer, as the pistols had fallen close by my side" (169) [152]. The Branghtons are so sure she is dead, they don't even bother to help her. Lest this seem an event enabling Evelina to purge a suicidal wish, reject a suicidal double, she concludes her letter on a pessimistic note: "The rashness and the misery of this ill-fated young man engross all my thoughts. If indeed, he is bent upon destroying himself, all efforts to save him will be fruitless" (169) [152–53].

Here, perhaps, is the excessive sentimentality that Austen's *Love and Freindship* would parody in scenes strewn with unconscious female bodies. But in a novel whose heroine purportedly enters the world, such an obvious staging of her exit by suicide/murder seems worth consideration. My sense that it signals despair of a proto-feminist kind is reinforced by another Burney character who attempts suicide: Elinor Jodrell of *The Wanderer*, a cross-dressing advocate of women's rights, is driven mad by a lover who prefers the more traditional heroine, Juliet. Evelina's attribution of her seeming death to either her own hand "or the cruelty of some murderer" would appear to support this reading. The double verdict specifies, too, the alternation I am tracking between reluctance and willingness in *Evelina* to accuse men of murdering female development.

That Evelina's engagement coincides with a form of death is written between the lines of the novel's closing pages. Villars's last letter is overwhelmingly morbid. Should misfortune mar Evelina's happiness, Villars protests, he would die. In any case, he prays only to live long enough to bless her, "closing these joy-streaming eyes in her presence, and breathing my last faint sighs in her loved arms!" (387) [336]. Whether happy or unhappy, Evelina's marriage means death to Villars, his defeat and replacement by a younger man. From this he proceeds to equally fond thoughts of Evelina's own death, wishing her an end propitious as his. "And mayest thou, when thy glass is run, be sweetly, but not bitterly, mourned by some remaining darling of thy affections—some yet surviving Evelina!" (387–88) [336]. Villars does imagine her a timely death, yet his vision of a "surviving Evelina" still serves to identify her with the ill-fated Caroline. What is more, his yen for a second, still-living Evelina has this one already buried. It makes sense for Villars to mourn Evelina, since he loses her twice (first to Belmont and now to Orville). Richardson's *Clarissa*, one might reason, helped to create an appreciative audience for novels concluding in this kind of sentimentalized grief. But if *Evelina* were all it appeared to be—a girl's growing up completed by marriage—it would still typically conclude with a hopeful account of vows, perhaps a hint of progeny to come. That it closes, instead, on a queerly elegiac note should alert readers to another developmental theme.

Evelina's (and the book's) last letter frankly conflates her marriage to Orville with her return to Villars at Berry Hill, sustaining the note of requiem where epithalamion should be. I quote the entire letter, which is addressed to Villars:

> All is over, my dearest Sir; and the fate of your Evelina is decided! This morning, with fearful joy and trembling gratitude, she united herself for ever with the object of her dearest, her eternal affection. I have time for no more; the chaise now waits which is to conduct me to dear Berry Hill, and to the arms of the best of men. (388) [336–37]

The sense of finality, of things being out of her hands, of eternity and time run out; the feelings of joy mixed with fear; the fact that neither Orville nor Villars is mentioned by name—these add up to an impression that Evelina is meeting her Maker instead of her lover. The very briefness of the letter suggests a shortness of breath, a running down of words, a laying down of arms. Words have been, throughout, Evelina's best defense against assaultive experience. As the novel's preeminent narrator, she wields more power than she herself knows. To a large extent, her meanings, both conscious and unconscious, have prevailed. The loquacious Sir Clement, by contrast, speaks for himself only once—in the short, rude letter that Evelina contains inside one of her own. Clearly letters give Evelina a kind of control that, away from her writing desk, she rarely has. Ultimately, they slip beyond her control, hazarding judgments, mounting oppositions, which may have more to do with the novel's intentions than they do with Evelina's own. In her opening letter, for example, Evelina means to remain a dutiful daughter, within the geographical limits Villars has set. But the appeal of transgression, the determination to see London, continually leads her pen astray.

> Pray don't suppose that I make any point of going, for I shall hardly sigh, to see them depart without me, though I shall probably never meet with such another opportunity. And, indeed, their domestic happiness will be so great,—it is natural to wish to partake of it. I believe I am bewitched! I made a resolution, when I began, that I would not be urgent; but my pen—or rather my thoughts, will not suffer me to keep it. (13) [18–19]

This has been my point about *Evelina*: that its heroine's pen is bewitched and her letters, like those of women conduct writers, haunted by dissident meanings. Though Evelina aims to tell a story of growth and fulfillment, her tale is countered by another of hindrance and frustration, and marriage to Orville does not break so much as chime with the gothic rhythms of this narrative. And if marriage serves to keep Evelina from getting anywhere, it also, by ending her letters, eliminates what has been her only mode of complaint. The heroine's amusing tongue-tiedness on first meeting Orville appears to have been prophetic, for that lord no sooner claims her—"You are now," he declares, "all my own!"—than Evelina's usual spring of words runs dry: "I could make no reply, indeed I hardly spoke another word the rest of the evening; so little talkative is the fulness of contentment" (386) [335]. Leaving its heroine in happy silence, *Evelina* challenges us to recuperate its other story of female destiny bound and abandoned, but not gagged—the story embodied by Madame Duval, feet tied and dumped in a ditch, yet "sobbing, nay, almost roaring, and in the utmost agony of rage and terror" (133) [121].

MARGARET ANNE DOODY

Beyond *Evelina*: The Individual Novel and the Community of Literature†

It seems a sign of our times that an issue of *Eighteenth-Century Fiction* devoted to Frances Burney should have arisen spontaneously—that is, not as a result of editorial long-term planning, but as an effect of

---

† From Margaret Anne Doody, "Beyond *Evelina*: The Individual Novel and the Community of Literature," *Eighteenth-Century Fiction* 3 (1991): 359–71. Reprinted by permission of *Eighteenth-Century Fiction*. The author's notes have been edited for brevity.

essays submitted. Obviously, there is real and growing interest in Burney's work. It is not now considered absurd to give detailed attention to such a lighthearted and flimsy novel as *Evelina*—for so it used to be considered. At one time—and a very recent time, too—it would have been ridiculous to offer a collection of *Evelina* essays: most would have been returned to their senders, on the grounds that "we already have one."

That the reputation of Burney's work has changed must inevitably be a matter for rejoicing for me personally. I feel that I can claim some credit for the change in attitude—as can Julia Epstein and Kristina Straub. The condescending tone has almost entirely vanished, a tone very audible even in the 1970s—e.g., in Patricia Meyer Spacks's *Imagining a Self* (1976). It is gratifying also to see signs that *Evelina*'s popularity has increased, since I am at the moment editing *Evelina* for Penguin Books. Yet, despite my own deep engagement with Burney, I am surprised—not that there should be a Burney issue of *ECF*, but that such an issue should be entirely given over *Evelina*. What is it about *Evelina* that calls forth all this attention now?

First—*Evelina* has always been the most accessible of Burney's novels. Burney's success in creating the naïve and charming seventeen-year-old narrator ensured the popularity of heroine and novel not only among contemporaries but among successive generations of readers. The book is unpretentious, or so it could be seen, a light comedy about courtship in which the female narrator (like the author) knows her place, speaks from acknowledged ignorance, never trespassing the boundaries of the female position. The strategy Burney chose in presenting her first published novel—the strategy of narration by the naïve character—worked perhaps too well. Critics, both friendly and hostile, identified Burney herself with the girl Evelina. Pierre Choderlos de Laclos's review of *Cecilia* begins with the current gossip about the author (almost entirely erroneous) which Laclos accepts as true history, including the idea that the author was just eighteen when she finished writing her novel. Later, Burney was going to be accused of having lied about her age—really on no better grounds than the fact that she was actually nearly twenty-six years old when she offered her seventeen-year-old heroine an Entrance into the World. Later still, when literary critics and historians alluded to Burney—and of course at the beginning of this century it was the harmless-sounding "Fanny" Burney—it was usually the Burney of *Evelina* that they meant, an author whose artistry was hardly greater than that of the nice little rustic Miss. The desire to sustain this unthreatening Burney meant that readers were prepared to prefer her journal-letters to her novels, once the Letters arrived on the scene edited into more charm and less disturbance than the raw manuscripts possess. To write letters to a sister seems more like the idea of an "Evelina" than to write mature satires.

Burney's strategy in some ways thus worked against her, and, I think, continues to work against her to some extent. But it did ensure that *Evelina* had a place (if not a very high place) in our vision of the eighteenth century. We must acknowledge that to give this novel a position is hardly to introduce a new outlook. *Evelina* has always been the Burney novel closest to the canon. It may indeed be seen as traditionally the most canonical of novels by eighteenth-century women. Modern styles of teaching literature in the academy in mid-twentieth century have helped to cement that position. The work most familiar to the teacher, and the most admissible of the women's fictions even to the conservative judgement, it is the female novel most likely to appear on a university course. That this novel is relatively short is an obvious advantage for the designer of courses, but modest length alone would not suffice—many novels by women, such as Inchbald's *A Simple Story*, are shorter yet, but have not yet been standardized fare in the classroom. So the specialist in eighteenth-century literature, once in graduate school or advancing in the academic career, can re-examine *Evelina* as a well-known work, encountered, like *The Rape of the Lock or Tom Jones*, fairly early during college education; the novel announces itself as happily familiar and yet freshly exciting because new things are being said about it, and about its author.

Here, then, are some of the reasons for the emphasis on *Evelina*. It is, however, evident in the essays in the present collection that the writers are drawn to the book because of certain elements in the story itself. It is interesting that all four critics here represented concentrate on the same kind of material, the same elements. These elements are aspects of the "plot" of *Evelina*, the story of the girl's relation to her dead mother and disowning father, and the ways in which that absent and rejecting father is brought at last to "own" her (Amy Pawl), or give her "recognition" (Gina Campbell), or "character" as "social identity" (David Oakleaf). All four essayists emphasize the question of *name* in *Evelina* (a hare which I credit myself with having started). Susan Greenfield gives the "naming" which Sir John Belmont the disowning father holds in his power a twist by insisting that it is the mother who is really the author of Evelina's identity (and that thus too the absent and un-nameable father is not the real author of the author's being). The mother has the power (through her written words and Evelina's role as her signifier) to create or extort a social identity that the repentant father simply validates. The novel's subtext is thus "subversion of the patriarch and insistence that naming and textual production are matrilinear powers."[1]

It is interesting and naturally gratifying to me to see that my approach in *Frances Burney: The life in the Works* has had a good deal of effect. The relation of Burney's works to her life has obviously illumined

---

1. Susan C. Greenfield, " 'Oh Dear Resemblance of Thy Murdered Mother': Female Authorship in *Evelina*," *Eighteenth-Century Fiction* 3 (1991): 316. [*Editor*]

these critics' own readings. They have freely drawn upon the biographical material that I related to *Evelina*, and upon my own commentary upon the novel, while amplifying and sometimes refining upon my suggestions, as Campbell does when, in analysing the father-figures in *Evelina*, she reinserts the dead Mr Evelyn (whom I had largely ignored) into the novel's system and relates him also to Charles Burney, who "marries a vulgar woman responsible for the misery of his children."[2] The biographical approach has offered a welcome mode of entry into the novel. The frame-story of *Evelina* is now visible as never before. In short, from having considered that frame-story meaningless and merely "conventional," criticism has done about-face and has come to see it as fraught with meaning, emotion, and tension, not a mere hackneyed convention but a story radically particular to Burney's own case.

The plot's story is a Fable of Identity, a fable that has not lost its power to provoke or disturb. It may be that this fable is the more interesting to us because, as we near the end of a century and of a millennium, we are less assured about the stability of social structures, or about the cultural philosophical frameworks that uphold social structures—both structure and philosophy conferring identity. Western cultural identity is no longer so stable that the identity and the subordinate identities it confers can go unexamined. Even Marxism, an ideology that could be used to probe other ideologies, has itself crumbled with the crumbling of the political arrangements of Eastern Europe. In such a time of instability we are going to be the more attracted to fables that ask questions about identity and identification. It may seem absurd to mention Burney's novel in the same breath as the fate of Warsaw Pact Nations in the revolutions of 1988–89—but *Evelina* was not written outside political time. The novel was written, or at least completed and published, during a war—the English war with the colonies (better known as the American Revolution). In that political conflict (long a-brewing), a daughter country defied identification with a Father (George III), a metaphorical parent who could be presented as either paternally concerned (a Villars) or harshly obdurate, unheeding and rejecting (a Belmont). One of the reasons for *Evelina*'s immediate popularity may have rested in the fact that novel was not just an escape from present troubles, but was also (if obscurely) an interpretation and investigation of those troubles. It offered its Fable of Identity (while representing that identity as problematic) during a crisis in which, challenged by colonists who refused to accept the definitions laid upon them, the English had to question their own identity, and to face the fact that the future would not be the same as the past.

It is a tribute to the power and persuasiveness of Burney as a novelist that her Fable of Identity has not lost its power to instruct or to provoke.

---

2. Gina Campbell, "Bringing Belmont to Justice: Burney's Quest for Paternal Recognition in *Evelina*," *Eighteenth-Century Fiction* 3 (1991): 329.

We in our time are much vexed with questions regarding personal identity, "self," personal subjectivity. Is there an inner stable individual? The
current study of cases of multiple personalities raises interesting questions about the limitations of the concept of the individual self. We also
continually wonder whether we have a personal subjectivity, whether
we are not the mere constructs of our culture. Such questions concerned Locke (often too easily blamed for setting up simple answers)
and Hume after him, as well as Swift and Richardson and other writers
of the eighteenth century. Burney's novel (as Oakleaf notes) raises questions about "character" as inner form or outer impression. The epistolary mode itself, of course, reassures us as to the individual "self," while
that self's difficulties in gaining recognition, and its repeated vulnerability to external control and explication, raise questions and supply perpetual tensions.

It may be surprising to some younger readers of this issue of *ECF* to
be told that sixty, or forty, or even twenty years ago most commentary
on *Evelina* would have dealt with the Branghtons and Mr. Smith. We
are seeing here an interesting example of canonical change within
canonical change, displacement within displacement. It is not a particularly striking move, as I have indicated, to put *Evelina* on the reading
lists. The real canonical change, it strikes me, is to be found in the
critical preference for those parts of the novel which used to attract no
commentary at all. One *Evelina* (the social comedy) is being put on the
back burner; another *Evelina* has come to the fore.

The danger is, of course, that we may become fixated upon this new
Evelina, unable to succeed in reuniting it with its partner—or partners—the other aspects of this novel. If we do not make such a reintegra-
tive effort, the criticism will quickly ossify, just as the "charming" school
of criticism, insisting on the novel's playfulness, hardened and turned
into a carapace that made much of *Evelina* invisible. None of these
present writers addresses the question "What made Frances Burney a
comic writer?" or that other question "How does her comedy work?" It
is true that we have recognized within the telling of our *Evelina* some
interesting problems and complex strategies, including the problematic
use of Evelina herself, so often speechless yet always an author. We
have gained some interesting new commentary. But we need to strive
perpetually to increase the depth of our commentary.

It concerns me that none of these writers seems interested in the
background of eighteenth-century literature (literature in its broadest
sense) which lies behind *Evelina*. True, Oakleaf points out that a quota-
tion from Swift escaped *Evelina*'s editors in the 1970s because they were
not accustomed to associate Burney with a major male writer of the
period.[3] But the critic does not carry his stricture so far as to question

3. David Oakleaf, "The Name of the Father: Social Identity and the Ambition of *Evelina*," *Eighteenth-Century Fiction* 3 (1991): 355. [*Editor*]

what he himself might be missing, nor does he carry the matter further to deal with Burney's relation to the Swift who is a *satirist*.

The lack of interest in Burney's comic effects seems sometimes an extension of a lack of interest in the eighteenth-century literature that preceded *Evelina*—literature that its author read. By taking everything in the fable *au sérieux*, critics may seriously miss what the author has to say. Attention to the literature does not mean disdaining the biographical approach (after all, what an author has read is an aspect of biography). But it does mean opening up the biographical approach, and not putting the entire emphasis, when discussing author or fable, on personal psychological material.

One happy example of the interworking of influences and references both public and private is the mock-Dedication of *Evelina* "To the Authors of the Monthly and Critical Reviews."[4] This Dedication has a deal of hidden comedy revealed only through knowledge of some facts of Burney's life. Frances Burney knew some of these reviewers personally (particularly Samuel Crisp, who wrote for the *Critical Review*). She knew also of her father's ceaseless efforts to cultivate the reviewers, and to ensure that his own works were reviewed by sympathetic and flattering friends. As she worked as her father's secretary and copyist, she had good reason to know what kind of secret activity goes into constructing the reception of a book. Publishing *Evelina* anonymously, Frances Burney was quite aware that she was forgoing this behind-the-scenes influence. But she knew quite well that such influence existed, that it was possible to work the periodicals, and her references to the Reviewers' "impartiality" and the "sacred ties of integrity" which bind them are loaded with the deepest irony. The Reviewers' "integrity" seems a source of private laughter, a laughter resulting partly from a disdainful suspicion of self-manifesting Censors of any kind (compare her reference to the Reviewers as "Censors for the Public" with her use of the character Censor in *The Witlings*). The sharp satire in this part of the Dedication is not available unless we know more than she wants to tell us here about the author and her life. But the overt satire is readily accessible, emphasized by the visible relationship of this mock-Dedication to Tobias Smollett's mock-Dedication of *Ferdinand Count Fathom* (1753) to himself.

Every novel is a crossroads of ideas, and a collection of what used to be called "influences." That is, the novel enters into dialogue with other works, or parodies or cannibalizes or subverts them. However we wish to speak of the complex relationships, every novel is intertextual, a tissue of allusions. The better we understand the allusions, the better (other things being equal) we should be able to read the novel. Let us take an

---

4. Frances Burney, *Evelina; or the History of a Young Lady's Entrance into the World*, ed. Edward A. Bloom (London: Oxford UP, 1968) 3–5. References are to this edition. [Bracketed page numbers refer to this Norton Critical Edition. *Editor*]

instance. Pawl coments upon the "fictitious relationship" of Evelina with Lord Orville as her self-proclaimed brother, and upon his calling her by "the affectionate title of sister"[5] (*Evelina*, p. 349 [259]). Lord Orville's assumed role of sibling represents to the critic only the novel's (and Evelina's) desire to reconstitute a family, and highlights the "desexualized nature of their later romantic relationship." But the matter of assumed brotherliness in *Evelina* seems more complicated than this. Within the novel itself, the presence of Macartney hints at other possibilities, and the mysterious attractions of incest can loom through the plot-line. If we look in a different direction, then we are sharply reminded of another hero, Sir Charles Grandison, who proclaims Harriet Byron his "third sister." Harriet is at first grateful for his tactful generosity, but comes to resent this interpolated relationship. When reminded by Charlotte Grandison of the hero's emphasis on this relationship Harriet looks "silly enough" and admits to herself "To say the truth, I *was* disappointed."[6] Later, when she finds that Sir Charles in Italy took up a similar fraternal relation to Clementina, Harriet reacts with shame and chagrin: "He has been *used* to this dialect, and to check the passions of us forward girls."[7] Lord Orville is a hero with obvious connections to Grandison, and contemporary readers would have picked up the fact that he uses the same technique for encouraging friendship and confidence between himself and the girl, while maintaining a distance. He can thus let himself off the responsibility of courtship. By becoming a "brother" he may in fact be increasing his sexual attractiveness (by increasing intimacy) while making himself unavailable, repressing the "passions" of a secretly "forward" Evelina. The assumed brother-sister roles are stimulating and frustrating, certainly not purely gratifying, to both heroines. An eighteenth-century reader, coming to *Evelina* from a reading of *Grandison* (and so much else) could pick that up almost at once.

The authors Burney summons in her Preface—Rousseau, Johnson, Marivaux, Fielding, Richardson, Smollett—are authors we are invited to dismiss and to retain, to cast out of mind and to keep in mind—for how can we measure the author's departure from their broad beaten track without knowledge of that track (or tracks)? That is, we must know both Burney and her predecessors in order to know differences—which is also to note similarities.

A reading of *La Nouvelle Héloïse*, for instance, may offer some precedent for the epistolary manner of *Evelina*, as well as some suspicion of all governors, masters, and Mentors of young ladies. This "Abelard" tradition (figured also by Grandison as Clementina's teacher) is recy-

---

5. Amy Pawl, " 'And What Other Name May I Claim': Names and Their Owners in Frances Burney's *Evelina*." *Eighteenth-Century Fiction* 3 (1991): 288.
6. *Sir Charles Grandison*, ed. Jocelyn Harris, 3 vols. (London: Oxford UP, 1972), I, ii, 424. References are to this edition.
7. *Grandison*, II, iii, 157.

cled, played with, partly overturned. Villars may be seen as a more virtuous St Preux grown old, in his multi-generational involvement with the
heroine's family and in his habit of affectionate eloquence. But Villars
is aged, and his possessiveness (which might once have been a real
threat to Caroline Evelyn) is evaded, even while ostensibly honoured.
Evelina, unlike the male suitors' heroines, is not to be readily over-
thrown by Mentors. Despite her apparently malleable and docile
nature, Evelina makes a major moral decision (not to tell Macartney's
story) in the face of her Mentor-brother-lover's disapprobation.

It is of course disingenuous of Burney to mention only male predecessors in her Preface—but in that curious manifesto she emphasizes her
departure from the road of all these men. She mentions none of the
female writers of fiction, and she has good reason to omit them, if only
because any such reference would have unveiled the gender of the new
author and put readers (and dangerous Reviewers) on the track of the
hidden identity. Although Burney mentions none of the women writers,
she is evidently in a relation with them also, perhaps a more sympathetic
connection than with those whom the anonymous author of the Preface
calls "great writers" (p. 8) [7]. Thanks to the recent (and, alas! brief)
appearance on the scene of the Pandora series (valuable despite error-
ridden typography), more readers have been able to read more eighteenth-century novels, and a number of students will now be acquainted
with Eliza Haywood's *Betsy Thoughtless* (1751). Like Evelina, Haywood's heroine finds it difficult for a young woman to enter society, to
pursue the limited freedom allowed her within the world of eighteenth-
century excursions and parties, and to get to know young men without
being misunderstood. Betsy, like Evelina, is often misinterpreted by the
company she keeps. If you are with a "whore" or even in a place frequented by "whores" you are in danger of being identified as a "whore."
So Betsy learns, and so too Evelina finds in the dangers of Marylebone
Gardens, where she momentarily seems to be one of a group of prostitutes.

There are many, many models for and influences on *Evelina* within
eighteenth-century English literature. But in order to understand the
novel and to make our commentary deeper, we should go deeper into
the literary tradition. The deeper structure of the novel comes from
traditions far back in time. It is not really right to take *Evelina* as its own
myth, if that means a myth complete on its own, discovered by its one
named author. In her Preface, Burney raises the question of "originality," that problematic idea, only to claim that she is not vain or foolish
or blind enough to have "an opinion of my own originality" (p. 9) [7].
If we read that careful sentence as carefully as it was crafted, we can see
that it is not quite a disclaimer of originality, but she must deny *herself*
the luxury of thinking of her own status as a source. The discussion here
is one of Burney's many riddles. We may believe that Burney does want

to indicate her originality. But I think she sees "originality" as possible in one sense, impossible in another. Readers coming fresh to *Evelina* and wishing to give at last full credit to this hitherto undervalued writer may indeed be inclined to stress the originality of the novel—to the point of overstating the case. That is not to say that *Evelina* is *less* original than other novels. But the "originality" of the Romantic cause is not now a necessary article of belief, and at times it can sadly obstruct the view. In the case of this novel—and as is true of all interesting novels—at the level of myth the novelist taps into something deep and old.

Much has been said (by myself among others) of the importance of the mother in *Evelina*, and of the place of the mother's transmitted text in giving identity and meaning to a heroine who has no name. But this is not fire-new. The mother's text that confers identity upon the heroine is a very old motif indeed. It is found, writ large (as it were) in one of the oldest novels of the Western tradition: Heliodorus's *Aithiopika* (c. 250–380 AD). This is a novel often translated and reprinted throughout the Renaissance, and it maintained currency in the eighteenth century. In this story the heroine's mother, Persinna, Queen of Ethiopia, was forced to abandon her baby daughter, but left with her as tokens not only precious gems but also a silken girdle embroidered in a script so exclusive (Ethiopian royal script) as to be decipherable by few. The writing tells the child her identity and the real story of her (legitimate) birth. The mother's story is thus both concealed and revealed. Suppressed in speech it emerges in writing—a communication whose final object or reader the mother-writer cannot know: "perhaps my writing may remain mute and useless, or perhaps it will be real of advantage to you, for the secrets of Fate are hidden from mankind. This writing will be to you . . . if you are spared, a token of recognition and if not, it will serve as my funerary inscription for you, and a mother's tears and funeral dirge at your tomb."[8]

Charikleia, the heroine, grew up in ignorance of her parentage—her very *name* is wrong, the name of her adoptive, not her true father. She learns of her legitimate birth and heritage through the care of the good Egyptian priest Kalasiris, who is able to read the writing and inform her who she is. Charikleia, like Evelina, has the guardianship of a good priest, her spiritual "father," to rely upon, though Burney's heroine, unlike her predecessor, does not have to endure the bereavement of this "father." In Heliodorus's novel, as in Burney's, the heroine has to wait

---

8. My own version of these passages (with citation of book and chapter number) is based on the Greek-French edition, *Les Ethiopiques*, ed. R. W. Rattenbury and T. W. Lumb, trans. J. Maillon, 3 vols (Paris: Les Belles Lettres, 1960), book IV, chap. 8. A new English translation by John R. Morgan of the novel can be found in the excellent *Collected Ancient Greek Novels*, ed. B. P. Reardon (Berkeley and London: U of California P, 1989). Note that the mother's gift, her written work, is ambivalent in its functions: it may identify the daughter, or it may bury her so that both women are silenced, save for the mother's (imagined) tears—but these are again merely silenced script.

for recognition until the end of the novel. As Charikleia explains to her sweetheart Theagenes, tokens must be presented at the right moment and in the right way. Without the proper introduction any and all tokens (including the writing) are mere objects. Identification takes time, and plots must be unravelled:

> A multiplex plot which from the beginning a demon has entangled—that cannot suddenly come to an end without many subordinate finishings. Besides, something which has become increasingly more complicated over a long period of time cannot suddenly be unveiled and unknotted, especially when the chief worker of the whole piece, the weaver of the web, the one on whom my recognition depends—I mean Persinna, my mother—is not there.[9]

In Heliodorus's use of the Mother-Daughter plot, the mother is still alive, and it is the mother's intuitive recognition (more gradual, however, than Sir John Belmont's) that reinforces the validity of her letter. Evelina has to rely on her father's perception and intuition as well as the mother's words that speak for her; like Charikleia she keeps her history and identification in the secret private writing that is also the mother's story.

I am citing Heliodorus here, but not in order to make a claim that Burney knew this novel and was drawing on it directly. Elsewhere, it is true, I do suggest a more direct connection, and offer a reading of *The Wanderer* as a female re-vision of the Heliodoran novel. Sir Philip Sidney's *Arcadia* and Richardson's *Clarissa* are other re-visions and new versions of Heliodorus's work. The *Aithiopika* (under many translated titles) was transmitted through numerous texts, and its myth(s) adapted and readapted. As a strong Mother-Daughter story it offered a sort of model to women writers, and it was one of the central examples of the tale of the mother who tries to transmit an identity through writing to the separated (and in some sense orphaned) daughter. There is an additional stress in the mother's fear, even as she writes, that her writing may be silenced, that her utterance will remain κωφά (dumb, mute). That same motif is exploited by Mary Wollstonecraft, for instance, in her unfinished *Maria, or The Wrongs of Woman*. To draw all these connections is not to cast aspersions on Sir Philip Sidney, or Mary Wollstonecraft, or Samuel Richardson, or Frances Burney. To suggest that Burney is enabled to write *Evelina* because there is a novelistic tradition conveying a strong and serviceable myth to her, thus enabling her to raise and cultivate her story in the seedbed of this archetype, is certainly not to belittle her. Still less is it to deny the dynamic present tense, the constant contemporary quality of *Evelina*—or that novel's value as a picture of social history in England in the 1770s. It is impossible for a novelist not to write myth; it is equally impossible for a novelist (whether

9. *Les Ethiopiques*, book IX, chap. 3.

dealing in realism or fantasy) not to write history. It is in each author's power to vary the myth he or she has received, and to introduce new and strong perceptions. The responsibility of the literary critic includes the responsibility of seeing the material on which the author draws, not being misled by the notion of an author—any author—as an entire and sole creator.

Feminist theory and feminism itself have made it easier for critics of all kinds to see beyond the idea of "original genius" serving up only itself, its wonderful original work. Almost everybody can now see the pitfalls in the view of literature as an archipelago, a series of Great Works by Great Men. It is necessary of course to guard against erring in the other direction, denying the individual writer any existence, any creative choices (that is to say, creative power) at all.

Burney did have creative power. But should we assume that a Burney novel can be read in the light of itself alone—or in the light of Novel + Biography—or even in the light of the triangulation of Novel + Biography + Theory. Nothing, I believe, replaces a full sense of the past—not as dead and dusty but as lively and stimulating. My biography itself was intended as a reclamation of the past, and not as a resting point. I believe I contributed something vital with the biography. Yet it would be a pity if we got stuck in the biographical reading of the kind I exemplify . . . or may *seem* to exemplify. Part of my purpose was to raise *all* of Frances Burney's works to view—to get away at last from the idea of her as a single-book author. Thus I find it particularly unsettling to look at a group of essays which reflect my own insights back at me very persistently, and yet persistently overlook or discount the novelist's works—save for *Evelina* the Inevitable.

We are all aware of a renewed conflict in our society between an ideal attention to the individual and an ideal attention to the generality, the community. At a political level this difference makes itself felt very sharply. It is a strong ideological and philosophical difference. For some, there exist only strong individual selves, and Society, if there is any such, is merely an aggregate of separate Individuals. There is no need to attend to the group—attend only to the Individual. For others, the idea of the Individual Person is at best dubious, and the true reality is the Community, that which truly lives on, the repository of culture, in which alone the momentary individuals cohere and make sense. The four articles on *Evelina* really reflect belief in the single subject, whatever the authors may think of their own personal theoretical orientation. In their attention to the one work they are in danger of throwing out the general and communal—to the extent of cutting out the rest of Burney's works. The community, that is, of the author's whole body of work is not only obscured but denied. The community which is eighteenth-century literature, or Western literature, is very largely denied—even if implicitly or unconsciously. And the community of *Evelina* with itself—or with "its selves"—is denied. The multiple personalities of that novel cannot function together yet. In a world where you cannot have chickens or eggs without having both chickens *and* eggs, we need both individual and community.

No—no. I do not want the old view of *Evelina* as a light comedy into which some melodrama and some horseplay has crept by mistake. My own book on Burney begins with a repudiation of that idea. I do not want commentary on the Branghtons and Smith such as we used to get. But—yes—I do want more attention paid to Burney the satirist. If she wanted to write about a disowned girl without a family, why does she place this girl, her Eve, her Charikleia, in a story that includes the Branghtons and Smith? What is the real place of Mme Duval?—who connects the girl not just with her mother but with the Branghtonian world.

We who are Burney critics (and how good to think that that is now a large plural, even a community) need to reintegrate the novel with itself, as well as with its world. So we need to integrate Burney's works (a considerable number if we include the plays) with themselves and with each other. (This does not rule out the discovery of differences, contrasts, and contradictions.) We must engage in this work if we are not to make of Burney again the one-book little novelist. I feel impatient, at last I must own, with too much *Evelina*. I have always liked *Cecilia* slightly better—but *Camilla* is so complex, so extraordinary. Yet think of *The Wanderer*, what a weird and challenging and poetic novel it is, with its play with the Gothic, with Romanticism, its representation of feminism in terms of an uncompromisingly gritty working world, combined with its fantastic images of human history.

Yes, we must look at the community too, not just the individual. And we should have regard to the community of the Burney works. No one should presume upon expertise in this novelist until all the four novels, at least, have been read. Burney replays her themes, reconsiders questions. She did not reach "an answer" in *Evelina*—she merely brought one book to a conclusion. From the sacred guardian Villars in *Evelina* we go to that unholy mess of guardians in *Cecilia*; it is not going to be so easy, after all, to make a quick generalization about Burney's attitudes to male authority. And what a contrast Mortimer Delvile is to Lord Orville. What one novel stabilizes, another knocks down.

And of course there is always that other community to which we must attend in seeking to understand any literary work. That is the community of all the books the author read, the traditions in which the work was done. Without a recognition of that community (as real as the author's relationships with the personal community of family friends and acquaintances) we will not get too far. And a lot of good jokes will be lost on us.

Frances Burney:
A Chronology

1752	Born in King's Lynn, Norfolk, June 13
1760	Burney family moves to Poland Street, London
1762	Esther Sleepe Burney, Burney's mother, dies
1767	Burns juvenile writings, June 13
1768	Begins journal, March 27
1778	Publishes *Evelina, or, a Young Woman's Entrance into the World*, January 29
1778	Begins close friendship with Hester Lynch Thrale and Dr. Johnson
1779	Completes *The Witlings, a Comedy* by May 4
1782	Publishes *Cecilia, or Memoirs of an Heiress*, July 6
1783	Samuel ("Daddy") Crisp dies April 26
1784	Hester Thrale and Gabriel Piozzi marry July 23; ends friendship with Burney
1784	Dr. Johnson dies December 13
1786	Becomes Second Keeper of the Robes to Queen Charlotte, July 17
1790	Finishes draft of *Edwy and Elgiva: A Tragedy* in August
1791	Completes draft of *Hubert de Vere, A Pastoral Tragedy*, June 1791
1791	Writes draft of *The Siege of Pevensey: A Tragedy*
1791	Begins tragedy *Elberta* in June but does not complete it
1791	Leaves Queen's service, July 7; receives £100 annual pension
1793	Marries Alexandre d'Arblay, July 28
1793	Publishes pamphlet, *Brief Reflections relative to the Emigrant French Clergy*
1794	Gives birth to son, Alexandre, December 18
1795	*Edwy and Elgiva* plays one night at Drury Lane, March 21
1796	Publishes *Camilla: or, a Picture of Youth*, July 6
1796	Elizabeth Allen Burney, Burney's stepmother, dies October 20
1799	Completes *Love and Fashion: A Comedy*, April
1800	Susanna Burney Phillips, Burney's favorite sister, dies January 6

1800–1 Writes *A Busy Day, or An Arrival from India* and *The Woman-Hater: A Comedy*

1802 Leaves for France, April 20; trapped in exile by outbreak of war between England and France

1811 Undergoes mastectomy, September 30

1812 Returns to England, August 16

1814 Publishes *The Wanderer; or, Female Difficulties*, March 28

1814 Dr. Charles Burney, Burney's father, dies April 12

1814 Returns to France, November

1815 Is in Brussels during the Battle of Waterloo

1815 Returns to England with husband, now Lieutenant-General, Count d'Arblay

1817 Reconciles with Hester Lynch Piozzi, November 17

1818 General d'Arblay, Burney's husband, dies May 3

1832 Publishes the *Memoirs of Doctor Burney*

1837 Alexandre d'Arblay, Burney's son, dies January 19

1840 Frances Burney dies January 6

Selected Bibliography

Novels

Camilla; or, A Picture of Youth. 1796. Ed. Edward A. Bloom and Lillian D. Bloom. London: Oxford UP, 1972.
Cecilia; or, Memoirs of an Heiress. 1782. Ed. Peter Sabor and Margaret Anne Doody. London: Oxford UP, 1988.
The Wanderer; or, Female Difficulties. 1814. Ed. Peter Sabor and Margaret Anne Doody. Harmondsworth: Penguin, 1991.

Plays

Complete Plays of Frances Burney. Ed. Peter Sabor, Geoffrey M. Sill, and Stewart J. Cooke. 2 vols. London: Pickering; Montreal: McGill-Queen's UP, 1995.

Letters

The Diary and Letters of Madame d'Arblay (1778–1840). Ed. Austin Dobson. 6 vols. London: Macmillan, 1904–1905.
The Early Diary of Frances Burney, 1768–1778. Ed. Annie Raine Ellis. 2 vols. London: Bell, 1913.
The Journal and Letters of Fanny Burney (Madame d'Arblay). Ed. Joyce Hemlow, et al. 12 vols. Oxford: Clarendon, 1972–84.

Biographies

Adelstein, Michael. *Fanny Burney*. New York: Twayne, 1968.
Doody, Margaret Anne. *Frances Burney: The Life in the Works*. New Brunswick, NJ: Rutgers UP, 1988.
Farr, Evelyn. *The World of Fanny Burney*. London: Owen, 1993.
Kilpatrick, Sarah. *Fanny Burney*. Newton Abbot, Eng.: David & Charles, 1980.

Criticism

• indicates works included in or excerpted for this Norton Critical Edition.

Bloom, Edward A., and Lillian D. "Fanny Burney's Novels: The Retreat from Wonder." *Novel* 12 (1979): 215–35.
• Brown, Martha G. "Fanny Burney's 'Feminism': Gender or Genre?" *Fetter'd or Free? British Women Novelists, 1670–1815*. Ed. Mary Anne Schofield and Cecilia Macheski. Athens: Ohio UP, 1986. 29–39.
Campbell, Gina. "Bringing Belmont to Justice: Burney's Quest for Paternal Recognition in *Evelina*." *Eighteenth-Century Fiction* 3 (1991): 321–40.
• ——. "How to Read Like a Gentleman: Burney's Instructions to Her Critics in *Evelina*." *ELH* 57 (1990): 557–84.

Cecil, David. "Fanny Burney." *Poets and Storytellers*. London: Constable, 1949. 77–96.

Copeland, Edward W. "Money in the Novels of Fanny Burney." *Studies in the Novel* 8 (1976): 24–37.

Cutting, Rose Marie. "Defiant Women: The Growth of Feminism in Fanny Burney's Novels." *Studies in English Literature 1500–1900* 17 (1977): 519–30.

Cutting-Gray, Joanne. *Woman as "Nobody" and the Novels of Fanny Burney*. Gainesville: UP of Florida, 1992.

Daugherty, Tracy Edgar. *Narrative Techniques in the Novels of Fanny Burney*. New York: Lang, 1989.

Deitz, Jonathan, and Sidonie Smith. "From Precept to Proper Social Action: Empirical Maturation in Fanny Burney's *Evelina*." *Eighteenth-Century Life* 3 (1977): 85–88.

Devlin, D. D. *The Novels and Journals of Fanny Burney*. London: Macmillan, 1987.

Dobbin, Marjorie W. "The Novel, Women's Awareness, and Fanny Burney." *English Language Notes* 22.3 (1985): 42–52.

• Doody, Margaret Anne. "Beyond *Evelina*: The Individual Novel and the Community of Literature." *Eighteenth-Century Fiction* 3 (1991): 359–71.

Dowling, William C. "Evelina and the Genealogy of Literary Shame." *Eighteenth-Century Life* 16 (1992): 208–20.

Eighteenth-Century Fiction 3.4 (1991). Special *Evelina* Issue.

Epstein, Julia. "Evelina's Deceptions: The Letter and the Spirit." *Fanny Burney's* Evelina. Ed. Harold Bloom. Modern Critical Interpretations. New York: Chelsea, 1988. 111–29.

———. "Fanny Burney's Epistolary Voice." *The Eighteenth Century: Theory and Interpretation* 27 (1986): 162–79.

———. *The Iron Pen: Frances Burney and the Politics of Women's Writing*. Madison: U of Wisconsin P, 1989.

Fizer, Irene. "The Name of the Daughter: Identity and Incest in *Evelina*." *Refiguring the Father: New Feminist Readings of Patriarchy*. Ed. Patricia Yaeger and Beth Kowaleski-Wallace. Carbondale: S. Illinois UP, 1989. 78–107.

• Fraiman, Susan. "Getting Waylaid in *Evelina*." *Unbecoming Women: British Women Writers and the Novel of Development*. New York: Columbia UP, 1993. 32–58.

• Graham, Kenneth W. "Cinderella or Bluebeard: The Double Plot of *Evelina*." *Man and Nature / L'Homme et la Nature* 5 (1986): 85–98.

Greenfield, Susan C. " 'Oh Dear Resemblance of Thy Murdered Mother': Female Authorship in *Evelina*." *Eighteenth-Century Fiction* 3 (1991): 301–320.

• Hemlow, Joyce. *The History of Fanny Burney*. Oxford: Clarendon, 1958.

———. "Fanny Burney and the Courtesy Books." *PMLA* 65 (1950): 732–61.

Malone, Kemp. "*Evelina* Revisited." *Papers on Language and Literature* 1 (1965): 3–19.

McMaster, Juliet. "The Silent Angel: Impediments to Female Expression in Frances Burney's Novels." *Studies in the Novel* 21 (1989): 235–52.

Montague, Edwine, and Louis L. Martz. "Fanny Burney's *Evelina*." *The Age of Johnson: Essays Presented to Chauncey Brewster Tinker*. New Haven: Yale UP, 1949. 171–81.

Newton, Judith Lowder. *Women, Power, and Subversion: Social Strategies in British Fiction, 1778–1860*. Athens: U of Georgia P, 1981.

Oakleaf, David. "The Name of the Father: Social Identity and the Ambition of *Evelina*." *Eighteenth-Century Fiction* 3 (1991): 341–58.

Olshin, Toby A. " 'To Whom I Most Belong': The Role of Family in *Evelina*." *Eighteenth-Century Life* 6 (1980): 29–42.

Parke, Catherine. "Vision and Revision: A Model for Reading the Eighteenth-Century Novel of Education." *Eighteenth-Century Studies* 16 (1982–83): 162–74.

Patterson, Emily H. "Family and Pilgrimage Themes in Burney's *Evelina*." *New Rambler* 18 (1977): 41–48.

———. "Unearned Irony in Fanny Burney's *Evelina*." *Durham University Journal* 36 (1975): 200–204.

Paulson, Ronald. "*Evelina*: Cinderella and Society." *Satire and the Novel in Eighteenth-Century England*. New Haven: Yale UP, 1967. 283–92.

Pawl, Amy J. " 'And What Other Name May I Claim?': Names and Their Owners in Frances Burney's *Evelina*." *Eighteenth-Century Fiction* 3 (1991): 283–300.

Poovey, Mary. "Fathers and Daughters: The Trauma of Growing Up Female." *Men by Women: Women and Literature*. Ed. Janet Todd. Vol. 2. New York: Holmes, 1981. 39–58.

Rogers, Katharine M. "Fanny Burney: The Private Self and the Published Self." *International Journal of Women's Studies* 7 (1984): 110–17.

Rubenstein, Jill. "The Crisis of Identity in Fanny Burney's *Evelina*." *New Rambler* 12 (1972): 45–50.

Scrutton, Mary. "Bourgeois Cinderellas." *Twentieth Century* 155 (1954): 351–63.

Shaffer, Julie. "Not Subordinate: Empowering Women in the Marriage-Plot: The Novels of Frances Burney, Maria Edgeworth, and Jane Austen." *Criticism* 34 (1992): 51–73.

Simons, Judy. *Fanny Burney*. Totawa, NJ: Barnes, 1987.

Spacks, Patricia M. "Dynamics of Fear: Fanny Burney." *Imagining a Self: Autobiography and Novel in Eighteenth-Century England*. Cambridge: Harvard UP, 1976. 158–92.

———. "Women and the City." *Johnson and His Age*. Ed. James Engell. Cambridge: Harvard UP, 1984. 485–507.

Staves, Susan. "*Evelina*: or, Female Difficulties." *Modern Philology* 73 (1976): 368–81.

Steeves, Harrison R. "A Young Lady's Entrance into the World." *Before Jane Austen: The Shaping of the English Novel in the Eighteenth Century*. New York: Holt, 1965. 204–22.

• Straub, Kristina. "*Evelina*: Marriage as the Dangerous Die." *Divided Fictions: Burney and Feminine Strategy*. Lexington: UP of Kentucky, 197. 53–77.

Tucker, Irene. "Writing Home: *Evelina*, the Epistolary Novel, and the Paradox of Property." *ELH* 60 (1993): 419–39.

Wagner, Jennifer A. "Privacy and Anonymity in *Evelina*." *Fanny Burney's* Evelina. Ed. Harold Bloom. Modern Critical Interpretations. New York: Chelsea, 1988. 99–109.

White, Eugene. *Fanny Burney, Novelist: A Study in Technique*. Hamden, CT: Shoe String, 1960.